THE NEW EUROPEAN SECURITY DISORDER

Also by Simon Duke

*US DEFENCE BASES IN THE UNITED KINGDOM: A Matter
for Joint Decision?

UNITED STATES MILITARY FORCES AND INSTALLATIONS
IN EUROPE

*THE BURDENSHARING DEBATE: A Reassessment

*From the same publishers

THE NEW EUROPEAN SECURITY DISORDER

The New European Security Disorder

Simon Duke

Assistant Professor
Political Science Department
The Pennsylvania State University

M

St. Martin's Press   in association with
ST ANTONY'S COLLEGE, OXFORD

First published in Great Britain 1994 by
THE MACMILLAN PRESS LTD
Houndmills, Basingstoke, Hampshire RG21 2XS
and London
Companies and representatives
throughout the world

This book is published in the *St Antony's/Macmillan Series*
General Editor: Alex Pravda

A catalogue record for this book is available
from the British Library.

ISBN 0-333-61764-9

Printed in Great Britain by
Ipswich Book Co Ltd
Ipswich, Suffolk

First published in the United States of America 1994 by
Scholarly and Reference Division,
ST. MARTIN'S PRESS, INC.,
175 Fifth Avenue,
New York, N.Y. 10010

ISBN 0-312-12371-X

Library of Congress Cataloging-in-Publication Data
Duke, Simon.
The new European security disorder / Simon Duke.
p. cm.
Includes bibliographical references and index.
ISBN 0-312-12371-X
1. National security—Europe. 2. Europe—Defenses. 3. Europe-
-Politics and government—1989– I. Title.
UA646.D87 1994
355'.0334—dc20   94-21686
                                                            CIP

To my parents

Contents

List of Tables and Figures   x
List of Maps   xii
Acknowledgements   xiii
Abbreviations   xv

Introduction   1
   Power and Security   3
   Which Europe?   10

PART I   ASSESSING EUROPE'S SECURITY CONCERNS

1   The Nature of Post-Cold War Security   17
   Smoke and mirrors?   19
   The search for a new 'ism'   22

**2   European Security Challenges in the
     Post-Cold War World**   29
   Weapons proliferation and the nuclear threat from the
     ex-Soviet Union   29
   Nationalism and irredentism   57
   Migratory pressures   69
   The role of Germany in any new European security order   82
   Implications for the security of Europe   83
   Conclusions   88

**PART II   LEADERSHIP ISSUES IN POST-COLD WAR
          EUROPEAN SECURITY**

3   European Leadership: A Ship without a Rudder   93
   France et l'Europe des patries   95
   France and the end of the Cold War   100
   Into the future   113
   Fog in the channel   117
   Conclusions   132

4   Germany, Security and the Post-Cold War World   135
   Basic law, basic problem   143
   Test cases: Bosnia and Somalia   150
   German security policy   154
   Common security policy?   156
   Conclusion   163

5   The US Role in Europe's Security   165
Primus inter pares   165
Underpaid, underloved, and on the way out?   170
The end of the transatlantic community?   186
Military options for the US in Europe   189
The Bush legacy   194
Conclusion   196

PART III   THE NEW EUROPEAN SECURITY DISORDER

6   The 'New Security Architecture'   203
The new security environment   204
A new security architecture?   208
Conclusion   214

7   Euro-Confusion   215
Building Euro-models: round one   215
Building Euro-models: round two   217
The European Community and the Maastricht process   224
The WEU: the EC's 'security branch'   231
The Franco–German Corps: an expensive language school? 241

**8   Pan-European Options: The Conference on Security
       and Cooperation in Europe   255**
From Paris back to Helsinki . . . and beyond   256
CSCE and Yugoslavia   267
Interlinking, but obstructive   269
Conclusions   272

9   The Transatlantic Option   275
Changed circumstances: new problems   275
The attempt to transform the Alliance   278
Changing the geographical focus   280
Au revoir or adieu?   286
The New Strategic Concept   288
The role of nuclear weapons   292
The out-of-area problem: NATO's Achilles heel?   295
The North Atlantic Cooperation Council   301
Command and Control   304
NATO revived? The 'Partnership for Peace'   305
Conclusion   311

PART IV   PAN-EUROPEAN SECURITY?

10   Democracy without Security   317
       Economic assistance and stability   333
       The European stability pact   340
       Peace by pieces   343
       Conclusion   345

**11   Lessons for European Security from the Yugoslav
       Conflict**   347
       Leadership and responsibility   351
       Institutional inertia   355
       Ramifications of the Bosnian crisis for European
          security   364
       Conclusion   366

12   Conclusions   368

Appendix I   382
Appendix II   385
Notes and References   391
Bibliography   433
Index   440

List of Tables and Figures

Tables

2.1	Ukrainian Nuclear Weapons (September 1993)	43
2.2	Kazakhstan Nuclear Weapons (September 1993)	48
2.3	Do you believe that countries should stop breaking up because it creates too much instability in the region, or that it is up to the people of each country to decide their own future?	59
2.4	Nationalities in the autonomous republics	61
2.5	Refugees from former Yugoslavia (April 1993)	70
2.6	How many people from non-EC countries reside in your country? (figures for EC 12)	77
2.7	How do you experience the presence of foreigners in your country? (figures for EC 12, poll taken January 1993)	77
2.8	What do you feel about the different groups of immigrants? (figures for EC 12, poll taken January 1993)	78
2.9	Have you ever seriously considered going to work in a country in Western Europe?	80
2.10	How likely is it that you will move to Western Europe to live and work?	81
4.1	Are you in favour of the EC being responsible for a common policy in matters of security and defence?	160
4.2	Assuming American forces left the FRG, could the country's military security still be guaranteed?	160
4.3	If tomorrow you were to read in the newspaper that the Americans were withdrawing their forces from Europe, would you welcome or regret this news?	161
4.4	Should US forces withdraw from Germany?	162
5.1	Options for US military representation in Europe	190
5.2	Planned cuts in US military forces	195
7.1	Are you in favour of the EC, as a political union, assuming responsibility for foreign policy towards countries outside the EC, or for a common security and defence policy?	227

x

7.2 European defence collaboration 242
9.1 Planned reductions in NATO forces by 1997 289
9.2 Changes in NATO defence budgets 280
9.3 Changes in NATO armed forces 281
10.1 Experience of multi-party democracy in Eastern Europe before 1992 332
10.2 Support for membership of the EC in Central–Eastern Europe 334
10.3 Responsibilities under the European Stability Pact 341
11.1 Do you feel that the following bodies have been on the whole rather effective or rather ineffective in trying to help resolve the conflict in former Yugoslavia? 362
11.2 Do you feel that the following bodies have been on the whole rather effective or rather ineffective in trying to help resolve the conflict in former Yugoslavia? 363
A.1 Attitudes towards non-nationals of the EC 385
A.2 Presence of people of another nationality, race or religion 386
A.3 Acceptance of people coming from south of the Mediterranean 387
A.4 Acceptance of people coming from Eastern Europe 388
A.5 Acceptance of people seeking political asylum 389
A.6 Acceptance of people from other EC countries 390

Figures

2.1 Defence structure of the CIS forces 40
8.1 The new structure of the CSCE 264
A.1 Overlapping membership in Europe's security institutions 382
A.2 EC (Common Foreign and Security Policy – CFSP) 382
A.3 WEU 383
A.4 CSCE 383
A.5 NATO 384
A.6 NACC 384

List of Maps

Map of the former Soviet military forces   32

Acknowledgements

This book was written largely as a result of the author's own efforts to teach students about European security in the post-Cold War world. Aside from articles, there seemed to be a need for a comprehensive book presenting an overview and critique of the main developments in European security in this period. It is not expected that this book will be definitive or the last word; it is, however, hoped that it will be a valuable contribution to the debate on European security issues. My first debt must therefore be to my students who, perhaps unwittingly, led me to write this book.

The New European Security Disorder was written in tranquil surroundings that were unfortunately far removed from Europe. The efforts of Helen Sheehy, in the Documents Section of the Pattee Library at The Pennsylvania State University, helped to keep me in touch with the world. My thanks are also due to Doug Royer who did a fine job of document collecting and critiquing early drafts of the manuscript. Daniel Else also provided copious amounts of NATO material and my thanks are due to him as well. The Atlantic Council of the United States also enabled me to participate in the 1992 NATO Discussion Series, which is designed to bring together members of the Council's Academic Associates Program with NATO's senior staff and decision-makers. The Discussion Series proved to be most stimulating and challenging and had a direct bearing on my decision to commit my thoughts to paper. Likewise, the discussions with colleagues who attended the National Faculty Seminar on Teaching International Security, at Bowdoin, Maine in the summer of 1993, did much to stimulate me and challenge some of my original notions. To them, my thanks are also due.

Many other people have made observations (sometimes harsh) and encouraged me along the way and, although they are too numerous to mention, my thanks go to them. A special word of thanks should, however, go to Roberta Haar who did much to improve the final drafts of the manuscript. Her patience and generous giving of time are much appreciated. Thanks are also due to Ian Thomas at St. Edmund's College, Cambridge, whose insightful comments on an early draft of the manuscript were of immense help. I also much appreciated the encouragement and academic camaraderie given by Professor Edward Keynes of the Pennsylvania State University. Even though I have had invaluable help from several sources, any errors and inadequacies of the book remain entirely my own.

State College, Pennsylvania	SIMON DUKE

Abbreviations

ABM	Anti-Ballistic Missile
ACE	Allied Command Europe
ANF	Atlantic Nuclear Force
ARRC	Allied Command Europe Rapid Reaction Corps
ASAT	Anti-Satellite Activities
ASW	Anti-Submarine warfare
AWACS	Airborne Warning and Control System
BAOR	British Army of the Rhine
BECR	Black Sea Economic Cooperation Region
CAP	Common Agricultural Policy (European Community)
C^{3}I	Command, Control, Communication and Intelligence
CD	Conference on Disarmament
CDU	Christian Democratic Party (Germany)
CENTCOM	Central Command
CFE	Conventional Armed Forces in Europe (Vienna negotiations)
CFSP	Common Foreign and Security Policy
CIS	Commonwealth of Independent States
CPC	Conflict Prevention Centre (CSCE)
CMEA	Council for Mutual Economic Assistance
CRF	Crisis Reactionary Force (Germany)
CSBM	Confidence and Security Building Measure
CSCE	Conference on Security and Cooperation in Europe
CSFR	Czech and Slovak Federal Republic
CSU	Christian Social Union (Germany)
DM	Deutsche Mark
DoD	Department of Defense (US)
EBRD	European Bank for Reconstruction and Development
EC	European Community
EDC	European Defence Community
EMS	European Monetary System
ERM	Exchange Rate Mechanism
ESI	European Security Identity
ESP	European Stability Pact
EU	European Union
FAR	Force d'Action Rapide (France)
FCC	Federal Constitutional Court (Germany)

FCO	Foreign and Commonwealth Office (United Kingdom)
FDP	Free Democratic Party (Germany)
GDR	German Democratic Republic (East Germany)
GNP	Gross National Product
GPALS	Global Protection Against Limited Strikes
G-7	Group of Seven (highly industrialized countries)
HEU	Highly enriched uranium
ICBM	Intercontinental Ballistic Missile
IEPG	Independent European Programme Group
INF	Intermediate-range Nuclear Forces
JDF	Joint Defence Council (Franco-German)
JNA	Jugoslav People's Army
MAPI	Ministry of Heavy Machinery and Atomic Industries (Soviet Union)
MLF	Multilateral Force
MTCR	Missile Technology Control Regime
NAFTA	North America Free Trade Agreement
NACC	North Atlantic Cooperation Council
NPT	Non-proliferation Treaty
NSC	National Security Council
OECD	Organization for Economic Cooperation and Development
OOA	Out of Area
OPEC	Organization of Petroleum Exporting Countries
PALS	Permissive Action Links
PHARE	Poland and Hungary Reconstruction Programme
POMCUS	Prepositioned Organizational Material Configured to Unit Sets
PSD	Peaceful Settlement of Disputes
RSFR	Russian Republic
SACEUR	Supreme Allied Commander Europe
SALT	Strategic Arms Limitation Talks
SAM	Surface-to-Air Missile
SDI	Strategic Defense Initiative
SED	Socialist Unity Party (East Germany)
SHAPE	Supreme Headquarters Allied Powers Europe
SIPRI	Stockholm International Peace Research Institute
SLBM	Submarine-Launched Ballistic Missile
SPD	Social Democratic Party (Germany)
SSBN	Nuclear-Powered Ballistic Missile Submarine
START	Strategic Arms Reduction Talks

TACIS	Technical Assistance to the Commonwealth of Independent States
UNPROFOR	United Nations Protection Force (Yugoslavia)
USEUCOM	US European Command
WETO	West European Treaty Organization
WEU	Western European Union
WTO	Warsaw Treaty Organization

Introduction

This study was embarked upon at a time of great changes in Europe, the implication of which are in many instances unclear. In spite of changes that may occur, the contention of this book is that the future stability and peace of Europe depends upon the construction of a pan-European security system. Such a system will include Central and Eastern Europe, Western Europe, as well as North America. It is recognized that there is currently no one institution that can provide ready-made answers to the security problems facing these countries. In the future, though, a system based around the Conference on Security and Cooperation in Europe (CSCE) would best serve Europe's security interests. The leitmotif of European security should therefore be to work towards a comprehensive security system for all of Europe that streches not just geographically but functionally beyond any current arrangements.

The enormousness of this task is not underestimated. It is explicitly acknowledged that there are daunting tasks ahead; the first of which is to bring about a fundamental change in the way that many Western leaders think of security. All too often lipservice is paid to the idea of pan-European security arrangements but security is defined increasingly in terms of the national interest with scant regard for wider regional or external concerns. The ongoing crisis in Yugoslavia, and the failure of the major powers to respond decisively, illustrates not only the need for a new 'Europe' in security terms but also points to the lack of leadership in post-Cold War European security.

The book consists of four interrelated parts which aim to offer a comprehensive critique of post-Cold War European security, as well as to provide some tentative suggestions. Part I examines the nature of the new security threats facing Europe. It is argued that there are two exaggerated threats to European stability; these are the threat of a 'back to the future' scenario and the threat posed by Islamic fundamentalism – also known as the Green Peril. On the first point it is acknowledged that although there are serious threats to Europe's stability, they are not of the nature of 1913 or 1936. The main powers are locked together in highly interdependent (if fractious) relationships. The likelihood of a war between the major powers in Europe leading to a general war is rejected. The second exaggerated threat, that of Islamic fundamentalism, exists largely because of a lack of knowledge about

1

the many strains of Islam, accompanied by the tendency to identify all Muslims as potentially threatening to non-Islamic culture and ways of life.

Three main challenges to Europe's security are identified: those of weapons proliferation (especially nuclear), nationalism and migratory pressures. Many of these threats demand non-military responses which, in turn, call for a wider-based conceptualization of security. Definitions of security that still centre around military notions of security are in-adequate in the European context. Thus reference to security problems does not necessarily refer to those problems which demand an immedi-ate military response (although in some instances they may). Instead it refers to developments which are considered to pose a *significant* threat to the stability, culture and well-being of a country or group of countries.

Part II considers the absence of coherent leadership. The three main European powers, Britain, France and Germany have all, to varying extents, failed to assume responsibility or initiative in security affairs that stretch beyond their own immediate concerns. Some of the factors behind this are held in common by all, such as the effects of economic recession, while others, like Germany's constitutional restrictions, are more particular. The factors shaping the respective defence policies in each country are considered in detail, as are their relations with the various regional or international organizations with security roles.

Since the US has been the centre of Western Europe's security and one of the main actors in Cold War Europe, a detailed examination of the US's future role in European security is necessary. The US will have a highly influential role to play in the design and configuration of Europe's security arrangements – and, it is argued, not necessarily a positive role. Part II concludes by arguing that there is *no* coherent leadership in European security. Each of the powers has, to varying extents, actively sought to avoid positions of responsibility and com-mitment in deference to national preoccupations.

Part III examines the euphemistically titled 'European Security Archi-tecture'. As a logical extension of Part II, the lack of leadership is reflected in the institutional chaos that currently presides in security matters. In theory, the institutions examined – the CSCE, the Council of Europe, the EC, NATO and the WEU – are supposed to form a 'network of interlinking institutions'. Instead of doing so, the new se-curity architecture that has emerged since the end of the Cold War is one characterized by overlapping responsibilities which may lead either to paralysis as each waits for the other to respond, or to institutional turf battles. Institutions in and of themselves have no life of their own. It is states, groups and individuals that give them life. Accordingly, the reasons why states wish to enhance or detract from the stature of a given institution is examined in detail.

The fourth, and final, section looks at developments in Central and Eastern Europe and the extent to which their security interests are (or are not) incorporated into existing or nascent security structures. In spite of the existence of institutional affiliations between these countries, such as the North Atlantic Cooperation Council, Europe is far away from a pan-European security arrangement. At best, the Central Europeans remain second-class citizens who are allowed to sit at the table but are given no formal guarantees and little hope of membership of the select 'clubs'.

Although the book was written during the struggles in Bosnia and the outcome or resolution of the conflict remains unknown, it was felt that it would be amiss not to evaluate the effects of the conflict upon European security. What the outcome may be is not particularly important since there are lessons that can already be drawn from the initial failure of any country or institution to respond decisively.

Before embarking upon the analysis outlined above, some initial definitions are essential. Since the end of the Cold War many fundamentals that underpinned assumptions about security have been undermined. Notions that are central to any study of international relations and conflict have changed, particularly what is understood by the terms 'power' and 'security'.

POWER AND SECURITY

The memorable scenes of Germans tearing down the Berlin Wall seemed to signify a time of hope, and it was this act, more than any other, that signified the end of the Cold War. For a brief period a feeling of euphoria swept over Europe and politicians began to spend peace dividends in their minds. The tearing down of the wall also signified the end of the confrontation between two military alliances, both of whom had faced each other across a divided Germany. It also heralded the end of an era of precarious stability but also one marked by a clear conception of threat.

Now that the euphoria has died down and some of the prognosticators are smugly looking at the resurgence of racially motivated attacks in Germany, the internal tensions within the European Community,

the economic woes of the US, and the threat of mass migration from
North Africa and the ex-Soviet Union, economic dislocation in the
former Soviet Union, and the dissolution of Yugoslavia, it appears
that the unctuous 'stability' that marked the Cold War years may have
been swapped for one that is very bit as unstable. This pessimistic
view of the Europe that emerged out of the Cold War needs to be
balanced by the optimistic stance which observes that the post-Cold War
Europe, featuring potentially huge reductions in the levels of conventional and nuclear armaments in Europe, is one where the chances of
major war have substantially diminished. The types of wars that have
created countries, destroyed others and moved borders in the past are
less likely to occur *between* countries but may happen *within* countries.

Of the many intellectual tasks confronting analysts trying to understand Europe's post-Cold War security, the first challenge is to reach
an understanding of what security has become in the post-Cold War
world. At the centre of any concept of security is the military and
their role in maintaining, or undoing, order and stability. However, to
define security solely in military terms would convey a profoundly
misleading impression of contemporary Europe. Instead of concentrating exclusively on military security, which was synonymous with the
idea of the national security state and defence, the concept must now
include far more diffuse threats to security posed by migratory movements, self-determination, economic disruption, and the spread of
nationalism or irredentism across borders. The incorporation of these
factors into an understanding of the term 'security' clearly makes security a more complicated notion than its Cold War variant.

This, in turn, raises the problem of how to prioritize threats to security;
in the Cold War it was clear that the biggest threat was that of a
global nuclear exchange. In the post-Cold War world a good case could
be made for arguing that economic and social challenges to societies
are as important, or more important, than those of a purely military
nature when considered in terms of the stability of a given state. The
'invaders' crossing borders into various parts of Europe are no longer
stormtroopers. Instead they are refugees stealing across borders and
nationalist or ethnic groups working with determination within borders for change. The nature of these, and other, factors making for
instability demand coordinated action. Aside from these broader security
questions, there are many problems that fit more easily into traditional
military notions of security. Perhaps the best example of this is the
uncertainty stemming from the appearance of three new nuclear powers
in close proximity to Central and Western Europe.

Security in the post-Cold War context also demands that we back away from the bloc-to-bloc approaches to security which characterized the Cold War years. Security now has to be seen in global or transnational terms since there are problems that are simply beyond the influence or resources of any one nation to solve. These problems include factors such as the environment, desertification, the world population problem and hunger. The Chernobyl incident perhaps did more than any other to promote the environment as a serious concern. This has been underscored by the demise of the Eastern bloc and the revelations of the atrocious environmental damage to the entire region. The signing of multiple arms-control treaties, such as START I, START II, and the Chemical Weapons Convention, may contribute to long-term stability, but will pose immediate problems regarding the effective and safe disposal of large amounts of weapons-grade nuclear material and other toxic substances. Although these are security concerns only in the broadest sense of the term, they demand the attention of the developed countries. The Cold War exigencies monopolized not only these countries' attention, but also their resources.[1] Thus, within any European security design, there should be an acknowledgment of Europe's wider international responsibilities, which include full participation in peace-making and peace-enforcement operations as well as humanitarian activities. Yet, what has emerged since the end of the Cold War is a security structure that is still largely Western European in its focus and one which has proven reluctant to incorporate wider concepts of security.

Many threats in the twenty-first century will be transnational threats and will not lend themselves to solutions at national or regional levels. As Jessica Tuchman Mathews has observed, 'our accepted definitions of the limits of national security as coinciding with national borders is obsolete'. She recognized at the same time that overcoming our tendency to think in terms of 'national' security preoccupations is not going to be easy and that we will require 'social and institutional inventions comparable in scale and vision to the new arrangements conceived in the decade following World War II'.[2] It should also be stressed that security is *not* an absolute term since a state may be quite secure in some senses and insecure in others. Germans, for instance, may feel secure from the threat of major armed invasion but simultaneously anxious that the country will be 'invaded' by thousands of asylum seekers.

Any new security architecture must reflect not only the traditional military preoccupations, but also be concerned with the construction of a viable economic order which safeguards the emergent democracies. A new understanding of security is therefore the first step in addressing various challenges, but this must then be complemented by a shift in policy – a move that has generally not yet been made. There is evidence at official levels that the meaning of security has broadened, but it still remains a somewhat imprecise term. For instance, the 1990 London Declaration by the North Atlantic Council stated that 'security and stability do not lie solely in the military dimension, and we intend to enhance the political component of our Alliance.'[3] Whether this has been done is open to debate. Other governments and organizations have adopted a more extensive definition of security, but their ability to incorporate changes that reflect new security challenges remains limited.

The shift away from traditional notions of security poses a second related problem, which is the nature of *power* in the international system. The neo-realist idea of a struggle for power is predicated upon a common understanding of the concept of power. Hans Morgenthau acknowledges the difficulty of defining power when he states that 'power may comprise anything that establishes and maintains the control of man over man'.[4] The Cold War criteria, which hinged primarily around military definitions, have been replaced by new criteria which emphasize other factors, such as economic power and membership of the select clubs, such as the European Union (EU).

The changed notions of security suggest that the currency of power has swung away from military comparisons towards a far more complex, multifaceted conception of power. In short, power has become 'less fungible, less coercive and less tangible'.[5] The rise to international prominence of countries like Germany and Japan, the collapse of the Soviet Union, the democratization of Eastern Europe, the advent of newly industrialized countries (NICs) in the Pacific basin, and the process of European integration, all suggest the need for a re-examination of those traditional notions of power that attribute primacy of place to military strength.[6] Events during the Cold War, such as the Arab OPEC members' 1973 oil embargo, or the Teheran hostage crisis of 1979, where the US was made to look impotent, have also aided this process.

Attempts at redefining the nature of power in the international system must also be wary of pointing to the forty-five-year post-war period as evidence of the decline in utility of military strength. The end of the Cold War has already seen several conflicts that have commanded international attention – the Gulf War, the Yugoslav and Caucasus crises stand out. The essentially anarchic nature of the international system, which underpins any bipolar or multipolar model, still means that military strength still has and probably always will have utility. The question is, what is its *relative* value?

Clearly military power continues to have some utility, for reasons of self-defence or collective defence related to guarding or defending territory, but the amount of forces required is less. The overt threats to territory, which characterized the Cold War years, have in many instances been replaced by claims to territory from *within* countries by ethnic groups. The major European powers, who formerly displayed a *penchant* for relieving neighbours of tracts of territory, are now woven together in collaborative patterns of behaviour that are most evident in the economic realm and are emerging in political and security areas. The use of force for territorial aggrandizement between these powers is most unlikely. Where territorial disputes do exist, due to vying claims, there is obviously the potential for conflict. These threats, however, do not exist between any of the major powers and, where they do exist, they do not threaten to destabilize Europe as a whole. This does not mean that Western Europe should not be concerned. On the contrary, ethnic disputes elsewhere will have effects for Europe that could be damaging while not necessarily destabilizing. The effects, however, could be sufficiently harmful to give the Western Europeans and their institutions a vested interest in the promotion of stability, democracy and prosperity to their east.

Stability has all too often been imposed by victors on the vanquished, normally by one power in particular. Such imposition was the cause of resentment and ultimately war in the case of Germany in the inter-war years. The relative peace that Europe enjoyed in the Cold War years was largely the result of superpower ability to impose or establish an armed standoff through the possession of enormously destructive military arsenals. In the post-Cold War period, the lack of a monopoly of economic, political and military pre-eminence by any one state, accompanied by uncertainty about what type of power is most relevant, has led not to a realist-type power struggle but, in the security field, to something more akin to a reverse-realist paradigm – a competition to avoid positions of leadership and responsibility and to shift the burden of responsibility to another party. An example of this type of behaviour was the lack of any coherent response or initiative on the part of Europe and North America to the deteriorating situation in Bosnia. It is against this confused background where military power has *less* sway, but still has some, that the issue of the future of European security must be considered.[7]

Power may be a vague term, having much to do with perception, but its diffuse nature has three important ramifications for European security:

1. Traditional notions of power measured mainly in terms of military muscle have given way to more complex measures and, as a result of this, the clear hierarchies between allies have either eroded (in the case of NATO) or disappeared (in the case of the Warsaw Treaty Organization). More specifically, the remarkable changes in Europe and the diminution of the importance of military power, in particular the attention given to nuclear armaments, demands a redefinition of the role of the only superpower to survive the Cold War – the US – and its relations to Europe. For so long the US was accustomed to play the role of *primus inter pares* but, faced with serious problems of its own, the US is now faced with the difficult task of coming to terms with its domestic woes whilst simultaneously redefining its post-Cold War interests.

2. International Relations scholars have habitually attributed notions of power and influence to the state. The state was seen as *the* actor to which responsibility for acts could be attributed. While some theories did advance beyond simplistic state-centric paradigms, such as regime theory, it has become increasingly unsatisfactory to think in these terms. In a global system that is highly interdependent and where there are many non-governmental and transnational organizations that wield considerable influence, a more sophisticated and complex view of who the actors are on the world stage is needed. Attributing notions of power and influence to the state is also inadequate in the light of developments in Europe since 1989. There are numerous states that may well be undermined from within and not, as the realists would have it, as the result of competition between states for power and influence.

3. The general recognition that there is less likelihood of conflict between the major European powers poses serious institutional questions. New instruments of cooperation and collaboration have to be designed or adapted from existing ones to reach cooperative solutions to problems that threaten instability. Since the Western Europeans are no longer artificially protected from the problems that beset Eastern Europe, any new security designs must be pan-European in scope and look beyond military notions of containment and defence to other tools that can be utilized to enhance the prospects for stability in Europe. Economics will be of particular significance.

Intellectually there is the challenge of identifying a paradigm or analytical framework with which to identify the security problems facing

Europe and their potential solutions. There would appear to be no all-encompassing model explaining European security in the post-Cold War world. Neo-realist ideas have probably done more to hinder our understanding of post-Cold War Europe since the constant references to nineteenth- and twentieth-century struggles encourage inaccurate historical assumptions, as well as serving to camouflage the fact that the Europe of 1914, or 1933, is a radically different Europe from that of the 1990s. Even other conceptual tools, such as regime theory, have become muddied as the distinctions between the regimes blur and lose the analytical clarity that they enjoyed in the Cold War years.

Concepts such as 'national interest' have also become immensely difficult to pin down, in large part because it has become virtually impossible to attribute actions to a state as a unitary actor. Thus the idea of the state having a clear monopoly on power and that states will compete for power in a competitive 'zero sum' manner is inaccurate. Networks of interdependence, the existence of multiple international governmental organizations and collaboration, make it difficult for states to monopolize power and to use it in a simplistic power-political competition with other states.

The immense changes in Europe and elsewhere since 1989 have outpaced the ability of scholars of International Relation to explain much of what has happened, or to predict what may happen. The realist–idealist debate has exhausted itself and there is, as of yet, no satisfactory paradigm to explain the immense changes of the past few years. Two approaches to post-Cold War European security issues seem to have become popular, one of which is not of central importance to this study, the other is.

The first, that of drawing historical comparisons with previous periods of European history which occurred just before or after a major war, is rampant – even among political scientists who may normally disdain such techniques. Most of these comparisons are confusing and do little to help our understanding of contemporary Europe. The second, arises from a fascination with the new European Security Architecture, based on the study of the internal and external dynamics of organizations.[8] This is a seemingly natural reaction to a time of upheaval. There are numerous examples of institutions encapsulating the aspirations of states and even individuals for a more stable and enduring regional or international system after a period of turmoil – such as the 1814 Congress of Vienna, the League of Nations and the United Nations. The Cold War became institutionalized through the Warsaw Treaty Organization and the North Atlantic Treaty Organization. It seems only natural that responses to security concerns in post-Cold War Europe will be sought through institutional arrangements.

There are, though, some important asymmetries between the situation of Europe in the 1990s and that of Europe, for example, in 1919 or 1945. All of the institutions mentioned above were created as the result of a war; whatever institutional structures emerge in the 1990s will not arise as the result of a war. This is a significant difference since it allows for careful reflection about the security order that is desired and also avoids the stigma of shaping a security order around what victors see fit to impose on the vanquished.

The emphasis in this study will be upon the examination of the various options based upon existing institutions that may be adapted, modified or scrapped. This does not specifically rule out the possibility of new organizations emerging, such as a European Security Organization[9] or a European Defence Organization.[10] However, many of the suggestions for 'new' machinery are derivative. In the examples above, they are conceptually and, to an extent, organizationally based upon the WEU and CSCE and the EC and WEU respectively. The object therefore will be to examine in detail the adaptability of the existing institutions and the positions of the main actors within the institutions.

So far the case has been made for the adoption of a wider definition of security, based on military, economic and political factors. It has also been argued that power is a diffuse term and, since it is closely related to security, it follows that power must also be considered in a highly diverse manner which also incorporates relative measures beyond crude comparisons of military hardware and numbers of troops. One further term deserves consideration: that is, exactly which Europe is being talked about in the security context.

WHICH EUROPE?

The artificial division of Cold War Europe into East and West, separated by Winston Churchill's 'Iron Curtain', established a precise picture of Europe. The 'security' Europe, which was the basis of the divide, was mirrored in the 'political' and 'economic' Europes. The picture in the West was only complicated slightly by the neutral and non-aligned countries. The countries were linked by institutional ties – NATO, the WEU, the Council of Europe and the European Community (EC) and European Free Trade Area (EFTA). In the same manner the 'Eastern' bloc had its security branch, the Warsaw Treaty Organization (WTO).

The economic counterpart to the WTO was the Council for Mutual Economic Assistance (CMEA). Much of the Cold War was spent bean-counting the military assets of respective military alliances, or calculating division equivalents with various weighted factors, to reach a quantifiable assessment of the threat and relative power. At least the Cold War had the underlying simplicity of the reassurance about whose gun muzzles were pointing where.

The end of the Cold War has meant confusion about what *European* security is – indeed, there is confusion about what Europe itself is. To some it is the area stretching from the Atlantic to the Urals, to others it is Brest to Brest, or Vancouver to Vladivostock,[11] and to some it may stretch as far west as San Francisco. But since when has the US been part of Europe? If the US is excluded, how can Russia be included? If Russia is obviously European, how can the US be excluded as a 'counterweight'? The eastern extremities are also problematical; should the five Asian republics of the ex-Soviet Union be included or not? Even if Europe is assumed to be the north-west portion of the Asian land mass, this still leaves the eastern boundaries vague. To reflect accurately what Europe has become in security terms we may have to borrow the geographers' term: Eurasia.

Even if one ignores the niceties of the geographical debate and concentrates on the *institutional Europe*, the 'boundaries' still remain obscure. In each case the Europes being referred to are different – ranging from the Europe of ten for the WEU, to sixteen for NATO with some East and Central European countries with quasi-membership which together form the North Atlantic Cooperation Council (NACC), to the Conference on Security and Cooperation in Europe (CSCE) which will doubtlessly expand beyond the current membership of fifty-three, which includes almost all of the ex-Soviet Union, the Baltic States, the rest of Europe and North America. This is the *institutional* Europe.

There is also the *cultural-historical Europe* which has evolved over four hundred years. This Europe will have a highly significant bearing on security issues since cultural and religious animosities are driving many of Europe's separatist groups. Virtually every European country has pressure from one or more separatist groups as the Basques, the Tyrolians, the Welsh, the Lombardi League or the Transylvanians, remind us. The weaker countries of Eastern Europe will find the competing demands of various cultural and religious minorities a serious challenge to their stability.

While disintegrative forces will have a hand in shaping Europe, so too will integrative forces. The existence of two political blocs, each headed by a superpower, served as a clear expression of Europe's subordination to the superpowers. The disappearance of one superpower and the decreasing influence that the US can bring to bear on European security affairs has led to a resurgence of interest in adopting a European identity. Although Europe will never exert the influence it did in 1914, when over 80 per cent of the world's surface was administered by one European power or another, the pull of a common European identity underpins much of the European integration process.

Gorbachev popularized the notion of Europe stretching from the 'Atlantic to the Urals', nominally as a cultural-historical entity but also as a *political entity*.[12] Although there may be a common cultural heritage based on the Renaissance and the Enlightenment, which may act as 'magnets' in the search for mutual understanding, it is also clear that the Europe from the Atlantic to the Urals was a notion that was promoted with some enthusiasm during the Cold War, since it was a version of Europe that excluded North America. This is clearly at variance with former-President Bush's insistence that Europe 'whole and free' includes active North American participation.

Europe can also be thought of in the *analytical sense*. This Europe is normally a fairly small one, confined in this century to the study of five main powers (Germany, France, Italy, Britain and Russia) and the balance of power between them. The latter lost much of its relevance as a strictly 'European' actor after the Bolshevik Revolution. Much of the academic discourse turned to the remaining four and the relative balance of power between them. Two world wars and the need for outside intervention destroyed the European balance of power irreparably. The world wars, especially World War I, also served to destroy Europe as a global actor and confined Europe henceforth to a regional or theatre actor. The Cold War era was marked by the ability of the two superpowers to bring a conflict to this theatre. During this period the impulses shaping European security were seldom of European volition. Some problems were incidentally solved, at least temporarily, by the partition of Europe – most notably the 'German question'.

The formation of two security blocs, built around NATO and the Warsaw Treaty Organization, reinforced the tendency to think in terms of theatres of operation, communism and capitalism, totalitarianism and democracy and, most apparent, East and West. The post-Cold War Europe, which may one day promise to be a 'Europe whole and free', requires an enormous psychological adjustment. The *idea* of an Eastern and Western Europe has to be undone, the grinding economic deprivation of parts of eastern Europe has to be eliminated, responsibility for the security of other European countries has to be assumed in the absence of superpower guarantors, the institutions which hark back to the Cold War (the EC and the WEU in the West and COMECON/CMEA in the East) have to be restructured to reflect the changes in Europe. The Yugoslav crisis serves as a sad example of the failure to make this transition on the part of most of the security-related European institutions. It also illustrates the extent to which Europe, at least in security terms, remains primarily a Western concept with an underlying unwillingness to address seriously the security problems of the neighbours to the east.

The idea of a European security identity, whatever its institutional base, is necessarily a fluid one and is normally a concept associated with the drive towards European Union within the EC/WEU framework. Until there is some consensus upon what Europe is in security terms, it seems logical to suggest that different problems demand differing responses from the various security institutions that are part of the erroneously named 'security architecture'.

What should be avoided in the various institutional versions of Europe is that Central and Eastern Europe be ignored or, if security guarantees are advanced, that they become a buffer for Western Europe; the impression should not be given to Moscow that NATO has merely moved east. The answer to what Europe will become in security terms may well depend on what the problem is and whether it is in the interests of the central actors to intervene. Here again, the Yugoslav crisis was assumed to be on the periphery and of no real concern to the main Western European countries or the US. Peripheral concerns, however, have a nasty habit of becoming central preoccupations.

The apparent straightforwardness of the Cold War and the assumptions that could be made about power, security and the shape of Europe have been replaced by a confusing and rapidly changing Europe. For the sake of clarity in the discussion which follows, some assumptions about post-Cold War Europe in the 1990s must be made. These are:

(1) The demise of the Cold War East–West confrontation calls for the construction of a pan-European security order. This is based upon the understanding that there are security concerns that cannot be confined to Western or Eastern Europe; nor can they be met with the resources of any one country. They therefore demand pan-European responses based upon non-violent mechanisms of conflict resolution. Any such order shall not deliberately exclude the CIS countries, particularly the RSFR and the Ukraine, nor those of North America.

(2) Security, as a term, must transcend the mere military connotations

to include the grave economic, social and human rights issues that underpin democracy and, ultimately, peace.

(3) The institutional representation of Europe's new security order will come from existing institutions or derivatives of existing ones.

(4) Europe will not be completely denuclearized.

Based upon these assumptions, an examination will be made of the willingness of the main security actors in Europe (including the US) to embrace new definitions of security and pan-European approaches. Few things can be certain in a time of such rapid change and transition, but one is: the challenges facing European security in the post-Cold War era clearly call for a different European security order, quite unlike that of the last forty years.

Part I
Assessing Europe's Security Concerns

1 The Nature of Post-Cold War Security

The end of the East–West struggle has upset the simple bipolar lens with which the major powers were used to looking at the world. The lack of a clearly identifiable 'enemy' figure has contributed to the profusion of new 'threats' and to the neo-realist assumption that a multipolar world is, of necessity, more unstable than the bipolar system typifying the Cold War era.

As has been discussed, the post-Cold War meaning of security is far more difficult to pin down and, for that reason, advocates of neo-realist approaches to international relations tend to assume that the disappearance of the bipolar Cold War structure has given way to what John Mearsheimer calls 'the anarchy of international relations'.[1] The realists are correct in predicting an era of instability, complete with violence and the likelihood of conflict – the fate of the Bosnians and the bloody conflict in the Caucasus being just two examples.

The end of the Cold War has yet to usher in an era of peace, let alone a 'peace dividend'. However, neo-realists tend to jump to the conclusion that because the international system has reverted to a state of anarchy, the prospect of major war and crisis in Europe 'is likely to increase dramatically now that the Cold War is receding into history'.[2] Neo-realist approaches suggest that Europe is faced with a myriad of threats that seem quite overwhelming. The new insecurity which, ironically, former-President Bush referred to as the 'New World Order', is characterized by vying territorial and ethnic problems as well as the emergence of organized terror. The Cold War seems, in retrospect, more stable than it actually was. It is worth briefly reviewing the 'stability' of the Cold War, since it is often used as the benchmark to explain the *instability* of the post-Cold War international system.

The stability of the Cold War was ultimately based on the threat of a cataclysmic nuclear exchange, in the event that deterrence broke down. Stability was, therefore, built upon the existence of two equivalent military arsenals and the threat of mutual annihilation.[3] Although a nuclear threat still exists, the nature of that threat has changed significantly. Total annihilation as the result of a strategic nuclear exchange does not loom large on the horizon, as George Bush indicated in his 1992 election campaign when he spoke of the absence of 'the nuclear nightmare'. The Intermediate-Range Nuclear Force (INF) and the Strategic Arms Reduction Talks (START I and II) treaties have taken substantial strides towards the removal of this threat.[4] This does not mean that a nuclear exchange is out of the question; it clearly is not. Nor does it mean that the problems posed by proliferation should not be treated seriously. It does mean that the post-Cold War world may offer an increased likelihood of conflict and violence, but *not* annihilation which, ultimately, is what the Cold War posited.

The nostalgia for the Cold War security system and the stability that it offered is also based upon questionable assumptions about the internal cohesion of the blocs. In spite of, or because of, the overwhelming role of the superpowers and their respective arsenals, there were signs of dissention within the blocs that were to play a dramatic role in the tumbling of the Soviet colossus and the weakening of transatlantic ties. If the bipolar system of the Cold War years was such a stable one, then why would lesser powers within the blocs wish to revise the system? It could be argued that the stability of the Cold War period was *imposed* on states that were economically weak and had little ability to bargain with their hegemons. With the growth in strength and assertiveness of Western European allies, accompanied by a relative decline in influence of the US over its allies, the artificiality of the East–West divide became apparent to the allies, as did the undesirability of basing a security system upon mutual annihilation. The Soviet Union maintained 'stability' in its sphere of influence by occasional but dramatic intervention, as in the Hungarian case in 1956 and Czechoslovakia in 1968. This version of stability may have avoided war, but it did so at an enormous cost to basic human rights and dignity. Stability was also built upon an economic base, in the case of the Soviet Union and to a lesser extent that of the US, that was of questionable durability.

The myth of stability in the Cold War era is also based upon the comparative notion that Europe is now faced with a bewildering array of new threats. However, on close analysis, many of the threats are not so much new but, rather, old concerns that were obscured by the preoccupation with the Cold War and authoritarian regimes. The illusion of a more insecure post-Cold War international system is also based upon broader post-Cold War interpretations of security.[5] For example, a few years ago not many would have considered environmental problems a 'security' threat, whereas now such problems have found a firm place in new security literature. The monopoly imposed by the Cold War on East–West issues obscured other transnational threats that were struggling to find a voice in the international arenas – and failing more often than not. With the end of the Cold War, these problems have begun to find a voice through international institutions, like the UN, that no longer find themselves preoccupied with, or paralysed by, superpower antagonisms. These suppressed 'new threats' have contributed to the illusion that the Cold War era was one of stability and that the post-Cold War world is one of instability.

Furthermore, ignorance or secretiveness can no longer serve as legitimate excuses to disregard other types of security threat that could be seen as spin-offs of the Cold War, such as the threats posed by pollution, the ex-Soviet domestic nuclear programme, the problem of toxic-waste disposal, the status of Russian minorities in the new Soviet republics (most notably in the Baltic republics), the threat of economic collapse throughout Eastern Europe, widespread black-marketeering and the potential for massive migratory movements fleeing from ethnic and religious persecution or economic hardship. This list is not exhaustive, but it serves to illustrate the immense diversity and complexity of post-Cold War security.

Harking back to the bipolar system as a period of nostalgic stability is misleading and may also have important ramifications for the design of Europe's security institutions. In the first place, there is nothing inherently stable about bipolar systems. It was, after all, the politics of bipolarity that induced the Peloponnesian war between Athens and Sparta.[6] Second, many of the problems that have been or are presently encountered in the post-Cold War period actually existed during the Cold War, or they were temporarily obscured by it, as has been discussed above. Third, other problems arose as a direct result of the Cold War; the most obvious example being the arms race between the superpowers and the resultant weakening of the Soviet economy. Fourth, the reluctance to let go of cherished institutions, like NATO, is partially based upon reference to the success of Western institutions in ultimately achieving peace and surviving the dangers of the Cold War. By extension, the logic is that such institutions can continue to play a successful and constructive role in a vastly changed security environment.

SMOKE AND MIRRORS

The danger of becoming swamped by the multifarious threats facing Europe, with the attendant risk of paralysis, can be avoided by distinguishing at an early stage between those challenges to security that deserve serious consideration and those that are either overpromoted or that are not urgent. Two in particular fall into the latter category. The first set of concerns arises from the historical parallels with the Europe of 1866, 1913 or 1933–38 which are trundled out to illustrate the point that Europe has been historically unstable and that many of the elements which led to instability are once again present. The second exaggerated threat is that of fundamentalism: this stems primarily from ethnocentric Western notions which assume that Islam and democracy are incompatible and that Islam must therefore be a threat to democratization. It is also based upon the general failure to differentiate between different strains of Islam. It is argued, in both cases, that these are exaggerated threats and that by focusing on them, other more important problems are not given the attention or emphasis they deserve.

One fallacy that should be dismissed early on is that there is any value in positing inaccurate historical analogies between present-day Europe and Europe in 1913, or even Europe at the turn of the century. The main cause of disintegration of order into war in these earlier periods was typically the failure of balance-of-power configurations. It was fashionable to blame Germany as the chief culprit in the Franco–Prussian War of 1870, World War I and even World War II. The Franco–Prussian War was, however, partly a result of French diplomatic meddling; to an extent, the French encouraged the war. World War I can be seen as the outcome of a prolonged struggle between Germany and Britain; and World War II can be attributed, in part, to the strictures of the Versailles Treaty, which were unacceptable and odious to the German people (especially the War Guilt Clause).[7]

Instability during the period 1870–1939 can be attributed to a perceived imbalance which, stated somewhat simplistically, threatened to pit two of the three powers (Britain, France and Germany) against a third. Russia also played an important part in the events leading to World War II. Imbalances in power distribution between states are no longer relevant for the above-mentioned powers. Individually they can no longer claim to be the strongest military or economic power. Interdependence between the first three has developed to the extent that war between themselves has become almost unthinkable. This does not mean that residual fears about Germany's role in contemporary Europe do not exist; however, these concerns tend to be about economic expansion and the possible pursuit of some historical variant of *Mitteleuropa*. The possibility of Germany again invading Belgium, Poland or France is highly fanciful.

The Europe that emerged from the Cold War is radically different from the Europe of 1870 or 1918. The main difference is the existence of a highly developed network of interdependent political and economic relations. This does not mean that clashes are unthinkable (Yugoslavia being a case in point), but major wars between the main European powers are unlikely. The complex institutional links which weave the European countries into integrative structures has blurred many of the traditional notions essential to the neo-realist tradition. Additionally it is increasingly difficult to identify clearly domestic policy from foreign policy, just as it is also becoming more difficult to distinguish national sovereignty from supranational power vested in the various European organizations. Indeed, the web of supranational institutions makes Post-Cold War Europe radically different from its historical antecedents.

The strongest facet of the historical analogies argument is in reference to Germany. The concern expressed by European powers about once again having a strong, unified Germany at the centre of Europe, pursuing its *Ostpolitik* to the detriment of its Western ties, is exaggerated. Clearly, the economic strains encountered because of unification, the less than enthusiastic reception given by German businessmen to investment opportunities in Eastern Europe, and the immense importance of EC markets to Germany, clearly identifies Western Europe as more important to Germany than any other actual or potential markets.

The post-unification, racially inspired violent incidents, coupled with the asylum problem, have given rise to legitimate grounds for concern about Germany's general direction, and reawakened historical doubts about German character. The growth of nationalism and neo-Nazi movements in Germany's main cities is a sinister development, but it is a problem that could have been alleviated by immediate tough action by the Kohl government. Unfortunately, not until the Mölln murders in late November 1992, were decisive countermeasures taken. In spite of historical fears provoked by these developments (complete with inaccurate analogies with 1933[8]), these incidents remain essentially internal problems that have not been reflected in German security or foreign policy. It should also be noted that there has been a resurgence of right-wing activity not only in Germany but in other European countries as well.

The realist's case for a 'back to the future' scenario rests upon the Hobbesian view that the international system is essentially anarchic, and will eventually result in a 'war of all against all'.[9] The system may well be anarchical, but this does not mean that it is totally bereft of order or notions of international society that modify the way that states behave; nor does it mean that the system is prone to irrevocable and bloody breakdown.[10] The existing network of European and international governmental organizations may not challenge the primacy of the nation-state, but they are sufficiently influential to modify the way states behave towards each other. The threats to stability, and particularly Mearsheimer's much touted hyper-nationalism, are indeed present; but they are present in the *smaller* powers, not in the main European powers to the extent that any would be willing to use aggression as a means of overthrowing the established system and replacing it with another. This at least is a lesson that Europeans have learnt following the experience and pain of two world wars.

THE SEARCH FOR A NEW 'ISM'

Inevitably, with the fall of communism and its Marxist ideological trappings in many parts of the world, there has been an almost subconscious search for the new 'ism'. The present 'ism' being touted about is Islamic fundamentalism, the worthy successor to Stalinism, Nazism and communism. As one author remarks, 'The specter is symbolized by the Middle Eastern Muslim fundamentalist, a Khomeni-like creature armed with a radical ideology and nuclear weapons.'[11] Islamic fundamentalism, it is feared, could make significant inroads into the world's fifty or so Islamic nations and lead to a confrontation with the incompatible Judeo-Christian democratic nations. If this is taken to be a real threat, the wars of the future will be more akin to the Crusades or *jihad*. After discussing the threats posed by the disintegration of the Soviet Union and especially the nuclear angle, one writer added that:

> The possibility that Islamic fundamentalism, albeit of a different var-iety than that of Iran, might gain the allegiance of the political elite and publics in Central Asia is also quite alarming. In the long run, what transpires there may well affect the destiny of such countries as Turkey and Pakistan, and of the Near East in general.[12]

Such statements are typical of the vague unease felt at the apparent growth of Islamic fundamentalism.[13] While there may be a threat posed by Iran's attempts to gain nuclear weapons and to become the regional superpower, this bid does not mean that, *ipso facto*, it will be able to export Islamic fundamentalism. As is argued in more detail below, the spread of Islam in Africa, the ex-Soviet republics of Central Asia, and south-eastern Europe is generally not of the militant Shiite variety. There may also be problems reconciling Sunni Islam with the *shari'a* and Western notions of democracy, but this does not necessarily imply a security threat to Europe nor the violent mobilization of the Muslim population in Europe. If there is gravity to the fundamentalist threat, then the lessons of the fight against communism should be applied: ideology cannot be effectively combatted with guns.

The attraction of labelling threats in terms of 'isms' is that these labels can quickly be applied and become synonymous with a particular threat or danger. For example, the positing of communism in the McCarthyite era had the desired effect of presenting a catch-all threat. As with other eras, the search for a new 'ism' runs the risk of over-simplifying the complexity of the threats.

There are a number of questions raised in the presentation of Islamic fundamentalism as a serious threat to the security of Europe. What is the 'variety' of fundamentalism that is being referred to? Need the spread of Islam be a security 'threat' (when there are numerous instances of Western nations having close relations with Islamic countries that are far from democratic). How is the West perceived by Islamic countries? To what extent does the export of Western political ideology pose a challenge to Islam? Finally, is there a double standard at work (for instance, when Islamic fundamentalists were engaged in the struggle against Soviet forces in Afghanistan they were lauded as 'freedom fighters')?

In the specifically European context, the origins of the Islamic 'threat' go back to the 1970s, when an influx of immigrants from Africa and west Asia led to the growth of an Islamic identity within Europe. No doubt much of the perception of a threat arises from the tendency to equate Islam with fundamentalism. This misperception partly explains the growth of extreme right reactions to Islam. Much of the misperception is understandable, since most Europeans are not exposed to Islamic thought in a systematic way. Instead, European attitudes toward Islam are formulated by episodes, such as the 1979 Iranian Revolution following the downfall of the Shah, incidents of terrorism such as the 1992 bombing of the World Trade Center, hostage-taking and the Salman Rushdie affair. Hysteria is also whipped up with exaggerations of immigration problems and 'threats' to European culture, for example, by Jean-Marie Le Pen's *Front National* in France. Immigrants from Islamic cultures account for a small proportion of the EC population – around 2 per cent. This may rise in particular countries to anywhere from 5 per cent to 20 per cent, depending on the population concentration in low-rent urban areas.[14] It is probably their relatively small numbers that make them an easy target for discrimination and scaremongering.

Islam is also portrayed as a growing force in world politics, covering the Middle East, North and West Africa, the former Soviet Asian republics,[15] India and Western China. However, there are still a very small number of avowedly Islamic states – only Iran, Morocco, Pakistan and Saudi Arabia meet the criteria of being states that are regulated by Islamic norms.[16] The instances of Islamic fundamentalist violence or terror that contribute to the equation of fundamentalism with threat do not necessarily stem from these avowedly Islamic states; the activities of Hizbollah in Lebanon and Dawa in Iraq being but two examples. But it is Shiite activism and violence that dominates Western minds, and out of this the new threat is extrapolated.

However, as Robin Wright has argued,[17] the growth of Islam has been more prevalent among the Sunni, who account for around 85 per cent of the world's one billion Muslims.[18] It is also the Sunni who are most prevalent in the area stretching from Africa to the Levant, the CIS, Western China and Indonesia. Wright sums up the difference between the resurgence of Shiite fundamentalism and the resurgence of Sunni activism as follows:

> Unlike the extremism that typified the first resurgence – in political upheavals as well as suicide bombings, hijackings and hostage seizures – the new Islamic activism is now characterized by attempts to work within the system rather than outside it.[19]

The problem of constructing pluralist states is not going to be easy for Islam since it is not only a set of spiritual beliefs but a system for organizing and ruling society based on a divine law or *shari'a*. The difficulties associated with reconciling Islam with the interests of minorities (particularly Jews in the Central Asian ex-Soviet republics) and independence will also not be easy. While the spectre of a series of *jihad* cannot be ruled out, the lessons have hopefully been drawn from past attempts at radical reform in Iran and Lebanon. The Islam facing the West now is not necessarily extremist. As Wright points out, there is tremendous diversity within Islamic activism, which does not seem necessarily to rely upon extremism. Even in those cultures that are commonly thought of as strictly Islamic there is enormous diversity.[20] The Saudi and Pakistani cases illustrate that the character of Islamic fundamentalism does not need to mimic the Iranian type. The US and other Western nations have had close ties with Saudi Arabia and Pakistan, which includes military assistance, and good relations have been maintained. The differences within Islam also illustrate that it cannot be a unified threat; nor can it be conceived of as a 'bloc', as communism was.

The fear that Iranian-type fundamentalism might be exported is a notion that is hard to support. The implication of such arguments is that Iran, as the first state wholly to embrace Islam as the basis of state policy, is worth emulating. As one writer suggests, 'So far it has not been a convincing model to the rest of the world, but neither has it had much chance to demonstrate its policies on anything other than a war footing.'[21] In the Iranian case the increasingly shrill anti-American sentiment may have backfired, as a process of 'quietly developing sympathy for the United States' is growing, 'precisely because the regime is anti-US'.[22] There is much that the US, in particular, and to a lesser extent its European allies, can do to alleviate the potential for Islamic radicalism. Much of the radical movement evolves from anti-Western sentiment which, in part, is a reflection upon the values and actions of these societies themselves.

The popularity of the Iranian model can be challenged. After fourteen years of fundamentalism in Iran, popular resentment is 'deep and widespread'.[23] During this period there has been an increasing dependence on imported basic necessities, a 50 per cent decrease in real income, the creation of a super-rich business class, 25 per cent unemployment, 20 per cent annual inflation, and a critical housing shortage for middle- and low-income people.[24] If these are the fruits of fundamentalism, it is hard to see why this would provide an example to emulate. The appeal of Islamic fundamentalism may well prove to be transitory since it promised to provide an answer to the failures of nationalism and socialism in the Middle East in the aftermath of colonialism. The dictatorial regimes that have promised societal restructuring and development have been generally unsuccessful in their attempts to deliver these promises.

The question of whether Islam is compatible with democracy is still open. A recent test case, that of Algeria, has been disheartening. It would seem that the West tends to have little interest in this problem. The lack of comment from the West following the overthrow of Algeria's fledgling democracy by a junta is surprising, especially when the West has been preoccupied for years with anti-democratic communist regimes in various parts of the world. This Western silence could be interpreted as tacit support for anti-Islamic elements. The struggles of Algeria with radical Islam and the potentially more serious struggles in Egypt will further test the West's true interests in democracy. The successful handling of these two cases would do much to downplay the threat and to drive home the point that Islamic fundamentalism, with its accomplice terrorism, are unacceptable to international society.

The problems surrounding Islam and its compatibility with democracy pose a horse-and-cart question. Is it despotism working *through* Islamic regimes that is antithetical to democracy, or is it Islam itself that is fundamentally undemocratic? Mansour Farhanq, a former Iranian ambassador to the UN, has suggested that, 'An examination of the empirical evidence strongly suggests that it is not Islam but the pervasiveness of despotism that hinders democracy's advance in the region.'[25] Most of the Middle East countries, whether avowedly Islam or not, could be characterized as autocratic, which in turn feeds the instability of the region as a whole. To attribute this instability to Islamic fundamentalism alone would be an error.

Even if democracy and Islam do turn out to be incompatible, this does not necessarily mean that Islam is a threat. There are several countries that enforce the *shari'a* with whom the US and Europe have close relations, Saudi Arabia being the best example. Even in countries that are Islamic republics (this need not imply a theocracy of the Iranian type) there are moves afoot (for example, in Central Asia and Africa) to design an Islamic model of democracy. In the Middle East the 1991 Gulf War prompted a call for more democracy. Youssef Ibrahim observed that, 'ever since Kuwait was invaded, the single theme on which Arab writers and commentators in the Arab media have almost unanimously agreed has been the need for democracy and freedom.'[26] Even former allies of Iraq, like King Hussein of Jordan, have begun to distance themselves from Saddam Hussein's Ba'ath party and demanded the replacement of the Baghdad government with a pluralist democracy.

The concerns voiced in the West about the compatibility of Islam with democracy, and hence about stability, point to a lack of tolerance and understanding. As one author has noted:

> The west still considers itself as deserving to set the tempo for the rest of the world to follow. Patent as this is in the title and basic premise of Fukuyama's best-seller or in Binder's acknowledged presupposition that the whole world – and especially the Islamic part of it – must become politically liberal, it also prevails in the analyses of those who seek to explain what is truly fearful about calls for political Islam.[27]

Part of the incompatibility of Islam with Western notions of democracy can be explained by the lack of a clearly delineated political process. The calls for Islamic politics, by Abd al-Salam Faraj and Saykh Kishk in Egypt, Rached Ghannouchi in Tunisia, Muhammad Hussain Fadlallah in Lebanon and Ahmad Yassin of Hamas, point not to structures but visions. Within Islamic politics is an explicit rejection of Nasser's modified socialism or Khomeini's capitalist consumerism. But, beyond the desire to move towards a system that respects divine laws, there is little political guidance. Even where Islam is the basis for political opposition movements, the aim of the movements is usually to go back to the principles of the *Quran* and the *sunna* and upon this base to build a new social organization and ultimately an Islamic state. Such aims may seem to Western observers overtly political, but they need not be, since they are 'not committed to particular institutions or to political principles such as democracy and equality. They are concerned rather with individual morality and ethical behaviour, and to them the state is simply the force that encourages or requires the people to adhere to Islamic norms.'[28] Tolerance on the part of the West could lead to the existence on the perimeters of Europe of Islamic societies that may not be close but whose aims are not inimical. Indeed, a lack of tolerance and understanding leads to the image of a 'threat'.

Fears of more strident types of Islam moving into the newly independent republics in Central Asia may also be exaggerated. Iran has established embassies in these republics, as has Pakistan, and the indications are that cooperation is preferable to confrontation. The threat of the Iranian model being exported and militant Islam spreading like wildfire also overlooks the weakened economic state of Iran after the Khomeini revolution and eight years of war against Iraq. One author, with considerable knowledge of Soviet Central Asia, has commented that:

> Assessing the situation as a whole, one should point out the following. First, Islam as the symbol of national identity, of the return to the original culture, became extremely popular among the peoples of the former USSR. Second, Islam is used as a means of political mobilization by various political forces, democratic, conservative, and nationalist. Third, the Islamicist movement as such still prefers to appeal to democratic or nationalist ideas. This last factor is due to an awareness of the sentiments of the masses of the population, who, in most Muslim areas today, are not ready to support the idea of an Islamic state in its direct form.[29]

The Yugoslav embroglio has also prompted concerns about the possibility of a militant Islamic role in defence of Bosnia's Muslim population. In June 1992, Suleiman Demirel, Turkey's ex-Prime Minister, offered military assistance in the event of a conflict erupting with Serbia over the ethnic Albanians (who are Muslim) in Kosovo. Iran's Ayatollah Emami Kashani proposed the creation of an 'Islamic army'. The proposal occurred during a visit of the Bosnian foreign minister to Tehran in August 1992. However, in spite of repeated concern by Muslim countries about the fate of the Bosnian Muslims and the threat to those in the Kosovo region, unilateral action has been ruled out by Turkey and Iran. Of interest in the Yugoslav case is the fact that it was not the Bosnian Muslims who defined the conflict in sectarian terms; rather this was a distinction forced upon them by Christian Serbs and Croats. The concern over the fate of the Bosnian Muslims is understandable and, in so far as their concern can be interpreted as anti-Western, this stems from the suspicion harboured by members of the Organization of the Islamic Conference (OIC) that the 'United States and the Europeans have been so dilatory to act over Bosnia because an independent Bosnia would have been predominantly Islamic.'[30]

There are two basic choices that confront the west vis-à-vis Islam.[31] One could lead to coexistence and the other could lead to renewed containment and maybe conflict. The first is to reject the antagonistic image of Islam, based on Shiite fundamentalism and the US's struggle with Iran, and to press Muslim-dominated countries to adopt democratic processes. The benefit of this course is that even if the attempts at constructing Islamic democracy are not always successful, the West has made a clear statement of interest in democracy, which could be used to hold Islamic countries accountable for any abuse of democracy. To remain silent, or disengaged, could be interpreted as being guilty of anti-Islamic sentiment.

The second, and least desirable, alternative would be to try and contain Islam. How this could be done is uncertain and, even if it were possible, the cost would be extraordinary. Unlike communism, which is a political belief and a fairly modern one at that, Islam is a religious conviction stretching back many centuries. By attempting to challenge Islam, the West could also provide the impetus to unite the Islamic world against what they may perceive as a common oppressor. A new divide based on religion could be far more dangerous that one based on political ideology. Thus, the contention here is that Islam is not a grave threat to the West, much less an urgent security threat. It is, however, something that does require diplomatic action and open encouragement, from the US especially, for these countries to pursue democratic ideals. Islam can be thought of as a challenge, but if it is presented as a threat there is danger of it becoming a self-fulfilling prophecy.

2 European Security Challenges in the Post-Cold War World

Having identified the exaggerated threats, the more difficult task of identifying those areas that may pose security concerns to Europe will now be undertaken. At this point the use of the term 'threat' will also be dropped in favour of the word 'concern' or 'problem'. The idea of threat is too closely bound up with the Cold War notion of 'military threat'. The slightly more neutral word 'concern' helps to signify challenges to security that go beyond the military environs and demand non-military solutions. Five overlapping problems are touched upon. Although the list is by no means exhaustive, it will serve as a backdrop for subsequent discussion. The five problem areas are:

1. Weapons proliferation and the ex-Soviet nuclear arsenal.
2. Nationalism and irredentism.
3. Migratory pressures.
4. The role of Germany in any new European security order.
5. Implications for the security of Europe.

1. WEAPONS PROLIFERATION AND THE NUCLEAR THREAT FROM THE EX-SOVIET UNION

Problems for any future European security order will arise from *within* the ex-Soviet empire. The most visible problem is the re-emergence of old ethnic rivalries which were merely suspended, but not forgotten, for the duration of the Cold War. These problems are exacerbated by the virtual collapse of the CIS economies, political instability and the ambiguous role of the military. In addition to the numerous ethnic rivalries within the CIS republics, there are problems of some urgency in Bulgaria, which is suppressing its Turkish minority, and in Romania, which has problems with its Hungarian minority and its claims to Moldavia, in addition to the well-documented problems of the Albanian majority and Serbian minority in Kosovo, and Croatian and Serbian separatism to the north. These are primarily security concerns threatening the domestic stability of the countries involved, but they may easily spill over the borders. One feature of particular concern in this unstable picture is the role of nuclear weapons.

Amongst the other reforms started by Gorbachev was the gradual dismantling of much of the Soviet military apparatus, encoded in treaties, such as the INF treaty, and expressed in unilateral reductions. The dissolution of the Soviet Union puts Europe in an awkward dilemma. The reforms started by Gorbachev and continued by Yeltsin suggest that Moscow's accommodating stance is genuine and that any cooperative security arrangements for Post-Cold War Europe must not exclude Russia. Against this consideration must be balanced the consideration that the Soviet nuclear arsenal has been split between four countries, which necessitates the maintenance of a military counterweight to these nuclear forces. It is to the latter problem that we now turn.

The creation of fifteen independent republics with large armies, four[1] armed with nuclear weapons (some 27 000 warheads), out of the Soviet Union has created a potentially unstable scenario – although it is unclear what this may mean in security terms for European countries.[2] Of the total number of warheads, approximately 12 500 are *strategic*, deployed on land, bombers and nuclear submarines. Seventy-five per cent of the strategic missiles are on Russian territory. The Russian strategic nuclear arsenal stands at 1064 ICBMs, 940 SLBMs and 69 SSBNs as well as 101 heavy bombers – together amounting to 7449 warheads. Even so, the nuclear arsenal outside the Russian Federation is still substantial enough to give cause for concern: the Ukraine has 46 SS-24s and 130 SS-19s in addition to 21 TU-95 Bear-H19 strategic bombers (with a total of 1408 warheads). Kazakhstan has 104 SS-18s and 40 TU-95 Bear strategic bombers (making a total of 1360 warheads), and Belarus has 72 SS-25s.[3] The SS-19 missiles are already scheduled for destruction under START stipulations, while the SS-25s, which are mobile, could be relocated to Russia. The bombers are more problematical since they would need support bases and infrastructure in Russia before they could be moved. Tactical weapons, of which there are around 15 000 warheads,[4] were removed from Belarus and the Ukraine by July 1992 and are in the process of being destroyed on Russian territory. No resistance to this plan was encountered.

The nuclear and conventional forces of the CIS must exist in a highly unstable environment marked by the possibility of conflict between the former Soviet republics, such as Russia and the Ukraine, or widespread civil war spilling over into other parts of Europe. The CIS is still based on the vestiges of the Soviet Union and may, therefore, be subject to further attempts at secession which may be attempted by force. Such use of force may harm the rights and lives of Russian minorities scattered around the CIS. Such fears may have partly justi-fied Yeltsin's decision to retain some Russian troops in the Baltic states.[5] Russia itself is faced with demands for autonomy from the Tartars and the Yakutians. The possibility of other fissures developing along non-ethnic lines must also be considered. For example, the Russian army could attempt to halt devolutionist tendencies by forming ties with political parties composed of former communists or nationalist elements.

The fragility of the CIS poses two specific concerns regarding nu-clear weapons: the threat of proliferation of existing systems to other parties, and the possibility of the loss of control over a portion of these weapons. These are reasons for concern, but there are also rea-sons for guarded optimism. The reasons for concern centre around the possibility of reform failing and of some kind of alliance forming be-tween the disgruntled military and political opposition groups. There is little that the US or Europe can do to influence such developments decisively. Yet cautious optimism is still possible. Two sets of agree-ments may lead to a dramatic reduction in the number of nuclear weapons on ex-Soviet territory, while a second group of agreements will stabil-ize the control of existing weapons. The first set of agreements are the START Agreements. START I was signed on 31 July 1991 by Presidents Bush and Gorbachev, after nine years of negotiation, and entailed reductions to 6000 accountable warheads for each country by 1999.[6] Its successor agreement, START II, was signed in January 1993. The Minsk Agreement establishing a Commonwealth of Independent States (8 December 1991), the Ashkhabad Declaration (13 December 1991), and the Agreement on Joint Measures on Nuclear Weapons signed at Alma-Ata (21 December 1991) form the second group of agreements.

The START I and II treaties will, *once ratified*, result in enormous reductions (by almost 70 per cent) in the US and CIS nuclear arsenals. It has been agreed, albeit with a measure of reluctance, that the Rus-sian federation (RSFR) will, after 1995, be the only nuclear power in the CIS. The removal of tactical nuclear weapons from the other nu-clear republics started in December 1991. However, this development has in itself caused security problems since there is a shortage of fa-cilities in Russia suitable for dismantling the weapons. There is also a scarcity of suitable facilities for safely storing plutonium and enriched uranium.

Map of the former Soviet military forces

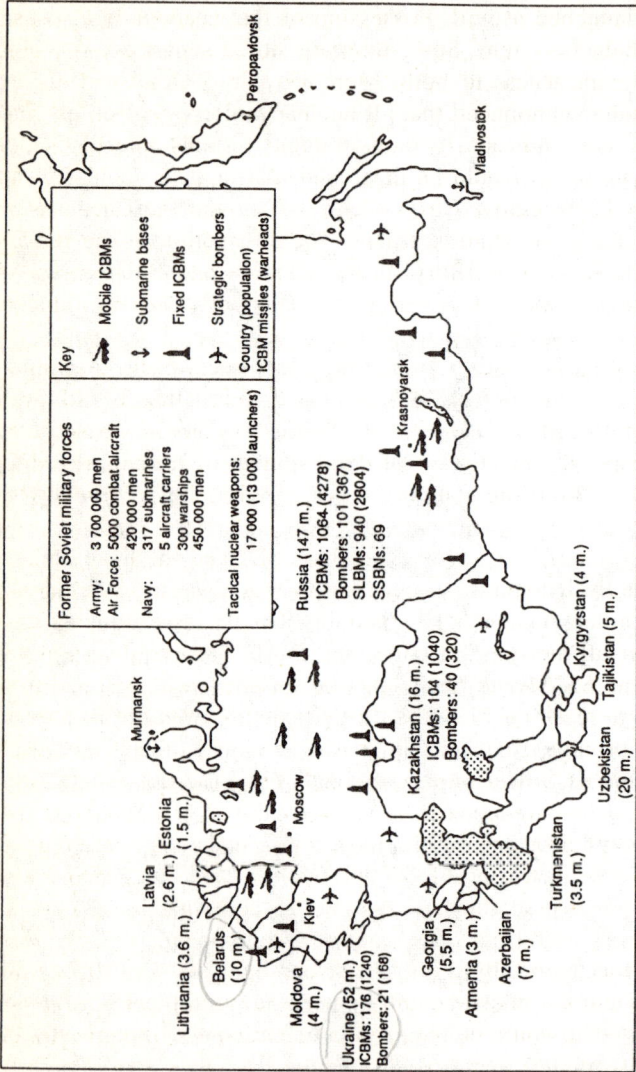

Key

- Mobile ICBMs
- Submarine bases
- Fixed ICBMs
- Strategic bombers
- Country (population)
- ICBM missiles (warheads)

Former Soviet military forces

Army: 3 700 000 men
Air Force: 5000 combat aircraft
420 000 men
Navy: 317 submarines
5 aircraft carriers
300 warships
450 000 men

Tactical nuclear weapons:
17 000 (13 000 launchers)

Russia (147 m.)
ICBMs: 1064 (4278)
Bombers: 101 (367)
SLBMs: 940 (2804)
SSBNs: 69

Kazakhstan (16 m.)
ICBMs: 104 (1040)
Bombers: 40 (320)

Ukraine (52 m.)
ICBMs: 176 (1240)
Bombers: 21 (168)

Belarus (10 m.)

Moldova (4 m.)

Lithuania (3.6 m.)

Latvia (2.6 m.)

Estonia (1.5 m.)

Georgia (5.5 m.)

Armenia (3 m.)

Azerbaijan (7 m.)

Turkmenistan (3.5 m.)

Uzbekistan (20 m.)

Tajikistan (5 m.)

Kyrgyzstan (4 m.)

Murmansk

Moscow

Kiev

Krasnoyarsk

Petropavlovsk

Vladivostok

Sources: For army air force and navy data see International Institute for Strategic Studies, *The Military Balance* 1991–1992; for strategic nuclear weapons see Pikayev, A. and Savelyev, A., *Nevavisimaya Gazeta*, no. 137 (2 November 1991), pp. 1–4. This map is reproduced from Landgren, S., 'Post-Soviet threats to security', in *SIPRI Yearbook 1992: World Armaments and Disarmament* (Oxford University Press: Oxford, 1992).

The chances of tactical weapons being misappropriated by a dissident or terrorist group and then being used for nuclear blackmail is not unimaginable, but is nevertheless exaggerated.[7] Tactical weapons, like strategic weapons, are linked to the CIS central command and *cannot* be launched at will. Possession of the weapons is also useless without a launch system. Since they are stored separately it would be difficult to gain access to both. Moreover, on 5 October 1991 President Gorbachev announced that all nuclear artillery projectiles, nuclear land mines and warheads for non-strategic systems (the FROG, Scud and SS-21 missiles) would be destroyed. All tactical nuclear weapons had already been removed from Central Asia and the Caucasus when Gorbachev made his announcement. The destruction of the remaining ones outside Russian territory, in the Ukraine and Belarus, was supported by their respective governments. The Gorbachev announcement followed a proposal by President Bush, made on 27 September 1991, for sweeping cutbacks to be made on a reciprocal basis. Amongst the cutbacks proposed on the US side were: destruction of all ground-based tactical nuclear weapons (2150) and all (250) sea-based tactical nuclear weapons; cancellation of development of the mobile MX and Midgetman ICBMs; the standing down of all strategic bomber forces from alert.

Some items were not touched, such as SDI and the development of the B-2. The Bush administration's clear intention was to force Gorbachev to make similar cuts, which would involve the assertion of Russian control over all missiles; in particular, Bush's proposal was aimed at scrapping the SS-24 and SS-25 mobile missiles, which were of sufficient range to reach the US. These proposals followed the August coup, which had prompted concern in Washington and other capitals about control of the ex-Soviet nuclear arsenal. The proposals effectively removed all nuclear weapons from the Korean peninsula and lopped off much of the nuclear arm of the navy and army, thus returning to the air force the main trusteeship of the nuclear deterrent forces, a position mirroring that of the late 1940s. The combination of cuts made within and out of formal arms control forums means that the chance of a tactical weapon falling into the wrong hands is slim. If one did, it is not clear that the missile could be used due to the permissive action links (PALs) that would be required to operationalize the missile. PALs are normally codes that have to be entered by several people to operationalize the warhead. This does not of course rule out the possibility to a nuclear missile being used in a non-nuclear mode, with the aim of causing radioactive contamination.

Strategic nuclear weapons remain the biggest area of concern to the west. The START I and II Treaties give some grounds for optimism; but there is still concern about whether the treaties will be ratified, the speed at which the systems covered by the treaties can be deactivated and dismantled, and the fear being that they may be overtaken by events. In response to this concern, President Bush used a significant portion of his 28 January 1992 State of the Union Address to speed up the 'build-down' by announcing significant reductions, in the expectation that Yeltsin would reciprocate:

> I have informed President Yeltsin that if the Commonwealth – the former Soviet Union – will eliminate all land-based multiple warhead ballistic missiles, I will do the following: We will eliminate all Peacekeeper missiles. We will reduce the number of warheads on Minuteman missiles to one, and reduce the number of warheads on our sea-based missiles by about one third. And we will convert a substantial portion of our strategic bombers to primarily conventional use.[8]

Yeltsin responded almost immediately by proposing further reductions in the number of strategic forces, but only to about half of what Bush had proposed, to about 2000–2500 on each side.[9] Also of interest in Yeltsin's speech was the announcement that strategic forces in the Ukraine would be dismantled sooner than planned under the START I Treaty and that the Russian Federation would accelerate the START Treaty implementation over the period of three years, instead of the seven specified. It was also suggested that Russia would not conduct exercises involving more than thirty heavy bombers and that the production of TU-160 and TU-95MS heavy bombers would cease. Production of nuclear warheads for land-based tactical missiles and nuclear artillery shells and mines was stopped and stockpiles of the same would be eliminated. Stocks of air-launched tactical nuclear munitions would be halved and those that remained, with US reciprocation, could be placed in centralized storage.

Yeltsin, in the same speech, announced Russia's intention of continuing the unilateral moratorium on testing (of October 1991), the ending of production of weapons grade uranium, the cessation of submarine combat patrols (provided that the US does the same), and an end to the US and Russia targeting each other. Yeltsin offered further reductions in the chemical and conventional areas as well. However, the entire success of both START and the unilateral cuts proposed by Yeltsin depends upon Russia not feeling threatened by the other nuclear CIS republics, and their subsequent cooperation to achieve Yeltsin's goals.

The competition that arose between George Bush and Boris Yeltsin to outdo each other in unilateral arms reduction means that both START agreements have been running behind. START I was soon outstripped by unilateral reductions in the number and readiness of both super-powers' arsenals.[10] In January 1992 an accord was agreed between Bush and Yeltsin, which led to a framework agreement between them on further reductions in June 1992. This, in turn, formed the basis for START II, signed by both leaders on 2 January 1993. The agreements were not reached without a good deal of compromise, particularly from the US. For example, the US superiority in strategic nuclear warheads shrank dramatically from a ratio of 8556 to 6450 under the SALT I agreement, to 4700 to 4456 in the January 1992 accords, to a pro-posed level of 3500 to 3475 by the year 2003 under the START II agreement. In spite of the flurry of activity, they remain paper agree-ments. START II is meaningless without ratification by all four So-viet nuclear successor states of START I as well as the 1968 Non-Proliferation Treaty (NPT). Until such ratification takes place, neither Moscow nor Russia will ratify START II. The Russian Supreme Soviet has refused to implement START I until Ukraine, Belarus and Kazakhstan become nuclear states. To make an already complicated situation more confused, there is the question of the fate of the NPT treaty following its final review conference in 1995.

One of the problems facing Boris Yeltsin was how to overcome the unpopularity of the treaty amongst his domestic opponents, who ob-jected to the US advantage in nuclear warheads. Several concessions have been granted to the CIS in order to make the agreement palat-able. For instance, under the June 1992 framework agreement all of the Russian multiple-warhead SS-18 silos were to have been destroyed. However, a special exemption has been granted whereby ninety will be permitted to house single-warhead missiles. START II was, in many ways, all that Yeltsin could have hoped for and certainly the best agree-ment he could take back to parliament. For the first time the US rec-ognized Russia as an equal by establishing the same ceiling on strategic nuclear weapons. All of this was at a time when Russia had little choice about whether to make cuts or not, since it could simply no longer afford such an arsenal.

The problems with the START agreements are twofold: first, how to destroy all missiles in a safe and rapid manner, and second, since not all of the strategic warheads are in the RSFR, the compliance of former Soviet nuclear republics, the Ukraine especially, has to be assumed for the agreements to be achieved. Until the Ukraine makes significant moves to surrender or destroy the 1656 strategic nuclear warheads on its soil, the likelihood of Russia or the US ratifying START II is low. The US aimed to help solve the first problem by announcing direct assistance to Russia at the mid-April 1993 Vancouver Summit between Clinton and Yeltsin. A portion of the $1.6 billion aid package to support Yeltsin's reforms was set aside to facilitate the destruction of nuclear weapons. However, any such assistance for this purpose is contingent upon the Russian parliament ratifying START II, which, at the time of writing, is unlikely.

Apart from internal problems in Russia, the Ukraine also poses serious obstacles to SALT II's ratification. The central difficulty appears to be the Ukraine's insistence that Russia's instability and historical tendency to be overbearing necessitates the retention of their nuclear arsenal.[11] This, in turn, makes the Russian Supreme Soviet reluctant to ratify START II, since the Ukraine has not ratified the original treaty nor has it become a non-nuclear signatory to the NPT. Ukrainian foot-dragging has been used by Russia as an excuse for not ratifying START II; and, in the event of an absolute refusal by the Ukraine to ratify, Russia would not feel legally bound by the stipulations of either START treaty. A resolution of the Ukrainian problem, which will result in their ratification of START I, appears to have been found with the Ukrainian endorsement of a US plan to put all warheads on Ukrainian soil under international control.[12] The difficulties of ratification also raise another more serious issue: who controls the ex-Soviet nuclear arsenal?

The Question of Control

Although little can be done immediately, or in the short term, about the potential loss of control of nuclear weapons in any of the four ex-Soviet nuclear republics, the assumption, which may be questionable, seems to be that the weapons would be safer in Russian hands. None of the other three nuclear republics are enthusiastic about giving up their strategic arsenals since they were regarded as valuable bargaining chips with Russia and, more importantly, for economic concessions from the US and Western Europe. The pressure to relinquish control over them comes most strongly from the West, where the offer of aid and recognition is explicitly linked to the surrender of such weapons and the assumption of non-nuclear status.

The outcome of Western and Russian pressure produced three agreements: the first was the Minsk agreement establishing a Commonwealth of Independent States of 8 December 1991; second was the Ashkhabad Declaration of 13 December 1991; and third was the Alma-Ata Declaration of 21 December 1991. The first stated that, 'The member states of the community will preserve and maintain under united command a common military-strategic space, including unified control over nuclear weapons, the procedure for implementing which is regulated by a special agreement.'[13] The Ashkhabad Declaration reinforced the Minsk Agreement by stating: 'In the interests of preserving strategic stability in the world, it is expedient to ensure common control of nuclear weapons and a unified command for strategic restraint troops and naval forces.'[14]

The final agreement, the 21 December 1991 Joint Agreement on Nuclear Weapons, is the most far-reaching. The agreement, between Belarus, Kazakhstan, the Russian Federation and the Ukraine, confirmed their adherence to the 'non-proliferation of nuclear armaments' and to strive towards the elimination of all nuclear weapons. The agreement also made reference to specific limitations:

> Article 4: Until nuclear weapons have been completely eliminated on the territory of the Republic of Belarus and the Ukraine, decisions on the need to use them are taken, by agreement with the heads of the member states of the agreement, by the RSFR President, on the basis of procedures drawn up jointly by the member states.

> Article 5: The Republic of Belarus and the Ukraine undertake to join the 1968 Nuclear Nonproliferation Treaty as non nuclear states and to conclude with the International Atomic Energy Agency the appropriate agreements-guarantees . . .[15]

> Article 6: The member states of this agreement, in accordance with the international treaty, will assist in the eliminating of nuclear weapons. By 1 July 1992, Belarus, Kazakhstan and Ukraine will ensure the withdrawal of *tactical* nuclear weapons to central factory premises for dismantling under joint supervision.[16]

Of note here is that Khazakhstan, represented by President Nursultan Nazarbayev, did not agree to join the NPT, nor did he commit the republic to surrender its tactical and strategic nuclear weapons until early February 1992 when he agreed to permit the removal and dismantling of all nuclear weapons by 1995. Thus, under the Alma-Ata agreement the nuclear weapons based in the Republic of Belarus, Kazakhstan and the Ukraine are under central control until they are removed to Russia for dismantling and destruction.

On 23 May 1992, the four ex-Soviet nuclear states and the US signed a Protocol to the 1991 Treaty on the Reduction of Strategic Offensive Weapons (START) in Lisbon. Under the terms of the Lisbon accord, all five signatories agreed to destroy or turn over to Russia all strategic nuclear warheads and to accede in the 'shortest possible time' to the 1968 Nuclear Non-Proliferation Treaty. The Ukraine, Belarus and Kazakhstan also agreed, in legally binding letters, to eliminate all nuclear weapons and all strategic offensive arms from their territories within the seven-year START reduction period. These obligations, assumed by the three former Soviet republics, were reaffirmed in the Moscow statement signed by the heads of the CIS states in July 1992. However, the Lisbon Protocol remains ambiguous in some significant ways; it failed to draw an explicit link between accession to the NPT and ratification of START I. Thus, like Kazhakstan, it is possible to ratify START I while remaining uncommitted to the NPT. Until the Lisbon Protocol was signed the Ukraine considered itself to be bound by the Minsk agreement, which specified that all nuclear weapons on Ukrainian soil should be eliminated by the end of 1994. Under the Protocol, the Ukraine now considers itself to be covered by the seven-year START I weapons reduction period. This interpretation has been rejected by Russian foreign minister, Andrei Kozyrev.

The four agreements establish some hope, but the dangers inherent in this still unstable situation need acknowledging. The assumption that, if the new ex-Soviet republics acceded to the Nuclear Nonproliferation Treaty (NPT), then peace and stability would be enhanced is open to debate. Due to the NPT's definition of a nuclear-weapon state, which is a state that has 'manufactured and exploded a nuclear device prior to 1 January 1967', it may be possible for Belarus, Khazakstan and the Ukraine to sign the NPT whilst *still* being in possession of nuclear weapons, since the weapons in these countries were manufactured in Russia and, as far as we know, none of the non-Russian ex-Soviet nuclear powers enjoys the ability to use the weapons unilaterally. Only if they could use the weapons with no veto being exercized from outside (that is, Moscow), would they be ineligible to join the NPT as non-nuclear states.

There has also been considerable speculation about the control of nuclear weapons, with the obvious concern that control could slip into unauthorized hands. This is not only of concern to European powers but also to the CIS republics themselves. As laid forth in the above agreements, control of nuclear weapons falls under joint CIS command, headed by (temporary) CIS Defence Minister Marshal Yevgeni Shaposhnikov and President Yeltsin of the Russian Federation. Shaposhnikov is in direct command of the specially trained forces whose job it is to guard, protect and maintain nuclear weapons.[17] President Leonid Kravchuk of the Ukraine has also alluded to the existence of a 'special communication system' which allows the presidents of Russia, the Ukraine, Khazakhstan and Belarus to keep in touch.[18] The fears that the generally low morale and the decline of discipline in the ex-Red Army will spread to these special forces cannot be discounted, but such forces are given special privileges and, to date, there has been no documented account of any signs of instability in them. Boris Yeltsin acknowledged the existence of this concern when in November 1991 he raised the salaries of all servicemen by 90 per cent, in an attempt to keep pace with inflation and to counter disaffection amongst the military. The well-publicized problems that Russia is encountering in its attempts to redeploy forces from Eastern Europe has overstretched the ability of the military to accommodate the returning servicemen. Even if they were demobilized, there would still be problems finding jobs and accommodation in the civilian sector. The possibility that the deteriorating situation of the military could lead to a backlash and another attempt at a coup makes the case for the centralization and destruction of all nuclear weapons even stronger. Much of the risk depends upon how long it takes to destroy the 15 000 tactical and strategic nuclear weapons that are due to be eliminated under Gorbachev's 5 October 1991 pledge. Soviet estimates, which were made before the additional burden of eliminating extra weapons under the START I and II treaties, indicate that it may take up to ten years to destroy these weapons and cost up to $2 billion.[19] US concern about the pace of the destruction has led to a grant of $400 million in FY1993 towards the cost of destroying the weapons, as well as pledges of technical assistance. Obviously the sooner the weapons can be safely destroyed the lower the chances are of nuclear weapons falling into unauthorized hands.

The centralized control of nuclear weapons has been complicated by feelings of resentment against Russia, most notably from the governments in the Ukraine and Kazakhstan. The RSFR is the only legally recognized nuclear successor state to the Soviet Union. On the basis of this legacy Russia has argued that all former Soviet nuclear weapons should remain under the *control* of the Russian High Command. Other CIS republics may participate in Russia's nuclear guarantee by subscribing to the joint CIS defence structures (see Figure 2.1). As has been observed, this claim rests partly upon the numerical distribution of nuclear weapons, but also upon additional claims: (i) Russia, unlike

Commander in Chief
of the CIS Armed Forces

High Command of the CIS Armed Forces

General Staff of the CIS Armed Forces

Joint Strategic Forces of the CIS

Joint General-Purpose
Forces of the CIS

Nuclear Forces	Homeland Air Defence	Naval Forces	Airborne Units	Transport Aviation	Air Forces	Ground Forces
ICBMs	Radar network	Surface fleets			Tactical fighters	Tank divisions
SSBNs/SLBMs	SAMs	Attack submarines				Motorized rifle divisions
Bombers	Fighter interceptors					
Ballistic-missile warning systems						
ABM system around Moscow						
ASAT systems						
Tactical nuclear weapons						

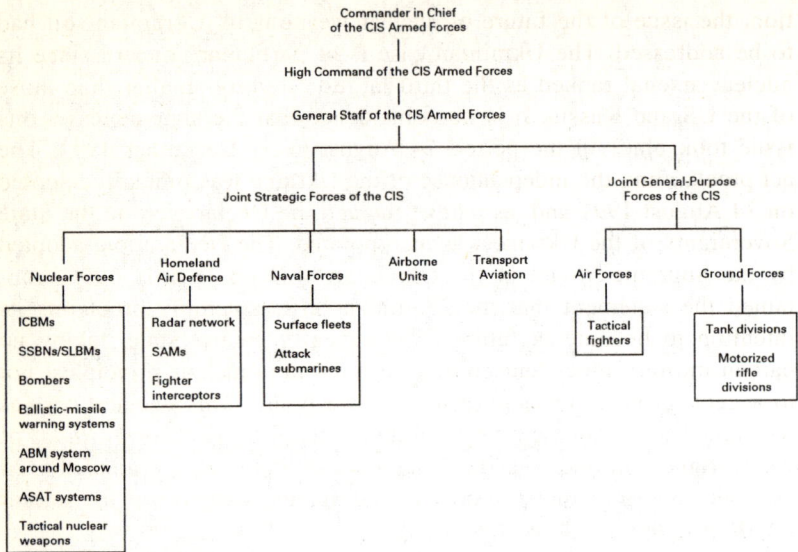

Figure 2.1   Defence structure of the CIS forces

the other nuclear republics, can provide efficient and reliable main-tenance, storage and control of nuclear weapons; (ii) Russia possesses the facilities to dismantle nuclear weapons; (iii) Future negotiation of arms-control agreements is easier with one power than between four powers.

The second of the above arguments is true, but raises doubts amongst the other republics that Russia will in fact dismantle the weapons and that it will do so in a safe manner. Accordingly, Ukraine has inde-pendently requested that the US provide assistance in the dismantling of weapons in the republic that are covered by the START Treaty. Leonid Kravchuk has resisted attempts to establish a broad military mandate for the CIS, which would include most aspects of the military apparatus. At Kravchuk's insistence, the joint strategic forces of the CIS consists of the unified strategic forces and a 'small central ap-paratus in Moscow to oversee them'.[20] Kravchuk has also made clear his unwillingness to have general-purpose commonwealth forces on its territory, beyond those directly associated with the tactical and stra-tegic nuclear units temporarily on Ukrainian soil.

Almost simultaneously with the Ukraine's independence proclamation, the issue of the future of nuclear weapons on Ukrainian soil had to be addressed. The Ukrainian case is of particular concern since its nuclear arsenal ranked as the third largest, slightly smaller than those of the US and Russia. It is no coincidence that the statements on this issue took place in the period 24 August to 31 December 1991. The act proclaiming the independence of the Ukraine was officially adopted on 24 August 1991 and, as part of the act, the Declaration on the State Sovereignty of the Ukraine was incorporated. The Declaration, adopted by the Supreme Soviet of the Ukrainian SSR on 16 July 1990, contained the statement that the Ukrainian SSR 'solemnly proclaims its intention to become in future a permanently neutral state, taking no part in military blocs and holding to three non-nuclear principles: not to accept, produce or acquire nuclear weapons'. This declaration was reinforced by a statement made in the parliament (*Verkhovna Rada*) of the Ukraine, entitled 'On the Non-Nuclear Status of Ukraine', on 24 October 1991, in which the presence of nuclear weapons of the former USSR was described as 'temporary'.[21]

The same commitment was reiterated in Article 4 of the Agreement on Strategic Forces, 30 December 1991, between the CIS participants. This stated: 'Pending their complete destruction, nuclear weapons deployed on Ukraine's territory are placed under the control of the united command of the Strategic Forces for their non-use and dismantling till the end of 1994 and as far as tactical nuclear weapons are concerned till 1 June 1992.'[22] As if to underline the Ukraine's seriousness about its non-nuclear option, Kravchuk insisted upon guarantees for the non-use of nuclear weapons before they were removed from Ukrainian soil. Perhaps due to the Chernobyl experience, Ukrainians more than most are aware of the supreme folly of nuclear war.

What, in legal terms, do these agreements actually mean? The agreements provide the necessary authority for the government to conduct negotiations and reach agreements. But, in spite of the fact that parliament empowered the executive to conduct negotiations, parliament retains the final right of say regarding the entry into force of any agreement. Thus, all of the above agreements have the legal status of a declaration of intent and cannot be considered as legally binding until voted upon (positively) by the parliament. In the words of the foreign minister of the Ukraine, Anatoly Zlenko, 'there are no obligations which would bind Ukraine to being a non-nuclear weapons state before the final decision of the Parliament to accede to the NPT is taken'.[23] To many observers of Ukraine, these commitments appeared to have full legal status. Accordingly, concerns about the sincerity of a Ukrainian non-nuclear stance were prompted by President Leonid Kravchuk's announcement at a press conference in Kiev on 12 March 1992 that the removal of tactical nuclear weapons was being 'temporarily suspended'.[24] This was, however, officially not prompted by any second thoughts but by concern about whether the tactical nuclear weapons that had been removed from Ukrainian soil were in fact being destroyed, and concern that, if they were, they were being destroyed in a controlled manner. Kravchuk therefore proposed that the Ukraine, with Western assistance, should become the centre for the destruction of nuclear weapons. The timetable established for the disassembly and destruction of the tactical and strategic nuclear weapons (by 1 July 1992 and the end of April 1994 respectively) prompted legitimate Ukrainian concerns about the safety of these procedures. The understandable haste to dispose of the bulk of the superpower nuclear arsenals needs to be moderated by the immense problems surrounding the unprecedented disposal of such a large number of weapons.

From the Ukrainian point of view, the disposal of nuclear weapons had to be accomplished in a manner that was not only safe, but also one that answers Ukrainian sensitivities and security concerns. Specifically, the right to be a nuclear weapons state was seen to be as legitimate as Russia's right. Thus, to 'surrender' weapons to Russia for disposal would also be an act acknowledging the falsity of the Ukraine's claim while confirming Russia's. There are also security concerns that have to be acknowledged; the desire to retain at least a portion of the missiles[25] on their soil was seen as a guarantee of independence from Russia. Furthermore, to surrender Ukrainian nuclear weapons to Russia with no guarantees that they wouldn't merely be incorporated into a Russian arsenal was seen as another justification for retaining some nuclear weapons. Anatoly Zlenko, Ukraine's foreign minister, argued that, 'We believe our country is an equal successor state to the former Soviet Union, has exceptional proprietary rights to fissile materials and other components of nuclear warheads, including both strategic – presently located on our territory – and tactical weapons, the latter having been removed from the Ukraine.'[26] In a partial response to Ukrainian anxieties, an agreement was drawn up in April 1992 by the presidents of the Ukraine and Russia. It was agreed that none of the nuclear weapons, or their components, withdrawn from Belarus, Khazakhstan or the Ukraine to Russian territory for dismantling and disposal, could be used to build up a Russian military arsenal. As a result of this agreement, the Ukraine consented to the removal of all tactical nuclear weapons to Russian dismantling facilities by 6 May 1992.

Like other republics, the Ukraine is not in a position to allocate substantial amounts of money to the elimination of strategic arms from its territory and it is reliant upon outside help to do so. The question of finance has placed yet another stumbling block in the path to the removal of nuclear weapons from the Ukraine. President Kravchuk outlined one possible solution to the problem when, during a statement at the International Economic Forum in Davos in February 1992, he proposed an International Fund for Nuclear Disarmament in the Ukraine. However, the terms on which aid is given to the Ukraine for disarmament remain to be worked out. The September 1993 agreement between Yeltsin and Kravchuk (see below) may provide a solution to the funding question but, the agreement has yet to be ratified by the *Verhovna Rada*. With all of the tactical nuclear weapons removed from the Ukraine, the problem of the removal of the 1656 strategic nuclear weapons still remained.

There are several possible motives behind the Ukrainian retention of strategic nuclear weapons; one is the need for a guarantee against potential aggression from Russia and, since the Ukraine could not possibly deter Russia with superior conventional forces, nuclear deterrence

Table 2.1 Ukrainian Nuclear Weapons (September 1993)

	Number	*Warheads (per missile or delivery vehicle)*	*Location*
Missiles			
SS-19	130	6	Khmelnitski
SS-24	46	10	Pervomaysk
*Bombers**			
TU-95(Bear)	21	16	Uzin
TU-160 (Blackjack)	16+	12	Priluki

* The TU-95 Bear strategic bomber can carry up to 19 ALCMs, while the Blackjack bombers can carry up to 12 assorted weapons. The Ukraine inherited virtually all of the Soviet TU-160s, but the operational status of only 16 is known.

Source: Compiled from Serge Sur (ed.) *Nuclear Deterrence: Problems and Perspectives in the 1990s* (New York: UNIDIR, 1993), pp. 33–4; *Military Balance 1992–3* (London: IISS, 1992), pp. 232–5; and *SIPRI Yearbook 1993: World Armaments and Disarmament* (Oxford: Oxford University Press/SIPRI, 1993) pp. 226–8.

seems like a prudent step. Another possible motive, as suggested by the Ukrainian defence minister, General Konstantin Morozov, is that the West will only take note of the Ukraine so long as they possess nuclear weapons.[27] This is in accordance with statements made (behind closed doors) by Leonid Kuchma, the Ukrainian ex-prime minister, who recommended that the Ukraine should keep a few nuclear weapons as a security guarantee.[28] This position is in contrast to that adopted by the Ukraine's president, Leonid Kravchuk, as well as the Ukrainian foreign and defence ministers, who are publicly in favour of eliminating the nuclear arsenal. However, Kravchuk's public protestations did not prevent him from announcing in May 1992 that all strategic nuclear weapons on Ukrainian soil were henceforth under Ukrainian *administrative* control. The question of who *actually* controls the nuclear weapons is ambiguous. Offically, the decision to use the missiles would be made by representatives from the CIS in accordance with the Minsk agreement of 31 December 1991. The Ukraine is a signatory to this agreement and it specifies joint command of the strategic forces of the signatories by the CIS and unified control by the CIS commander and the Russian president, in consent with the heads of the CIS states. Since the Minsk agreement mentions the word *consent*, the Ukraine, like other CIS republics, would have the right but not the capability to veto a launch decision. However, as John Mearsheimer argues, the Ukraine probably controls the bombers on its territory. Kravchuk has also suggested that his country has the ability to fire the Ukrainian made SS-24 missiles, and that 'Kiev is developing a command and control system of its own that could be used to launch the weapons without Moscow's permission'.[29] If this is the case, it would obviously complicate Ukrainian accession to the NPT as a non-nuclear state.

By the spring of 1992 Ukraine had secured administrative control over the nuclear forces on its territory, which means that all the personnel manning the nuclear forces are under the direct administrative conrol of Kiev and almost all have taken an oath of allegiance to Ukraine. In mid-July 1993 the Ukraine's parliament declared sole ownership of the nuclear warheads based on its soil. This evoked immediate concern in the West that the Ukraine would renege on its commitments and retain the weapons indefinitely. The Russian minister of defence, General Pavel Grachev, observed that the weapons are under the operational control of Russia and that the Ukrainian declaration was meaningless. Kravchuk was only willing to dismantle its strategic weapons if there was substantial financial assistance from the US. The Clinton administration's position was that aid would be forthcoming, but only after the Ukraine had ratified the NPT. By the end of that month the Clinton administration had backed down on its position when, during a visit of the Ukrainian minister of defence, General Kostiantyn Morozov, to Washington it was revealed that the Ukraine had begun to dismantle SS-19s in the Pervomaysk region. This led to a pledge of $175 million to hasten and help in the dismantlement of the weapons. Morozov demanded a total package of $3 billion for the dismantling of the warheads, their shipment to Russia and compensation for the enriched uranium.

The problem of what to do with the warheads still remained. For the meantime they are being stored in the Ukraine, but in the long term the US has agreed to the purchase of uranium from the warheads *provided* that the four CIS nuclear republics can agree on a method of apportioning the funds from the sale and that the silos housing the missiles are also destroyed. Talks between Russia and the Ukraine, that commenced on 15 January 1993, recognized that the Ukraine would be compensated for any sales of highly enriched uranium extracted from warheads withdrawn to Russia for dismantling and disposal. However, as a concession it was insufficient to overcome the basic mistrust that exists between the Ukraine and Russia. In Russia's case the strategic missiles have become the focus of political opposition to Yeltsin and, in the Ukraine, they have become a symbol and guarantor of the country's new found independence.

A further bone of contention in Russian–Ukrainian relations concerned ownership of the Black Sea Fleet. President Yeltsin and President Kravchuk met at Yalta, Crimea, on 3 September 1993 to discuss this issue. According to the *Russian version* of the meeting, as the result of considerable pressure, Yeltsin persuaded the Ukraine to give up its claim to its half-share of the ex-Soviet Black Sea Fleet in return for the amortization of its debts to Russia. Kravchuk also agreed that *all* nuclear weapons on Ukrainian soil would be transported to Russia for dismantlement and, in return, Russia would supply nuclear fuel for the Ukraine's nuclear reactors. The *Ukrainian interpretation* of the meeting is at varience with the Russian interpretation; at a press conference on 6 September, Kravchuk described the Russian terms as an 'ultimatum' and that 'if we do not find the means to start repaying our debts right away, Russia will turn off the oil and gas supplies'.[30] The Ukrainian version of the agreements reached at the meeting was that a joint commission would be formed to study the feasibility of the proposals.

The Ukraine has, on paper, agreed to the removal of all nuclear weapons from its soil by 1994 (the Ukraine is committed to eliminate all of its nuclear missiles by the end of 1994, in accordance with the Minsk Agreement between the CIS states. The Ukraine has however asserted that it is not bound to elimiate its nuclear weapons until the end of the seven-year reduction period outline in the START 1 Treaty).

The question of the future of the Ukraine's nuclear weapons came one step nearer to a solution on 14 January 1994 when a trilateral agreement was signed between the US, Russia and the Ukraine. Under the agreement the Ukraine is to transfer its nuclear weapons to Russia for dismantling. It marks, as President Boris Yeltsin observed, 'The last full stop to the last chapter of the cold war.' Under the terms of the agreement the Ukraine has agreed to transfer at least 200 warheads (which, significantly, include the accurate SS-24 warheads) to Siberia over the next ten months for dismantling by Russian technicians. The Ukraine will eliminate all nuclear weapons from its soil within seven years.[31] Russia will then extract and reprocess the highly-enriched uranium (HEU) and supply 100 tonnes of low-enriched uranium to the Ukraine for use in civilian nuclear power stations. The US will pay $60 million to Russia for the cost of reprocessing the HEU and at least $155 million in economic aid to the Ukraine. Leonid Kravchuk also received security guarantees from Russia and the US[32] which are 'essentially those already available to it as a member of the Conference for Security and Cooperation in Europe and as a signatory to the Non-Proliferation Treaty.'[33]

In a separate agreement the US will pay $11.9 billion to Russia over the course of the next twenty years for 500 metric tonnes of HEU. The purchase and the transfer of the HEU will be coordinated by the US Enrichment Corporation. The agreement was careful to include up-front all forty-six of the ten warhead SS-24 missiles. The agreement is encouraging since it opens up the way for implementation of the START I and START II treaties that will lead to a reduction in the US and Russian nuclear stockpiles by up to two-thirds by the end of the century. However, the optimism surrounding the agreement between Yeltsin, Clinton and Kravchuk must be tempered by some cautionary observations. Two in particular stand out: first, that the agreement may not be ratified by the Ukrainian parliament and; second, developments in Russia since the December 1993 elections may cause a reconsideration of the Ukraine's promises.

On the first point, there is vehement opposition within the Ukraine to the agreement, especially from opposition nationalist leader, Vyacheslav Chornovil. Chornovil has denounced Kravchuk's signature of the agreement as an act of 'treason,' while others have called for Kravchuk's impeachment.[34] Doubt about whether the agreement will actually be upheld have also been voiced, based on the Ukraine's past tendency to renege on agreements. One reason to suggest that the agreement will go through is that, unlike past agreements, this agreement has incentives attached to it that would be hard for Ukrainian politicians to resist in the midst of a grim economic struggle. On the second point, a more real danger to the Ukraine's willingness to abide by the agreement may be posed by the rise to power of Vladimir Zhirinovsky, who secured twenty-three percent of the vote in the December 1993 elections. The ultranationalist tendencies that Zhirinovsky represents, alongside his erratic and threatening comments, could have the effect of building support for Ukrainian resistance to the agreement and its implementation.[35]

The status of the Crimea and the ownership of the Black Sea Fleet remain highly contentious issues. A nationalist-minded parliament in Russia could easily engender fear in the Ukraine and a reversal of their position on nuclear weapons. The security guarantees, given by Clinton and Yeltsin, are vague and certainly do not amount to a guarantee of the Ukraine's independence or sovereignty.

The stability of the Ukraine is of critical importance to Europe. A denuclearized Ukraine would lessen the chance of a nuclear exchange between Russia and the Ukraine. Vigilance should however be paid to the considerable conventional forces that the Ukraine and Russia possess. Even in the event of a conventional clash there may still be nuclear risks – the Ukraine alone has fourteen operating nuclear reactors which could cause untold destruction and death in the event of their destruction. It is clear that the Ukraine could not hope to match Russia in conventional force terms, which may increase the Ukraine's resistance to surrender all of its nuclear weapons.

The understandable concentration on the Ukraine has often overshadowed important developments in the other ex-Soviet nuclear republics. In a meeting between President Nazarbayev and the French foreign minister, Roland Dumas, the former let it be known that nuclear arms will remain in Kazakhstan until the year 2000, unless the republic receives suitable reimbursement for the damage caused by nuclear testing since 1949 at the Semipalatinsk site. In spite of Nazarbayev's posturing, Kazakhstan ratified START I in July 1992 and has also promised to sign the NPT – but has yet to fulfil its promise.

Kazakhstan has been far less confrontational than the Ukraine on the question of the future of nuclear weapons on its soil. It is in a somewhat unusual situation since neither START I nor the Lisbon

Table 2.2 Kazakhstan Nuclear Weapons (September 1993)

	Number	Warheads (per missile or delivery vehicle)	Location
Missile			
SS-18	104	10	Derzhavinsk
Bomber			
TU-95 (Bear)	40	–	Semipalatinsk

Source: Compiled from Serge Sur (ed.) *Nuclear Deterrence: Problems and Perspectives in the 1990s* (New York: UNIDIR, 1993), pp. 33–4; *Military Balance 1992–3* (London: IISS, 1992), pp. 232–5; and *SIPRI Yearbook 1993: World Armaments and Disarmament* (Oxford: Oxford University Press/SIPRI, 1993) pp. 226–8.

Protocols mention the dismantling of nuclear weapons on Kazakhstan's territory. The SS-18s would have to be dismantled under the provisions of START II. Nazarbayev signed an accord with Boris Yeltsin in October 1992, on the occasion of the latter's visit to Kazakhstan, which confirmed CIS control over nuclear forces. In January 1993, at the CIS Minsk Summit, Kazakhstan and Ukraine both rejected a Russian motion to place command of strategic forces in their hands. Exactly who has control over the forces in Kazakhstan is, as in the case of Ukraine, open to debate. It is likely that Kazakhstan has administrative control, but operational control rests with Moscow. It is also evident that Nazarbayev has been monitoring developments between Russia and Ukraine very closely and this has led to demands for security guarantees and US financial assistance for the dismantling of the heavy ICBMs. Unlike the Ukrainian position, there seems to be little chance of a reversal of the basic commitment to nuclear disarmament and membership of the NPT.

Belarus, with eighty-one mobile SS-25s (possessing one warhead each) based at Lida and Mozyr, acceded to the NPT on 4 February 1993 and, at the same time, ratified START I and the Lisbon Protocols. In the same closed session of parliament Belarus reconfirmed the status of nuclear weapons on its soil, as laid out in the 1991 Minsk Agreement. Unlike the other republics, the SS-25s will not be dismantled but will be redeployed to Valdai (Russia) to replace the ageing SS-17 missiles. This is entirely in accordance with the START treaties. Belarus has been strongly supportive of the CIS command and highly critical of Ukraine's stand. The Chairman of the Supreme Soviet of Belarus,

Stanislav Shushkevich, was the first of the ex-Soviet heads of state to be invited to the White House by President Clinton. In a measure that was clearly designed to send a message to Ukraine and Kazakhstan, the US granted $59 million to clean up Belarus's missile bases and convert them into civilian use. In June 1993 Pytor Kravchenko, Belarus's foreign minister, pleaded for another $232 million to help in the denuclearization and cleaning-up process.

Russia itself is already a member of the NPT and ratified START-I on 4 November 1992. However, the Russian parliament added the proviso that implementation of the agreement would only start when the three other CIS nuclear powers have transferred all of their nuclear weapons to Russia in addition to acceding to the NPT. The US Senate has not yet ratified START I and is unlikely to do so until the three non-Russian nuclear republics have transferred all of their nuclear weapons to Russia. START II, signed by Bush and Yeltsin on 3 January 1993, has run into stiff opposition in the Russian parliament. The treaty enjoys support from the Russian defence minister, Pavel Grachev, as well as from the foreign minister, Andrey Kozreyev. Within the Russian parliament START II has become a rallying point for the opposition. Lieutenant-General Boris Tarasov, a prominent hardliner, leader of the Fatherland Opposition party and instigator in the failed attempt to impeach Yeltsin, commented that, 'Strategic nuclear weapons gave the Soviet Union the status of a superpower. Ratification of START II would mean Russia loses this status.'[36] Exactly the same argument is used in the Ukraine by those opposed to surrendering all of their nuclear arsenal. Specific objections are voiced against the dismantling of SS-18 heavy missiles, which are seen as the most important and impressive part of the land-based arsenal. If Russia destroys the SS-18s and the US continues to research GPALS, it is argued by those opposed to START, Russia would have a decisive inferiority. In order to shore up feelings of inferiority or vulnerability and observe treaty stipulations, Russia would have to develop SSBNs rapidly, an option that is clearly unrealistic given the shape of the economy. As with the other three ex-Soviet nuclear republics, the cost associated with dismantling weapons in a safe manner is also daunting for Russia, especially given the numbers of warheads and missiles involved. On 8 September 1993 ex-US Secretary of Defense, Les Aspin, pledged $85 million in aid to Russia, on top of existing aid (making a total of around $370 million). The aid is mainly designed for the construction of sites for the safe storage of nuclear materials.

The chances of the three non-Russian CIS nuclear powers transferring their weapons to Russia depend not only upon overcoming governmental or parliamentary resistance, especially in the Ukraine's case, but also upon public opinion. The administrations in Kiev and Minsk face strong anti-nuclear movements which had initially been galvanized into action by the Chernobyl accident. Similar public sentiment has been brought to bear in Alma-Ata where there is public resentment at the environmental damage caused by the underground tests there, which were carried out with inadequate safeguards.

Even if one works on the assumption that all CIS nuclear weapons are surrendered to Russia, there are still formidable problems to be addressed. For instance, what will become of the five hundred tons of enriched uranium that will result from the dismantling of Russia's nuclear weapons under START-I stipulations? One possible solution would be to downgrade the uranium and utilize it in domestic nuclear reactors. However, given the lack of secure storage in Russia a better option may be for another country, such as the US, to purchase the enriched uranium. At around $800 per kilo, this may cost the US up to $13 billion, as well as the predictable political problems of whose back yard to put the waste into. There will also be other highly dangerous materials to be disposed of, such as plutonium. In April 1993 a US–Russian agreement was signed to co-develop a plutonium-fuelled reactor.[37] The agreement soon became bogged down over disputes about the budget for the programme. Even if these bureaucratic hurdles can be overcome, it will take a minimum of ten years for such a reactor to become operative.

If we assume that the Ukraine and the three ex-Soviet nuclear powers surrender their weapons to Russia and that they are then dismantled in a safe and prompt manner (assuming the two are not incompatible), would Europe be safer? Some evidence points to a positive response, especially the 'Moscow Declaration' signed by Yeltsin and Clinton on 14 January 1994. The declaration stated that, by May 30, Russia and the US would no longer target each other with intercontinental range nuclear weapons which, together, amount to almost 8000 warheads. Although the agreement is chiefly symbolic, since both sides could retarget their missiles in a matter of minutes, it lessens the chance of accidental launch or over-hasty actions. The agreement has obvious side-benefits for Europe which would suffer enormously in the event of a nuclear exchange between the powers. The negative response has everything to do with the intangibles of Russian politics, such as the future of Yeltsin following Yegor Gaidar's resignation and the unpredictable antics of Vladimir Zhirinovsky who, in spite of being a clownish figure, deserves to be treated seriously. Gaidar was joined a day later by Boris Fyodorov, Russia's Finance Minister, who resigned in protest at Yeltsin's economic policies. The loss of two key figures will weaken Yeltsin and may lead to an increasingly bitter struggle between the Parliament and Yeltsin, the security implications of which, remain unclear.

Proliferation

Concerns regarding control go beyond the weapons themselves to include the control and ownership of all fissile materials, equipment and technology. Export control of Soviet nuclear materials was previously under the control of the Ministry of Heavy Machinery and Atomic Industry (MAPI), the specialized export control agencies and the Foreign Ministry. This bureaucratic machinery is currently in the process of being decentralized. An indication of the future control regimes that will regulate the export of fissile materials has been hinted at by the creation of Chetek in December 1990. Chetek is a 'semi-private company consisting mainly of nuclear scientists, including nuclear weapons experts, offering a whole spectrum of nuclear and other advanced technologies to the international market'.[39] The first service offered by Chetek is the use of underground nuclear explosions for the purpose of specialized waste incineration. Such explosions, it is argued, could be used to vaporize nuclear and chemical weapons. This would have the obvious attraction of ridding the CIS of such weapons quickly and thus lessen the chance of these systems falling into unofficial hands. This service was offered to the UN and subsequently declined.[40]

Chetek underwrites work for MAPI and the All-Union Scientific Research Institute of Experimental Physics (Arzamas 16) to the tune of 130 million roubles per annum. The activities of companies like Chetek give reason for concern, and disorganization in Moscow gives rise to the possibility that export controls, no matter how rigid, may be unenforceable. The problem of export controls is one that is relevant not just to Russia but to most of the CIS republics; and, although unproven, it has been claimed that small batches of uranium and plutonium have appeared in Switzerland and Italy from (former) Soviet, Bulgarian and Romanian sources.[41]

Prior to the break-up of the Soviet Union, exports were controlled by Technabexport which was, in effect, MAPI's export division. The end of Technabexport's monopoly on the export of nuclear material has opened the way for private companies and the possibility that export could get out of hand. There is already an active export market in high-tech space-related and military equipment at moderate prices. Amongst the items on sale is plutonium 238, for use as a compact power source in space programmes.[42] The tightening of export controls, as promised by President Yeltsin to US Secretary of State James Baker III on 16 December 1991, has been largely unimplementable. However, even international expressions of concern about the problem may fall second to the need for hard currency and shortages of alternative fuel sources.[43]

Most of the potential trade in nuclear material would emanate from Russia since nearly all of the nuclear warheads were manufactured in Russia and tested in Khazakstan. Russia was, however, highly dependent upon other parts of the former Soviet Union for its access to uranium which, at its height, amounted to half of the world's known reserves. Only Russia, though, had the facilities to enrich uranium. Kyrgyzstan, Tajikistan, Ukraine and Uzbekistan had the ability to make uranium hexafluoride, used in some enrichment processes. Several republics also have research reactors which may have the ability to make plutonium and zirconium. Since these republics are not signatories to the NPT, they obviously fall out of the 'safeguards' system. Nor are they members of the Nuclear Suppliers Group; only Russia is a member. Thus, in terms of bureaucratic restraints, there is little that can be done to contain the export of potentially dangerous nuclear materials to those who are willing to pay. Even if there were effective safeguard arrangements, the desperate plight of many of the economies, accompanied by rife black-market activities, could lead to covert nuclear export activity.[44] Although there have been reported attempts at, or incidents of, smuggling of nuclear material from Belarus to Poland, from Russia to the Ukraine, and from Russia to Slovakia, there is no evidence to suggest that this is organized in a systematic way or state-sponsored.[45] Furthermore, it is not certain that all of the nuclear material that was intercepted could be used in weapons-related programmes. As a precaution against the possibility of unscrupulous states exporting nuclear material, it would obviously be prudent for the international community to bring pressure to bear on the non-Russian CIS republics to accede to the NPT and, where relevant, to join the Nuclear Suppliers Group.

Aside from the leakage of nuclear material, a far more intractable problem concerns the nuclear weapons experts themselves. Few expenses were spared on training world-class nuclear experts in the former Soviet Union. With the collapse of the Soviet nuclear-military industrial complex there were an estimated one to two thousand persons with relevant knowledge about the design and engineering of nuclear weapons, and a further two to five thousand who may have some specialized knowledge about the production of weapons-grade fissile material.[46] The announcement of a unilateral moratorium on testing by Mikhail Gorbachev on 5 October 1991 and the closure of the Semipalatinsk test site in Kazakhstan on 29 August 1991 means that most of the nuclear experts are no longer needed.[47] This opens up the possibility that weapons experts will be encouraged, with the inducement of attractive salaries and benefits, to move to countries with an interest in utilizing their knowledge in a nuclear-weapons programme. The severe economic conditions prevailing in much of the CIS may make this an attractive option for scientists. Russia is plainly aware of the potential dangers stemming from the flight of scientists to nuclear aspirant countries. In January 1993 the Russian parliament passed legislation stating that those who had access to state secrets were forbidden to leave the country for a period of five years after their last contact with such information. Whether this is enforcable is an open question.

There are several plans in existence to help employ these scientists with funding from Germany, Japan and the US. Most of these plans involve employing the scientist to help in the dismantling and safe disposal of nuclear weapons and material, as well as enhancing the safety of domestic nuclear plants. Much, for instance, could be learnt from detailed scientific studies of the faults associated with Chernobyl-type (RBMK) reactors, as well as from study of the effects of nuclear accidents, such as those at Chernobyl and Kyshtym.[48] Such plans do not, however, rule out the possibility of lucrative financial offers luring nuclear scientists into nuclear projects in existing nuclear states, such as China, or to those countries that require technical expertise to establish a nuclear-weapons programme.[49] Such concerns, though, should not just be applied to Russian scientists. Many other countries have also scaled back their nuclear-weapons programmes, along with their defence industries, and these experts must also be considered as potentially 'on the market'.

Consideration of the problems aroused by proliferation must go beyond the ex-Soviet republics and include the more general problem of ballistic missile proliferation in the Third World and the Middle East.[50] Nuclear, chemical and conventional threats to the south of Europe will have to be taken seriously in the light of the Gulf War. The threat of such proliferation is not of such immediacy for the US.[51] The concern expressed about the potential use of nuclear weapons by Iraq during the 1991 Gulf War illustrates the relative ease with which powers (with acquiescence) can gain weapons of mass destruction. Iran poses the latest proliferation threat in the Middle East with its attempts to gain a nuclear deterrent force. North Korea has also reminded us of the problem in Asia. While this may be a threat, it must also be seen as part of a wider historical picture of the West attempting to balance the military forces of the powers in the region. The 'Iraqgate' hearings in the US and the Matrix-Churchill scandal in Britain can be seen in terms of these two countries' concerns that Iran was becoming too powerful in the latter days of the eight year Iran–Iraq war, with the result that the US and Britain (and other European countries) helped to rectify the balance in the vain hope that this would stop any one country from becoming too powerful. The defeat of Iraq in the 1991 Gulf War and the destruction of much of its military strength has had the effect of making the Iranians appear as the new threat in the region. They may well be, but this is a familiar game of balancing one against the other that outside powers have been engaged in for the entire post-World War II period.

Such weapons may be acquired for many reasons, amongst them being aspirations of regional hegemony or concerns prompted by proliferation in neighbouring countries. Libya and Pakistan serve as examples of these respective pressures. Such developments, once started, are enormously difficult to control. For instance, in response to the rumour about Libyan attempts to acquire a nuclear capability, Algeria felt compelled to achieve similar capability and secured Chinese assistance in building a large research reactor. A research reactor of Chinese design is also being constructed in Syria. The accession of China to the NPT on 9 March 1992, which followed the accession of France and South Africa to the Treaty, is an encouraging step. However, the Gulf War and the break-up of the Soviet Union have highlighted the dangers of proliferation and the need for active control to halt the spread of ballistic missile technology and weapons of mass destruction. The most helpful step in this regard would be the continuation of the NPT beyond its 1995 expiry date and the strengthening of the Safeguards system (the latter point being particularly poignant in the light of Iraq's initial ability to hide large facilities for the enrichment of uranium and, after the Gulf War, to obstruct the IAEA in its task of identifying all significant nuclear-related facilities in accordance with the mandate granted under UN Security Council resolution 687).

The still relatively new Missile Technology Control Regime (MTCR), formed in 1987, may have a decisive effect in limiting the spread of ballistic missile technology.[52] However, before the MTCR becomes a significant actor some weaknesses have to be ironed out, like the problem of 'dual-use' technology. Many components used in a ballistic missile, such as computer components used in the guidance systems, fuel technology, thruster systems, and so forth, may also be used for civilian purposes. The MTCR shares information on all the technical aspects of ballistic missile production and research, but it is ultimately up to the individual members to determine what is prohibited technology, and consequently may not be exported. In spite of the fact that membership of the MTCR has expanded since 1987, the main countries engaged in ballistic missile proliferation are outside the MTCR. The Soviet Union was a major arms supplier to the Middle East, but since its demise sales from that region have plummeted and Russia has agreed to abide by MTCR guidelines. When China acceded to the Non-Proliferation Treaty in March 1992, it also gave verbal assurances about its compliance with MTCR export guidelines, yet China has continued to market nuclear missile technology to other countries, including those with nuclear ambitions.[53] The unchecked sale of ballistic missiles of inter-continental range (around 2800 km) by Russia or China, who are the only known sources of such missiles, could have serious effects on peace and stability, particularly amongst the nuclear-aspirant or chemical weapons states who do not have the capability to develop such missiles themselves. The imposition by the US of a ban on the export of high-technology to China, worth almost $1 billion, following revalations in August 1993 that China was exporting missile technology to Pakistan in violation of the MTCR, may serve to reinforce the MTCR.[54]

Conventional Force Problems

The tendency to focus on the nuclear aspects of the ex-Soviet Union has helped to distract attention from potential problems posed by *conventional* forces. During the Cold War era the Warsaw Treaty Organization amounted to an enormous force of some five million men. The disintegration of the Soviet Union has split up this force. The Minsk Agreement Establishing a Commonwealth of Independent States, signed on 8 December 1991, was noticeably vague on the question of security. The only hints were vague obligations to 'serve the cause of peace and security', 'to respect one another's territorial integrity and the inviolability of existing borders within the Commonwealth', and the statement that 'the activities of the former USSR are discontinued on the territories of the member states of the Commonwealth'. The

Agreement did, however, significantly commit member states to 'preserve and maintain under united command a common military-strategic space, including unified control over nuclear weapons'.[55] What is
meant by a 'common military-strategic' space is ambiguous. Even when
this agreement was signed by representatives from the Republic of
Belarus, the RSFR and the Ukraine, the latter had taken the decision
two months earlier to establish its own national forces. Does this
conform to the idea of a common military-strategic space?

The Ukraine was soon joined in this decision by other new CIS
members – Belarus, Turkmenistan and Uzbekistan. Those who expressed
some interest in becoming members of a unitary CIS force were, in
addition to the RSFR's forces, the forces of Armenia, Kazakhstan,
Krgyzstan and Tajikistan. However, there has been no agreement on
how such forces should be organized. This does not rule out the possibility of a unitary CIS force being established at some time in the
future, but *only* after the formation of national forces. For many of the
new, larger republics national military forces are one of the cherished
symbols of independence from Russia and they will be loath to surrender these forces to a unitary force commanded by a Russian. Even
the suggestion of a two-year reorganization of the former Soviet forces,
which would take place under CIS direction, was hastily rejected by
Azerbaijan and the Ukraine.

There is danger in the lack of organization of the ex-Soviet forces.
The lack of centralized organization will allow disaffected elements
within the military to have a greater impact upon their respective national military apparatus. The clashes in Nagorno-Karabakh have also
prompted similar questions for the ex-Soviet countries, as Yugoslavia
has for NATO. Who should take responsibility for intervention in disputes which may destabilize a region? Would Russian intervention be
counter-productive and be perceived as an attempt to reassert hegemony
over their old vassals? The resentment against the 'Soviet' forces still
in the Baltic States is an indication of an extreme form of this sensitivity. There is also the problem of the status of returned military and
demobilized military personnel (especially officers). Prior to the break-
up of the USSR, military officers enjoyed many privileges with the
intention of ensuring loyalty to Moscow. Yeltsin's careful treatment
of the military and the extremely close relationship between Pavel
Grachev, Russia's defence minister, and Yeltsin, have ensured close
army support for his policies.

The military-industrial complex, previously the backbone of the Soviet
economy, has been scaled down. This, too, creates the potential for

discontent amongst those who have been laid off. Two speculative results may arise from this: first, elements of the military may find natural
allies in not only ex-communists or nationalists, but also among the
leadership of the defence industries who are also anxious to return to
the status quo and their position of relative privilege.[56] The second
danger is that, in an attempt to revive some of the ailing defence industries, politicians or industrial leaders may be more willing to violate
export controls, thereby contributing to the general process of proliferation and undermining international efforts to control exports of high-
tech weaponry. Even Gorbachev's much heralded conversion programme
(whereby defence industries are converted to civilian production) has
not yet produced significant profits. The programme has been criticized in some circles because it has not led to any appreciable 'peace
dividend'. These problems may not pose direct military threats but
they are part of a general threat to the stability of the CIS and, as
such, there is little that outside nations can do, except try and enforce
the stipulations against the export of high-tech items – which is in
itself a Herculean task.[57]

2. NATIONALISM AND IRREDENTISM

The second threat is that of *nationalism and irredentism*. The redrawing of maps since the end of the Cold War has seen the emergence of
numerous new countries, many of which are units that may prove
unsustainable economically and politically. The Cold War concern about
conflict *between* states has given way to concern about conflict *within*
states, which could then spill over borders, fuelled by vying claims to
national self-determination. At the very point when Western Europe
seems to be overcoming some of its preoccupations with the nation-
state, Eastern Europe is firmly entrenched in the process of reinventing
the nation-state based on the 'rights' of certain national minorities which,
by distinction, deny others theirs.

The Post-Cold War variant of national self-determination bears little
resemblance to its distant cousin of 1919. Instead of being based on
the concepts of popular sovereignty and democracy, it is often based
on racial, religious and linguistic factors. The changed nature of self-
determination makes it a far more insidious force, since none of the
European or CIS countries can be regarded as homogeneous in a racial,
religious or even linguistic sense. The savage fighting between the
Serbs and Croats serves as an extreme example of the new brand of

self-determination which, in this case, has led to the attempt by one party to eradicate another as a means of asserting their rights. There are counterpoints to this, such as the peaceful division of Czechoslovakia into two republics, which illustrates that maps can be redrawn peacefully.

The predominant tendency in Central and Eastern Europe is that states belong to 'peoples' or nations and not, as was assumed until recently, vice versa. An example of this tendency is the Estonian case where the government represents a 'people' that comprises 60 per cent of the population – the remainder of the population are mainly Russians and are excluded from citizenship.[58] The root of much of the resentment against non-Estonians lies in the forced repatriation of people from other parts of the Soviet Union into Estonia, in an attempt to 'Russify' Estonia and other countries. Other examples of peoples defining the state as belonging to a particular ethnic group are the Lithuanians and the Croats.

In a survey carried out in *Central and Eastern Eurobarometer* in Autumn 1992, an absolute majority (53 per cent) of Central and Eastern Europeans considered that it was up to people to decide their own future, even if this entails the break-up of the state. There was nonetheless a significant minority (38 per cent) who consider that the break-up of countries causes too much instability and that they should not, therefore, break-up. A majority in the CIS countries believe that it is up to the people to determine their own future.

The figures in Table 2.3 suggest that those countries that had a prolonged struggle for independence and those that have a sizeable Russian population are more in favour of the people's will being the decisive factor. Absolute majorities support this view with the exception of Belarus, Moldova and European Russia, where the issue divides people almost equally. Although the figures must be interpreted carefully, the data suggest that attempts to deny other ethnic groups citizenship or territory, or intervention to protect the rights of one people or the other, will be a cause of instability for Europe as a whole. The crisis in Yugoslavia started in this manner when supposedly neutral forces were sent in to keep order following a declaration of independence by Serbs in Croatia. Another example is that of Moldova where Russian-speakers proclaimed independence under the 'protection' of Russian forces. Self-proclaimed neutral forces sent to quell minority differences may, as in these cases, be far from that.

The revolutionary changes that were started under the leadership of Mikhail Gorbachev remain unfinished and unpredictable. At worst, there

Table 2.3 Do you believe that countries should stop breaking up because it creates too much instability in the region, or that it is up to the people of each country to decide their own future? (%)

Country	Stop breaking up	People's choice
Belarus	49	46
Moldova	46	50
European Russia	45	47
Czech Republic	43	54
Ukraine	41	53
Slovakia	37	59
Romania	35	59
Poland	29	58
Georgia	28	59
Bulgaria	26	50
Hungary	25	66
Armenia	23	65
(Macedonia)	22	67
Latvia	17	74
Estonia	16	78
Lithuania	14	83
Albania	12	81
Slovenia	13	82
Region Total	38	53

Source: *Central and Eastern Eurobarometer* No. 3 (Brussels: Commission of the European Communities, February 1993).

is a real likelihood of a backlash against *glasnost* and *perestroika* and the reimposition of undemocratic regimes, perhaps spearheaded by nationalist elements and a discontented military. Such backlashes clearly pose the potential for civil war and the possibility of massive population dislocation – the three million displaced by the Yugoslav crisis may look small in comparison. Anti-Russian sentiment could also act as the catalyst for bloodshed, particularly in the Ukraine or the Baltic States. The open rifts and bloodshed between supporters of President Boris Yeltsin and Vice President Aleksandr Rutskoi, following Yeltsin's dissolution of the Communist-dominated legislature on 21 September 1993, served as a reminder of how short and how fragile the democratic tradition is in Russia.[59]

However, if the potential for further instability in Russia, prompted by the reversion to some type of authoritarian regime, is taken as a threat by the Europeans, it is also a risk to those who may wish for such a regime. In the event of this happening, the new leaders would still have to face objective constraints, such as the economic situation, the hostility of others to Russia, the decline in the armed forces and the lack of any immediate allies. Self-determination movements will undoubtedly further divide the new states that have emerged since the end of the Cold War. Consider the former Soviet Union which, through independence movements and fragmentation, may well produce a collection of 'twenty to thirty more or less independent states' in the region between the NATO area, the Caucasus and Vladivostok.[60] Even this estimate may be conservative when one considers the fact that the RSFR itself is made up of sixteen autonomous republics, five autonomous provinces and nine autonomous districts and that, in the fifteen republics of the CIS, there are over one hundred ethnically distinct peoples.[61] Within the CIS there are an estimated seventy-two territorial claims, many of which are fundamentally incompatible. Of these conflicts, forty have reached the 'acute' stage.[62] In ten of the RSFR's sixteen autonomous republics the titular nationality constitutes a minority (see Table 2.4).

Clearly the ethnic composition of these ten autonomous regions is of immense concern to the stability of the RSFR. Of the remaining six autonomous regions that have a titular ethnic majority, there may be further grounds for concern since three (Dagetan, Chechen-Igush and Kabardin-Balkar) have Muslim majorities, while North Ossetia has a Muslim minority. The likelihood of further fracturing in the RSFR is high: one can only hope that it will be by peaceable, constitutional means. However, the violence witnessed so far in Osh, Kyrgyzstan, Nagorno-Karabakh, Georgia (with its three civil wars), the North Caucasus and Moldova's Trans-Dniester region, may be the tip of the iceberg. Other areas advancing claims of regional self-assertion which are currently non-violent, but may change to the use of force, are:[63] (i) Sverdlosk and its neighbouring *oblasts* (provinces) in the Urals region. Boris Yeltsin is from Sverdlosk and it is therefore expected that there will be Russian resistance to any secessionist movement. (ii) The Irkutsk region where there have been frequent demands for closer relations with Japan and the Pacific Rim. Moscow has failed to foster these relations. (iii) The Far Eastern regions, which share similar frustrations to those of the Irkutsk region. (iv) Yakutsk. The Yakuts, who have enormous mineral deposits, are anxious to exploit this wealth for themselves, a move that also has some popularity among Russians in the region.

Many of the regions that are potential flashpoints have also made the decision to establish national armed forces. Given the lack of cen-

Table 2.4 Nationalities in the autonomous republics

Autonomous Republic	% Titular Nationality	% Russian	% Other
Bashkir	21.9	39.3	38.8
Buryat	24.0	69.9	6.1
Kalmyk	45.3	37.7	17.0
Karelian	10.0	73.6	16.4
Komi	23.3	46.5	30.2
Mari	43.2	47.5	9.3
Mordov	32.5	60.8	6.7
Tatar	48.5	43.3	7.2
Udmurt	30.9	58.8	8.3
Yakut	33.4	50.3	16.3

Source: Paul B. Henze, 'Ethnic Dynamics and Dilemmas of the Russian Republic', *RAND NOTE*, N-3219-USDP. Figures used are complied from the 1989 census.

tralized control that existed in the Soviet system, this means that these new national forces could themselves become involved in an armed struggle. They, in turn, could be seen as partisan and encourage other groups outside the region to side with those who are under attack, and thus conflict could spread over borders. The dangers of this type of conflict are most obvious in Central and Eastern Europe, where political passions have been held in check by repressive regimes but never disposed of. The combination of peoples unused to exercising their democratic rights and a bureaucracy with little or no experience in managing public affairs could lead to the collapse of fledgling democracies and the re-emergence of semi-authoritarian or even dictatorial regimes.

The dispute between the rival factions in Yugoslavia serves as a warning of other potential trouble spots, such as the dispute between Hungary and Romania over the two million ethnic Hungarians in Transylvania. In addition, Eastern Europe is still fragile enough to be easily disrupted by events in the CIS, such as migratory movements and the ambiguous question of the involvement of the remaining Soviet forces in Eastern Europe.[64] Even if Eastern Europe does not succumb to external pressures, there are the risks arising from the patchwork of minorities throughout Europe – the break-up of Yugoslavia being the most powerful reminder of this. The following are amongst the minority-risk areas that will have to be monitored very carefully:[65]

Countries	Minority Dispute
Poland/Belarus, Lithuania/Ukraine	Territories lost by Poland in World War II left around 1.2 million Poles scattered throughout the former USSR.
Hungary/Romania	Hungary claims that between 1.5 and 2.3 million ethnic Hungarians have been denied economic and political rights. Romania denies this. There are also competing claims to Transylvania arising from the 1920 Treaty of Trianon that took it from Hungary.
Bulgaria/Greece, Macedonia	Bulgaria claims Macedonians are Bulgarians. Twice in the twentieth century it has occupied Macedonia and parts of Serbia.
Albania/Serbia	Albanian minorities make up almost 85 per cent of the Kosovo and Metohia region, with strong separatist tendencies. Initial demands are for the creation of a Kosovo Republic which would be unified with Albania. Although never part of Albania, it was part of the medieval Serbian empire and the cradle of Serbia's spiritual and political identity.
Greece/Albania	With around 350 000 Greeks in south Albania (known as North Epirus by Greeks) and an Albanian minority in Northern Greece, there have been 'spontaneous' exoduses across the borders.
CIS/Romania	Within the former Soviet Union there are around 3.3. million 'Moldovians' and 145 000 Romanians. Nationalists on both sides of the Prut river want a unified Romanian–Moldovian state.
Bulgaria/Turkey	Around 10-14 per cent of Bulgaria's 9 million population are Turkish Muslim or Bulgarian Muslim (Pomaks). Efforts of Turks, who fled communist suppression in 1984–85 and 1989, to return and resume their occupations are creating severe tensions.
Bulgaria/Romania	Territorial disputes stem from the divided territory of Dobrudja adjacent to the Black Sea, most notably from the Bulgarian minority in the Romanian portion.

While the list of potential flashpoints is clearly not exhaustive, it does point to the fact that internal threats should be taken very seriously in the design of any new security order. While bilateral contacts will be an important aspect of stability, such as those between Romania and France, or Greece and Bulgaria, there is a need for an overall structure to monitor and identify trouble spots at the earliest moment.

The existence of nationalist pressures in Central and Eastern Europe poses the obvious dilemma for the Western European institutions to whom many of the *states* of Central and Eastern Europe wish to accede. Does one admit potentially unstable countries and therefore risk destabilizing the entire institution, or does one not admit them and risk exacerbating potential conflicts which could have deleterious effects on the institution and its members? By itself, Eastern Europe is too fragile to withstand these pressures, and so far there has been no formal commitment to Eastern European security by its Western neighbours. The results of any of these scenarios could be serious for Europe – the loss of markets, the triggering of mass movements of people towards Western countries, the denunciation of fledgling democracies and the re-establishing of hostile totalitarian regimes. While such threats do not call for a direct military response, they would seem to call for a concerted peace-keeping role in those European countries who are not directly involved but who border on volatile trouble spots.

Similar historically based nationalist pressures are being felt in the ex-Soviet Union as well. Sometimes the nationalist or separatist pressures in Central or Eastern Europe can exacerbate the problems within the ex-Soviet territories. For instance, the overthrow and execution of Ceauşescu in Romania encouraged the aspirations of the Moldavian separatist movement, which led to ethnic clashes in Moldavia during October–November 1990. The transformations in Eastern Europe also emboldened the Poles in the Ukraine and Belarus. Although it is impossible to foresee all of the potential trouble spots, the following (on page 64) represent some that could lead to the escalation of conflict:

Area	Nature of Forces	Dispute
RSFR	CIS	Attacks on Russian population (Baltic, Tartarstan, Tajikistan etc.). Disputes with Ukraine over ex-Soviet territory.
Ukraine	National	Ukraine claims former Soviet territory in Poland, Czech, Hungary and Romania. Dispute with Russia over division of the Black Sea fleet. Ukraine unable to finance its obligations under CFE and START.
Belarus	National (maybe later CIS)	Over-deployment of ex-Soviet forces. Decision that all military forces, except strategic, fall under national command.
Moldova	National	Potential reunification with Romania will cause severe problems with Russian population. Above may also bring conflict with the Ukraine. Russians in Dnestr established a break-away republic and want to transfer to RSFR. Gagauz minority also declared an independent republic and want to transfer to RSFR. Dnestr Republic formed its own military forces with compulsory military service.
Caucasus		
Armenia	National	Multiple disputes over borders.
Azerbaijan	National	Further break-up of republics on ethnic lines.
Georgia	National	Strong opposition to Soviet forces. Plans to create a Caucasus Republic independent of the RSFR.
Soviet Asia		
Kazakhstan	National/CIS*	Possibility of union with other Islamic nations and destabilization.
Kyrgyzstan	National	
Tajikistan	CIS	Differing attitudes regarding integration with CIS.
Turkmenistan	National/CIS*	
Uzbekistan	National/CIS*	

* Interior troops only under national control.

The table above suggests that the current configuration of the CIS will change further and include the formation of more fragile republics or autonomous regions. The Caucasus shows signs of particular instability with an immensely complicated ethnic mix and unresolved conflicts between Armenia and Azerbaijan over the Armenian-populated enclave of Nagorno-Karabakh. It is beyond the scope of this brief examination to provide all of the details, but what stands out as potentially destabilizing is the role of the Russian forces in the dispute. The Russian military command of the Transcaucus Military District was originally under instructions to fight back. In February 1992 Marshal Yevgeni Shaposhnikov, commander-in-chief of the joint CIS forces, ordered a withdrawal from Nagorno-Karabakh. In a close parallel to the 14th Army in Trans-Dniester, Moldova, the Russian forces then became a target for both sides while individual units decided to join one side or the other. Fears that the conflict would spill over into Turkey prompted large manoeuvres by the Turkish 3rd Field Army and pointed at the very real possibility of elements of the former Soviet 4th Army in Armenia or the 7th Army in Azerbaijan clashing with Turkish forces. Following an offensive in May 1992, in which Armenian forces managed to take nearly all of the land between Nagorno-Karabakh and Armenia, Turkey intervened on the side of Azerbaijan and demanded US intervention.[66]

The North Caucasus has also posed challenges to the stability of the federation. War erupted in the North Caucasus, which is part of the Russian Federation, in 1992. The conflict arose when the re-established Ingush Republic demanded parts of its original lands back from North Ossetia.[67] This resulted in conflict in October, leading to many deaths and refugees. After six days of fighting, Russian paratroopers were deployed to quell the fighting. Chechnia[68] mobilized on 11 November in response to Russian intervention and threatened to attack Russian troops in Ingushetia on the grounds that they were on Chechnian territory. In spite of Russian attempts to play a peace-keeping role, its forces were allegedly supporting the orthodox Ossetians against the Sufi Muslim Ingush. Although both North Ossetia and Ingushetia remain part of the Russian Federation, the turbulence of the North Caucasus, alongside that of Nagorno-Karabakh, stands as testimony to the weakness of Russia to control or halt the spread of violence.

Georgia has also been the scene of bloody clashes between Georgian forces and two autonomous provinces (South Ossetia and Abkhazia) who are demanding secession from Georgia and the right to be independent republics. In the case of South Ossetia, a similar picture can be traced as that in Nagorno-Karabakh. The Russian forces in Georgia failed to convince the parties to the conflict that they were neutral, and came under attack from both Georgian and Ossetian forces. Fighting in Abkhazia followed soon after the declaration of independence in July 1992, but was soon quelled by the Georgian National Guard. The uneasy peace was short-lived since Abkhazia mobilized and fought back, which was interpreted in Georgia as evidence of Russian aid to the secessionists.[69] A declaration made on 25 September 1992 by the Supreme Soviet, led by Ruslan Khasbulatov, demanded that all forces surrender their arms to Russian troops. The Georgian leader at that time, Eduard Shevardnadze, was quick to point out the threat to Russia of an independent Abkhazia: it has a large Russian population, it connects the North Caucasus to the Black Sea, and it is a major exporter of citrus fruit. Deadlock ensued – Abkhazia vowed to continue the war until all Georgian troops left; Georgia remained adamantly opposed to Abkhazia's independence, and Shevardnadze demanded the withdrawal of all Russian troops from Georgia.

The above cases illustrate three important points: first, the Russian Federation is composed of far more nationalities than republics, and without tight central control further unrest is highly likely. Second, in both cases Russia has failed to convince the parties to the disputes that they are impartial and interested in peace keeping. Third, the conflict in these areas has shown an alarming tendency to spread over international borders, either literally or in the sense that the results of such conflicts impose strains upon other countries, especially through refugee movements. The last point is of special concern to those Eastern and Southern European countries who face the ramifications of unrest in Moldova as well as of the disputes in Armenia and Georgia, Turkey's neighbours.

The 'threat' posed by these various conflicts is diffuse and difficult to plan a response to. There are many conjectural effects of these conflicts for Western Europe, and potential pitfalls include the following: refugee movements prompted by war and economic depravation; human rights abuses; violation of arms control agreements; the decision to renege on the 30 December 1991 Minsk Agreement and to retain a number of nuclear weapons for internal security or to use against secessionist groups; the formation of anti-Russian blocs (for instance between the Ukrainians, Slovaks and Romanians) which could exacerbate Russian fear of being 'alone' with no buffer; the spread of conflicts in the RSFR to the Middle East or Southern Europe, which could trigger demands for NATO or WEU involvement.

Ethnic conflict and strife in several different locales could become linked and spread across national borders. The Russian Federation is therefore an area that demands careful attention on the part of Western countries and their security organizations. The examples discussed above illustrate very clearly that few governments, let alone Moscow, have complete control over their armed forces and little power to halt secession or insurrection. In spite of this, the situation would look a good deal bleaker if Russia were able to exercise *no* influence over the Federation. The fall of Yeltsin or the splintering of Russia itself would lead to a chaotic situation where it is possible not only to imagine independent republics being torn apart, but also fledgling democracies in Central and Eastern Europe being overwhelmed by the knock-on effects of the conflicts on their borders. For instance, a flood of refugees fleeing conflict in the ex-Soviet territory could severely strain already delicate Eastern European economies. It is also worth briefly reiterating that aside from the problems faced by the RSFR, there are more than enough disputes within Central or Southern Europe to give cause for concern. In addition to the former Yugoslavia, the disputes in Transylvania, Kosovo or Silesia could pose grave security problems for Europe.

This rather doom-laden examination of Europe in the late twentieth century may well evoke comparisons with the chaotic state of Europe at the start of the century. However, unlike earlier periods, the major powers have by and large remained aloof from conflicts. This can undoubtedly be explained in terms of national self-interest – none of the conflicts described above poses a threat to the survival, prosperity or the general well-being of these states. This attitude is, however, both short-sighted and unwise for several reasons.

First, the assumption that no conflict will pose a serious challenge to the well-being of the prosperous Western European or North American countries is questionable. By planning ahead, allowance can be made for potential problems, thereby incurring less expense and upset than waiting for the effects of conflict to become evident. Although it would be unrealistic to expect that it is the duty of the affluent Western countries to address all of the conflicts in Europe or elsewhere, certain steps that could be taken but have not been. For instance, a greater emphasis should be paid to developments in the south of Europe and especially along Turkey's borders. The use of available organizations should be emphasized and encouraged, such as the CSCE's monitoring efforts in Georgia and Moldova. Security guarantees cannot be extended to all, but they should be to those whose interests are most directly linked to Western Europe's.

Second, Europe is still in transition. What may initially have appeared to be optimistic models of peaceful change are now open to challenge. For instance, on 1 January 1993 Czechoslovakia split into two separate republics: the Czech and Slovak republics. Within the space of six months Slovakia began to slide towards one-party rule. In the same period of time the Czech economy, which had been regarded as the strongest in Eastern Europe, declined rapidly. Part of the decline of the Czech economy can be accounted for by the decline in trade between the two republics, as well as the breakdown of the system for settling trade payments. Furthermore Slovakia had a greater concentration of defence industry than the Czechs, which has hindered the growth of the economy – a problem compounded by a stubborn refusal to devalue Slovak currency. In the event of acute economic difficulties turning into civil unrest, the sizeable Hungarian minority in Slovakia (who account for around 10 per cent of Slovakia's population) could be at risk. Relations between the two are already tainted by mutual accusations of discrimination. An appeal by the Hungarian minority to Hungary could cause yet further unrest.

Third, it is also worth reassessing the stability of Western Europe itself. Although Western European countries do not share problems of the same gravity as their neighbours to the east, there are potentially fractious influences that could pose problems. One such example is the ongoing dispute in Belgium between the Dutch-speaking Flemings and the French-speaking Walloons. The former represent approximately 60 per cent of the Belgian population and in the last few years the Flemish economy has enjoyed an upswing. By way of contrast, the Walloon economy, based on coal and steel, has declined to the extent that it has been reclassified by the EC as amongst the poorest regions in the Community, on a par with Eire, southern Italy or Portugal. This trend has fuelled Flemish demands for separatism and led Luc van den Brande, the leader of the Flemish regional government, to publicly support separatism.[70] The Belgian case merely serves as a reminder that although Western Europe is not torn apart by nationalism to the extent that Eastern Europe or the ex-Soviet Republics are, the assumption that Western Europe is immune from pressures related to self-determination is erroneous.

3. MIGRATORY PRESSURES

The immense migratory pressures that are presently being felt in Western Europe represent a security problem that was perhaps not anticipated. The migration problem can be seen as an ironical comment upon the strenuous efforts by the West to include the principle of open borders in the 1975 Helsinki Accords. So long as Europe was divided and the Berlin Wall stood, '[The EC] could complacently preach the inalienable right to freedom of movement'.[71] The threat of invasion by the Warsaw Pact has been replaced by the prospect of masses of hungry and homeless people fleeing to Western Europe.

Migration, both legal and illegal, to Western Europe is a pressure not only from the east but also from North Africa. The pressures created by *illegal* immigrants are particularly worrisome. There are an estimated 2.8 million persons living illegally in the seventeen Western European countries. Unemployment in these same countries is expected to creep up to an average of 12 per cent by 1994, or around 19 million unemployed people.[72] Although not a traditional national security problem, illegal immigration obviously has ramifications for the economies of the host countries. Having a large number of illegal immigrants changes the Western 'host' countries' relations with their Eastern and Southern neighbours and, ultimately, their internal and external security. External problems relate to the ability of migrants to cross borders and, once inside a country, the internal problems relate to the willingness of indigenes to accept people from diverse economic, cultural and religious backgrounds. Migration problems have assumed serious proportions in the last decade, especially during the last two years, since the Yugoslav conflict erupted. Over the last ten years the number of migrants seeking asylum[73] in Western European countries has risen tenfold. In the decade up to 1992, nearly three million asylum seekers were received by Western European governments. From a total of 67 400 in 1983, the figure has leapt to nearly 700 000 in 1992 alone.[74] What is recognized in official circles as a 'refugee crisis', was further exacerbated by the conflict in the former Yugoslavia. The civil wars fought there have given rise to over one million Muslim and Croat refugees. One quarter of Bosnia's pre-war population of 4.3. million has fled. Neighbouring Croatia and Serbia have absorbed nearly 500 000 refugees (271 000 Muslim and Croat refugees from Bosnia are in Croatia, and 302 000 Bosnian Serb refugees are in Serbia and Montenegro) and around 650 000 people have fled to Western Europe

Table 2.5   Refugees from former Yugoslavia (April 1993)

Country	Refugees
Germany	300 000
Switzerland	80 000
Austria	73 000
Sweden	62 202
Hungary	40 000
Turkey	18 060*
Italy	16 000
Czech Rep./Slovakia	10 000
Denmark	7 323
Netherlands	7 000
Spain	4 654
Britain	4 424
France	4 200
Norway	3 674
Belgium	3 371
Albania	3 000*
Poland	2 100†
Finland	2 050
Luxembourg	1 618
Ireland	187
Bulgaria	185*
Portugal	250
Greece	7
Others	30 000
Total	643 205

* not confirmed
† may be as high as 3000

Source: UN High Commission for Refugees, quoted in *The Washington Post: National Weekly Edition*, 23–29 August 1993, p. 11.

– many displaced by 'ethnic cleansing.'[75] Most have fled to Germany, Austria and Switzerland. (See Table 2.5)

The displacement caused over the course of two years in the former Yugoslavia is a reminder of one of the effects of conflict. There may be other 'Yugoslavias' waiting to happen in, for example, the Caucasus, which may spark off more waves of refugees. The adoption of restrictive immigration legislation, which is examined below, is an answer to the short-term problems that many European countries face in absorbing refugees. It does not, however, address the longer-term questions of where uprooted people go and what effect these people may have on the chances of establishing some semblance of order in strife-torn countries. The new asylum laws adopted by Germany, Austria and other countries have restricted the number of immigrants to the extent that most are refused entry on the grounds that they arrived from 'safe countries'. This leaves Croatia itself facing the daunting task of coping with 271 000 Bosnian refugees, in addition to the 254 000 Croats who fled from the portion of the country occupied by Croat Serb forces. The cost of caring for these displaced people was estimated to be $746 million in 1993 – out of a total government budget of $1 billion.[76] This desperate situation led Vladimir Seks, Croatia's vice prime minister, to observe that, 'Croatia is the only European country whose borders are still open'.[77]

The situation in the former Yugoslavia raises the question of why many European governments have adopted such restrictive practices? Western Europe was able to absorb almost twenty million migrants in the first three decades after the end of World War II. With the economic downturn of Western European economies following the 1973 oil embargo, the demand for alien labour decreased. The attractiveness before the early 1970s of Western Europe to migrants and the demand for them meant that the distinctions between genuine political refugees seeking asylum and those who were primarily 'economic refugees' who sought better standards of living were not vigorously enforced. Until the mid-1970s there were around 30 000 political refugees seeking asylum in Europe each year. With recession in all of the economies and the need for 'guest workers' greatly decreased, the distinction has become a critical for all Western governments.

The popular, and often ill-informed, notion that 'foreigners' are ruining the indigenous cultures and depriving the indigenous people of 'their' jobs has had dramatic political ramifications (see Appendix II, Table A.1 and Table A.2). Almost every Western European country has some form of Far Right party expounding a mixture of racist, anti-foreigner or anti-Semitic ideas. Examples include the Freedom Party in Austria, the Republican Party in Germany, Vlaams Blok in Belgium, Falangists in Spain, the British National Party, the Front National in France and the Northern League in Italy. As in well-publicized incidents in Rostock, Mölln and Solingen, it is not always possible to attribute racially inspired violence to specific parties. While such extreme parties demand vigilance, in most cases they remain small bodies that do not enjoy representation in national legislatures and largely remain isolated from the 'responsible' political Right.

An irony of the 'refugee crisis' is that Western Europe will in fact need immigrants. The populations of the EC countries shaw little projected growth between 1992 and 2025. Some countries, like France, Italy and Germany, have come close to zero population growth rates. As a whole, the EC countries have a birth *deficit* of around 1.2 million per annum. By way of contrast, in the same period the population of North Africa is expected to grow from 147 million in 1992 to 274 million in 2025; put another way, the average Western European woman has an average of 1.5 children, while women in North Africa have 6 or more.[78] This fact is of special concern to France who had substantial colonial holdings in North Africa and already has a sizeable North African immigrant community.

Not only is Europe's population not reproducing itself, it is also 'greying.' Only fifteen years ago Europe and Africa had approximately the same number of people (around 75 million) in the age bracket 15–25; by the year 2025, Europe as a whole will have only 50 million people in that age category, while Africa will have six times more. By that same date, the population in the whole of Europe will be smaller than the population of sub-Saharan Africa alone. The result of this 'greying' is that between 1990 and 2020 the EC labour force will decline from 145 to 137 million.[79] The shortage of workers will have to be made up predominantly from North Africa or perhaps the Middle East, where there is also a high population growth rate. Eastern Europe has similar population growth patterns to Western Europe and so cannot be counted on to make up the deficit in the workplace. With an earnings ratio of 1:7 between Africa and the EC countries, there will be considerable attractions for migrants from Africa.

The cost to Western European economies of asylum seekers is another important factor driving Germany, France and other countries to adopt more restrictive asylum laws (see Appendix II, Table A.5). The cost of housing, feeding and caring for applicants and those who have been rejected but not yet deported, amounted to $8.3 billion in 1992 (by way of contrast it was $2.1 billion in 1988).[80]

The problem has been highlighted in a particularly ugly way in Germany, where in 1992 neo-Nazi groups carried out racially motivated attacks that left sixteen dead and many injured. Racially inspired attacks again resurfaced in the spring of 1993. These attacks in Germany have been against *Ausländer* generally and not specifically immigrants, but clearly immigration is exacerbating existing tensions. Germany is not alone in its treatment of immigrants and foreigners. The Italian treatment of Albanians; the French treatment of Algerians; the Kohl administration's earlier efforts to extradite Romanies; the Italian,

Spanish and French problems stemming from the Maghreb; Britain's problems with its Indo-Pakistani population – all are examples of Europe's struggle with immigration issues. Although immigration also have security dimensions, especially for those countries with common borders to Eastern Europe, like Germany, they beg for a political solution that is based on *jus soli* rather than *jus sanguinis*.

Germany has been at the centre of the migrant issue because of its proximity to Eastern Europe. Over 2.5 million immigrants have entered Germany since 1989 – which gives Germany an immigrant–indigenous population ratio several times that of any other West European country and twice that of the US during the 1920s.[81] Article 16 of the Basic Law grants 'persons persecuted on political grounds' the right of asylum. This catch-all phrase served as a symbol for Germany's openness during the Cold War years and enabled Germany to distance itself from its xenophobic history. This same phrase became the cause of political concern and popular resentment in Post-Cold War Germany until it was eviscerated on 1 July 1993. This clause brought in 438 000 immigrants in 1992 alone, threatening not only Germany's political stability but also economic stability in a country that was already trying to cope with the demands emanating from unification.

The growth in asylum-seekers has been staggering. Germany is host to approximately 1.4 million refugees from around the world and, of these, around 500 000 have applied for asylum. A total of 368 536 sought asylum in Germany in the first ten months of 1992, a figure that is 81 per cent higher than the corresponding figure (203 321) for the first ten months of 1991 (256 112 sought asylum in the whole of 1991).[82] Of these, a small number can expect to be granted asylum (a decision made on 16 362 cases in October 1992 resulted in favourable outcomes for 702, which means that 70.9 per cent were rejected). However, it can take up to thirteen months for a case to be considered and only some 200 000 cases can be processed in a year. One estimate suggests that there could be as many as 630 000 outstanding cases in Germany alone.[83]

Chancellor Kohl's government has had to cope with not only the formidable task of integrating seventeen million former East Germans but also the flood of refugees. Some of the racially inspired violence was undoubtedly due to a decision by the government to spread the refugees evenly throughout Germany; the theory being that they would be integrated into German society with greater ease. However, with unemployment running at an average of 17 per cent, and in parts of the eastern *Länder* reaching 30 per cent, the seeds of discontent and resentment were sown.

The Bundestag debated an amendment (*Begleitgestez*) on the asylum issue in March 1993. Several proposals were forwarded to amend Article 16 of the Basic Law which would reduce the number of foreigners able to enter Germany and claim asylum. The proposed amendment, specifically excluded those who were not 'politically persecuted' but merely sought a better standard of living. Accordingly, a list of 'safe countries' was proposed where political persecution was deemed not to exist and from which persons would not be eligible for asylum: the countries include most of Eastern Europe, India, Ghana and Senegal. Those who enter by land from neighbouring 'safe' countries, such as Austria, Switzerland, Poland and the Czech and Slovak Republics, are also not eligible for asylum. The controversial article was eventually dropped from the constitution on 1 July 1993. Immediately the number of asylum seekers in July was 10 000 lower than in June.[84] By August, the number of asylum seekers was half that of June and several refugee camps stood empty.[85] As a result of the amendment, Germany's immigration policies went from being amongst the most open in Europe to the most restrictive.

The attention paid to Germany's migration problems might create the false impression that other European countries are not also faced with grave problems and that German public opinion is more hostile to immigrants than other European countries. This is not the case. Due to its geographical location, Austria also finds itself a convenient target for refugees from the former Eastern bloc. Historically Austria has absorbed considerable numbers of refugees: 12 000 Hungarians in 1956, a smaller number from Czechoslovakia during the Prague Spring in 1968, and then Poles fleeing in 1981, following the imposition of martial law. Since the 1950s, more than two million refugees have arrived in Austria and around 600 000 have remained. In 1990–91 the number of foreign labourers doubled, following an influx from Hungary, Poland and the Czech and Slovak republics.[86] Austria's influx has dramatically increased since the war in Yugoslavia which, like the upheavals referred to above, has left Austria as an attractive target for those fleeing from danger or persecution – Austria has officially registered 47 000 Bosnians, but the real number is over 70 000.[87] The absence of anti-foreigner agitation, of the kind witnessed in Germany, has enhanced the country's attractiveness. As a result, Austria's interior minister, Franz Loschnak, has expressed growing agitation with the refusal of other Western European countries to share the problem.[88] Austria also adopted new, stringent laws in June 1992 which were designed to make political asylum difficult to attain. Like the revised German laws, the new laws refuse to accept asylum applications from those who have come through 'safe' countries. The new Austrian laws would appear to have been effective. In the first six months of 1992 there were 11 875 applications for asylum. In the first six months of 1993 that number had dropped to 2490.[89] The numbers have also been kept lower than they might have been due to the fact that the principal transit countries into Austria – Hungary and Slovenia – require proof of a visa to a third country before a transit permit can be issued.

The south of Europe also faces severe migratory pressures from North Africa and the Maghreb (see Appendix II, Table A.3). Take the example of Cadiz, which is a scant nine miles across the Straits of Gibraltar from Morocco. In the first eight months of 1992, 1500 immigrants were arrested in the province of Cadiz.[90] The majority of those emigrating to Spain come from Morocco, but substantial numbers are beginning to come from Liberia, Senegal, Ghana, Ethiopia, Somalia and the Sudan. Spain already hosts around 300 000 illegal immigrants and the prospects for more are high, especially from Morocco which has around three million of its twenty-six million population unemployed. The prospects of civil unrest, spiralling population growth, and stagnant economies could lead up to twenty-five million people from the Maghreb region to enter the EC through Spain.[91] Nevertheless, Spain also has a substantial influx from Eastern and Central Europe. Of the (legal) immigrant population in Spain, around 9 per cent are Asian, 55.1 per cent are Africans, 27.8 per cent are from Latin America and 7.5 per cent are Europeans.[92]

Greece, to take another example, has employed the most drastic solution to the immigration problem to date. Over the course of the last three years an estimated 200 000 Albanians have slipped over the border. As a result of the expulsion of a Greek orthodox priest from Albania, the Greek government took this as a pretext to round up and expel 25 000 Albanians.[93]

The immigration problem in France, and particularly that associated with the Maghrébins, accounts for the rise in popularity of Jean-Marie Le Pen's Front National and its anti-immigrant strains. The appeal of the Extreme Right has been aided by remarks made by ex-Prime Minister Edith Cresson, to the effect that 'special planes' would be used to deport illegal immigrants, as had been done in 1986 to return 101 illegal immigrants to Mali.[94] Jacques Chirac, the mayor of Paris and leader of the neo-Gaullist Rassemblement pour la République, also made some ill-timed remarks about the plight of a hypothetical French couple of modest means living in a public housing project in Paris who are confronted with a large immigrant family with a 'father, three or four wives and twenty or so children, getting 50 000 francs in welfare payments, naturally without working. If you add to that the noise and the odour, the French worker on the landing goes crazy.'[95] Although Chirac never provided examples of such families, his ratings in the opinion polls rose. The rightist interior minister, Charles Pasqua, has also declared a goal of 'zero immigration'.

Britain is in a slightly different situation since, as an island, it does not face the same direct pressure from illegal immigrants who demand asylum. However, with a large ethnic minority – an estimated 2.6 million out of a population of 56 million (compared to 4 million out of a population of 57 million in France) – and a gloomy economic situation, incidents of racially motivated incidents have increased from 4383 in 1988 to 7793 in 1992.[96] Much of the violence was not systematically organized. The British National Party (BNP) has adopted an open anti-immigration stance, but has neither a national following (there are approximately three thousand BNP members, the majority around the Milwall area of London), nor is a serious contender for seats in parliament. The BNP has also been unsuccessful in making immigration its issue; nearly all of the mainstream British parties have tacitly supported the whites who feel engulfed by immigration. Much of the urgency attached to the British debate about the effects of immigration results from misrepresentation. For instance, Winston Churchill, the wartime leader's grandson, made a plea in the House of Commons for a halt to the 'relentless flow of immigrants' so that the 'British way of life' may be preserved. He also misrepresented immigration in some towns in Britain, such as Bradford and Leeds, when he claimed that half of the population were immigrants – 15 per cent is nearer the mark.[97] Nevertheless, as a result of his plea he received 7500 letters, with a ratio of 100:1 in support.[98] In spite of the popular impression of Britain being invaded by immigrant hordes, Britain's primary immigration from its ex-colonial possessions ceased years ago. In 1992, only 52 000 immigrants were admitted on the grounds of their special skills.[99] The feelings of insecurity arising from immigration are thus attributable to a lack of impartial information in the first place and, secondly, to the general economic depression that has engulfed the developed countries.

Public opinion within Western Europe illustrates some interesting, and sometimes puzzling, trends. For instance, a majority of people in the EC countries feel that there are too many people living in their country who are not nationals of any of the EC states (see Table 2.6).

Table 2.6 How many people from non-EC countries reside in your country? (figures for EC 12, %)

	Too many	A lot, but not too many	Not a lot
January 1991	50	34	9
January 1992	50	35	9
January 1993	52	34	9

Source: *Eurobarometer*, No. 39 (Brussels: Commission of the European Communities, June 1993) p. 86.

Table 2.7 How do you experience the presence of foreigners in your country? (figures for EC 12, poll taken January 1993, %)

	Disturbing	Not disturbing
Other nationality	13	83
Other race	16	81
Other religion	13	82

Source: *Eurobarometer*, No. 39 (Brussels: Commission of the European Communities, June 1993) p. 86.

In countries where immigration has been traditionally high, such as Belgium, Germany, France and Britain, there has been a long-held opinion that there are too many immigrants. The biggest increase in those who believe that there are too many immigrants can be found in Greece and the former East Germany, while Luxembourg shows the biggest decrease in this belief (for details on individual countries, see Appendix II).

At the same time as there is a consensus that there are too many non-EC nationals living in the EC countries, polls suggest that large majorities (for details see Appendix II) are *not* bothered by the presence of residents of other nationalities, race or religion (see Table 2.7). The poll data also suggest that the origin of non EC-nationals who come to work in EC countries has little impact upon the welcome given by EC citizens, with the possible exception of immigration from other EC countries, where there is a higher acceptance of immigrants (see Table 2.8).

There are, however, some significant differences on a country-by-country basis (see Appendix II). The data suggest that since the spring of 1992 Spain, Portugal, Ireland and Italy have been the most open-minded. However, this has changed, especially in Spain and Portugal,

Table 2.8   What do you feel about the different groups of immigrants? (figures for EC 12, poll taken January 1993, %)

	Welcome	Welcome with reservations	Not welcome
S. Mediterranean	15	57	24
E. Europe	12	59	25
Political Exiles	24	51	19
Other EC countries	35	46	14

Source: *Eurobarometer*, No. 39 (Brussels: Commission of the European Communities, June 1993) p. 88.

which face severe immigration pressure from North Africa.

It is clear that, apart from adopting highly restrictive legislation, the solution to the problem of migration from and through North Africa lies largely in that region itself. In spite of the anticipated population growth rates, the area is overpopulated in relation to its resources, but not its area. For example, Morocco is five times larger than Italy but has only half the population; Algeria is four times larger than France but has only half the population; Tunisia is five times larger than the Netherlands but has half the population. The EC could, do much to solve migratory pressures from the south and stabilize the area politically by encouraging private investment in these countries. The continuing existence of a relatively affluent EC which, according to World Bank figures, enjoy a per capita GNP over ten times that of its southern Mediterranean and North African neighbours, will act not only as a reminder of the very real North–South divide but also will continue to be a magnet to those fleeing poverty and instability.[100] Many of the Maghreb countries face challenges to democracy, but countries like Tunisia have demonstrated that it is possible to pursue democracy and economic reforms in the face of these challenges. Regional integration, such as the formation of the Arab Maghreb Union in 1988, offers further bulwarks against extremism and opportunities for economic reform.[101]

In security terms the formation of a Mediterranean imitator of the CSCE, the Conference on Security and Cooperation in the Mediterranean (CSCM), should also be encouraged as a highly positive development. There is already an established dialogue between the Arab Maghreb Union states and the five southern Mediterranean states (France, Italy, Malta, Portugal and Spain), but this should be expanded to the

EC as a whole. There is clearly a need for northern European countries to enhance this dialogue and to strive towards practical measures
to enhance stability and productivity in the south of Europe and North
Africa. This would not only benefit these countries, but be in the self-
interest of the more affluent European countries.

The immigration wave from the east has been exacerbated by the
reform of Soviet passport laws, which now allows millions of people
to move around Europe. These people could head towards Finland and
Germany as well as Hungary, Poland and the Czech and Slovak Republics. The strain on the fragile economies of the latter countries could,
at best, put tremendous pressure on the already scarce resources and,
at worst, cause the collapse of their fragile democracies and economies.
The potential for this to happen has resulted in the decision by the EC
to delay until 1 July 1993 the implementation of the Schengen Agreement (it was due to be implemented at the beginning of 1990), which
removes all border controls between France, Germany, Italy and the
Benelux countries.[102] Even with the implementation of the Schengen
Accords, a significant number of people in the EC as a whole are only
willing to accept immigrants from other EC countries (see Appendix II).

The delay in the implementation of the EC's Schengen Accords,
which would allow the free movement of people between nine countries (as in the US between states), was largely prompted by fears of
influxes of migrants and secondary concerns about terrorism and narcotics – these latter in particular being the grounds for Britain's and
Denmark's non-participation in the Accords. As has been observed,
the primary migratory pressures come from North Africa, but there are
also significant ones emanating from the PHARE/TACIS countries.[103]

A majority of those interviewed in the *Central and Eastern Eurobarometer* survey, conducted in the autumn of 1992, have seriously
considered moving to Western Europe (see Table 2.9). However, there
may be something of the 'grass is greener on the other side of the
fence' syndrome since, when asked a variation of the question above,
the response is slightly different (see Table 2.10).

The figures in Table 2.10 would obviously require some adjustment
since the poll does not allow for the full effects of the war in Bosnia.
Nevertheless, there is a surprising consistency, since almost as many
TACIS (28 per cent) as PHARE (30 per cent) citizens would consider
moving; a similar pattern emerges with their concrete intentions to
live in Western Europe (8 per cent and 10 per cent respectively). In
terms of numbers of people, the number who say they will definitely
go (1.2 per cent) amounts to 2.7 million. The more vague category of

Table 2.9 Have you ever seriously considered going to work in a country in Western Europe? (%)

	Considering	Not considering	Already*
Albania	54	39	1
(Macedonia)	44	46	5
Armenia	40	53	1
Slovakia	37	60	1
Georgia	36	58	2
Slovenia	32	63	3
Belarus	32	65	3
Romania	32	65	2
Estonia	31	64	3
Czech Republic	30	69	1
Poland	29	65	4
Ukraine	28	69	1
Latvia	27	68	1
European Russia	27	70	1
Bulgaria	25	67	1
Hungary	24	74	1
Lithuania	23	75	1
Moldova	16	79	1
Region Total	29	68	1

* Already = already worker in that country.

Source: *Central and Eastern Eurobarometer,* No. 3 (Brussels: Commission of the European Communities, February 1993).

those who would consider going (6.1 per cent) would amount to around 16.7 million (the definites, plus the 'consider' category, amount to approximately the size of the population of the former East Germany).

The immigration problem has a pernicious nature: on the one hand it often feeds people into economies to do jobs that citizens of the country in question prefer not to do. On the other, it breeds resentment, xenophobia and violence. There are no traditional solutions, and what solutions may be advanced fall outside the scope of the existing security institutions, except maybe the European Union. The best solutions lie in a combination of economic and political suasion. Most immigrants are fleeing from economic deprivation or political persecution, or a combination of the two. Logic suggests that solutions to this problem lie primarily with the European Community, who should create incentives for these people *not* to leave. This is clearly a mammoth task and involves a combination of strengthening economic collaboration

Table 2.10 How likely is it that you will move to Western Europe to live and work? %

	Emigrate*	Not emigrate**	Certain
Albania	53	29	33
Georgia	26	45	6
(Macedonia)	22	54	5
Armenia	21	69	4
Romania	17	79	3
Latvia	12	82	2
Estonia	12	82	2
Ukraine	12	83	1
Bulgaria	11	82	2
Lithuania	9	88	1
Slovenia	7	89	1
Belarus	7	89	1
Slovakia	6	89	1
Czech Republic	6	93	1
European Russia	5	90	0
Poland	5	90	2
Hungary	4	94	1
Region Total	9	86	1

* Emigrate Considering or probably.
** Not Emigrate = Probabiy not or definitely not.

Source: *Central and Eastern Eurobarometer* (Brussels: Commission of the European Communities, February 1993).

with the countries of Eastern Europe in particular. The EC should also adopt common rules for the granting of asylum, which would simplify the processing of requests for asylum. A significant, but unquantifiable, number of immigrants arrive in Western Europe via Eastern and Central Europe. The adoption of tougher immigration rules by these countries would alleviate some of the pressure, but would run the risk of sending back asylum seekers to possible death or encouraging the formation of small nucleii of radicals dedicated to the overthrow of regimes by violent means. Lastly, those countries that pose major immigration headaches for European countries should be given economic incentives to stem their own migratory flow. Those that make a concerted effort to do so should be proportionately rewarded.

The irony, as has already been pointed out, is that Western Europe does need immigrants to buoy up its falling birth rates and its greying population. The issues are how they will attract the right number, how they will assimilate immigrants who will come from North Africa in particular and who, more likely than not, will be Muslim. One solution would be to answer Western Europe's need for workers and alleviate some of the immigratory pressures by adapting the German *Gastarbeiter* model. Under this model, work permits (not citizenship) could be granted to immigrants with strict conditions attached which guaranteed that the workers would return to their country of origin at the expiry of their permit. This would allow the EC countries to exercise some control over the influx of immigrants and, more importantly, would act as a valuable source of earnings and stability for other countries – as in the case of Turkey where earnings from workers in Germany have helped development significantly.

The immigration problem calls for a concerted effort to be made through national governments, the EC, and even the CSCE, which could act as a forum to discuss progress on the issue. Progress will have to be made on the immigration issue for European Union to have any real substance. Since it remains primarily a political issue, with security ramifications,[104] immigration will not be discussed at length here; but to exclude it as an area of concern would have been short-sighted.

4. THE ROLE OF GERMANY IN ANY NEW EUROPEAN SECURITY ORDER

The East–West divide of the Cold War period effectively restricted not only Germany's military power but also its influence in Europe. The reunification of Germany and its restoration to full sovereignty has once again placed Germany at the centre of Europe. This, in turn, has given rise to the 'new German question', which concerns the direction that unified Germany will adopt. Will Germany adopt an independent role, perhaps deepening its ties to the East and to the detriment of those with the West? Will Germany pursue some historical vision of *Mitteleuropa?* What effect will unification have on the attempt to create a European Union, as posited by the Maastricht Treaty? What role should Germany play in the new security order?

The role that Germany presently plays in Europe, and could play in the future, are examined in detail in a later chapter. Suffice it to say at this stage that any new or adapted European security structure would clearly be incomplete without Germany. The initial fears associated with post-unification Germany, particularly those associated with Germany's economic might, have proven to have had some basis with the near collapse of the ERM in the spring of 1993. When faced with a conflict between stabilizing German interest rates, or following the ERM guidelines, the Bundesbank insisted that it was its constitutional responsibility to take care of its national interests before those implied by the ERM. In the security realm there are concerns associated with this type of decision-making: namely, the potential for Germany to drift towards a pacifist or neutral stance.

While Germany has in many ways been the most influential European actor in its efforts to support the fragile democratic regimes to its east, including the CIS countries, its military policies are dated. Germany still clings to conceptions of self-defence based on Cold War notions of the defence of NATO territory against aggression. Clearly these notions are dated since, as is argued below, many of the security challenges facing Europe will emanate from outside the NATO area. Chancellor Kohl missed an opportunity during the Gulf War to demonstrate solidarity and support his European partners when Germany declined to become involved in the coalition forces, preferring instead to give financial aid.

Germany is central to any attempt to form a European security identity as part of the ongoing Maastricht process; and, with one of the largest and best trained armies in Europe, German participation in out-of-area contingencies is paramount. While there are signs that the Kohl administration is slowly prompting the German public to accept a wider international role in peace-keeping operations, there is still political opposition from the SPD and historical qualms about Germany assuming such a role. Germany's reluctance to redefine its military policies in a manner more fitting to the exigencies of the Post-Cold War world has met with criticism from other European countries. Germany was also criticized for its assertive behaviour when, in December 1991, it prematurely recognized Croatia and Slovenia, contrary to the wishes of the other EC members. The criticisms of Germany's non-role in the Gulf War and those following the recognition of Croatia and Slovenia illustrate the fact that there is still a residual concern about Germany's Post-Cold War role. In defining this role, Germany will shape the future of the European security order.

5. IMPLICATIONS FOR THE SECURITY OF EUROPE

Europe, much as it may wish it were, is not an island. The demands made upon the main European powers in the maintenance of peace and stability will undoubtedly exercise most of their energies. However,

Europe exists in a global context as well, with obligations to the international community. Many of the 'Twenty-first century threats', which include the pandemic AIDS, drug trafficking, pollution, human rights, environmental problems, and so forth, may have important ramifications for Europe. All of these problems have security implications for the European countries, but are best suited to political negotiations at an international or regional level.

Some of the existent European security institutions are suited to addressing aspects of these questions; for instance, the record of the Council of Europe and the CSCE have been impressive in the area of human rights, while the EC and UN have made slow but significant steps on environmental questions. The pandemic AIDS will continue to be addressed by a combination of national resources and international aid coordinated mainly through the UN. It is clear that those countries most threatened by AIDS, such as Uganda or Thailand, need more help from developed countries and international bodies.

The Iraqi invasion of Kuwait in August 1990 serves as a reminder that there is always the possibility of conflict outside of Europe which may have serious security implications for the region. The construction of a European security order that is intended to enhance peace and stability in Europe may still face challenges from elsewhere on the continent. The emphasis upon the ability to intervene outside the traditionally defined area of security interest must therefore be maintained. Other potential sources of instability that may arise from outside Europe are touched upon in the above section. Two in particular, those of weapons proliferation in the Third World and Middle East, and migratory movements, need careful monitoring.

The implications of the new security challenges facing Europe are many. There will be obvious effects upon military force levels as well as upon the designation of those forces. For example, more emphasis will have to be put on highly mobile forces; there will need to be on defence, while more will have to be put on *early* intervention with the aim of stopping a conflict from spreading. It is this last point that may imply the most profound change of all: the way in which we think about sovereignty.

European concepts of statehood, and thus sovereignty, evolved from the 1648 Treaty of Westphalia, which ended the prolonged miseries of the Thirty Years' War. A combination of secularism and absolutism made the state the primary focus of the individual's loyalties. From the end of the Thirty Years War onwards, the nation-state achieved an unassailable position above the law. Article 2 (7) of the UN Charter enshrined the primacy of the state in international affairs when it stated:

> Nothing contained in the present Charter shall authorize the United Nations to intervene in matters which are essentially within the domestic jurisdiction of any state or shall require the Members to submit such matters to settlement under the present Charter . . .

However, there has long been an inherent tension in the role of the state and the legal rights of groups and individuals as subjects under international law. For instance, the UN Charter appears to confirm the primacy of the state, but the Preamble also recognizes the 'faith in fundamental human rights . . . equal rights of man and women and of nations large and small . . . and to establish conditions under which justice and respect for the obligations arising from treaties and other sources of international law can be maintained'. Article 1 (3) states that the purpose of the UN is to 'achieve international cooperation in solving international problems of an economic, social, cultural or humanitarian character'. Rights, aside from those pertaining to the state, are also established elsewhere, such as in the 1948 Universal Declaration of Human Rights. The question of whose rights prevail, whether it is those of the individual or group, or those of the state, is open to debate. Much of the international system is based on the idea of a state-centric order where, in the positivist tradition, international law evolves primarily from the state and 'rights' exist because the state wishes them to. In a differing tradition, natural law, stemming from the thoughts of Augustine or Thomas Aquinas, argues that there is a higher authority than the state evolving from human nature and understanding.

Clearly the nation-state's near monopoly on aggression has changed, with an increasing number of non-state actors involved in conflict. According to SIPRI data, there were thirty major armed conflicts in the world in 1992, with most in Asia (eleven) and relatively few in Europe (four).[105] Under the SIPRI counting rules, conflicts must be prolonged and involve two governments, or a government and at least one organized armed group; of the thirty conflicts identified, most fall into the latter category. Many of the conflicts do not involve the stronger powers directly, but the suffering caused to civilians and those who are the object of hatred opens the question of the obligation of the stronger powers to help the innocent.

The debate over individual or group rights versus those of state sovereignty is not just a matter of legal niceties; it is a debate that will assume increasing importance for international and European security issues. There are several ways in which this may be of particular importance for Europe: (i) The 'new' security challenges facing Europe, and indeed those in other parts of the world, will pose problems that may well fall within the domestic jurisdiction of a state; yet these new security challenges may well have grave consequences for other countries as well. (ii) The intrusiveness of modern satellite systems and global communications has literally opened states up to international purview. (iii) Many European countries are signatories to major international treaties recognizing the rights of individuals and groups. (iv) Violent acts may emanate increasingly from non-state actors (ethnic groups, religious groups, terrorists, and so on). (v) Poverty and treatment of ethnic minorities may make 'humanitarian intervention' increasingly necessary.

Delicate areas, such as human rights abuses against Kurds in northern Iraq which led to UN Security Council Resolution 688 in April 1991, have the potential to pose a head-on clash between state sovereignty and the rights of individuals.[106] The fate of former Yugoslavia yet again serves as another disturbing example of the problems of reconciling state sovereignty with the security concerns of the international community. Unfortunately, the Kurdish example is an atypical example of a group of countries being in a position to force compliance, whereas in other cases, such as in Bosnia or Cambodia, international responses were not forthcoming.

What is required is a balancing act between the concept of sovereignty and the need to protect minorities and groups who may be subject to victimization by undemocratic regimes. The concept of sovereignty will have to be balanced with growing international ties, an idea forwarded eloquently by Boutros Boutros-Ghali in his 'Agenda for Peace' speech in the United Nations General Assembly:

> Respect for [the state's] fundamental sovereignty and integrity are crucial to any common international progress. The time of absolute and exclusive sovereignty, however, has passed; its theory was never matched by reality. It is the task of leaders of States today to understand this and to find a balance between the needs of good internal governance and the requirements of an ever more interdependent world.[107]

Finding this balance will not be easy. Clearly, in a highly interdependent world the domestic affairs of one state are of interest to others. But at what point do the potentially deleterious effects of the domestic affairs of a particular state give another state the right to intervene? Does the proven abuse of human rights in a particular state give the international community the duty to intervene?

There are no easy answers to these questions. Two possible approaches that would begin to answer some of these questions, would be a re-definition of 'aggression', as defined by the UN General Assembly in 1974, and a clear distinction between collective security and multi-lateralism. The General Assembly's definition of aggression is insufficient largely because it omits important types of conflict, such as intra-state hostilities and terrorism.[108] A more comprehensive definition of aggression would extend the meaning of 'acts of aggression' as they appear in Article I and Chapter VII of the UN Charter, and would extend the range of threats to international peace and security that would invoke a UN response.[109] A clearer understanding of collective security and multilateralism may also help. The UN has never functioned as a true collective security operation. It has been heavily reliant upon regional organizations for the use of force. As a result of this, multi-lateral uses of force are often used in lieu of collective security. The coalition assembled after the Iraqi invasion of Kuwait serves as an example; it used the twelve Security Council resolutions as the legal basis for the force, yet the force was not under UN command, and the extent of reporting back to the Security Council was minimal. The confusion between multilateralism and collective security has led to a situation where there would appear to be no *obligations* to intervene, unless it is in the national interest of a great power or group of powers. This explains, in part, the reason why swift and decisive action was taken against Kuwait, but not in the Bosnian case.

A move towards strengthening collective security, which means prior agreement that operating procedures to be used in the event of a crisis are *consistently* implemented, would have important effects for Europe. There may also be some more direct implications for European security organizations, such as the CSCE. They would be faced with greater demands for security assistance, but there would at least be an alternative to *ad hoc* responses of the Bosnian type, which in that case left thousands of innocent people dead. Although such an agreement may cost more, it would seem to be a prudent investment in peace and stability, and preferable to hoping problems will go away, because if they don't they may become far more intractable, difficult and costly to solve.

CONCLUSIONS

Contrary to the views of many realists, who argue that the Cold War period, marked by a bipolar system, was one of immense stability, and that the current multipolar order is one marked by instability, there are strong arguments that suggest that the stability of the Cold War world has been exaggerated. The incidence of conflict may not have diminished significantly but the *type* of conflict, involving major powers, that could lead to global wars, has lessened. No matter how grave the problems are that face Europe today, the division of the continent and its ultimate threat of destruction no longer hangs over Europe. This is the most important and encouraging change in post-Cold War Europe.

The post-Cold War world will see more conflicts concerned with state formation: these will involve non-governmental opposition forces that are in favour of changing the constitutional status of a territory, either by seceding or by gaining territory.[110] The Yugoslav crisis falls under the latter category, but nevertheless poses problems for the international community, since it is not clear if such conflicts fall under the aegis of international security bodies, such as the UN, or whether they are internal matters. Conflicts within states and over the issue of state formation have the potential to be destabilizing for a region but need not threaten the international system.

A qualification needs to be added to the above observation: Russia is still a major military power and therefore needs to be treated with caution. There are numerous scenarios that could be conjured up, ranging from Russian military intervention in the Baltic States to 'protect' the rights of the Russians there, to the possibility of the disgruntled heads of the ex-Soviet military allying with ex-Communists to form the bulwark of an undemocratic opposition group that may have aspirations of regaining some of their empire. In spite of the various arms-control treaties that the Soviet Union signed, and the more recent December 1991 Alma-Ata Declaration between the RSFR, Ukraine, Belarus and Kazakhstan, and the START agreements, there are still thousands of nuclear weapons in the former Soviet Union. The impossibility of deterring an irrational or unauthorized use of nuclear forces underlines the importance of, in the first place, maintaining a minimal deterrent force in Europe and, second, of pursuing arms control more vigorously, at the negotiating table. The precise nature of the deterrent force maintained in Europe matters less than ever before – that there is *something*, is the important point.

All of the challenges to European security outlined above suggest that there are some essential tasks that the affluent industrialized nations of Western Europe and North America should address:

(1) Germany must be anchored in Europe and be encouraged to continue its role as a major force in European integration, which should become a pan-European movement.

(2) The idea of Europe, in security terms, being confined to the NATO area is clearly passé. Europe in security terms must be expanded to include Russia, and it must address those threats which may arise from neighbouring areas, such as the Middle East. Although Russia need not be a member, any new security order in Europe must be constructed in such a manner that the Russians do not feel excluded or isolated. Any new or evolving European security order that excluded Russia and ignored threats from adjoining regions would clearly be constructed on shaky foundations.

(3) The further proliferation of nuclear weapons within the ex-Soviet Union or involving other areas should be prevented by collaboration, including curtailing the export of applicable technologies and using international bodies and arms control negotiations to further reduce the number of such weapons.

(4) The existing institutional structures in Europe can be used to promote links and ties between countries and groups. These ties should be designed to counter nationalist or ethnic impulses by demonstrating the benefits of collaboration across borders and divisions.

(5) A preventative mechanism must be designed that will intervene at the *earliest* hint of conflict, before it spreads to neighbouring countries. Similarly, efforts should also be made to halt the spread of security problems from North Africa, the Middle East and other neighbouring regions, that might become European problems.

(6) While the state will remain the primary building-block of the international community, but the growing interdependence of the global community and the effects of domestic actions upon other states must be recognized; eventually provision should also be made for intervention in cases involving the abuse of citizens by their government or upon humanitarian grounds.

(7) The international obligations of Europe, especially those concerning the environment, should be given equal priority with domestic and regional agendas.

Underlying all of the security issues outlined above, there is a common denominator – economics. Many of the problems are driven by economic factors; for example, the migratory movements from the Third World to Europe are largely economic in character, as are some of the same movements from Eastern and Central Europe to Western Europe. Economic health is a critical underpinning in the construction and maintenance of democracy. Democratic institutions, in turn, form strong disincentives for aggression. Economics may also be behind weapons proliferation, as major arms suppliers struggle to keep ailing defence industries open by searching for new markets. The global recession has affected the US, Japan and Western European economies means that a 'Marshall Plan' for the 1990s is out of the question. The post-Second World War Marshall Plan was launched at a time when the US had by far the largest economy in the world, representing almost half of the world's GNP. Clearly, no one power has this economic leverage in the 1990s.

A rethinking of the term 'threat' may also be constructive. The word 'threat' is linked to military connotations (such as NATO's Cold War use of the word in the context of 'threat perception') and, since many of the threats outlined above do not demand an obvious military response, it may be more accurate to think in terms of *challenges* or *problems* which demand responses beyond those of a military nature. By thinking in terms of challenges to security, a response is demanded that involves societies as a whole and their assets, not just the military and their arsenals.

Part II
Leadership Issues in Post-Cold War European Security

3 European Leadership: A Ship without a Rudder

Institutions are useful only as tools through which states or organizations work. By themselves they are inert. The success of any institution depends upon two factors: first, the willingness of the major powers to work through the institution, and, second, leadership and initiative within a given institution. As has been argued in the previous chapter, there is a willingness on the part of all the major powers to work through institutions – albeit differing ones in some cases. The problems lie in the second factor: there is an unwillingness on the part of the major powers to take the initiative in a security environment that is much more unpredictable than that of 1945, and there is little consensus about which institutions to work through.

In the immediate post-World War II period, the US emerged as the undisputed Western leader in the economic and military realms. This capacity was soon backed by a political resolve. In spite of it being fashionable to describe the post-Cold War world as 'unipolar', it is not clear that the Europeans can rely upon the US for leadership or initiative in the same way that they could in 1945. The US has neither the money nor, arguably, the political resolve to assume an unequivocal leadership role; nor do the European powers wish to subsidize the US to carry out such a role. Yet, at the same time, the main European powers seem reluctant to take the initiative themselves and assume full responsibility for their own security affairs. Excuses for this are often based upon the argument that the necessary institutional machinery for a common foreign and defence policy is not yet in place.

The lack of any clear European security identity can be attributed to several reasons. The first rationale may be found in changes in the definition of security itself and the tendency for security not to assume the high priority position that it once occupied. Those powers who could, in concert, play a leading role, have become preoccupied with other more pressing problems now that the overarching threat, which challenged their very survival, has disappeared. The primary concerns are now domestic and, in particular, economic. The initial expectations amongst the Western publics that there would be a 'peace dividend' following the end of the Cold War has also engendered the attitude that security is less important than it was in the Cold War.

The second explanation, based on past historical experience, encompasses the neo-realist approaches to post-Cold War Europe which have led us to expect competition within Europe for leadership.[1] The fact that this has not happened indicates that there is something at fault with these expectations. Since the 'currency' of power has changed and the amassing of military might no longer has the attraction that it used to, there is a disincentive to compete for leadership on the battlefield, which has been the conclusion of past European power struggles. The obvious expectation would be for competition to be transferred simply to those areas of central concern to European states. However, the existence of the EU acts as a built-in disincentive to pursue competitive strategies within the Community (especially since Germany, as the strongest economy, is an export-driven economy).

A more accurate way of explaining the apparent lack of leadership or initiative in European security is something more akin to a *reverse-realist* paradigm, where, instead of a competition for power and influence, states attempt to *avoid* positions of leadership and responsibility because such positions may imply commitments and obligations that individual states or groups are unwilling to assume.

Realist-type power struggles, in the traditional sense, are unlikely in Western Europe, as the potential rivals (Germany, France, Britain and Italy) are interdependent economically. Economic interdependence and the lessons learnt from Europe's experiences in two world wars act as strong disincentives to rivalry. Interdependence also breeds complacency in the form of an unwillingness to accept wider international responsibilities that stretch beyond the immediate concerns of the group of states or, in this case, the EU. This too is reflected in the security field. Since there is little in Europe that will fundamentally challenge the borders or sovereignty of the main Western European powers, most 'new' security challenges will appear far more remote. Only in the advanced stages of fighting in Bosnia, when evidence of ethnic cleansing and mass rape became widespread, alongside fears that the conflict could spill into Kosovo, did such activities become uncomfortable enough for the major powers to consider action. The same potent beliefs in racial, ethnic or religious superiority, which could be used as the basis for a campaign to exterminate those who are seen as inferior, can be found in other parts of Europe, such as the Caucasus or Georgia. These cases have invoked little concern or interest primarily because no one person or country has chosen to take the lead and make it an issue which demands collective action.

The third explanation rests upon the fact that not all of the European powers are free to 'compete' in the way the realists would assume. There are severe economic and political restrictions which modify the behaviour of states and preclude competition in the security realm. The tying together of the major European economies in the EU may also reinforce the tendency to define interests primarily in terms of the Community of Twelve. Neither France nor Germany nor Britain has exhibited any willingness to assume prime responsibility for the collective defence of pan-European security interests, with the result that the European security agenda lacks clarity and definition.

The US has been swift to point to the Yugoslav crisis as an example of how the Europeans are incapable of reaching a consensus on security issues or taking effective action. This, in turn, acts as the basis for the argument that the European NATO members still need the US. Yet, attempts on paper to move toward a more clearly defined European security agenda, which would relieve the US of much of the burden associated with the defence of Europe, have caused consternation in Washington.

A fourth explanation is the 'Euro' propaganda associated with the move towards European Union. This propaganda has created the false impression that there is a common foreign policy – quite apart from a common security policy. The reality of Europe's actual progress towards union lags behind the aspirations, and a common foreign policy, the prerequisite for a common security policy, simply does not exist.

The lack of leadership in Europe has institutional ramifications which are examined in a subsequent chapter. At this stage it is important to recognize the individual preoccupations and problems faced by the primary actors in Europe. The countries examined are France, Germany and Britain. In each case the factors that function as significant constraints upon the state's ability to act and assume a leadership role will be examined. The differing constraints help to define national interest and conceptions of security which, in turn, may lead to the advocacy of one institution over the other.

FRANCE ET L'EUROPE DES PATRIES

The one country that has a desire to redefine its security relations with Europe and North America in the post-Cold War era is France. For almost the last three decades French security policy has been based on three platforms. The first is resistance to American overbearingness within NATO; the second is development of close security relations with Europe, especially those with Germany; and the third is the preservation of an identifiably French foreign and security policy. As with many other European powers, French security policy was also geared to the maintenance of a sphere of influence overseas, primarily in North Africa and the Middle East.

The first trend manifested itself most dramatically in President de Gaulle's decision to withdraw France from NATO's integrated military command in 1966. The ostensible cause was de Gaulle's consistently voiced doubts about the US's nuclear umbrella over Europe – doubts about whether the US really would risk retaliation against its own soil by using nuclear forces based in Europe to strike against the Soviet Union. Such a course of action could conceivably escalate to an all-out strategic exchange with incalculable results for the US. Would, the US, as de Gaulle posited, be willing to exchange 'Chicago for Paris'? In addition, the decision to leave NATO was motivated by de Gaulle's own vision of France's grandeur and its relations vis-à-vis the US. Jean Lacouture has commented that, 'if there was one thing de Gaulle hated at least as much as the subjection of France to another power, it was the direct, exclusive dialogue between superpowers, avoiding the smaller states.'[2] The result of the 1966 decision was to force France into a position of adopting alternatives to the US-led NATO, which partially explains why France has consistently been an advocate of European security options.

What of French security policy? During the Cold War period French security policy rested upon two beliefs: that nuclear weapons could only be used in the defence of one's own country, and that while states endure, institutions are transitory. The assumption that the US's commitment to Europe was not indefinite made the advocacy of a European security option a rational choice, which would also answer concerns about the traditional French preoccupation with Germany. Ironically, the French independent nuclear force, the *force de frappe*, in large part depended for its effectiveness upon the continued existence of a US nuclear presence in Europe. The French nuclear programme was motivated, amongst other factors, by a frustration at the political outcome of World War II, which had left France without recognition as a 'great power'.[3] Nuclear weapons were also the most visible sign of Britain's special relationship with the US, and in both the Fourth and Fifth French republics this was seen not as the result but rather as the cause of their special relationship. The pursuit of nuclear prestige also led France to opt out of NATO's integrated military command in 1966, only to discover in later years that the emphasis placed on the development of a French nuclear deterrent in the Cold War era meant that the depleted conventional forces had difficulty in intervening in out-of-area concerns, such as the Gulf War.

In spite of France's nominal independence in security issues, it was the link between the French force and the US deterrent forces that gave credibility to the French doctrine of proportional deterrence; only by making the implicit link between the French deterrent force and the larger ones of the US, could France's deterrent be considered credible. The presence of US nuclear and conventional forces in Germany, which was part of the integrated Alliance structure, in effect formed a protective barrier for France itself. This factor explains why France, although often hostile towards US foreign and security policies, is a strong defender of a US military presence in Europe.

The second strand guiding French security policy, that of the development of close ties with Germany, was motivated out of historical concern regarding German militarism, as well as an exploitation of French relations with Germany in a diplomatic tug-of-war with the US. Perhaps the best example of the complex relations between France and its NATO allies is the background to the 22 January 1963 Franco–German Treaty. In the aftermath of the 1963 Nassau meeting, where President Kennedy persuaded the British prime minister, Harold Macmillan, to support the proposed Multilateral Force (denounced by General Pierre Gallois as the 'Multilateral Farce') in exchange for the delivery of Polaris missiles under American control, de Gaulle saw little choice but to cultivate closer relations with Germany. De Gaulle may also have been personally slighted by Kennedy's extension of the offer of Polaris missiles to France, in the full-knowledge that they were not compatible with France's strike force. The resultant Franco–German treaty 'appeared from the outset as an attempt by Paris to snatch Germany away from American influence, just as the Nassau accords had turned Great Britain away from offers of association with France'.[4]

To interpret the 1963 Treaty simply as a riposte to the Kennedy–Macmillan agreement and their closeness, would be inadequate. A pattern of close Franco–German defence cooperation already existed; it can be traced back to the September 1958 Colombey meeting between the German chancellor, Konrad Adenauer, and de Gaulle. These close connections between France and Germany led France to promote European defence options that were not so much motivated by anti-American or pro-German sentiments as a feeling that European strategy needed a firm French guiding hand. Jean Lacouture has eloquently summarized how de Gaulle envisaged the French role in Europe: 'With [German] Reunification postponed indefinitely, the Federal Republic would be linked first to the West through the French umbilical cord, Paris ensuring the nuclear cover of her special ally. In this way the General acted as a kind of hinge between Germany and the West, which gave him an eminent position on the Rhine, a central role in Europe and a vital function in relations between that Franco–German Europe and the United States.'[5]

The urge to give French security policy a firm European basis was underlined in the post-de Gaulle era with the advent of the new German *Ostpolitik* and the normalization of German relations with the Soviet Union. As perceived from Paris, *Ostpolitik* gave Moscow additional leverage over Bonn, which meant that Paris would be less important to the Soviet Union since they could have a direct bearing on European security by operating through Bonn. French concern also grew with the advent of the hard-line Reagan administration: the enunciation of the Strategic Defense Initiative was seen as a sign of growing US insularity. The 'Dual-Track' decision of the NATO Council in 1979 and the hot debates about the wisdom of pursuing simultaneous deployment and arms-control options were also seen by the French as destabilizing for European security and, more important, particularly injurious to French interests which depended upon a strong US nuclear presence in Europe. These perceptions help explain why the French were the most enthusiastic advocates of the deployment of Pershing II and Ground-Launched Cruise Missiles in Europe.

Further concern arose in Paris, as well as in other European capitals, as a result of the 1986 Reykjavik Summit between Reagan and Gorbachev. The promise to cut strategic nuclear forces by up to half stunned the French leadership, since there was no prior consultation and the French doubted the wisdom of major nuclear cuts. The growing concern over the worsening US economic situation, which was evident by the second Reagan administration, also led to fears that the US would resort to cutting overseas forces as a way of halting the precipitous economic decline; a recrudescence of the burden-sharing debate seemed to be looming on the horizon, except this time it promised to be more of a *burden-shedding* debate. All of these factors, when combined, led to a grim outlook: the US seemed to be losing its interest in sustaining a strong military commitment to Europe, Germany had become the main conduit for conducting West European relations with the Soviet Union, demonstrations against the deployment of INF missiles in Europe threatened the credibility of NATO's nuclear deterrent and, by extension, France's *force de frappe*. The result of these developments was to push French policy clearly towards advocating a strong European security option which would contain a potential German slide towards pacifism and neutralism. This new security option would bring France back into the security dialogue with Moscow and provide an alternative security choice in the event of continued US insularity.

Close German relations with the US acted as an irritant to France; yet, at the same time, they served French interests by guaranteeing them an influential hand within the EC. It should also be noted that there was on inherent contradiction in French eyes in pursuing of national independence alongside the advocacy of a European stance in economic, political and security affairs. The apparent contradiction can be explained, first, by the type of integration that France envisaged for Europe, which was far short of a federal Europe, and second, by the fact that the integrative process in Europe was seen as a vehicle for promoting French interests. With the absence of Germany as a decisive leader in this field, as well as Britain whose attitude towards European integration has been historically ambivalent,[6] France was free in many respects to mould a French model of Europe.

In military terms these concerns led to some fundamental restructuring of French forces and, under Giscard d'Estaing's presidency, the beginning of a move away from the Gaullism which had hitherto dominated French security policy. Giscard broadened the definition of French interests to include its immediate neighbours, with a particular emphasis on forming strong ties with Germany in the military and non-military spheres (the European Monetary System hatched by Giscard and his German counterpart, Helmut Schmidt, being the most important non-military development). The structure of the army had changed little since de Gaulle and Pompidou, but in 1975 it was overhauled under Giscard. The most notable change was to break up the large divisions into smaller divisions which could fight alongside the forces of its neighbours. In a significant move, which was designed to maintain an active US role in Europe and to demonstrate a break with the Gaullist policies of the past, a number of agreements were made which gave the US access to French ports, airfields, pipelines and other logistical facilities, so that the central front could be reinforced effectively and more safely.[7]

The last feature of post-war French diplomacy, the preservation of a sphere of influence overseas, became less relevant as time went on. The independence of Algeria, the defeat at Dien Bien Phu in 1954, and the considerable costs associated with supporting French colonies in Africa and cultural clashes in the Muslim world, led to the downgrading of the necessity of preserving such spheres of influence.

FRANCE AND THE END OF THE COLD WAR

The end of the Cold War and Germany's reunification presented France with numerous headaches – a fact borne out in floundering French foreign policy in the period following the collapse of the Berlin wall up to the Maastricht Summit at the end of 1991. As has been argued, the maintenance of an overseas sphere of influence had long ceased to be a high priority, which left France with the problem of promoting its independence while simultaneously trying to deal with a united Germany – since Germany had been assuming an increasingly important role within the EC and was in many senses the dominant power. President Mitterrand promoted the 'deepening' of the EC as a way of dealing with a powerful Germany. Part of the 'deepening' process included the construction of a foreign and security policy component in the European integration process.

Once the unification of Germany was accepted by Mitterrand as a *fait accompli*, French security preoccupations revolved around designs for building a close security relationship with the Germans and ensuring the maintenance of a US military presence in Europe – which are not necessarily complementary tasks. The former, in policy terms, has been seen as a way of buttressing the European pillar of the Atlantic Alliance with the eventual aim of developing a European defence policy. The development of a European security identity was given its most visible symbol in the formation of the Franco–German brigade. The formation of the brigade was the culmination of years of careful diplomatic manoeuvring, starting in 1982 with the Franco–German Joint Committee for Security and Defence and the annual Franco–German summits held three times a year since 1985. French designs are based upon its traditional preoccupations with Germany and the belief that a Germany that is enmeshed in economic, political and security relations with other states is less likely to pursue distinctly nationalist policies. The French still have to overcome the dilemma of how to convince the US that the formation of a distinct European security identity is not aimed against NATO or the US, and how to convince Germany that aspects of French security policy are not inimicable to Germany's interests. The bulk of French efforts have been directed towards the latter objective.

(1) In 1983 France embarked upon a major restructuring of its armed forces, which included the formation of the *Force d'Action Rapide* (FAR). This force was designed mainly with the defence of Germany in mind. It consists of 47 000 troops who can provide 'hard-hitting, air-transportable, conventional forces 250 kilometers forward along the central front in the FRG as an important supplement to the First French Army'.[8] The 'Kekker Spatz–Moineau hardi' (Bold Sparrow) exercises held in 1987 involved German and French forces, including the FAR.

(2) In February 1986 Mitterrand stated that he was willing to consult on the use of the pre-strategic weapons, 'time and circumstances permitting'.[9]

(3) In June 1987 Chancellor Kohl suggested the formation of a Franco–German military unit, which, with French agreement, began operating in late 1989.

(4) In the 1988 French white paper on defence[10] it was agreed that the Hadès missile, scheduled for deployment in 1992, would have its range increased from 350 to 500 kilometres, in response to German anxieties. This reinforced Mitterrand's pledge, made the previous year, that French nuclear weapons would not fall on German soil.

Sentiments in Germany are counter to those in French security policy, especially on the question of the use of nuclear weapons; the Germans are strongly in favour of reducing the role of nuclear weapons in Europe, while French energies seem to be directed toward the modernization of its nuclear forces. This discrepancy of nuclear weaponary becomes especially problematical when considering the relationship between the Euro-brigade and the French national forces, the latter having a nuclear component.

The post-1985 developments in the Soviet Union had profound effects on French security policy. In many ways they challenged the fundamentals of Defence Minister Jean-Pierre Chevènement's strategy, which was to build a European security consensus and maintain a US military presence. The gradual demise of the Soviet Union and the collapse of the Warsaw Treaty Organization in 1991 not only left a strategic vacuum in Europe, but also gave rise to French fears that Germany would feel a strong urge to concentrate its interests on its traditional area of concern, Central Europe, and thus pay less attention to Western European integration. Memories of Germany's penchant for wandering to the East have led to concerns that Germany may adopt an increasingly independent policy towards the former Soviet Union – fear of a 'new Rapallo' has reinforced French attempts to enmesh Germany in a European *'confédération'*. Chevènement voiced these concerns in mid-1990: 'The rebalancing between these two powers, readily expansionist, one to the detriment of the other when their respective weight is unequal, can lead in the following period to a sort of entente; there is between these two peoples an old connivance, which has known many forms.'[11]

Such a 'connivance' would obviously have the effect of marginalizing France and isolating it politically. French support of German membership in NATO, the formation of the 'Euro-corps' and the Maastricht process, complete with its foreign and security policy stipulations, mark a concerted effort to avoid this eventuality. French suspicions and concerns about being marginalized have some basis, since there have been numerous examples of Bonn making decisions of fundamental importance to Europe with little or no consultation with Paris. Two examples stand out in particular: first, Chancellor Kohl's announcement of a ten-point plan on 28 November 1989 for the reunification of Germany, with no prior warning to Paris; and, second, in July 1990, Kohl's direct negotiations with Gorbachev over German membership of NATO, which effectively bypassed the Two-plus-Four forum.

Relations between Bonn and Paris have not been all smooth, especially in the period preceding reunification. To Bonn, Mitterrand appeared to be less than enthusiastic about the prospect of reunification, and his visit to East Berlin, on 20–22 December 1989, at the invitation of Erich Honecker, seemed calculated to insult Bonn. The visit has also been explained not as an attempt to perpetuate the division of Germany but 'rather [a reflection of] the will to contribute to an orderly transition towards national unity following modalities to be agreed upon by the governments of East Berlin and of Bonn'.[12] There were serious divergences between Paris and Bonn on the question of the western border of Poland. A particularly strong speech by the French Minister of Foreign Affairs, Roland Dumas, in Berlin on 1 March 1990, reminded Germany of the need to settle such questions as a condition of reunification. The issue was settled soon after the legislative elections of 18 March in the GDR. Although the Polish border issue was no longer contentious by the time of the 55th Franco–German consultation in Paris on 25–26 April 1990, it served as a reminder of the historical nervousness felt by France at the prospect of a unified Germany. With the acceptance of the inevitability of reunification, a prime aim of French policy became the rapid construction of a European Community able to *contain* Germany. In April 1990, Kohl and Mitterrand agreed that the unification process should be 'embedded' in the process of European integration, which included the goal of working towards a political union.

In December of that same year, Mitterrand met with Gorbachev and confided his hope that the pace of unification could be slowed down. However, in public Mitterrand insisted that France was 'not afraid' of German unification and that '[France] would enhance future relations if Germany's leaders carried forward the unification process in a spirit of close consultation'.[13] What could be interpreted as reticence towards the unification issue could also be interpreted as concern not with unification *per se,* but with the fact that it should materialize peacefully and democratically.[14]

When the unification of Germany became a question of when, rather than if, Paris championed the extension of the EC's purview into the realms of foreign and security policy; but, in a caveat that is significant, such common policies should be made by national leaders,[15] not by supranational EC institutions, thus maintaining France's cherished independent stance whilst also seeming to promote integration. Paris also favoured the adoption of common foreign and security policies *before* any actual or potential enlargement of the European community. An enlarged EC could refocus interest in the Community to the north and east and away from French areas of interest and towards Germany's.

The reduction in the level of confrontation in Europe also meant that the need for the US to maintain expensive military forces in Europe was also challenged. This provoked concern that with fewer US and allied forces in Germany, the ties keeping Germany in the fold would be all the more loose, leaving Germany to follow its own aspirations. Thus France found itself in the curious position of supporting the continuing presence of US forces in Germany (but not, of course, on French soil) and supporting German membership in NATO, whilst *simultaneously* building independent and 'Euro' ties with Germany, such as the Franco–German corps. The two aims are inherently contradictory; if the Franco–German corps is the basis of a Euro army, this will make the need and relevance of the US forces in Europe look all the more questionable. In the event of a US withdrawal, this could leave France alone with Germany – given the distinct lack of enthusiasm in Britain for European security integration. Conversely, by supporting the continuing presence of US troops in Germany and German membership of NATO, France is effectively relinquishing any effective control or influence it may have over Bonn to Washington. Karl Lowe captured the essentially paradoxical nature of French security policy when he wrote:

> France sees declining American influence as heightening its own leadership prospects. In every forum, the pragmatic French are busily putting together a framework of economic, political and military co-operation which supports a European pillar based more on equality than junior partnership . . . France sees the United States as an essential account balancer, not only in the security sphere, but in political and economic matters as well.[16]

Other contradictions abound; for instance, there have been numerous French calls for the promotion of the WEU as the EC's security arm while, simultaneously, preserving French military independence. The anti-American vein which runs through much of French post-war diplomacy is still present but, in spite of this, Mitterrand saw no contradictions with putting substantial French military forces under US command during the Gulf War.

Yet, in the absence of a significant US military presence in Europe, France would be hard pressed to assume the leadership mantle for several reasons. First, the defence expenditure level which was considered necessary in the Giscard years and the early Mitterrand years to maintain a credible nuclear and conventional deterrent force, has not been attained. The effects of the global recession alongside low growth in the French economy and expectations of a 'peace dividend' have all led to cutbacks in some of France's more conspicuously high-tech ventures, such as the S-4 missile, which was plagued by cost overruns, and the Rafale fighter, which has been delayed.[17] If France is serious about its 'containment' role of Germany, in the event of a significant decline in US force levels below CFE limits there would be substantial costs involved in those areas where the US, sometimes exclusively, provided for Europe's defences – areas such as command, control, communication, air defences, air transport and electronic interdiction capability.

It could also be argued that the 'currency' of military hardware, especially nuclear forces, has declined with the demise of the Cold War. The independent *force de frappe* was seen as one of the significant differentiating factors between Germany and France. With the decline in the political value of military assets, French policy-makers will be faced with the challenge of finding other means of influencing Germany. Unification of Germany and the changed nature of Post-Cold War security challenges to Europe also raise the possibility that Germany is well placed to provide for itself and has no need to rely upon

French, or other, military contributions. The overall effect of the decline in the political value of military assets may tend to stress the
significance and importance of developing ties in other fields. It is
not obvious, though, in *what* other fields France could assert its influence
over German policies. Since Germany's economic prowess is no longer
linked to heavy dependence on the allies for security, France will find
it difficult to have any decisive influence over Bonn.

Second, the changes in Europe present many political minefields
for Mitterrand which could further reduce France's stature in European security affairs. For instance, the wisdom of maintaining and expanding an independent deterrent force could be challenged, and moves
towards its allies in the defence field may lead to charges from Gaullist
stalwarts, like Jacques Chirac, that France is going soft on NATO.
The continued investment in the *force de frappe* and the reduction in
the US nuclear presence in Europe has underlined some of the va-
garies of French nuclear policy and when nuclear weapons may actually be used. On this question France has proven itself to be out of
step with the other main powers. Mitterrand's preference for the post-
Cold War *force de frappe* was to continue to rely upon the threat of
an early use of nuclear weapons – the NATO nuclear powers agreed
in July 1990 that nuclear weapons should be 'truly weapons of last
resort'.[18] The French desire to use their close relationship with Bonn
to further European integration in the economic and political spheres
may also prove to be at variance with the modernization of the French
nuclear force and especially the deployment of Hadès, which, with a
range of around 500 kilometres, was unpopular with Germany. Various
methods were employed to assuage the Germans, including the argument forwarded by Jean-Pierre Chevènement in 1990, then minister of
defence, that Hadès could enhance Europe's security as a whole.[19] The
argument is particularly interesting in the light of later statements that
Hadès could not be considered as part of a Euro-deterrent force because of its limited range.

The difficulties encountered between France and Germany over the
role of French nuclear forces relate mainly to differing perceptions of
the utility of the weapons. With the reduction in US nuclear weapons
in Europe, the intentions of the French and British became all the more
important to Germany. Prime Minister Jacques Chirac gave his vision
of the future of French nuclear forces at the end of 1987:

Who could doubt now that if Germany was the victim of aggression, France's engagement would be immediate and unreserved? There
cannot be a battle for Germany and a battle for France . . . In the

same spirit, France must be able to deliver her pre-strategic warning as soon as the Head of State judges that our vital interests are at stake, i.e. if necessary, well before the invasion of French national territory.[20]

Such statements have caused immense concern in Germany. The concern was heightened by ambiguous statements from Mitterrand about whether Hadès will be equipped with an enhanced radiation (neutron) warhead. French statements were intended not just to influence German policy but to be heard in Moscow as well. The demise of the Soviet Union and the vast reductions in nuclear armaments in Europe, as a result of the 1987 Intermediate Range Nuclear Force Treaty, the 1991 START Treaty, and the signature of the January 1993 START II agreement, have challenged the rationale behind the French modernization programme and made the consistent French refusal to put nuclear arms on the arms-control negotiating table increasingly difficult to defend.

Third, France must pursue an active *Ostpolitik* that is carefully co-ordinated with Bonn. The rationale driving this is that it would be unwise to leave Germany free to create *Mittleuropa* in its traditional area of influence; yet the east is an area in which the French do not enjoy the same influence or popularity as Germany. Mitterrand's idea of a European *confédération* was supposed to offer a solution to this dilemma, by promoting both deepening and widening of the EC simultaneously. The deepening part (the promotion of European Union) of the agenda seemed inherently contradictory to the idea of widening (extending membership to new countries). Neither policy seems to have worked.

The policy of 'deepening' is in trouble, in part because of the collapse of the ERM, but also because of French attempts simultaneously to promote its own interests, and those of the EC as well as the WEU, alongside its support of the US in the Gulf War, which in turn hinted at collaboration in the NATO context. However, France has thus far failed to persuade either Germany or Britain that there are serious 'Euro options' to NATO that do not smack of French opportunism and self-promotion.

The widening aspects of *confédération* would also seem to have come to grief, most notably in Prague in June 1991. Mitterrand was opposed to any sudden influx of new members into the EC, especially from Central or Eastern Europe. It was feared that this would increase Germany's influence in that area at the cost of French influence. The

Central Europeans were quick to spot that they were being offered second-class membership, if even that. As a consequence, France did not emerge as a champion of the Central and Eastern Europeans but was shown to be their detractor. The idea of *confédération* was also unappealing to the Central Europeans since it explicitly excluded the US, meaning they would have to deal without a significant counter-weight. The French refusal even to discuss tentative EC entry dates for the Czech republic, Hungary and Poland, serves as a gauge of French apprehensions about Germany. Unfortunately there are many fallacies in the French position on the widening of the EC. Space prohibits a comprehensive examination of these arguments, but two deserve high-lighting. First, German influence within these countries could be as-sured independently of the EC or any other structure. In order to halt this, France should have taken the lead in investment and rebuilding in the east. Rather than France or any other country, doing so, Ger-many did. Second, the notion that Germany would exert *more* influ-ence over Central Europe if these countries were EC members is questionable. Might not Germany be able to exert more influence by dealing with these countries on a one-to-one basis?

As to which institutional affiliations France wishes to promote, the picture is complex. Perhaps the clearest statement is to be found in the Franco–German proposals forwarded at the Inter-Governmental Con-ference of the Twelve on Political Union in Rome on 21 February 1991.[21] At the conference French backing was given to the develop-ment of a Common Foreign and Security Policy (CFSP), which would have the following essential features: (i) the setting up a common Eu-ropean defence system; (ii) both NATO and a continuing US military presence were recognized as 'indispensable' for European security and stability; (iii) the WEU should become the 'cooperation' channel be-tween Political Union and NATO to 'reinforce European *or* trans-At-lantic security structures'. The WEU was also recognized as an 'integral part of the European unification process'; (iv) disarmament and con-trol of armaments will be of particular importance to the CSCE; (v) a CFSP should include the definition of common positions in debates on armaments and disarmament in the UN; (vi) economic aspects of security, such as cooperation concerning arms production and control, should take place within the CFSP context.

The attempts to create a CFSP, spearheaded by France, complement Mitterrand's idea of a *confédération* which includes the EC, Central and Eastern Europe as well as the former USSR. The *confédération* was intended to cover such issues as the environment, energy, transport, cultural affairs, the movement of peoples, and so forth. The purpose of striving towards *confédération* and, more explicitly, the purpose of the French initiative launched at the Inter-Governmental Conference can be summarized as:[22] (i) the maintenance of France's established security position in Europe, which also includes upholding its autonomy; (ii) to sustain France's leadership position within the EC; (iii) to tie Germany to the existing institutional structures in Europe (CSCE, EC, NATO and the WEU); (iv) the retention of US military forces in Europe; (v) to encourage the democratization and stability of Eastern Europe and the CIS; (vi) to maintain a dialogue with Moscow to prevent either a German–Russian dialogue that may exclude France, or to prevent Moscow from feeling isolated.

Alongside the preoccupation with Germany has been that of avoiding US domination of Europe.[23] In institutional terms this has led to some strange twists. It has led, on the one hand, to the stubborn defence of French interests when they clashed with those of the US; for example, the French position on agriculture within the GATT Uruguay round. On the other, the French have promoted their vision of Europe by staunchly defending the WEU against any attempts at linking it explicitly with NATO, as the British wish to do. French policymakers have also advocated the idea of a European force within the WEU that could, somehow, be differentiated from NATO. These 'Euro forces' could also be used in distinct WEU out-of-area operations – which conveniently sidesteps the question of how such forces may reach out-of-area contingencies. French designs have been thwarted, and antagonisms with London deepened, by the British-inspired initiative forwarded at the June 1992 North Atlantic Council meeting. The Oslo meeting welcomed the development of the WEU as 'the defence component of the European Union and as a means of strengthening the European pillar *of the Atlantic Alliance*'.[24] As far as Britian and Germany were concerned, this placed the security aspects of the Maastricht Treaty ultimately within the NATO context. The French remain convinced that the development of a European security identity within the WEU is an *alternative* to the US-dominated Atlantic Alliance.

France has been unsuccessful at persuading Europe, especially Britain, that the brigade is not the beginning of a 'Euro' alternative which may drive the US from Europe. For example, the Franco–German invitation in May 1992 for other WEU members to contribute forces to a joint European army corps has been met with little enthusiasm. If anything, the 'Eurocorps' has been perceived as a rival to NATO's Allied Command Europe Rapid Reaction Corps (ARRC). In an attempt to clarify any hint that the Eurocorps was being forwarded as an alternative to the ARRC, the former French defence minister, Pierre Joxe, reassured other WEU and NATO allies in September 1992 that the corps would be placed under NATO command if Article 5 of the North Atlantic Treaty were invoked. Joxe also forwarded the hope that France might assume a role in NATO's decision-making bodies, mentioning specifically the Military Committee.[25] In November a Paris–Bonn agreement to put the Eurocorps under NATO command was presented by General Wiesmann, the German Defence Ministry representative in the negotiations on the future of the Eurocorps. Under the new agreement the Eurocorps will be able to call upon the joint forces to repulse attacks on the NATO area, or at the request of either France or Germany. The switch to NATO operational control would have to be sanctioned by Bonn and Paris.[26]

Although France has shown a willingness to work through NATO,[27] as shown by Chevènement's restructuring of the French Army, enshrined in *Plan Armée 2000*, there is no significant move in France to reintegrate fully into NATO. The *Plan Armée* will involve the reduction of the first corps from three to two corps, with the loss of about 7000 troops. As with former restructuring of the French forces in 1975 and 1981, the slimmed down corps are designed to enhance the 'interface' with the redesignated NATO forces. Mitterrand has also tried to strengthen ties with NATO by promoting a European Security Identity (ESI) within NATO. Although this is presented as a compatible development, which would enhance the European role in NATO, it remains unclear that this is what will happen in practice. François Léotard, the current French Defence Minister, indicated in front of both the Assemblée and the Sénat that France was willing to work with NATO but there was no intention of reversing de Gaulle's 1966 decision. The growing willingness to work with NATO, without re-joining, can be understood largely in terms of the huge geostrategic changes since the end of the Cold War and in particular the decline of US influence within NATO, which modifies the equilibrium of the Alliance. As Léotard pragmatically observed, 'Le bon sens, la lucidité, la prudence nous amenent à nous adapter à cette réalité nouvelle.'[28]

As is often the case in politics, public pronouncements and resultant actions can be different. Instead of the desired patterns of collaboration with NATO emerging, there appear to be signs of estrangement from NATO following France's open doubts about the wisdom of NATO's decision to 'rely increasingly on multinational corps made up of national units'.[29] As David Yost has observed, French officials see the creation of multinational units under the Supreme Allied Commander in Europe as 'not only operationally problematical but also politically undesirable'.[30] The multinational units could, according to French concerns, increase integration under US authority and guidance and thus postpone a long overdue redress of European–American security relations.

The largest area of difference between France and the revamped NATO was over the role of nuclear weapons. The London declaration declared that there should be 'an appropriate mix of nuclear and conventional forces, based in Europe, and kept up to date where necessary'.[31] It also stated that, in the future, NATO should move towards a strategy making 'nuclear forces truly weapons of last resort' and that increasing reliance will be placed upon multinational corps.[32] Mitterrand enthusiastically welcomed the endorsement of the EC's movement towards political union but was less enthusiastic about the description of nuclear weapons as weapons of 'last resort'. French nuclear strategy is explicitly linked to a deterrence strategy where nuclear weapons have the mandate to prevent war. Thus the notion of using them as a last resort after a period of prolonged conventional warfare was contrary to French wisdom. To add to the doctrinal confusion, in February 1992 Mitterrand vetoed the construction of mobile ground launchers for strategic weapons, but not for the short-range *pré-stratégique*[33] weapons. It is also in the area of nuclear strategy that the most serious contradictions are to be found in the French pursuit of a distinct European defence identity, when there seems to be a reluctance to provide a nuclear deterrent force for any such organization.

In a policy document adopted by the ruling Socialist Party in December 1991, the increasing difficulty of conserving the purely national character of French defence policy was acknowledged. Mitterrand suggested one possible solution to the dilemma at a conference on 10 January 1992.[34] He proposed an enlargement of the role of France's *and* Britain's nuclear forces, which would include an extension of France's 'vital interests' to the frontiers of the twelve EC countries. The seriousness of such a suggestion can be challenged since it rests upon the knowledge that the British are unlikely to be enthusiastic about such a 'Euro-deterrent' outside of NATO's parameters. By floating the idea, Mitterrand did serve to sharpen the party lines on the issue. The centre-right *Union pour la Démocratie Française* is strongly in favour of a European defence organization that could include the extension of the French nuclear deterrent, while the neo-Gaullist *Rassemblement pour la République* is adamantly opposed to any extension of France's nuclear deterrent that may erode France's sovereignty and control over its nuclear forces. French public opinion polls also illustrate the same ambiguity; a majority are in favour of the adoption of a common European defence, but many are reluctant to surrender their national nuclear deterrent.[35]

The British reaction to Mitterrand's suggestion was to continue to press the essential contradiction between France's pursuit of a European security identity, with France at the centre, and a strategic and pre-strategic nuclear doctrine that centres entirely on the defence of France with no consideration of its friends or allies.[36] By way of contrast, the British independent deterrent is designed to enhance the Alliance's deterrent force, as well as safeguarding vital national interests. One of the arguments forwarded in defence of the Gaullist role for the French nuclear deterrent forces has been to observe that the bulk of the French nuclear forces, the pre-strategic systems, are of such short range that they could not serve as 'Euro-deterrents'.[37] The maintenance and modernization of France's nuclear deterrent force has been given high priority and remains the centre of French defence policy. François Léotard made the point forcefully in an interview:

> La dissuasion reste le fondement de notre défense, et il n'est pas question de mettre en case, de quelque manière que ce soit, cette realité. Dans cet sprit, la modernisation constante de nos forces de dissuasion ne peut souffrir la moindre inattention.[38]

The issue of the modernization of France's nuclear forces is problematical since the French Prime Minister, Edouard Balladur, announced to the Assemblée Nationale on 8 April 1992 that France would desist from testing in the south Pacific in that year. Modernization without testing is difficult, unless alternative testing grounds are found.

France's continued alienation from NATO poses an uncomfortable problem: of the existing institutions, of which France or Germany are members, only NATO is in a position to act as a brake on Germany. The other institutions, which were supposed to contain Germany, are instead dominated by it. The ERM was clearly built around the German mark, Germany is the largest military force in the WEU and also has considerable influence within the CSCE. These factors explain why, in the Bosnian context, France preferred to work through the UN or the EC rather than the CSCE or NATO. The same tendencies can be seen in other areas of state activity. For instance, in the economics field France has promoted the EC and the European Bank for Reconstruction and Development (EBRD) rather than GATT, the World Bank, or even the OECD. In the security realm the hope was that France could attract Germany away from NATO to a European security system in which Britain and France could constrain Germany if need be. As is argued below, this is a design that the British have proven to be distinctly unenthusiastic about.

French security policy is full of apparent paradoxes and contradictions. David Yost caught the essence of these essential contradictions when he wrote:

> The French want a U.S. military and nuclear presence in Europe, but not on their soil. They want a united Germany to be in NATO – and to avoid a 'strategic vacuum' in Central Europe, and to minimize the risk of Germany seeking neutrality, a special security relationship with Russia or security through its own means. Yet the French oppose the multinational corps approach that could be of great political utility in keeping American and allied troops in Germany, and they place great emphasis on bilateral cooperation vehicles and exclusively European institutions rather than on renovating the Atlantic alliance.[39]

The contradictions can largely be explained in terms of internal political disagreements between the parties. The Rassemblement pour la République, under Jacques Chirac, has attempted to move France away from overt dependence upon nuclear weapons, which posit the all or nothing dilemma. Chirac has also been the most forward about the French commitment to forward defence and about the wisdom of coordinating French and American strategy. Even during the period of *cohabitation* with Mitterrand, Chirac continued to use defence policy as a means of challenging Mitterrand and the Socialists. The Socialists themselves have held contrary positions, particularly with regard to French relations with the former Soviet Union and the plans to modernize the French nuclear force. There has also been a strain within the Socialist Party that supports a greater reliance upon 'existential' nuclear deterrence and on disarmament, in contrast to the majority who remain if not opposed to, at least suspicious of, arms control.

In spite of Chirac's attempts to weaken Mitterrand's position by attacking Socialist defence policies, his success has been limited. Mitterrand has, on the whole, successfully balanced internal French security needs with those of the evolving post-Cold War Europe: he has maintained the independence of the French nuclear forces; he has successfully resisted pressures that may have further estranged France from its European colleagues; he has shown a willingness to enter conventional arms control (through the CFE process) but resisted pressures to put French nuclear arms on the negotiating table, except in the case of his stiff demands being met. Chirac could challenge Mitterrand on the grounds that he has 'sold out' French interests by enmeshing France in the Political Union process, but even here it would be difficult to make the challenge stick. To mount an attack on Mitterrand by arguing that he had abrogated French interests would therefore be difficult.

The French Prime Minister, Edouard Balladur, remains an advocate of not just the formation of a European security organization but also of pressing Western Europe's wider responsibilities. In an address to the European Council on 9 June 1993 Balladur spoke of the lessons to be learnt from the paralysis of the EC and the international community in Yugoslavia.[40] Balladur specifically recognized the important role that the US, Canada, Russia, Belarus, the Ukraine, Moldavia, and the three Baltic republics, have, in collaboration with the EC members, in ensuring stability in Europe. Specifically, Balladur advocated a European Stability Pact which would be drawn up between these countries addressing minority issues and border disputes within the region. The Balladur design for a European Stability Pact (ESP) was publicly unveiled at the 20–21 June 1993 European Council Summit in Copenhagen. Briefly, under the ESP, those nations aspiring to join the EC would settle their minority and territorial disputes through the mediative assistance of other nations, particularly the twelve EC nations (for more details on the plan, see Chapter 10). Mitterrand lent his support to the plan. However, the Balladur plan, as it stands, will do little to convince other European powers or the US that it is not merely another veiled attempt to reorganize Europe on French lines. Jean Musitelli, in an interview with *Le Monde*, went so far as to suggest that, 'l'un des objectifs majeurs de la politique étrangère de la France devait être d'organiser l'Europe'.[41] In principle, the problems identified and the need to think and talk in pan-European terms, are sound. What is still open to doubt is the willingness of France's European colleagues to collaborate in the thinly veiled attempts to assert French leadership in Europe.

INTO THE FUTURE

The future of French defence policy is unclear, largely because of the contradictions that have been built into it. A delicate balancing act will have to be attempted, avoiding the dangers of alienating the US, of bringing too much pressure to bear on Germany, and of promoting a European security identity as an alternative to NATO. French security policy will also have problems consolidating its relations with other Western European powers, especially Germany, while simultaneously trying to achieve pan-European stability. If there is a key to French security concerns and therefore a priority, it is surely in the maintenance of close relations with Germany and the objective of tying Germany to a European *confédération* in which France plays the leading role.

That France continues to see its role in post-Cold War Europe as that of a leader is beyond dispute. Pierre Lellouche caught the flavour of what sounded almost like manifest destiny, when he wrote, 'no other European nation but France has the desire, the ambition or the means to play a decisive leading role in redrawing Europe's security order'.[42] The question of whether France could assume a 'decisive' role is perhaps less relevant than the question of *how* France could assume this decisive role. The Raynaud report, named after a Commission report chaired by Jean Reynaud, sheds some light on the future direction of French security policy.[43] As with other defence reviews, there is an overall concern with budgetary factors. This aside, the report reconfirms that French security policy will be framed within a European network, which includes the maintenance of a sufficient nuclear arsenal. The question of how France will simultaneously push for the evolution of a European security network while leaving the precise relationship between any 'Euro forces' and the independent *force de frappe*, remains unresolved.

France will have to shape any future security order for Europe *in conjunction* with the US, assuming that the US continues to play a role in European security. This will necessitate a purge of Gaullist attitudes towards the US which, although not an easy task, would have the benefit of making any new or adapted European security order attractive to Britain and maybe to the Central Europeans as well. Although this may seem like an enormous task, the animosities between France and the US on security issues are based largely on disputes from the mid-1960s, fuelled by Gaullism. The evidence of continuing Gaullist tendencies in French defence policy, manifest most noticeably in the preference for unilateral or multilateral contacts over organizational ties, points to a continued reluctance to associate with any organizations that lack a decisive French influence – especially if there is a strong American influence evident in a given organization. Forming exclusive ties with Germany may not be the best way of containing the new Germany; it may push Germany into an unwilling and unwelcome position between Paris and Washington and, ultimately, alienate one or the other.

It has already been stated that France shows few signs of wishing to rejoin NATO, but this does not rule out the possibility of an integration between the various security institutions, in some of which the US will enjoy influence and some of which will have a preponderant French influence. Since NATO's geographical delineations are becoming increasingly irrelevant, the US will be forced to look to other institutions to 'give NATO legs' – possibilities include the WEU and the CSCE. The declining relevance of NATO serves as a disincentive for French membership, but may also lead to a subtle reversal of US–French relations. Instead of remaining outside the 'main game' (which was NATO), France may inadvertently assume crucial roles in other institutions, which may place the US in the position of going to Paris for cooperative measures – a situation that would presumably appeal to Paris. Since the French, like other European countries, will still remain dependent upon the US for significant logistical assistance, an increase in the pooling of resources and command responsibilities is an obvious must. The Eurocorps, which could be used for Euro-pean or NATO contingencies, serves as one example of this type of flexibility.

The collaboration described above will demand adjustments from the US as well. In a later chapter it is argued that the decline in the number of US forces in Europe and the disappearance of an overt threat demand a redefinition of US–European relations. There are dangers of such a redefinition being carried out in negative or uncooperative ways. Negative or uncooperative measures will have to be guarded against, since alienation of the US by Paris may well prompt a US withdrawal, which would not serve French interests.

There are also practical considerations that point towards the retention of active US military involvement in Europe, at least in the immediate future. France, like the other European NATO allies, would be heavily dependent upon US for much of its observation and intelligence capacity in the event of a crisis. In the French case, this was borne out in the Gulf War when the American capability made air and land battle plans possible through information gleaned from observation satellites, which intercepted Iraqi communications, guided French and allied forces through NAVSTAR navigation satellites, and warned of SCUD attacks. French troops had only the Syracuse telecommunications network running on TELCOM 1 satellites. In addition, commercial SPOT satellites were used to update Iraqi maps. Although ex-Defence

Minister Pierre Joxe increased expenditure in this area, the sums involved are miniscule compared to the US (over a ten-year period France invested Ffr. 16 billion in space and communication programmes, compared to Ffr. 760 billion for the US). Even if the Helios I and Helios II photographic observation satellites live up to French expectations, they will not be fully operational until the end of 1998.[44] Without massive investment by France and other European partners, America's European allies will remain heavily dependent upon the US in unseen but important ways.

By reversing the traditional animosity of France to the US, the interests of France, its allies and the US would be served. France, on its own, is simply not strong enough to stand up to the problems of the post-Cold War world. It needs the US as a counterbalance to Germany, at least while suspicions and reservations about Germany remain. Collaboration with the US would actively involve Britain in the design and construction of a European security order and, once again, help avoid the potentially difficult scenario of France being left alone with Germany in a security relationship.

A further reason for the need for a *rapprochement* is the battered state of the Maastricht Treaty. Although the treaty has been ratified by all twelve EC members, it is a treaty with many holes and reservations. One of the many problem areas is clearly the commitment to work toward a common defence policy. Although this may remain a desirable long-term objective, there is a lack of support for a purely 'Euro' option. If France prosecutes this option, they may well find themselves, once again, on the outside.

The doctrinal debates that had in the past separated France and the US have diminished – most notably over the compatibility of NATO's flexible response doctrine and French notions of pure deterrence and in the field of arms control, where France has shown a willingness to take an active role – but there are still significant differences. The potential exists for a realignment of Europe's security along lines that involve the US as well as giving France a decisive role. For France to exclude the US at this time, which still leaves open the question of the US's long-term interests in Europe, would be a mistake. Without the US, there will be no decisive French role.

France's best hope for exerting its influence is, therefore, through the existing institutions, most notably the UN and the EC. To forsake completely the other international security and economic institutions, such as the CSCE or GATT, on the grounds of pernicious German or American influences would be short-sighted. Above all, France's tendency to pursue an independent role that, either deliberately or accidentally, sabotages the existing institutions would help nobody and could lead to destructive nationalism. Finally, as a matter of speculation, defence will play an important role in the 1995 elections for the French presidency. One of the leading Socialist candidates is the current president of the European Commission, Jacques Delors. Delors is on record as stating that, 'If we really are on the way toward a political entity with a common foreign policy on basic issues, then I consider that France's nuclear force should be available to serve that policy.'[45] The presidential elections in 1995 will do much to set the tone and content of Europe's future security designs, as well as transatlantic relations.

FOG IN THE CHANNEL

Britain is unlikely to assume a leadership role. In many ways the role of Britain since 1989 is reminiscent of the 1950s when, at the beginning of European economic integration, under Ernest Bevin's guidance, 'it had been the godfather of NATO but then parted ways with the continent as economic integration began'.[46] Britain, while not completely unsympathetic to the strengthening of the European pillar, has tended to continue to look towards the Atlantic pillar for guidance. This reflects the role that Ernest Bevin, Clement Attlee's foreign secretary, is often credited with – that of creating the 'entangling alliance' whereby the security of the US was seen as inextricably linked to that of Europe. Although it is acknowledged that NATO must adapt to the changed circumstances of the Post-Cold War world, any radical reassessments have been firmly resisted by Margaret Thatcher and John Major. Ironically, those institutions that may now pose an alternative to NATO, such as the WEU, were created largely as a result of British initiatives designed to demonstrate that the Europeans were sincere about their own defences, and thus attempt to avoid an 'agonizing reappraisal' and a potential US loss of interest in Western Europe's security.

In historical terms Britain has often played the role of mediator, albeit reluctantly, between the US and its European allies. While this role may be dated, Britain could play a crucial leadership role in the security arena in concert with either France or Germany. However, as with the other main European powers, Britain has been slow or reluctant to grasp the implications of integration in other areas of state activity. Thus, in security terms the traditional preference for the special relationship with the US seems to prevail; one need only consider the frequent divergence of continental European security stances and US–British postures[47] to see the inherent bias in British defence policy towards the US and NATO. This bias can be traced back to the beginning of the nineteenth century when George Canning turned to the 'New World' to redress the balance of the 'Old World'.[48] Historically, Britain has also shown an unwillingness to intervene in European entanglements, preferring instead 'splendid isolation'. Historically, Britain's best interests were served by a weak and divided Europe; intervention only being considered when a strong continental power endangered Britain's security and overseas interests.

The emphasis placed by Britain upon its relations with the US, and with NATO, were further emphasized by the downturn in Britain's post-war economy.[49] It was not, however, a relationship without discord. The 1946 McMahon Act, passed by Congress in August, marked a low point in Anglo-American relations. By this treaty the US banned any exchange of atomic information, which to the British, who had been close collaborators in the Manhattan Project, appeared to be a slap in the face.[50] Prime Minister Attlee and Foreign Secretary Bevin both understood that, according to the terms of the 1943 Quebec Agreement and the 1944 Hyde Park Agreement, Anglo-American nuclear cooperation would be continued after the war. In spite of this setback, and others to follow, it remained true that throughout the Cold War period British defence planning was based on the assumption that 'the US and Western Europe would be allies and that they would jointly resist aggression'.[51] Throughout this period British officials in the Foreign Office and Ministry of Defence showed less interest in European defence integration, although they were involved, than they showed concern with enmeshing the US into the Atlantic Pact.

The setback induced by the McMahon Act reinforced prior British resolve to acquire nuclear weapons. As a result of this determination some of the barriers to nuclear cooperation between the US and Britain were dismantled. In January 1948, a *modus vivendi* was agreed upon between the two governments, which opened up nuclear collaboration in specific fields.[52] More importantly, in the Atomic Energy Act, passed by Congress in 1954, collaboration was undertaken in several significant fields. By 1958 the restrictions of the McMahon Act seemed unnecessary since Britain was clearly able to attain an independent nuclear capability and the Soviet Union had long ago demonstrated a thermonuclear capability. Accordingly, it was repealed in 1958 and followed shortly thereafter by a new Atomic Energy Act, which allowed for intimate collaboration between the US and Britain. No other

European power was to be party to such a relationship, which, in turn, was reflected in Britain's loyalty to the US. The importance of the domestic and military nuclear programmes as the underpinning of the special relationship was underlined in 1958 by the Anglo-American Agreement on the stationing of IRBMs in Britain, followed by the Skybolt Agreement of 1960, and the Polaris Agreement of 1962.[53]

Events like the Eden plan, presented at the Nine Power Conference and subsequently adopted in the 1954 Paris Accords, by which Britain committed forces to the European continent, marked not so much a shift by Britain towards Europe, but a commitment to retain US forces in Europe. In Foreign Secretary Anthony Eden's own words, the commitment was designed to 'bring the Germans and the French together, and keep the Americans in Europe'.[54] Similarly, the move to scupper the Multilateral Force (MLF) by proposing the Atlantic Nuclear Force (ANF) in the mid-1960s was an attempt to solidify US–British relations while retaining influence over the British independent deterrent force. The decision to commit Britain's Polaris submarines to NATO (unless 'supreme national interests' were at stake, in which case they would be reserved for exclusive British use) also signified a further deliberate move to cement Anglo-American defence relations.

In spite of the closeness between Britain and the US, stemming from what Winston Churchill described as the 'English-speaking alliance', Britain also found itself ineluctably drawn towards greater integration with the continental European powers. Britain was initially unimpressed by the early advocates of European integration, such as Jean Monnet, Paul-Henri Spaak, Robert Schuman and Ernesto Rossi. In spite of Churchill's wartime enthusiasm for confederal models of Europe after the war, Attlee's post-war Labour government was more concerned with domestic concerns, including the construction of a welfare system. As with other post-war goverments, British foreign policy under Attlee was a case of balancing Britain's three areas of interest: the Commonwealth, the special relationship, and Europe. At best, Britain was an awkward partner in the European context and only half-heartedly adopted a role in Europe. Britain's lead in establishing the European Free Trade Area (EFTA) illustrates the recognition that Europe had some importance but, at the same time, Britain remained initally reluctant to embrace the federalist ideals of the European Economic Community established in 1957. Only with the decline in the significance of Britain's Commonwealth countries and the comparatively quick growth of the EEC economies, did EEC membership begin to appear more attractive to Britain. De Gaulle resisted two attempts by Britain to join, and only after his fall from power in 1970 was the way open for eventual British membership, which took place in 1973.

Britain's adoption of a European identity, through participation in the EC, has not been without complications. Initially Britain insisted on preferential trade quotas for its Commonwealth trade partners, thus illustrating continuing concern about where the focus of British foreign and security policy should lie. The disparities between growth rates in the British economy and those of the other EEC countries arrested the attention of the British government. This disparity, alongside a general malaise in British defence policy and Anglo-American relations following the Suez crisis, led to a greater European orientation. British membership of the EEC, which took place after two failed attempts in 1962 and 1967, marked an economic and political commitment to Europe. Significantly, there were no parallel security ties to Europe, apart from those to the somnabulent WEU. From the British point of view, the EEC was exactly what the middle 'E' suggested – primarily an economic institution. Thoughts of dropping the middle 'E' and furthering integration to include political, foreign policy and security, ran counter to the confederalist approach adopted by successive governments. Thus a commitment to the European Community did not, as a corollary, necessarily mean that Britain was duty-bound to support the eventual establishment of a European Defence Community; this had been tried once, in 1954, and failed.

British behaviour just before and after EC membership continued to show a predilection for close defence relations with the US, although it was never to be as close as the pre-1970 era – a fact signified in Prime Minister Harold Wilson's preference for the term 'close' relationship rather than 'special' to describe Anglo-American relations.[55] Britain's failure actively to support America in Vietnam was to be a blow to Anglo-American relations and again signified a gradual move away from an Atlantic-oriented security stance to a more European one.

Under Prime Minister Edward Heath's guidance, Britain eventually acceded to the EEC in 1973. Heath was determined to advance Britain's European identity and role, which included the defence realm. As if to stress the changed nature of Britain's defence relations, the Heath government rejected an American application to utilize bases on Cyprus for the reinforcement of the Israelis in the 1973 Arab–Israeli war. The 1973 war also had the effect of stressing Europe's pro-Arab sentiments in a marked contrast to the US's pro-Israeli stance. Continuing economic difficulties led to defence cutbacks in 1975, which had the effect of curtailing Britain's ability to intervene out-of-area and, therefore, stressed the importance of European defence in British defence policy.

By the end of the Heath government in 1974, Anglo-American defence relations had changed dramatically. The 'special relationship'
had certainly cooled but not as the result of a deliberate anti-US stance;
it was merely a matter of prudence.

The 1974–9 Callaghan government helped to revive some of the
warmth of the special relationship, although it was never to be as intimate as during the Wilson and Heath governments. James Callaghan's
government tried to respond to Washington's fears of atrophy in the
European allies defence budgets. In 1977, President Carter launched
the Long-Term Defense Plan, part of which was a commitment by
NATO allies to an increase in defence expenditure of three per cent
per annum for the period 1979–84. Although in retrospect the case
could be made that these were aspirations rather than realistic targets,
Britain was one of the few European countries to actually take the
commitment seriously.[56]

The advent of the first Thatcher government in May 1979 was to
redress what was perceived to be an imbalance towards Europe to the
detriment of transatlantic relations. Rather than reach a balance, Mrs
Thatcher and President Reagan established close relations while those
with the European leaders cooled. On paper, the Thatcher government
stressed the importance of a British commitment to Europe's defence;
this was stressed in the 1981 Defence Review as well as in subsequent
years. In practice, the close defence ties with the US were of abiding
importance. As if to underline their importance, the Trident agreement
of 1982, alongside the US assistance given to Britain during the Falklands war, served as reminders of the enduring importance of the transatlantic ties. It should also be noted that the Thatcher government was
an unwavering supporter of the NATO Council's 1979 Dual-Track
decision, under which cruise missiles were to be deployed at RAF
Greenham Common and RAF Molesworth. Other European governments, such as those of Belgium and the Netherlands, were distinctly
unenthusiastic about the deployment of such missiles on their soil.

Attempts to expand European integration in political union, complete
with its defence component, met with little support amongst the conservative party. This lack of enthusiasm can largely be explained in terms
of Britain's historically ambivalent attitude towards European integration
generally and, more specifically. Mrs Thatcher's own personal leanings.
Hugo Young, a British journalist, has commented on this issue:

> By articulating the British sense of distance from Europe, she rein-
> forced it. She was not interested in expanding the European idea
> beyond the narrow ground of Britain's economic advantage. . . .[57]

Anti-integrationist forces, anxious to confine integration to the economic realm, found an ally in Margaret Thatcher, who was willing to take well-publicized stands against encroaching supranationalism, most memorably in a famous speech to the *Collège d'Europe* in Bruges, on 20 September 1988. In this speech Mrs Thatcher 'appeared to repudiate the commitment in the Single European Act to a European union, presenting instead the neo-Gaullist idea of a Europe of independent states which would cooperate closely but not submit to any central control over economic policy, nor move to any sort of political union.'[58]

During the Thatcher era the revitalization of the WEU was broached. Initially it was the French who forwarded the idea of using the WEU as a forum for reaching a common position on such things as the USSR, Afghanistan and SDI. A meeting between the seven members in 1984 resulted in an agreement to awake the sleeping institution, although the British expressed reservations. The 1985 Defence White Paper declared that the European effort (which included the works of the Eurogroup, the IEPG, WEU and unilateral efforts) is 'not an alternative to transatlantic cooperation.'[59] The 1986 Reykjavik summit, in which Reagan and Gorbachev agreed to extensive cuts in strategic arms without consulting their allies, led Geoffrey Howe, the Foreign Secretary, to call for a revival of the WEU as 'a forum for defining European defence priorities *within* NATO', in a speech given to the Belgian Institute of International Relations in March 1987.[60] Although Howe was careful to stress this process as falling within the NATO structure, Thatcher warned of the dangers of 'sub-structures in Europe which could unwittingly, unintentionally have the effect of undermining links across the Atlantic'.[61] Mrs Thatcher's reaction to the rejuvenation of the WEU, while positive, also illustrated ambivalence towards European defence cooperation, which, it was feared, could either demonstrate to the US that Europe could provide for its own defences and the US was thus redundant, or that an independent European security entity would not be able to agree on a common security policy, by which time the US would have been alienated and reluctant to maintain a sizeable military presence in Europe. At the same time that Britain has shown a keen interest in keeping the US involved militarily in Europe, there was also concern that if Britain does not collaborate in the European defence fora, France and Germany will be left, by default, to take the critical decisions regarding Europe's future security.

More recently, the fundamental ambivalence of Britain towards a stronger European defence entity, which is one of the goals of the Treaty on European Union, has led to a general reluctance to see the

European integration process proceed rapidly to full European union (that is, union that goes beyond economic union to include foreign and security policy). The lack of enthusiasm for deep integration can be seen both in Mrs Thatcher's attempts to renegotiate Britain's payments to the common agricultural programme and John Major's subsequent negotiation of two opt-out clauses for Britain in the Treaty on European Union: the 'social chapter' and European Monetary Union. Prime Minister Major claimed that the Treaty on European Union (and, more specifically, the terms that he negotiated for Britain) marks the point at which, 'For the first time, we have begun to reverse that centralizing trend. We have moved decision-making back towards the member states in areas where Community law need not and should not apply.'[62] Contrary to French interpretations of the same treaty, which they claim heralded more integration extending, eventually, to European Union, the British interpretation would appear to be the opposite. The reluctance to see a greater European role in foreign policy and security issues that has been evident in the late Thatcher years and under Major, would not appear to be backed by public opinion (see Table 7.1). The doubts about extending the European Community to full union, which would mean embracing a common foreign and security policy, under Thatcher and Major has put Britain in the position of being advocates of 'widening' the Community to include some of the Central European states. The backing for widening the Community, which means extending membership beyond the twelve members of the Community, can be explained as an attempt to slow down or halt the 'deepening' of the Community into full union.

Since the advent of the momentous changes in Europe that ended the Cold War, Britain has made a concerted effort to keep the US involved in Europe. The significance and importance of NATO to Britain has also been underlined when, in May 1991, it was decided by the organization that Britain should command the Alliance's Rapid Reaction Corps (ARRC).[63] Since the corps will also draw heavily upon European forces, it could be argued that the ARRC has also emphasized Britain's links with Europe in the defence field as well. Britain occupies a somewhat precarious position between its American ally and the European allies; it plays a bridging role between North America and Western Europe – explaining European policy to Washington and defending the US to its European allies.

In spite of Britain's differences with some of its European colleagues over security, there are common concerns that could serve to draw them together, most notably with France. Britain and France share concerns regarding the following security matters: Germany's post-unification foreign and security policy (or, to be more specific, Germany's non-role); the possibility of a US withdrawal from Europe; and maintaining independent nuclear deterrents.

There are also other links between France and Britain. For example, they are both UN Security Council members, who will presumably have a large role on defining extra-European relations. Britain and France are both nuclear powers who show little enthusiasm, thus far, for sharing their deterrent forces with other European allies. Additionally, inaccurate comparisons have been drawn between post-Thatcherism and neo-Gaullism. While there are indeed superficial links, such as the preoccupation with '*grandeur*,' or 'putting the "Great" back into Britain', a deeper comparison shows some fundamental differences. Unlike de Gaulle, who had a well-developed vision of '*l'Europe des patries*,' which extended beyond Western Europe to Eastern Europe, the Thatcherite view of Europe was never that specific. If anything, the Thatcherite view of Europe was based primarily upon protecting Britain's national interest and not in extending a British vision of Europe. Mrs Thatcher was openly suspicious of moves towards European Union suspecting, among other things, the existence of a 'Franco-German axis with its own covert federalist and protectionist agenda'.[64] She was also suspicious of Franco-German support for political union: the 'French wanted to curb German power', while political union for the Germans was 'the price of achieving quick reunification with East Germany on their own terms and with all the benefits which would come from Community membership' and it was also a demonstration that 'Germany would not behave like old Germany from Bismarck to Hitler'.[65] There is little evidence to suggest that Britain's position has markedly changed under John Major.

The possibility of nuclear collaboration between the two European nuclear powers, which could lead to a 'Euro-deterrent,' has been suggested in some quarters. However, in spite of cooperation on non-strategic nuclear systems, such as the co-development of an air-launched missile, wider collaboration seems unlikely.[66] The deterrents, in spite of changes in Europe, remain *national* deterrents and the psychological leap required to dedicate these forces to uses beyond the purely national has not been made. Any such collaboration will not be the result of any desire to create a European defence entity with France at the head, but the result of necessity, in the event of a life-and-death situation. As far as British forces are concerned, the 'independent' nature of the British deterrent force can be questioned. The British independent nuclear deterrent, comprised of four Trident D-5 nuclear submarines,[67] relies heavily upon US support and expertise for servicing and maintenance. In the event of the (unlikely) creation of a 'Euro' deterrent force, or further arms cuts beyond START II that may put pressure upon Britain to put its strategic nuclear forces in the table, the US may decide to rescind some of its commitments to the British government regarding its supply of warheads and their servicing. If the US were to take such action, the British deterrent force would be severely compromised.

Among the commentators on post-Cold War European security there seems to be a consensus that Britain and France should retain their nuclear weapons. The reasons for this seem to be unclear since, as weapons, they have utility only if they are explicitly linked to a threat. Possible justification for the short-to-medium-term retention of independent nuclear deterrents are twofold: first, although much of the immediate danger of a nuclear exchange has been removed, there is still the possibility of residual threats arising from within the ex-Soviet Union; second, presumably it would be unacceptable to leave France as the sole nuclear power in Europe – logic that would presumably work in reverse as well!

At the conventional level there have been significant changes in Britain as well. In 1990 the government launched a major overhaul of its defence forces, the first significant one since *The Way Forward* in 1981 under the then Secretary of State for Defence, John Nott. The new review, coordinated by Tom King, announced significant cuts in force levels – the army was cut from 160 000 to 120 000 (mainly by withdrawing the BAOR from Germany), the Royal Air Force was cut by 14 000, the Royal Navy by 3000 and a cut of 21 000 civilian personnel employed by the Ministry of Defence. The King review was also significant in several other ways: it committed the government to acquiring a fourth Trident submarine (which was bitterly opposed by the Labour opposition); it created a special force designed to be able to respond rapidly to out-of-area contingencies; and it failed to decommission any of Britain's three aircraft carriers.

The dramatic cuts in British defence expenditure, which amounted to a cut from 5.1 per cent of the GDP in 1985 to 3.9 per cent in 1990[68] (compared with 4.0 per cent and 3.6 per cent for France in the same years, and 6.5 per cent and 5.6 per cent for the US) reflected not only the changes in the security environment but the depressed state of the British economy. For economic reasons alone, Britain is unlikely to want to step into a leadership role that may entail more costly commitments overseas. It is the political reasons that are the strongest factor for doubting that Britain will assume an assertive role on European security issues.

Unlike France, Britain has been exceptionally slow in reacting to the changes in Europe and what that implies for the US military presence. The unwavering support that successive British governments have shown to NATO and the US, most notably in the Reagan–Thatcher years, have made the British slow to entertain seriously the notion of European defence. Even under John Major's leadership there is still a suspicion of European or pan-European challenges to the familiar transatlantic security arrangement. Mrs Thatcher was one of the most outspoken critics of any hint of excessive European defence collaboration and, most noticeably, of Franco-German cooperation, which she warned could give the impression to Washington that its defence contribution to Europe has become superfluous. Just as the French have to cope with some Gaullist spirits in their defence planning, there remain Thatcherite ones lurking in British defence policy today.

John Major came to power in November 1990 and, although there is certainly a marked difference in leadership style, the underlying Thatcher ambivalence regarding political union remains. Major inherited Defence Secretary Tom King's July 1990 White Paper *Options for Change*,[69] which emphasized the inherent uncertainties that may result from the upheavals in Europe and the former Soviet Union; although it was also perceived no urgent threats to the United Kingdom from the former Soviet Union existed, and those risks that may arise were 'diffuse and ill-defined'. The emphasis was put upon maintaining existing security structures at a time of uncertainty. The White Paper commented that, 'Defence arrangements . . . cannot sensibly be made the leading agent of political change.'[70] In contrast to the French advocacy of enhancing European integration to include defence arrangements, the Thatcher and Major governments have preferred to stress the importance of continuity. In institutional terms this obviously translates into strong support for the primacy of NATO and a continued US military role in Europe.

A review of 'options' appeared in the July *1992 Statement on Defence Estimates*, which stressed the uncertainties and risks in both Europe and internationally. The strategy stressed Britain's determination to play a 'wider role in seeking to maintain international stability'.[71] The 'wider role' was to be supported by a defence budget that had been reduced by almost 5 per cent in real terms over the period 1989–92. 'Options' also committed Britain to the purchase of a fourth Trident submarine and to keep its nuclear forces as the 'ultimate guarantee.' Within NATO the British role was expanded to include military training and assist-ance, deployments and support for peace-keeping and other operations. These operations could also be carried out through the aegis of the WEU or the UN.

Tom King's White Paper marked the first attempt to come to terms with the changed security environment of the post-Cold War world. King's 'Options' had cut Britain's armed forces by around 25 per cent, while promising 'smaller but better' defence systems, but by 1993 it became obvious that further adjustments would have to be made. A further defence review, entitled *Defending Our Future*, appeared on 5 July 1993 and was carried out under the guidance of Malcolm Rifkind, Secretary of State for Defence, and aimed to prune at least one billion pounds from the defence budget.[72] Prior to the review, Rifkind had been given the almost impossible mandate of cutting defence spend-ing, while at the same time upholding the operational capacity of the services.

Defending Our Future cut deeper and further than the original had been prepared to, due to the 'inherently cautious' nature of the orig-inal cuts, which were made in accordance with other allies' plans as well as the uncertainties of the immediate post-Cold War security en-vironment.[73] The main changes outlined in the 1993 white paper are a reduction in the number of ASW aircraft and the overall number of aircraft provided for the protection of UK airspace; the Eurofighter 2000 was heralded as the 'cornerstone of the RAF's future capability', while, by the mid-1990s, the army would be increased from 116 000 to 119 000. Under *Defending Our Future*, the most severe cuts were sustained by the Royal Navy.[74] These forces are assigned three main defence roles; namely protection of the UK and its dependent terri-tories, defence of the UK against major external threat and international security interests.

In spite of Tom King's promises of no further cuts following those in *'Options for Change'*, Rifkind felt able to carry out further cuts, for, as *The Times* commented, '[he] is able to make cuts to please the Treasury because he has the luxury of planning a defence programme without having an identifiable enemy.'[75] The 1993 white paper recog-nized that, in the absence of an overarching threat to Britain's se-curity, there would be increased pressure for Britain to assume an active role in international peace-keeping missions through NATO, which 'is now in a position to support UN or CSCE operations'.[76] As a con-tinuum, this projected role for NATO meant that the distinction between 'in and out of area' was no longer deemed relevant for British defence planning. Instead, the criteria to be applied to security problems will be the 'depth of British and allied interests involved and the implications of the crisis for international peace and stability, while recognizing our continued commitment to collective defence through NATO'.[77]

There are many apparent awkwardness with the White Paper's seeming predilection to work through NATO and for NATO to assume new roles. Many of these problems are covered in more detail in Chapter 9. Briefly, there appear to be two general problems: First, NATO is designed as a collective defence organization, yet one of the roles identified for NATO is essentially that of peace-keeping, a role for which it is not well suited. As is argued elsewhere, collective defence and peace-keeping are quite different concepts; the former demands a response to an act of aggression, while the latter may demand long-term commitments of the Lebanon or even Northern Ireland type. To add to the confusion, the White Paper welcomes the willingness of the UN and CSCE to 'prevent or contain' conflict, which appears to point toward a 'peace-making' or 'peace-enforcement' role. Again, these are different concepts from collective defence. Second, the disposal of 'in and out of area' terminology makes sense in the post-Cold War era, but by replacing it with new criteria (the depth of British and allied interests) there is no automaticity about any response and the reference to 'allied' seems to primarily cast British defence interests within a Eurocentric NATO role and not necessarily a pan-European one.[78]

Under the provisions of '*Defending the Future*', the bulk of the forces are assigned to the first two of the three roles outlined above. Defence role three, addressing the somewhat vague international security interests, is regarded as a 'free good' since for costing purposes the division-sized force earmarked for this role would be drawn from existing forces that have other functions. The division-sized contingent would be designed with an Operation Granby-type scenario in mind (Granby being the code name for Britain's contribution to the Gulf War).

Although both Tom King and Malcolm Rifkind have resisted the notion that the reshaping of Britain's defence forces was driven primarily by Treasury demands, it was clearly a significant component. Defence expenditures will drop by roughly 12 per cent in the period 1990–91 to 1995–96, which, by the later date, will leave Britain with combined forces of around 240 000 (52 500 Royal Navy, 119 000 Army and 70 000 Royal Air Force). The shrinkage of the armed forces has elicited charges from the political opposition that, in the quest for budgetary cuts, the government risks overstretching the armed forces.[79] Rifkind has rebutted such charges with the observation that, since there is no need to have forces specifically dedicated to unexpected contingencies, all the forces that could be used in a crisis are used in peacetime for other roles.

What is abundantly clear from the post-Cold War defence reviews is that NATO is still the centre of Britain's defence efforts, but with an implicit recognition that Britain may be willing to assist in operations coordinated through other agencies. Furthermore, NATO serves to ensure 'the firm commitment of US conventional and nuclear forces to common security'.[80] Less clear is the continued need for nuclear deterrence as the 'ultimate guarantee' – against whom will it be targeted, and how independent will the Trident force really be, if and when an ultimate force is needed? Furthermore, does the US role in maintaining Britain's Trident fleet make Britain even more uneasy about any of the 'Euro' options?

Within the British bureaucracy there are some subtle differences of opinion which could be significant. While the Ministry of Defence remains wary of attempts at European defence collaboration, the Foreign and Commonwealth Office (FCO) remains more open to persuasion. The FCO has been traditionally more sympathetic to the idea of strengthening the second pillar of Kennedy's two-pillar model of the Atlantic alliance and has also backed efforts to revive the WEU as a way of achieving this end, yet this backing was also as a means of preventing the EC from assuming political, and particularly security, functions.

The cuts made in Britain's defence budget since 1990 could easily leave the impression that they are primarily driven by national concerns, with relatively little thought given to the subject of Britain's wider security functions. While there is an explicit acknowledgment of Britain's international security obligations in the 1993 White Paper, the physical manifestation of these obligations would appear to be of an *ad hoc* nature. The argument forwarded by Rifkind that, in the event of a crisis, Britain's international obligations could be met from peacetime forces raises questions about training and readiness, as well the wider questions of what exactly the 'depth of British and allied interests may be'. The Bosnian example, referred to as an example of a low-intensity operation (to borrow the outmoded American concept), points in the opposite direction to the one adopted in the White Paper. The situation in Bosnia has demonstrated the inadequacy of merely drawing from regular, peacetime forces and transferring them to a dangerous and foreign environment. Bosnian-type scenarios point to the need for dedicated, highly skilled troops who, if need be, can react swiftly. The forwarding of Operation Granby as a model for the fulfilment of

Britain's wider security interests is perhaps an unfortunate one, since the British contingent sent to the Gulf was cannibalized from the remains of the British Army of the Rhine.

The advent of a Labour government could, however, change the picture radically and lead to full British cooperation with France and Germany in defence matters. This need not necessarily imply a stark choicè between Europe and the US either; there are arguments from the US perspective that may mitigate in favour of a strong British role in this process since it would give them an 'inside line'. This could also open up the historical suspicions of the type held by de Gaulle that Britain was, in effect, the US's Trojan Horse. Such an eventuality could best be managed, as is argued below in more detail, by an institutionalized process of transparency and complementarily which involves the main European actors as well as the US.

Britain's economic weaknesses and its traditional preference for close relations with the US mitigates against any expectation that Britain will be inclined to pursue a leadership role in Europe. It will, moreover, remain for the immediate future a staunch defender of NATO and a US military presence in Europe. In contrast to France, Britain has been enthusiastic to see an expansion of NATO's role into political roles; and, at the same time, Britain has sought to ensure active American participation in European security. By supporting NATO so staunchly, Britain has been able to secure two objectives which, on their own, would have been impossible: first, the continuation (for the foreseeable future) of an American role; and, second, anchoring Germany to a European security system built primarily around NATO. Britain's support of NATO has underscored its command role for the new Allied Rapid Reaction Corps (ARRC).[81] The 1993 White Paper stated that NATO 'remains essential to peace and stability in Europe', as well as being 'the principal guarantor of our security'.[82]

There are potential hazards arising from Britain's staunch defence of NATO which, as is suggested below, is in many ways an outmoded institution. In the event of the demise of NATO, Britain would be left with a second-string role to play in Europe. It may also be hazardous if the US independently decides to phase out its military presence in Europe. This would have the effect of leaving Britain without a coherent security policy and with potential difficulties in integrating into European security structures.

British backing of NATO has had knock-on effects for its relations with the various 'Euro-options'. At the time of the WEU's resurrection in the mid-1980s, other options were being forwarded, such as the West European Treaty Organization (WETO), which were resisted by Britain on the grounds of the uncertain role (if any) that the US would play and the central role that Germany would assume in any such institution. The Eurogroup until recently a part of NATO, was ruled out because it would exclude and thus alienate the French. The WEU was backed only in so far as it served as a device for building up the European pillar of NATO; here again is a contrast with French policy, which saw the WEU as an alternative to NATO, not just an adjunct. For example, Douglas Hurd referred to the WEU as a 'bridge' between NATO and the EC. The WEU also had other positive aspects from the British perspective, especially the non-membership of Denmark, Greece and Ireland (although this changed in June 1992 with the addition of Greece as a full member and the remaining two as observers). By viewing the WEU as a means of 'strengthening the European pillar of the Atlantic Alliance',[83] the British government was also sending out the message that, in spite of the Maastricht process, security issues were not to be left in the hands of the EC Commission.

Britain's attitudes toward the security aspects of European Union have been opposite to those of France. For instance, the Gulf War and the sizeable British contribution were seen as symbolic of the necessity and strength of Anglo-US relations, while Germany's failure to send any forces was taken as confirmation of the weakness of any ideas of European security organizations which excluded the US. The wording of the Maastricht Treaty allowed both the British and the French to feel reassured about their respective outlooks on European security collaboration. For the British the most relevant stipulations were those *requesting* the WEU, 'which is an integral part of the development of the European Union, to elaborate and implement decisions and actions of the Union which have defence implications'. The same article stated that, 'The policy of the Union ... shall not prejudice the specific character of the security and defence policy of certain member states under the North Atlantic Treaty and be compatible with the common security and defence policy established within that framework.'[84] The idea that any European security arrangements should be compatible with NATO was inserted at British insistence. Thus, from the British perspective this seemed to confirm that any European security integration would take place within the WEU and, more importantly, with the intention of reinforcing NATO. The British interpretation was supported by the Italians. The French and the Germans took comfort from the same article which, at the beginning, stated, 'The common foreign and security policy shall include all questions related to the security of the European Union, including the eventual framing of a common defence policy, which might in time lead to a common defence.'[85] This seemed to hold out the promise of a common *European* defence which was not necessarily based on the WEU or NATO.

The complex British relations with the WEU can be explained in terms of an insurance policy. While there is little doubt about the primacy of NATO in Britain's defence planning, there is, nevertheless, enough concern at the growth of a European voice in security affairs that makes it a prudent move to have a British voice in that movement, so that Britain could promote the idea of the EC and the WEU being a bridge to NATO. The dissolution of the Soviet Union, hints of neo-isolationism in the 1992 US Presidential election campaign, and the advocacy of European Union by France and Germany in particular, reinforced the perceived need for a British voice within the WEU. As has also been argued, Britain's active role within the WEU served both to promote the links with NATO while also serving to monitor ties with the EC Commission.

Other institutions, such as the CSCE, are greeted with little real enthusiasm as the basis for a pan-European security organization. The 1993 White Paper offers no commentary or evaluation of the CSCE's effectiveness, but simply limits itself to a description of the CSCE's functions and suggests that 'forces deployed under CSCE auspices could help to supervise and maintain ceasefires, monitor troop withdrawals, support the maintenance of law and order, provide humanitarian aid and assist refugees'.[86] Although these roles are recognized as significant, they are seen primarily as support roles to the UN and the CSCE may, if need be, request the support of the EC, NATO or the WEU.

CONCLUSIONS

British security policy, as reflected in 'Options for Change' and 'Defending Our Future', suggests a somewhat cautious, and in some areas ambiguous, security policy. The three defence roles outlined in the 1993 White Paper make Britain's own defence and that of its NATO allies paramount. As with other NATO countries, Britain's defence forces have been cut largely in response to national interest and budgetary considerations. In institutional terms, British defence is defined primarily in terms of NATO, the main objective being to ensure a continued US military presence in Europe as well as the maintenance of close Anglo-American relations.

Although there may appear to be superficial evidence of an interest in pan-European initiatives, most of the British responses to the post-1989 events in Eastern Europe have been economic. For instance, Britain has backed the EBRD and launched its 'Know-How' scheme for Eastern Europe with an initial starter fund of 25 million pounds. In terms of private investment there would appear to be little enthusiasm for ventures in Eastern Europe; only one of the top twenty investors was British, compared to four German and six American groups.[87] Mrs Thatcher is on record as supporting Eastern European membership of the EC, presumably with the intention not so much of helping the ailing economies of those countries, but as a means of keeping in check the power of the EC commission.[88] In most other respects Britain remains profoundly anti anything that smacks of federalism, as seen in the opposition to the single currency, majority voting in the Council of Ministers, to a stronger legislative role for the European parliament and to close links between the WEU and the EC.

Since British policy vis-à-vis Europe is for the most part at variance with that of the other main European powers, especially on the issue of 'deepening the community', it is logical to conclude that British defence policy will remain firmly embedded in NATO and, more profoundly, in a close Anglo-American partnership. Continued resistance to the deepening of European integration could have some deleterious effects for Britain. Amongst these could be the gradual alienation of Britain as 'the odd-one-out' (instead of France) and perhaps the accomplishment of the opposite to what was intended: namely, instead of binding Germany to a Europe with a strong US influence, it may alienate Germany and lead to more independent actions by Germany in its relations with the east. Thus, rather than preventing deepening as a means of keeping a check on Germany (and maybe French federalist designs as well), the opposite may be achieved. In a similar fashion, British resistance to deepening in the security realm and its dogged loyalty to NATO may also prove disadvantageous at a time when the future relevance of NATO is under scrutiny.

There are many loose strings that remain in this brief survey of French and British security policy which, when tied or cut, will have an important effect on European security. To start with the obvious, the basic thrust of British and French security policies are at variance. Britain remains adamant that any new European defence or security identity must remain linked to the US through the Atlantic Alliance and that this identity must be expressed through the WEU and not the EC. The French continue to have a preference for promoting a security identity independent of the US with an institutional base in the EC. If movement is possible, the easiest alignment is to focus the emerging European security identity on the WEU, which would partially satisfy the French desire to have a 'European' identity, as well as British concerns that a link be preserved to the US and NATO. It would also serve as a link for French collaboration with the US which, as has been argued, is an essential ingredient of post-Cold War European stability. This will not be an easy task, but to continue a struggle over *who* defines the emerging 'security identity' would be to miss a historic opportunity.

A further loose end is the question of the purpose and functions of the two nuclear deterrents. Both France and Britain have compelling internal reasons for retaining their deterrent forces. The French nuclear deterrent remains committed to purely national uses, while Britain's strategic and sub-strategic deterrent force is committed to NATO's Strategic Concept.[89] This immediately creates some interesting and currently unanswered questions. France, as has been discussed, has not accepted that nuclear weapons should be 'truly weapons of last resort' as agreed by Britain and the other NATO members at the London meeting of the North Atlantic Council in July 1990. This situation obviously creates some serious asymmetries for the potential use of nuclear weapons. A second area of issue is the relation, if any, of French nuclear weapons to the Eurocorps and any emergent European security organization. A third area that could prove to be of concern is the possibility that, in the light of any post-START agreement, Britain and France may feel pressurized into putting nuclear weapons onto the negotiating table.

This brief survey of British and French security policy has attempted to show that the two countries remain, in security and other senses, at loggerheads. France has pursued a post-Cold War security policy that is intended first, to be self-serving and, second, to promote a European security alternative to NATO. Britain has pursued a traditional security policy which puts national interest first and allegiance to the Alliance a close second. 'Euro-options' are regarded with suspicion by London, which puts any foreseeable British defence policy at varience with that of France. As countries that still assume the status of major powers, through the retention of seats on the UN Security Council and membership of the élite international clubs, both may believe that they have leadership roles, but the directions in which they wish to lead Europe are quite different.

4 Germany, Security and the Post-Cold War World

Hans J. Morgenthau noted that European history can be summarized by two overriding concerns, 'One is the natural superiority of Germany among the nations of Europe; the other is the unwillingness of the other European nations to accept that natural superiority. Since 1870, the great convulsions on the European continent, and the diplomatic moves preceding those convulsions, have all been dominated by those two facts.'[1]

Traditionally, the natural superiority of Germany has been dealt with by a series of alliances designed to counter this preponderance. The failure of the European balance-of-power mechanism to contain German militarism led eventually to two world wars and to the imposition on Europe of 'order' by outside powers, who divided Germany. The division was reluctantly accepted, although reunification remained a goal that was never dropped. The division itself may have provided a solution to the problem of Germany's predominant role in Europe – but it was to be a temporary one. The US, Britain and France were all formally committed to the unification of Germany, as enshrined in the 1955 Paris Treaty and in the 1967 Harmel Report.

The continuation of the German Democratic Republic (GDR) was unacceptable to the people of East Germany. Impositions both from Moscow and the SED were seen as increasingly repressive in the late 1980s. The eventual collapse of the Berlin Wall on 9 November 1989 was due, in large part, to the pressures from the East Germans themselves, for example in the huge rallies in Dresden, Leipzig and Berlin. Some credit also has to be given to other countries, like Hungary, who acted as a thoroughfare for East Germans seeking a new life in West Germany. The opening of the Berlin Wall was a last-ditch attempt by Egon Krenz, Honecker's successor to the SED leadership, to stem the flow of people from the East to the West. It proved futile: the streams of people heading into West Germany could not be halted. On 3 October 1990 the five East German *Länder* were incorporated into the FRG.

Germany's reunification has prompted concerns that, once again, Europe has Germany as its central actor. This in turn evokes historical comparisons with the past when Germany was strong, unified and

135

aggressive. The inapt historical comparisons made between the present Germany and the Germany in 1848, 1871 or 1933 have led some to conclude that there is a new German question or, more accurately, a new-old German question. These anxieties have been exacerbated by the re-emergence of neo-Nazi movements. Germany's new economic and political position has also engendered concern about where Germany's real interests lie – are they with its fellow EC and NATO colleagues, or do they lean more toward historical notions of *Mitteleuropa*? Speculation is also rife regarding what role Germany may assume on issues of international peace and security.

What is radically different about Germany today and what many overlook is the interdependence of Germany economically and politically with the other main European powers. By creating structures within which Germany can play a role, such as the European Coal and Steel Community and the European Economic Community, Germany's traditional superiority has been checked. However, it is worth noting that the very institutions that were intended to constrain German expansionism have also served to promote it to its current position within Europe. In spite of Germany's central role in Europe, there seem to be four reasons to suggest that the historical analogies involving the late nineteenth or earlier decades of the twentieth century are inappropriate.

First, the interdependence of Germany economically with its EC partners makes any realistic German threat to the security of Europe an illusion; and, with that, it also poses some awkward questions regarding the continued necessity of the US military presence as 'insurance' within the Alliance. The notion of history being a didactic cycle, where people are doomed to repeat variants of the same mistake, also ignores the changes in the German people themselves. The emergence of neo-Nazi groups in Germany may lead some to suspect that little has changed, yet neo-Nazis mark a small segment of the population. On the contrary, many Germans are acutely aware of their history; furthermore it is difficult for them to forget when institutions, such as the US Holocaust Memorial Museum, serve as constant reminders of a bleak period in German history. As a result of these constant reminders and the sincere regrets there is little inclination towards militarism.[2] If anything, there is an inclination in the opposite direction, toward pacifism, in the German public. This tendency can make the concerns of other Europeans, like France, look strange. There is concern on the one hand about Germany's new central role in Europe; yet, at the same time, there is concern that Germany may 'go soft' under the influence of pacifists.

Second is the fact that many of the historical causes for dispute have, by and large, been laid to rest. Perhaps the most spectacular example of this was the vote taken on 21 June 1990, which indicated that an overwhelming majority in both parliaments (the FRG's and GDR's) would confirm in a treaty that the existing Oder-Nisse line is the 'irrevocable' boundary of Poland and Germany. This pledge was later solemnized on 14 November in the course of the 'Two plus Four' talks on the unification of Germany.[3]

Third, the FRG is far less politically centralized than it was in the past. Increasing powers have been devolved to the *Länder*, as well as outside of Germany, to the EC and other supranational organizations. The different distribution of power in Germany would seem to militate against military revanchism.

Fourth, unlike the 1918 Treaty of Versailles and its notion of collective guilt, the conditions that were imposed upon Germany as a result of the Yalta Treaty demanded a peaceful solution. The guilt for the Second World War was assumed, at least in the formal sense, by those tried at the Nuremberg Trials. The immense dissatisfaction felt with the Versailles Treaty eventually proved to be a fertile breeding ground for nationalism and national socialism. Although the division of Germany was far from ideal and emotionally wrenching for many Germans, the grounds for nationalism and attempts to rewrite peace treaties by force were not present in the Cold War years. The dramatic changes that have been provoked by Germany in the past have been due to the use of military force. In contrast, the 1989 'revolution' was peaceful and promoted not by extremist parties within the two Germanies, but by the centre parties. Nor was the revolution a top-down one that was led from above with the people, however reluctantly, following; instead, this revolution was fostered by trade union and religious organizations that eventually percolated through to the higher echelons of political leadership. These four differences make direct historical comparisons with Europe's past inaccurate and misleading.

The ahistorical nature of these comparisons should not leave the impression that there is no longer a German problem. Indeed, one still exists, but it is a different problem. The concerns posed by unification (*Vereingung*)[4] seem to be twofold: first, the impact of the creation of a Europe with Germany at its centre; second, the concern that Germany will diverge in its foreign-policy interests from those of Britain, France and the US.

In terms of the first concern, a united Germany with around eighty million people at the centre of Europe led to the common assumption that the German economic powerhouse will drive the European agenda, with the attached suspicion that Deutsche Marks will do what Panzers did not. The economic prowess of Germany has led to further suspicions being unjustly attached to the FRG. During the euphoria surrounding unification, few were prepared to express any suspicions they may have had, with the possible exception of some well-publicized remarks by Nicholas Ridley, a member of Thatcher's Cabinet, to *The Spectator*.[5] These harboured concerns have since become outright alarm, with the re-emergence of neo-Nazi groups in most of the main German cities.[6] The ugly developments in Germany were initially not adequately addressed by Chancellor Kohl and, as a result, exacerbated doubts about Germany's direction and the extent to which it has forsaken its Nazi past. The expression of hatred against *Ausländer* by extreme right-wing Germans served to re-create the spectre of German nationalism for apprehensive Europeans.

Contrary to the common hyperbole, the German economic miracle has been exaggerated. Furthermore, if the economic strength of Germany is put into perspective, many of the former concerns abate. Pre-unification fears that a German economy, which could be 50 per cent larger than that of France, swelled by seventeen million East Germans, would dictate Europe's economic interests have proven unfounded. Germany's economic growth for the financial year 1992 was near zero, the first time it had been so for many years. Such low economic growth can be accounted for by the global recession and the immense costs of unification, the latter having amounted to over $90 (DM 150) billion per annum. Of the annual expenditure on the costs of unification, a staggering DM 100 billion is going towards benefits, unemployment pay and wage subsidies; this in turn reflects the fact that it costs approximately 80 per cent more to produce a unit of output in eastern Germany than in the west.[7] Aside from chronic underestimation of the costs of unification, other burdens such as those associated with absorbing 500 000 refugees per annum have assuaged concerns that a runaway German economy would dictate Europe's economic interests. Many of the present economic problems predate reunification and have structural roots. From the mid-1980s on, (West) Germany had been losing its attractiveness as a place to invest. The combination of high taxes, stiff regulation and some of the highest labour costs in Europe led an increasing number of German companies to look overseas for production facilities. In the period 1986–91 German companies invested DM 166 billion overseas and foreign companies invested only DM 13 billion in Germany. As a result Germany's current account moved from a healthy surplus of DM 108 billion to a deficit of DM 33 billion between 1989 and 1991.[8]

The German economy accounts for around a quarter of the EC's GDP, whereas Britain and France combined account for around 40 per cent.[9] The export-driven nature of the German economy is, at that same time, a strength and weakness. The relative, but declining, strength of the economy obviously gives Germany considerable leverage within the EC and the international market. The benefits to other EC countries of Germany occupying this position were to be found in Germany's role as an underwriter of the EC which, to take an obvious example, has positive effects for French farmers even though other sections of the French economy may make a net loss under the EC. Germany's ability and willingness to subsidize French agriculture is of immense importance for France and, as a consequence, the German position within the EC is supported. How long Germany will be able to afford this position, in light of its internal economic troubles, remains open to question.

The British relationship with the EC and the FRG has been a slightly different case. Unlike with the French, there was no obvious sector that benefited from EC membership, which, considering Britain was the second largest financial contributor, became a source of tension. The deadlock over British budgetary contributions under Mrs Thatcher focused on expenditure on the Common Agricultural Policy (CAP), an issue that was only resolved at a special meeting of the European Council in Brussels in February 1988. It was largely at Kohl's initiative that British budgetary contributions to CAP were reduced, but in return an increase in the general availability of funds was agreed upon, as was a doubling of the regional and social fund by 1992 – measures that may well end up costing Britain more.[10]

Ultimately, the questions regarding Germany boil down not so much to Germany's economic position or its influence within the EC, but to the question of its national character. Some, like Josef Joffe, have argued that even if Germany is Europe's economic hegemon, it is still a country whose foreign policy is not based on aggression or economic imperialism.[11] This view is not, however, unanimous. Simon Reich, for instance, questions the extent to which contemporary Germany can be divorced from its history and earlier behaviour.[12] A relatively new development is the rise of a new division in Germany: that of Germans against Germans. Now that the euphoria associated with reunification has worn off, it has been replaced by antagonisms between the 'Ossis' and their western counterparts.[13]

The second concern, that Germany will be pulled away from Western Europe towards its neighbours in the east in pursuit of the historical notion of *Mitteleuropa*,[14] is only partially justified. Germany has
been investing considerable amounts in Eastern Europe as well as being the main donor of aid to the former Soviet Union. The German
purchase of Skoda, the Czech car maker, in the face of stiff Franco–
Swedish competition, serves as a striking example of Germany's growing
economic interest in Eastern Europe.[15] Germany is Russia's largest trading
partner – trading more to Russia than the closest three partners combined (China, France and Italy) – and has also made significant inroads into Central European economies. Germany has also been the
largest donor of aid to the CIS, contributing over 50 per cent of all the
aid to the former Soviet Union; in financial terms this represents over
$50 billion since 1989 (compared to $9 billion and $3 billion commit-
ted by the US and Japan respectively, up to the end of 1992).[16] However, the investment in Eastern Europe does not change the fundamental
observation that the German economy is firmly grounded in Western
Europe – something that reunification has not weakened but stressed.
If there is a concern about the direction of the German economy, it is
that Eastern European exports will be shut out of Western Europe.
The decision to delay the move of Germany's capital from Bonn to
Berlin is indicative of Germany's hesitation to adopt an east-facing
identity.[17] What may be interpreted in some quarters as the rejuvena-
tion of *Mitteleuropa* may only be recognition of the simple fact that
Germany's geographical position gives it a vested interest in Eastern
Europe and in enhancing stability there.

The uncertainties and costs associated with reunification have overshadowed German foreign and security policy. The military has been
so unassertive that it has left Germany's allies wishing that they would
do more to share the burdens associated with world peace. The ambivalent role played by Germany in the 1991 Gulf War illustrated a
degree of uncertainty in Bonn about what response would be appropriate for Germany.[18] The wavering over what would be an appropriate
role for Germany during the Gulf War, is highly significant; it illustrates the deep-rooted resistance to war in German society, even amongst
the post-war generation who do not wish to be associated with, or
seen as culprits for, any war involving Germany. Germany is, therefore, highly unlikely to push for a hegemonic role in the security field
without the support of the French, British or the WEU. Because of
their deep-seated cultural objections to war and any hint of German
militarism, Germans have a compulsion to seek security through col-

lective security arrangements. These arrangements are intended to halt the development of strategies that are inimicable to German interests and also to reassure neighbouring countries of Germany's desire to cooperate fully. However, the reassurance provided through common membership of the EC and other institutions also has a high degree of altruism to it (such as the linking of the economic elements of the EC with political union in the Maastricht Treaty).

The key to European security has traditionally been stable relations between France and Germany. While relations are stable, significant differences still remain between the two that demand a solution; examples include the French resistance to admitting new members to the EC, France's desire for a common European security identity that is not linked to NATO, the French concern about surrendering more power to the European Parliament, and the French criticism of the *Bundesbank's* apparently selfish attitude towards interest rates, exemplified in their shift in interest rates on 12 September 1992, which triggered a fiscal crisis in the EC.

Germany's reaction to the Gulf War, the substantial problems that exist between Germany and its European allies, and the heightened anti-Americanism as a result of the Gulf War and the incorporation of seventeen million East Germans into a unified Germany, have posed some fundamental questions about the reliability of Germany. Close security ties with the US and the European allies had been the central feature of post-World War II German national security policy. The significance attached to these ties have eroded in the post-Cold War years, partly as a result of the demise of the Warsaw Treaty Organization and the Soviet Union's disintegration. However, the ties between Germany and the US had in fact started to crumble long before the radical changes of the post-Cold War world. Although it is difficult to pinpoint an exact time for the beginning of the erosion, it seems to stem from the decision in 1967 to adopt flexible response as NATO's official strategy.[19] Flexible response relied upon a graduated response to aggression, by way of contrast to mutually assured destruction (MAD) which relied upon a massive nuclear response to aggression (or, as Herman Kahn aptly called it, a 'wargasm'). In spite of the incredibility of MAD, it put the primary emphasis on deterrence and not on the ability to actually conduct a war. Flexible response, from the German perspective, implied a decoupling of the US from its guarantee of extended deterrence. The willingness of the US to fight a war in Europe *before* they would consider the use of strategic nuclear weapons, which would involve the possibility of an exchange between Russia and the US, concerned Bonn. Flexible response also implied that the US was willing actually to fight a war on German soil and use nuclear weapons on German soil, all in the name of the common defence. In short the split between Germany and the US came down to a difference between war-fighting and deterrence. While Bonn valued deterrence, it did not share Washington's enthusiasm for a strategy based on war-fighting.

The early seventies, during the Carter administration in the US, saw more severe fissures in German–US relations. While Bonn actively pursued détente with the Eastern bloc, the Carter administration adopted a hard line on human-rights violations, of which the Soviet Union was seen as the chief culprit. The differing foreign-policy approaches were exacerbated by the Reagan administration which deepened the divide in German and US foreign policy, as well as security policy. The announcement of the Strategic Defence Initiative (SDI) by Reagan was seen in Bonn as another weakening of extended deterrence and a potentially inflammatory measure that could redirect the arms race into new and harmful avenues.[20] In the event of SDI coming to fruition, Germany and other European allies would be left vulnerable to nonballistic missile attack, while the US would have been less vulnerable. Anxiety about extended deterrence was compounded in Reagan's second term.

In 1986, Reagan met with Gorbachev in Reykjavik and agreed to dramatic cuts in the strategic nuclear arsenals. Once again, this had the effect of provoking fears in Bonn that the US was beginning to decouple its forces from Europe. These anxieties resurfaced the following year with the signature of the Intermediate Nuclear Force (INF) Treaty. The INF Treaty removed an entire 'layer' of nuclear weapons from the NATO arsenal, and thus gave rise to questions in Germany about the linkage between the short-range missiles and the strategic missiles. The INF Treaty was interpreted as another attempt by Washington to decouple its strategic nuclear forces from Europe. By the end of the second Reagan administration in 1988, the actions of the US had contributed to a fundamental shift in the orientation of German foreign and security policy away from the US.[21] The change in orientation was aided by evident tensions in the Warsaw Treaty Organization and the pro-democracy movement in Eastern Europe.

The precise nature of the reorientation is still not clear; the formation of the Franco–German corps would seem to indicate a primary role within the context of Western European integration, but with interests to the east as well, while being careful to maintain cordial relations with Washington – a balancing act that will not be easy. Before Germany's final orientation becomes transparent, whereby political direction is matched with the will and ability to carry out those desired roles, there are three more general problems that Germany may have to face, whatever foreign policy direction it chooses.

BASIC LAW, BASIC PROBLEM

The first policy mire is that Germany must still resolve its constitutional debate and reconsider its staunch refusal to involve German units in operations beyond the traditionally delineated NATO area. This refusal, presumably, would be a significant barrier to any effective European peace-keeping operations that Germany may pursue unilaterally or collectively. German participation in NATO has been accepted as falling within the constitutional stipulations of the *Grundgesetz*, the German constitution (this being supported by a government declaration to that effect in 1982), and thus activities out of the NATO area (OOA) have been traditionally viewed as constitutionally suspect. As long as Germany was able to define its main foreign and security policy preoccupations in NATO terms, the constitutional issue was not pressing. However, the end of the Cold War, the questionable relevance of NATO, and external pressure on Germany to assume a heightened profile in collective security operations, has made this an extremely pressing question and, perhaps, the most pressing question in European security.

The contention elaborated upon below is that the questions surfacing about the nature of the Bundeswehr's future role have been buried in the constitutional debate. The debate is a legal fig leaf that hides the underlying problem, which is a political one, that goes right to the heart of German sensitivities about their wartime experience.

What does the Basic Law permit and forbid? The framing of the *Grundgesetz*, a mere four years after the defeat of Germany, was designed primarily to stop Germany from conducting a war of aggression as well as to restore sovereignty to the West German people. In terms of *intent* the Basic Law was designed to create a defensive front of sufficient strength to make Russian aggression impossible and, second, to grant the same rights to the FRG as to the other participating countries in the newly formed North Atlantic Treaty Organization.

The intent is spelt out in the Basic Law itself, which forbids the preparation for or the conduct of a war of aggression, which constitutes a criminal offence.[22] As an extension of this, the function of the armed forces in the FRG is for defence. The most important article in this respect, and the focus of the debate, is Article 87a which states:

1. The federation shall build up armed forces for defence purposes. Their numerical strength and general organizational structure shall be shown in the budget.
2. Apart from defence, the Armed Forces may only be used to the extent explicitly permitted in this basic law.

Since 'defence' is specifically referred to, it has been assumed by Bonn that this refers mainly to NATO, which is a self-proclaimed defence organization. However, as long as military operations are of a defensive nature, there is nothing specifically binding the use of German armed forces to NATO territory. Those who supported the more conservative interpretation also invoked the Final Act of the 1954 Nine Power Conference which binds the Federal Republic to refrain from any action 'inconsistent with the strictly defensive character' of the North Atlantic Treaty and the Brussels Treaty.[23] Confusion regarding the extent of the FRG's security obligations remained until 1982 when, at Hans-Dietrich Genscher's behest, Bonn argued that German military activities were restricted to those obligations appearing in the North Atlantic Treaty and, beyond this, assistance could only be given to an alliance partner if facilities or property belonging to the Federal Republic were threatened or attacked.[24] This argument, however, was never subject to a ruling by the Federal Constitutional Court. There is nothing, aside from political convenience, that legally limits German military actions to NATO operations within the prescribed Treaty area. Active participation in collective security organizations, like the UN, limitations on national sovereignty, and transfer of sovereign rights to international organizations, are all permissible under the Basic Law. In the course of the last few years the Kohl administration has tried to distance itself from the 1982 interpretation, since it drew heavily upon the wisdom and expertise of the previous Social–Liberal coalition.

Amongst the other legal uses of the armed forces contained in the Basic Law are those enshrined in Article 24 of the Basic Law, which grants the Federation the power to transfer sovereign powers to intergovernmental institutions. And, for the maintenance of peace, 'the Federation may enter *a system of collective security*; in doing so it will consent to such limitations upon its right of sovereignty as will bring about and secure a peaceful and lasting order in Europe and among the nations of the world.'[25] It has been assumed by many that 'collective security' is a reference to NATO, but there is nothing to support this in the constitution – it could just as well refer to the CSCE or the UN.

There are significant definitional problems with the position that restrict the interpretation of Germany's security commitments to NATO. Article 24, as stated above, refers to 'collective security'; and it should, therefore, be noted that the North Atlantic Treaty does not describe NATO as a collective security organization, but rather as a 'collective defence' organization.[26] The differences are not just a matter of legal pickiness, since the two concepts imply quite different obligations. The obligations imposed by collective *defence* were unambiguous in the Cold War years; in the event of an act of aggression against any Alliance member, the automatic right of individual or collective self-defence under Article 51 of the UN Charter could be invoked. The obligations imposed by collective *security* are far more diffuse, as the Gulf War illustrated. In the Gulf War case, the support of a NATO ally (Turkey) was invoked, although there was no direct threat endangering the direct security of Germany. The fate of former Yugoslavia also illustrates the definitional problems associated with the Basic Law and what is, and is not, permitted. As the Yugoslav crisis worsened, pressure mounted within Germany for some kind of action but, once again, there was confusion about whether 'defence purposes' referred to German and NATO territory, or to wider obligations.

The crisis in Yugoslavia marked a small, but significant, test case for the constitutional debate. The passage of a UN Security Council Resolution, on 31 March 1993, in favour of military enforcement on the ban on flights over Bosnia, provoked the charge from the SPD that further German involvement in AWACS operations would be tantamount to participation in a combat role, which would be allegedly unconstitutional. Through an unusual device, the junior party in the governing coalition, the Free Democrats (FDP), agreed to challenge their coalition partners (the CDU and CSU) on this issue and thereby force a ruling from the Federal Constitution Court (FCC). The FCC rejected the application from the FDP to block German participation in the AWACS flights on 7 April. Of particular significance in the FCC deliberations was the argument that German non-participation may result in significant foreign-policy disadvantages, including the loss of trust in Germany on the part of NATO members. The ruling, however, only dealt with the specifics of the AWACS dispute; a more general ruling will be forthcoming in 1995.

In purely legal terms there would seem to be nothing to stop active German military participation in collective security operations beyond the NATO area, or to stop Germany playing a major role in the UN or a new European security organization. The 'official' Bonn interpretation of the Basic Law is based upon self-interest as well as oversensitivity to potential reactions to German military involvement in out-of-area activities. Past German involvement in out-of-area activities – such the Gulf War in 1991, when Germany contributed minesweepers *after* the end of the war, and the enforcement of the naval embargo in the Adriatic and the flight ban over Bosnia – have been gestures but not serious contributions. Nor will the substitution of in-kind assistance be a substitute for actual physical involvement. The benefit to German politicians of hiding behind this constitutional fig leaf is that it postpones the inevitable debate about what the larger political aims of unified Germany are; a debate that certainly would take place in the event of a reinterpretation of the Basic Law. The constitutional debate has given politicians a paper wall to hide behind and avoided the awkward questions about Germany's security policy beyond the confines of NATO's area of interest.[27]

The AWACS dispute, described above, is only one of a number of cases challenging the constitutionality of German military involvement in operations outside the FRG's borders. The low-level German involvement in the 1987–88 Iran–Iraq War, the German contribution to help in the monitoring operations regarding the UN embargo against Serbia and Montenegro, and the freight (*Transall*) flights from Kenya into Somalia, alongside the contribution to a 1500 strong 'security force' for Somalia (*Kampfeinsätze*) in June 1993, all involved or assumed the use of non-combat forces.[28] Soon after the Kohl administration's August 1991 announcement of the dispatch of the *Bayern*[29] and two naval 'Breguet Atlantic' reconnaissance aircraft to the Adriatic in response to the Yugoslav crisis, Hans-Ulrich Klose, the chairperson of the SPD's parliamentary group, threatened to bring a suit against the government at the Federal Constitutional Court, claiming that the deployments were in violation of the constitution which only permitted 'defensive' military action. The threat was not fulfilled, but it does serve as notice of the extreme sensitivity of this issue.

The announcement by Chancellor Kohl on 17 December 1992 that Germany would increase the number of humanitarian aid flights from Kenya to Somalia from two to eight, and that the UN would be offered a battalion of Bundeswehr troops to help in the reconstruction of the country after 'Operation Restore Hope' had been concluded, provoked immediate charges from Björn Engholm, the ex-SPD chairperson, of unconstitutionality. Although Kohl had stressed that the forces, which were composed of medical personnel, engineers and security forces, would only be used in a non-combat role, some in the FDP and SPD charged that a constitutional change was necessary to allow such 'out-of-area' operations. Kohl enjoyed support for his position from most of the CDU and the CSU. The general secretary of the Christian Democrats, Peter Hintze, declared that it was 'barely tolerable and hardly responsible if Germany would still not be in a position to participate completely in (a Somalia-like) operation'.[30]

Kohl's defence was twofold: first, that the forces were being used for defensive purposes within a 'system of collective security', as stipulated by the constitution; second, in an essentially political argument, that 'Germany's international situation will become untenable if it removes itself from the community of nations in these questions... we would become more and more isolated – and that is the last thing we can afford.'[31] Kohl's announcement and the predictable resistance from the FDP and the SPD led to agreement on 13 January 1993 that a constitutional amendment should be drafted to Article 87a of the Basic Law which would permit German troops to participate in international peace-keeping operations sanctioned by the UN or other international organizations.[32] The amendment was designed to permit German participation in 'peace-keeping' and 'peace-creating' (*Friedensschaffende*). The amendment laid forth the terms under which Bundeswehr forces could be deployed in OOA contingencies: (i) for *peacekeeping missions* approved by the UN Security Council or within the framework of regional organizations of which the Federal Republic of Germany is a member; (ii) for *peacekeeping missions* based on Chapters 7 and 8 of the UN Charter and approved by the UN Security Council; (iii) in *collective self-defence* roles in accordance with Article 51 of the UN Charter, together with other nations within the framework of alliances or regional organizations of which the Federal Republic of Germany is a member.[33]

In the bill's first reading on 15 January it failed to reach the two-thirds majority required for a change in the constitution. Chancellor Helmut Kohl and the CDU have made plain their desire to make it possible for Germany to aid its allies against threats that may arise outside the NATO area, as illustrated by the AWACS dispute in relation to 'Operation Deny Flight'. Karsten Voigt, the defence spokesman for the SPD, opposed any attempt to change the constitution and, in an interesting twist to the debate, argued that what is important is the public consensus, which is firmly in favour of the current (restrictive) interpretation of the Basic Law.

In party political terms, any change of the Basic Law would require a two-thirds majority in the *Bundestag* and the *Bundesrat*. In order to achieve such a majority, the CDU would have to count on support from the SPD, the largest opposition party, controlling about 34 per cent of the seats in the *Bundestag*. Such support is unlikely to be forthcoming.[34]

The SPD itself is split. The Social Democratic leadership, including ex-party leader Björn Engholm, supported the idea of German participation in UN peace-keeping activities under special conditions; while others, to the left of the party, were opposed to any involvement with the UN, including peace-keeping. In the spring of 1992, the SPD proposed that the Basic Law be changed to support German participation in UN peace-keeping activities, that any such commitment should involve only the professional (non-conscript) element of the Bundeswehr, and that any such commitment should be agreed upon by a majority vote in the *Bundestag*. Others within the party stipulated that the forces should only be deployed in non-combat, unarmed roles. Some, such as Engholm, specified that the forces could only be deployed under UN command and not, as in the Gulf War, under foreign command which was operating on behalf of the UN to enforce resolutions. In a meeting of the SPD held on 22 August 1992, Engholm also specified that any such involvement should involve the maximum number of nations possible and not just the major powers.

The complexity of the debate illustrates cause for both optimism and pessimism. On the former there seems to be recognition within the SPD that some type of German commitment to the UN, and maybe other organizations like the CSCE, is desirable if Germany is to assume its international responsibilities and become a responsible and significant member of the international community. The grounds for concern stem from the immense difficulty encountered in deciding what type of commitment is appropriate. Those to the left of the SPD continue to oppose any Bundeswehr involvement out of the NATO area. The lowest common denominator may be a commitment that is of little real significance and smacks of mere symbolism.

Aside from the SPD, the other parties have adopted a less restrictive approach to the question. The main parties in the ruling coalition, the CDU and CSU, are in favour of a constitutional amendment which would permit German involvement in UN operations. Volker Rühe, who was CDU General Secretary and then Defence Minister, was highly critical of the SPD tokenism and advocated a more substantial commitment to the UN, one befitting Germany's status and position in the

Post-Cold War world.[35] Kohl's party, the CDU, has argued that Bundeswehr units should be able to participate in UN operations, including those mandated by the UN but not under direct UN military command. The CDU/CSU have advocated that, in the first place, peace-keeping operations should be permitted and then, later, combat operations should be sanctioned – the former would require a simple majority in the Bundestag, the latter a two-thirds majority.

During a visit to Washington D.C. in February 1993, Volker Rühe confirmed to ex-Secretary of Defense, Les Aspin, and Secretary of State, Warren Christopher, that German participation in AWACS operations would continue and was within the German constitution. Such opinions were not shared by the junior partner in the coalition, the FDP, headed by Count Otto von Lambsdorff, who opposed any involvement in the AWACS operations over Bosnia. Lambsdorff drew not only upon legal arguments but also historical sensitivities pertaining to Germany's past role in the region, when he observed that, 'We were there fifty years ago, that's enough.'[36] Klaus Kinkel, Foreign Minister and the highest placed Free Democrat, stated on 17 January that, according to the interpretation of the Basic Law that has prevailed since 1982, Germany may only participate in non-military actions and that he would 'not be part of violating the constitution'.[37] Kinkel and Lambsdorff have threatened to leave the coalition if airborne German forces were involved in the monitoring of direct military operations over the Balkans – a threat that was not carried out in the light of the ruling made by the FCC.[38]

Kinkel's own position on the issue reflects some of the wider ambivalence felt on the subject of German OOA participation. In his first address to the UN on 23 September 1992, Kinkel stressed the need for Germany to assume all the rights and obligations of UN membership, including a supporting role for the Bundeswehr within the UN and assistance in the administration of humanitarian aid and the implementation of embargoes. Kinkel's statement was made to the UN General Assembly and followed a hint made by Michio Watanabe, Japan's ex-Foreign Minister, that Japan was interested in a permanent seat on the Security Council.[39] It would appear that statements made to an international audience on this issue may be at varience with those intended for a domestic audience.

Above all, it would appear that the constitutional debate is about Germany's own sensitivities stemming from the Second World War. The notion of sending German troops outside the European area is one that creates distinct nervousness amongst the German public (mirrored by the concern voiced about Japan's UN involvement in Cambodia). The reservations against the use of force by Germany can be attributed in part to a general opposition to the use of military force; the massive anti-war demonstrations during 'Operation Desert Storm' and the preference to defuse the Yugoslav crisis by political means bear testimony to this. During the 1991 Gulf War, Bonn attempted to balance its constitutional restrictions and its international obligations by contributing some $11.4 billion in direct and indirect aid (out of a total of $80 billion) to the coalition forces and Israel. Bonn, mistakenly, saw this cash outlay as an appropriate response. Many others, including some European allies, saw the need for more active German participation, which would include more than just cash contributions (captured in the sarcastic comment by one senior NATO official, 'They buy, we die').

In a survey carried out in both the eastern and western parts of Germany in March 1991 a majority of those interviewed agreed (54.8 per cent agree, 42.6 per cent disagree) that Germany should take on more responsibility in world affairs, yet a vast majority (73.8 per cent againts 21.5 per cent) were against changing the constitution.[40] These trends, alongside an all-time post-war high in the number of conscientious objectors (150 000 in 1991 alone),[41] make any rapid resolution of the constitutional question unlikely. The public might be swayed if Germany assumes small roles at first and then gradually builds up to a commitment that is more of the type that Kohl has been advocating.

TEST CASES: BOSNIA AND SOMALIA

Events in former Yugoslavia have divided the political parties deeply. A Serbian anti-aircraft attack on a German cargo plane on 6 February 1993 underlined the fact that the legal niceties of combatant and non-combatant status do not necessarily matter to the parties in a conflict.[42] In spite of the potential dangers, the German cabinet agreed on 24 March 1993 that German armed forces should step up their involvement in ex-Yugoslavia. Three points were agreed upon: (i) Three German transport aeroplanes should assist the US in the airdrops to the Muslims in Bosnia. Following the US practice, the drops would be made from a safe 10 000 feet. (ii) Two Federal Border Police launches would join boats from other countries in patrolling the Danube in the section where the river flows through Serbia, the objective being to stop goods reaching Serbia. (iii) To continue AWACS flights along the Adriatic coast until such time as there may be a Security Council resolution on the (military) enforcement of the ban on air flights over Bosnia. The final point was the most contentious since the CDU/CSU and the FDP were split on what to do in the event of a Security Council resolution calling for the enforcement of a flight ban over Bosnia. In such an eventuality, the CDU/CSU agreed to vote for continued participation while the FDP would abstain from voting and would then appeal to the FCC for a ruling upon whether the action was constitutional or not. The proposed action would force the Court to make a definitive statement on the issue. The unusual mechanism of a member of the coalition, in this case the FDP, appealing against the larger members of the coalition was agreed upon since the SPD would otherwise have blocked the move to take the issue to court.

What was a theoretical debate became reality on 31 March 1993 when the UN Security Council voted for the military enforcement of the ban of flights over the Republic of Bosnia and Herzegovina. The new Security Council resolution authorized member states to use 'all necessary measures' to ensure compliance with the ban. Concerns were immediately voiced that, as a result of the resolution, Germany could be involved in an unconstitutional combat role. The semantics of Operation 'Deny Flight', which commenced on 12 April 1993 as a result of Security Resolution 816, stood in marked difference to Operation 'Sky Monitor' which had preceded under the aegis of Security Council Resolution 781 of 9 October 1992.[43]

On 2 April, in accordance with the agreement with the CDU/CSU, the FDP called for a temporary injunction on German participation in AWACS flights over the Adriatic and appealed to the FCC for a ruling on whether German participation in a 'combat' role was constitutional. The FDP were joined by the SPD in pressing for an injunction until a decision on the matter was reached by the FCC. In a ruling delivered on 7 April (the day Security Council Resolution 816 was to become operative) the FCC rejected (by a vote of 5 to 3) the injunction based upon both their interpretation of the constitution and broader international factors. The ruling applied only to the specific issue of the AWACS flights and was *not* a general constitutional ruling on the OOA issue. The arguments hinged around the issue of whether German AWACS crews were involved in a combat role as a result of Resolution 816.

The FCC decided that the AWACS crews were in little immediate danger and, since they are fully integrated (around 30 per cent of the crew were German), the withdrawal of the German component would harm the overall effectiveness of the AWACS operations and the ability of the UN to enforce the flight ban. The FCC observed that if the German flight crews were withdrawn, the Alliance (and presumably the UN) would have to accept the German position.[44] But this would take place at the cost of a loss of faith in Germany and the subsequent damage might be irreparable. To protect the individual German servicemen involved in AWACS operations the FCC observed that the service personnel involved cannot be held legally responsible. Only the government can bear legal responsibility for their deployment. The FCC argued that there were several instances where the government had committed, in principle, to collaborate in OOA activities – as in the case of the UN Charter, the CSCE's Charter of Paris for a New Europe, the Franco–German Proposals at the Intergovernmental Conference of the Twelve (EC) on Political Union, or the WEU's Petersberg Declaration. Finally, the FCC forwarded the notion of the 'common good' whereby neither the constitution nor the political system were damaged by the FCC decision; nor would the decision prejudice future decisions.

The second challenge arose from the deployment of Bundeswehr personnel to Somalia. The principal challenge, once again, came from the SPD, which since 13 June 1993 had been under the leadership of Rudolph Scharping, following Engholm's resignation the previous month. In party-political terms, his appointment seems to have done little to change the SPD's position on the OOA issue. The worsening situation in Somalia was to provide the first test case for the new leadership when, in the light of clashes between Somali rebels and UN Soldiers in Mogadishu, the SPD parliamentary group announced in early June that they would petition the FCC to rule on the constitutionality of the deployments.[45]

The Federal Cabinet voted on 21 April 1993 in favour of sending some of the Bundeswehr to Somalia, which then received approval from the *Bundestag* (341 for, 206 against, 8 abstentions), but only as a humanitarian mission. On the same occasion, the *Bundestag* also approved German participation in AWACS operations (338 for, 208 against, 9 abstentions). Following the submission of an SPD-sponsored petition to halt deployments to Somalia until the constitutional questions were settled, the FCC ruled on 23 June that the Bundeswehr deployments to Somalia were in accordance with the constitution. However, as in the Bosnian case, the ruling applied only to the deployments to Somalia. The Somalia question was less controversial since, unlike the AWACS case, the 1640 strong Bundeswehr force would be participating in humanitarian tasks, in peaceful areas protected by armed infantry.

The reluctance of the FCC to reach a general ruling (one is expected in 1995) points to the sensitivity and complexity of the subject. If the FCC eventually decides upon a restrictive interpretation of the Basic Law and the Federal Republic's security obligations, it could conceivably be challenged under the *rebus sic stantibus* terms of Article 62 of the Vienna Convention on the Law of Treaties, which argues that a fundamental change in circumstances has taken place, thus acting as grounds for the amendment or alteration of legal documents.[46] The prevailing circumstances that existed in the period 1949–55 were largely coloured by fears of German remilitarization and hence led to the emphasis upon defence in the Basic Law and the Nine Power Agreement. The reunification of Germany and the disappearance of the Warsaw Pact constitute a fundamental change in the circumstances now surrounding these treaties. Although the *rebus sic stantibus* argument is a device relating to international law, and thus unlikely in and of itself to lead to an amendment to the German constitution, it may be used to change international legal documents, such as the North Atlantic Treaty, the London and Paris Agreements or the Brussels Treaty. A change in these treaties, such as a redefinition of NATO's area of interest outlined in Article 6 of the North Atlantic Treaty, may have the effect of pressuring the FCC to make a less restrictive interpretation of the Basic Law.

It should also be observed that there may be serious contradictions between those obligations that Germany has entered into under international law and the restrictive interpretations of Germany's constitutional obligations stemming from the Bonn government's 1982 judgement. For instance, in NATO's Strategic Concept, agreed upon by the Heads of State and Government participating in the meeting of the North Atlantic Council in Rome on 7–8 November 1991, Article 42 stated that the 'Allies could... be called upon to contribute to global stability and peace by providing forces for United Nations missions'.[47] In a communiqué issued by the North Atlantic Council meeting in Brussels on 17 December 1992, to which Germany was also a signatory, it was stated that '[the Alliance] supports the further strengthening of CSCE structures and the extension of the CSCE's authority and operational involvement in the prevention of conflict'.[48] The FRG was also signatory to the WEU's Petersberg Declaration in which it was agreed that the WEU would take part in 'peacekeeping and humanitarian operations only at the request of other international organizations such as the United Nations and the Conference on Security and Cooperation in Europe'.[49]

The constitutional debate will obviously be of critical importance to any future European security designs. Unless the debate is resolved, it is unlikely that any such designs will be pan-European; it may also tie down one of Europe's largest and best-trained militaries to the defence of an area that has lost much of its strategic rationale. Without active German military participation, any prospective European security organization will be difficult to envisage.

GERMAN SECURITY POLICY

The end of the Cold War and the diminution of threat perceptions vis-à-vis Germany's eastern neighbours prompted a fundamental review of German security policy that would seem to pitch strategy at variance with the constitutional debate described above. In a press conference on 15 December 1992, the German Defence Minister, Volker Rühe, outlined plans for the future of the German armed forces. The plans included a 'strategic reorientation of the armed forces' which will promote military stability and integration in Europe, and will serve world peace in harmony with the UN Charter.[50]

In practical terms this involves the division of the Bundeswehr into two components: the first is the main defence force which will be mobilizable for joint allied ground defences of NATO territory; the second, smaller, component is the crisis reactionary force (CRF) which would 'carry out its international missions in the United Nations and the CSCE frameworks'.[51] General Klaus Naumann, chief of staff of the German armed forces, has been charged by Volker Rühe with responsibility for preparing forces for UN peace-keeping operations.[52] This charge has been reflected in Bundeswehrplan 94 which places primary emphasis upon rapid reaction forces for use within the UN and NATO contexts.

In compliance with the CFE Treaty, Germany will reduce the size of its armed forces to a combined total of 370 000 (compared to pre-unification levels of 450 000 for the Federal Republic), but it will still remain a highly significant military force in Europe. The cuts in other NATO members' force levels, including the reduction on US force levels in Europe from 326 000 to 100 000 (by 1995), may emphasize the importance of German forces for OOA roles. However, even if the constitutional debate is resolved and the German military is able to assume an OOA role, two potentially serious problems still remain. The first is that of lift capacity. Germany, in common with other major

European powers, lacks sea and air lift capacity, which is needed to make an OOA role feasible.[53] The lack of any serious lift capacity can be explained by Germany's location on the 'central front', in Cold War NATO parlance. The emphasis was therefore upon other powers, especially the US, developing their lift capacities to reach NATO's central front.

The second problem relates to the fact that the German military was designed entirely with NATO contingencies in mind and thus has neither the training, experience or weaponary best equipped for an OOA role. The adoption of a serious OOA capability by Germany, and other European powers, will entail investment in lift capacity and training for such eventualities. The alternative is to continue to rely upon the US, with its shrinking military presence in Europe, for lift capability in OOA interventions. This, as is argued below, is an unwise option at a time when there are divergencies of opinion between the US and its European allies on many OOA questions. Reliance upon the US may mean sanctioning US policy, which may be at odds with that of the European powers, especially policy concerning the Middle East.

Last, in the event of the successful destruction of the ex-Soviet strategic nuclear arsenal, in line with the START I and START II stipulations,[54] there is the possibility of nuclear weapons losing much of their 'currency'; the possession of nuclear weapons by France and Britain used to be one of the important distinguishing points between these countries and Germany, who had pledged in 1954 not to manufacture weapons of mass destruction.[55] Although there is no evidence to suggest that Germany wishes to acquire nuclear weapons, European defence collaboration, like that entailed in the Franco–German corps, will raise the question of the relationship between 'Euro' forces and the French and British nuclear deterrents. This, in turn, may raise the possibility of a 'Euro deterrent' accompanied by a German finger on the button. Such an eventuality could have fractious outcomes for European defence collaboration.

The end of the Cold War nuclear standoff between the two alliances has led to an increased emphasis being put on rapidly deployable conventional forces. In spite of the reductions in the size of the *Bundeswehr*, which formed part of the Two-plus-Four agreements, Germany will retain a larger military than Britain or France. Sheer numbers and the quality of the forces make the role of the German military a critical component of any future European security entity.

COMMON FOREIGN POLICY?

Germany's main preoccupations are domestic, particularly after incorporating the eastern *Länder*; the reunification process has proven to be more time consuming and expensive than anticipated. In so far as general foreign policy priorities are discernable, keeping the doors open for the Czech Republic, Poland and Hungary's entry into the EC and eventually NATO, has assumed high priority. This has led to speculation that Germany is pursuing its mythical *Drang Nacht Osten*, whereby Germany fulfils some manifest destiny to lead Central Europe. The reality is, however, nearer *Zwang nach Osten*, meaning Germany feels compelled out of morality and historical ties to intervene to its east, with the objective of bringing stability to its eastern neighbours. Germany has not only invested more in Eastern Europe and given more aid, it has also adopted a surprisingly assertive role in the foreign-policy realm. Evidence of Germany's vigorous new foreign-policy role can be seen in Kohl's criticism of the indifference displayed by the Western powers towards Yugoslavia – whilst judiciously hiding behind the constitutional fig leaf described above. The decision by Kohl and Genscher to recognize Croatia and Slovenia before the EC was ready to is evidence of a new assertiveness at the very same time that Germany was adopting the Maastricht goals of moving toward European Union, of which common foreign and security policies are integral parts. The decision to support Croatian and Slovenian independence involved an open challenge to British and French leadership and, in a less direct sense, the US as well. Following the recognition of Croatia and Slovenia, accusations followed of German attempts to regain influence in the western part of Yugoslavia. For their part, Britain and France pursued a policy of hidden support, or at least non-condemnation of the Serbian regime. It seems that Britain and France were, if necessary, willing to sacrifice the pro-democratic and intensely nationalistic part of Yugoslavia for the sake of maintaining a strong and dominant Serbia. The result of the split over the recognition of Croatia and Slovenia was to serve as a reminder that the achievement of a common European foreign or security policy may be a difficult undertaking and certainly not a 'natural' progression from economic integration.

   The idea of Germany exhibiting leadership qualities, particularly in the Balkans, gave rise to some inappropriate, but significant, references to the Ustashi.[56] By way of contrast to Germany's apparent assertiveness in the Croatian case was the extreme reluctance of the German public or leadership to become involved in the Gulf War. The widespread media coverage of the German anti-war demonstrations gave the appearance of a country that appeared to be going pacifist and was self-absorbed in its own internal problems arising out of unification. The contrast may be explained by the fringe role that Germany plays in the Middle East and its sensitivities toward Israel. In the Croatian case, Germany has a strong historical link with Eastern Europe as well as a sizeable Catholic Croatian community amongst the Yugoslav *Gastarbeiter* in Germany. It would be wrong to account for the German initiative in recognizing Croatia or Slovenia as an overt bid for leadership. The recognition reminded fellow Western Europeans of Germany's close ties with Central and Eastern Europe; the main pressure within the Kohl administration came from the CDU's sister party, the CSU, which is composed mainly of Catholic Bavarians with close ties to Catholics in both Croatia and Slovenia. A sizeable Croatian community in Germany also applied significant pressure.

Germany was most affected by the crises in Eastern Europe and has the closest links geographically, culturally and politically with the Eastern neighbours. Bonn has felt a special responsibility for Eastern Europe, stemming from its historical role in the region. This responsibility was first expressed in Willy Brandt's *Ostpolitik* of the early 1970s. German unification was largely made possible by the changes in Poland and Czechoslovakia which led to the eventual collapse of the GDR. German preoccupations with its eastern neighbours are also determined by the geographical situation of Germany itself. The effects of political and economic reform failure in Central and Eastern Europe would be grave for Germany – perhaps more so than any other Western European power. This explains, in part, why Germany has provided much of the aid going to Eastern Europe and the ex-Soviet Union. In the period 1989–91 Germany provided 56 per cent of all the Western aid to the Soviet Union and 32 per cent of the aid to other Eastern European countries.[57] The reluctance of other Western European countries to make comparable investments in Central and Eastern Europe has left some uncomfortable options, with equally disconcerting security implications:

(1) Germany will be forced to commit significant resources to its European neighbours to the east and to the ex-Soviet republics, which, it is hoped, will stem the tide of migrants and asylum seekers.
(2) The channeling of resources to the East will stunt the growth of the European Community or it will divert much needed assistance from the southern members of the EC toward the east.

(3) The failure of the US or its Western European partners to take a significant role in Central or Eastern Europe may lead to the German decision to go it alone. This may lead to bilateral relations with Russia or other Central European countries displacing those with the Western Europeans.

(4) The complete collapse of the CIS and maybe Russia itself, into multiple Yugoslav-type wars, based on hyper-nationalism, may overwhelm Germany with refugees and migrants.

(5) The collapse of Russia and other CIS states may lead to calls from the fragile Eastern and Central Europeans for some type of emergency security guarantee from Germany. The existence of a power vacuum further to the east of these countries could suck Germany into commitments that would overshadow Germany's commitments to the EC or even NATO.

(6) There are no satisfactory institutional answers to these security dilemmas. The EC, WEU and CSCE remain too young to be able to deal with these problems. NATO has failed to resolve its 'out-of-area' problem, which, combined with the weakness of the other security institutions, may lead to increased German pressure to resolve this question through other institutions.

The public utterances by Kohl, Genscher and Kinkel suggest that German foreign policy will be made within the context of German–US and German–European ties. Kohl has observed that, 'the Atlantic Alliance remains the foundation for peace and freedom in Europe', and that 'The closer we come together in Europe the more effectively we will be protected from relapses into national or even nationalistic rivalry and into the hegemonic thinking of the past.'[58] In spite of public utterances, Germany may find itself irresistibly pulled toward the east, either in an attempt to stop instability from spilling over into Germany, or in an attempt to fill a potentially dangerous power vacuum. The concern in Germany over this issue was initially muted, mainly confined to the debate about the wisdom of admitting new members to the EC in an attempt to broaden the community and thus head off potential instability. The tone became less muted with the debate between the CDU and the SDP over changes to the Basic Law which would restrict the number of asylum seekers (see Chapter 2). Chancellor Kohl warned the minister of the interior, Rudolf Seiters, that the failure to do this could result in a state crisis.[59]

As a result of concerns from all of the main German political parties a constitutional amendment was passed in May 1993 that restricted the number of asylum seekers coming to Germany. The coalition parties and the opposition SPD agreed that the amendment would stop the 'massive abuse' of the right to asylum which, until the amendment, was guaranteed in Article 16 of the Basic Law. After 1 July 1993, the date on which the new legislation became effective, no person entering Germany from a list of secure third countries (incorporating all of the EC and Germany's neighbours) would be granted the right of asylum.

The concern in Germany over security threats that could arise from political and economic threats from the east has important security implications. The failure of Germany to obtain support for its concerns amongst the other Western European countries and the US could result in Germany being faced with some stark choices between pursuing its interests in Central and Eastern Europe, or buttressing its relations with its western neighbours within the EC and CSCE and hope that these institutions address some of their eastern concerns. Although there is no public statement that currently reflects the starkness of this choice, the lack of support for Germany's concerns to the east, which have a direct bearing on German interests, may make such stark choices a reality. Germany has also shown that when a chance to enhance its security arises, it will try to do so multilaterally but is still quite prepared to do so unilaterally if need be. For instance, the deal struck between Chancellor Kohl and Mikhail Gorbachev to accelerate the timetable for the withdrawal of Soviet forces from the eastern portion of Germany, in return for credits to Russia, caused consternation in other Western capitals.

Of critical importance to the Cold War security of Europe was the sizeable US military presence. Aside from the obvious military role played by these forces against the opposing Warsaw Treaty forces, they played a secondary function of reassuring Western European allies about Germany. The US presence acted as a brake on any potential German revanchism (the 'keep Germany down' part of Lord Ismay's famous quip). The end of the Cold War has challenged the need for security guarantees against the defunct Warsaw Treaty Organization. It has also raised the possibility of ascendant American neo-isolationism complementing the position of those in Germany who favour moving prime responsibility for a common security policy to a European-led institution and a substantially reduced US military presence.

The figures in Table 4.1 suggest that the EC publics are in favour of the EC having greater responsibility in security and defence matters. As one would expect, the figures are higher in the former East

Table 4.1 Are you in favour of the EC being responsible for a common policy in matters of security and defence? (%)

	Yes	No
Germany	73	13
eastern	71	14
western	83	9
Britain	55	31
France	73	17
Italy	78	7
EC 12	70	16

Source: *Eurobarometer*, No. 37 (Brussels: Commission of the European Communities, June 1992) A.49.

Germany. Although conjectural, one possible explanation for the figures is the perception that the US is losing interest, or at least scaling down its military contribution to Europe, which therefore makes greater European self-reliance the obvious option. In the German case, there may also be more complex explanations, having to do with the restoration of pride and identity in the security realm, which could best be accomplished in a European framework rather than a Transatlantic framework. Also of interest is the variance between the statements of the policy élites, who are avowedly pro-NATO, and public opinion, which may not be anti-NATO but which certainly reflects a high degree of self-reliance and a reduced US role. Public opinion research carried out by the *Institut für Demoskopie Allensbach* indicates that support for the maintenance of US troops in Europe has also dropped as a result of the end of the Cold War and unification:

Table 4.2 Assuming American forces left the FRG, could the country's military security still be guaranteed? (%)

	Guaranteed	No longer guaranteed	Impossible to say
July 1988	37	37	26
December 1988	34	34	32
July 1989	43	32	25
March 1990	54	21	25

Source: *Institut für Demoskopie Allensbach*, quoted in R. Asmus, 'A Unified Germany', in Robert A. Levine, ed., *Transition and Turmoil in the Atlantic Alliance* (New York: Crane Russak, 1992) p. 91.

Table 4.3 If tomorrow you were to read in the newspaper that the Americans were withdrawing their forces from Europe, would you welcome or regret this news? (%)

	Welcome	*Regret*	*Undecided*
July 1988	36	34	30
December 1988	33	33	34
July 1989	38	30	32
March 1990	49	22	29

Source: *Institut für Demoskopie Allensbach*, quoted in R. Asmus, 'A Unified Germany', in Robert A. Levine, ed., *Transition and Turmoil in the Atlantic Alliance* (New York: Crane Russak, 1992) p. 91.

Although the figures may be effected by those who are undecided, they nevertheless indicate that the end of the Cold War has eroded public support for a continued US presence in Germany. Survey data from other sources indicate that not only are a higher number of east Germans in favour of the US withdrawing its troops from Germany, but they are in favour of Germany adopting a neutral status (see Table below). Nevertheless, there is some concern expressed that, if the US withdraws all of its troops from Germany (nearly half of those questioned in western Germany and over three-quarters of those questioned in the former East Germany are in favour of them doing so), then Germany would be inadequately defended in the event of worsening East–West relations. There is, unsurprisingly, more support for Germany's continued membership of NATO in the west of Germany than in the east.

The ambivalence reflected in German public opinion regarding the need for a future US military presence in Germany places the onus on the Clinton administration to come up with a convincing rationale for a continued US presence in Europe. Policy disagreements between the US and Germany, concern about the future size and composition of US military forces in Europe, and public opinion have led to a delicate balancing act between the government and public opinion as well as trying to square Germany's security concerns with those of London, Paris and Washington. Kohl's security policy shares London's anxiety that the US should not feel alienated, while, for different reasons, sharing France's ambitions to establish a coherent European defence entity at some point in the future. As a result, Bonn has become caught in the trap between Paris and Washington it had thus far avoided. On the one hand, some kind of European defence organization is the logical extension of the integration process as well as being a way of

Table 4.4   Should US forces withdraw from Germany?

The Soviet Union is withdrawing all its troops from a united Germany. The US has declared its willingness significantly to reduce its troops as well. Do you think the US should also withdraw all of its troops from Germany or should a limited contingent remain? (%)

	West	East
US should withdraw all troops	46	79
A limited number should remain	41	13
Don't know	12	8
No Comment	–	–

Many people believe the total withdrawal of US troops might leave Germany insufficiently defended in the case of an eventual worsening of East–West relations. Do you agree? (%)

Strongly agree	18	5
Partially agree	46	34
Strongly disagree	35	60
No comment	1	5

What type of alliance should a united Germany pursue in the future? (%)

United Germany should remain in NATO	74	31
Adopt the status of military neutrality	25	68
No comment	1	1

Source: Survey data prepared by the Infratest Kommunukationsforschung GmbH, which appeared in Ronald D. Asmus, 'German Perception of the United States at Unification', *RAND*, R-4069-AF (Santa Monica: RAND, 1991) pp. 50–51.

compensating for the US's relative weakness in being able to influence developments in Eastern Europe; while, on the other hand, for political reasons Germany is unwilling to act 'out-of-area' and needs the US to protect its wider interests. Until there is a resolution of the bogus 'paper wall' issue of whether it is legal to use German forces for 'out-of-area' collective security efforts, Germany cannot be counted on as the nucleus for a Post-Cold War security organization.

There are undeniable forces pulling Germany towards *Mitteleuropa*, as well as some incoherent, but repugnant, extremist political forces at work in Germany. These may well give cause for concern about the drift of Germany. It is, however, worth observing that there are stronger forces pulling Germany towards its western colleagues. The German 'economic miracle' and the FRG's seemingly invincible economy has been dealt a severe blow by the costs of unification. The unforeseen expenses of German unification in an export-driven market, which for the first time in post-war history is showing a zero growth rate, means that Germany will have to safeguard its markets to get out of the economic malaise it now finds itself in. The most important markets are clearly the EC partners who in 1989 accounted for 54.8 per cent of the German export market – under 5 per cent going to the former Soviet countries.[60] For pragmatic reasons alone, it seems reasonable to suggest that, in the short-term at least, Germany will remain firmly committed to its EC partners. Conversely, Germany's historical interests to the east may persuade the EC to show an interest in Eastern and Central Europe. The FRG also remains firmly committed to the process of European integration – the large majority in the Bundestag on 2 December 1992 in favour of adopting the Maastricht Treaty indicates that the FRG's primary interests remain in the west.[61]

Even those influences pulling the united Germany to the east need not be pernicious or injurious to Western European interests and the process of integration. The process of finding a balance will not be easy, but it seems clear that for reasons of self-interest alone Germany's closest economic and political ties will remain those with France, Britain and the US.

CONCLUSION

The developments in French, British and German security policy in the post-Cold War world merit only tentative conclusions since there will be further future changes. The first tentative conclusion is that, while there is no overt bid for leadership by any of these powers, there is at the same time the recognition that Germany should be tied into any emerging security order. Germany has an immensely important role to play in the post-Cold War Europe. However, the notion of a powerful Germany, once again at the centre of Europe, forming some sort of Fourth Reich is fanciful. It is also recognized that Germany will be in a transitional period for some time, between the old divided Germany and that of a state which has a foreign and security role commensurate with its economic and political weight.

The concern that Germany may drift eastward in pursuit of *Mitteleuropa* will be countered by growing economic malaise, which will underscore the links with the EC countries. The precise foreign and security policy Germany will adopt remains unclear in its details; in general, though, it will continue to be tied closely to those of its European colleagues within an institutional framework provided by a modified NATO, the EC, WEU or CSCE, either collectively or singly. Those who still harbour concerns about the direction in which Germany may go, which could be revanchist, neutral, Atlanticist or Europeanist, can exert some control over Germany by ensuring that the institutional ties between Germany and other European countries are strengthened. The post-World War II era saw the creation of an 'entangling alliance' with the objective of ensnaring the US. In the post-Cold War era it must be Germany that is ensnared into economic, political and security networks.

Second, the post-Cold War security policies emerging out of France, Britain and Germany do not seem to indicate the evolution of a pan-European security policy. The emphasis seems to be very much on *Western* European security. Germany, as has been argued, has security interests that reach to the east but, in the event that circumstances call for it, is unwilling or unable to back up these interests with military force.

Third, the emergence of a European leader or collective leadership that would assume responsibility for European security challenges, has yet to take place. The French are actively promoting a stronger European security identity; the Germans still have to solve the constitutional debate about their ability to take an active role in out-of-area operations; and Britain remains in favour of strengthening the European flavour of its defences provided that this is not done at the expense of the links to the US and to NATO. Some of the lack of leadership or initiative can be accounted for by the factors above, which are essentially internal European factors; but there are also external factors which act as significant brakes upon the development of a European security identity. The main external limitation is the US itself, which has yet to define a clear line on the extent to which it is in favour of Europe assuming more responsibility for its own security. It is to this issue that we now turn.

5 The US Role in European Security

At the heart of Europe's security dilemma is the US itself. Successive US administrations have insisted that the security of the US is intimately linked to that of Europe, and therefore the US, almost by right, should continue its leadership role in the Alliance. The paranoia that the development of a strong European pillar will weaken the Atlantic pillar, and therefore the US's position, is an ironical twist on the Cold War demands from Washington for the Allies to assume a fairer share of the defence burden. Although all of the European NATO allies have rejected the idea of a complete US military withdrawal from Europe, a reduced US military role will lead to pressure for a different kind of relationship between the US and its allies. This pressure calls for a new understanding between the US and its European allies; an understanding which should explicitly accept a stronger European identity in security affairs. As has been suggested already, adjustments will have to be made on the part of the Europeans, especially by the French, who will have to be open-minded to realignments in US defence policy.

PRIMUS INTER PARES

On Christmas Day 1991, the red Soviet flag was lowered from the Kremlin for the last time. A few days later, on 28 January 1992, George Bush addressed a joint session of Congress in his annual State of the Union address. President Bush captured the historical flavour of the occasion by announcing that, 'By the grace of God, America won the cold war'. He went on:

> A world once divided into two armed camps now recognizes one sole and pre-eminent power, the United States of America. And they regard this with no dread. For the world trusts us with power, and the world is right. They trust us to be fair and restrained. They trust us to be on the side of decency. They trust us to do what's right.[1]

This speech reflected many of the changes that had taken place in the world but it also, unintentionally, reflected a lack of graciousness and perspective. The US may have been the main 'winner' of the Cold War but the very use of the word 'won' reflects both an American obsession, as well as implying something finite about the world around the US.[2] In reality, we do not know who won the Cold War. Even if the notion of winning the Cold War has any credence, the victory would be pyrrhic if the collapse of the Soviet Union were considered to be the decisive point, with no regard for the ensuing international system and its stability.

The natural leadership qualities of the US seem to be part of a historical process dating from the assumption of the 'global policeman' role, albeit with some reluctance, under Franklin Roosevelt's presidency. The continuation of this role seems not only natural, but just, in American eyes. Indeed the US has become accustomed to this role, although the current heads of the US armed services are distinctly nervous about open-ended commitments. However, the assumption of this role in the 1990s is more difficult than it was in 1945. The economic power of the US in the 1990s is simply not that of 1945, nor can it afford its global role without making some difficult prioritization decisions and showing a willingness to share power or even to leave some regions alone. Nevertheless, the untidiness of the balance ledger does not detract from the zeal shown for the US's destiny to remain leader and defender. Similar thoughts as those expressed by Bush have been put by General Colin Powell, the former chairman of the Joint Chiefs of Staff. Powell wrote:

> No other nation on earth has the power we possess. More important, no other nation on earth has the trusted power we possess. We are obligated to lead. If the free world is to harvest the hope and fulfill the promise that our great victory in the Cold War has offered us, America must shoulder the responsibility of its power. The last best hope of earth has no other choice. We must lead.[3]

Rhetoric aside, the comments of both Bush and Powell have pertinence for Europe. While it may be true that no single nation has the power that the US possesses, it is clear that as an economic actor Europe has enormous potential – the European economic area, of some 380 million people, is potentially a bigger market than the US.[4] The combined military forces of Europe would also pose a formidable array of military power. In spite of the potential strength of Europe, or Asia, the 'new world order' is seen as an American preserve.

The underpinnings of the new world order are twofold: first, the maintenance of a network of military bases which obviate the need for historically fractious powers (such as Germany or Japan) to build up large armies which could upset regional balances of power; and, second, the use of these bases to protect crucial US trade and economic relations. From this it follows that if the US did *not* exercise leadership, in the form of preponderant military forces within alliances, which ensures its leadership role, latently fractious powers would once again build up military forces which, in turn, would probably lead to war and once again to US intervention. Furthermore, any power that destabilizes Europe (or Asia) poses a threat to US economic interests – leading to the conclusion that the US views its military forces as a *means* of protecting its economic interests. Thus, far from economic interdependence obviating the need for such military arrangements, it would appear actually to reinforce the need for them. An internal Department of Defense document, *Defense Planning for the Fiscal Years 1994–1999*, which was leaked in February 1992, caught the flavour of the Bush administration's belief that, for the sake of peace and stability, the US has to lead. The document, which created storms of protest in Europe, stressed that new world order was based on 'convincing potential competitors that they need not aspire to a greater role or pursue a more aggressive posture to protect their legitimate interests'.[5] Thus, with the end of the Cold War the second strand of the US's double containment strategy has moved to the fore: the containment of potential competition – most notably from Germany and Japan. This, in turn, goes some of the way towards offering an explanation for Washington's often awkward post-Cold War relations with Bonn and Tokyo. Even with the end of the Cold War it would seem that NSC-68, which articulated America's Cold War strategy in 1950, is still essentially intact since the fundamental purpose of US foreign and security policy is still to 'foster a world environment in which the American system can survive and flourish'. Furthermore, it was a policy that the US would pursue 'even if there were no threat'.[6]

The type of leadership that the US can offer in the 1990s is clearly different from that of the 1940s. For one, the economy of the US in the 1940s was by far and away the strongest. The US's economic strength was reflected in its military might and its global network of bases. By way of contrast, the economy of the 1990s is beset by the twin deficits, while the global network of military bases has shrunk dramatically. During the Cold War the US was willing to contribute vast amounts of its GNP, which could have been as much as $5–6 trillion, to contain the Soviet threat; NATO alone accounted for some $2.5 trillion of expenditure. The enormous military cost has had deep effects upon the

US. One commentator observed that, 'NATO not only has contributed to debilitating the American economy but has helped to warp American society and skew its domestic governance'.[7]

The amounts contributed by the US since the end of the Cold War to ensure that the international system will enjoy some stability have been minuscule by comparison. With the exception of Germany, this picture is typical of many Western countries, which have been reluctant to consolidate the claimed victories of the Cold War. This reluctance to continue spending money on security and stability can mainly be accounted for by the fact that the publics have been falsely encouraged to expect savings in their national budgets as a result of the end of the Cold War. The appeal for more aid for the ex-Soviet republics and Eastern and Central Europe is falling on deaf ears, as there is no political lobby advocating a new *Ostpolitik*.

The world created by this victory is insecure and has costs as well as opportunities for the US and its allies. The Cold War was not just won by the US. Would the end of this era have been possible without Willy Brandt's *Ostpolitik*? Would it have been possible without the remarkable and historic contribution of Mikhail Gorbachev? Would it have been possible without the crusading spirit of Lech Wałesa or Vàclav Havel? The Cold War was not a victory for America, it was a victory for common sense and rationality.

The second significant claim, regarding the implicit trust that other countries vest in the US, made by Bush who was harking back to his major foreign-policy achievement, was the successful conduct of the 1991 Gulf War under American leadership. In this specific context, the US demonstrated that if its own national self-interest was at stake, which it was in the Gulf, then the US would act. Those same interests were not at stake in Yugoslavia; there was no oil, only 'ethnic cleansing', and the Bush administration decided initially to 'take a pass'. Yet the US had been anxious to exercise leadership and use the UN to right an injustice in the case of Saddam Hussein's invasion of Kuwait. In the case of Yugoslavia, the US stood by and watched the EC and the UN attempt to deal with the problem, while they failed to give the CSCE any meaningful chance of addressing the problem. The Bush administration was reluctant to intervene in Bosnia, and it wasn't until mid-June 1992 that the US agreed to take part in a UN-sponsored airlift of food and humanitarian supplies to the beleaguered city of Sarajevo, which was under siege by Serbian forces opposed to Bosnian independence. Perhaps the most important feature of these comments is the implicit assumption that the US knows what the 'will' of the

free world is. Was it, therefore, the will of the free world to intervene
in the Persian Gulf in 1991, an area with two-thirds of the world's oil
reserves, but not in Yugoslavia, with no strategically important reserves? How does the heavy US involvement in Somalia square with
the low-key involvement in Bosnia – what *essential* national interests
are at stake for the US in Somalia?

Aside from the Yugoslav crisis, which said as much about European
leadership (or lack thereof) as it did about US leadership, there are
other grounds for concern about US leadership. The much-highlighted
problems of the US economy, which were laid out in the US presidential race in 1992, have posed problems for how the US will balance its
overseas leadership role while simultaneously finding solutions to its
troubling economic woes and other domestic problems. This balance
was not established in the first one hundred days of the Clinton administration. The swing from Bush, who may be portrayed as a foreign-
policy president, to Clinton, who seems most comfortable dealing with
domestic issues, has led to a lack of consistency and predictability in
US foreign policy. The failure to exercise any leadership in the deteriorating situation in Bosnia and the open differences between Washington and the other European capitals, including unusually London, sets
a worrying precedent for the Clinton administration.

There are also opportunities that have been presented to the US as a
result of the end of the Cold War. The biggest constraint upon the US,
which was the need to restrain the Soviet Union and its allies, has
been removed. The US is therefore free, in theory, to address issues of
importance in a more logical and consistent manner. The twin deficits
have understandably given the Clinton administration a domestic bias,
but at the same time it should be recognized that the amounts of money
required for the maintenance of the military and the costs of intervention will pale by comparison with those projected during the Cold War
years.

It would be unfortunate and unwise to see the changes in the international system as an opportunity to retreat into a form of isolationism. While arguments about the costs of commitment are bound to
arise between allies, the US cannot afford *not* to be the main actor in
the international system. The America of 1919 that slid into a form of
splendid isolationism, as a result of the Senate's failure to ratify League
of Nations membership, is vastly different from that of today. With
over 15 per cent of the US's GNP being accounted for by export earnings, it is clear that the US has a considerable financial motive to
remain actively involved in the international system.

Underpaid, Unloved and on the Way Out?

In European terms the debate about the role of the US has come to
focus on the future of NATO. In his last State of the Union address
President Bush spoke of the Alliance as being 'indispensable both for
the creation of a stable new world order and the building of a new
Europe whole and free'. The references made by Bush to a 'Europe
whole and free' raise the question of which Europe Bush was referring to. Certainly the US inaction over Yugoslavia and the failure to
define any coherent out-of-area policy for NATO, coupled with a lack
of enthusiasm about working through the CSCE, provokes legitimate
questions about what may happen in the event of a crisis in, for example, Poland, Moldova or Hungary.

President Clinton has also refuted those critics of NATO's future
utility when, on 17 June 1993, he observed that, 'I do not agree that
NATO is dead'.[8] While NATO is certainly not dead, the end of the
Cold War has led to the need for a thorough review of NATO's functions and utility, which includes the US role within NATO. Since US
military commitment to the Alliance has dropped dramatically with
the demise of the Cold War, any review should include the apportionment of responsibility and leadership. As a result of the CFE agreement it was agreed that the Soviet Union and the US would reduce
their troop levels in Europe to 195 000 each by the mid-1990s. The
CFE agreement was soon overtaken by events and a unilateral agreement between Chancellor Kohl and President Gorbachev who made an
agreement that all troops would leave the former East Germany by
1994. As a result of these developments, US troop levels in Europe
have dropped to 150 000 and will in the future, according to promises
made during Bill Clinton's electoral campaign, drop well below that.
The US Army in Europe's headquarters in Heidelberg estimated that
forces will be cut by a further 12 000 in the period October 1992 to
September 1993. Eventually force levels are expected to reach 92 000
by 1995.[9] It would seem logical to suggest that, as a result of these
cuts, the US will have to accept a different role within NATO, one
based on equality, with the US no longer being the dominant partner.
In spite of the fact that other NATO allies have also been scaling
down their forces, no reductions in Europe have matched those of the
US. In spite of the significant reductions, it would appear to the Clinton
administration that this does not fundamentally alter the US role within
the Alliance or call for a new bargain. Secretary of State Warren
Christopher wrote:

The United States will sustain its unparalleled military strength [in Europe], and we will continue to maintain substantial, effective forces in Europe – about 100 000 troops – to ensure our ability to meet our security commitments. The end of the Cold War is making American leadership even more important – and we accept the challenge.[10]

Such statements reflect not only the assumption of a 'natural' US leadership position but also reflect Washington's fears of being sidelined by the attempts of the European allies to institutionalize their security concerns into a predominantly European setting. The key instigators in this respect are the French who, for example, proposed that a European rapid-reaction force should be ultimately responsible to the EC. Washington countered, in this instance, by warning Bonn and Paris that any such action could have the effect of driving the US from Europe. French resistance against US-inspired initiatives to transform NATO, plus their consistent advocacy of Euro-options, will have the effect of sinking the Alliance and, more speculatively, it may reinforce neo-isolationist tendencies in the US and leave France adrift in an increasingly unstable Europe with an independent Germany at its core. A Franco–US *rapprochement* is essential both in attempts at reinvigorating the Alliance as well as in attempts eventually to construct a European Security Organization (ESO), which may not include North American participants but should at least be done in a manner that reassures the US that its allies can take care of their own security. Clearly the formation of any type of ESO is a considerable way down the road, and, for the foreseeable future, a US military presence in Europe is in the interests of both the US and the Europeans.

At the centre of the transatlantic security debate is the role of NATO, for this is the main vehicle of US influence in Europe. For this reason Washington has maintained an adamant line that NATO be preserved and that all other institutional affiliations on the part of its European allies should be seen as attempts to strengthen NATO's European pillar. It is worth quoting President Bush at length to illustrate the fact that, to Washington, the move towards a greater European voice in security matters was an adjunct and not an alternative to the transatlantic partnership embodied through NATO. The statement below was made in the immediate aftermath of the European Council's Maastricht summit:

Europe's steps toward unity will strengthen our renewed Atlantic Alliance. NATO's endorsement at the Rome summit of a 'European pillar' underscores the additional responsibilities which the European allies are assuming in the protection of shared vital interests and values. At Maastricht, the EC requested the Western European Union, whose members are in both NATO and the EC, to serve as the vehicle for increased European responsibility on defense matters. We are pleased that our allies in the Western European Union in turn decided to strengthen that institution as both NATO's European pillar and the defense component of the European Union. NATO will remain the essential forum for consultation among its members and the venue for agreement on policies bearing on the security and defense commitments of the allies under the Washington [NATO] Treaty.[11]

This statement was designed to remind European leaders in pursuit of enhanced European integration that transatlantic links are still of immense importance. The clear or wilful conception of the process of forming a European security identity as a process that happened within the transatlantic framework is one that is obviously in the US's interest to promote – a view that was not shared in some of the European capitals, most notably Paris.

The sensitivity of the US to allied attempts to define a European security identity, either within or outside NATO, emerged in spectacular style in 1991, first in the form of a memorandum from the State Department to the European capitals and then at the Rome Summit. In February 1991, what became known as the 'Bartholomew Memorandum' was sent to the governments of the EC as well as to the WEU secretary-general. The memorandum, sometimes in undiplomatic language, criticized developments within the EC as posing a challenge to the integrity of NATO and hence to the US as well. The apparent change of position on the part of the Bush administration, which had hitherto supported the development of a European security identity within the transatlantic context, caused confusion in the European capitals. Behind the Bartholomew memorandum and subsequent elaborations by Secretary of State James Baker III was the growing fear that the scramble towards a European defence identity could pose a challenge to the US's leadership position and prestige, and that any designs that contributed to an authoritative decision-making mechanism at the European level would lead to the 'us and them' problems of the type encountered in the Uruguay GATT round.

Later that same year these anxieties re-emerged at the North Atlantic Council's Rome summit, which was held on 7–8 November 1991. At the summit, Mitterrand reminded Bush that the end of the Cold War and the disappearance of the Soviet foe meant that NATO was no longer a 'holy Alliance'. Bush, in a departure from the script, expressed his mounting exasperation with the European allies, when he commented that, 'If, my friends, your ultimate aim is to provide individually for your own defense, the time to tell us is today.'[12] Whether it was this exchange or others that prompted Bush's ad-lib remarks, is unclear. Bush's remarks soon evoked reassurances from all the allies, including France. Prime Minister John Major quickly reassured Bush of the 'primacy of NATO'. Yet, in spite of the reassurances, US anxiety and suspicions about allied intentions had come into the open. Further, it was obvious to all that, while the European allies tried swiftly to assuage American doubts, they continued to march toward greater European collaboration.

The lack of clarity about what the US's role should and ought to be in the radically changed Europe has resulted in an almost paranoid devotion to NATO. The Atlantic Alliance was seen not just as a symbol of stability but also of American munificence and success. Any moves toward a common European foreign and security policy (CFSP) could therefore be perceived as posing problems for NATO, and thus potentially for the US. Whether the advocacy of a CFSP will be seen as a threat to US interests or whether it will be seen as the butressing of the European pillar within NATO depends upon the twin concepts of transparency and complementarily between the emerging European security and defence identity and the Alliance.[13] Thus far, neither concept is self-evidently present.

The US remains ambivalent about European attempts to organize their own defence for fear of having its role as *primus inter pares* challenged. Terms such as the 'European pillar' or talk in the early 1950s of a 'European Defence Community' had been translated in Washington as attempts by European allies to organize their defences more efficiently so that they may act in US interests more effectively – indeed, the whole process in the 1950s took place with the blessings of Washington. In 1953, in an attempt to persuade the French National Assembly to adopt the European Defence Community, Secretary of State John Foster Dulles spoke of an 'agonizing reappraisal' of the US military commitment to Europe. In the event of a failure to ratify the EDC, Dulles warned that there would be concern 'as to whether Continental Europe could be made a place of safety. That would compel an agonizing reappraisal of basic United States policy'.[14] The failure of the French *Assemblée Nationale* to ratify the EDC Treaty was evidence both of the failure of Dulles's heavy-handed approach as well as the fact that the European North Atlantic Council members were tired of such approaches. This was not the first, or last, time such actions would be threatened. To European ears it began to sound like Aesop's Fable of the shepherd and the wolf.[15]

The Kennedy administration also voiced support for the development of a European pillar, albeit with an overarching US nuclear component. Indeed official statements of US support for a stronger European contribution to the common defence of the Alliance can be found from Truman to Bush. These statements are tempered by an equal concern that the European pillar may develop into a third force, of the type advocated by de Gaulle, which Washington would be unable to influence decisively; an anxiety shared by the British who do not relish the prospect of being confronted with a European security order that excludes the US.

Differences in security-policy direction also became evident in 1973, during and after the Middle East war, where the Europeans, most notably the French, refused to act in accordance with US desires. US–European differences were fuelled by the US's failure to consult with their allies when US forces were put on a heightened state of alert without consultation. Kissinger reminded European leaders that 'imminent danger did not brook an exchange of views and, to be frank, we could not have accepted a judgement different from our own'. Kissinger did acknowledge, in the light of complaints from the European capitals, that the complaints were 'abstractly' justified.[16] In the mid-1980s the WEU awoke from a prolonged slumber and considered a response to Reagan's SDI proposals. This prompted a reminder from the assistant secretary for European affairs, Richard Burt, that NATO was the proper forum for such discussions and not the Eurocentric WEU.

The US ambivalence towards European cooperation on security issues turned into action in early June 1991, when the European allies discussed the need for coordination of European foreign and security policy and, in time, defence. The WEU was the chosen vehicle for this role. The US promptly informed the European leaders that nothing they did independently in the security field should disrupt or endanger NATO's future well-being.[17] The US warning led to a dilemma for US policy on European security – the professed enthusiasm from Washington for enhanced European security and defensive efforts were matched by efforts to ensure that the US maintained its leadership and influence in Europe, particularly on security issues. The Bush administration, like others before it, continued to assume that in the post-Cold War world it is the duty of the US to provide the 'leadership needed to promote global peace and security'.[18] The Bush administration was also just as adamant that NATO was the only forum capable of addressing the multifarious security challenges of post-Cold War Europe. Bush's insistence on this reflects his sincere belief that the US is a European power sharing the interests of its allies, while also recognizing that NATO is the only institution which formally links North America to Western Europe.

Washington's repeated insistence that NATO is the only forum for dealing with European security issues reflects the concern that other forums, such as the WEU, threaten to exclude the US from its preeminent position and maybe representation altogether. This is also tied to America's self-image as the world's only superpower; challenge NATO and you challenge the status of the US itself. While it is possible that other institutions could act as valuable adjuncts to NATO, the interpretation of what those institutions stand for may not be the same for all actors. For instance, the French interpretation of the WEU's function is at odds with the German or British understanding. Mitterrand proposed a *confédération* which extended beyond the EC to include Eastern Europe and Russia (and maybe other CIS members). Washington was adamant that it would support the WEU only within the context of NATO (as a European pillar), although there has been considerable vagueness about what constitutes the permissible geographical confines of the US's area of interest. Moreover, the attempt to place twenty-first-century security on a pillar from another era may prove to be futile – clearly a 'defensive' alliance like NATO is a difficult foundation on which to start building a collective security structure. As it is, NATO's Rome summit ended with no clear idea about what NATO would be doing in five years time, and the US left the summit with an unclear idea of its role in the new Europe.

While there has yet to be a clear European security identity, defined in terms of agenda and responsibility, the significance of the growing clamour for a 'European' voice in security affairs cannot be ignored. The likelihood of a serious rift between the US and its European allies, especially France, is present if this European pillar is not able to develop at its own pace and define its own agenda. The security changes since 1989 make the idea of the 'Atlantic Community' a questionable concept at a time when Europe is integrating rapidly and the US is reinterpreting not only its global role but its ability to act on a global level (in other words, it is redefining its 'power'). Michael Vlahos describes these developments in sibling terms:

What is happening in Europe is real fraternity; the sibling rivalry European Community revealing true family ties. By contrast, they also reveal the Atlantic Community for what it was: a live-in relationship; more than a fling – like 1918–19 – but something less than a marriage; perhaps a conjugal partnership – intimate and intense and demanding but without enduring bonds. Because it was never a marriage, there need be no divorce. The partners can remain friends, but talk of a closer union is over.[19]

Washington has handled the emerging 'European' identity clumsily, especially its security dimensions. The US opposition to a formalized link between the WEU and the EC was largely futile and ended in a back-down when it became evident, at the NATO Council meeting in June 1991 and at Maastricht in December 1991, that it was pointless arguing about whether something was desirable in theory when it appeared to be happening in practice.

The US continues to assume that it will provide 'the leadership needed to promote global peace and security', without being specific as to how this will be done with the budgetary constraints that exist.[20] There is merely a mention in the *National Military Strategy of the United States* (1992) that the new strategy is designed to be implemented 'within a significantly reduced defence budget'.[21] The problem of implementing a new strategy while maintaining leadership at a time of budgetary stringency is one that may be insurmountable. It is clear that merely cutting with no regard to the threats being faced will result in military forces that are ill-prepared to face the challenges of the post-Cold War world. It would be unrealistic to expect instantaneous matching of domestic needs with security imperatives. The immediate post-World War II era was also a time of immense upheaval and it took several years for this process to be worked out. Only with the shocks of 1949 – the 'loss of China', the Soviet explosion of an A-bomb, and interservice wrangling over strategy – did Truman authorize a 'single, comprehensive statement of interests, threats and feasible responses, capable of being communicated throughout the bureaucracy'.[22] At present the *National Military Strategy of the United States* is the closest that the US can come at the moment to a comprehensive military strategy.

The new strategy, as it relates to Europe, is covered in the strategy's Base Force framework. The Base Force is divided into four areas: Strategic Forces, Atlantic Forces, Pacific Forces, and Contingency Forces. The Atlantic regions include Europe, the Mediterranean, the Middle East, Africa and Southwest Asia.[23] Within this region the US will maintain 'forward stationed and rotational forces, a capability for rapid reinforcement from within the Atlantic region and from the United States, and the means to support deployment of larger forces when needed'.[24] This new military strategy for the Atlantic regions poses several problems:

(1) The lack of base access in many of the Atlantic regions means that there will be a heavy reliance upon the European bases as staging posts, as in the Gulf War.
(2) The New Strategy opens up many important problems for NATO since the use of forces in non-European sectors of the Atlantic Regions may lead to out-of-area disputes.
(3) The use of US forces based in Europe and in other Atlantic regions may be done on a bilateral basis. However, there is a general reluctance in Europe to permit *carte blanche* use of bases for such operations.
(4) Desert Shield and Desert Storm may have provided the models for the Atlantic Forces, in as much as Europe was used as an important staging area. This may, however, be an atypical example and should not be used as a model for future operations.

The new US national military strategy emphasizes the importance of collective security and hints at a more collaborative role for the US in the international community:

> Increasingly, we expect to strengthen world response to crises through multilateral operations under the auspices of international security organizations... While support of formal alliances such as NATO will continue to be fundamental to American military strategy, the United States must be prepared to fight as part of an ad hoc coalition if we become involved in conflict where no formal security relationships exist.[25]

The commitment to multilateral operations has been underlined by the Clinton administration, particularly by working with the United Nations. The issue of the serious budget arrears faced by the UN, and the US's major role in creating this situation, sits uneasily at odds with the renewed commitment to multilateralism. The US has historically preferred to work through organizations in which it enjoys an unambiguous leadership role.

The three major post-Cold War crises, in the Gulf, Yugoslavia and Somalia, have illustrated that, when the US chooses to become involved, the superior military power of the US creates the assumption of a leadership role. The Gulf War coalition was formed in response to the twelve UN Security Council resolutions that required Iraq to restore invaded territory to Kuwait. Once military operations began, there was little UN control over the military aspects of Operation Desert Storm. Indeed, at times one could have been forgiven for wondering if the UN was involved at all. The US 'humanitarian' intervention in Somalia, in December 1992, also put the US in the leadership role but with one important difference: the US commander was directly account-able to the UN Security Council, which demanded tight control over Operation Restore Hope. In the Yugoslav case, there are no clear US interests at stake and it may also have been anticipated that this was a purely European problem that demanded a purely European response. The piecemeal responses by the US (and other leading Western powers) opens the question of the criteria for intervention. Operation Desert Storm, launched with the objective of restoring democracy, merely restored a hereditary emir to his throne and allowed a dictator to re-tain power. The fundamental issues of the Somalia crisis remain yet unresolved at the time of this writing; evidence of 'ethnic cleansing' in Bosnia-Herzegovina has elicited no clear US response to date. For the US and its NATO allies it has become a question of whether col-lective security is now replaced by 'selective security'.[26]

In light of the domestic problems that beset the US, the impulse to hand global responsibilities to the UN may become stronger. How-ever, without simultaneously restoring funding and devoting forces to collective security operations, the UN will be swamped by the de-mands made of it.[27] By using the withholding of funds as a means of inducing reforms, the US not only sets an appalling example, but weakens the very organization of which it was a founder and backer. The lack of an effective international organization will have deleterious effects upon regional security organizations, such as NATO, most of which were founded under the aegis of Article 52 of the UN Charter.

The ambivalence that the Clinton administration has shown about matching deeds with words, and thereby making the UN a realistic and effective collective security organization, stands in marked con-trast to the continuing preference for regional or unilateral arrange-ments. In the European context this can be explained by the following factors: (i) The traditional leadership role enjoyed by the US. (ii) The US has a vested interest in European security. (iii) In spite of the burden-sharing debate, the costs of the common defence were more evenly assumed amongst European NATO countries than in, for example, Asia. (iv) The security of Europe in the Cold War period *was* international security. The focus of post-Cold War security has yet to change to stress other areas.

Most of the these points were underlined and reinforced by the existence of the Cold War, but, with its demise, there is less validity to nearly all of these points. For instance, the US's leadership role in Europe rested primarily upon its nuclear role. One commentator observed that, 'Nuclear technology allowed the United States to dominate NATO in a way that would have been impossible under a nonnuclear regime... Leadership in nuclear affairs almost automatically gave the United States the priority position in shaping NATO decisions and studies through the power of the US-uniformed Supreme Allied Commander in Europe (SACEUR) and through the ability to chair all of the key groups and committees within the Alliance.'[28] Much of the Alliance structure was determined by nuclear weapons; the Anglo-American 'special relationship', the French decision to withdraw from NATO's integrated military command structure in 1966, and Konrad Adenauer's attempts to include Germany in the nuclear planning process, all stress the critical importance of nuclear weapons within the Alliance.

The decline in the number of nuclear weapons in Europe and the importance attached to them in the post-Cold War world will have significant implications for leadership. No longer will the US have a clear 'right' to the leadership mantle, and without this clear role the US will have to adjust to having less leverage and influence within NATO. This, then, poses the question of the extent the US is able to be, or wants to be, a team player instead of captain.

Assumptions that the leadership role would be provided by the US were reinforced by the Gulf War where European troops were deployed 'behind' US leadership. The Gulf War also served to propagate the myth that US and European interests are synonymous. With the disappearance of the Soviet threat it is difficult to see why foreign policy interests are necessarily synonymous any longer; the Soviet threat was *the* common interest.

The crisis in Yugoslavia provides the counter-example whereby 'American interests do not require the nation to continue in the active, leading political role it has played in Europe for the last four decades'.[29] The US's initial non-involvement in Yugoslavia is the clearest indicator that the US's European allies should assume more responsibility, initiative and leadership in their own security affairs since what is important to the Europeans may not be significant to the US, or vice versa.

In part, the leadership role of the US can be explained in terms of differing international perspectives; the key one being the US still seeing itself (at least on paper) as a global actor[30] in a unipolar world versus the European preference for an essentially regional role in a multipolar world. No European power has the global interests of the US, nor do they aspire to an international leadership role. The diversification of US interests may well lead some European leaders to gain the impression that Europe is less important to Washington, particularly in light of the fact that the Pacific Basin is of growing importance as an overseas trading area, and therefore the pursuit of a more active European voice and agenda seems logical. For the US it may be difficult to relinquish the leadership role it has assumed for four decades in Europe.

The advocacy of a natural leadership role by the US administration rests upon another questionable assumption: that the American public will indefinitely endorse this role. This endorsement can no longer be assumed, especially if the perception exists that the US is assuming an unfair part of the burden – in Warren Christopher's words, 'President Clinton must be able to show the US Congress that our allies are contributing commensurately'.[31] The burden-sharing debate, a child of the Cold War, may yet reach sturdy maturity in the post-Cold War world. Signs that the US leadership role may not be quite as 'natural' as the Bush or Clinton administrations assume, can be found in the GATT Uruguay Round, which began in the fall of 1986. The long-drawn-out dispute between the parties was nominally about subsidies;[32] but, in the wider context, it is about protectionism and power. Domestic support for a continued US role in Europe will depend in large part upon US perceptions of Europeans and their trade practices. A substantial public perception that the EC is unfair in its trade practices could present a major – or perhaps *the* major – threat to Alliance cohesion.

The trade war focused upon agricultural subsidies,[33] but there are also problems in the industrial field following allegations that the Europeans are not trading fairly or negotiating in good faith. The same charge could, however, be aimed at the US, who passed The Omnibus Trade and Competitiveness Act in 1988, which provided for penalties against those who were deemed to be using unfair or discriminatory trading practices. Washington subsequently identified several problem areas and presented them as a package for GATT consideration. The package included agriculture, investment and intellectual property rights; areas commonly viewed as benefiting the US and not the Europeans. The GATT discussions overall also have a direct bearing on European security and the US role in Europe. This was evidenced by the discussions between the German and US leaders: Chancellor Kohl refused to give way on the agricultural subsidies issue without US concessions; but, at the same meeting with President Bush at Camp David, he emphasized that 'European freedom and security will be safeguarded by the transatlantic alliance which... includes a substantial presence of American troops in Europe'.[34]

The need for the US taxpayer to maintain forces in Europe may also be questioned in light of Congressional disillusionment with EC '92 and the perception of a 'Eurofortress' that competes successfully against the US and discriminates against imports from outside the European Trade Area, while simultaneously anticipating that the US will subsidize European defences.[35] As the EC continues on its path towards an integrated market, characterized by the absence of tariff or customs barriers and the free movement of capital, goods and people, the potential for US disillusionment is high. The GATT Uruguay round assumed a high-profile in US–European relations because the European partners have broken one of the unwritten rules stemming from the Marshall Plan years: *that the Europeans support the US on economic goals in return for security guarantees.* In an international economic system that is increasingly becoming defined by trade blocs, such as the EC and the North American Free Trade Area (NAFTA), the likelihood of Western security collaboration being disrupted and of a US withdrawal from Europe is heightened. *In extremis*, 'the regional trading blocs of the new economic world order may divide into a handful of protectionist superstates. If by the new political world order we mean increased American hegemony disguised as international cooperation, we may come to know the new economic world order as regional hegemony disguised as free trade.'[36]

Up to now, where commercial disagreements have occurred between the EC and the US, the issues have been amicably resolved, with the exception of the impasse over agricultural subsidies. In the Cold War era the Europeans have 'always had at the backs of their minds the fear that the United States would lose interest in their security, and Washington (in particular, Congress) has sometimes found it necessary to remind their allies of their dependence'.[37] The threat of cuts obviously holds less sway in the changed security environment. Furthermore, the EC had a series of trade dispute successes against the US, ranging from the failure of the US to get the European allies to agree to its response to OPEC in 1973–74, the Reagan administration's backdown over the Siberian gas pipeline dispute in 1982, and the failure of the US to limit allied trade links with Eastern Europe in the 1970s and 1980s. However, none of these disputes challenged the fundamental basis of US–European relations until the Uruguay-round agricultural subsidies dispute. The challenge to CAP is one disagreement that the EC is unlikely to back down on, nor will the Cold War leverage that the US exerted through security policy (by threat of withdrawal or 'agonizing reappraisals') carry the same weight.

The Post-Cold War security scenario demands a delicate balancing act between the European allies and the US. The former must be careful not to alienate Capitol Hill and force further US military cuts in Europe; cuts which may force the European allies prematurely to construct a European Defence Community of some kind before an agreed agenda and a leader exists. The US, must continue to encourage the development of a European defence dialogue, one in which it cannot expect to wield the same influence as in the Cold War years and one in which the US can expect to lose, as well as win, security disagreements. To alienate the Europeans at this delicate stage by 'getting tough' would be dangerous and counter to the US's long-term interests. Hardest of all would be for the US to make the painful adjustment of withdrawing from Europe altogether, particularly so when the presence of US troops overseas is inextricably tied up with the image of being a superpower.

Much of the US resistance to a military withdrawal from Europe is based on the assumption that for the US to be 'in' Europe there have to be military forces there. Surely, if the State Department is so anxious to remain 'in' Europe it could be accomplished by the forging of other links? A strong argument, for instance, could be made that the US could demonstrate its concern for stability in Europe not by maintaining expensive US forces in Europe but by helping alleviate non-military threats to European stability, such as economic dislocation which may endanger fledgling democracies and, ultimately, peace. One analyst observed that the US could 'double its aid to all of Central and Eastern Europe for half the $4 billion a year it costs to keep each of the five US army combat divisions in Germany, poised to meet a short-warning Soviet attack that isn't going to come'.[38] Although US military commitments have changed, the point about alternative forms of demonstrating commitment to European security remains.

The fears expressed by the former secretary of state, James Baker III, in a speech on 21 September 1990, that Europe would become 'insular' and 'absorbed' with the process of integration, points not only to the administration's need for European support within the Alliance, but also externally, for the broader objectives of US foreign policy. The extent of this need for support was reflected in the German press:

> [I]t has become clearer than ever that Germany is the most important partner for the US in Europe. This is even more true since, as a result of the electoral campaign in the US, the change in the domestic mood has limited Bush's foreign policy potential. It is therefore important for him to have a system to pave the way in Europe. He needs it in his dealings with the EC, France, and above all with Eastern Europe, where Bonn is the most active agent for change. This new and close partnership is important for Bush, and Kohl has become a key figure for him. The only danger is that expectations are too high. Kohl, too, has his priorities; most important is that he is first and above all chancellor of a republic which is burdened by growing internal problems.[39]

The internal problems alluded to in Germany and the US may lead to introspection in the political sense. The same pattern is evident in France, following the 1992 regional elections.[40] Britain is also obsessed by worsening internal problems, chiefly the dismal state of the economy and John Major's tenuous hold on power. In these circumstances no one state has made a bid for leadership in European defence planning. Instead, there seems to be an optimistic expectation that somehow an institutional solution to the problem will materialize.

Indeed, an institutional solution to the problem is possible, but will require changes on the part of the US and its allies. The US is firmly rooted in NATO and, as has been argued, has regarded other institutions as challenges to NATO. Other institutional security arrangements would radically change the US's relationship with the EC as well as redefine the US's global role and identity. The official line has been that NATO is 'Europe's only time-tested security structure' and that NATO should seek to 'find ways to fill the security vacuum in Europe'.[41] This was exactly the task of the North Atlantic Council's meeting in Rome in November 1991. The Rome meeting was designed to reinforce the 'integrity and effectiveness of the Alliance as a whole'. It did this by weakly acknowledging the role of the WEU, CSCE and the EC as valuable efforts that buttress the European pillar within the Alliance. The meeting also ended, it should be noted, without the US finding its place in the new Europe. The stress placed on the 'permanent link' by which the security of the North America is tied to the security of Europe seemed almost shrill – a desperate attempt to continue to control an organization based upon a profound belief that America knows best what is good for the European allies.

The assumed permanence of that link is a relatively recent development stemming from the Reagan and Bush years. Earlier administrations, such as those of Roosevelt and Eisenhower, assumed that NATO
was intended to give Europe security guarantees *until such time* as the
Europeans could assume responsibility for their own defences. Richard
Nixon wrote, 'I vividly recall a meeting of the National Security Council
when President Eisenhower said that he intended this to be only a
temporary measure needed until our allies in Europe recovered from
World War II.'[42]

The need for NATO permanence can be traced to three beliefs: first,
the belief that the Europeans are fundamentally incapable of speaking
with a coherent European voice on security affairs or of organizing
their own defences, as shown in Yugoslavia; second, the complete removal of US forces from Europe would sooner or later lead to conflict in Europe, and yet again the US would be forced to bail Europe
out; third, the belief that the US is in many ways European and that
the US and Europe share many common values and trade links and a
common fate.

There is much truth to the first point: there *is* no coherent European
voice. The lack of an adequate response to the Yugoslav crisis, which
Warren Christopher portrayed as a 'European' problem, would seem
to prove conclusively that the US should continue to act as the 'cement' of the Alliance and keep the fractious Europeans from each
other's gizzards. While there is undoubtedly some truth to this proposition, there are also some problems with it. The lack of a coherent
voice on security affairs does not mean there is *no* voice. The importance of the political side of European union in the Maastricht Treaty,
which calls for the *eventual* framing of a common defence policy that
'might in time lead to a common defence', means that there is an
obvious desire to work towards this end. The lack of a coherent voice
could also be *caused* by the presence of the American voice in the
dialogue, whereby the US has actually obstructed the development of
a coherent European security identity. Common opposition and resistance to US policies in the Cold War years – over the neutron
bomb fiasco under Carter, the Libyan raid and the Lance modernization debate under Reagan, and the raid conducted against select targets in Baghdad by the Clinton administration, following revelations
of an Iraqi plot to assassinate George Bush while he was on a visit to
Kuwait – have helped to forge a delicate European identity, yet opposition to US policies is not a solid foundation for such an identity.

The ambiguous messages emanating from successive US administrations regarding the extent to which the US supports a distinct European security identity have not been helpful to the European allies. The Alliance is effectively split between the British, Dutch and Italians, who are sceptical of a European defence identity which excludes the US, and the French and the Germans, who are in favour of a far more assertive European defence identity which does not necessarily exclude the US, but does involve a substantial change in the US's position in the Alliance. If the Clinton administration gives a clear line of support for the development of a European security identity, consensus and coherence would probably be easier to achieve.

The second point, that the removal of US forces from Europe would lead to conflict, has already been challenged in an earlier section, on the grounds that Europe in the 1990s is fundamentally different than that of 1919 or 1945. The purpose of retaining US forces in Europe may have more to do with US policy considerations rather than the good of Europe *per se*. The purpose of a continued US presence in Europe is twofold, according to Lieutenant-General William Odom: first, to serve as a 'hedge against undesirable developments in the east', and, second, for making old adversaries – the Germans, British, French, Poles, Czechs, and others – 'continue to trust one another. Put bluntly, a US corps will defend the Germans against their neighbors and their neighbors against the Germans. By keeping the United States engaged in Europe, these troops will place limits on transatlantic quarrels and competition.'[43]

Such views are not untypical, yet they square awkwardly with post-Cold War Europe. For instance, the main threats to European security are likely to come from the south, not the east, as the Bosnian imbroglio has illustrated. Furthermore, the chapter of security challenges to Europe argued that there are many problems facing Europe that do not call for a military response and require diplomatic action by the European partners themselves. The logic of the second part of Odom's argument is perhaps the most puzzling: it seems to suggest that, in the absence of a US military presence, the 'old adversaries' would resort to stereotypical behaviour and, therefore, that the US military presence in effect *imposes* harmony. This argument runs counter to the entire logic of European integration, which was to create interdependent structures, especially economic ones, that would make warfare unthinkable. Although there are undeniable problems with the European integration process (many are no surprise), it has advanced sufficiently far to make a US military presence redundant if it is justified on the grounds of imposing 'order' on Europe. The only possible exceptions to this argument are potential conflicts in the south and east of Europe; here again, the US reaction to the Bosnian crisis has been sufficiently ambiguous that the European allies could be forgiven for questioning the extent to which the US is prepared to become involved in out-of-area disputes that do not directly affect US interests. In reality, the US military presence in Europe can be justified more accurately on grounds of mutual self-interest – they protect vital US economic interests in Europe and allow the allies to subsidize their defence expenditure. There is, furthermore, an important asymmetry in the justification for a continued US military presence in Europe: if the main threats are to the south of Europe, shouldn't there be a concentration of force in that region? The answer, it would appear is no, since America's main interests lie elsewhere, in Germany. It is the protection of vital US economic interests that ultimately lie behind the US military presence in Germany and, for that matter, Japan.

THE END OF THE TRANSATLANTIC COMMUNITY?

The third point, that the US is in many ways European and that its fate is intimately bound up with that of Europe, is also open to challenge. Europe's origins were those of tribes who over the millennia have defined (and defended) their identities in relation to a particular piece of land; and only recently, through the experience of two hugely destructive wars, has integration been taken seriously. Europe remains far from a United States of Europe and will, in all probability, never become one. The end of the Cold War has emphasized national interest amongst the European countries, which complicates the integration process as well as inducing resistance to US hegemony. The notion of a transatlantic community was built primarily upon close defence ties between the US and Western European countries. The unravelling of much of that security relationship has challenged the extent to which the US and its European allies share common values and interests.

The US is, of course, much different from its European allies. Americans do not generally have existential tribal roots but rather are unified by their polity and a shared devotion to common ideas enshrined, most obviously, in the constitution. To become an American citizen you do so by a process of self-proclamation – by promising to uphold the constitution of the United States of America. The belief in the invincibility and essential good of the American model of democracy could be seen in the almost messianic zeal with which constitutional experts departed to the new democracies in Europe to persuade them to adopt a US-type constitution. Europe, on the other hand, is still deeply rooted in the evolutionary process starting from tribes settling on distinct lands – a fact sadly exemplified in the savagery in Bosnia, which, when stripped of the modern verbiage, is essentially a tribal war. This does not mean, as argued above, that these 'tribes' will revert necessarily to war, but it does explain the immense importance to Germany of the lands to its east and the need to incorporate not just Central Europe into the new and established institutions, but also Russia, which is part of the Eurasian land mass.

The differences in background are also manifest in the historical perspectives of Europeans and Americans. Many of the latter are only cognizant of American history from 1945 on, while their European counterparts are aware of their own turbulent history. Awareness of this history, however vague, is also one of the strongest reasons for avoiding wars that have rent the continent asunder many times in the past. Even Britain, seen as the stalwart defender of the US in Europe and its most valuable ally, is quite different and is currently feeling torn between its allegiances to Europe (which may be pragmatic) and its ties to the US.

The cultural characteristics outlined above are important and feed directly into the current European security situation. The US continues to see itself as a model society whose values and norms should be upheld by others. The belief in the 'American way' and leadership is reflected in the earlier extract from Bush's State of the Union address, as well as in President Clinton's observation that 'We are after all the world's only superpower. We do have to lead the world.'[44] The implicit belief that America can be trusted and that America will 'do what's right' drives not only foreign policy but serves as the foundation for a further belief: that stability and justice can be defended only with US involvement. The new commonwealth of freedom, resting on common values, represents values that the US thinks the rest of the democratic world should uphold.

To many Americans it may be surprising, or even abrasive, to suggest that there are plenty of examples of disquiet amongst the European allies stemming from US actions that found no, or little, support in European capitals. The ham-fisted attempts at handling state-sponsored terrorism in the Libyan raid of April 1986 or, in the same year, the Reykjavik Summit at which Reagan negotiated away 50 per cent of the US's strategic arsenal with Gorbachev, with no consultation with the allies, serve as examples of the US assuming it knew best or, more worrying, not really caring what the allies thought. Domestic crises, such as Watergate, the Iran-contra affair, Iraqgate and the mining of Nicaraguan harbours, have shaken confidence in US leadership and tainted the brightness of the 'City on the Hill'. Above all, the end of the Cold War means that many of the shared concerns and the common culture will begin to disintegrate. There are essential differences between Europe and the US that should be acknowledged, and these differences may well lead to different policy outcomes and, eventually, the formation of different security emphases which need not be fractious.

It has already been argued that the US wishes to maintain NATO since this organization, more than any other, symbolizes the US's superpower status and influence (it was intended initially that the United Nations be this symbol for the US which, like the League, was primarily a US initiative; however, the UN was discreetly dropped as the US lost control of the organization to Third World countries). Yet, the general reluctance on the part of the European allies to see NATO fade away is not a confirmation of the US's position within the Alliance. The allied support of NATO is due to two factors. On the one hand, there is a dependency amongst the European members; they are used to the security and sense of order that has been instilled through the US presence. In spite of the emergence of a European Security Identity, there is insufficient coherence to this identity to pose a serious alternative to US hegemony. On the other hand, the rapid changes in the Soviet Union, the unification of Germany and the lingering doubts that surround these changes have reinforced the tendency to cling to American commitment and leadership. Since the world is still remarkably unstable after the end of the Cold War, it may seem like a matter of prudence to hold on to the one surviving superpower.

The European tendency to cling onto the US could be part of a transition, rather than a reconfirmation, of the US's role. Unless a new overarching threat emerges that challenges the security and well-being of *all* the Alliance members, it is difficult to see how the gradual erosion going on in the trade fields, differences in relation to Central and Eastern Europe and the integration process underway through the EU, will not eventually challenge the stability of the entire NATO edifice and the position of the US. The transatlantic Community, as we know it, is changing. It could evolve along one of two paths: either, it could evolve from its collective defence role into a role whose prime goal is to encourage democracy and stability and to manage crises at the earliest moment; or, the decline of the transatlantic community could simply signify a period of destabilizing introspection where NATO remains an arcane collective defence organization, as the US attends to its domestic woes and the Western Europeans fret about the path to European Union.

MILITARY OPTIONS FOR THE US IN EUROPE

Any future US military presence in Europe will have to be decided upon with these three considerations in mind: (i) internal US considerations (budgetary, demands on US forces elsewhere, and public/Congressional sentiment); (ii) military strategy (MC 14/4) and threat perceptions in Europe; (iii) the competing demands made upon US military and its resources from other parts of the globe. The likelihood of instability in Europe or surrounding regions is high; yet, as discussed, it no longer calls for the deployment of vast forces. Still, it is agreed in Washington and the European capitals that for the foreseeable future some US military representation in Europe is necessary. The questions of how many, at what cost, and with what political ramifications, obviously depend upon a number of variables ranging from threat perceptions, domestic support, economic factors and so forth. Four alternatives are outlined in Table 5.1. The options outlined represent distinct choices in terms of policy, strategy and capability. In the case of forward strategy, this implies a sizeable US military presence which would perform the same basic duties as the Cold War presence: those of a sizeable ground force that, with its air support, could halt an offensive attack and hold until reinforcements arrived. However, due to the changes in Europe and the CFE agreement, this option has been precluded since force levels are already well below the level required for forward defence, and the likelihood of a major offensive is low.

The second option, that of dual basing, involves the continued presence of a substantial portion of a corps formation in Europe, but with elements deployed in the US which in time of crisis could be relocated back to Europe. The third option, that of a limited presence, provides for 70 000 troops, a single army division, as well as a skeletal support structure. The final option merely provides for the essential personnel to run the logistical networks as well as command, communication, control and intelligence networks. The combat element would be extremely small and would be designed mainly with a symbolic function in mind.

Table 5.1 Options for US military representation in Europe

US force posture in Europe	150–165 thousand forward presence	100 thousand dual-based presence	70 thousand limited presence	40 thousand symbolic presence
Central Europe				
Ground HQ	Corps	Corps	Division	Division
Basing mode	Forward	Dual-based	Forward	Dual-based
Forward brigades	7	4	2.4	0.5
Tactical fighter wings	2.5	1.7	1.2	0.6
POMCUS*	2–3	2–3	2–3	2–3
Southern Europe				
Ground forces	Battn	Battn	0	0
Tactical fighter wings	1	0.6	0.3	0
Naval bases	3	3	2	2

*POMCUS = Prepositioned Overseas Materiel Configured in Unit Sets.

Source: Richard Kugler: 'The Future U.S. Military Presence in Europe: Forces and Requirements for the Post-Cold-War Era,' *RAND Report*, R-4194-EUCOM/NA, 1992, p. vi.

Of the options in Table 5.1, the first has already been discounted. This is in part a result of the changes in Europe and the CFE agreement, but also a result of successive cuts in US force levels since those announced by Secretary of Defense Dick Cheyney in 1991.[45] The depth of the cuts has been dramatic, from 326 000 US military personnel deployed in Europe in 1988, to around 167 000 in 1992. Pressure to go below those numbers under the Clinton administration is fierce.[46]

The second option fits the existing force presence in Europe, but the dual-based presence is an expensive option, and it is unclear that the will exists in Congress, given the strictures of the Gramm-Rudman-Hollings Deficit Reduction Bill, to support such a presence. One argument that is sometimes forwarded in favour of the second option is that, in the light of the 1991 Gulf War, the European bases provide valuable jumping-off points for US forces to mount operations in the Middle East/Persian Gulf areas. Indeed the assumption that US forces in Europe have tasks beyond Europe is built into the command structure; for instance, USEUCOM has responsibilities not only for the European area but also for the Middle East and Africa. The critical role played by European-based US forces in Operation Desert Storm serves as a striking example of the utility of forward basing for rapid intervention purposes. However, this particular case was atypical and exemplified an unusual degree of cooperation in response to a particularly blatant violation of international law, where the direct interests of the US and the European allies alike were endangered. More generally, such support cannot be counted upon from America's NATO allies, most notably in the Middle East, and the US should not consider European bases as tools to be used in pursuit of US policy goals in adjacent areas. It is also possible that the 100 000 US troops who remain in Europe after 1996 may be considered to be too intrusive a presence by the European host countries.

The third and fourth options depend heavily on future developments in Europe. The limited presence option would still present the US with an operationally effective force but may, from the US perspective, have some political liabilities. There is no magic figure for the ideal US military presence in Europe; however, compared with other European force levels, any US contribution under 100 000 loses much of its political weight. Arguably, it was not so much force levels that gave the US its leadership position within the Alliance (there was no perceptible change in US leadership within the Alliance when US force levels dropped by almost 30 000 from the 1950s to the mid-1980s) but its nuclear role. The nuclear role 'impose[es] upon the U.S. government a need to maintain the kind of influence and presence that allows it to help manage potential crises before they spiral beyond recall'.[47] The scaling down of the nuclear threat and the shrinkage in conventional force levels throughout Europe obviously removes much of this imperative. The exact importance that should be attached to the link between military presence and political influence is difficult to quantify in any situation. That there is a perceived link, however, is beyond dispute. One author, quoted above, makes the point that while influence is difficult to measure, as well as subtle, its absence is 'normally transparent'. He continues:

> Military forces, to be sure, are not the only vehicle by which the United States gains influence. Nevertheless, U.S. military forces, when continually deployed in Europe, do buy a particular kind of influence there. Whereas diplomacy and economic instruments have realms of their own, military forces buy leverage in the unique, hard-to-crack realm of European defense relationships and security affairs. This was the case during the Cold War, and it is likely to remain true in the coming era.[48]

The logic of such arguments is that a large force in Europe carries significant political leverage, and a smaller force a lesser amount of political leverage. NATO has clearly moved to smaller numbers in conventional and nuclear forces, and even if the US still enjoys a *proportionate* amount of influence it is worth less in the Post-Cold War world. The threats to Europe are now of a less cataclysmic nature and the US cannot under these circumstances expect to exert the same degree of leadership and influence it did in the past. This, at root, is the fallacy of a symbolic US military presence. What does the force symbolize? If it cannot symbolize leadership, would there be interest in retaining US forces in Europe?

The symbolic presence of 40 000 troops may not comprise a combat force but would represent sufficient personnel to operate the command, control, communication and intelligence assets. In this case it is difficult to see on whose behalf these assets would be operated. It is highly unlikely that they would be run as the infrastructure for European forces. If, on the other hand, the US used these assets as support for US forces that would be transported from the US in time of emergency, this would stretch slim air- and sea-lift resources to breaking point. The symbolism at this, or other, levels is also questionable since it is no longer obvious that this is the best means of demonstrating the shared interests of the US and Europe or of symbolizing the US's status. If the US government continues to emphasize its national interests and superpower status, 'it may reduce, rather than enhance, the respect and influence it seeks'.[49]

Of the options outlined above it seems clear that in the period 1992–95 the second option is preferable. The period will be one of instability, although the likelihood of a full-frontal invasion of Germany or any other part of Europe does not warrant the retention of a forward presence of the type outlined in option one. As the remaining Soviet forces complete their withdrawal from Eastern Europe by 1995, the need and justification for a US military presence in Europe may become less pressing.[50] Within this period many other decisive factors will become clearer, such as: (i) the threats that face NATO and, more generally, Europe; (ii) the shape of European integration, especially in the security realm; (iii) the budgetary strictures faced by the US and its allies; (iv) the progress of Eastern Europe towards economic stability and truly democratic forms of government.

Although conjectural, it seems a reasonable argument that US policy should substantially reduce the amount of forces with the aim of *eventually withdrawing all US forces from Europe*. This would be in the *long-term* interests of both the Europeans and the US, but would involve adaptation and tolerance from all. For the Europeans it would mean formulating a security policy and building up areas where they are heavily reliant upon the US – most noticeably in the C^3I and logistics areas. This would entail heavy expense but would not be beyond the European economies; in addition, the development of such a system could have advantageous export potential.

The usual objection to the withdrawal of US forces from Europe is the historical observation that the US has on two occasions had to bale out the Europeans. This observation assumes, though, that Europe has not changed and that there will be another European conflagration that will demand US intervention. The likelihood of a major European war has been rejected already. The 'let's stay put because if we don't they'll fight' argument is one that has become less and less persuasive to the post-1945 generation. The continuing presence of a large number of US servicemen in Europe could have quite the opposite effect from the reassurance it is meant to symbolize. The retention of small, non-combat forces for symbolic purposes could be misconstrued; the assumption is that they would demonstrate transatlantic solidarity, but they could easily demonstrate other things to the European allies who may feel that the US is trying to set the pace of, or disrupt in other ways, European integration.

From the US perspective the concern about force levels, which played a role in the 1992 presidential election debates, reflected a preoccupation with numbers. Part of the reason why there seems to be a consensus emerging that a US military presence in Europe of between 100 000 and 125 000 seems to be about right is because the US has traditionally accounted for about 18 per cent of NATO's active manpower. Thus, if allied manpower shrinks by around 20–25 per cent, the US can comfortably reduce its forces and retain the same proportion. A larger reduction, to say 70 000, would account for only 7 per cent of the allied forces, and would 'alter the traditional burden-sharing arrangements and possibly the command relationships that flow from them'.[51] It is this fear, that the US would lose much of its influence over its allies, that seems to motivate the numbers issue. Beyond the numbers themselves, there seems to be little vision of where the remaining US forces should be allocated. There is, for instance, no suggestion of relocating US forces to the north and the south (Norway and Turkey) to meet the security concerns of NATO's peripheries.

THE BUSH LEGACY

In an extensive, six-month review of America's defence needs, the Clinton administration eventually adopted a defence doctrine that is similar to Bush's and with force levels only slightly below those of the Bush administration. The cuts announced by the Secretary of Defense, Les Aspin, in early September 1993 will result in the shrinking of the military from 1.7 million to 1.4 million over a five-year period.

The underlying military strategy governing the use of US military forces (shown in Table 5.2) was much the same as that of the Bush administration, largely because of the guiding hand of the chairman of the Joint Chiefs of Staff, General Colin Powell, who served under both presidents until the end of September 1993. The strategy is sometimes called the 'win–win' strategy. The object of the strategy is to be able to fight two almost simultaneous (non-nuclear) conflicts. To pare US forces further would have made this an unrealistic objective; and, in the event of this, it was thought that the outbreak of aggression in one place would absorb the majority of US forces and thus provide the opportunity for another aggressor to exploit the US's preoccupation with a conflict elsewhere. Thus, in theory the US should be able to fight simultaneously in, for instance, the Persian Gulf and North Korea.

The Clinton defence plan may have some interesting ramifications for Europe. First, the plan stresses a heavy reliance upon POMCUS stocks that are in theatre. The role of US bases in Europe would therefore be that of a springboard for operations in neighbouring areas and, most probably, the Persian Gulf area. Such a plan assumes that the European host nations share the same goals and concerns as the US in the Gulf and other areas. It also assumes that host nations are willing to let bases on their territory be used for operations for which, even if they are not directly involved, they may nevertheless become legitimate targets for retribution. The use of bases as out-of-area springboards may pose particular difficulties in the south of Europe where Turkey and Italy have shown considerable nervousness in the past about such use. The plan will also revive the interminable OOA debate within NATO. If the main purpose of the US maintaining forces in Europe is to be the policing of surrounding areas, with or without European assistance, the extent of NATO's interests must be addressed. The argument that OOA collaboration is permitted under Articles 2 and 4 of the North Atlantic Treaty, and thus that the dispute over Article 6 is a red herring, will not carry much weight amongst the US's European allies if this is perceived merely as a vehicle to exer-

Table 5.2 Planned cuts in US military forces

	Current forces	Clinton plan	Old Bush plan
ARMY	14 active divisions	10 active divisions	12 active divisions
	6 reserve divisions	15 reserve brigades	8 reserve divisions
NAVY	13 carrier battlegroups	11 carrier battlegroups	12 carrier battlegroups
	1 training carrier	1 reserve and training carrier	
MARINES	182 000 active	174 000 active	159 000 active
	1 reserve division	1 reserve division	1 reserve division
AIR FORCE	16 active fighter wings	13 active fighter wings	14 active fighter wings
	12 reserve fighter wings	7 reserve fighter wings	10 reserve fighter wings

Key: A division comprises 18 300 soldiers and 324 tanks. 3 brigades equal one division. Each brigade is comprised of 3 battalions or regiments. A battlegroup is 1 aircraft carrier and cruiser and destroyer escorts. A fighter wing consists of 3 squadrons of 18–24 aircraft.
Source: Department of Defense, reproduced in *New York Times*, 2 September 1993, A.18.

cise US influence in adjoining areas in the name of 'promoting conditions of stability and well-being'.[52]

If the prevailing tendency is to use overseas bases as springboards, the French may become unwilling to collaborate with NATO. The use of bases for OOA contingencies may only add venom to French charges that NATO is a US-dominated organization that does not have the interests of the European allies at heart. Open differences in opinion between the US and its European allies in the Persian Gulf region (the Gulf War collaboration standing as a notable exception) may make the use of bases in Europe for 'power projection' not only controversial, but the surest way to ensure the disintegration of the Alliance.

Criticisms of the Clinton defence plan have focused on the question of whether his strategy tries to do too much with too little. The fact that the Clinton administration has not cut the Marine Corps as much as the Bush administration planned to, is indicative of the important role that they could play in trouble spots around the globe. The ability of the US to intervene in trouble spots in a timely fashion depends not only upon air- and sea-lift capability, but also upon the political compliance of host nations near the trouble spots. Such compliance could almost be assumed in the Cold War period, but in the post-Cold War period, where the US has a significantly reduced base network overseas, such compliance may be more difficult to secure – including in Europe.

In its first year the Clinton administration concentrated on domestic issues to the detriment of foreign policy. The Bosnian crisis is discussed in more detail later, but it did illustrate the extent to which the European allies had come to rely upon the US for leadership. The Clinton administration failed to do this. A significant shift in US foreign policy took place in the first year of his administration; not so much by what was done but by what was not. Clinton's first visit to Europe took place only after a whole year in office, when he attended the NATO summit in Brussels on 10–11 January 1994. The Brussels summit is discussed in greater detail in Chapter 9 but, at this stage, it should be observed that Clinton's efforts to reestablish a leadership role in NATO through The Partnership for Peace and renewed threats of air strikes against Serb held positions in Bosnia, have left many unconvinced. The summit was marked by Clinton's emphatic support for NATO's continued importance as well as the enduring nature of the transatlantic ties. By putting his support behind an institution which appears to be flailing around for a convincing *raison d'etre*, he may only encourage the European allies to enhance European security alternatives. Partnership for Peace, which Clinton heralded as a great success, was not greeted with much enthusiasm by the leaders of Central Europe and it certainly fell short of the security guarantees that they anticipated. The claimed success of the summit was tarnished further by the resignation of Clinton's Secretary of Defense, Les Aspin, shortly after the summit as well as enduring rumours (which were dutifully reported in the European press) of Clinton's personal infidelities and financial irregularities. When combined, these factors leave a picture of a President who has no clear foreign or security policy and one whom the European allies should not expect too much of. Difficult choices have to be made between domestic reinvigoration and fulfilling the US's self-proclaimed global leadership role. The choices are complex and immensely difficult and point, from the European perspective, to the need for the European allies to reduce their dependence on the US and to not expect decisive leadership. This need not, and hopefully will not, mean an antagonistic relationship, but it does mean redefining the relationship. The US is clearly no longer *primus inter pares*, which may not be a bad thing for either the US or the European allies.

CONCLUSION

The arguments presented above suggest two conclusions about the role of the US in Europe's security. The first is, that the US *does* have a valuable role to play in helping its European allies and others to make the transition from a transatlantic security system to one which reflects the changes in Europe and elsewhere. The transition does *not* necessarily mean that North America will have no role to play; few are advocating that. It does, however, mean that there will have to be a new security bargain in which the US is not necessarily the hegemon and in which US values and interests may not be paramount. Whether the American people would support this remains a moot point.

By sending out highly ambiguous signals to the European allies about the Franco–German corps or the enhanced role of the WEU, the US merely compounds tensions across the Atlantic. Much of the adversarial relationship that exists between those who suspect that the US is itching for the opportunity to derail European security integration, and those who believe in a Franco–German plot to destroy NATO and the transatlantic connection, stems from the consistent refusal of Washington to outline explicitly its perceived role in a vastly changed Europe.

The leaders of the EU countries can also be criticized for their failure to acknowledge the US's role in the EU. The US is, in all but name, a member. Certainly if assets and investments are considered, it is one of the more influential members. The apparent breakdown of communication in the GATT Uruguay Round risks not just serious clashes in trade policy, but also places at stake the security relationship at a time when there is no effective European leadership in this field.

The second conclusion is that if the transition is resisted by Washington, the Atlantic Alliance may well fall apart and with it may go the US's ability to have an important say in Europe's affairs. By fostering the transition, the US may witness the demise of NATO, but it would not lose its say in European affairs or all of its influence. The US could get in through the 'back door' by developing strong ties with the EU or by encouraging the Europeans to coordinate their policy through the CSCE, where the US could also play a significant role. The option of continuing the Alliance as it is and imposing US leadership and visions, based on historical and cultural baggage emanating from the Cold War years, will cause resentment.

This chapter has already argued that much of the institutional confusion about which organization speaks for European security concerns stems from the US insistence that its security is intrinsically linked to the security of the Europeans and, on the other hand, to its resistance to Europe's attempts to build a European Security Identity which carries any hint of endangering the transatlantic security structure. The insistence that NATO remains the paramount security organization could be counterproductive for the US, since although NATO is flushed with success, that same success has planted the seeds of its irrelevance. As NATO struggles to find a role that is relevant to the post-Cold War world, so too must the US redefine its relations with Europe.

The Atlanticist/European debate may be resolved through the growing economic deterioration of the US and differences of opinion between the US and its European allies over Bosnia, under the Clinton administration. The trip made by Bush and twenty-one prominent industrialists to Japan in January 1992 was a noticeable example of the way in which national economic woes are beginning to drive foreign and security policy – a link that has been emphasized by President Bill Clinton's formation of an Economic Security Council. The clashes with the EC over agricultural subsidies also serve as an example. It seems logical to expect this line of behaviour to carry over into NATO where, in return for a continued US military commitment, greater economic contributions will be expected. The response to this could be twofold: first, to accept the proposition but with the condition that the US's leadership role in NATO be downgraded, in which case the appeal of NATO may diminish in the US; second, demands from Washington for increased contributions could swing those European countries who are Atlanticists towards a European security stance. The differences of opinion between the US and its European allies regarding the wisdom of intervening militarily in Bosnia, which arose in the spring of 1993, may also have the effect of strengthening European consensus and lessen dependency on the US for leadership and initiative.

The first one hundred days of the Clinton administration showed an unwillingness to deal with complex foreign-policy issues and a preference for domestic issues, such as the health-care system and the budget deficit. The state of the US economy has focused attention on a distinctly American set of interests and, as a part of this realignment of interests, the paring of overseas military commitments has radically reduced the military options available to the US. The question that arises with the apparent shift in focus of the Clinton administration, is the length of time that Americans will perceive that they continue to have vital interests at stake in Europe? So far, the reaction has been to cling to NATO as the strongest and most visible link, not just as the US's commitment to Europe, but as a symbol of its influence in Europe. Clearly, with the changed circumstances of the post-Cold War world there will have to be a rethinking of the US role in Europe. The crisis in Bosnia, still unresolved at the time of writing, will also have an important impact upon US–European relations. Both Bush and Clinton have proclaimed loudly and visibly that the US is the world's leader, yet in the Bosnian case the US's allies have waited for the US to lead. Western Europe has refused to take punitive military action against Serbia without US leadership and backing. For Warren Christopher to turn around and tell the European leaders that this is a 'European problem' both undermines the US's credibility as a leader and causes confusion about the future of collective security in Europe and surrounding areas. For the US to be a leader, rhetoric must be followed by action. Failure to do so can only result in disillusionment and recriminations between Europe and the US.

The domestic agenda of the Clinton administration, and those after, will have an important bearing on the future involvement of the US military in Europe. Precisely what this bearing may be has yet to be seen. While there may be no obvious institutional panacea to the question of direction and emphasis in European defence planning, there are some institutions, or mixes thereof, that appear to offer more hope than others. These options are examined in the next section.

Part III

The New European Security Disorder

Part III
The New European Security Disorder

6 The 'New Security Architecture'

The security challenges facing Europe, outlined in the previous chapter, call for cooperation and collaboration through institutions devoted to the maintenance of peace and stability. What appears to be happening, both in their insistence and the manner in which the Western countries are approaching them, is the opposite. The removal of the overarching nuclear threat and the opposing alliances, which were the main features of Cold War European security, has weakened the perceived need for collaboration on security matters. Instead, the *relance* of the nation-state, contrary to earlier postulating about the decline of the nation-state and the emergence of regimes, has been the salient feature of the post-Cold War international system.

The re-emergence of clearly defined national security goals, in the absence of an overarching security threat, means that the appeal for broad security commitments is unlikely to be as persuasive as in the Cold War years. Cooperation is most likely to appeal to individual countries if it is made on a regional basis, particularly with neighbouring countries; the Hexagonal Initiative, the Black Sea Economic Cooperation Region (BECR), and the Council of Baltic States serve as examples. The building of economic ties may, in time, give rise to the perceived need to protect shared economic interests through security arrangements (although this need not be the logical progression, as the faltering moves of the European Community towards European Union, with its foreign and security policy components, illustrate).

The apparent tendency to define security interests in primarily national terms need not necessarily be viewed as a negative development if it is part of a more general reassessment of security concerns, which should, logically, start with the individual states and expand outwards to neighbouring states, the region and so forth. Hans J. Morgenthau related the concept of national security to national interest when he observed:

The concept of the national interest presupposes neither a naturally harmonious, peaceful world nor the inevitability of war as a consequence of the pursuit by all nations of their national interests. Quite to the contrary, it assumes continuous conflict and threat of war to be minimized through the continuous adjustment of conflicting action by diplomatic action.[1]

This observation serves as a reminder that the existence of two highly armed alliances in the Cold War years, both of whom defined their rationale for existence in terms of the other, also served to subsume the essential differences between alliance members. As has been argued earlier, the re-emergence of nationalism has prompted comparisons with the immediate period before World War I. The key difference between this period and that of the post-Cold War world is that, although national interest plays a heightened role in shaping a new security agenda, other areas of state activity where a high degree of interdependence is to be found, such as the economic integration represented by the European Community, impose significant limitations upon an individual state's security choices. Thus the eventual emergence of a new security order for Europe will evolve out of an assessment of national security concerns, balanced with the protection of extended state interests, expressed through interdependent relations with other states – the latter often being expressed in institutional terms.

THE NEW SECURITY ENVIRONMENT

The European security environment has changed beyond recognition when compared to that of pre-1990 Europe. The main changes can be summarized as: (i) The end of the forward deployment of armoured units capable of short-warning offensives in Central Europe. (ii) The end of the bipolar structure, symbolized by the dismantling of the Warsaw Pact and the reduction in numbers of US forces deployed in Europe by 50 per cent to around 150 000 and the closure of 381 bases. The cutbacks include drastic reductions in the numbers of nuclear weapons. (iii) The failure of authoritarianism in Eastern Europe. (iv) A more assertive and cohesive Western Europe. (v) The end of unproductive posturing at the arms-control table.[2] (vi) Confusion at the institutional level about which institution, or institutions, should represent European security concerns. (vii) A decreased role for nuclear weapons in Europe. (viii) Significant budgetary strictures that seem to drive threat assessment and strategy. (ix) A stronger role for national self-interest. (x) A reduction in arms markets. The list could go on, but suffice it to say that virtually every fundamental precept of European security has been challenged. Amidst the speculation about the shape and nature of the new European security architecture, there is only one certainty: it will not be like the architecture of the previous forty-five years. The Cold War world from the Western perspective was, in retrospect, an ordered and more predictable world. In the words of Lord Ismay's oft-quoted observation, it was a security structure that served to keep the Russians out, the Americans in, and the Germans down. It was these three factors that drove European security and prosperity in the post-war era.

The Cold War era was one that gave the Western European powers an incentive to integrate and grow economically. The overarching Soviet threat and the US military presence served respectively to diminish differences between the European powers and spared the US's European allies of some of the burdens of self-defence. For the smaller European states, such as the Benelux countries, there was comfort in the military guarantee provided by a superpower that was distant and not, as had been their historical experience, on their borders. The US military presence also served to tie in, however tentatively, the Southern European powers, who otherwise may have been ignored or even ostracized, bearing in mind the distinctly undemocratic nature of their post-war regimes.

The US presence in Western Europe was also viewed as a convenient mutual justification for the Soviet military presence in Eastern Europe and vice versa – although the nature and involvement of the respective militaries in the internal affairs of the host nations were remarkably different. The division of Germany was also a matter of convenience for the Soviet Union, who was deprived of a historical adversary, and thus permitted them an almost unhindered hand in both Eastern Europe and the vast Soviet empire. So, too, was the Cold War distribution of forces convenient for the US. The US's active involvement in Western European defence made the defence of Europe the forward defence of the US itself, as well as ensuring the protection of US interests in Europe.

With the demise of the Cold War these certainties disappeared and new uncertainties emerged: a united Germany resumed its position as a major power once again in the centre of Europe; an independent Eastern Europe free of Soviet purview; a fractured Soviet Union with fifteen unstable pieces; and a diminished US military presence. These uncertainties give rise to many interlinked questions. For example, what are the security ramifications of these changes? And what organizations should be charged with responsibility for Europe's security (however Europe may be defined)?

Characteristic of much of the thinking concerning the above questions has been the *institutional bias* to the analysis. There is a deeply embedded historical tendency to think in institutional terms, or what Richard Ullman calls the 'architectural imperative'.[3] Most of those who study various aspects of European security share the common assumption that some institutional representation of security interests embodied in a supranational organization is a starting point for any new or revised security regime. In the case of the post-World War II security architecture, the design was prompted not just by concern regarding the Soviet Union but also as a response to fears of German remilitarization (the Pleven Plan for the construction of an EDC being the most notable example of concern regarding the latter).

There are grounds on which architectural or organizational approaches can be challenged. The record of security organizations, with the exception of NATO's history in the Cold War era, has not been inspiring. Even if NATO is taken as the model security organization, it must be remembered that NATO's forty-five years of history is a tiny part of Europe's history, most of which has taken place without any form of regional security organization. Although speculative, it may be worth pondering whether any regional security organization could have stopped the Franco–Prussian War, World War I or World War II. It could also be argued that the need for regional security organizations in the European case has diminished since interdependence has developed to an extent never seen before, and the risks and costs of war are well known to all parties. Does Europe need a new or revised security order based on a supranational body, or any number of them?

Supranational organizations have been generally poor at preventing conflict until the Cold War and the formation of NATO and the WTO. However, there may be other useful functions that such bodies could carry out, such as the resolution of conflict, with the aim of containing wars and stopping a general war. The more substantive argument for rejecting a return to a balance-of-power system is that, in spite of the EC rhetoric, there is still a residual suspicion about Germany and its intentions. Germany has risen as indisputably the most powerful European country in post-Cold War Europe. The fear associated with Germany's new position are real, yet also incoherent. It may not be true that Germany will once again give way to its habitual desire to go on the rampage through adjoining lands, but there is nevertheless unease. At least the presence of Germany in the major security organizations gives the impression that Germany is fettered and less likely to go off at a tangent.

Successive efforts to institutionalize security arrangements have usually been motivated by fears that one or more states would threaten or use force as a means of challenging the existing order. Although the threat of war between the major states of Europe is unlikely, and thus may seem to challenge the necessity of such institutional representations of security concerns, there are several counters that can be offered in favour of an institutional approach to contemporary European security challenges: (i) Institutions slow down tendencies to define security in completely nationalistic ways. They serve as a constant reminder of shared concerns that are beyond the capacities of any one state to address. (ii) The history of Western European institutional collaboration has conditioned not only state behaviour but also thinking about security. To undo this would be difficult and of questionable merit. (iii) The negotiation and implementation of arms-control agreements would be well nigh impossible. For example, the CFE agreement is dependent upon the existence of such organizations for its implementation. (iv) Traditional enmities, such as those between Greece and Turkey, may well flare up (as they did over Cyprus and mineral exploitation rights in the Aegean Sea) in the absence of any institution to contain such pressures. (v) Security institutions have until the late 1980s been concerned with various aspects of containment (both internally and externally). The end of the Cold War is a chance not to dismantle institutions but to extend them for the first time into a structure that stretches across Europe.

Although diminished military threats to European countries may well justify reductions in their respective militaries, and may even seem to challenge the need for the existing security institutions, new and traditional challenges facing Europe still demand a collaborative answer. The question thus becomes not so much one of *whether* institutions are desirable, but *which* may address the different security threats that now face Europe. Adapted or entirely new institutions may face demands for earlier intervention and in non-traditional security roles. As argued in Chapter 2, the main security problems facing Europe are likely to be those of migration, economic disruption, the re-emergence of non-democratic regimes, nationalism or irredentism spilling over into Western Europe and the new democracies to the east. The identification of these new threats and any ensuing course of action would be virtually impossible to achieve on a unilateral basis. The nature of the problems demands close cooperation between the European countries within an institutional structure, with the proviso that different problems may well demand collaboration within different organizations, because just as it is beyond any one country to answer all of these problems it is also clearly beyond any one institution.

The institutional representation of security interests is also vital for giving coherence to the *idea* of Europe. Without the institutional structure provided by NATO, the EC, or the myriad of other organizations, the idea of 'Europe' and its security interests would quickly dissolve under vying national claims for resources. This explains the Eastern European insistence that NATO not be disbanded. In the absence of such institutions, the ability of Eastern Europe to remind its neighbours to the west of their security concerns would be largely lost.

The above arguments are intended to make the case for the institutionalization of European security interests which may, or may not, require the support of the North Americans. It is not, though, an argument for the *status quo*. The new security challenges in Europe clearly need a new or modified institutional response. This will involve the redefinition of the existing organizations' roles and, in some cases, the recognition that they may be moribund. With these arguments in mind, what should the purpose of a supranational security organization be in the European context? The purpose of any new security design seems to be the following: (i) To act as a safeguard against threats to international peace and security and to uphold international norms and principles. (ii) To provide an effective collective response to potential and actual conflict by intervening at the *earliest* practicable time based on a clear mandate. (iii) To provide solutions to the *root causes* of potential or known states of conflict. (iv) To construct a security network that is pan-European. (v) To provide adequate monies and resources to carry out the above.

Some of the purposes of the new European security architecture may appear to be contradictory or even impossible. They may well be; but, without a clear framework of aims or goals to act as the underpinning for the institutional representation of European security interests, the architecture lacks form or structure and will not last. Without a clear sense of purpose, any new or revamped security architecture will resemble a tent rather than a grand building.

A NEW SECURITY ARCHITECTURE?

As was observed in the previous chapter, there seems to be an almost natural tendency to cope with periods of transition in the international system by institutionalizing the emerging order and the aspirations held by the main actors – the League of Nations, founded in

1919, and the United Nations, founded in 1945, serve as the obvious examples. In modern European terms, the genesis of the search for a new European security architecture probably stems from Mikhail Gorbachev's idea of a 'common European home'.[4] Since Gorbachev's musings the idea of a 'new security architecture' has been bandied around, often with no attempt at being specific. However, in an important extension of Gorbachev's metaphor that is normally overlooked, he stated that:

> the home is common, that is true, but each family has its own apartment, and there are different entrances, too. But it is only together, collectively, and by following the sensible norms of coexistence that the Europeans can save their home, protect it against a conflagration and other calamities, make it better and safe, and maintain it in proper order.[5]

Since the coining of the term 'common home', considerable interest was shown in the structural aspects of it. The rapid pace of events since 1985 often overtook planners, yet the structures, being more inert, were subject to more scrutiny and redesigning and the 'common home' was soon replaced with talk of 'pillars' and 'bridges'. The idea of a European pillar dates back to President Kennedy, who envisaged a pillar that would remain indefinitely a close transatlantic partner. From the European standpoint, 'pillar' can carry the obvious meaning of something that supports a common structure or it could mean a pillar that has more in common with the majestic, isolated columns of a Greek ruin.

Talk of *new* European security architecture is generally one that is unhelpful and confusing. It is a phrase which implies something that has been conceived, designed and constructed rather than an essentially *ad hoc* response to new security challenges.[6] Stanley Hoffmann's observation regarding foreign policy is appropriate in this context: that it is more like gardening than building. Institutions tend to evolve, given the investment of authority and responsibility, and in the absence of such qualities the institution will wither. Gardening metaphors may be more appropriate to describe the process of institution building. Nevertheless, the architectural metaphor has shown considerable persistence.

The specifics of the 'new architecture' were outlined by former Secretary of State James Baker III, in a Speech to the Berlin Press Club. In the speech he specified that,

This new architecture must have a place for old foundations and structures that remain very valuable – like NATO – while recognizing that they can also serve new collective purposes. The new architecture must continue the construction of institutions – like the European Community – that can help draw together the West while serving as an open door to the East.[7]

Baker also stressed that an essential element of the new architecture is that 'America's security – politically, militarily and economically – remains linked to Europe's security. The United States and Canada also share Europe's neighborhood.'[8] The metaphor seems to be here to stay since it reappeared in Baker's speech to the Aspen Institute in Berlin on 18 June 1991. In the Aspen speech he elaborated upon the architecture for a new Europe and a new Atlanticism. The goal of the new architecture was outlined as fulfilling the 'long-established NATO goal, from the 1967 Harmel Report, of achieving a "just and lasting peaceful order in Europe"'.[9] In order to achieve this goal Baker specified three tasks: (i) to promote Euro-Atlantic political and economic values; (ii) to establish the components of cooperative security for a Europe whole and free; (iii) to demonstrate how integration can cope with new dangers from old enmities.

Although the idea of security architecture seems to have appealed mainly to American writers and commentators, this is by no means exclusive. For instance, Johan Jørgen Holst, Norway's Defence Minister, used the idea of an open village in Europe, 'where inhabitants choose their preferred dwellings, and where life depends on cooperation, tolerance, division of labour, mutual respect and restraint; a village where serfdom has been abolished and which maintains open gates to the outside world, rather than the forbidding walls of a fortress Europe'.[10]

What is striking about the various renditions of the new security architecture is the implicit assumption that European and Atlantic values are necessarily synonymous. There is a strong argument to be made for a future role for the US in Europe but it is one that will be radically different from the role it occupied in the Cold War years. There are two reasons for this: first, Europe still needs the US for the immediate future, but as European strength and confidence grows with further integration and the construction of a distinct European security voice, so too will the need for an active US military role decline; second, the major area of US foreign and security policy concentration in the Cold War era was largely upon Europe – Europe was the 'prize' in the Cold War struggle. Now US attention is far more diffuse and is leaning towards the Pacific rim.

Beyond the generalities of the catch-all phrase, there appears to be little coherence about the exact nature of the architectural design. Documents from the State Department and other official bodies, such as NATO, content themselves by talking of a 'network of interlocking institutions'. Normally this involves specific reference to NATO, the EC and the CSCE, although others are sometimes thrown in for good measure, such as the Council of Europe, the WEU, NACC and even the OECD.

What is *not* discussed within the parameters of the design is the UN. This can largely be explained in terms of US objections to the voting system in the UN and the funding assessments. Seven UN members contribute just over 70 per cent of the budget, while 150 smaller contributors account for just under 30 per cent of the budget. Yet, the seven main contributors have only nine votes, while the small contributors account for 150 votes, on budgetary matters.[11] In spite of President Bush's proclamation of a 'new world order', of which the UN is a central feature, there would seem to be a general preference on the part of the US and its allies to work through alternative international organizations such as NATO or the CSCE.[12] The new world order would seem largely divorced from the European security architecture.

The new European security architecture is uneasily constructed around a group of institutions whose aims are converging (see Appendix I, Figure A.1); yet, at the same time, each institution is fighting to preserve its specific area of competence. Above all, the US's conception of the architecture is that it should build a structure around NATO and thus guarantee the US's self-appointed role as leader. Other institutions either offer the US a vastly diminished role, such as the CSCE, or no role at all, as in the case of the WEU or EU. For this reason, the US is particularly enthusiastic about ensuring that NATO provides 'the core security functions in a new Europe'.[13] While the Bush and Clinton administrations have responded to some of the changed circumstances in Europe, with changes in force levels and strategy, the more significant reassessments regarding the US role in Europe have been resisted. By way of contrast, the conclusions reached in many Western European capitals about the post-Cold War security agenda and institutional representation are more fundamental.

The precise role of NATO is one that has been subject to much scrutiny in the last few years.[14] Most of the literature on NATO in the post-Cold War era recognizes the need for a thorough revamp. The assumption is that, whatever NATO's shortcomings, it is still of use and can be adapted to the changed security circumstances of post-Cold War Europe. Such assumptions are most closely held by American thinkers who, in some cases, reflect an attachment to NATO which derives from the fact that it is the US that has run it. The literature devoted to the study of European defence initiatives is much smaller and tends to be either historical, focusing upon the attempts to establish a European Defence Community in 1954,[15] or the more recent studies[16] that focus upon attempts to construct a European security identity, more often than not within NATO, but sometimes as a deliberate alternative.

Advocates of NATO tend to point to its success in maintaining the peace for forty-five years, while failing to acknowledge that it may not be the most suitable organization to meet the very different security challenges posed by post-Cold War Europe. NATO is first a military alliance and is therefore ill-equipped to deal with more general security problems; and, second, it is an organization that risks becoming anachronistic in the light of the stubborn refusal to make NATO relevant to the post-Cold War world by redrawing its area of interest. The very success of NATO in containing the Soviet military threat has become its biggest weakness.

The end of the Cold War clearly makes the idea of adversarial blocs outdated, yet such blocs remain the basis of NATO. Far from acting as a catalyst for knitting the blocs together, NATO may become a major impediment to attempts to form pan-European security ties. Furthermore, the idea of 'interlocking institutions' as the basis of the new security architecture is acceptable only with the assumption that the various institutions are complementary. This is debatable: NATO has become closely associated with advocates of transatlanticism and thus is a challenge to European options. In the wider context, NATO may not be the most suitable vehicle for expanding security to the pan-European context, since it remains an alliance and represents, particularly for Russia, significant adverserial images.

What should the role of NATO be in relation to the other components of the European Security Architecture? NATO has an essential role to play as a transitional manager between the current *ad hoc* security arrangements and an institution that will eventually put responsibility for Europe's defence in European hands. The argument that NATO should be a transitional manager is based upon two notions: first, that the European and CIS countries are not in a position to adopt a security policy independent of the US at this time; and, second, that the US cannot rely indefinitely upon the unwavering support of all of its allies for help in its wider global concerns. It has become almost sacrilegious to suggest that NATO has limited utility in the long term, but it is an institution that was intended to answer the exigencies of the Cold War world and was not intended to be a permanent institution – that accolade went to the United Nations.

It would, however, be premature to rush immediately into a European security organization that excluded North American participation. The dangers of placing too much hope in the Maastricht Treaty's foundations for a future common defence were well illustrated by the Danish referendum of 2 June 1992, where Denmark refused to ratify the Treaty of Maastricht and thereby threatened the whole process of European integration.[17] In spite of the eventual passage of the Maastricht Treaty through all twelve members' legislatures, the enthusiasm for integration in sensitive areas, such as security and immigration policy (often referred to as areas of 'high politics'), is not shared equally. The initial Danish rejection of the Maastricht Treaty illustrates something that had hitherto been ignored, or at least downplayed, by many European leaders: that there is a fundamental lack of unity in European security. Both the Gulf War and the ongoing civil war in the former Yugoslavia serve as examples of disunity and impotence respectively. The Gulf War saw the Belgians refusing to sell 155mm ammunition to the Gulf-bound British forces, and German prevarication about what role, if any, was appropriate for Europe's strongest power. The Yugoslav crisis, which included a Dutch initiative for an EC sponsored 'peace force', was hastily undermined by early German recognition of the breakaway Yugoslav republics of Croatia and Slovenia – a move which created irritation in several European capitals.

While reliance upon a European security order is premature, long-term reliance upon the US for leadership and major financial and military contributions would be just as unwise. The successful cooperation of the coalition forces during the Gulf War has lulled some into a false sense of security. Notwithstanding the coalition cooperation in the Gulf, the overall history of collaboration between the US and its European allies in out-of-area conflicts has generally been unhappy. The fact that the US still holds global foreign and security policy goals alongside severe domestic economic malaise means that the US will rely increasingly upon its allies for political and financial support for goals that they may not be willing to share. In this sense the 1991 Gulf War must be regarded as an exception to the rule, and there is nothing to suggest that future coalitions will be formed behind the US with finance coming from other sources with the same ease – the paralysis in Bosnia serves as a fitting counterpoint.

CONCLUSION

Institutions by themselves cannot provide the answers to Europe's security challenges, but they can provide a framework for discussion and collaboration. The initiative and will to make an institution work must come from states' willingness to work through institutions and not to circumvent or ignore them. The fact that there is an ongoing discussion about designing and building institutions which represent a collective desire to face the security challenges of the post-Cold War period is highly significant. The considerable volume of articles and books devoted to various types of security architecture suggests that there is a strongly entrenched need to find collective solutions to security problems which can best be addressed in an institutional setting.

The use of the term 'new security architecture' is widespread but confusing. There is little that is new; most architectural designs are based upon adaptations of existing institutions. Even 'new' organizations, such as the suggestions for a European Security Organization,[18] or a West European Defence Community,[19] are either based upon existing institutions or owe a conceptual debt to existing institutions such as the CSCE and WEU.

The advocacy of one institution against another reflects an individual state's conceptualization of security challenges and its envisaged role within the structure. James Baker III and Warren Christopher's advocacy of NATO's central role had as much to do with the Bush or Clinton administration's assessment of NATO's utility as it did with the US's self-appointed leadership role. The problem of leadership and initiative is one that will to a large extent influence which of the various security institutions will flourish and which will wither, as well as the extent to which they reflect a transatlantic or European bias in terms of membership and agenda.

7 Euro-Confusion

BUILDING EURO-MODELS: ROUND ONE

The first coherent post-war voicing of a 'European' attempt to gain a security identity was made by René Pleven, the French prime minister, in 1950. The impetus for the initiative was the problem of how to rearm Germany and how to design an institutional setting that would satisfy German demands to be able to provide for their own defence (or at least make a contribution), while also assuaging French fears of a recrudescence of German militarism. An additional area of uncertainty was how long the US would maintain troops in Europe, for until 1950 the assumption in Washington was that the presence of US military personnel in Europe was a temporary measure, pending the creation of a Western European defence entity.[1] Although the emphasis has changed, the same basic concerns can be found in the early 1990s.

The Pleven Plan called for the creation of 'the common defence of Europe by a European Army under political institutions of a united Europe'. Pleven's plan emanated from the Assembly of the Council of Europe's resolution of 11 August 1950, that there be the immediate creation of a unified European Army.[2] Significantly, the plan called for contingents to be supplied by those participating 'on the level of the smallest possible unit'.[3] The integrated forces would be controlled by a European minister of defence who, in turn, would be responsible to a Common Assembly and a Council of Ministers. The European Army would, according to Pleven, operate in accordance with the undertakings of the Atlantic Pact.

Whilst it seemed perfectly reasonable to expect Germany to eventually assume some of the burden for Europe's defence, the French nevertheless remained nervous about the prospect of rearming Germany so soon after a major war. After seemingly endless debates, the EDC, along with its often forgotten companion, the European Political Community, became a victim of the French Assemblée Nationale on 30 August 1954.

There are many reasons for the failure of the EDC, amongst them being the problem of relations between the EDC Council and NATO, the Truman (and later Eisenhower) administrations attitudes toward European integration, and French nervousness at the prospect of German

215

rearmament. Perhaps the most important reason to emerge was that a European Army, which included a German contribution, was unappetizing without active British involvement as a counterweight to Germany. In a precursor to the debates about European security in the Post-Cold War world, Britian played a pivotal role, balancing between Europe and the US. In a revealing meeting in November 1951 between Prime Minister Winston Churchill's Foreign Secretary, Anthony Eden, and General Eisenhower, then SACEUR, the ambiguity felt by both countries toward the EDC was captured in a description of the meeting given by Eden to Churchill:

> I met with General Eisenhower on the morning of November 27th...
> He thought we should do all in our power to encourage the European Army, but, if we were to offer to enter it at this stage, we should further complicate the budgetary and other technical arrangements and would delay rather than hasten a final solution. Moreover, in his view, we and the United States could be more effective as elements supporting the European army within [NATO].[4]

Britain did offer 'association' and 'close relations' with the EDC, but full membership was resisted on the grounds that the EDC was a vehicle, at least to French and Italian minds, paving the way toward full federation. The debates taking place over the EDC between 1951 and 1954 provide an interesting parallel to the debates arising from the Maastricht Treaty and the resolution to move toward a common European defence as part of European Union. The position of the individual countries toward the EDC has changed surprisingly little. The eventual failure of the EDC also swung the general pattern of integration away from the federalist model towards a functionalist one, whereby integration would take place by functional areas, commencing with those areas of *least* direct threat to state sovereignty.

The failure of the EDC left Germany's security role unresolved. In order to address this problem a conference was convened, on the initiative of Sir Anthony Eden. The Nine Power conference, convened at Lancaster House on 28 September 1954, proved to be historical.[5] The Final Act of the London Conference was signed at the Paris Conference, held on 20–22 October 1955. The most significant features of the Paris Accords were:[6] (i) The governments of the UK, France and the US ended the Occupation Regime, revoked the Occupation Statute and abolished the Allied High Commission. (ii) Germany (and Italy) were invited to accede to the Brussels Treaty – which became the Western European Union. (iii) The German Chancellor agreed to a voluntary self-imposed restriction upon the *manufacture* of specified types of armaments, which included nuclear, chemical and biological weapons, missiles, warships and strategic bombers. (iv) The NATO members present at the conference undertook to recommend German membership of the Alliance at the next Council meeting. In accordance with the final point, the North Atlantic Council met on 23 October and voted for German membership to NATO. German membership was subsequently formalized on 5 May 1955. The WEU assumed primary responsibility for the legal and political facets of German rearmament, while NATO assumed responsibility for the military and operational aspects of the German military.

French acquiescence to Germany's membership of the WEU and NATO was not a simple task. The French prime minister, Pierre Mendès-France had been determined to extract every concession for French sensitivities. It was a surprise announcement by the British Foreign Secretary, Sir Anthony Eden, that ultimately swung French approval. During the London Conference Eden gave an assurance that Britain would maintain on the mainland of Europe four divisions and a Tactical Air Force 'for so long as the majority of the Brussels Treaty powers desired it'. He added, that: 'My colleagues will realize that what I have announced is for us a formidable step to take. You all know that ours is above all an island story. We are still an island people in thought and tradition, whatever the modern facts of weapons and strategy may compel.'[7] It was this commitment that changed the way the French thought of a German military contribution to the defence of Europe. A further comfort to the French was the fact that all of the German forces were to come under the authority of the Supreme Allied Commander, Europe (SACEUR).

The division of responsibility between the WEU and NATO ensured that for most of the period from 1954 until the late 1980s the WEU would be condemned to obscurity and NATO would become the only serious security game in town. The WEU was to remain dormant for much of the Cold War and it was not until the mid 1980s that the WEU, along with the other 'Euro' institutions (CSCE, the Council of Europe, the IEPG, the Eurogroup, and the EC) began playing a more assertive role. NATO is now struggling to retain its centre-stage position and to justify its existence in a changed Europe.

BUILDING EURO-MODELS: ROUND TWO

The history of European defence integration is of relevance to the current discussions promoting the creation of a European security identity since themes seem to be reappearing. The French position regarding the EDC seems to echo their nervousness over the post-Cold War European security picture with a strong Germany at the centre, Britain as the reluctant ally (at least in European ventures), and the US rapidly scaling down its commitment to Europe. However, the parallels should not be overdrawn since it has already been argued that there are significant differences between Germany in the 1990s and in the 1940s. It was the presence of a significant, overbearing military threat to Western Europe that led to the British commitment and to the earlier US military presence in Europe. The questions regarding Germany's role were certainly important, but secondary. With the virtual disappearance of this threat the questions of 'European defence' have re-emerged. With the tentative pushes toward the definition of a European security identity, much confusion has also been generated; not the least of the problems is which country(ies), working through which institution(s), should be empowered to represent 'European' defence interests.

NATO has been joined by a host of other institutions, all vying for a role – the choices range from the CSCE, the WEU, the EC, the Council of Europe, or a combination of any of these. The Rome Declaration on Peace and Cooperation, issued by the North Atlantic Council in November 1991, recognized the contribution that other bodies could make but was not forthcoming about how responsibilities should be apportioned:

> The challenges we will face in this new Europe cannot be comprehensively addressed by one institution alone, but only in a *framework of interlocking institutions tying together the countries of Europe and North America* ... The development of a European security identity and defence role, reflected in the further strengthening of the European pillar *within* the Alliance, will reinforce the integrity and effectiveness of the Alliance. The enhancement of the role and responsibility of the European members is an important basis for the transformation of the Alliance.[8]

The implicit assumption of the interlocking institutions model is that NATO should be the centre and that any enhanced European security collaboration should take place within this setting. Furthermore, the primary responsibility for enhancing the role of the Alliance was placed upon the European NATO members. This assumption may be flawed in several ways: the assumption of a greater role by the European members could well result in demands for commensurate leadership roles or could lead to a move away from the Alliance towards the adoption of a separate European security identity. It is also assumed that the institutions, in the structural sense, can be 'interlocked'; however, this too is an assumption worthy of challenge.

Perhaps the greatest problem with the idea of interlocking institutions and an enhanced European security role is that it assumes the existence of a European consensus. Although it is true that with the demise of the Soviet Union, the Europeans could for the first time entertain the notion of a European security entity, this has been seen by some as an adjunct to NATO, and for others a replacement. A brief period of 'Euro-optimism' following the end of the Cold War – when the idea of European security integration in the context of European Union seemed feasible – was interrupted abruptly in June 1992 when the Danish 'brake' on European integration reminded Europeans of two factors: first, that integrative efforts were easier to entertain and agree upon in a hostile Cold War environment; and, second, that change in the security environment has removed much of the urgency to integrate and collaborate. The Danish vote also seemed to confirm suspicions in Washington that the Europeans were incapable of organizing a coherent security organization which, *ipso facto*, proved the need for NATO backed by a strong US commitment.

The post-Cold War history of the institutional struggle for primacy of place is confusing, and ultimately inconclusive. However, en route, several landmarks seem to stand out: first, the June 1991 Copenhagen summit which appeared to assert the primacy of NATO; second, a setback in October 1991, in the form of an announcement by Bonn and Paris that they were creating a Eurocorps (which was seen by NATO advocates as a challenge); third, the North Atlantic Council's meeting in Rome in November and the announcement of the New Strategic Concept that seemed to reassert NATO's primacy; fourth, the following month's European Council's Maastricht meeting reopened the debate about the role of a distinct European security identity. Within each of the resultant documents arising from these meetings there is a sufficient degree of latitude of interpretation to have fuelled the institutional debate.

At the Copenhagen meeting, the Bush administration assumed that it had firmly asserted NATO's key role, and that any other European initiatives were in support of and subordinate to NATO. In a statement issued by the North Atlantic Council at Copenhagen on 6–7 June 1991, it was agreed that 'NATO is the *essential forum* for consultation among the Allies and the forum for agreement on policies bearing on the security and defence commitments of its members under the

Washington Treaty'.[9] But, far from being definitive, the Copenhagen meeting merely prepared the way for the ensuing debates about NATO's role. For example, the following passage also appeared in the Copenhagen statement:

> A transformed Alliance constitutes an essential element in the new architecture of an undivided Europe; we are agreed that the Alliance must have the flexibility to continue to develop and evolve as the security situation dictates. An important basis for this transformation is the agreement of all Allies to enhance the role and responsibility of the European members. We welcome further efforts to strengthen the security dimension in the process of European integration and recognize the significance of the progress made by the European Community towards the goal of political union, including the development of a common foreign and security policy. These two positive processes are mutually reinforcing...[10]

However, the Bush administration's understanding of the Copenhagen statement was soon upset in institutional terms by a joint letter from Chancellor Helmut Kohl and President François Mitterrand on 14 October 1991, proposing that a European force be built out of the existing 4200-man Franco–German brigade. At the same time they also proposed that European security be strengthened by the enlargement of the WEU to include Greece, Denmark and Ireland, the latter in observer status.[11] There was also talk of a European *corps*, which created the impression that there would be a joint Franco–German force of some 40 000 to 50 000 troops[12] which, it was hoped, would form the crux of a European *army* to which other WEU members would contribute.

The meeting of the North Atlantic Council in Rome in November 1991, where the Alliance's New Strategic Concept was outlined, seemed to represent a swing of the pendulum back toward NATO. The language of the Rome Declaration leaves no doubt about the importance of this partnership when it states, 'NATO embodies the transatlantic link by which the security of North America is *permanently* tied to the security of Europe', and that 'the presence of North American conventional and US nuclear forces in Europe remains vital to the security of Europe, which is *inseparably* linked to that of North America', that 'NATO is the essential forum for consultation among the Allies and that '[the Alliance] provide[s] one of the *indispensable* foundations for a stable security environment in Europe'.[13] Not only was the New Strategic Concept intended to confirm NATO's primacy, but it was also intended to limit the potential security role of the EC.

While the New Strategic Concept may seem to have asserted NATO's primacy, it also encouraged the development of a European Security Identity (ESI) which would have an 'important role to play in enhancing the Allies' ability to work together in the common defence'.[14] The endorsement of the necessity for ESI would seem to challenge NATO's continuing primacy, particularly since such an identity seems to imply a consultative mechanism that would encourage pre-shaped 'European' and 'American' positions within NATO's consultative organs.

The failure to establish a network of interlocking institutions could be seen in the lead up to the Maastricht Summit of 9–10 December 1991. Prior to the meeting the British were enthusiastically promoting the WEU, as a way to keep the EC *out* of security issues while the French were promoting the WEU with the objective of using it as a conduit to get the EC involved *in* security matters.

Any hope that the European Council would resolve the NATO/ESI struggle dissipated with the publication of the Maastricht Agreement. On foreign policy all agreed to closer cooperation, but also agreed that foreign policy should be left outside the formal EC structure. On defence it was agreed that there should be, at some unspecified point in the future, 'the framing of a common defence policy, which might in time lead to a common defence'.[15] It was also recognized that the WEU is an 'integral part of the European Union' that may 'request... the WEU to elaborate and implement decisions and actions of the Union which have defence implications'.[16] This sufficiently ambiguous outcome left the security implications open to interpretation; the French arguing that this clearly meant that the WEU is subordinate to the European Union and the British taking the opposite view. In addition to the British preference for preserving the special relationship with the US, other reservations about a common foreign and security policy were voiced by Denmark and Portugal.

The Provisions on a Common Foreign and Security Policy agreed upon by the European Council at Maastricht were sufficiently vague to placate the British, Italians and Dutch, who were afraid of anything that may be openly perceived to be a challenge to NATO. The provisions also satisfied the Franco–German aspirations for an extensive European policy coordination mechanism. The Provisions stated, amongst other things, that:

> Member States shall support the Union's external and security policy actively and unreservedly in a spirit of loyalty and mutual solidarity. They shall refrain from any action which is contrary to the interests of the Union or likely to impair its effectiveness as a cohesive force in international relations.[17]

It also stated that:

> Member states shall inform and consult one another within the Council on any matter of foreign and security policy of general interest in order to ensure that their combined influence is exerted as effectively as possible by means of concerted and convergent action.[18]

The wording of these two key articles was made suitably innocuous to please everyone, but it also reassured Washington that the Rome Declaration still held true – that NATO was still the essential forum for consultation.

In spite of the ambiguous outcome of the Maastricht summit, the WEU emerged as the basis for the organization of a European security identity – with a lesser, but significant role being prescribed to the CSCE. In spite of its ambiguities, the Maastricht Treaty established the momentum for a move towards ESI of which the Franco–German corps was to be the practical embodiment.

The Rome Declaration on Peace and Cooperation of November 1991, as well as the Declarations of the WEU at Maastricht, led the North Atlantic Council at Oslo to support the 'objective of developing the WEU as the defence component of the European Union and as a means of strengthening the European pillar of the Atlantic Alliance'.[19] This still leaves open the potential for disharmony; the development of the former and the formulation of a specific European security agenda will not necessarily complement the security concerns and issues of the North American NATO members. Optimistically, the Oslo communiqué declared that the 'common understanding laid down in the Rome Declaration on Peace and Cooperation, and the agreement reached by the member states of the European Community and in the Declarations of the Western European Union at Maastricht, establish the basis of the future relationship between the Alliance and the emerging European security and defence identity'.[20] There may be 'common understanding' in the sense that the papers have been signed and filed, but in practical terms it seems that there is a distinct *lack* of common understanding, let alone complementarily and transparency.

The confusion about what exactly was implied by the Maastricht Treaty for European security was further muddied as a result of a meeting at La Rochelle, in May 1992, between Kohl and Mitterrand. It was agreed at this meeting that the new 'Eurocorps' (as it was optimistically referred to in Bonn and Paris) would be based in Strasbourg and be ready by October 1995. The idea met with uneasy reactions in London and Rome where the Eurocorps was seen not as an adjunct but as a potential rival to NATO. Kohl has added to the confusion by referring to the Corps as being 'complementary to NATO' as well as 'part of the way to a European defence identity'.[21]

The Franco–German corps has an ambiguous role. To Germany it is a way of bringing France closer to NATO and the European pillar; to France it marked the foundation of a European force quite distinct from NATO. On balance, the French conception of the corps seems closer to reality since the accord charges the corps with primary responsibility for the support of the WEU; and, somewhat more vaguely, it 'can be used' to support NATO. It also can take part in peace-keeping missions outside Europe, although this obviously raises the aforementioned problems of German constitutional restrictions.

The subsequent Kohl/Mitterrand letter caused immediate consternation in Washington and London; and, contrary to earlier speculation, it became clear that the new force was not intended only for 'out-of-area' use but for use within Europe. This letter, alongside the fact that there was no consultation, caused outrage in Washington and London and seemed, once again, to pose a direct challenge to NATO. The ultimate effect of the letter was to put the WEU back into the fore-front of the dialogue and, unwittingly, to posit the WEU not as a complement to the Atlantic Alliance but as a competitor.

Britain felt in a particularly uncomfortable position vis-à-vis the 'Eurocorps' since John Major's government found itself torn between the need to guard against any weakening of NATO and the need to be seen as championing pro-European causes. The result of this dilemma was a plan announced by the Defence Minister, Malcolm Rifkind, on 14 May 1992, that would require WEU members to provide contingents from their national forces to cope with challenges outside the NATO area. Under this proposal there would be no standing forces, and contributions would be made only in time of emergency upon the collective authorization of the WEU Council of Ministers. From the British point of view such a design had the advantage of avoiding any permanent WEU forces or structure, of which the Franco–German corps would be a part, which could pose a challenge to NATO. The Rifkind plan came too late to influence decisively French or German attitudes toward the corps. The US continues to be suspicious of any hint of a

European security and defence identity and they have some support in these concerns from Britain, Italy and the Netherlands. Germany and France would appear to entertain the notion of a far more expansive European role.

The differing national positions on security matters is reflected in the advocacy of one security-oriented institution against another by European nations. The result of the institutional advocacy has been the opposite of the intended 'interlocking institutions'. The institutions are used for competitive ends to serve individual or group interests, which often results in needless and wasteful duplication of institutional functions. Thus, far from being interlocking, the institutional mish-mash that has resulted is one that appears to be capable of reacting to security challenges only on an ad hoc basis.

The next section examines the institutional structure of European security and considers the extent to which the institutions, individually and collectively, are equipped to meet the new and emergent challenges of the post-Cold War world.

THE EUROPEAN COMMUNITY AND THE MAASTRICHT PROCESS

The European Community has been hyped as an alternative security organization since the 1986 Single European Act (SEA) explicitly empowered the EC to deal with the 'political and economic aspects of security'.[22] A notable omission was any mention of the military aspects of security. The idea of security collaboration within the EC arose out of the process of political cooperation, going back to the 1969 Hague Summit, the 1981 London Report, and the Genscher-Colombo Plan which eventually led to the SEA. The SEA itself was soon overtaken by the Inter-Governmental Conference on political union which led up to the Maastricht Summit of December 1991. The idea of forming a Common Foreign and Security Policy (CFSP) is therefore one with a well established history and does not present a new and startling break with the past. If anything, the CFSP that has emerged out of the Maastricht Treaty is watered down compared to the proposals of the 1950s and the mid-1970s.

In spite of the long-held interest in a CFSP, which harkens back to the ill-fated EDC/EPC experiment of 1954, the process of European political cooperation has been slow to emerge. The first real milestone on the road to a CFSP was the 1986 Single European Act (SEA). The

SEA requires EC members to 'inform and consult each other' and to 'take full account of the positions of the other partners' so that they may 'endeavour jointly to formulate and implement a European foreign policy'.[23] Progress toward a CFSP then sped up dramatically as a result of, first, a series of intergovernmental conferences discussing the future of European integration after the SEA and, second, the Iraqi invasion of Kuwait in August 1990. The conferences took place not in a mood of enthusiasm, but of exasperation at the slow progress toward integration. The drawing up of the Maastricht Treaty with its economic and political components, which would hopefully fuse together to make the European Union, was an attempt to kick-start the Community back into life (see Appendix I, Figure A.2).

The Iraqi invasion of Kuwait accelerated the discussions on the formation of a CFSP, but reservations were soon shown about the speed and depth of integration in these areas: the Benelux countries, Germany, Greece and Italy were enthusiastic supporters of a common foreign policy, with some reservations about security policy; and the Irish were concerned that a common foreign policy may be tied to a common security policy, which would compromise their neutrality. Although the concept of neutrality has since lost much of its meaning with the demise of the Warsaw Pact and the Soviet Union, it may still become an issue as other neutral or non-aligned nations apply for EC membership (Austria, Finland and Sweden). Other countries, such as Britain and Denmark, expressed reservations that the political aspects of European Union were running ahead too fast and that a common European security policy may be seen as an open challenge to the US.

The results of the intergovernmental conference and Operation Desert Storm gave coherence to the CFSP, which found expression in the 1991 Maastricht Summit, the main features of which can be summarized as: (i) CFSP is to include all questions of foreign and security policy. (ii) CFSP is to include the 'eventual framing' of a common security policy which 'might in time' lead to a common defence. (iii) CFSP would make allowance for the specific character of member states' security and defence policies. (iv) Cooperation on issues of defence are to take place only on the basis of unanimity. (v) The WEU is to be an integral part of the European Union which may carry out decisions and actions with defensive implications. The above points appear in Title V, Article J of the Maastricht Treaty, entitled 'Provisions on a Common Foreign and Security Policy'. The CFSP forms one of the pillars of the European Union.[24] Article J.1 is careful to point out the intergovernmental nature of the CFSP when it states that, 'The

Union *and its Member States* shall define and implement a common foreign and security policy.' The CFSP is also somewhat unusual since, unlike the other components of the union, it is not officially part of it since it is not subject to the same decision-making procedures, nor is it subject to judicial review by the European Court of Justice.

The objectives of the CFSP are laid out in Article J.1. These include the safeguarding 'of common values, fundamental interests and independence of the Union', to strengthen 'the security of the Union', to 'preserve peace and strengthen international security', to 'promote international cooperation', and to 'develop and consolidate democracy and the rule of law, and respect for human rights and fundamental freedoms'. The coordinating role for joint action 'in matters covered by foreign and security policy' falls to the Council. The Council (of the Union) decides, 'on the basis of general guidelines from the European Council, that a matter should be the subject of joint action' (Article J.3). Under Article J.6 the president of the Council shall 'represent the Union in matters coming within the common foreign and security policy'.

Most significant of all, it was agreed in Article J.4 that the CFSP shall include 'all questions related to the security of the Union, including the eventual framing of a common defence policy, which might in time lead to a common defence'. The somewhat curious wording of this important article recognizes the aspirations of those who are willing to coordinate foreign and defence policy but who wish to retain control over their foreign-policy apparatus and their armed forces, and those with more federalist aspirations. The Maastricht Treaty also 'requests the WEU to 'elaborate and implement decisions and actions of the Union which have defence implications'. The WEU is considered to be an integral part of the development of the Union and, as such, is expected to play an important role. As is observed in the section below, this is a relationship that is not without its difficulties and weaknesses. In terms of public opinion and support for the EC assuming responsibility for foreign and security policy there are some notable trends (see Table 7.1).

A majority in the EC seems to place more confidence in the EC assuming a security role, rather than a foreign-policy role. This could perhaps be explained by the tendency of Europeans to think in terms of foreign policy as a national preoccupation, while the likelihood of any one EC country using its military alone seems slim and thus lends itself more readily to integration. There are in some cases significant majorities in favour of the EC assuming more responsibility for secur-

Table 7.1 Are you in favour of the EC, as a political union, assuming responsibility for foreign policy towards countries outside the EC, or for a common security and defence policy? (%)

Country	Foreign		Security	
	yes	*no*	*yes*	*no*
Belgium	62	17	72	13
Denmark	48	43	52	40
Germany				
West	61	23	71	14
East	61	25	83	9
FRG	61	23	73	13
Greece	58	23	65	20
Spain	56	18	65	12
France	59	27	73	17
Ireland	49	24	47	29
Italy	73	8	78	7
Luxembourg	66	18	72	13
Netherlands	64	24	82	10
Portugal	58	14	68	8
UK	44	38	55	31
EC 12	59	23	70	16
EC 12+	59	23	70	16

Note: Difference between 'yes' and 'no' columns is the percentage of 'don't know's'.

Source: *Eurobarometer*, No. 37 (Brussels: Commission of the European Communities, June 1992) A.49.

ity policy, especially France, Italy and the Benelux countries. As one would expect, there is less enthusiasm for such a development in Ireland, due to their neutralist sentiments, and in Britain. There are also notably more people in Ireland and Britain who are unsure about the wisdom of a CFSP. Table 7.1 indicates overall a strong public preference for the adoption of a CFSP.

The adoption of a CFSP has pros and cons. On the pro side, the CFSP provides a necessary complement to the economic and political integration between the twelve EU members. The adoption of a CFSP may also provide the best response to the problems of accommodating Germany, tying German power to other European powers, and providing a forum for discussing Germany's foreign-policy concerns, such as Eastern Europe's desire for a closer relationship with the EC.

Although full membership of the EC, or NATO, is on the cards for the Eastern European aspirants, the EC is critical to providing a supportive environment for these countries and for advancing the dialogue within Europe.

Another positive aspect of a CFSP is the potential for developing non-military schemes. As 'security' moves away from its traditional links with the military towards a far wider conceptual basis, the EC has an important role to play in promoting awareness of non-military aspects of security and particularly those with an economic bias. The importance of the EC in this regard was recognized in July 1989, when the EC Commission, under Jacques Delors, was given prime responsibility by the G7 for the coordination of OECD aid to Hungary and Poland. Other EC bodies with a pan-European flavour, such as the European Environmental Agency and the European Energy Community, complement the EC's security role. The formation of the European Bank for Reconstruction and Development (EBRD), which was the first major post-Cold War pan-European institution to be established, also serves to underline the importance of the link between economic stability and security.[25] Freer access to the EC countries by the Eastern and Central European countries would undoubtedly help to stabilize their fragile economies but would pose serious problems for the EC and, in particular, the Common Agricultural Policy (CAP).[26]

The consultative machinery that exists at ministerial level in the EC is far more advanced and developed than that of NATO. The Davignon report and the move towards creating a European Political Community in the 1970s bore fruit in the 1986 Single European Act (SEA). The regular consultations in the EU are complemented by the biannual European Council meetings, which have played an important role in shaping the political and foreign policy stance of the twelve members since 1974.[27] The Council has assumed increasing importance within the EC, making decisions that the Council of Ministers has been unable to make. The Council has not only initiated major changes within the EC, but has acted as a foreign-policy coordinator, even coordinating security issues. It could be argued that the basis for a CFSP has in fact existed in the European Council for almost two decades and that Maastricht goals merely gave *de facto* recognition to the process.

The overall logic of the CFSP is that the close integration of the economies of the EC (and maybe the majority of the EFTA members) provides the impetus or 'spillover' for integration in other areas, namely security. To integrate economic and fiscal policy without the eventual

framing of a CFSP seems to make little sense to functiona
EC already coordinates its policies on external trade relatio
the GATT negotiations or economic relations with the Africa
bean and Pacific countries under the Lomé Convention, and ι ᴜnds
the collective interests of member states.

However, the problems with the CFSP also have to be acknowledged. While the biannual European summits have served a useful purpose
for defining broad goals, the EC has proven ponderous and indecisive
when decisions have to be taken rapidly – the wavering over what
should be done following the Iraqi invasion of Kuwait in August 1990
and, more recently, in the Yugoslav crisis,[28] are not encouraging por-
tents. In both cases it was the WEU that gave the strongest lead in
responding to these incidents. The functionalist theory that integration
spills over from one area of state activity into another can also be
challenged. Areas that have traditionally been regarded as 'high politics', such as defence and security policy, have met with far more
resistance towards integration than other areas, such as trade; the idea
that because individual countries accept the integration of their economies they will therefore accept the integration of their national armies
into a European army, is one that must be treated with scepticism.

Even if spillover is treated at face value, spillover from one area of
state activity to another depends upon the success of the initial stages
of integration. Thus the move towards a CFSP depends upon the success
of economic integration and the formation of a single market. The
virtual collapse of the European Monetary System, the delayed and
incomplete implementation of the Schengen Accords, which were intended to guarantee the free movement of people, the decline in the
German economy and the negotiation of opt-out clauses on major areas
of economic and social policy,[29] puts the future of European economic
integration in doubt – and thus that of the integration process as a whole.

The features of the projected CFSP, outlined in points (iii) and (iv)
above, also give cause for concern. By making allowance for the specific
security interests of individual states *as well as* stressing that cooperation on defence should only take place on the basis of unanimity, many
of Europe's more pressing security concerns would be precluded. Even
these seemingly simple prerequisites may prove immensely difficult
for the EC to fulfil, given the different historical and geographical
preoccupations of its individual countries. The formation of a CFSP
would incorporate many of Europe's problems, such as the Irish quag-
mire with Britain, Denmark's irresolute attitude towards NATO, and

Greece's defence policies, which seem to conflict with most other EC members'. Consensus may be virtually impossible to achieve on many issues and, even if a common position is found, disagreement on who should finance the resultant course of action and who should donate what forces (which may again come up against the German constitutional problem) may hobble the chances of action actually being taken.

Another problem area is the relationship between the WEU and the EC. This is touched upon in more detail below, but suffice it to say at this stage that the adoption of the WEU as the EC's 'security arm' at the Maastricht summit was not supported enthusiastically by all members. The current WEU/EC relationship is a compromise between the British, who wanted to keep them apart, and the French and Germans who wanted a closer relationship between the two.

Whether the bid to create a CFSP will be successful depends not only on internal factors, but also upon external pressures. The profound changes in Europe caught the European Community at a point of transition in its history away from its image as the 'Common Market' toward something far more profound – a European Union with federalist underpinnings. The collapse of Communist regimes in Eastern Europe and beyond poses the 'deepening' or 'widening' dilemma for the Community.[30] Should the Community deepen, in other words, to push political and economic integration between the existing twelve members? Or should it widen, that is, admit new members from elsewhere in Europe and risk ending up with a diluted Community?

The choices between widening or deepening have been modified by the reforms in Eastern and Central Europe. Often they are presented as mutually exclusive; resistance to widening Europe is often justified on the grounds that deepening must assume priority. It may be possible to combine elements of both by moving towards an expanded Community and include the former EFTA members as well as some Eastern European countries, while also pursuing the Maastricht goals leading to European Union. The newer members could be included in the strictly economic aspects of the EC's work, while decisions on participation in other areas of the Community's activities could be postponed until a later date. The chances of many current EC members achieving the rigorous economic terms laid down in the SEA for the creation of the single market are slim; for the prospective Eastern European members the chances are even slimmer. The solution to the deepening or widening dilemma is to create a two-tier Europe (which is happening anyway) that moves at different paces towards a single market. The core group of twelve could at the same time pursue integration beyond the economic arena, to include political and security integration.[31] The deepening aspect of the Community's work is not of utmost importance to the Eastern Europeans. For them it is more important to be given guaranteed access to the EC markets by a certain date. Failure to do this on the part of the EC may well crush any hopes of overcoming the challenges the fragile democracies have with their parlous economies, which may result in further disintegration and violent ethnic struggle in the east.

The Community also finds itself in the strange situation of preaching the Delorsian creed of integration and pushing federalism within the community when, at the same time, the changes in Eastern Europe have given nationalism a new respectability. It is by no means clear how the Eastern Europeans and some of the new ex-Soviet republics will balance their apparent enthusiasm for integration with Western Europe with their desire to guard their new found freedoms jealously. Membership of any European 'club' carries with it costs which have to be acknowledged and faced early on by each Eastern European country.

The positive and negative aspects of the CFSP seem to lead to the conclusion that the EC is not a particularly effective actor in the narrower sense of security – when defined in its military way – but is an immensely important actor in every other meaning of the word. Military security would best be left, at least for the moment, to those security organizations that have forces dedicated to them, such as NATO or the WEU. It is these organizations that should explore ways of working through the CSCE. In many senses the military security worries are lesser worries than those of managing change in Eastern Europe. If the transition to democracy and economic stability fail, then the questions of military guarantees become relevant. Of greater importance to the stability of Eastern Europe is a closer association with the EC, for economic stability, backed by security guarantees from NATO.

THE WEU: THE EC'S 'SECURITY BRANCH'

The problems with the EC adopting a security role, some of which have been touched on above, led to a compromise between those who were less than enthusiastic about the political union part of European Union, and those who wanted to emphasize the political aspects of the EC. The result of the compromise was the incorporation of the WEU into the European integration process in the Maastricht Treaty. By this treaty the WEU became the EC's security branch. The merger, however, is not formal since full integration depends upon a review which will take place in 1996, two years before the WEU Treaty expires.

The WEU assumed importance as a security actor with the advent of the operations in the Gulf following the Iraqi invasion of Kuwait. Several countries, such as Belgium, Italy, the Netherlands and Spain, insisted that any military action be coordinated by the WEU. By the second week of August, there was 'a general expectation in Europe that the WEU would be the pivotal European organization with regard to the military aspects of the question, taking the place of the defence arm that the EC lacked in reconciling British and French positions, in providing a focus for states' contributions and in coordinating the activities of NATO's European members'.[32] The WEU, it was argued, was also more suited to play the role of a 'pivotal' organization, since the EC was burdened with differences over whether the formation of an EC security identity would be seen as a challenge to the US and an attempt to undermine NATO (see Appendix I, Figure A.3).

The WEU, in its 1987 *Platform on Security Interests*, had given itself the task of reinforcing the European pillar within NATO. To others, particularly the French, the WEU was a symbol of an existing institution which, if closely allied to the EC, could eventually serve as the foundation for a European security identity. It was as a result of the EC's failure to deal with the security issues posed in the period following Saddam Hussein's invasion of Kuwait that the WEU became the existential security identity of the EC. There were those who clearly hoped to promote this linkage as a deliberate policy while others hoped that, by working through the WEU, the European pillar of NATO would be strengthened at a time when it seemed to be crumbling.

The WEU was especially helpful as far as the French were concerned. It offered a solution to the problem of how the French could contribute to any military operations in the Gulf without openly giving the appearance of following US leadership. As is their usual practice, Paris insisted that all French forces be under French command and serve only French national interests; that stated, the French could comfortably follow the overall US leadership in the Gulf. By chance, France also happened to hold the WEU presidency at the time. Operations Desert Shield and Desert Storm enabled France to promote the WEU and to forge explicit links between the EC and the WEU. By inviting the EC members to attend a WEU meeting on 21 August 1990 (the three non-WEU members at that time being Denmark, Greece and Ireland) the links were reinforced. The number of occasions on which foreign ministers went immediately from meetings in one forum to meetings in the other forum as they attempted to show that Europe was a significant element in the international response to events in the Gulf'.[33] As a result of the expanding links between the two organizations, the WEU ministers agreed in February 1991 that, *in principle*, the WEU should become a bridge between NATO and the EC.

The Yugoslav crisis also served to solidify the EC–WEU links. The EC initially enjoyed more success in coordinating its action than did the WEU in the Yugoslavia crisis. Part of this was due to the fact that the EC had more leverage with Yugoslavia than it did with Iraq. For instance, in the spring of 1991 the EC notified the Yugoslav federal authorities that any intervention could lead to the cancellation of EC credits and assistance. In spite of attempts from May to November to exert pressure through the threat of sanctions, that resulted in the removal of Yugoslavia from the EC's general preference system, there is little evidence to suggest that sanctions had any significant effect upon the behaviour of the various parties to the Yugoslav conflict. The EC also attempted to broker a ceasefire, initially headed by Lord Peter Carrington and later by Lord David Owen and Cyrus Vance. However, there was no agreement on a further course of action beyond these mediatory attempts.

When the issue of military intervention was broached, it was again to the WEU that the EC turned. The EC foreign ministers and the WEU met in the Hague on 19 September 1991, with the intention of finding ways to strengthen the monitoring operations. Trevor Salmon noted that this meeting was of special significance, since it 'broke new ground in the relationship between the EC and the WEU, and it became clear over the next few weeks that the WEU was, on this matter at least, becoming the military arm of the EC'.[34] There was little agreement at the meeting about what kind of strengthening and intervention would be appropriate. Britain drew the provocative analogy with Northern Ireland and the fear that this could bog down forces in an interminable conflict. This position elicited sympathy from other countries with separatist problems, such as Spain. Proposals that the WEU could be used to open land corridors for the relief of the Bosnians were rapidly dismissed by Britain as well. Germany advocated military intervention but was unclear about what its own role would be, given the constitutional restrictions on its own involvement (see Chapter 4). Germany further alienated its EC colleagues by prematurely recognizing Croatia and Slovenia. In the end, both the Gulf and the Yugoslav crises had the effect of reinforcing the role of the WEU as the somewhat ineffectual security extension of the EC.

By the Maastricht Summit in December 1991, the idea of the WEU as 'an integral part of the development of the Union' was firmly embedded. Under Article J.4(2) the WEU was charged with responsibility 'to elaborate and implement decisions and actions of the Union which have defence implications', and it was agreed that the Council shall in 'collaboration with the WEU, adopt the necessary practical arrangements'. The tasks with defence implications were outlined as: humanitarian and rescue tasks; peace-keeping; crisis management, including peace-making; implementation of UN/CSCE resolutions or decisions. The wording of Article J.4(2) is curious since it gives the WEU responsibility 'to elaborate and implement', but leaves open the question of who exactly takes the decisions. Furthermore the idea of the WEU being an 'integral' part of the development of the Union may create problems for the WEU's relations with NATO. Since the re-awakening of the WEU in 1984, there have been attempts not only to make the institution an adjunct of the EC but also to portray it as being intimately linked to NATO, as the embodiment of the 'European pillar' of the Alliance.

Article J.4(4) specified that the CFSP of the Union shall not prejudice 'the specific character of the security and defence policy of certain Member States and shall respect the obligations of certain Member States under the North Atlantic Treaty and be compatible with the common security and defence policy established within that framework'. The reference to certain members largely points to present or future neutral or non-aligned members of the Union, such as Ireland. They shall have the right to continue their defence stances, but it remains unclear how they fit in with this pillar of the Union. Article J.4(5) stated that the development of closer cooperation between 'two or more Member States on a bilateral level, in the framework of the WEU and the Atlantic Alliance' is permissible, 'provided such cooperation does not run counter to or impede that in [Title V]'. This article does little to resolve one of the central problems of the idea of a 'common defence' which is that some members, like Ireland or France, will inevitably prefer to work through one or none of the institutions. Furthermore it is difficult to see how member states shall 'support the Union's external and security policy actively and unreservedly in a spirit of loyalty and mutual solidarity' (Article J.1(4)), without contradicting those rights laid out in Article J.4(5).

Under the terms of the Maastricht Treaty the WEU is an 'integral part' of the development of the Union. At the same time as the Maastricht Treaty was signed, the WEU agreed to a 'Declaration of the Member

States of the WEU which are also members of the European Union on the role of the WEU and its relations with the European Union and with the Atlantic Alliance'. Under the terms of this document it was agreed that the objective is to 'build up the WEU in stages as the defence component of the European Union, as well as to 'develop the WEU as a means to strengthen the European pillar of the Atlantic Alliance'. Also worthy of note is that the WEU agreed to 'act in conformity with the positions adopted in the Atlantic Alliance'.[35] In order to achieve these aims the WEU proposed to synchronize its meetings with those of the Union, to establish close relations between the Council and Secretariat-General of the WEU on the one hand, and those of the Council of the Union and the Secretariat-General of the Council on the other. Efforts will also be made to harmonize the sequence and duration of the respective presidencies. Having agreed to these changes, the WEU also agreed in the Declaration to synchronize dates and venues of the WEU with those of the Alliance where necessary, as well as establishing closer cooperation between the Secretariats-General of the WEU and NATO. In order to facilitate the strengthening of the WEU's new role the seat of the WEU Council and Secretariat will be transferred to Brussels. The dual loyalty to both the Union and the Alliance leaves the Maastricht Treaty in an unhappy dilemma: is the goal eventually to change the defence relations of the WEU from the Alliance to the Union? If not, does the WEU assume that in every circumstance it will be able to represent the interest of *both* the Alliance and the Union? These are unresolved questions and could lead to acute institutional schizophrenia in the WEU or, worse, the collapse of the WEU as it is torn between conflicting loyalties.

It would be unfair to attribute the WEU's potential institutional schizophrenia solely to the Maastricht process. Since the WEU was been awoken from its prolonged slumber in the mid-1980s it has been pulled in various directions. In 1987, when the WEU Council was extended to include not only foreign ministers but defence ministers as well, the WEU became an important discussion forum. That same year saw the Hague meeting and the announcement of the WEU's programmatic basis in the Platform on European Security Interests. This document made it abundantly clear that the WEU was in no way, shape or form intended to be an alternative to NATO, when it stated that, 'The security of the Alliance is indivisible. The partnership between the two sides of the Atlantic rests on the twin foundations of shared values and interests.'[36] The seeds of possible institutional schizophrenia were sown in the same document when it stated that the WEU Council intended to develop a 'more cohesive European defence identity which will translate more effectively into practice the obligations of solidarity to which we are committed through the modified Brussels and North Atlantic Treaties'.[37]

Historically, the evolution of the WEU has also been more closely tied to that of NATO than to European integration. The Convention on the Presence of Foreign Forces in the Federal Republic of Germany, signed on 23 October 1954, stated that, 'The present convention shall enter into force when all of the signatory states have made such deposit and the instrument of Accession of the Federal Republic of Germany to the North Atlantic Treaty has been deposited with the government of the United States of America.'[38] A subsequent document, the Protocol of the North Atlantic Treaty signed on the Accession of the Federal Republic of Germany, stated that the entry into force of the protocol was dependent upon acceptance by each of the parties of the North Atlantic Treaty, successful ratification and deposit of the Protocol Modifying and Completing the Brussels Treaty with the Belgian Government, and ratification by all parties of the above Convention on the Presence of Foreign Forces in the FRG.[39] The intention, at least legally and historically, therefore seems to have been to build the WEU as an adjunct to NATO. However, the precise purpose and identity of the WEU, if it was indeed intended to be a mere extension of NATO, was never spelt out. The prolonged thirty-year period of WEU inactivity can largely be accounted for by the failure of the WEU to establish a clear sense of purpose and identity or, some would argue, NATO's reluctance to allow the WEU to assume a distinguishable role.

With the awakening of the WEU in the mid-1980s, the debate over its purpose and its relations with other organizations arose. In a Europe that was much changed from the 1950s, the WEU began to be pulled between those determined to use the WEU to promote a distinctly European security entity and those determined to use the WEU to strengthen the European pillar of the Alliance. The British and the Dutch are champions of the latter position, while the French and some of the Benelux nations have been more in favour of the former. Some, like Germany, appear to waver between the two positions.

Putting to one side the concerns about the relationship between the WEU and other institutions, there are also potential problems within the WEU related to membership. The WEU has extended to ten full members, three associate members, and two members with observer status.[40] With a largely overlapping membership, the tendency for the

WEU to be used to present NATO with a *fait accompli* as a way of advancing a 'Euro' agenda or securing North American compliance is a real danger. The process could, of course, work the other way around as well, with the US presenting the WEU with a *fait accompli*.

On the strictly military level the WEU's links with NATO have been forged through the proposed WEU Rapid Reaction Force which, it is hoped, could become the out-of-area legs for NATO. The benefit of this design is that it would bring France back into the fold. It is possible that the WEU Rapid Reaction Force could be the same as the NATO one, minus the US and Canadian contributions and adding a French one. The commander, if from a WEU country, could also be the same person in different 'hats'.[41] The idea, whilst it may have a superficial appeal, would involve considerable investment in infrastructure and equipment (such as lift capacity). In the absence of such investment the WEU would, ironically, be heavily reliant upon NATO and especially American logisitical capabilities to intervene anywhere outside of the NATO area.

The Petersberg Declaration attempted to answer some of the shortcomings of the WEU.[42] The declaration emphasized the interdependent nature of the European Security Architecture, especially the 'importance of strengthening the role and institutions of the CSCE for peace and security in Europe'.[43] The declaration also stressed that the WEU, 'together with the European Union, was ready to play a full part in building Europe's security architecture'.[44] At several points in the declaration, the integral role of the WEU in the Maastricht process leading to European Union was stressed, as was the need for close working relations with the Atlantic Alliance. It was also agreed that WEU members could not invoke the military assistance clause of the revised Brussels Treaty (1954), nor could Article V of the North Atlantic Treaty be invoked against a WEU member. The assumption that the various institutions are complementary was assumed throughout.

On the issue of membership there have been some advances. On the afternoon of the Petersberg meeting the foreign and defence ministers of the nine WEU members were joined by those of Czechoslovakia, Hungary, Poland, Bulgaria, Romania and the Baltic states. The ministers of the nine, along with those from Central Europe agreed that, 'In view of the profound changes in Europe of the last few years, intensifying the relations between WEU and the States of Central Europe will contribute to stability and the emergence of a new peaceful order in Europe based on partnership and cooperation, greater security and confidence, as well as disarmament.'[45] The dialogue between the WEU members and Central and Eastern European countries was formalized in a Forum for Consultation, consisting of the WEU Permanent Council and the Ambassadors of non-member Central European countries.[46] The forum meets at least twice a year (it met at Ambassadorial level in October 1992 and in April 1993). The forum is designed to: (i) explain the WEU's role and activities; (ii) provide a *specifically* European framework for the discussion of security issues of common concern; (iii) build cooperation with Central Europe.

Whilst helpful, the forum runs the risk of, first, duplicating some of NACC's tasks and, secondly, offering a discussion forum but not membership. The risks of creating a dialogue with no commitments may eventually endanger the entire process. It is difficult to persuade Central European officials that WEU members are sincere, especially when they show no compunction to do anything, except in self-interest.

The Petersberg Declaration also attempted to clarify the WEU's role as the defence component of the European Union and as the European pillar of the Alliance. All members agreed to make available military units from 'the whole spectrum of their *conventional* armed forces for military tasks conducted under the authority of the WEU'.[47] Decisions to use military forces answerable to the WEU will be taken by the WEU Council in accordance with the UN Charter. The military units will be drawn from the forces of the members states, which includes those forces with a NATO mission, but only 'after consultation with NATO'.[48] Furthermore, all forces will be organized on a multinational and multi-service basis and member states will designate which of their units and headquarters they are willing to make available to the WEU for its possible tasks. The tasks, which merely reiterate those applying to the Maastricht process, are identified as humanitarian and rescue tasks, peace-keeping, crisis management and peace-making. However, the Petersberg Declaration contains some carefully worded language that suggests that there is nothing automatic about WEU intervention and that special efforts have been made to accommodate the constitutional sensitivities of the Germans, the bristles that the French demonstrate towards NATO, and the British devotion to the transatlantic alliance:

> Ministers acknowledged that the WEU will be one of the essential elements of the future European security architecture in accordance with the decisions taken by the European Council in the Maastricht Declaration. We are prepared to support, on a case-by-case basis

and in accordance with our own procedures, the effective implementation of conflict prevention and crisis management measures,
including peacekeeping activities of the CSCE or the United Nations
Security Council.[49]

The number of caveats in the Declaration suggests that, far from
implying any automatic response to conflict, there may (or may not)
be a response, depending upon where the conflict is and whose interests
are involved. The considerable problem of how the WEU would be
able physically to move military forces without logistical assistance
from NATO was only briefly addressed when the declaration stated
that the WEU members 'intend to develop and exercise the appropriate capabilities to enable the deployment of WEU military units by
land, sea or air to accomplish these tasks'.[50]

Stipulations regarding WEU membership were also outlined in the
declaration. Full membership of the WEU is only on offer to states
that are members of the European Union – this led to Greece assuming full membership in November 1992, and Ireland and Denmark
becoming observers at the same time. Other European member states
of NATO were invited, at the 23 June 1992 Bonn meeting, to become
associate members of the WEU 'in a way which would give them a
possibility of participating fully in the activities of the WEU'.[51] This
offer led to Iceland, Norway and Turkey becoming associate members
of the WEU. Limited membership or even observer status was not on
offer to the Central Europeans. The issue of membership raises the
interesting question of whether Greece, with full membership, will block
Turkey's accession to full membership.

As part of the implementation of the Maastricht Declaration the IEPG[52]
and the Eurogroup had agreed to analyse their respective roles in the
new European Security Architecture and the possibility of moving these
institutions to the WEU from NATO.[53] In November 1992 the WEU
ministers agreed to transfer to the WEU the role of the Independent
European Programme Group (IEPG), with the eventual aim of creating a
European Armaments Agency. The activities of the Eurogroup were transferred to the WEU at the same time as the IEPG, a move which started in
1994. The move of the IEPG to the WEU outlines the importance and
significance of collaborative arms reductions and, as a result, the need
for careful control of where arms are sold to. There are potentially
negative aspects to this move; one in particular deserves mentioning.

The move of the IEPG and Eurogroup from NATO to the WEU in
effect further 'Europeanizes' the WEU, and places what has traditionally

been a contentious field between the US and its European allies into a specifically European network. Removing the IEPG from NATO may lead to an increased tendency to think in terms of 'European' and 'American' interests and to think of NATO as the Atlanticist institution, and the WEU as the European institution. An example of this is the WEU's attempt to establish a WEU Satellite Centre at Torrejon (Spain). The contract for the feasibility study was awarded to a 'consortium of firms from WEU member states led by Germany'.[54]

The removal of the IEPG from the NATO context may frustrate US attempts to compete for arms contracts in Europe and elsewhere. The growth in the number of collaborative European arms production projects (see Table 7.2) may pose serious competition for the US in the world's dwindling arms markets. Competition in this field, exacerbated by the more general strains within GATT and the G7, may have deleterious spin-offs on security relations between the US and Europe.

The future development of the WEU and its relations with other security institutions depends largely upon whether it is perceived as an adjunct to NATO or the centre of a Euro-alternative to the transatlantic ties. The evolution of the WEU–NATO relationship should, in theory, complement the 'network of interlocking institutions', but for several reasons it may work in the opposite way. The WEU *and* NATO operations in the Adriatic in 1992, serve as an example not only of wasteful duplication, but of the potential for institutional turf fights, in which all institutions suffer. Some of the potential problem areas between the WEU and NATO are as follows:

(1) The evolution of the WEU as an alternative to NATO and US influence, where the WEU becomes an adjunct or pillar within NATO. Much of this problem stems from the confusion about whether the move towards European Union, of which the WEU is an integral part, involves the adoption of a European security *policy* or the construction of a European security *structure.*

(2) The non-WEU members of NATO may feel compelled to follow the Alliance for the sake of solidarity. This could breed resentment and distrust. The opposite must also be guarded against.

(3) The granting of associate WEU status to Iceland, Norway and Turkey could exacerbate tendencies for those who are not full members to play off one organization against the other. Similarly, membership of one organization, and not the other, could be highly destabilizing.

The avoidance of these problems will involve close collaboration and consultation. Embarrassing and counterproductive incidents such as the

WEU and NATO deployments to the Adriatic need to be avoided. Some of the problems faced by the WEU and NATO are shared, especially that of membership. The reluctance to extend WEU membership to the east poses the question of the utility of the *Western* European Union covering ten full members who pose no threat to each other, when the threat of instability comes from outside these countries? In common with other institutions, the WEU has been reluctant to extend security guarantees eastwards and remains primarily geared towards meeting military threats to security.

Even in the military realm, there are some severe shortcomings. Two in particular stand out:

(1) The scaling down of the European militaries will mean increasing reliance upon active German participation. Any such reliance may run into problems with the aforementioned constitutional issue.
(2) The British, French and Germans possess little in the way of air and sea lift. There has been a traditional reliance upon the US for the bulk of Western Europe's lift capacity. To give the WEU the 'legs' to intervene in trouble spots will require either a considerable investment in lift capacity at a time when military budgets are being cut, or the use of the WEU as an instrument to arrive at agreed positions which will then be presented to NATO.

The next section considers the role of the nascent Franco–German corps, sometimes dubbed the 'Eurocorps'. The corps will have a direct bearing on the effectiveness and even the future of the WEU since the primary role of the corps falls within the WEU context.

THE FRANCO–GERMAN CORPS: AN EXPENSIVE LANGUAGE SCHOOL?[55]

Much media space and discussion has been devoted to the Franco–German corps. It is seized upon either as a symbol of European defence cooperation and the way of the future, or as an attempt to undermine NATO. Furthermore, it is often presented as a sudden, audacious step which has posed a direct challenge to the US and more generally NATO. However, there is a history of French initiatives aimed at building a West European consensus on European security issues. This history stems from the special position of the French vis-à-vis NATO and the need, since 1966, to work through distinctly European channels.

Franco–German security collaboration is a relatively recent phenomenon.

Table 7.2 European defence collaboration

	UK	France	Germany	Belgium	Netherlands	Turkey	Spain	Italy
Aircraft								
European fighter aircraft	*			*				*
European future large aircraft	*	*	*			*	*	*
Tilt rotor technology	*	*	*				*	*
Multi-role combat aircraft (Tornado)	*		*					*
Helicopters								
NH-90 (naval)		*	*		*			*
Light attack helicopters	*	*			*		*	*
Euro consortium helicopters (Tiger, formerly PAH-2)	*	*	*					
Missiles								
3rd generation anti-tank	*	*	*	+	+		+	*
Family of anti-air system	*	*						
Modular surface-to-air		*						
Anti-tank		*	*					
MILAN, anti-armour		*	*					
ROLAND, surface-to-air		*	*					*

RM-5, surface-to-air		*	*	
Point defence missile system		*	*	
Hypervelocity missile		*	*	
Other				
EMPAR	*	*		*
BREVEL	*	*	*	*
MLRS	*	*	*	*

* = committed
+ = uncommitted

EMPAR: European multifunctional Phased-array radar
BREVEL: Reconnaissance drone
MLRS: Multiple Launch Rocket System

Source: Issue Paper, 'US and European Defense Industries: Changing Forces for Cooperation and Competition', 1992 (Washington D.C.: AAAS Program on Science, Arms Control and National Security) p. 6.

244 The New European Security Disorder

The 1963 Elysée Treaty, which provided for extensive consultations between France and Germany on security matters, is taken as evidence that security relations were close.[56] In spite of the superficial closeness of Franco–German relations in this period, there were severe differences until the 1980s. Throughout the period from the 1960s to the 1980s their respective security policies were pulling in diametrically opposed directions. The differences included the following:

(1) German integration into the NATO framework, compared to French attempts to distance itself from NATO and the US as much as possible.
(2) Differing visions of European integration, with Germany in favour of extensive integration with federal overtones and France in favour of collaboration through national authorities but not necessarily full supranational integration.
(3) Germany actively cultivated close ties with the US, whereas France remained cold and, on occasion, hostile to Washington.
(4) Relations between Britain and France were strained through most of the 1960s and 1970s. De Gaulle portrayed Britain as being America's 'Trojan Horse' while Germany supported Britain's two unsuccessful attempts to join the European Community.
(5) Germany's long-term aim, as enshrined in the Basic Law, was to unify the two parts of Germany. France saw unification as a development to be discouraged.

Differences aside, integration at the foreign policy level was pursued quietly between President Valéry Giscard d'Estaing and Chancellor Helmut Schmidt. Integration was facilitated by détente which opened a vigorous dialogue with the Soviet Union. For Giscard d'Estaing, détente was a chance to rid French foreign policy of some of its Gaullist vestiges as well as intensify French relations with Germany. However, relations in the security area were not as close as they could have been due to French criticism of London and Bonn's desire to avoid a direct confrontation with Washington and Franco–German differences over the utility of France's Hexagon nuclear forces.[57]

Attempts at constructing a Franco–German platform on defence and security issues had to wait until the early 1980s. Two factors induced a significant change in the dialogue which led to the intensification of Franco–German security relations: first, the debate over the Dual Track decision made by the North Atlantic Council in December 1979 provoked a crisis in East–West relations as well as a crisis between the US and its European allies; and, second, Helmut Schmidt and Giscard d'Estaing were replaced during this crisis by Helmut Kohl and François Mitterrand respectively. The latter manoeuvre was determined to intensify relations with Kohl both as a means to resist Soviet pressure and to curtail US influence within NATO. Thus the French used the INF dispute as a vehicle for intensifying European links. Kohl, for his part, was anxious to use Mitterrand's support for the INF deployments as a means of defeating the West German Socialists, who were bitterly opposed to the deployments. In return, Mitterrand saw his support for Kohl as a chance to take away some of the US influence over European security policy.

The year after Mitterrand was elected, 1982, the defence component of the 1963 Elysée Treaty was eventually implemented.[58] As a result of mutual anxieties felt by Bonn and Paris that the US was reducing its commitment to Europe, Mitterrand agreed, at a Franco–German summit held on 24–25 February, to intensify bilateral defence coordination in view of worsening East–West relations.[59] A further meeting was held in October of that same year and, as a result of this meeting, the defence clauses of the Elysée Treaty were implemented. The agreement effectively extended the French national sanctuary to include virtually all of (West) Germany.[60] The implementation of the Elysée Treaty and the 1982 agreements had three significant consequences. First, the conventional shortcomings of the French forces and their ability to intervene rapidly were improved by the 1983 Defence Programme Law for the years 1984–88. Under this law, the Force d'Action Rapide (FAR) was created.[61] The force of around 45 000 troops was intended to intervene rapidly into the FRG, to a distance of up to 250 kilometres, where it would reinforce the French First Army. Since it also had Third World intervention ability, FAR was not exclusively for German deployment, yet the timing of its formation indicated a clear nod in the German direction.

Second, the implementation of these agreements led to the creation of a Joint Committee for Security and Defence, which was later upgraded by a supplementary protocol to the Elysée Treaty for a Joint Defence Council (JDC) on 22 January 1988.[62] The JDC first met in April 1989 and has been meeting continuously since then with the objective of harmonizing national military policy and operational plans. It has also served to underline areas of common security interest as well as areas of discord between the countries. A dramatic example of the lack of closeness on essential security issues was illustrated by the fact that shortly after the first JDC meeting, unknown to the French, Foreign Minister Hans-Dietrich Genscher and Defence Minister Gerhard

Stoltenberg made a trip to Washington with the purpose of inducing the Americans to begin negotiations as soon as possible on the reduction of short-range nuclear weapons in Europe.[63] The lack of consultation led to a crisis in the Alliance, which was defused by the May 1989 NATO Summit in Brussels. The incident served to illustrate that as long as France remained outside NATO's integrated military command, they could have little real influence upon nuclear policy.

Nuclear questions remained the most divisive ones in the JDC, but did not, however, hinder integration in the conventional sphere. Under the auspices of the JDC the idea of a joint Franco–German brigade was first discussed, and it was decided that, by the end of 1990, a joint brigade should be formed consisting of 4200 soldiers with its headquarters in Baden-Württemberg and under rotating German and French command.[64] Indeed, since 1985 the foreign and defence ministers of the two countries have met at least three times per year to discuss matters of common security concern.

Third, these agreements have meant that under Mitterrand and the conservative prime minister, Jacques Chirac, some of the Gaullist tenets of French security have been undone. The idea of national autonomy has been rejected in favour of a commitment to the forward defence of the FRG. The reversal of Gaullist tendencies in French strategy was to make explicit the ties between France and Germany, which in turn would serve three purposes. It would (i) firmly anchor Germany in Western Europe; (ii) provide France with its traditional shield against the east; (iii) contain any German tendencies to drift towards Central Europe and away from the West.

The commitment to a forward defence of the FRG raised problems for France regarding the French nuclear forces: would they too be included in the guarantee and, if so, what kind of consultation over their use could Germany expect? Laurent Fabius, the president of the Assemblée Nationale, argued that it was 'now necessary to consider the extension of our strategic nuclear guarantee to German security'.[65] Following the reorganization of French nuclear forces in 1983, under Defence Minister Charles Hernu, the non-strategic forces had been placed directly under the orders of the chief of joint staffs. This move was either intended to reassure the allies (particularly Germany) that intervention on their behalf would be conventional, at least initially, or it was intended to heighten the deterrent effect of the nuclear forces by signalling that the deployment of conventional forces could be independent of the use of its nuclear forces. The issue of whether a French nuclear guarantee could be extended to Germany was one that had been raised by Helmut Schmidt who was in favour of uniting the militaries, including the nuclear forces, under French leadership.[66] Under Hernu's reorganization, the French tactical weapons (renamed *armes pré-stratégiques* in 1984 in order to stress the link between tactical and strategic weapons) were virtually independent from the land forces (*Corps de Bataille*) to whom they had formerly been linked. In response to German anxieties about what the reorganization may mean for the defence of the FRG, an agreement was reached on 28 February 1986, by which President Mitterrand promised:

> within the limits imposed by the extreme rapidity of such decisions, the President of the French Republic is prepared to *consult* the Chancellor of the Federal Republic of Germany on the possible use of French pre-strategic weapons on German territory.[67]

Although the agreement did little more than apply the terms of NATO's 1962 Athens Guidelines, which specified the conditions for the use of US nuclear weapons from NATO host countries, it was nevertheless a significant gesture. The nuclear guarantees given to Germany were greeted enthusiastically by conservatives within the Ministry of Defence since they signified the potential for a significant shift away from dependence on the US, with whom they found themselves increasingly at loggerheads. Hans-Dietrich Genscher and the Free Democrats (FDP) were also anxious to use the intensified Franco–German security relations to increase their room for manoeuvre vis-à-vis Washington – although this did not go as far as endorsing a European defence system run along French lines. It should be noted that Mitterrand disliked the idea of explicit and binding agreements which could compromise the ability of France to use the weapons in its own self-defence, as did the US with those host nations with US nuclear weapons.

The agreement was not seen to restrict French options since there was a promise only to consult, not to seek consent and, even then, only if time and circumstances permitted. The policy relevance of the agreement was soon apparent to all when on two separate occasions, both in front of the Institut des hautes études de défense nationale, Jacques Chirac made an explicit statement about the security ties between the two countries. In September 1986 Prime Minister Chirac stated that, '[France's] increased awareness of the European dimensions of her security, allows her to explore independently the ways and means of a strengthening of deterrence in Europe ... If our nation's survival is at stake at our frontiers, our security is already at stake at the frontiers of our neighbours.'[68] Later in December 1987, Chirac was more specific about which neighbours he had in mind, when he stated, 'Were West Germany to be the victim of aggression, who can now doubt that France's commitment would be immediate and whole-hearted? There cannot be a battle of Germany and a battle of France.'[69]

Charles Hernu's reorganization of the French nuclear forces was also a response to German anxieties about the short-range Pluton missile. These anxieties led France to decide to replace the Pluton missile with the Hadès missile.[70] The replacement had a range of around 350 kilometres, which was still not enough to alleviate the German anxieties that, in the event of war, they would be the unhappy recipients of nuclear missiles that were intended for their defence. This led, in 1988, to the extension of the range of Hadès to a range of 500 kilometres, accompanied by a guarantee from President Mitterrand that the use of *armes pré-stratégique* would not take place on West German soil. The role of nuclear weapons will continue to be a problem since the French still view them as a positive contribution to European security, especially in light of US drawdowns. The Germans, as argued above, have not been enthusiastic about nuclear weapons that would potentially be used on their soil, yet the value of their deterrent effect was recognized during the Cold War years.

In military terms Franco–German cooperation continued into the late eighties. In 1987, during the *Kecker Spatz* military exercises, which involved the joint manoeuvres of 75 000 troops (55 000 German and 20 000 French), French rapid reaction forces (*force d'action rapide*) served under German command. The formation of the Franco–German brigade in 1990 was a formalization of cooperation and collaboration that had already started. The Franco–German brigade, soon to be corps, did not however exist in isolation. It was part of a wider attempt to build a European security identity that would be compatible with NATO as well as meet some of the anticipated changes of the Post-Cold War period.

The US reductions of its military forces in Germany, along with those of the other NATO allies, left France with the problem of dealing with Germany's three 'isms': nationalism, neutralism and pacifism. Since the tearing down of the Berlin Wall and the unification of Germany, these three 'isms' have been very much in evidence. The formation of close diplomatic and military ties between France and Germany is aimed at restricting these three tendencies. The security ties that have been formed between Bonn and Paris will become all the more important to Paris in light of the US force reductions in Europe.

Of great significance to Franco–German security relations was the advent of Mikhail Gorbachev to power. In the period 1985–89, Gorbachev was fundamentally to reorient French and German foreign and security policies in the following ways: (i) The gradual diminution of direct military threats reoriented attention away from the Soviet threat and, in the German case, led to preoccupation with the possibility of unification. (ii) The reforms in the Soviet Union and Eastern Europe meant that the US no longer held as much influence as it had enjoyed over European security affairs. (iii) The general process of European integration beyond the economic aspects could be accelerated, which included the formulation of a stronger European security identity.

In spite of the significant changes and the dramatic downgrading of the military threats to Western Europe, neither France nor Germany is willing to advocate the removal of US troops from Europe. German concerns relate to the fact that Germany was not ready to assume an active security role without the US. Kohl has stated on numerous occasions that the North American military presence in Europe is 'of vital importance', and that it provides an 'indispensable security link between Europe and North America'.[71] French concerns in relation to US troops in Europe stem from historical discomfort at being left alone with Germany.

While France and Germany intensified their bilateral ties, they were also active in promoting the WEU as the European embodiment of a common security identity. The rejuvenation of the WEU in 1984, which met at the defence and foreign minister level, arose out of the controversy surrounding the GLCM and Pershing II deployments, which had been agreed to as a result of the 1979 Dual Track decision. The 1986 Reykjavík summit between Gorbachev and Reagan prompted concerns about US–European decoupling and also strengthened the WEU. Prime Minister Chirac observed after the Reykjavík summit that the superpowers were making decisions which could have significant effects upon European security with scant regard for European opinion on the issues involved. The March 1987 *Platform on European Security Interests* (discussed in more detail above) maintained that European integration would remain incomplete until a security dimension was added; this would later be reflected in the 1991 Maastricht Treaty.

The revival of the WEU and the 1987 *Platform* were the multilateral justifications for the formation of a close security relationship between France and Germany, although cooperation was not intended to be exclusive but was intended to extend to other European allies. That the WEU had become the multilateral embodiment of the European security identity idea was left in little doubt when, in early November

1991, the French and Germans announced a major increase in their troops committed to the WEU from 5000 to 30 000.[72]

The increasingly visible role of the WEU and the formation of the Franco–German brigade did not initially provoke much public comment. Soon after its formation private concerns turned into consternation when, on 22 May 1992, Chancellor Kohl and President Mitterrand announced at the conclusion of a meeting in La Rochelle, France, that they had approved the formation of a 35 000 strong joint army corps (consisting of one French armoured division and two German mechanized brigades) with the eventual aim of turning it into the nucleus of a European army. The corps, with its new headquarters in Strasbourg will become active on 1 October 1995. It is charged with three main responsibilities: (i) European defence; (ii) peace-keeping outside Europe; (iii) humanitarian tasks. The announcement also contained an invitation for any of the other WEU members to join. Only three, Spain, Luxembourg and Belgium have shown interest, while Britain remains resolutely critical. The Netherlands has also raised doubts that the new corps would duplicate existing NATO functions and raise defence expenditure at a time when reductions are being sought. Fears that the Eurocorps would create a head-on challenge to NATO have been refuted by both Mitterrand and Kohl. The former stated, 'We want the presence of Americans in Europe. We know what we owe NATO.' Kohl, using a more forceful answer, replied that, 'We're doing what the Americans have asked us to do for years – be able to assure our own defences.'[73]

It would appear, at least judging from a note that President Bush's National Security Adviser, Brent Scowcroft, sent to his counterpart at the German Chancellery, that this development was not entirely welcome.[74] Washington's objections were varied. The first charge was that the formation of the corps violated the Rome Agreement, signed by NATO members the previous November, which endorsed the idea of a European identity in the security and defence realms which would 'underline the preparedness of the Europeans to take a greater share or responsibility for their security and will reinforce transatlantic solidarity'.[75] In Washington's opinion the corps violated the last part of the statement: the corps did not demonstrably reinforce transatlantic solidarity. There were also private warnings that the construction of such a corps outside of NATO could result in the weakening of US domestic support for NATO and encourage a withdrawal. Warnings have also been given from Washington about trading US guarantees for French ones. One US official, without sparing words, said, 'The French have a second-rate nuclear deterrent, a third-rate real-time intelligence capability and a third-rate conventional army... For years to come, European security will exist only with the Americans in place.'[76]

The British line has not been as outspoken as Washington's. The Defence Minister, Malcolm Rifkind, merely commented that 'the criteria we will apply is whether it will strengthen or weaken NATO'.[77] The issue caught the British at a difficult time since it presented the Prime Minister, John Major, with the simultaneous tasks of backing the Maastricht process (an issue that put his political head on the block) and sustaining the vestiges of the special relationship with the US. Italy, too, has voiced concern about the developments but is more likely to wait and see which way the wind blows before making a decisive pronouncement.

The furore surrounding the announcement of the Franco–German corps is interesting since it illustrates Washington's almost paranoid fear of real challenges to NATO arising. The French have been painted by the US as the Machiavellian plotters who are determined to undermine NATO and the US's position in Europe at almost any cost. The *National Review* showed one of the most alarmist responses of all:

> As American policy has become more conciliatory to the idea of accommodating the famous 'European identity', French policy has become worse. The French have flaunted the fact that the new Franco–German corps is outside the NATO command as a contribution to European independence from the United States and as a hedge against the day (which the French seem determined to hasten) when the Americans leave Europe... For forty years, the fact that the Bundeswehr was embedded in NATO's integrated military command has been a source of reassurance to all of Germany's neighbours. The French are deluding themselves if they think they can be an adequate counterweight to German power by themselves, without the United States.[78]

The US governmental response has not been untypical of those expressed in the above extract. Aside from factual problems, the spectre of a Europe having to face a powerful Germany on its own is once again trotted out. But, is this not exactly the point of the Franco–German corps? Was that not the point of trying to form a European Defence Community in 1954 (on that occasion with US blessing)? The French desire to find a cooperative defence arrangement with Germany is one that is understandable from historical and geographical perspectives. There has been no attempt in the criticism to move away from the actors involved, and what that may mean for NATO and the US, and to consider why the Eurocorps was felt to be necessary in the first place.

The corps was formed as a continuum in Franco–German relations and not a sudden or abrupt event. Furthermore, membership was open to all WEU countries. The necessity was predicated upon a perception of a growing (but not necessarily fatal) difference of opinion between the European allies and the US on a number of issues. These were most evident from 1985 on and did not just start in 1991. The French saw the Eurocorps as a way of involving themselves in the building of a new security arrangement that would represent European interests. The failure to modify NATO radically at the November 1991 summit also acted as an impetus to transform the brigade into a corps. The Yugoslav crisis taught a bitter lesson to Europeans, and Germans in particular, about where US interests started and stopped.

The corps, which has put Bonn in a difficult position between Paris and Washington, is not as much of a threat to NATO or US interests as is commonly portrayed, since there are still three unresolved problems that surround the corps:

(1) The relationship between the corps and NATO is ambiguous, as is that between the corps and the WEU. The accord reached between France and Germany was vague since it stated that the Eurocorps *could* be used in the NATO context, but that its *primary* role was within the WEU context. This opens up the possibility of the Germans wishing to use some of their Eurocorps forces for a NATO contingency and the French being opposed to any such use. In the event of such a situation emerging, this would raise the possibility of Bonn being torn between Paris and Washington.

(2) The second problem relates to the invitation to other WEU members to join the corps. There are significant reservations from some of the other European powers about joining the corps. The Netherlands, for example, has significant reservations about joining a corps that would be dominated by France and Germany. A major, and unlikely, contribution by the British could alleviate this problem. The term 'Eurocorps' may be very evocative, but it scarcely deserves the European adage yet.

(3) The third problem relates to the problem of Germany's constitutional restrictions (see Chapter 4). Until this problem is solved, there will be no actual Eurocorps that can achieve its mandate. Germany has framed its constitutional geographical limitations regarding the use of force specifically in terms of Article 6 of the North Atlantic

Treaty. The WEU, unlike NATO, has no specific geographical limitations on its potential area of intervention. By placing the Eurocorps unambiguously in the WEU camp, a constitutional crisis would be provoked. If agreement is not reached by the October 1995 deadline, the Eurocorps will be stillborn.

The debate over the Eurocorps has created some false assumptions about the extent to which the European militaries are integrated and the extent to which they can be integrated. There are practical problems with integration that also need to be acknowledged. Virtually every French and German weapon system is made to different specifications, which makes interoperability largely a dream. There is, however, the possibility that defence collaboration could encourage joint ventures in the defence industries.[79] The Franco–German Tiger attack helicopter, which is being co-developed and built by MBB and Aerospatiale (with Rolls-Royce engines) could be a sign of the future.[80]

The Franco–German brigade has illustrated more about US policy and attitudes than about anybody else's. The US alarm that resulted from the expressed intention to extend the Franco–German brigade from 4200 to around 35 000–50 000 reflected a primary concern of US leadership and its ability to influence European allies. The corps seemed to be sending a message to the US that it had lost its overarching influence in Europe. The puzzling part about the US's attitudes is that European self-sufficiency is exactly what successive US administrations over the last forty years had wanted. Yet, at the same time the Europeans assume more of the burden, they are supposed to recognize the US's position as *primus inter pares*. While French and German leaders are on record as supporting a continued US presence, they are also aware that through CFE and unilateral cuts the number of US troops deployed in Europe will shrink to a low level, which may imply the need for a redefinition of alliance roles and responsibilities. Thus, the Franco–German corps does not signify opposition or a conscious alternative to NATO, but merely a matter of prudence to create such a force. Washington has failed to provide an adequate answer to the Eurocorps by helping to restructure NATO, or any other organization, which would alleviate German and French security concerns that lie outside the traditional NATO area of interest. By attacking Paris and Bonn and denouncing the Eurocorps, the gulf between these European capitals and Washington can only widen.

The lack of constructive criticism and adjustments within existing organizations has also left Britain out in the cold. A clear indication from Washington that the Eurocorps was a valuable complement to

NATO – by giving the Europeans 'legs' outside of the NATO area – may help to, first accelerate a resolution of the constitutional debate in Germany and, second, involve the British and other Euro-waverers. The alternative is that NATO must *publicly* agree to use its forces in peace-keeping roles beyond its borders, which would help to alleviate German concerns.[81] Unless such a commitment is made, NATO will remain of questionable relevance to European security and initiatives and may be seen as contrary to US interests.

In an attempt to provide reassurance to European and US concerns about the Eurocorps, Mitterrand and Kohl announced on 30 November 1992 that their forces in the corps would be placed under the 'operational command' of the Atlantic Alliance in the event of a threat to Western Europe's security.[82] This position is entirely in line with Germany's position that the corps should be an adjunct to NATO. The French position remains more obscure. Presumably it could be seen as an attempt to slow down US force reductions from Europe while reassuring Britain of French intentions. Full acceptance of the corps by NATO would make it substantially easier to make progress on general French relations with the Alliance. In spite of the Franco–German efforts to reassure their NATO colleagues, the more general problems of defence integration remain, as does the constitutional problem for Germany, and the vague relation of French nuclear weapons to the corps.

8 Pan-European Options: The Conference on Security and Cooperation in Europe

The CSCE has emerged as an important security organization and deserves attention mainly because the breakdown of the bipolar confrontation in Europe has made the concerns of NATO and the WEU, organizations that evolved as a result of the instability of the early Cold War years, seem outdated.[1] To some, the CSCE promises a more representative basis for planning *European* security since it encompasses all of Europe (including the CIS) rather than just Western Europe, as well as Canada and the USA. The refusal of other European institutions to consider full membership for Eastern Europe will probably lead to pressure on the CSCE to take on much of the burden for non-military threats to European security. The CSCE is the only institution that can lay claim to being pan-European. The Prague Council meeting of January 1992 granted 'participating state' status to all former Soviet republics – thus creating a security area from Vancouver to Vladivostock which goes far beyond North America or Europe, to include Central Asia and the Far East. Significantly, the Helsinki summit of the same year took the decision to invite Japan to participate, as a non-participating state, in CSCE meetings, thereby tying together aspects of European and Asian security.

The CSCE is an institution that, in the words of the Helsinki Summit Declaration of July 1992, is devoted to 'forestall[ing] aggression and violence by addressing the root causes of problems and to prevent, manage and settle conflicts peacefully by appropriate means'. Unlike other European security institutions, the CSCE places its emphasis on the prevention of conflict – a role stressed by the addition of important new structures to CSCE over the last three years. While other institutions, like NATO, are gradually moving away from a defence-oriented mandate, they have neither the breadth of mission nor the geographical spread of CSCE; factors which could be read both as strengths and weaknesses.

FROM PARIS BACK TO HELSINKI ... AND BEYOND

The CSCE has assumed increased prominence since the Charter of
Paris for a New Europe was agreed to by thirty-four heads of state
during a meeting in November 1990 – the first summit meeting since
the historic 1975 Helsinki meeting. The Charter outlined an extra-
ordinarily wide mandate, ranging from collective security to problems concerning migrant workers. The Paris meeting was notable for
giving the CSCE process a wider institutional base (outlined below).
The new security arrangements have the fundamental objective of presenting Europe 'whole and free' with a new beginning.[2] The CSCE
was also to provide a framework for the long-term democratization
of Eastern Europe and be the future forum for the conduct of US–
European relations.

The revitalized CSCE has had enthusiastic backing from many of
the Eastern European countries, such as that given by Vàclav Havel,
the Czech President and, more recently, Jiří Dienstbier, the Czech and
Slovak Republic's foreign minister.[3] In security terms the aim of the
Paris Declaration was to move decisively away from the bloc security
system towards a collective security system and, beyond that, into something approaching President Mitterrand's somewhat elusive European
confédération which would feature a mandatory mechanism for the
peaceful settlement of disputes and the replacement of national military forces by CSCE peace-keeping forces.[4]

The CSCE has also been given backing by other institutions including NATO. In the North Atlantic Council's July 1990 London Declaration it was urged that the CSCE should 'become more prominent in
Europe's future' and that the CSCE's institutions should provide 'a
forum for wider political dialogue in a more united Europe'.[5] The London
Declaration made suggestions for the institutional machinery that they
would like to see, most of which was implemented soon after in the
Charter of Paris. In an interesting aside, the North Atlantic Council
suggested that 'the sites of these new institutions should reflect the
fact that the newly democratic countries of Central and Eastern Europe form part of the political structures of the new Europe'.[6] By the
time the CSCE met, four months after the North Atlantic Council's
London Declaration, the atmosphere was highly supportive of the extension of the CSCE's mandate and institutional apparatus.

Until the Paris Summit of 1990, the CSCE was very much a paper
organization. Only since the Paris Charter has it, in a meaningful sense,
become a permanent organization. The Charter created a Committee of
Senior Officials which meets in Prague, the Centre for Conflict Preven-

tion in Vienna, an Office for Free Elections in Warsaw, a Secretariat
in Prague and, shortly, a secretary-general. The Paris Charter of 19–21
November 1990 gave the CSCE the following institutional shape:

Institution	Function
Assembly	Delegates from the national parliaments (Strasbourg) meeting in the Council of Europe's Assembly building.[7]
Council	Ministers of foreign affairs who (variously) comprise the central forum for consultation, who consider all issues relevant to the CSCE and take appropriate decisions. Meetings held at least once a year or in emergency situations.
Committee of Senior Officials (Prague)	Prepares work of the Council, carries out the Council's decisions, reviews current issues considers relations with other international forums. Committee meetings chaired by a representative of the state whose foreign minister chaired the preceding Council meeting.
CSCE Secretariat (Prague)	Provides administrative support to the meetings of the (Prague) Council and the Committee of Senior Officials. Consists of a director, three officers and other administrative staff.
Consultative Committee	Responsible to the Council; holds meetings of the participating states which may be convened under the mechanism on unusual military activities; prepares seminars on military doctrine; holds annual implementation assessment meetings; provides a forum for the clarification of CSBMs and works under the direction of the Council, or the CSO as its agent.
Secretariat (Vienna)	Responsible to the Consultative Committee; maintains a data bank compiled on the basis of exchanged information under agreed CSBMs.
Conflict Prevention Center (Vienna)	Assists Council in reducing the risk of conflict and supports the implementation of CSBMs, exchanges military information, and helps cooperation on avoidance of hazardous incidents of a military nature.
Office for Democratic Institutions and Human Rights	Facilitates contacts and the exchange of information on elections within participating states. Facilitates implementation of the Copenhagen Document's stipulations on free and fair elections (see also Appendix I, Figure A.4).

The Paris Charter heightened the profile of the CSCE as an increasingly important security organization. For some, it has become *the* security organization; certainly in terms of scope the CSCE is the most extensive. The Paris Charter appeared at a time of relative euphoria, when the Warsaw Pact appeared to be disintegrating and the unification of Germany was still relatively fresh. The rhetoric of the Charter catches some of this optimism when it speaks of a 'new era of democracy, peace and unity in Europe' and states that the CSCE will commit the peoples of Europe to shared values – 'the steadfast commitment to democracy based on human rights and fundamental freedoms, prosperity through economic liberty and social justice, and equal security for all our countries'.[8] The Charter also claimed that the CSCE commitments must form 'the *basis* for the initiatives we are now taking to enable our nations to live in accordance with their aspirations'.[9]

Such was the enthusiasm surrounding the Charter of Paris that it was seen as a threat to other institutions, most notably NATO. Since the CSCE's Paris meeting there were frequent warnings from the British and the US that the CSCE must complement, not challenge, the core security functions of NATO. This same warning has also been stressed in subsequent North Atlantic communiqués. In an interesting mirror to the language used in the Paris Charter, the North Atlantic Council stated a year later that the core security functions of the Alliance provide 'an essential *basis* from which the Allies will be able to take full advantage of new opportunities in building the new Europe'.[10]

At a summit meeting on 9–10 July 1992 in Helsinki, the fourth follow-up meeting since the signing of the CSCE final Act in Helsinki in 1975, fifty-one heads of state[11] gave the CSCE another important boost by agreeing to transform the CSCE from a forum for East–West dialogue into a primary guarantor of stability in Post-Cold War Europe. The resultant 75-page Helsinki Summit Declaration established a four-point plan to enhance the CSCE's ability to avert crises amongst its members.[12] The four points were:

(1) The early warning phase: this concentrates on human rights issues and the building of democratic institutions as a way of forestalling conflict situations.
(2) Political management: the focus in this stage is upon measures that can be taken to encourage a non-violent end to a dispute.
(3) Specific instruments: this stage involves the use of fact-finding missions and the identification of mechanisms for the peaceful settlement of a dispute.

(4) Formal peace-keeping operations: in the event of failure of the above stages, the CSCE will agree on procedures to initiate peace-keeping operations *drawing upon the resources of other organizations, such as NATO or the WEU.*

The last point was not without contention and ambiguity. The question of control the peace-keeping forces became a heated issue. France argued that operational control should be exercised by the CSCE, while the US insisted that it should rest with NATO. The result of the debate was a messy compromise: the US is to be involved in peace-keeping operations through NATO but with the organization's authority significantly limited. Those CSCE members who are not NATO members (the majority) would be able to participate in peace-keeping operations and would not have to report to NATO commanders.

The June 1992 Helsinki Summit also saw several additions to the CSCE in addition to those outlined in the Paris Charter; the most important innovation was the creation of a High Commissioner on National Minorities.[13] The High Commissioner's mandate is to provide early warning and, in some cases, early action, in the case of tensions involving national minorities that have the potential to develop into a conflict within the CSCE area. The High Commissioner's activities will draw upon the resources of the Office for Democratic Institutions and Human Rights in Warsaw.[14] The Summit also approved of the formation of a 'Green Helmet' force which could respond to environmental disasters in Europe.

The Helsinki Summit also attempted to give substance to the idea of a network of 'interlocking institutions'. The Helsinki document laid down guidelines for the CSCE's relations with European and international organizations, but in so doing it merely confirmed that all other institutions apparently had important roles *as well*. It would obviously have been counterproductive to promote one institution or demote another, but the document promises to do little to change the basic pattern of post-Cold War state behaviour, which is to promote the institution that represents national self-interest most effectively, and not necessarily the common good. More significantly, the CSCE confirmed that it is a 'regional arrangement in the sense of Chapter VIII of the Charter of the United Nations, and as such provides an important link between European and global security. The rights and the responsibilities of the United Nations Security Council remain unaffected in their entirety.'[15] The explicit linkages between European and international security was not only important, but long overdue.

The July 1992 Helsinki Declaration represented a general outline of CSCE aims in the post-Cold War world. These general aims were to be given form in three follow-up meetings: the September 1992 Vienna Meeting launching the Forum for Security Cooperation; the October 1992 Geneva Experts' Meeting on Peaceful Settlement of Disputes; which put forward mandatory third-party conciliation; and the December 1992 Stockholm CSCE ministerial meeting.

The Vienna meeting (then consisting of 51 members) saw an ambitious development in the CSCE's Post-Cold War role, in the form of the Forum for Security Cooperation (FSC). The FSC's mandate is to promote an enhanced dialogue on military issues, defence conversion, non-proliferation, and regional disputes; to harmonize arms control and disarmament obligations between the CSCE members, and to promote CSBMs and transparency between the members respective militaries; to promote conflict prevention.[16] The FSC set itself ambitious goals at the meeting, where special attention was paid to proliferation issues. In addition, global exchanges of military information were agreed upon, and enhanced transparency in force planning and structure. The exchange of information on defence conversion and promoting regional security information, was also discussed. The meeting reached a general consensus that a new generation of CSBMs are required for crisis-management purposes. The aim is to move towards automatic application of the consensus-minus-one principle in all cases involving a clear and persistent violation of the CSCE commitments regarding military security, which presumably would include not just interstate behaviour but intrastate as well. The success of the FSC obviously depends upon the cooperation of all its members as well as the ability to oversee a broad range of activities.

The Vienna meeting stressed the CSCE's arms-control role, most notably in the context of the CFE talks which were held between the WTO and NATO through the CSCE. The FSC will play a leading role in future arms-control discussions – a role reflected in the Helsinki Summit which specifically called for the CSCE to play a major role in pan-European arms-control agreements – and also ensure that there is congruence between arms-control measures and CSBMs. This will pose problems; for example, the CFE Agreement stipulates that there should be prior notification of the call-up of reserves. Such notification is a valuable CSBM, but whether it will be accepted by those CSCE members with strong neutralist traditions remains open to question. The general agreement at the Vienna meeting, that a new generation of CSBMs were needed, may also meet problems in practice since it is unlikely that all parties will agree upon which CSBMs are fitting. Since much of the CSCE's CSBM work will involve conventional force-generating capabilities amongst the CSCE members, manpower and cost may also become issues.

Non-proliferation will also occupy much of the FSC's attention. Amongst the many issues that could appear before the FSC under this heading is the issue of the future of the Ukraine's strategic nuclear arsenal. In addition, the issue of conventional arms transfers will also be in the forefront. Proposals forwarded on 18 November 1992 by Iceland (on behalf of NATO), Bulgaria, the Czech Republic, the Slovak Republic, Hungary, Ireland, Poland, Romania and Sweden, may help to enhance this aspect of the FSC's work. Specifically, the proposals forwarded for discussion were: (i) membership of the NPT and agreement on the need for its continuation beyond the Final Review Conference in 1995; (ii) observance of the Missile Technology Control Regime; (iii) ratification by all of the Chemical, Biological, and Toxic Weapons Conventions; (iv) full exchange of information and date on arms transfers, including the register of all conventional arms transfers with the UN Register of Conventional Arms; (v) the drawing up of common criteria for the restriction of arms transfers within the CSCE framework, including the use of embargoes.

The need for new CSBMs to match the changed circumstances of post-Cold War security will require more *transparency*, which could include the exchange of information on defence capabilities and defence doctrine, observation of military exercises and manoeuvres, collaborative training, and regular consultations between military and civilian authorities. Obviously, cooperation in the arms-control field is assumed within the overall context of CSBM, especially the sharing of verification tasks.

The Geneva Peaceful Settlement of Disputes (PSD) experts meeting, held on 12–23 October 1992, acting on a mandate from the Helsinki meeting and a Franco German initiative, drew up a mechanism for the peaceful settlement of disputes in the form of a Court of Conciliation and Arbitration and a Conciliation Commission – which would give the CSCE an international legal identity. Prior to the Geneva experts meeting, mechanisms for the settlement of disputes had been somewhat *ad hoc*. Under the Paris Charter, it is the Conflict Prevention Centre (CPC) that will 'assist the Council in reducing the risk of conflict'.[17] However, the CPC was charged originally with the task of promoting the exchange of information on CSBMs and other tasks concerning 'the conciliation of disputes as well as broader tasks relating to dispute settlement'.[18] There was no guidance beyond the general talk of conciliation and dispute settlement, due in large part to disagreements about the appropriateness of adding such roles to the CPC's technical CSBM function. An attempt to solidify the content of this secondary function was made at the January 1991 Valetta Meeting on the Peaceful Settlements of Disputes (PSD). Agreement was not forthcoming, in part due to the lack of consensus about whether a dispute settlement mechanism should fall under the CPC or be housed elsewhere.[19] Furthermore, the projected Valetta 'mechanism' for the peaceful settlement of disputes not only relied upon a request for third party assistance, it also allowed any party to the dispute to ignore comment or advice if the dispute involved territorial sovereignty, national defence, title to land, or jurisdiction over maritime and air space. The list of exceptions excludes nearly every conceivable reason for a dispute likely to lead to conflict!

In agreement with the proposed structural modifications forwarded at the Geneva meeting, the Council noted at the Stockholm meeting that there was a need for an 'impartial third party' to aid in the peaceful settlement of disputes in line with Principle V of the 1975 Helsinki Final Act.[20] This led to the Stockholm Convention on Conciliation and Arbitration, signed by the CSCE participating states on 14 December 1992 (and already adopted at the Geneva PSD Experts Meeting). Under this convention the Council formally established a Court of Conciliation and Arbitration and a Conciliation Commission, and empowered the Committee of Senior Officials to 'direct' any two participating states to the commission by a consensus-minus-two mechanism (that is, all CSCE members with the exception of the two parties to a dispute). Conciliation and arbitration is undertaken on a case-by-case basis and the resultant deliberations are *not* binding unless the parties to the dispute have agreed to be so bound. Article 18 lays down the competence of the commission and the arbitration tribunal; under this article, 'Any State party to this Convention may submit to a Conciliation Commission any dispute with another party which has not been settled within a reasonable period of time through negotiation'.[21] The commission will issue a *report* suggesting how the parties to a dispute may settle their differences. Any parties to a dispute may also, *by mutual agreement*, bring their dispute to binding arbitration. However, the same exceptions regarding the Court's competence may be made by the parties as exist in the Valetta mechanism.

The Court is still fledgling and, at the time of writing, only thirty-four of the fifty-three CSCE members have signed the Stockhom Convention on Conciliation and Arbitration, and fewer than the required dozen have ratified in order to activate the commission and court (which may be a relief, considering that Armenia, Bosnia-Herzegovina, Croatia, Russia and Ukraine have all signed). Aside from the severe limitations placed upon the court's competence, there are also questions about the need for such a court. The Convention establishing the court stated that it was not the aim of the court to infringe upon the competence of the International Court of Justice, the European Court of Human Rights, the Court of Justice of the European Communities and the Permanent Court of Arbitration. Although the CSCE's new Court has yet to prove itself, there seems to be an element of needless duplication. For instance, many of the functions of the Court of Conciliation and Arbitration overlap with those of the International Bureau of the Permanent Court of Arbitration. The CSCE's first venture into international law may have improved international conciliation mechanisms, but the arbitration mechanisms leave much to be desired. The problem may not be the need for more courts, but the general problem of the observance of international law.

The Stockholm Council meeting was also notable for a further innovation: the creation of the post of Secretary-General of the CSCE.[22] The Secretary-General's post is intended to support the chairman-in-office in all activities that fulfil the goals of the CSCE, which includes the oversight of all of the CSCE's bureaucracies and operations. Eventually the Secretariats in Prague and Vienna will be placed under a single structure under the secretary-general. Thus, the new structure of the CSCE will be as shown in Figure 8.1.

The Secretary-General will derive his or her authority from 'the collective decisions of the participating States'[23] and will act under the guidance of the chairman-in-office of the Committee of Senior Officials in Prague. The new post marks a welcome development and gives the CSCE a visible face, which is of particular importance given the burgeoning size of the CSCE and the high visibility given to the UN Secretary-General, the Chairman of the Commission of the European Communities, and the Secretary-General of the North Atlantic Treaty Organization.

As a result of a series of meetings since the Paris Summit, the CSCE has vastly expanded the range of its activities as well as its structure. The following missions were referred to at the 22nd meeting of the Committee of Senior Officials in Prague on 29–30 June 1993:

Heads of State and Government

Court of Conciliation
and Arbitration
(Geneva)

Parliamentary Assembly
(Secretariat: Copenhagen)

Council
(rotates)

Ad hoc Steering Group

Committee of Senior Officials

Chairman-in-Office

Secretary-General

FSC
(Vienna)

CPC
(Vienna)

Secretariat
(Prague)

ODIHR
(Warsaw)

Special Committee

Consultative Committee

Mission Support Groups

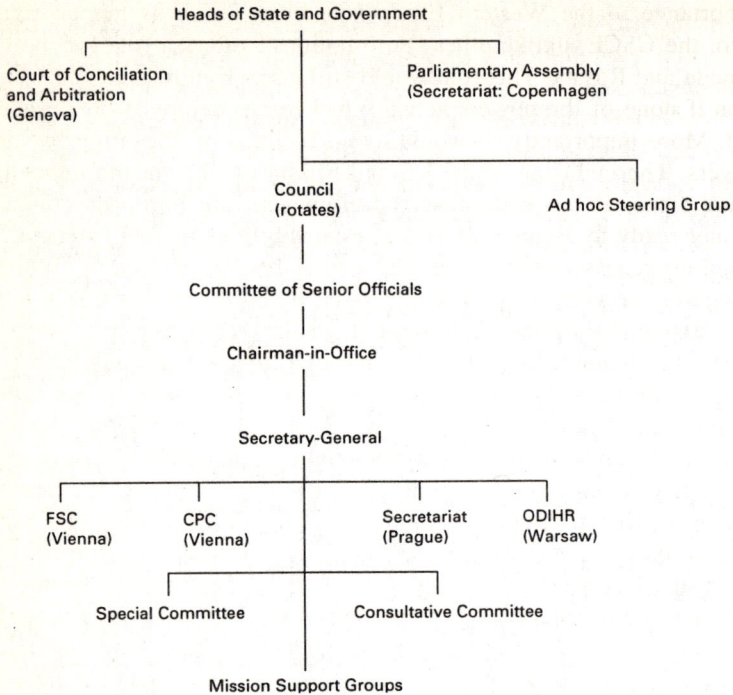

Figure 8.1   The new structure of the CSCE

(1) Long-term mission to Kosovo, Sanjak, Vojvodina.
(2) Monitor mission (carried out with the EC) to Skopje.
(3) Observation mission to Estonia, Georgia.
(4) Rapporteur mission to the Former Yugoslav Republic of Macedonia.
(5) Chairman-in-Office visit to Kazakstan, Kirgistan, Tajikistan Turkmenistan and Uzbekistan.
(6) Pending mission to Nagorno-Karabakh.

There are arguments both for and against this expansion. The arguments in favour are, one, none of the other existing institutions really address Europe's security problems which extend beyond the purely military and beyond the narrow confines of Western Europe. The wider definition of security represents not only a more realistic assessment of post-Cold War security in Europe, but also keeps at the forefront of the security agenda aspects of security which may not be of central importance to the Western European powers, such as human rights. Two, the CSCE, unlike other 'Euro-options', offers a role for the US, Canada and Russia. This role would still carry significance and weight even if none of the powers actually had forces deployed on European soil. More importantly, it would avoid feelings of alienation by these powers. The inclusion of the US and Russia is vital for the immediate future since, as has been observed elsewhere, the European countries are not ready to assume all of the responsibilities related to post-Cold War European security. Three, the artificiality of the idea of 'Western Europe' in security terms has already been addressed. The CSCE is the only existing European institution to address pan-European security issues. Its membership and the range of subjects that come under its purview are more extensive than that of any other body or institution. In time, the distinction between European and other regions' security may also become artificial. The potential to expand the CSCE to other adjacent areas may be an attractive feature – in which case the final 'E' would need to be dropped. For instance, the CSCE could offer Japan a potential role in European affairs. The eventual tying together of Asian and European security interests may also help to overcome the artificial divides that are currently imposed on the various Europes – whether it be the WEU's Europe of nine, the EC's twelve, or the CSCE's fifty-three. These various versions of Europe's security interests are incongruous when compared to economic areas of interest that are inter-regional or global.

The positive aspects of the CSCE's role must be balanced by some negative observations. One, the CSCE has been seen by many as providing the framework for a pan-European security organization.[24] Its very strength, that of its pan-European nature, may also be its Achilles heel. The expansion of its membership, alongside the structural modifications, poses the dual risk of overbureaucratization and paralysis in the decision-making forums. The security role of the CSCE also rests upon cooperation between the major powers within the CSCE framework. Britain and Italy remain sceptical of such schemes, while Germany has still to resolve its constitutional issue; which leaves the somewhat unlikely prospect of the US, Russia and France as the initial crux of the organization. The correlation, or lack of, between economic and security areas of interest may also pose some fundamental problems. For instance, the existence of the EC (or European Trade Area) within the CSCE could lead to resentment amongst those other CSCE members who may be willing to make mutual security guarantees but who are simultaneously excluded from participation in the select economic organizations. The immense disparity between the economic levels of the CSCE countries will be difficult to reconcile with the adoption of common values and standards. Two, the CSCE has some valuable functions, such as crisis consultation,[25] but as a collective security organization it is open to many of the criticisms that have plagued the United Nations for most of its life. These issues revolve around what form of action should be recommended, who should contribute what and when, and who should pay. Even if answers are found for these problems, the voting system in the CSCE may prove to be problematical since unanimity may prove virtually impossible to achieve – a case in point being the CSCE's inaction following the killing of unarmed civilians in Lithuania and Latvia by Soviet Interior Ministry forces in January 1991.[26] This raises the question of whether the CSCE is able or willing to tackle infringements by its more powerful members.

In a further parallel to the UN, there are also financial concerns plaguing the CSCE. Those that are the main financial underwriters of the CSCE may find themselves resenting the lack of weighted voting rights – with similar grave results that have been witnessed in the UN. At least the UN attempted to circumvent this problem by the creation of the Security Council. However, the CSCE allows for no special position, reflected in practice, leadership or voting rights, to be accorded to the main powers. Even if it did, it is not clear what criteria should be used to decide who, to paraphrase George Orwell, would be more equal. In this sense the organization may be more democratic than the UN or NATO, but the absence of such privilege may give the major powers an added inducement to work through other organizations that recognize their special position. It is also worth noting that the Helsinki Final Act, as well as other CSCE documents, are *not* legally binding but are considered to be politically binding.[27]

Specific problems concerning the CSCE may also arise for the US, which may feel that the CSCE is not as relevant to its direct interests in Europe as, for example, NATO. Furthermore, Congress may object on legal and policy grounds to an organization that is theoretically able to commit US troops to combat with no effective veto. From Capitol Hill's standpoint it may be difficult to persuade the American public that their tax dollars are being well spent overseas by an organization many have probably never heard of.

Even if all the above problems could be resolved – by the adoption of weighted voting, the creation of an Executive Committee (paralleling the UN Security Council, which should be a warning in and of itself!) or other such devices, there still remains a fourth problem: how does the CSCE *enforce* any actions to be taken against a recalcitrant state? In spite of the fact that the CSCE's missions have expanded greatly in the last three years, especially in the fields of early warning, conflict prevention and crisis managements, the lack of any enforcement mechanism gives rise to questions regarding the overall utility of the CSCE.

Herein lies one of the central dilemmas of the CSCE: the question of its identity. Is it an alliance or a security organization? While the CSCE is engaged in security-related issues the lack of any defence counterparts to compliment existing CSCE machinery is a grave flaw. Thus, if its prime utility is as a conciliation and arbitration mechanism in support of the UN, there is also the need for modification. Two concerns in particular need addressing: one, the still relatively new conciliation and arbitration mechanism is a welcome development, but while almost half of the CSCE's members are not parties, it will be of questionable utility; and, two, a voting procedure must be adopted that no longer requires 'consensus-minus-one'. The CSCE has evolved very rapidly over a three-year period and is, as a result, a far more useful institution with vast potential. It is up to member states to use that potential.

THE CSCE AND YUGOSLAVIA

As with the other institutions discussed here, the CSCE faced a major challenge as a consequence of the Yugoslav conflict. At an early stage, in the summer of 1991, the CSCE was actively involved in promoting a diplomatic solution to the constitutional crisis in Yugoslavia. In July of the same year the EC evoked the CSCE's brand new emergency consultation and cooperation mechanism. The Committee of Senior Officials (see above organizational chart) adopted a resolution, matching the EC's, which requested that all military forces subordinate themselves to political authority and requested a three-month stay of any declarations of independence. Like the EC, the CSCE could do little beyond these measures. Other parts of the new CSCE machinery were also activated at Austria's request, such as the CPC. The CPC's prevarications resulted in yet another call for the cessation of conflict. The procedure for the peaceful settlement of disputes was not, however, activated since, at that time, no mediators had been appointed. There were several meetings of the CPC, but these additional meetings had little effect on the Yugoslav crisis for three main reasons. First, the methods and structure were new and, as such, untested. Nils Eliasson, the director of the CSCE Secretariat, observed that, 'The crisis came a little early – the new structure has not matured. One delegate joked that we needed a nice little conflict we could settle easily and show the world.'[28] Second, the CSCE was not designed with Yugoslav-type crises in mind. The Charter of Paris made it clear that the CSCE was primarily a conflict-prevention institution, where by promoting human rights, economic cooperation and confidence, and security-building measures (CSBMs), the reasons for conflict would be avoided. Furthermore, the CSCE was also designed to deal with disputes *between* countries and not within them (the same argument could be made in reference to the UN). The principle of non-intervention in the internal affairs of a member state is enshrined in the Helsinki Final Act[29] as well as in the UN Charter.[30] Because of the recognition of this principle, gross violations of human rights, 'ethnic cleansing' and genocide can go on within the confines of a country and be subject to no legal intervention from outside. Clearly there is a need in the light of Bosnia's recent history for the creation of a legal mechanism that would permit intervention in the event of such violations taking place.

Third, the biggest area of weakness in the CSCE structure to be exposed by the Yugoslav conflict was is the unanimity voting rule. Since the CSCE is an intergovernmental organization, its membership is drawn from national governments which are represented as sovereign and independent actors with full equality. The fact that Yugoslavia, represented by the federal government in Belgrade, enjoyed membership ensured that only resolutions that were in its interest would be passed. Independent Croatia and Slovenia have had to rely upon proxy powers within the CSCE to represent their interests. The CSCE process is also supposed to take place outside the formal military alliances. While this may seem laudable in the context of post-Cold War Europe, where many of the alliances have disappeared or are crumbling, the remaining alliances are often instrumental in reaching coordinated positions and consensus within the CSCE.

While the crisis in Yugoslavia made many of the CSCE's imperfections clear, the case against the future development of the CSCE is not a logical corollary, since *all* of the institutions that were involved proved to be, in one way or the other, wanting. The non-involvement of NATO was just as damning as the involvement and failure of the EC or CSCE.

INTERLINKING, BUT OBSTRUCTIVE

The construction of an ever more complicated security architecture based on supposedly overlapping institutions has made the differences between these various interlocking organizations – the WEU, NATO, the Council of Europe, the CSCE and the EC – difficult to distinguish. Not only are there problems of distinction, there are also cases of wasteful duplication, such as the involvement of NATO and the WEU in the Adriatic, the Council of Europe and CSCE in Yugoslavia, UN and CSCE involvement in Nagorno-Karabakh and Georgia. Furthermore, overlapping or interlinking institutions have consistently failed, time and again, in Yugoslavia. These failures are not so much a fault of the institutions, but of the apparent inability of governments to work through institutions and to utilize them to their fullest extent. This does not mean, however, that the institutional structure of European security could not help or encourage governments to use their mechanism. There is, for instance, much overlap between the respective institutions, which results not only in waste and duplication but in confusion for the member states themselves. Simplification of Europe's security structures could do much to encourage states to work through the institutions to prosecute a given course of action.

In the case of the first two organizations, NATO and the WEU, the notion of having a 'two-hatted' force (a notion explicitly rejected by France) is one that could well lead to confusion.[31] The WEU in this context would become the out-of-area branch of NATO, which would in effect extend the geographical legs of NATO while also preserving it. However, there are obvious difficulties with such plans; the main one seems to be that the WEU would still be reliant upon the US for the airlift of large items (such as a main battle tank) and technical support. In the event of a sincere European effort to develop the WEU into an organization capable of acting independently from the US, the costs (which are generally not discussed in the literature) need to be acknowledged.

Institutional confusion also exists between the North Atlantic Cooperation Council (NACC) and the CSCE (for a detailed discussion of NACC see Chapters 9 and 10). Following proposals in the North Atlantic Council's Rome Declaration, the NACC was created.[32] At the NACC's June meeting, which followed immediately after the North Atlantic Council's meeting, the function of NACC was outlined as, 'to contribute to the building of a new security architecture based on cooperative relations among states and a network of mutually reinforcing institutions'.[33] The statement issued from this June meeting by the NACC highlighted the CSCE as one of the mutually reinforcing institutions aiming for a secure Europe and devoted a considerable amount of space to it (almost half of the paragraphs in the statement mention the CSCE). It is not, however, immediately clear what NACC does that the CSCE does not; and, as NACC grows in membership, the differences between the two organizations will probably become even more difficult to distinguish (there are currently 53 CSCE members and 39 NACC members; all NACC members are CSCE members). However, the new NACC has very few powers, since it is primarily a consultative body designed to make Eastern European and CIS countries feel involved without really giving them legroom under the table. NACC is certainly not what some, like Lech Wałesa, had hoped for, which was a NATO II, presumably designed to offer NATO security guarantees against mutual Polish, Czech and Hungarian suspicions of one another. NACC has essentially left the Eastern Europeans out in the cold by providing them with a 'table', thus fulfilling the political mandate of NATO's new role, but completely failing to address their very real security anxieties.

The strongest justification for NACC's existence seems to be that it reinforces NATO's central role in the building of a Post-Cold War Europe and gives the US a voice in the political reconstruction of the continent. The US has changed its attitude towards CSCE, which, prior to 1990, enjoyed little popularity in Washington. The end of that year and early 1991 marked the development of the debate between NATO and the European Community in the security realm. In this context the CSCE served as a hedge for the US so that, if the EC prevailed, Washington would still be able to exercise some influence through the CSCE.

The Council of Europe, founded in 1949, also overlaps with other institutions. Similarities and duplication of tasks are also evident between the thirty-two-member Council and the CSCE; for instance both are simultaneously involved in Estonia. The Council has two roles: the first is to foster Europe's common heritage, and the second is to promote human rights and social progress. Two of the Council's organs, the European Commission on Human Rights and the European Court of Human Rights, investigate and rule on alleged violations of the European Convention on Human Rights. The newly established CSCE Court of Conciliation and Arbitration is not intended to overlap with the Council's organs. Yet it is conceivable that they may well do so – if not with the Council's, then with those associated with the UN or the European Community. All of the Council's members are also CSCE members. The CSCE is also a forum for human rights and the East–West dialogue. There would seem to be no obvious case for such duplication of these particular tasks.

The Council of Europe does have some unique features that deserve mention.[34] Its role in promoting Europe's common heritage is an important task. The Council is the only organ that actively safeguards minorities from exclusion, which includes the right to political participation as well as the protection of cultural and linguistic identities. The Council is ill-equipped to deal with what is perhaps a more serious form of exclusion – that which takes place on economic grounds. This problem can only be addressed within the general process of European integration.[35]

Institutional guidance on European security issues seems vague, and more often than not is designed to justify the existence of a particular institution or to preserve an individual state's position within an institution. This has led to several proposals for the design of new institutional structures, which could be designed around post-Cold War realities and not be encumbered with historical and associational baggage. Richard Ullman, for instance, argues that NATO is an institution that is in 'atrophy', and that any further division of Europe into 'adverserial groups' based on the old military blocs is potentially harmful. He therefore proposes a European Security Organization (ESO), 'linking together the members and former members of both alliances'.[36] The conceptual basis of such an organization, he proposes, should be the CSCE and the WEU. The Institute for Peace Research and Security Policy at the University of Hamburg has proposed a European Security Community, based upon existing CSCE machinery, with the exception of a Security Council. While there is nothing intrinsically wrong with the idea of a European Security Community or Organization, or an Alliance for the Development of Europe, or any other of the myriad of proposed structures, they posit a *structural* solution to the numerous security dilemmas faced by Europe. It remains unclear how any organization built around, or adapted from, existing ones, would avoid merely reinstituting the structural defects that have been outlined above. As Ullman correctly points out, the defects of past collective security organizations, such as the League of Nations, should not be attributed to the organization *per se* but to the governments of the era who failed to uphold the Covenant of the League and the principles upon which it was based. That said, it unclear that there is the will and leadership to make any new organization work, particularly if it is a 'European' organization with an ill-defined or dramatically reduced

US role.[37] Instead, the preference may be for *ad hoc* solutions where in some instances a decision may be made to work through one institution and in another case a different institution. Eventually the organizational basis of European security will emerge *from* this process as some institutions prove to be of more value than others.

While there are no easy answers to the security dilemmas facing existing institutions, it may be useful to remind ourselves that all the above institutions exist to promote the principles of the Charter of the United Nations.[38] This reminder serves a two-fold function: first, it reminds NATO members of their wider international obligations and the fact that the end of the Cold War has security ramifications beyond the NATO area; second, the UN's high profile role in the Gulf war, as well as in Yugoslavia (where NATO initially declined to become involved and the EC failed to reach any settlement) and Somalia, has stressed the critical role the UN has to play in the post-Cold War world. The rationale behind many of the regional security organizations during the Cold War years was the inability of the UN to function as intended. This position no longer applies, and in the midst of the institutional wrangling in Europe it is essential to remind Europe of the wider international picture and of its obligations to make the international collective security machinery work as a prerequisite to any new or adapted regional security designs.

CONCLUSION

The EC, the WEU and the CSCE are the 'Euro options' that are promoted with varying degrees of enthusiasm in European circles. It should be apparent that all have their strengths and weaknesses. The EC has been given considerable publicity as a result of the protracted debates in Denmark, France and Britain over the Maastricht Treaty. Since the WEU's revival in 1984, it has moved closer to the EC and has been promoted as the security arm of the EC. The CSCE has also grown in stature with the addition of new permanent machinery and stands out as the only truly pan-European institution of those discussed.

The invasion of Kuwait by Saddam Hussein's forces has renewed interest in the WEU as a European security actor. The WEU, however, is being pulled in two directions simultaneously, which may eventually harm the institution itself. The two forces are those that wish to promote the WEU as the European pillar *within* the Alliance (the British and the Dutch mainly, and to a lesser extent the Germans) and those who wish to promote the WEU as the European option (mainly the French), which could eventually form the basis for a coherent Western European security organization.

The CSCE has grown to fifty-three members and enjoys the distinct advantage of being not just a European body but one that involves Russia, the US and Canada. The CSCE could, therefore, be promoted as a 'European' option that does not exclude the North American or CIS partners. The limitations, though, are apparent; in spite of the new permanent machinery, the CSCE is still a fragile organization. Unlike NATO, the CSCE has no forces specifically at its disposal; nor does it have any guarantee that forces will be forthcoming. Reaching consensus on controversial matters may also be extremely difficult in light of the existing voting rules. The CSCE also has its strengths: it deals with far wider aspects of 'security' than NATO or the WEU, both of whom remain primarily devoted to security in its direct military sense. Yet, the broadening of the CSCE's mandate and the expansion of its membership have contributed to its institutional schizophrenia, whereby it is neither an alliance nor a security organization, but tries to be both at once.

When the overall European 'security architecture' is considered, there seems to be an unnecessary amount of overlap between the institutional mandates, which is bound to encourage counterproductive turf battles. Yet, it also seems that there is scope for constructing a rudimentary European security agenda around these existing institutions, with the EC and CSCE assuming responsibility for many of the non-military aspects of security – especially economic stabilization, arbitration and conciliation alongside CSBMs. The WEU and NATO are best suited to military aspects of security. This division of labour is assumed to be temporary, pending the evolution of an entirely new European security structure through which the main powers are willing to work.

The emerging 'European' security identity is still fragile. It does not yet engender sufficient confidence amongst the Europeans for them to make any institution redundant. It is clear that a coherent and viable self-sustaining pan-European security structure will not emerge unless there is the underlying willingness to work through it and to delegate power to it. The competition between the institutions for influence and responsibility has been counterproductive, since it has focused attention on institutions and processes rather than on the issues of importance such as the stabilization of Central and Eastern Europe and much of the ex-Soviet Union. The reliance on *ad hoc* solutions to the institutional wrangling suggests one further observation: the sum of the parts may be less than the whole. Even if all the institutions pull together to provide responses to security dilemmas, there are still areas of grey where no one institution, or combination of them, has a satisfactory answer. The Yugoslav crisis illustrates this problem and also suggests that where divisions of responsibility are not clearly delineated the outcome tends to be one of two extremes: either a vigorous and impressive response, such as that following the August 1990 Iraqi invasion of Kuwait, or indecisiveness and paralysis, of the type witnessed over the former Yugoslavia.

While there is certainly scope for criticizing the European response to the unrest in the Balkans, it would be unjust to conclude that the failure to respond in a timely and decisive manner means that a European security organization is doomed. The US must also accept some of the blame for the failure to create an effective regional security organization. Their dogged insistence that NATO is the only true security institution has given the Europeans the unenviable task of coming up with an alternative in the midst of a crisis. In the long term there seems to be scope for consolidating many functions of these institutions and for the eventual formation of a new European security body. In the short term, emphasis must be put on avoiding the conditions which lead to conflict and not on designing responses to conflicts that have already started.

9 The Transatlantic Option

CHANGED CIRCUMSTANCES, NEW PROBLEMS

NATO was formed under a bipolar system, with the primary objective of managing tensions and perhaps conflict on the inner German border. These basic foundations have changed. More than any other organization, the Alliance has the difficult task of retooling itself to the Post-Cold War security environment or, alternatively, admitting gracefully that it is an institution that is gradually becoming otiose.

NATO's success, although untried in the military sense, lay in its ability to dissuade the Warsaw Pact from acts of aggression. This success and NATO's credibility can therefore be attributed to the *existence* of the Soviet threat. The future utility of NATO is often based on NATO's historical record, which, in US Secretary of State Warren Christopher's words, is 'the most successful alliance in history'.[1] NATO, though, needs to be more than a historical success; the conspicuous failure of NATO and other institutions to halt the bloodshed in Bosnia serves as a reminder that it is an organization that has many difficult transitions to make in the post-Cold War world.

On paper NATO has claimed to be more than a military alliance, a claim that is all the more important in an era when non-military aspects of security are being stressed. The political aspects of NATO's vocation, always rather obscure, have now been put forward as the main feature of NATO's work and thus its institutional justification. Yet, for all intents and purposes, NATO was primarily a military alliance, with highly trained forces at its beck and call who would counter a Soviet attack on Alliance territory. The central features of NATO's military strategy were a reliance upon deterrence, and linear defences, which were supplemented by arms control negotiations and political negotiations between the leaders of the two blocs. The end of the bipolar system and its replacement by a multipolar one has negated the Alliance's central functions: the reliance upon deterrence has diminished vastly; the need for linear defence has disappeared with the end of the Warsaw Pact and the reunification of Germany, and the Europe that NATO operates in is no longer bifurcated between East and West. All these changes mean that a wider geographical focus than that of the Cold War years is now demanded from a European–Atlantic Alliance,

275

as well as a broader understanding of the meaning of security.

The track record of NATO is not in dispute in this chapter, for it has undoubtedly been a significant factor in maintaining the peace in Europe. It does not follow that because NATO has been the 'most successful defensive alliance in history' it will *ipso facto* continue to be.[2] What *is* in dispute is the ability of NATO to adapt to the new post-Cold War security environment. For example, Warren Christopher stated that, 'Above all, safeguarding the security of *our* countries and maintaining stability *throughout* Europe remains NATO's core responsibility.'[3] The role is not contradictory, but there is a notable gap between rhetoric and substance. So far, NATO's role in Bosnia and refusal of full membership to Eastern European countries has failed to persuade all that it has an interest in security throughout Europe, and the question of whether NATO has either the will or the means to make this a reality is also open to question.

Defenders of NATO, such as Manfred Wörner, have argued that there are still compelling justifications for NATO's continued existence. Four are forwarded in defence of this argument:[4] (i) NATO is the main transatlantic link which unites North America and Europe. (ii) Diplomacy, without military backing, is doomed to failure. (iii) NATO has put an end to European power politics, which have resulted in war. The disengagement of the US and the dissolution of NATO would endanger the European integration process. (iv) NATO is the key forum for coordinating transatlantic policies. The contention that NATO's continued usefulness can be justified on the basis of these four criteria can be challenged from several angles. In the first place, NATO may be the main transatlantic link but it is not the only one. The security link rose to primacy largely due to the exigencies of the Cold War. It thus follows logically that the demise of the Cold War no longer means that this link has to be *the* main transatlantic link. Indeed, it is a sad commentary on transatlantic relations that there is still an insistence on demonstrating the main link through the presence of armed forces and nuclear weapons on European soil. Second, the argument that diplomacy without military backing is doomed to failure is correct, as far as it goes (again, Bosnia has illustrated the self-evidence of this position). As Manfred Wörner has argued, 'NATO is the only organization that possesses the right package of political-military tools for effective crisis management . . . only NATO has the means to turn political declarations into coherent action.'[5] This capability is, according to Wörner, what demonstrates not NATO's irrelevance but its vitality and potential. However, if these observations are applied to Bosnia, there are grounds for doubt. NATO's role in Bosnia has been supportive: it has enforced a sea embargo and a no-fly zone; it has supplied UNPROFOR with command and control equipment and has coordinated its military planning and operations with the UN. However, at the same time that NATO has been supportive it has also failed to deal with the crisis in Bosnia beyond rhetorical and symbolic gestures. The military options presented by the crisis are insufficient and have not resolved the issue. The armed esorts of humanitarian aid have, in light of the high casualties, proven themselves to be an unpopular use of military force. The threat to use air strikes against Serbian targets has had little discernible effect, other than for a day or two. The ability of air strikes, when used against ground targets, to hit highly mobile, difficult-to-see, artillery and forces must be doubted. Nor has the no-fly zone had any striking effect on the war on the ground. Although NATO has played an important role in providing military backing, it has been to little effect. Furthermore, severe disageements within the Alliance make the task of designing coherent plans for out-of-area eventualities most difficult. If NATO forces are to be used primarily for peace-making, there must be a willingness to put NATO forces at the disposal of the UN (unlike projected military ground operations in Bosnia which, President Clinton argued, would have to fall under NATO command), and there must be more certainty that NATO would intervene at an early stage and that there would be support within the Alliance for this type of operation. These are big assumptions to make.

Third, the notion that NATO and the US presence somehow acted as a check upon Europe's habit of slipping into power politics, and even war, is also persuasive as far as it goes. However, whether NATO will *continue* to do so is open to dispute. The continuation of a US hegemonic role within NATO could lead to friction rather than harmony. A reorganized NATO which specifically recognizes a greater European role would encourage greater French participation in NATO, but may make the organization less attractive to the US. Ironically, the continuation of NATO in its current configuration could have a negative effect on transatlantic relations.

NATO's success in the Cold War has become a liability since it makes the Alliance all the more resistant to change. It is this last point, regarding NATO's ability to change and to provide an insurance against new risks, that is the most stimulating and, it is argued, the most flawed.

THE ATTEMPT TO TRANSFORM THE ALLIANCE

The transformation of the Alliance started with the London meeting of the North Atlantic Council on 5–6 July 1990 (see Appendix I, Figure A.5). In light of the unification of Germany, the North Atlantic Council proclaimed that, 'We recognize that, in the new Europe, the security of every state is inseparably linked to the security of its neighbours. NATO must become an institution where Europeans, Canadians and Americans work together not only for the common defence, but to build new partnerships with all the nations of Europe.'[6] In spite of the acknowledgement of the existence of a 'new Europe', the same document stated that NATO remains a '*defensive* alliance' and pledged to continue to defend the 'territory of all of *our members*'.[7]

The most interesting, and far reaching, outcome of the London Summit was the role of nuclear weapons, which, upon the complete withdrawal of Soviet forces and the full implementation of the CFE[8] agreement, would become 'truly weapons of last resort'.[9] This meant that NATO should maintain 'a conventional defense that by itself can blunt non-nuclear aggression'.[10] At the same time, the Declaration noted that NATO would move toward smaller and restructured active forces; that the active units would be less ready with reduced training and exercises; and that NATO would rely more heavily on the ability to build up larger forces if they are needed.[11]

Part of the conservatism evident in the London Declaration can be explained by the still sizeable Soviet forces in Germany and elsewhere in Europe. The declaration promised that, 'As Soviet troops leave Eastern Europe ... the Alliance's integrated force structure and its strategy will change.'[12] The promised changes had to wait until the North Atlantic Council's November 1991 Rome Summit, where the Alliance's new Strategic Concept was to be unveiled.

The Rome meeting fudged many issues, amongst them being the precise relationship between NATO and the other European security institutions, the whole question of the relevance of NATO's area of interest, and the question of how a defensive alliance could *simultaneously* safeguard the security of its members and establish a just and lasting peace in Europe, was also not touched upon beyond the barest generalities. The chance to transform the Alliance into a collective security organization relevant to contemporary Europe was missed. The post-Cold War focus on trade, reform in Eastern Europe, and containment of ethnic conflict has made NATO's concerns with territorial defence look archaic. A 'defensive' alliance is not well equipped to reach out to fledgling democracies and the free markets of Eastern Europe, in spite of the attempt at Rome to transform the Alliance into a security organization by 'enhancing the political component'[13] and constructing 'new partnerships with all the nations of Europe'.[14] No attempt to redraw NATO's area of interest[15] was made, which makes it difficult to understand how NATO will cope with non-military security threats.

One can sympathize with the enormous task of trying to respond to the multifarious security challenges present after countries have dismantled their Cold War military apparatus according to a set of national priorities (see Table 9.1). The absence of a shared threat has heralded disintegrative tendencies, as well as the belief that the end of the Cold War entitles powers that hitherto supported sizeable forces overseas not only to withdraw or substantially reduce their forces, but also to redefine their defence and security postures in nationalistic ways. Since 1989, the response to the end of the Cold War has not been coordinated institutionally, and what defence planning there has been has tended to be justified on the basis of actions already taken. The substantial reductions in the defence budgets of the NATO members, often made in the name of an illusory 'peace dividend', reflected a similarly chaotic reduction in the numbers of NATO's armed forces.

In the absence of any clear definition of threat or strategy, the most important consideration driving NATO and other European defence planning staffs would appear to be budgetary constraints. Fiscal constraints in turn impose significant political limits on future planning; the main political constraint is that the reduction in the size of NATO troop levels means that the remaining forces tend to receive a higher priority for national uses over those related to Alliance or other commitments further afield. Most types of military cutbacks can be made with almost immediate effect, especially those involving operations and maintenance, the cancelling of contracts, and retiring weapons systems. However, strategy takes longer. It may take up to five years for strategy to have an impact, if the time lag from Secretary of Defense Robert McNamara's Athens speech in 1962 until the adoption of MC 14/3 in 1967, is any indicator. Force structures in the post-Cold War world seem to be driven independently from strategic changes and assessments. There is therefore the real danger of NATO, and other organizations, producing hollow armies.

Clearly, dwindling defence budgets will put a greater emphasis upon collaborative projects and multinational forces, such as the Eurocorps. The planning of future defence budgets should also be done in

Table 9.2   Changes in NATO defence budgets

	1991 (in 1990 constant $ billion)	1989–92 (% change)
United States	314.0	−7
Canada	11.4	−5
United Kingdom	43.6	−7
France	37.3	−1
Germany	34.4	−5
Belgium	3.3	−21
Netherlands	8.3	−5
Luxembourg	.1	+?
Denmark	2.9	−1
Norway	3.8	−1
Turkey	4.4	+12*
Greece	4.5	−3
Italy	21.3	−8
Portugal	1.5	+?
Spain	9.0	−15

* Turkey plans an increase of 3% per annum in the period 1991–95.

Source: Congressional Quarterly Researcher, vol. 2, no. 31 (21 August 1992) pp. 724–5.

collaboration. If it is not, no institutional representation of shared security concerns will be possible.

CHANGING THE GEOGRAPHICAL FOCUS

South

The security exigencies of post-Cold War Europe have pushed to the fore traditional security concerns, that were hitherto subsumed by super-power rivalry, that had a primary focus on the 'central front' and a lesser emphasis on the flanks. The Cold War geographical focus was also built into the training apparatus: the Soviet forces were the enemy. Armed forces assiduously studied the strategy and tactics of their Warsaw Pact counterparts and trained to defend against acts of aggression. NATO was, in effect, a single-threat alliance and all of its resources and energies were geared towards countering that threat. This single-threat preoccupation explains the primary focus on the FRG as

Table 9.3 Changes in NATO armed forces in Europe

United States	30% cut in no. of divisions in Europe
	42% cut in no. of brigades Europe
	Troops will be cut from 307 000
	(1991) to : 150 000 (1995)
Canada	All 6600 troops to be withdrawn
United Kingdom	21% cut in total forces by 1995
	29 000 troops will remain in FRG
France	Army reduced by 60 000
	Conscription cut from 12 to 10 months
	10 000 troops will remain in FRG (part of the
	Eurocorps)
Germany	Active forces cut to 370 000 by 1995
	Conscription cut from 15 to 12 months
Belgium	Troop levels cut by 18% by 1995
	3500 troops will remain in FRG
	Conscription cut from 12 to 8 months
Netherlands	Troop levels cut by 17% by 1995
	Conscription cut from 14 to 12 months (all
	volun teer force anticipated)
Denmark	No immediate changes (mainly reserves)
Norway	Undecided on changes
Turkey	Substantial cuts planned
Greece	Increase in sea/air forces for NATO
Italy	Troop levels cut by 25% by 1995, with 40% cut in
	conscripts (all volunteer force anticipated)
Portugal	Dismantling garrison army; change to mobile
	brigades
	Planned conscription cut from 15 to 8 months
Spain	Planned reductions
	Conscription cut from 12 to 9 months
	(50% volunteer army anticipated)

Source: *Congressional Quarterly Researcher*, vol. 2, no. 31 (21 August 1992) pp. 724–5.

the 'central front' – others being considered the 'outside zones'. However, the flanks were also kept in the Alliance by the presence of the Soviet threat. With the change in the nature of the threat, the 'glue' that kept the flanks attached to the central portion is no longer so potent. Traditionally there has been little enthusiasm for the southern flank of NATO (comprising Greece, Italy, Portugal, Spain and Turkey) an area with its own fractious tendencies. Jed Snyder commented that:

The nations of Southern Europe have historically found it difficult to pursue defense and foreign policies on the basis of regional collaboration. Indeed, postwar Southern Europe has been characterized more by political, economic, and security fragmentation than by any sense of regional alliance.[16]

The countries of Southern Europe have just cause for feeling abandoned and neglected. The focus on Eastern Europe and its stability is often pursued at the cost of the south. For instance, the unification of Germany and the economic aid and investment flowing to the east, often does so at the expense of the south. The grandiose promises made in the Single European Act about eliminating the wealth disparities between the EC's north and south have proven to be false (not just because of monies flowing east, but because of an increasing amount of aid going to regions within the northern European EC members themselves). In security terms Southern Europe has been neglected as well. South-western Europe in particular remains an area of crises and instability which, while posing security concerns, are perhaps neglected because they do not represent a direct military threat.

It is essential that the southern region be fully integrated into any new European security arrangement and that the traditional preoccupation of the central region be dropped in favour of an increased focus on the south. The Gulf War of 1991 and the turmoil in Yugoslavia should have alerted security analysts to the critical strategic importance of this area, especially Turkey, which is justly concerned about ethnic conflicts spilling over its borders. At the same time, the larger European powers should support unilateral initiatives by the southern countries to secure peace in their adjoining areas by, for example, the creation of cooperation treaties like the Balkan Pact. Many of the cooperation schemes in the south of Europe, such as the Group of Nine,[17] are not primarily concerned with security issues but may have important security implications. The Gulf War of 1991 and Turkey's invaluable role in the war reminded NATO officials of the vulnerability of the southern region. The break-up of Yugoslavia provides the most dramatic example of the potential pitfalls awaiting those who consider Southern Europe as peripheral and of little interest to NATO.

Turkey has yet to become the security focus of Post-Cold War Europe, but it should be. Turkey has traditionally been part of Europe, yet simultaneously outside Europe. It is a valued member of NATO, yet at the same time it has been denied entry to the other 'European clubs' – the WEU and the EC. Since the end of World War II, Turkey has simultaneously sought closer relations with the Middle East countries and Europe. It was accepted as an associate member of the European Community in 1963 and formally applied for full membership in 1987. The refusal of the European Commission to consider the EC application before 1993, at the earliest, was taken as a rebuff by Ankara. Greece, an EC member, was remarkably successful in tying Turkish admittance to the Cyprus issue. In spite of attempts by the late Turgut Ozal to improve Greek–Turkish relations, most notably in the 1988 Davos meeting where Ozal and Prime Minister Andreas Papendreou met to discuss Cyprus among other issues, there is little likelihood of a quick solution to this issue. The pressure to admit Turkey into the EC will become more acute now that other European countries have made formal applications to join the EC. A decision to admit one of the other applicants and not Turkey could be regarded as most unjust in light of Turkey's valuable support of the coalition during the Gulf War.

Turkish involvement in the Middle East, which was most noticeable in the 1950s, was inspired by the desire to promote Turkish leadership aspirations in that region, as well as Ankara's desire to play a key role in the Baghdad Pact and to contain Soviet expansion into Syria. Turkey has also been anxious to cultivate its ties with Europe; consequently, it has been faced with an often difficult task of balancing its interests to the east with those to the west – at least until the invasion of Kuwait by Iraq in August 1990. In spite of Turgut Ozal's hopes that Turkey's role might lead to heightened chances of being fully accepted into the WEU and the EC as a result of Turkey's Gulf War role, there were few concessions.[18] At the end of the Cold War, Turkey was left with a foot in both camps, but it would appear that it is being pushed away from the European camp as a result of concerns in other European countries about Turkey's Islamic identity and the rise of anti-immigrant sentiments throughout Western Europe, especially in Germany.

The tendency for Turkey to be pushed to the periphery is also evident in the security realm as well. Ozal's main concern was that NATO would crumble and a new security system would supplant it, the most likely contender being the WEU, and would exclude Turkey. President Ozal's response to this fear was twofold: first, to attempt to strengthen bilateral ties with the US, and, second, to strengthen ties with the Turkic countries. It is in the second development that potential risks to European security lie.

With the break-up of the Soviet Union, Turkey has expanded its economic and political ties with the Central Asian republics – Azerbaijan, Kazakhstan, Kyrgyzstan, Turkmenistan and Uzbekistan. The efforts to build closer relations with the Turkic groups in these countries is primarily motivated by economics, but there is also a growing awareness that Turkey will become an important regional leader for these countries because of their cultural and ethnic ties. The danger posed by this development is that Turkey may unwittingly find itself involved in conflicts in the region – such as the Armenian–Azerbaijani dispute. Turkey may also clash with Iran over Azerbaijan, as Tehran sees Azerbaijan as important to its economy and politics. A further clash may ensue if Turkey unwittingly creates a divide between those Islamic countries that are interested in developing along Turkish lines (which combine elements of secularism and pluralism) and those countries that are interested in the more extreme Islamic model epitomized by Iran.

The elections in October 1991 saw the late Turgut Ozal's Motherland Party lose its eight-year majority in parliament.[19] The new coalition government, comprised of the True Path Party and the Social Democrat Populist Party (SDPP), is headed by Suleyman Demirel. Demirel and the SDPP were opposed to Turkey's involvement in the Gulf War and have also been vociferous critics of the close ties between Ankara and Washington. Turkey, once again, is the linchpin of Europe's security. A drift into further involvement with other Turkic groups could eventually entangle Turkey in ethnic issues, with resultant problems for NATO. A refusal from NATO to become involved, because of out-of-area concerns, could have the effect of driving Turkey from Europe towards a greater role in the still-volatile Middle East.

The debates within Europe about the role of the WEU, the role of the Franco–German corps, future US involvement and so forth, threaten to continue to focus attention on the centre of Europe and not on the North–South, or Barents–Mediterranean, perspective. Perhaps one of the few constructive outcomes of the crisis in Yugoslavia is that it has had the effect of changing the European security focus to the south, although in *NATO terms* the 'South' comprises Greece, Italy, Portugal, Spain and Turkey, thus excluding the source of unrest in that region emanating from the Maghreb, North Africa and, most importantly, the Balkans. A visit by NATO's Military Staff Committee[20] to Turkey, Greece and Italy in September 1993 is one encouraging sign that the south of NATO will begin to be given the attention it deserves.

The security concerns emanating from the south of Europe, North Africa and the Maghreb have already been addressed in Chapter 2. Clearly, the concerns voiced in Northern Europe regarding immigration and the potential for religious extremism emanating from this region have much to do with the economic plight of these countries.

Many of the potential security concerns could be answered by fairly straightforward measures, such as making sure that the region is not excluded from Northern European markets and direct investment in these countries. NATO's role is therefore limited, but if the problems of this area are not addressed urgently and at high levels it may become a matter of major, costly involvement.

East

Aside from the well-publicized woes of former Yugoslavia, which has historically been regarded as the 'powder keg' of Europe, there needs to be more attention paid to other potentially explosive regions that could pose serious security-related problems for Western Europe. The Caucasus is one such area. As an area that can be considered on the frontiers of Europe and Asia, east and west, north and south, it is extremely important. Yet, the conflicts around Nagorno-Karabakh, Abkhazia, Azerbaijan, North Caucasus and South Ossetia are given cursory attention in the NATO context. While such observations may be open to the retort that this is not NATO's problem, it leaves open the question of whose problem it should be? If the answer is that the Caucasus region is the responsibility of several international organizations, what role would NATO play?

Western policy-makers have also been slow to recognize the importance of Central and Eastern Europe to Europe's security equation. In particular, there has been a reluctance to recognize the link between security, democracy and security guarantees. The formation of NACC is not a serious attempt to offer any such guarantees. The absence of security guarantees may well undermine progress in Central and Eastern Europe towards security and democracy. As is argued in a later chapter devoted specifically to this area, the insistence that these countries pass certain 'democractic' tests is in many ways counterintuitive. Two criticisms can be levelled at this: first, the same stipulations were not made of Portugal, Spain, Greece or Turkey, none of whom were exactly democratic upon their entry into NATO; second, the need for security guarantees is greatest when a country is fragile, not when it has proven credentials. A crisis in any of the Central or Eastern European countries will most probably involve NATO countries directly or indirectly, whether they are members or not. Membership may have the effect of enhancing stability. The fate of former Yugoslavia stands as mute testimony to what may happen in the event of failure to agree on effective security structures. These arguments are expanded in Chapter 9.

AU REVOIR OR ADIEU?

NATO has evoked two strains of thought: one is that the Alliance can be modernized to accommodate the security demands of the post-Cold War Europe, and that it provides the main forum for discussion in the new Europe; the other is that NATO has outlived its usefulness and has become a fossil left over from the Cold War days.[21] The recently revived political aspects of the 1967 Harmel Report, which stressed NATO's traditional deterrence and defence roles, alongside those concerning the management of detente, would seem to have given NATO a new lease of life. The confidence that NATO could expand and assume new duties was forwarded by Presidents Bush and Clinton and strongly backed by Margaret Thatcher and John Major. The underlying hope was that through NATO the US would continue to exert a strong influence in European security affairs.

The communiqués resulting from the North Atlantic Council London, Rome, Copenhagen, Oslo and Brussels summits all assumed that NATO remains the underpinning for the new European security order and that other organizations were adjuncts. Furthermore, the summits and their resultant communiqués embodied the assumption that the transatlantic partnership is the immutable foundation for European security. Gregory Treverton summarized the dilemmas eloquently:

> The Alliance has been one of the great postwar successes, so some nostalgia for it is understandable, all the more so for Americans who have dominated it. But it is fruitless in the long run for American policy to acknowledge, on the one hand, that the Soviet threat which NATO was constructed to contain is no more and yet insist, on the other, that NATO must remain the preeminent European security institution.[22]

Attempts have been made to justify NATO's continuing relevance to Post-Cold War European security through claims that NATO is more than a military alliance.[23] However, NATO remains *primarily* a military alliance; attempts to justify its continued existence on the grounds of other areas of NATO activity seem thin. For example, the November 1991 Rome Declaration on Peace and Cooperation stressed that the 'political approach' to security will become increasingly important.[24] The precise nature and meaning of the political approach remained obscure until the Alliance's Strategic Concept stated that it featured preventive diplomacy and the successful management of crises affecting its *members*.[25] The effectiveness of the first component rests upon consensus and unanimity within the Alliance. This, in turn, rests upon the individuals involved, the nature and location of the crisis, and the nature of any potential commitments involved. An emerging 'Euro' agenda and the potential for a US increasingly involved in its own domestic woes might make preventive diplomacy less easy than is assumed. The fate of the former Yugoslavia is a – hopefully atypical – reminder of the failure of preventive diplomacy and crisis management. The adoption of crisis management as a major part of its strategy is also a significant departure for NATO and overlaps with the CSCE and UN mandates. The assumption that consensus will be easily reached within NATO is questionable; even with an overarching common threat, consensus was not always easy to achieve.

Aside from the efforts to give NATO a heightened political role in Europe, attempts were made to redefine NATO's area of interest. Margaret Thatcher was one of the first to suggest that NATO's security would be vitally affected by events taking place outside the NATO area.[26] The most obvious problem with any 'rehashed' NATO would be its extent of operations, since any attempts to redefine NATO's mandate outside the traditional treaty area, to include Eastern Europe and the Middle East for example, would meet with objections from some Alliance members. However, to continue with the current geographical confines would make little sense either. The core problem with NATO in the post-Cold War era is how to reconcile the US's desire to continue its Cold War position vis-à-vis its allies and the post-Cold War preference of the European allies to redefine their relationship with the US and to subordinate that relationship to the integration process in Europe.

NATO has attempted to revamp itself to meet the challenges of the post-Cold War world. Part of the transition involves an active role in political dialogue as well as a major restructuring of the military. The latter, however, may pose some serious operational headaches for NATO. For instance, the NATO Defence Planning Committee designed a new force structure which emphasized multinational units; the size of these units was to amount to about 50 per cent of the previous force structure. The committee, however, had little choice but to accept the force levels designated to them. The committee report states:

> The new force structure will reflect the characteristics of flexibility, mobility, and multinationality identified in the London Declaration. We noted with satisfaction that both the future national plans and the work done on the new NATO force structures will enable us to maintain a coherent and effective collective defence posture at lower overall force levels.[27]

In reality, though, the multinational corps were no more than the recognition that NATO had to find a way of maintaining its cohesion, with the recognition that several NATO members, such as Britain and the Netherlands, no longer had enough forces to form purely national corps. The plans were to form a multinational 'immediate reaction force' comprising one or two brigades and a 'rapid reaction corps' which would be drawn from the European militaries. An additional four or five multinational corps were also called for. Overall, this means that about one half of NATO's early available forces will be multinational, consisting of about one-third of its fully mobilized posture. The only countries maintaining forces of sufficient size for purely national contingents are France, Germany and the US. The changes in force structure were made public in Rome on 8 November 1991, when the North Atlantic Council outlined its 'New Strategic Concept'.

THE NEW STRATEGIC CONCEPT

The two biggest changes contained in the New Strategic Concept were the move away from forward defence towards a 'reduced forward presence' and the modification of the principle of flexible response principle to reflect a 'reduced reliance on nuclear weapons'.[28] However, the overall character of the armed forces continued to reflect 'its strictly defensive character'.[29] The adoption of a New Strategic Concept was not only a response to NATO's changed security circumstances, but also to the prospect of substantial force reduction. Overall there will be a force reduction of around 25 per cent across the board by 1997. Broken down into services, the *planned* reductions in NATO's forces by 1997 are as shown in Table 9.1.

In the Alliance's New Strategic Concept[30] it was agreed that, 'The forces of the Allies must... be able to defend Alliance frontiers, to stop an aggressor's advance as far forward as possible...'[31] Yet the basic commitment to forward defence still remains, somewhat surprisingly in the light of past heated debates over the force-to-space ratio in the early days of the CFE negotiations. The wrangling over this issue was pushed aside in 1989–90, when the CFE cuts went far deeper and were more extensive than many European allies had thought initially possible. Thus the force levels are lower, the borders are generally the same (although not in the political sense), and the threats remain undefined, or at least unspecified, yet NATO remains wedded to the principle of being a defensive organization and still tacitly endorses

Table 9.1   Planned reductions in NATO forces by 1997

Force	Reduction by 1997
Land	25% reduction in combat units (45% in central region)
Sea	10% reduction in naval combat units normally assigned to the NATO area, including aircraft carriers, submarines, destroyers, and frigates
Air	25% reduction in combat aircraft assigned to NATO and stationed in Europe (45% in the central and northern regions and 25% reduction in reinforcements from North America)

Source: Basic Fact Sheet No.5: 'NATO's New Force Structure', (Brussels: NATO Information Service, September 1993).

the idea of forward defence, albeit with a reduced forward presence.[32]

The concept of forward defence is clearly one that is open to serious challenge and it remains, arguably, what it has always been: a political concept. The object of forward defence was to defend the territorial integrity of NATO at the point of penetration, which precluded other defensive notions, such as defence-in-depth. The Cold War advocacy of forward defence by the European allies was clearly an expression of self-interest, whereby the amount of damage that might be caused in the event of aggression would be limited. It was also a recognition of basic geographical factors: densely crowded European countries simply did not have the option to withdraw into their interior, like the Soviet Union, or to contemplate trading territory for time.

Under the New Strategic Concept the old layer-cake concept of forward defence, consisting of army corps which were normally composed of troops from one nation, has been abandoned in favour of a forward presence.[33] The size of NATO forces in Europe no longer permits forward defence, layer-cake configurations; instead, the forces have been rearranged into six multinational corps (with little apparent regard for the difficulty of integrating troops of different cultures and languages), whose peacetime distribution would reflect a military presence throughout the territory of the Alliance. To use the food analogy again, this has been referred to as a 'currant bun' defence.[34]

The moves from a linear defence to a 'currant bun', or echeloned defence, are in part a response to the new force levels, but they can also be explained in terms of German unification. Upon unification, Articles 5 and 6 of the North Atlantic Treaty obliged other members to defend Germany along its new borders – the Oder-Neisse rivers.

Under the Two-plus-Four agreements, NATO is prohibited from moving large forces into the eastern part of Germany until ex-Soviet forces have completely withdrawn. Thus, a linear defence of Germany's eastern border is out of the question, and even if there were no legal limitations there would still be practical difficulties with NATO's ability to conduct a linear defence of the eastern border. For example, the existing logistical lines, command, control and communication facilities stretch only to the old inner German border. The cost of enhancing these facilities to provide for the linear defence of the new border would be prohibitively expensive and complicated. Thus, the option of a forward-deployed force, backed up by tactical air support and a strong 'wall' behind it, makes more sense.

The supposition behind NATO's multinational main defence corps is that they will pursue the same operational doctrines, command procedures, logistical coordination and so forth. However, the lowest level of coordination is the corps level; this raises the problem of how brigade-level contingents communicate (assuming they are using a common language) even though they may be part of the same corps. Training could also present some horrific nightmares. If the lowest level to be coordinated is the corps level, this would entail moving thirty to forty thousand troops to a training area. This is clearly ridiculous for several reasons, ranging from cost, public opposition, and the scarcity of large areas of training land needed to carry out such manoeuvres.[35] However, without such exercises it is difficult to imagine that the multinational corps will ever be integrated. If the logistical problems do not prove insuperable, and if the public opposition is not overwhelming, then the legal objections imposed on training exercises in a CFE follow-on agreement may prove too much. With the severe cuts in defence budgets, there is also the question of how some of the smaller nations, like the Netherlands, are going to support some of the logistical and training tasks given to them.

In addition to the Main Defence Forces (the six corps), it was also agreed that there should be multinational rapid-reaction air, ground and sea forces. There are two types of rapid reaction force: the Immediate Reaction Forces, which are brigade-size formations, and the Rapid Reaction Corps for Allied Command Europe, under British command, to be stationed at Bielefeld, Germany.[36] The Allied Rapid Reaction Corps (ARRC) came into existence on 2 October 1992, and has contributions from twelve of the sixteen NATO countries.[37] Manfred Wörner, NATO's Secretary-General, described the ARRC as the 'centerpiece of the alliance's changed military posture, capable of confronting every kind of security threat'.[38] ARRC also features an Immediate Response Force of around five thousand which would be able to deploy anywhere within seventy-two hours. However, in spite of these changes, ARRC will be deployed primarily within the geographical confines of NATO, and for deployments outside the area they would have to be deployed on a bilateral basis in conjunction with, for example, the UN. The enhanced flexibility and mobility of the NATO forces was designed to 'deter a limited attack and, if required, to defend the territory of the Allies against attacks'.[39]

Under the New Strategic Concept the main emphasis remains that of defence, with a few units at a high state of readiness and a greater emphasis on mobilization and reserves. It would appear that in practical terms the Alliance is moving towards something that looks more like the US Army's AirLand Battle 2000 (ALB) concept, which emphasizes the positioning of mobile reserves away from the front that can be used to contain the advances of the enemy and take advantage of potential weaknesses.[40]

The New Strategic Concept reinforced the Harmel Report by stressing the political as well as security aspects of NATO's tasks – referring to it as the 'broad approach to security'.[41] The New Strategic Concept acknowledges in several places that the threats to NATO are multi-faceted and multidirectional.[42] Yet, in spite of the changed security environment in which NATO is expected to operate, the concept concluded that this 'does not change the purpose or the security functions of the Alliance'.[43] In order to build genuine peace and stability in Europe there should be a correlation between the military and political aspects of NATO's work. It would seem, however, that the political track of NATO's new strategy is out of sync with the military track.

The reorganization of the forces still leaves NATO as a military defensive Alliance when it is not clear who intends to provoke NATO with an aggressive act, or how NATO will cope with threats to its territory which may emanate from outside of the NATO area. The November 1990 CFE Treaty, which entered into force in June 1992, would seem to challenge the need for the continuation of a defensively driven Alliance. Any attempt at an aggressive act against Western Europe would require elaborate and transparent redeployment of conventional forces. With the loss of the element of surprise, quite apart from the question of motives, the possibility of an attack against NATO seems highly unlikely.

The overarching problem with the New Strategic Concept remains the question of parameters. While acknowledging that the threats in the new security environment are multifarious and that the security of NATO is 'inseparably linked to that of all other states in Europe',[44] there has been no attempt to change (and hence make relevant) the new area of geographical concern to NATO. The Defence Planning Committee confirmed in May 1992 that the 'Alliance's core security functions remain unchanged, including NATO's fundamental responsibility for the defence of Allied territory'.[45] As is argued below in more detail, so long as the territorial extent of NATO's area of interest remains locked into Cold War parameters, it is difficult to see how the new force structure will be relevant, and ultimately how NATO will be relevant.

THE ROLE OF NUCLEAR WEAPONS

The nuclear deterrent forces, which amounted to some 7000 nuclear warheads in Western Europe alone in the Cold War years, were justified on the grounds of the nuclear Armageddon spectre. Since the end of the Cold War, dramatic reductions in the number of nuclear weapons have taken place, to the extent that the likelihood of any use of nuclear weapons has been significantly downgraded. The reductions that have taken place as a result of the 1987 Intermediate Range Nuclear Forces Treaty (INF), which removed an entire category of weapons globally, and the 1991–92 START I and II treaties, which are probably the most intricate arms control treaties ever negotiated, have been phenomenal. The START reductions, which are to take place over a seven-year period (assuming ratification), limit the US and Russia to 1600 Strategic Nuclear Delivery Vehicles (SNDVs). Moreover, there are signs that both sides wish to move beyond the reductions proposed in the treaty. The Conventional Forces in Europe (CFE) treaty has dramatically reduced the conventional force levels in Europe, and the Conference on Disarmament (CD) in Geneva may yield further reductions in the chemical weapon arsenals. Moscow has also expressed renewed interest in renegotiating the 1972 Anti-Ballistic Missile (ABM) Treaty. While other threats to NATO countries exist (there is a slim possibility of nuclear terrorism, which would probably not be directed at NATO states anyway), the nuclear threat has declined dramatically.

The role of nuclear weapons in post-Cold War Europe was first addressed at the North Atlantic Council's London meeting in July 1990. The London Declaration stated that the Alliance 'must maintain for the foreseeable future an appropriate mix of nuclear and conventional forces', and that NATO should seek the 'lowest and most stable level of nuclear forces needed to secure the prevention of war'.[46] In spite of the 'reduced reliance' on nuclear weapons, the London Declaration also stated that, '[nuclear weapons] will continue to fulfil an essential role in the overall strategy of the Alliance to prevent war by ensuring that there are no circumstances in which nuclear retaliation in response to military action might be discounted'. The declaration then added that NATO's new strategy would make 'nuclear forces truly weapons of last resort'.[47]

What, therefore, is the role of nuclear weapons under NATO's New Strategic Concept? The strategic concept did not renounce the principle of flexible response,[48] although it was agreed to 'modify the principle of flexible response to reflect a reduced reliance on nuclear weapons',[49] with 'continued widespread participation in nuclear roles and peacetime basing by the Allies'.[50] The reduced reliance reflected a 'very substantial reduction in NATO's sub-strategic nuclear stockpile in Europe'.[51] The reduction of NATO's sub-strategic nuclear stockpiles by 80 per cent means that the only remaining US nuclear weapons in Europe are the dual-capable aircraft. Aside from these, there are also the British and French independent nuclear deterrents (it should again be noted that the French have rejected the notion that nuclear weapons are truly weapons of last resort). The retention of a nuclear deterrent force under the Alliance's New Strategic Concept has been justified on two levels: first, nuclear weapons provide the 'essential political and military link between the European and the North American members of the Alliance',[52] and second, the purpose of the forces remains political, to 'preserve the peace and prevent coercion and any kind of war'.[53] On the first point, it is no longer clear that nuclear weapons are an essential political or military link between the US and its European allies. In part, this is due to the fact that the value attached to nuclear weapons in the public's mind has changed dramatically since the early 1980s. Vehement anti-nuclear sentiments may make it difficult to justify not only the preservation of NATO's nuclear deterrent posture but also the independent deterrents of France and Britain. Aside from public opposition to continued nuclear deployments in Europe, there is the more serious question of military strategy: under what strategy and scenarios would nuclear weapons be deployed and to what end? As mentioned above, the only US nuclear weapons actually deployed physically on European soil are dual-capable aircraft.[54] In the event of emergency these could be supplemented by offshore systems (that is, strategic systems). The New Strategic Concept argues that these systems continue to provide 'the necessary political and military link to NATO's strategic nuclear forces and an important demonstration of Alliance solidarity'.[55] There are some foreseeable problems associated with dual-capable aircraft related to their nature.

The effectiveness of deterring any potential enemy relies upon the clear and unambiguous potential to use nuclear weapons. While it could be argued that dual-capable aircraft do this, it should also be pointed out that they may also be potentially escalatory. If an enemy is faced with a retaliatory air raid in response to a conventional attack (assuming they are a nuclear power), should the enemy anticipate that the response will be conventional or nuclear? Nor, with a growing clamour in Europe for a European defence identity, is it as certain that the presence of US dual-capability aircraft provides the necessary political and strategic link to ensure Alliance solidarity. The 'escalation ladder', to be utilized in case of some (as yet unclear) attack is hazy – the gap between conventional response and retaliation with tactical nuclear fighters and the employment of strategic forces is wide.

While flexible response has not been entirely refuted, neither has the general belief that some kind of nuclear deterrent is desirable. The new deterrent force is less flexible than its predecessor and this, in turn, could renew the debates of the early to mid-1960s about the willingness of the US to use its nuclear weapons in the defence of Europe. The main problems with NATO's revised nuclear strategy relate to the murky picture of who the 'enemy' is. Until this picture is clear, who to target (countervalue versus counterforce), with what, and what is meant by 'minimum unacceptable damage', all remain moot points.

As war-fighting weapons, nuclear armaments have less utility today than ever before. With the fatal weakening of flexible-response strategy, there are legitimate grounds for concern amongst the European allies about the deterrent and war-fighting roles of these weapons. The declining US conventional force levels in Europe will also lead to mounting unease regarding the remaining US nuclear forces in Europe: does the lower level of US conventional forces mean that there is a greater reliance upon the remaining nuclear weapons? Or, is the withdrawal of US troops a prelude to the phasing out of the remaining US nuclear forces in Europe?

All these factors aside, many of the efforts to revamp NATO structurally do not answer some essentially political difficulties. NATO, at least in the early 1990s, remains the only nuclear alliance. This therefore raises the question of what would happen in the event of another European security organization, such as the WEU, that operates outside of NATO's traditional area of interest, calling upon NATO for the release of nuclear weapons in support of its operations. Although this may fall into the realm of fanciful speculation, there exists nevertheless the problem of NATO's nuclear relations with the emerging European security organizations.

THE OUT-OF-AREA PROBLEM: NATO'S ACHILLES HEEL?

The end of the Cold War and events since then, such as the Gulf War and the Yugoslav crisis, have had the effect of concentrating security questions on the most controversial area of NATO activity – the out-of-area issue. Historically there has been a general reluctance to coordinate out-of-area roles through NATO, and cooperation on such issues has not been good – the disputes in Indochina (1954), Suez (1956), Portuguese Africa (1949–54), the Middle East (1973) and Libya (1986) serve as examples of occasions where no agreement by Alliance members was reached.[56] It would be unfair to paint too bleak a picture of NATO's ability to cooperate since there are examples of bilateral collaboration, such as US aid given to the United Kingdom in 1982 during the Falklands/Malvinas conflict, or the collaboration between France and the US against Muammar Gaddafi's attempts to overrun Chad in 1983. The collaboration of British, French, Italian and US forces in Lebanon also serves as an example of multilateral cooperation. Nevertheless, these cooperative efforts do not present a basis for planning out-of-area operations within NATO and presently there is no apparent agreement on which areas should be included within any redefinition of NATO's area of interest.

With a few exceptions the US has been the power most inclined to call on the support of its NATO allies for out-of-area problems. More often than not, allied refusal led to a recrudescence of the burden-sharing debate. Nevertheless, in spite of allied intransigence the US normally pursued its global interests, with or without allied support. This single-handed approach has changed, as the 1991 Gulf War illustrated; the US is simply no longer able to contemplate major intervention without allied financial support and, to a lesser extent, manpower contributions. The out-of-area problem has focused heavily on the Middle East. While there have been instances of out-of-area collaboration, there have also been numerous occasions on which collaboration failed to take place. There are numerous reasons behind such failures, amongst them being policy or political differences, questions of resource allocation, differing perceptions regarding the significance and gravity of a threat, and, on the part of the Europeans, an occasional inclination to distrust US leadership.[57] While the argument here is *not* supposed to suggest that all cooperation on out-of-area issues is impossible (the allied assistance in patrolling the Gulf in 1987–88 and during the 1991 Gulf War demonstrate that it is possible), the chances of redefining NATO's area of geographical responsibility, as outlined in Article 6 of the North Atlantic Treaty,[58] are slim. France, above all, would resist attempts to define a wider geographical mandate for NATO, especially a mandate that would make French reintegration into any European security network, centred around a revamped NATO, almost impossible.[59]

The out-of-area issue is likely to be the one issue that could eventually render NATO ineffective for two main reasons: one, the existing area of concern has become increasingly irrelevant, yet there is no consensus on expanding the Alliance's area of interest by amending Article 6 of the North Atlantic Treaty, or admitting new members; two, the US will most likely call upon its European allies for assistance as it tries to maintain its global security interests with a declining economic base. These two factors only partially explain the resistance raised by Alliance members to a redefinition of NATO's area of concern. Other objections that have been voiced are that: (i) NATO is unwilling to extend any guarantees eastward when the situation in those countries remains fluid and unpredictable. (ii) Many of the problems encountered by the Central and Eastern Europeans, Middle Eastern countries and Southern Europeans are not strictly of a military nature, and therefore do not call upon NATO's area of military competence. (iii) The end of the Cold War has been marked by open disagreement between the US and its European allies on the question of where NATO should/should not be involved. (iv) There are physical limitations on the number of troops, airlift and sealift capacities available to NATO, which, in turn, prescribe limitations on NATO's area of interest.[60]

One possible solution to the out-of-area problem was the use of other institutions, like the CSCE or the WEU, as existential alliances. However, this solution remains flawed since these institutions are still subject to an effective NATO veto, and in reality they remain reliant upon NATO for many operational military matters. The insistence by some, like the British and the Dutch, that the WEU is intended primarily to strengthen the European pillar of NATO may also meet the same reservations held about a WEU role that differs too dramatically in scope from the parent organizations.

Since the end of the Cold War there has been a concerted effort to transform NATO's security mission to one that fits the new security environment. The first notable milestone in this process was the 1990 London Declaration, which proclaimed that, 'The Atlantic Community must reach out to the countries of the East which were our adversaries in the Cold War, and extend to them the hand of friendship.'[61] In a similar vein, a year later, the Rome Declaration stated that NATO had the task of acting as 'one of the indispensable foundations for a stable security environment in Europe'.[62] NATO's New Strategic Concept, unveiled at the Rome Summit, acknowledges that the new threats are 'multi-faceted in nature and multi-directional, which makes them hard to predict and assess'.[63] Some of the multifaceted threats are mentioned as those 'arising from the adverse consequences of instabilities that may arise from the serious economic, social and political difficulties'.[64] Also at Rome a special emphasis was placed upon the importance of stability in the countries on the southern periphery of Europe for the security of the NATO Alliance.

The threats identified at the Rome Summit clearly acknowledge the existence of significant concerns emanating from outside the traditional Alliance area as well as a recognition that the nature of these threats has changed. Having made these observations, the New Strategic Concept reaffirmed the 'defensive nature of the Alliance and the resolve of its members to safeguard their security, sovereignty and territorial integrity'.[65] There was, however, no attempt to realign the Alliance's area of geographical interest and, as far as forming contacts with the Central and Eastern European countries was concerned, the responsibility seemed to be handed over to the CSCE and the EC. The only passing discussion of the out-of-area question, or about threats arising from proliferation, from disruption of the flow of vital resources or terrorism, was encapsulated in the observation that arrangements exist for consultation under Article 4 of the North Atlantic Treaty.[66] The fact that preserving collective defence while simultaneously building cooperative Europe-wide security may be contradictory does not appear to be of great concern.

The extent-of-limits debate within NATO reached an ambiguous solution in June 1992 at the Oslo Summit. In the communiqué following the summit, it was agreed that NATO would contribute to the effectiveness of the CSCE, and in this regard:

[NATO is] prepared to support, on a case-by-case basis in accordance with our own procedures, peacekeeping activities under the responsibility of the CSCE, including by making available Alliance resources and expertise... This will be done without prejudice to possible contributions by other CSCE countries and other organizations to these operations.[67]

In spite of the importance of this statement, the exact significance that should be attached to it remains uncertain. The operational details that lurk behind the phrase 'case-by-case basis' are unclear, and it could be uncharitably observed that the communiqué really makes little difference to the existing system. The making available of 'resources and expertise' is also unclear, but presumably refers to NATO's C3I and logistics which played an important, but low-key, role in the Gulf War. At least the statement does open up the possibility of NATO actually doing something in future Balkan-type conflicts, rather than merely insisting that such conflicts fall out-of-area and are therefore of questionable concern.

Six months after the Oslo Summit the Council agreed on an even more qualified out-of-area role at their Brussels meeting:

> The Allies recognize that certain events outside the Treaty area may affect their common interests as members of the Alliance. Allied consultation on such events will be based on the recognition of those common interests. Those Allies in a position to do so may respond to requests by sovereign nations whose security and independence are threatened...[68]

In essence, the Brussels communiqué does little more than state the obvious: that individual nations may unilaterally or multilaterally carry out-of-area operations. Furthermore, the communiqué endorses the idea that it is sovereign nations that are most at risk in the new security environment. This frame of thinking omits the issue of Yugoslav-type situations arising elsewhere in the world. Aside from the lukewarm endorsement of an out-of-area role, the inclusion of the phrase that Alliance members 'may respond' to requests for assistance points to the fact that there are more examples of rifts being caused by potential involvement in out-of-area disputes than through collaboration.

Operations Desert Shield and Desert Storm may seem to prove that collaboration is possible. The coalition forces deployed to the Gulf included 530 000 US, 40 000 British and 20 000 French personnel. However, any aspirations of extending such collaboration to a NATO-wide feature have to take into account German constitutional deliberations, which eventually led them to make substantial budgetary contributions accompanied by low-scale military assistance to Turkey (air cover) and Cyprus (minesweeping, to relieve other NATO allies for operations elsewhere). The German public was adamantly opposed to any contributions of service personnel to Gulf operations. The success of Operation Desert Storm led many to overlook the fact that in nearly every area adjoining NATO territory there are substantial policy differences between the US and its European allies, not to mention the fact that there are also differences between the Europeans themselves. The 1990 crisis, triggered by Iraq's invasion of Kuwait on 2 August 1990, and the cooperation that followed, marks not a pattern but an unusual and atypical event. The success of Desert Storm certainly does not suggest that NATO members could adopt common regional policies with ease since, in this case, it is virtually impossible to separate Gulf policies from the wider Middle East concerns, which include European doubts about the US's pro-Israeli stance.

The Gulf crisis was unusual in three ways. First, the violation of Kuwait's territory and sovereignty was an unambiguous violation of international law. Few cases are so clear-cut. Second, the invasion of Kuwait posed a common problem for the US and its European allies – safeguarding the access to oil supplies. Third, the Middle East was not only known to be a volatile area (the eight-year Iran–Iraq war had reached a tentative conclusion in 1988) but also very heavily armed. Thus the potential for large-scale destruction and the spread of the conflict to adjoining countries was a possibility. For these three reasons the 1990–91 Gulf crisis serves as a weak basis on which to build any general observations about NATO's out-of-area potential.

The Yugoslav crisis may seem to offer similar legal grounds for intervention, but access to vital raw materials is not at stake. The willingness of NATO powers to become involved, in the absence of any strong self-interest, is weak in the Yugoslav case. Yugoslavia does, however, pose one interesting development for NATO's out-of-area role; a precedent was established when the UN asked NATO to draw up a detailed scheme for the enforcement of a no-fly zone over Bosnia. In December 1992, NATO offered the use of NATO aircraft and C^3I assets for the enforcement of a no-fly zone. On 31 March 1993, the UN Security Council passed Resolution 816, which authorized the enforcement of the no-fly zone. A week later NATO fighter aircraft and AWACS aircraft began enforcement activities, thus becoming the first NATO forces involvement in an out-of-area role combat role. Whilst undeniably welcome, NATO's participation came late, and it is also involved in the least controversial and safest way – the enforcement of a no-fly zone, where there is no serious competition for control of the air and where NATO's engagement rules are so restrictive, remains a far cry from a commitment of substantial forces on the ground.

The US, understandably, wishes to preserve its freedom of action in foreign policy; the Clinton administration is no exception to this. A relatively new development stemming from Clinton is the beginning of a series of policy differences between the US and Britain, which has traditionally been the US's strongest backer in out-of-area issues. Differences have become evident over the Vance–Owen plan, which the British were far more enthusiastic about than the US State Department. US policy in the Middle East and North Africa has also brought differences between the countries to the fore. The British backed World Bank loans to Iran, while the US were reluctant to do so; on the other hand, the US was more willing than Britain to see sanctions against Iraq eased. US and British interests also clashed on the issue of the oil embargo against Libya.

NATO's Existential Alliance?

Where out-of-area collaboration has taken place, the European allies have generally preferred to coordinate cooperation through other European institutions, such as the WEU or the EC. This has led to the logical advocacy of the WEU as the unofficial out-of-area working arm of NATO. This connection, though, is fraught with difficulties. Indeed, the WEU role in out-of-area operations has been of limited value and has generally been overstated. The examples of the WEU's role escorting oil tankers in the Iran–Iraq war or that of the WEU's coordinating role in the Gulf War are limited.[69] Furthermore, the WEU has only had experience in naval operations; it remains to be seen how air or ground operations would fare under its guidance. These factors aside, there still remains the same central objection: the fundamental unwillingness of any WEU member to commit forces to the WEU other than on a case-by-case basis.[70] There are also practical objections that can be raised against the WEU as an out-of-area actor. For example, how does the WEU operate out-of-area? The Cold War reliance of Europe on the US for reinforcement capability, based on the assumption that Europe was the battlefield, means that most of the airlift and sealift capability is American, not European.[71] Moreover, the European allies have no airlift capability designed to carry a full-size battle tank. The WEU would therefore have to rely upon the US to 'donate' the use of transport and refuelling aircraft, which defeats the very purpose of having the WEU, or build up its own indigenous capability by purchasing US made C-17s or produce their own line of transport aircraft. Both options are highly questionable at this time of cutbacks and defence budget stringency.[72] Aside from the WEU having no effective infrastructure to conduct an out-of-area campaign, there is the problem of the potential role of nuclear weapons where, presumably, NATO would be the existential nuclear alliance for the WEU.

Within NATO the out-of-area issue will probably continue to be met on a case-by-case basis, according to whether Articles 2, 4, 5 or 6 of the North Atlantic Treaty can be invoked. Although a move beyond the traditionally delineated NATO area of interest would seem to be desirable, particularly in relation to the Visegrad countries, efforts to extend it southeast ward would meet opposition from some countries, which, in turn, could test the cohesion within NATO beyond breaking point. The dilemma that faces NATO is that consensus on an out-of-area role may well be easiest to reach amongst the European NATO members, most notably on incidents in the Gulf area; however, for any meaningful out-of-area operations to be mounted, US assistance will be required for the immediate future.

The possibility of the British and the French forming a joint out-of-area force, maybe with Italy, cannot be completely discounted. Such a force could imitate CENTCOM and would involve those European powers that are most concerned about out-of-area issues. A more general out-of-area role for NATO will have to be coordinated with the CSCE and the UN. Encouragingly, following the NATO Council meetings in Oslo and Brussels, there are signs that relations between these institutions are becoming closer.

THE NORTH ATLANTIC COOPERATION COUNCIL

The North Atlantic Cooperation Council (NACC) is discussed in more detail in Chapter 10. The NACC was founded mainly in response to pressure from Central and Eastern Europe, as well as from the Central Asian ex-Soviet republics, who started a programme of diplomatic visits to Brussels in June 1990. The first formal meeting of the NACC, between NATO members and the Central European countries, was held in December 1991, a month after it was established at the Rome Summit (see Appendix I, Figure A.6). At this meeting, the NACC pledged to deepen cooperation within the framework of the CSCE process. The second meeting, held in March 1992, included not just the participants who had attended the first meeting, but the CIS states as well – eventually membership would climb to thirty-eight (the sixteen NATO members and twenty-two non-NATO members). This second meeting produced a 'Work Plan for Dialogue, Partnership and Cooperation' that broadened the consultative procedures between members and between NATO and other organizations. The third meeting took place in Oslo in June 1992; it applauded the closer cooperation resulting from the Work Plan, but otherwise really said little of substance. The Oslo meeting acknowledged that, 'Our Council contributes to the building of a new security architecture based on cooperative relations among states and a network of mutually reinforcing institutions.' It also stated that, 'The CSCE has a vital role to play in achieving a more peaceful and cooperative Europe', expressed 'deep concern at the dangers of nuclear proliferation' (and therefore recommended the preservation of the NPT and the speedy ratification of START), and stressed the importance of 'the consolidation and implementation of existing arms control, disarmament and confidence-building measures'.[73]

The December 1992 Brussels meeting proposed a vigorous exchange of information regarding the planning and preparation of peace-keeping operations, including joint training exercises. As a result of this meeting an *ad hoc* Group on Cooperation in Peacekeeping was established. Their deliberations have, so far, established that peace-keeping should be carried out only under the supervision of the UN or the CSCE. Presumably this leaves NATO with the task of being the military training and support framework for UN/CSCE operations. Although superficially attractive, any such use of NATO forces will inevitably run into thorny legal questions, such as the out-of-area question discussed above, the question of command and control, and the role of France. It may make much more sense to coordinate such activities within the CSCE context, thereby avoiding these problems while making the CSCE a viable security organization with truly pan-European roots. The NACC, at root, is still firmly embedded in Western Europe.

In addition to the NACC there are other links with Central and Eastern European countries, some less formal, such as a series of seminars designed to help the establishment of defence-oriented military forces and the successful implementation of arms control and civil-military relations. There is also more formal cooperation at the military level: namely the Group on Defence Matters (GDM), established on 1 April 1992 at a meeting of the fifteen NATO defence ministers (minus France) and those of the Central and Eastern European countries. The GDM was charged with responsibility for coordinating information exchanges on all matters dealing with multilateral or bilateral defence activities.

NATO's Military Committee, the highest military committee in the NATO structure, met with their GDM counterparts from the Central and Eastern European countries for the second time in April 1993, which resulted in several senior officers from non-NATO countries being invited to courses at the NATO Defence College (Rome) or at the SHAPE College (Oberammergau).

Although the NACC and the collaboration framework is still very new, its prime value seems to be as a consultation forum. This is obviously an important role, but does it go far enough? The NACC is in many ways a half-way house: the non-NATO members have their feet under the table, yet they are not fully-fledged members. In spite of the rhetoric and ambitious agenda outlined for members at its meetings, the NACC is pitifully funded: the FY 1993 budget for example amounted to $1.5 million. The NACC also has no formal security guarantees, and, beyond the list of supportive statements, possesses few functions that are really concrete. Full membership of NATO for NACC members is clearly a long way off. However, there are four reasons why it may be prudent to offer membership of NATO to NACC states:

(1) The collapse of the Warsaw Pact and the Soviet Union has removed the alliance system to which most had belonged. Although not lamented, its absence does pose the problem of what should take its place. Uneven military arsenals and potential rivalries could lead to the search for new alliances which in turn would beget a rival alliance. NATO membership could alleviate this tendency.

(2) Some states in the former Warsaw Pact have little or no indigenous military forces. Attempts by these states to build up forces for defensive purposes could easily be misinterpreted. Again, NATO membership may remove much of the incentive to devote precious resources to regional arms races with the resultant risks of destabilization.

(3) In contrast to (2), there are many states, mainly in Central Europe and the former Soviet Union, that are still heavily militarized, that depend heavily upon their defence industries for economic well-being, and that have military officers who could form the caucus for opposition to fledgling democratic regimes. By incorporating new members into NATO, these militaries could also be included and, if not neutralized, at least involved in the process of ensuring stability in their country and region.

(4) Membership would remove any stigma of being 'second-class' states and involve all in a collaborative effort rather than leaving some as the passive (and maybe resentful) recipients of assistance.

The refusal to advance membership to the non-NATO NACC members poses further problems of exactly what guarantees should be forwarded to them, and what NATO would do in the event of a conflict in one of these countries. The assumption by the NACC of a peace-keeping role (endorsed emphatically at the NACC meeting in Athens on 11 June 1993),[74] the collaborative military training programmes within the NACC, the exchanges of military officers, the support of arms control, and the central role that the CSCE plays in NACC's schema, all beg the question of whether these resources are not being misdirected. Should not these resources be put into the CSCE itself? If they are not, there is the potential danger of the NACC being hobbled by the parent organization, namely NATO. The disputes over out-of-area intervention, the specific constitutional strictures of Germany, the question of French relations with NATO, and differences of perspective between the US and some of its European allies may confound the effectiveness of the NACC. The transferral of resources and collaborative spirit to the CSCE would circumvent many of these issues and make a viable peace-keeping organization for all of Europe a real possibility.

COMMAND AND CONTROL

Following the reorganization of NATO's force structure, changes are underway in NATO's command structure that should be in place by July 1994. There will be a reduction in main commands from three to two, European and Atlantic; Allied Command Channel will be absorbed into Allied Command Europe (ACE). There will also be three new, subordinate commands to ACE, responsible for the south, central and north-west NATO regions.

The reorganization of NATO has meant that, in effect, NATO is a new organization in the operational sense and is therefore as unproven as any other alternative European security organization. The reorganization into multinational corps does away with the operational doctrine of NATO, which was organized around nationally homogenous corps whose training and equipping was the responsibility of national commands and who, in time of war, were deployed in national corps sectors. While the system had undeniable flaws, such as the lack of standardization of weapons and communication systems, it also had strengths that may not be immediately apparent. The operational doctrines of the European allies have largely been shaped by history (sometimes going back for centuries), culture and national quirks.

The reorganization of NATO also poses the question of command

and control in the new security environment. During the Cold War the hegemonic position of the US was reflected in the disproportionate number of US commanders in NATO, including SACEUR's position – largely due to the control and release procedures for nuclear weapons. With the scaling down of the US contribution to NATO from 326 000 to around 100 000 (and maybe lower) by FY 1996, and the dramatic reduction in the number of US nuclear weapons in Europe, the US's preponderant command role is no longer justified. The reallocation of command and leadership responsibilities within NATO should be part of a general streamlining of NATO's decision-making apparatus. There are few compelling reasons to have SACEUR always be an American, or for NATO's Secretary-General to be a European. The appointment of a European to SACEUR's position would do much to counter anti-American sentiment and simultaneously encourage the European allies to assume more leadership responsibilities.

The deliberate 'dual-hatting' of SACEUR and the Commander of US Forces in Europe serves to reminds one of yet another aspect of command and control: the release of nuclear weapons. The structure of NATO reflected and made credible the concept of extended deterrence in the Cold War alliance. While nuclear weapons are clearly not irrelevant or redundant, the thorny issues of who is in the command structure and who should request and be granted authority to release nuclear weapons could be raised as an objection to the appointment of a European SACEUR. One study has suggested that the problem may be solved by 'vesting such authority with an American deputy with separate channels to US officials for release authorization'.[75]

The role of nuclear weapons vis-à-vis rapid reaction forces also leaves room for concern. Of the three components of the new force structure – Main Defence Forces, Reaction Forces and Augmentation Forces – only the second component is intended to be ready for deployment without major mobilization. This also assumes that there will be a measure of predelegated release authority in the case of nuclear forces. If NATO continues to rely heavily on US nuclear forces for such eventualities, the question must be raised of whether allies will unwaveringly follow the US lead in time of crisis.

NATO REVIVED? THE 'PARTNERSHIP FOR PEACE'

The 'Partnership for Peace' was unveiled to the public at a NATO Summit, held on 10–11 January 1994 at NATO's headquarters outside Brussels. It also marked the occasion of Clinton's first trip to Europe as President. Partnership for Peace was first proposed by US Secretary of Defense, Les Aspin, at the NATO Defence Ministers meeting in Travemunde, Germany, in October 1993. Secretary of State, Warren Christopher, presented the Partnership for Peace to the North Atlantic Council at the beginning of December 1993. Its formal unveiling took place in the January 1994 summit.

The 'Partnership for Peace' could be seen as a last-ditch effort to save NATO from obsolescence or, alternatively it could be regarded as proof of NATO's continued vitality; before assessing which it may be, an explanation of the Partnership for Peace is appropriate (especially as it seemed to engender much confusion following its public unveiling). The Partnership is an attempt to 'build a new comprehensive Euro-Atlantic architecture of security with, and not without or against Russia'.[76] The opening statements of the Brussels summit appeared to be hopeful as far as aspirant members were concerned since it stated '*When* we extend membership of NATO to new countries, it will again be to help stabilize Europe and not divide it again.'[77] As far as the existing European NATO members were concerned, the most important part of the opening statements was that pertaining to the US forces in Europe; this stated that 'A significant level of forces permanently based in Europe will remain an indispensable component of our common security.'[78] According to the declaration of the heads of state and government participating in the Brussels meeting, which was released on 11 January 1994, the Partnership for Peace goes 'beyond dialogue and cooperation to forge a real partnership'.[79] Does it?

The invitation issued by the NATO heads of state and government to participate in the Partnership for Peace was made with the overall objective of 'enhancing the security and stability in the whole of Europe'.[80] However, the next sentence mentioned NATO's desire to strengthen its ties with the 'democratic states to our East.'[81] This was little more than window dressing, since it merely reconfirmed the right of other European states to join NATO if it was felt they enhance the security of the Alliance, enshrined in Article 10 of the North Atlantic Treaty.

The invitation is extended to those countries who are 'able and willing' to contribute to the security of the Alliance. Assuming a given state is able and willing, then:

(1) Partner states will participate in political and military bodies at NATO headquarters with respect to Partnership activities.
(2) Partners will expand and intensify military cooperation through-

out Europe, increase stability, diminish threats and build strengthened relationships by promoting the spirit of practical cooperation and commitment to democratic principles.

(3) All will work towards transparency in defence budgeting, promotion of democratic control of defence ministries, joint planning,
joint military exercises, and create the capacity of NATO forces
to carry out peace-keeping, search-and-rescue missions and humanitarian operations (which includes a proposal for peace-keeping field exercises beginning in 1994).

(4) Partners will be invited to send permanent liaison officers to NATO
Headquarters and a *separate* Partnership Coordination Cell at Mons
(Belgium) will be established to carry out military planning for
Partnership activities.

The specifics of the plan are laid out in detail in an accompanying
framework document.[82] Those states accepting the invitation will have
to agree to abide by the principles laid out in the UN Charter, the
Helsinki Final Act and the Universal Declaration on Human Rights,
with special mention of the need to refrain from the use of force against
the territorial integrity of any state, to respect existing borders and to
settle disputes by peaceful means. Partner states will then draw up and
provide NATO authorities with Presentation Documents which identify their willingness to contribute to the Partnership goals as well as
what military and other assets might be used to this end. NATO will
then propose a programme of partnership exercises and other activities
based on the Presentation document. The partner states may, *at their
own expense* and in consultation with the relevant authorities in Brussels, establish liaison offices at the NATO headquarters. Furthermore,
Partners 'will fund their own participation in Partnership activities,
and will endeavour otherwise to share the burdens of mounting exercises in which they take part'.[83]

The Partnership for Peace offers no security guarantees to any of
the central European states; the closest that the Partnership comes to
this is when it promises to 'consult with any active participant in the
Partnership if that Partner perceives a direct threat to its territorial
integrity, political independence, or security'.[84] NATO had made it clear
before the summit that the Ukraine would be excluded from the Partnership unless its pledges to dismantle its nuclear arsenal were upheld
and that it join the NPT as a non-nuclear state. President Clinton left
the NATO Summit and embarked immediately upon a whistle-stop tour
to persuade the leaders of the Czech Republic, Slovakia, Poland and

Hungary to accept the Partnership terms. Once the details of the Partnership for Peace became available those states who were most interested in the design were generally disappointed and the Partnership fell well below their expectations (for a discussion of this point see Chapter 10).

The Partnership for Peace falls short of its real goal, which was stated to be the forging of a 'real partnership.' A real partnership would involve full and equal membership of the Alliance with full security guarantees. These are patently not on offer although the message behind the summit seems to be that those states participating in the Partnership activities may be on a fast track to membership. The principal objection to admitting, say, the central European states (the Visegrad four) to full NATO membership seems to be the fear of alienating Russia. If these state were admitted to full NATO membership the potential is there, so the argument goes, for Russia to feel alienated, which would run the risk of re-establishing divisions or blocs in Europe, this time further to the east. There are two objections to this line of reasoning: first, by refusing to extend guarantees to (at least) the Visegrad countries for fear of alienating Russia, NATO has effectively established a buffer-zone where Russia, not the US, appears to have the upper hand; and second, warnings from Russia in November and December 1993 that any attempts to expand NATO's membership would lead to a fundamental reappraisal of Russia's security policy, could be interpreted in some west European capitals (notably Paris) as signifying that the US is more concerned with safeguarding its relations with Russia, than it is with maintaining those of its European allies with their neighbours. By refusing to address the issue of membership in a direct manner, the Partnership for Peace has merely added to the security concerns of Central Europe. As Senator Richard Lugar has observed, NATO risks 'exacerbating the current security vacuum in Central Europe by a policy vacuum'.[85]

Defenders of Partnership for Peace will doubtlessly observe that it does not entirely rule out the possibility of expanding membership, even it is vague about the specific procedures for aspiring members to follow. What terms and guidelines there are remain extremely general. Moreover, to succeed and to impress NATO members will also take a considerable investment on the part of aspiring members, since they have to fund any Partnership activities. This may be an intolerable strain upon their fragile economies. The Partnership invitation also hints that aspiring members must convince NATO members that they are democratic and stable – such arguments seem counterintuitive. The aspiring members *need* security in order to complete their transitions to democracy. Offering security guarantees after democracy has been well established, misses the point entirely. Security is a *prerequisite* for the successful completion of the democratization process.

The Partnership was designed to prove the relevance of NATO to Post-Cold War Europe. However, the vagueness regarding membership issues and the unrealistic stipulations may well encourage the further disintegration of NATO and the active pursuit of 'Euro options' at the expense of Alliance solidarity. The Partnership represents in many ways a lowest common denominator that all can live with, but does not hide the tension within the Alliance that, ultimately, will determine the success or failure of the Partnership. For instance, Germany has seen the extension of security guarantees eastward as a matter of some urgency, while it appears that the Clinton administration is content to put off such decisions for a considerable time. The Clinton administration's pledge to retain a 'significant level of American forces permanently based in Europe' poses two problems: first, there is the issue of whether the US public are willing to burden the costs of a 'permanent' presence in Europe; and second, the issue of what a 'significant level' amounts to is left open. Some may regard this as a crude means of ensuring a level of control and influence over European foreign and security policy on the cheap – a view that has already emanated from Paris. Nor does the Partnership settle the issue of where the 'Euro alternatives' fit into the Partnership. By failing to offer specific conditions for membership, NATO may have inadvertently made membership of the WEU and EU far more attractive and thus have proved its own irrelevance.

The Central and Eastern Europeans are understandably dissatisfied with the Partnership proposals. It may also prove unsatisfactory for the west European allies. The January 1994 NATO Summit was a chance for Clinton to reassert US leadership within the Alliance and to take a historical opportunity to shape Europe's future security design. By failing to demonstrate a clear American commitment to Europe (not just Western Europe), the US has exacerbated the Euro-Atlantic debate and has not presented the Alliance as a clearly more attractive alternative to European options, such as the CSCE or WEU. Furthermore, the extreme care exercised by Washington not to alienate or upset the Russians has created the unfortunate impression that, to the US, Russia is more important than Eastern Europe – this is the basis for the charges that the Partnership is in fact a 'Yalta II.' The clear choice made by Washington in favour of a 'Russia-first' stance will have repercussions within

Europe and, most notably, Paris. The chances for a *rapprochement* between France and NATO are slimmer and will serve only to exacerbate French suspicions that the security of Europe cannot be entrusted to the Americans. It can be entrusted only to the Europeans themselves.

Much of the centre stage at the summit was occupied by the Partnership for Peace. The summit was notable for the position adopted regarding the Bosnian crisis. The failure to address the crisis in Bosnia was the catalyst behind the debate on NATO's relevance to the post-Cold War world. The opening statements at the January 1994 summit included the claim that NATO is the 'only functioning collective defence organization on the globe.' If this claim is true, it raises the question of why NATO has not been more active in Bosnia. One answer to this question is supplied in the opening statement when it is observed that, 'NATO has done everything which the United Nations have asked of it in the former Yugoslavia.' This is certainly true, but sidesteps the issue of whether these actions have been effective or enough. The Summit 'reaffirmed' NATO's readiness to carry out airstrikes – for the third time – in order to prevent the 'strangulation of Sarajevo.'[86] The only new development in the case of Bosnian has been the extension of the use of NATO airpower to help relieve the beleaguered UNPROFOR contingent in Srebrenica, and to help open the airport at Tuzla for humanitarian relief operations.

It remains to be seen whether the third threat of airstrikes against Serb positions is taken seriously, or whether it is seen as another empty threat. The Brussels summit marked one new development that suggests that NATO's resolve to carry out the airstrikes, given UN consent, may be real; this is the shift in Britain's position from being opposed to airstrikes, on the grounds that UNPROFOR lives may be endangered, to support for airstrikes. Whether they take place or not is out of NATO's hands. The UN's Secretary General, Boutros Boutros-Ghali remains opposed to airstrikes and is critical of NATO's position. Unless he changes his mind, NATO's threat will have little effect and may lower NATO's credibility once again.

The overall purpose of the Summit was to reinvigorate NATO, give it direction, purpose and leadership. The key vehicle for doing this was the Partnership for Peace, the emphasis upon peace-keeping, and some supposedly tough statements on Bosnia. NATO has failed in almost all of these respects, in spite of the claims that the summit was a success and, for Clinton, a virtuoso performance. In reality, it was a clear indication that the US would like to continue to exercise leadership in the Alliance with the minimum commitment possible. The failure to provide guidance to aspiring members about specific criteria for membership may only damage NATO and certainly does little to stabilize the fragile democracies of Eastern Europe. Security is not a by-product of democratization: it is a prerequisite. This point seems to have been missed. The summit failed to answer two pressing issues: it neither proved NATO's relevance, nor did it solve the European security identity crisis. Clear US leadership and specific guidelines for membership of any non-NATO CSCE country would have solved these problems. The failure to do so may have proven NATO's essential irrelevance.

CONCLUSION

NATO is an organization that was designed with the immediate problems of the Cold War in mind. Historically NATO has been a self-proclaimed collective security organization as well as a political organization. With the end of the Cold War, NATO has embarked upon an ambitious plan to retool itself to cope with the new challenges of post-Cold War security. In the Cold War period NATO's main emphasis was placed upon its military role, particularly the US military presence in Europe. The demise of the Cold War has shifted that emphasis to a broader political mandate, while not excluding its defensive obligations.

In spite of the efforts to reshape NATO, it is still an organization that fits awkwardly into the post-Cold War world. One of the most notable challenges to this reshaping has been the growth within NATO of an increasingly assertive European voice since the 1970s. The exigencies of the Cold War and the reliance of the European NATO members upon the US's military presence helped to downplay the importance of this voice. Throughout the late 1970s until the present there has been a growing interest amongst the European NATO members to coordinate their wider security policies through the general process of European Political Cooperation – decisions on defence remain with NATO. The end of the Cold War means that the wider aspects of security policy are arguably as important or more important than purely defensive questions. NATO does not have a history of dealing with these wider problems, while other institutions have made non-military aspects of security their preserve.

NATO's rejuvenation does not go far enough and fails to provide a new or imaginative answer to European security problems. Of most concern is NATO's failure to answer the out-of-area question. The confines of NATO's area of interest remain as they were in the Cold War years, as defined in Article 6 of the North Atlantic Treaty. Of course there is nothing stopping *ad hoc* discussions of problems outside this area, as was the case in the Gulf War of 1991. The Yugoslav crisis revealed the shortcomings of NATO's reliance upon *ad hoc* decision-making; a system that defends one state's sovereign rights (and strategic resources), but stands by and does nothing in another case, is an inadequate basis for a new European security system. There is at present little likelihood of a negotiated settlement to the out-of-area issue, since France and Germany will be unable to agree in the foreseeable future.

The role of the US in NATO has been that of the hegemon. The Alliance has served as a vehicle for more general US influence over European affairs. This gives rise to two possible scenarios for the future. The first is that, since the US's role in NATO has acted as the 'cement' of the Alliance and has given Western Europe cohesion, the absence of a sizeable US military presence and involvement in NATO will *ipso facto* lead to the unravelling of Western Europe and the gradual decline into internecine squabbling that has characterized much of Europe's history. On the other hand, one might alternatively conclude that the US role in NATO has actually been a brake upon the development of European cohesion. Indeed, the second argument is gaining ground. For instance, the latter stages of the Cold War saw vociferous objections to the US nuclear role in Europe, as well as the recognition of increasingly divergent sets of interests between Europe and the US. This is not meant to imply that there is no scope for transatlantic cooperation, but it does challenge the notion that transatlantic cooperation and collaboration require a US military presence or US hegemony. The adaptation of NATO to the post-Cold War world has still left the US with the leadership role, but this will become increasingly incongruous as the need for greater European autonomy increases.

It would appear that NATO has attached much importance to the NACC as a way of rejuvenating NATO and making its role more relevant to post-Cold War Europe. The question posed above is whether the NACC eventually will be constrained as a result of the internal difficulties within NATO? In response to this question, it was suggested that the NACC is an immensely important development, but it would fit better within the CSCE's organizational umbrella, which in turn would lead to the creation of a truly pan-European security organization.

NATO *does* have a valuable role to play in the future of Europe's security as a transition organizer, where it can help and encourage the development of a coherent and effective European security body which, in time, could assume the responsibilities of NATO as well as address the wider challenges of post-Cold War European security. Stalwarts will doubtlessly rejoinder that NATO could be adapted to meet these future challenges. Yet this is questionable since any adaptation involves not just tinkering with the NATO apparatus but a substantial overhaul. It would also involve a redefinition of the US's relations with its European allies.

With the exception of the CSCE, NATO and the other institutions discussed so far have failed to provide any coherent pan-European security agenda or to encourage Eastern Europeans to assume a significant role in European security issues. In spite of the creation of the NACC, NATO remains a select club open only to a few; the WEU remains what its title suggests – Western; the EC, with its grandiose goal of European Union, is another primarily Western-centric club. The institutions and the national agendas discussed so far leave those Europeans who are not lucky enough to be in these select clubs in a dilemma: the Warsaw Pact and the Soviet Union have dissolved, yet Eastern Europe remains an insecure place and there is little apparent interest from the Western Europeans or the US to consolidate their 'victory' in the Cold War by stepping into the breach. It is to this problem that we now turn.

Part IV
Pan-European Security?

10 Democracy without Security

Instability in Central and Eastern Europe, especially southeastern Europe, has been the *casus belli* of two world wars as well as other smaller wars – the fate of Yugoslavia providing the most striking present example. Yet no security guarantee of either a unilateral or a collective nature exists for these countries in the post-Cold War period, beyond those of the UN Charter. There may be agreement on paper that the security of Western Europe is 'inseparably linked' to that of other European countries, but in practical terms deeds do not match words. If historical comparisons are at all appropriate, the West seems to be seeking a new brand of containment. But this time it is not incipient communism that is the menace; it is the turmoil of Central, Southern, and Eastern Europe that has to be contained.

In institutional terms this new kind of containment can be seen in the stressing of the value of defence and national security to the detriment of collective security. The US has remained committed to the former and has shown little interest in collective security; this in turn is reflected in the US's predilection towards maintaining NATO at all costs. By stressing the sanctity of NATO or the potential of the WEU, Western European security concerns are emphasized while pan-European concerns are not. The resistance to forward security guarantees to Eastern Europe does not stem from ignorance about the threats faced by these countries, nor does it stem from Western European failure to integrate reforms in that part of the world; it stems from a fundamental unwillingness on the part of Western leaders to admit that the security of Eastern and Southern Europe is part of *their* security. While it has to be acknowledged that there are no simple formulaic answers to the security problems besetting these parts of Europe, there are measures that Western Europe should take to bolster the stability of the fragile democracies in other parts of Europe.

Part of the early post-Cold War resistance to assume security responsibilities for other parts of Europe stemmed from the difficulty of actually identifying the legitimate authorities in the newly independent countries of Europe. James Baker III expressed this idea in his July 1991 Aspen speech:

Perhaps the most striking phenomenon across all of Europe today is
the combined and simultaneous devolution and evolution of the nation-state... In Western Europe, evolution has been accompanied by
the devolution of power to the state and local governments, to regions that sometimes cross national borders, and to the private sector. In Central and Eastern Europe, on the other hand, devolution is
certainly the more prominent phenomenon. With the collapse of
communism, ethnicity has re-emerged as a powerful political force,
threatening to erect new divisions between countries and, even more
acutely, within multinational states.[1]

Baker was correct to observe that ethnicity is a powerful force in
European politics, as well as elsewhere. His observations have, however, become dated in two significant ways: first, the evolution of
the nation-state into federalist structures in Western Europe is exaggerated; and, second, the devolution of the nation-state in Central and
Eastern Europe is also exaggerated. With the benefit of hindsight we
can see that support in Western Europe for defence and foreign policy
integration (and indeed the whole Maastricht progress towards European Union) has waned. In spite of the still fragile nature of regimes
in Central and Eastern Europe, along with Czechoslovakia's 'Velvet
Divorce', the rudiments for stability and prosperity are present. Contrary to Baker's observations, the difficulties of extending security
guarantees do not stem from devolutionist tendencies in Eastern Europe, but from those very same tendencies within the EC. It is not
Eastern Europe that is a threat to Western interests; it is the latter's
negligence that is a bigger threat to the fragile countries of the former.
   The image of Central and Eastern Europe as an area of instability,
and a 'threat' to Western interests, is arcane but explains NATO's
continuing role as the prime 'defender' of the territory of the Alliance
members, as well as the lack of a coherent out-of-area policy. Talk of
constructing a Europe 'whole and free' rapidly becomes fanciful if the
alleged instability of Central and Eastern Europe is used as the rationale for not providing security guarantees. Although NATO, or other
Western organizations, can clearly not guarantee the survival or stability of regimes, it is the fragility and potential instability in these countries that should provide the rationale for advancing guarantees. This
point was nicely captured by the ex-foreign minister of the Czech and
Slovak Federal Republic, Jiří Dienstbier, who noted during a visit to
London in 1990 that, 'There's nothing wrong with NATO except that

we don't belong to it.'[2] A similar comment was made by Eduard Shevardnadze, chairman of the parliament and Georgia's head of state:

> Those who led and participated in the peaceful European revolution of 1989–91 were right to count on the great solidarity of the Atlantic Alliance. We have begun the process of freeing Europe and the world from the nightmares of the Cold War and the threat of thermonuclear annihilation; for this, we have paid a very high price. The West has got what it wanted – the elimination of a concentration of powerful force in Central Europe, and so got rid of enemy number one. As a result, Europe was united, but many of us – I mean the Eastern part, the new states and their peoples – were left alone, exposed to numerous threats and misfortunes.[3]

Proposals for new pan-European security organizations have been forwarded from Poland, Romania, Czechoslovakia and Hungary, as well as from CIS republics. One of the Soviet foreign policy goals, enshrined in the 1955 Warsaw Treaty, was the eventual creation of 'a collective security system in Europe based on the participation of all European States, irrespective of their social and political structure, whereby the said States may be enabled to combine their efforts in the interests of ensuring the peace of Europe.'[4] More recently, in April 1990, Vàclav Havel, President of the Czech republic, proposed moving away from the old bloc system to a collective security system. In the same month, Valentin M. Falin suggested that Germany's role would be that of a motor to help extract the best out of NATO and the now defunct WTO and 'then meld them into an all-European security organization'.[5] In 1991 Hans-Dietrich Genscher spoke of the importance of developing a 'comprehensive partnership for security' between the former members of the Warsaw Pact, including the Soviet Union. He added that, 'If we together learn to guarantee our security from one another, we in Europe will be on the way to a collective system of security.'[6]

In spite of the well-meant protestations of 'equal security for all countries', proclaimed in the November 1990 Charter of Paris for a New Europe, or Warren Christopher's claim that 'maintaining stability *throughout* Europe remains NATO's core responsibility',[7] such slogans may well ring hollow for the Eastern and Central Europeans. The reaction of the various security organizations and individual countries to the Yugoslav crisis can scarcely be of much comfort. Attempts by Central European governments to design themselves a pan-European security structure have been of limited significance. In January 1990,

Vàclav Havel, in a speech before the Polish Sejm, emphasized the importance of trilateral cooperation between Czechoslovakia, Hungary and Poland. In April of that same year leaders of the three countries met in Bratislava to discuss Havel's initiative and to try and identify areas of common concern and interest – a process that soon took its name from the meeting place. Havel proposed a three-stage transition from the bloc system to a collective security system. The proposed stages were:

(1) 1990–91: The creation of a European Security Commission, comprised of foreign ministers of the CSCE. The Commission would consist of an Executive Secretariat and a Military Section, which was subordinated to the Advisory Committee of the Foreign Ministers.

(2) 1991–96: An Organization of European States (based on the Helsinki Final Act (Decalogue)) would coordinate relations with the eventual aim of securing a common defence guarantee amongst the members.

(3) 1996–2000: A European Confédération (along the lines of Mitterrand's suggestion) would be established which would incorporate the European states into a commonwealth of nations.[8]

These proposals were presented to the CSCE in June 1990, with the clear intention that the CSCE would be responsible for developing the mechanisms for the peaceful settlement of disputes between its members and, eventually, create a peace-keeping force. At the CSCE summit in November 1990 there was broad agreement on the need to institutionalize the CSCE and to promote its visibility in European affairs. This had been agreed upon by the NATO members in the London Declaration of 6 July 1990. At the same meeting, the leaders of Poland, Hungary and Czechoslovakia agreed to coordinate policies on economic, political and humanitarian issues and all resolved to withdraw in unison from the Warsaw Treaty Organization by June 1991. As a result of pressure from these three countries, Gorbachev accelerated the dissolution of the military arm of the Warsaw Treaty Organization by a few months, bringing the deadline to 1 April.

At the February 1991 Visegrad summit, between the leaders of these three countries, it was agreed that they had to find a place and identity in the region and that they should become sovereign actors within the bounds of the Helsinki Final Act and the CSCE's Charter of Paris. In addition to the Visegrad goals, a number of bilateral security agreements were made around the same time. Hungary signed a bilateral military cooperation agreement in December 1990 with Romania; just before the Visegrad summit Hungary also signed a similar agreement with Czechoslovakia and one with Poland in March 1991. The importance of the 'Bratislavia process' lies in the emphasis placed by these countries upon the adoption of a Central European policy initially by themselves and then in seeking external security guarantees. To seek economic stability and security within Central Europe alone would offer little promise without the eventual aim of wider integration. Jiří Dienstbier argued:

> The systematic evolution of trilateral cooperation must be developed and intensified, however, in a manner compatible with the pan-European process, so as to facilitate eventually wider cooperation mechanisms on a continental scale... Any other path of development would run counter to the interests of the Central European states and of Europe as a whole.[9]

By the beginning of 1991 it was obvious that the requests from new non-communist governments in South-East and Eastern Europe for security assistance of various kinds were falling on deaf ears in Washington, in spite of the support for these proposals given by Genscher. The CSCE became a victim of its own popularity, since the enthusiasm with which the CSCE and the Charter of Paris were greeted amongst the NATO governments posed the problem of whether the CSCE was an adjunct or replacement for NATO. There were also growing doubts about the viability of a pan-European security organization, expressed mainly by James Baker III.

The continuing decline of the Soviet Union throughout 1991 emboldened the Central European powers to form closer relations with NATO. Poland's case is illustrative: although Poland's stance was defined by Defence Minister Kolodziejczyk as one of 'armed neutrality', there was a clear move towards alignment with the Western European countries. At the same time that Kolodziejczyk clarified Poland's defence stance, the Polish foreign minister, Skubiszewski, stated that Poland had an 'implicit' security guarantee from NATO and that the expansion of NATO to include Poland is an 'explicit Polish foreign policy goal'.[10]

In the light of Western doubts about the viability of pan-European security structures, the Eastern European countries were forced to consider more immediate answers to their security dilemmas – a closer relationship with NATO appeared to be the only option which reflected a slim chance of a US-backed security guarantee. Thus, during the year a whole series of Atlantic-oriented groups emerged, often prompted by US embassies. During this time, the Visegrad countries were also subject to pressure from conservative forces in the Soviet Union. These conservative forces tried to persuade them to sign special security guarantees that would have effectively prevented them from joining Western institutions that did not coincide with Russia's interests.

In October 1991 the Visegrad countries met in Cracow, Poland, and reconfirmed their desire to integrate into Europe's political and economic institutions, as well their security institutions. Realizing that full membership of these organizations was not yet negotiable, the aim was to establish minimal security guarantees for 'as long as they remain outside those organizations' formal security arrangements'.[11] Jozsef Antall, Hungary's prime minister, made it clear that eventually NATO's security umbrella should be extended to cover Central and Eastern Europe and that full membership of NATO should not be ruled out. Formal approaches designed to secure NATO membership were accompanied by bilateral attempts at forming security relations with various NATO members as well as neutral European countries. However, in spite of their efforts, it became clear that NATO membership was not on offer.

Attempts to join other institutions, like the EC, have met with partial success. The Visegrad countries have managed to negotiate association accords, but even these have been of mixed value. Jerzy Lukaszewski, the Polish ambassador to Paris, observed that in 1992 EC exports to the Visegrad countries rose by 31 per cent, those from the Visegrad countries to the EC by under 10 per cent. Financial assistance, according to Vàclav Klaus, the Czech Republic's prime minister, has also been disappointing when compared to the potential trade benefits that could accrue to the EC, leading him to the conclusion that 'Western Europe has put a note on the door: do not disturb.'[12]

Since it is to NATO that Poland, the Czech and Slovak republics and Hungary have looked to for security guarantees, what are the objections to extending membership to these countries? There are six main arguments:[13]

(1) Extending NATO eastward would promote anxiety in the Russian federation. This in turn could slow down the critical defence spending cuts that are necessary to rejuvenate their economy. It may also have negative effects on Russia's willingness to carry out its arms control obligations (START and CFE).

(2) Admittance of Central European members would disrupt the Alliance machinery. An extension of membership would lessen the credibility of existing defence commitments and it would also dis-

rupt Alliance integration (both in the political and military senses). Even half-way measures, such as associate membership, are not realistic since there is no such entity as an 'associate' member of the North Atlantic Treaty. If there were, such membership could run the danger of creating a 'two-class' membership which could cause friction.

(3) NATO simply does not have the capital, equipment or manpower to extend its commitment east, particularly at a time when NATO members are cutting defence budgets.

(4) An intensive debate about membership and who should, and presumably who should not, be admitted could split the Alliance.

(5) If NATO admitted the Visegrad countries there would be immense pressure from others to join. If these countries were admitted, NATO could find itself pulled into insuperable ethnic conflicts which may spill over frontiers.

(6) The Visegrad countries are in no apparent danger. Nor is there any foreseeable danger which could warrant a formal NATO commitment.

There are several retorts to the arguments aimed against the extension of NATO eastward. In partial response to the first issue, Yeltsin has stated that NATO membership for Russia would be a 'long-term political aim'.[14] This proclamation followed those of all the other Central and Eastern European countries. Until Yeltsin dissolved the Soviet parliament on 21 September 1993, there seemed to be no overriding objections to Eastern European membership of NATO or other organizations. In a visit to Warsaw on 25 August, Yeltsin had expressed understanding of Poland's desire to join NATO and acknowledged that membership would not threaten Russian interests; the same sentiments were then expressed in the Czech Republic and Slovakia. Yeltsin's speech was taken as a green light for an intensive effort by President Lech Wałesa to gain Polish membership of NATO. Nor were there any signs that, if admitted, the Visegrad countries would prevent other European or CIS countries joining. The direct effects upon Russia's security, following membership of some of the Central European states, would also appear to be few. The only common CIS/NATO border in an extended NATO would be in the Kaliningrad enclave, unless Russia managed to create a truly unified defence structure within the CIS.

In a sudden and unexpected volte-face, Yeltsin, under pressure from the armed forces, reversed his position and objected to the extension of NATO to include Eastern European countries in a letter to President

Clinton (also sent to Mitterrand, Kohl and Major). Part of Yeltsin's reversal can undoubtedly be explained by the victory of the former Communist Party (known as the Democratic Left Alliance) in Poland in elections in October 1993. The letter reminded Western leaders that Russia had also expressed an interest in joining NATO and that membership for Poland, the Czech Republic or Slovakia, should not be considered without simultaneous membership for Russia.[15]

Objections to extended membership on the grounds that it may create anxiety in the Russian Federation could be reversed. If reforms in Russia do not succeed and more conservative elements seize power, one of their main objectives may be to extend *their* defence arrangements into the European heartland. The proposition is therefore simple: if NATO, or other bodies based in the West, do not extend into Central and Eastern Europe, then an unstable Russia may. In a worst-case scenario, which is not totally implausible, an authoritarian regime in Russia may maintain good relations with the West while simultaneously attempting to subjugate, for example, the Ukraine with the goal of forcing it into a new 'federation'. Such a development would make the Central Europeans understandably nervous, and for them may well carry hints of 'Yalta revisited'. By observing Russian sensitivities and anxieties, those of the Central and Eastern Europeans seem to be downplayed. Perhaps one of the strongest arguments to be made on behalf of immediate expansion to include Eastern European members is that this would strengthen democratization in Russia, not weaken it.

There is also evidence that Russian resistance to Central European membership of NATO is waning. The most spectacular example of this occurred during Yeltsin's first visit to Poland as leader of Russia. After the August 1993 meeting, President Yeltsin and President Lech Wałesa issued a joint statement repeating Poland's determination to join NATO and pointed to Yeltsin's 'understanding' of the policy.[16] With an unsettled Ukraine on its border and poor relations between that country and Russia, Poland may be expected to press its case for membership all the more vigorously, presumably closely followed by Hungary and the Czech Republic.

The second argument, that extended membership would be disruptive of the Alliance's machinery and arrangements, is one that does not really answer the problems of security elsewhere in Europe. NATO will have to go through major disruptions as a result of the end of the Cold War, quite aside from the question of new membership. The cohesion that has been built up over nearly four and a half decades was based upon a common threat perception which dictated everything from the shape and size of the infrastructure elements through to the multi-national exercises. The cohesion can no longer be taken for granted in the absence of a common threat, nor does the carefully constructed infrastructure necessarily have that much relevance any more – pipelines lead into the middle of Germany, airfields were built away from the inner-German border, exercises were built around heavily mechanized divisions, and so forth. There is nothing set about NATO's infrastructure and it has survived enormous disruptions in the past, such as that provoked by the French decision to withdraw from the integrated military command of NATO in 1966. At that time nearly all of the logistical lines ran through France to the Central Front.

An extension of this argument is that the Visegrad countries are themselves in danger of fracturing. In that case, membership of NATO, associate and eventually full membership of the EC and the WEU (in which case the 'Western' would have to be dropped) may help to keep these countries together. The disintegration of the Czechoslovak federation has threatened the future stability of the Visegrad triangle, which was widely viewed in Western Europe as a valuable instrument of regional stability within the region. It also served as a point of contact for many Western European institutions: the assumptions made by the new Czech Republic seemed to be that if it could extricate itself from its local tangles and those in the federation the new republic would be more readily accepted by the Western Europeans. The opposite has proved to be the case. Since the dissolution of the Czechoslovak federation, the Poles and Hungarians have made a concerted effort to strengthen Visegrad collaboration. The motives for keeping Visegrad collaboration close were particularly strong in the Hungarian case, since it represented a way of containing the historical disputes with Slovakia over the Hungarian minority in Slovakia[17] and the dispute over the control of the Gabcikovo (Danube) dam. Ironically, the separation from the Czechs could help the Slovaks identify more areas of common interest with Hungary. The future of Visegrad cooperation is obviously bleak without the active participation of the Czech Republic. Again, it is within the powers of NATO, the EC and other 'Euro' organs to persuade the Czech Republic to work through the Visegrad network rather than around it. Germany may play an especially important role in this respect, since the Czech Republic's largest trade partner is Germany.

The third concern, that NATO would have to invest in the forward stationing of US and Western European defence forces on the soil of the new members at a time of economic stringency and reductions in all the militaries, is a valid objection. But it is an objection predicated on a *defensive* approach to security problems. New defence commitments need not involve huge increases in defence budgets, nor in the build-up of forces, if a collective security approach is adopted whereby military forces are deployed to contain and head off crises rather than to intervene after a crisis has developed. The budgetary stringencies faced by the NATO members do not even begin to compare to those faced in the east. Bulgaria's military, under a civilian minister of defence, Dimitar Ludzhev, has been forced to stop payments to those industries providing goods and services to the military. Hungary received only 56 per cent of the money its defence minister claimed it needed to survive. The Czech republic warned that it needs at least half as much again as its current military budget, in order to be able to restructure the armed forces. Poland also has chronic problems with its military – ranging from lack of spare parts, which has grounded many of its MIG-29s, to lack of capital with which to buy new or used equipment.[18] The associated problems of civil–military relations could also exacerbate stability in these countries. Although there is a general trend towards civilian control over the militaries, problem areas still remain, such as civilian control over defence ministries – an area where there is no civilian experience. The same observation could be made of defence industries. Disenchantment amongst the displaced officer corps and unemployment resulting from closures in the defence industries could be a volatile combination that could undermine liberal governments.

Concerning the fourth argument, the debate about who should and who should not be admitted as new members, could indeed split the Alliance. However, it is worth observing that NATO's liaison programme, outlined in the London Declaration, invited specific governments to establish 'regular diplomatic liasion with NATO' and to 'share with them our thinking and deliberations in this historic period of change' (the governments invited were those of the USSR, the Czech and Slovak Federal Republic, the Hungarian Republic, the Republic of Poland, the People's Republic of Bulgaria and Romania).[19] The criteria for membership should, if specified, be open to all of those countries who are participants in the liaison programme. The argument that NATO should not admit new members because debate over who to admit would split the Alliance could also be seen as a condemnation of NATO itself and its relevance to the post-Cold War security of Europe.

The fifth proposition, that membership of Central and Eastern Euro-

pean countries will mean that NATO will be dragged into ethnic disputes that cross state borders, is likewise spurious. Continuing refusal
to admit new members or to acknowledge that the ethnic problems of
Central Europe are linked to Western Europe's security leaves Manfred
Wörner's claim that 'security in Europe is indivisible' as an empty
phrase.[20] Perhaps the most uncomfortable conclusion that can be made
about the wisdom of extending NATO membership to the east is that
if NATO is so fragile that its infrastructure and machinery wouldn't
survive, if consensus is so hard to reach, if NATO is unable to afford
to extend any guarantees, if NATO is really not interested in ethnic
disputes which may cross borders, and if Central European membership would alienate Russia, then maybe NATO is the wrong organization to offer any guarantees to the east. Maybe the countries of Central,
Eastern and Southern Europe should look back to those organizations
to which they already belong for their security.

It would be unjust to argue that NATO and other organizations have
done nothing for security elsewhere in Europe; but what has been done
simply does not go far enough. The process of dialogue and liaison,
laid out at the North Atlantic Council's Copenhagen and Rome Summits, has promoted better understanding and built trust. But, by resolutely not offering any kind of formal guarantees or full membership,
NATO has left Central and Eastern Europe with no clear idea of how
to reintegrate into a Western security system or, more generally, the
Western economies. The lack of guarantees and the growing concerns
in Central Europe about the volatility in parts of the former Soviet
Union has intensified the search for formal ties. Presumably the same
volatility gives NATO members an even bigger incentive for not admitting any new members, since admittance may mean making awkward choices about whether to defend European countries against the
effects of violence spilling over from the CIS.

The visits of Vàclav Havel and Lech Wałesa to NATO were in themselves remarkable testimony to the changes of the last few years. Both
leaders recognized clearly that full membership for their countries was
out of the question, but they encouraged the further pursuit of liaison
with NATO. Both also issued warnings about the potential dangers of
leaving Central Europe in limbo. Vàclav Havel commented, in his address
to the North Atlantic Council:

> our countries are dangerously sliding into a certain political, econ-
> omic and security vacuum. The old, imposed political, economic and
> security ties have collapsed, yet new ones are developing slowly

and with difficulty, if at all. At the same time, it is becoming evident that without appropriate external relations the very being of
our young democracies is in jeopardy.[21]

At the end of his visit, Vàclav Havel proposed a joint CSFR/NATO
statement on basic principles of relations. This was resisted since any
such statement could be construed as a 'guarantee' to the CSFR. A
few months later, on 3 July, Lech Wałesa reminded the same audience
that, 'Without a secure Poland and a secure Central Europe, there is
no secure and stable Europe.'[22] Significantly, Wałesa did not press for
any kind of joint statement at the end of his visit. Havel's and Wałesa's
visits prompted concerns in Central and Eastern Europe about how
sincere NATO is in its desire to help the Eastern countries emerge
into full-fledged democracies, or the extent to which NATO is anxious
to reassure the former Soviet states.

Concern about security in Central Europe is not just confined to the
leaders of the Central and Eastern European countries. One of the most
eloquent, and strongest, criticisms of NATO's failure to forward any
meaningful security guarantees was given by Senator William Roth:

> I have been struck repeatedly by the strong support which NATO
> enjoys in Eastern Europe. Some of the newly elected governments
> even wished to seek membership in NATO. They believed, quite
> rightly in my opinion, that membership in a new alliance with a
> broadened mandate would dampen potential ethnic and regional dis-
> putes, consolidate their membership in the democratic community
> and generally deter the violence and instability which was endemic
> to the region before it fell under the cold hand of communism.
>
> But NATO, rather than seeking the fruits of victory, forsook the
> initiative and instead chose to abrogate the expanded new role that
> it could have played in Eastern Europe, choosing instead to stay
> with its now outdated mandate. East European applicants to the al-
> liance were fobbed off on the basis that their membership in the
> alliance would offend the Soviet Union. As the Soviet Union ceased
> to exist that excuse faded and, instead, they were informed that their
> concerns would be addressed by a new, unspecified security organ-
> ization.[23]

The 'new, unspecified security organization' was the North Atlàntic
Co-Operation Council (NACC). The NACC resulted from deliberations
between US Secretary of State James Baker III and German Foreign
Minister Hans-Dietrich Genscher in early October 1991. The delibera-

tions were in large part prompted by pressure from the Central European countries for an extension of the London Declaration's liaison programme.[24] The liaison relationship had been informal, and in their October meeting Baker and Genscher agreed on the need to formalize the relationship. It was at this meeting that the NACC was first suggested and subsequently adopted at the Rome Summit. In addition to the NACC it was also suggested at the October meeting that NATO would welcome 'periodic' liaison participation by Central and Eastern European countries in NATO Political and Economic Planning Committees, the Atlantic Policy Advisory Group and other lesser bureaucratic bodies.

The advancement of liaison, as specified in a joint statement by Baker and Genscher on 2 October and the Rome Declaration of 8 November 1991, was undoubtedly a welcome development to Visegrad heads of state, but it was still not a security guarantee, nor was it membership of NATO. NATO also sought to recognize some sort of vague commitment to other parts of Europe through the NACC. The New Strategic Concept, adopted at the North Atlantic Council's Rome meeting held on 7–8 November 1991, stated that the new situation in Europe had 'multiplied the opportunities for dialogue on the part of the Alliance with the Soviet Union and other countries of Central and Eastern Europe'.[25] Indeed, the Rome Declaration built on earlier London Declarations by pledging to 'increase transparency and predictability in security affairs, and thus to reinforce stability'.[26] Promises were also made to increase bilateral and multilateral cooperation in 'all relevant fields of European security' (leaving out a definition of 'relevant') with the overall aim of 'preventing crises or, should they arise, ensuring their effective management'.[27] The intent of all these proclamations was to express the 'inseparability of security among European states. It is built upon a common recognition among Alliance members that the persistence of new political, economic or social divisions across the continent could lead to future instability, and such divisions must this be diminished.'[28]

Proclamations are fine; commitment is another matter. Again, the Rome Declaration is illuminating: having stressed the importance of dialogue and cooperation between NATO and its neighbours to the east, with the objective of defusing crises and preventing conflicts, the Declaration then shifts the prime responsibility to the CSCE. The Declaration states: 'To this end, the Allies will support the role of the CSCE process and its institutions. Other bodies including the European Community, Western European Union and the United Nations may also have an important role to play.'[29] Perhaps with even more significance, the Declaration soon thereafter reconfirms that 'the Alliance is purely *defensive* in purpose'.[30] The overall impression is therefore that of an Alliance which, on paper, is willing to make noble sounding statements but which, in practice, has the expectation that other security institutions will intervene in the event of a crisis that does not directly involve NATO members. The reconfirmation that NATO remains a 'defensive' alliance seems also to mitigate against NATO being transformed into a collective security alliance that would assist its eastern neighbours in the early stages of a crisis.

The Rome Declaration highlights one of the paradoxes of post-Cold War European security: there is recognition that the political cohesion of NATO must be maintained for the stability of Europe, yet the cohesion is to be maintained by making no binding commitments to Eastern or Central Europe, not even the much-routed Partnership for Peace. Furthermore, beyond NACC, the Alliance has never explained when and under what conditions new members could be admitted to NATO under Article 10 of the North Atlantic Treaty.[31] The 1993 North Atlantic Assembly Presidential Task Force on America and Europe was notable for its silence upon the issue of membership under Article 10, except for mention that 'public discussion of these issues is not helpful at present.'[32]

The membership issue poses two problems. First, if as Manfred Wörner has suggested NATO is to become the centre of a European security network, this implies that NATO has to address the question of how to move away from being a purely defensive alliance, towards the centre of a pan-European collective security organization. Clear and realistic guidelines therefore have to be given in a timely fashion on conditions for membership. Second, there are problems with the CSCE Charter of Paris and the Declaration of the twenty-two NATO states and members of the former Warsaw Pact, which was adopted in November 1991. This states that:

> The unprecedented reduction in armed forces resulting from the Treaty on Conventional Armed Forces in Europe, together with the new approaches to security and co-operation within the CSCE process, will lead to a new perception of security in Europe and a new dimension in our relations. *In this context* we fully recognize the freedom of States to choose their own security arrangements.[33]

Since all sixteen NATO nations and the seven ex-WTO countries are signatories to the Charter, does this imply that the right to choose membership of NATO exists? Several criteria that could be applied to membership have been suggested.[34] Usually these criteria involve stipulations regarding democracy, the renunciation of all territorial claims, recognition of the principle of self-determination for subnational groups, adherence to the Helsinki Final Act, and so forth. It is worth noting as an aside, that such rigorous criteria were not applied to many of the original NATO members – as has already been noted in the cases of Greece, Portugal, Spain and Turkey. There are more recent examples of stalwart members of NATO and the EC who have been racked by political scandals, like that in Italy in the spring of 1993 that eventually led to the resignation of Guiliano Amoto. Events such as this suggest that not all Western European countries are paragons of democracy. The democratic criteria idea is questionable since it appears to confuse the horse with the cart: peace, or the absence of an overt threat, is a necessary *prerequisite* for the process of democratization in the European ex-Warsaw Pact countries. The insistence that the Eastern European countries prove that they are sufficiently strong and democratic before admittance to the select clubs of the West – such as NATO or the EC – seems counterintuitive.

A rigorous set of criteria that would have to be proven to meet the criteria of a democratic polity, which would then act as an entitlement for membership, may pose problems for Turkey, which in the last two decades has exhibited occasionally unconventional means of dealing with domestic opponents. Turkey has also been the subject of investigation by Amnesty International for persistent human-rights violations.

The democratization of Eastern Europe is still in its infancy and many teething problems must be expected. Many of the Eastern European states are young, most originating in the early twentieth century; consequently they have little experience with democracy (see Table 10.1).

The expectation that the fall of communism in Eastern Europe would rapidly lead to the reinstatement of democratic regimes proved mistaken, mainly because there is a notable lack of a democratic tradition to reinvoke in these states. Even where democracies were nominally established, such as Bulgaria or Romania, they tended to be corrupt and unstable. Tensions between the Czechs, the Slovaks and the ethnic Germans ended democracy in Czechoslovakia. The present 'democracy' that has emerged in these countries is still of a questionable nature; the May 1990 elections in Hungary, where the leader of the National Salvation Front, Ion Iliescu, won 85 per cent of the popular vote amidst allegations of intimidation, illustrates some of the difficulties. The lack of a democratic tradition is also evident in the political structures that

Table 10.1   Experience of multi-party democracy in Eastern Europe before 1992

	Year of independence or creation of modern state	Number of years of multi-party democracy before 1992
Poland	1918	10
Czechoslovakia	1918	25
Hungary	1918	4
Romania	1878	12
Yugoslavia	1918	13
Bulgaria	1908	7
Albania	1912	3

have arisen. For example, Romania has seen fit to invest most power in the presidency, Hungary in the parliament. Hungary has two main parties, the Democratic Forum and the Free Democrats; the Polish parliament (Sejm) has twenty parties, no one with more than 13 per cent of the vote.[35] Along with the beginnings of multi-party democracy, there have emerged parties based on historic nations, whose primary purpose is the protection of the rights of national minorities such as the Macedonians in Bulgaria, the Hungarian minority in Transylvania, the Albanians in Kosovo, the Turkish minority in Bulgaria, the Macedonian minority in Bulgaria; a further example is the Romanian dispute with Moldova and Ukraine over Bessarabia and Bukovina. Pressure from minorities and the fear of ethnic conflict may also act as a brake upon the demilitarization of these countries, and thus also, in turn, slow the conversion of large parts of their economies into producing export goods.

The collapse of communism and centrally controlled economic planning has posed considerable problems for the southeastern and Eastern European countries. If the Western European economies discontinue 'pump-priming' the post-communist economies, neither economic recovery, nor democracy, will be attained. Similarly, the extension of security guarantees to provide assurance against attacks on the state may also help to redress the heavy emphasis on defence production in the east and allow for much needed economic diversification.

There are many sources of conflict in Eastern Europe that could lead to further splintering in Europe, but all too often these sources are concentrated upon to the exclusion of the sources of cohesion. It is tempting to think in terms of the Yugoslavization of Europe, but the assumption that the Serb–Croatian–Bosnian and Muslim struggles in the former Yugoslavia will set examples for other historically based wrongs to be righted may be flawed. The tragedy of Yugoslavia may carry the opposite message. Many European countries have seen war in their own land, which makes its re-emergence a very unappealing option. Some, like Poland, the Czech and Slovak republics and Hungary are anxious for admittance into the Western European 'club' precisely to be able to avoid war spilling over their borders.

ECONOMIC ASSISTANCE AND STABILITY

Clearly economic stability will play an important role in stabilizing Eastern European and CIS states. In this respect the EC has done some valuable work through its PHARE and TACIS programmes. Clearly the EC alone cannot solve the economic troubles of these countries, but they can do much, especially in Central Europe, to prompt them along the right path. Failure to do this will condemn the EC to remain a latter-day neo-Carolingian empire with all of the attendant weaknesses.

Several events arose during 1992 that may be of significance. The early reforming countries, the Czech Republic, Hungary and Poland, have established sufficiently stable economies which may yield growth in late 1993–94. These three countries have Europe Agreements with the EU; Romania also achieved this status on 17 November 1992, followed shortly thereafter on 22 December 1992 by Bulgaria. The Europe Agreement signatories are entitled to send delegations to the EC where, although they have no voting rights, they do enjoy visibility and EC assistance.

Elsewhere in Europe the picture is not as encouraging. There is commitment to the market economy in Central and Eastern Europe, but it is not universal. Amongst the PHARE countries, there is more than two-to-one support (57:25) amongst those who believe that a free market economy is right for their country's future.[36] Amongst the TACIS countries there are more against a market economy (36:45). With the exceptions of Latvia and the Former Yugoslav Republic of Macedonia, there are more people in the PHARE states for, rather than against, the market economy. In the TACIS countries there are majorities against without exception – the greatest doubts being expressed in Armenia and Belarus. Georgia recorded the highest percentage of the TACIS countries in favour of a capitalist economy. The negative attitude towards the market economy evident in the TACIS countries is obviously due

Table 10.2 Support for membership of the EC in Central–Eastern Europe (%)

	Europe agreements		EC membership	
	For	Against	For	Against
Albania	92	0	91	1
Armenia	76	7	82	5
Belarus	72	4	81	5
Bulgaria	68	2	73	2
Czech Republic	76	5	84	7
Estonia	74	2	79	5
European Russia	55	3	70	4
Georgia	79	5	82	5
Hungary	76	4	83	4
Latvia	67	3	72	5
Lithuania	76	6	86	5
(Macedonia)	83	6	87	6
Moldova	82	6	85	6
Poland	75	6	80	7
Slovakia	77	5	86	7
Slovenia	86	4	92	4
Region Total:	68	4	78	4

Source: *Central and Eastern Eurobarometer* No. 3 (Brussels: Commission of the European Communities, February 1993).

to the pain and frustrations associated with the attempts at creating free markets. However, throughout the Central–Eastern European region there is strong support for membership of the EC as it is evidently seen as a significant factor in helping economic recovery – perhaps too significant (see Table 10.2).

With the collapse of the former Soviet Union the amount of trade between the countries of Central and Eastern Europe and the EC has expanded enormously. Severe problems still remain with intra-CIS trade. The existence of a (relatively) prosperous Central and Eastern Europe is obviously of enormous importance to the EC countries since it will help solve some of the immigration problems that Western Europe is now facing. There are associated economic dangers that should also be recognized, such as the existence of wide disparities in standards of living between the EC and PHARE/TACIS countries. In the case of Central and Eastern Europeans this may breed resentment of the type witnessed in the former East Germany against their Western counterparts. The relative improvement of standards of living in the Central

European economies may also move some of Western Europe's current problems to the east. Instead of Germany being the object of massive migration, the combination of rigorous migration rules in Germany, France and Spain, may move the influx of people to the Central and Eastern European economies (see Table 2.10).

The Costs of Non-involvement

There is a generally shared belief amongst Western European powers that the Central European powers and eventually Russia and some of the core republics should eventually be encouraged to integrate into the political and economic organs of democratic Europe. The question of access to European security organizations is far less clear. While the debate rages across the Atlantic, between the Western European capitals and Washington, about the new security architecture, the other 'Europeans' are being forgotten. Fears of the US being caught in a 1945 position, where it becomes the main guarantor of European security with an open cheque book, has created a strong resistance in Washington to extending security guarantees eastward. The cost of such an easterly commitment would be heavy, and it is one that should be borne by the Western Europeans as well -- but the cost of going in to try and clear up a bloody mess, of the type witnessed in Bosnia, may be far heavier.

The refusal of NATO to resolve the out-of-area debate and to insist that Eastern and Central Europe are still 'out-of-area' is a narrow assessment of Europe's security concerns. Threats to the security of the fragile Eastern European democracies are not 'out-of-area' – they are threats to pan-European security. Hungary's Minister of Foreign Affairs summarized the concern of many new democracies when he wrote:

> Having won the Wild West, the new frontier is moving eastward. The emerging new world order will neither be a Pax Germanica, nor a Pax Americana. It can be a Pax Democratica, if all of us want it but are ready to make some sacrifice for it. NATO has won the Cold War and thus averted the Third World War, but it has yet to win the peace. If you in the West fail, all of us may become losers.[37]

At present however, it seems that the Central European countries must remain in an awkward limbo: not fully members of the Western European security organizations and not completely left out of them either. In the event of a crisis in Central or Eastern Europe, the issue of what assistance NATO might give and what kind of guarantees against further crises it would forward, will inevitably arise. Prevarication on these issues and vague promises of something beyond liaison is a luxury that NATO cannot afford; there is simply not time, and Europe cannot afford another Yugoslavia. Indeed, it would be morally indefensible to stand by and watch more 'ethnic cleansing' take place.

The formation of the NACC is an attempt to paper over some of these concerns by making the Eastern European members feel involved with, but not part of, NATO. In spite of the fact that the 1993 NACC Work Plan, adopted on 18 December 1992, vastly expanded the scope of NATO/NACC activities – which now include political and security related topics, defence planning and military matters, defence conversion, economic issues, challenges to modern society, and the dissemination of information – NACC remains largely a paper organization with little real impact, for the following reasons: (i) NACC has no budget. Committees decide individually how much of their own budget should be devoted to a particular activity. (ii) There is no formalized NACC managerial structure – efforts to construct one have broken down due to economic disagreement. (iii) There is no dedicated NACC Secretariat. (iv) There is no Central NACC doctrine, concept or statement of purpose except the very general aim of 'contributing to the establishment of an irreversible and effective democratic process in the new republics'.

NACC suffers from acute institutional schizophrenia; the Central European powers have pushed for NACC to become something far more than a means for pursuing a 'dialogue [which] will provide a foundation for greater cooperation throughout Europe'.[38] NATO members, particularly Britain, have pointedly reminded these countries that NACC is not a security institution in its own right, but a forum for cooperation. The 1993 NACC Work Plan serves as an accurate gauge of NACC's actual potential. The plan pushed NACC in the direction of peace-keeping and inaugurated a consultation procedure on peace-keeping, commencing at ambassadorial level, followed by the relevant political-military experts and eventually cooperation amongst the NACC members. This was heralded as an important step forward for NACC, but did little more than apply principles that had already been agreed to in the CSCE's 1992 Helsinki Summit. The consultation–cooperation procedure takes place with NATO's encouragement, but little more. The few examples of NACC requests for NATO assistance have met with little enthusiasm. For instance, in summer 1992 Romania requested assistance in monitoring its borders with the former Yugoslavia, the Baltic countries and Moldova requested NATO assistance to monitor

Russian troop withdrawals, and in March 1993 Georgia requested NATO representation in Tbilisi. Although there may have been legitimate grounds for concern in every case, there still remains the point that however close and enthusiastic NACC consultation may be, they do not have the resources to make peace-keeping work. NATO's reluctance to take on board the concerns of NACC members serves as a reminder that the bloc-to-bloc structure is in some ways still intact.

The solution to the problems of Central and Eastern European security may be beyond NATO or any single organization. If so, NATO should be honest about what it is willing or unwilling to do, so that false hopes are not entertained by these countries and that scarce resources can be invested in collective security organizations. There are some signs of hope that attitudes are changing within NATO. For instance, the Deputy Commander In Chief, US European Command, James P. McCarthy, made the plea for NATO to extend itself east:

> Having defended its Cold War borders so successfully, NATO needs to look East and extend Europe's security environment in response to the shift of political gravity on the continent. It is now logical for NATO to strengthen stability and security beyond its borders, to those states which are rapidly expanding relations with NATO allies in the political and economic arenas. By bringing in the East, NATO offers the opportunity for a broader European security, and serves as the catalyst for fostering democratic values. This is the best possible protection of the peace we have won.[39]

The Central European states may yet face their biggest challenge from threats from within, a by-product of the attempts to transform totalitarian countries to democracy and centrally planned economies to market economies. Although there are inherent dangers built into this democratization process, and there may be no absolute security guarantees that NATO, or the CSCE, can give to these countries going through it, the dangers of doing nothing should also be stressed. Jiří Dienstbier made this observation with force:

> In a period when democratic political structures are immature and adequate political management is in short supply, social pressures that lack outlets or viable solutions can give rise to tension, disappointment, and ultimately to anger and instability. This negative spiral would be accelerated if Western governments, fearing economic refugees, decided to build a 'new wall' in response to social conditions in Central and Eastern Europe. Such actions would erode the

confidence of these countries in the West's democratic institutions. More clearly than anything else, the flight of citizens across borders demonstrates the inability of traditional security institutions such as NATO or the WEU to cope with nontraditional security challenges.[40]

The reference to nontraditional security challenges bears out the findings of previous chapters: there are no institutions that effectively address the wider security problems facing Europe today. That said, membership of these inadequate institutions still remains an important aim of many Eastern European countries. Association, with the eventual goal of full membership of the these institutions, still represents a source of stability for these countries, no matter how imperfect the institutions. Being associated with the EC, NATO and the CSCE may not *guarantee* active involvement on the part of Western Europeans, but it does make the plight of the Eastern European countries more awkward to ignore.

The NATO Council's summit in Brussels on 10–11 January 1994 (discussed in Chapter 9) launched the Partnership for Peace plan which many Eastern European leaders had hoped would set down specific terms and conditions for membership of NATO. The Partnership was far from this and made no security guarantees whatsoever, except the vague promise to 'consult' in the event of a threat to the integrity or territory of a Partnership country. In spite of the fact that the leaders of the Visegrad countries endorsed the Partnership for Peace, there was general disappointment that membership, let alone specific guidelines to attain it, were not on offer. Poland's President, Lech Wałesa, summarized the sense of frustration when he described the Partnership as 'an insufficient step in the right direction'.[41]

The rationale for not offering specific NATO membership terms to Eastern European countries was the fear of isolating Russia. By not offering membership, NATO would be able to avoid giving the CIS countries that NATO was moving eastward. This same logic created fears that the Partnership was, in effect, a Yalta II arrangement over and above the heads of the Eastern Europeans. The alienation argument is a problematical one since, by being sensitive to charges of alienating Russia, NATO may well have alienated Eastern Europe – in effect, Eastern Europe has been left in a security limbo facing what some perceive to be pernicious and maybe dangerous influences at work in Russia, especially in view of the prominence of Vladimir Zhirinovsky's far-right Liberal Democratic party in Russia. If specific conditions had been laid out for NATO membership for all non-NATO

CSCE members, the charge of building blocs would be difficult to sustain. Failure to specify membership terms may have endangered the fragile democracies of Eastern Europe; in which case, they then become a security headache for Western Europe. In short, it would have been wiser to offer membership terms to CSCE members and, depending on the terms, Eastern European countries may well have been the first to attain membership. In the event of attaining membership the appropriate Article 5 security guarantees would have to be advanced. To leave Eastern Europe in a security vacuum and to pretend that these countries are not intimately linked to the security of Western Europe is illusory. Clearly the Partnership for Peace had to consider the security interests of Russia *as well as* Central and Eastern Europe into consideration. The Partnership avoided one of the main pitfalls, which was to give the impression that it was aimed against Russia, but at the same time it failed to make clear what it is directed towards – except possibly the rejuvenation of NATO. Yeltsin's enthusiastic endorsement of Partnership for Peace not only dispelled fears of neo-containment but also, in effect, served as assent to Yeltsin's free hand in the 'near-abroad' – a term that has proven to be highly elastic.[42] Of notable contrast to Yeltsin's enthusiastic endorsement of the Partnership for Peace is the grudging endorsement given by the Visegrad leaders. The clear choice made by Washington in favour of Russian interests over those of Central and Eastern Europe may well lead to a renewed interest amongst these countries in European alternatives to NATO. What are these alternatives?

In security terms, it would seem that the CSCE and the Council of Europe have much more to offer these countries, as their main security challenges are from within, particularly the threat of ethnic conflict within these countries. The CSCE is the only existing institution that can address the problems of refugee movements, while the Council could be of immense value as a forum for the discussion of similar problems. However, the CSCE remains unwieldy and it offers no military guarantees, and even if it did it is highly unlikely that there would be sufficient consent to lead to any coherent action. This does not preclude the possibility of the CSCE developing into a far stronger organization, backed by security guarantees and a voting system that allows for a realistic chance of aid. Whether the security threats to many of the newly democratizing countries allows the time for such institutional developments is open to doubt.

The possibility of the Visegrad countries being incorporated into the EC and the WEU is an alternative suggested by German Defence

Minister Volker Rühe. During a visit to Hungary in early April 1993, Rühe suggested a two-pronged strategy: first, the acceleration of membership of the EC and the WEU for the Visegrad countries; and, second, the provision by the Western countries of 'comprehensive political and economic assistance to Yeltsin's reform policy'; and the West should 'not forget about the other CIS member states, primarily the Ukraine, either'.[43] Critical to Ruhe's suggestion would be to convince Russia that such a step would serve its interests and add to the stabilization of Europe.

To counter these arguments, it could be suggested that the Central and Eastern European countries should be encouraged to form collaborative security organizations of their own, organizations that mirror Western institutions, such as the WEU. This is an idea that has little documented support, nor does it address the economic dimensions of security. The establishment of such a bloc could elicit strong criticism from the CIS countries, which may see this as an attempt to re-create the old bloc system between Europe and the Russian area of influence.

THE EUROPEAN STABILITY PACT

On 21–22 June 1993 the European Council discussed a French proposal for a European Stability Pact (ESP), forwarded by the French prime minister, Edouard Balladur. The proposed pact is being considered not just by the European Council but also by the CSCE. In essence, the pact draws upon the Maastricht Treaty's guidelines for progress toward a European Union and is designed to ensure observance of borders and minority rights throughout Europe. Balladur's plan also aims explicitly to set clear standards for non-EC European countries to meet in order to qualify for membership.

The membership qualifications were enunciated at the European Council's Copenhagen Summit. In order to qualify for membership of the European Union candidates must:[44] (i) have achieved stability of institutions guaranteeing democracy, rule of law, human rights and the rights of minorities; (ii) have a functioning market economy and the capacity to deal with 'competitive pressures' within the European Union; (iii) be able to assume the obligations and costs of membership.

The CSCE and the Council of Europe would also assist in the task of designing rights that would protect minorities. Membership is open to any whose relations have 'not yet stabilized through membership in one of the major European political institutions', and who 'wish to

Table 10.3 Responsibilities under the European Stability Pact

Task	Institution
Consolidation of Frontiers	Agreed at signing of European Security Pact and drawn up by CSCE Committee of Senior Officials
Minority Rights	Council of Europe (European Convention on Human Rights) CSCE Court of Conciliation and Arbitration CSCE High Commissioner for National Minorities European Council
Inducements and Support	European Union/WEU
Military Cooperation	EU, NATO and WEU

belong in the relatively near future to the European Union'.[45] The twelve EC countries would consider membership in the EC for these countries on 'the express condition that they *first* settle problems that could threaten European stability'.[46] The EC would also consider associate membership of the WEU, economic assistance and military cooperation as well. Optimistically, the Pact is anticipated to be signed in 1994.

The ESP is therefore designed to avoid future Bosnian-type situations in Europe by encouraging non-EC members to recognize common principles regarding frontiers and minorities. Its secondary role is to structure the roles and functions of the existing European security machinery (EU, CSCE, WEU and the Council of Europe) into a more coherent and efficient unit. The proposed division of labour looks roughly as shown in Table 10.3.

Balladur's proposed ESP will commence with a conference where the initial agreements on frontiers and criteria for membership will be formalized. Since the primary aim is to bring peace and stability to Central and Eastern Europe, the initial conference will have to include representatives from the EU, US, Canada, the Nordic countries, Albania, Austria, Finland, Iceland, Switzerland, Turkey, Russia, Belarus, Ukraine and Moldova and the Baltic states, as well as those from Central and Eastern European countries. The questions of representation from former Yugoslavia depends upon the outcome of the civil war.

The ESP is encouraging because it marks one of the few constructive efforts to think and plan in pan-European terms. It also provides some potentially useful divisions of labour for the various institutions, which would overcome the problems of needless duplication and turf battles. But it also has its potential faults. The entry stipulations for the ESP are problematical. An argument that has been made earlier on in relations to NATO bears repeating at this point in reference to Balladur's ESP. By insisting that a country must have 'achieved stability of institutions guaranteeing democracy, the rule of law, human rights and respect for and protection of minorities', the main causes of instability will have been eradicated. Having achieved these stipulations, what then is the purpose of a security pact? The economic criteria for (EU) membership are perhaps the most fanciful of all. In the absence of substantial assistance from the US and Western Europe it is unlikely that any aspirant member will achieve a 'functioning market economy', much less one that is able to cope with the 'competitive pressures and market forces' within the European Union. The series of conferences leading up to the eventual signing of the Pact will hopefully be able to provide guidance, but many of the problems facing Eastern Europe will require more than guidance and ambitiously high hurdles that aspiring members will have to jump over. The question of what happens to those members that do not attain the criteria for membership is left unanswered. Those that fail may still pose consider-able security problems for neighbouring countries and may, ultimately, necessitate intervention by the institution(s) to which they were denied membership.

A more general set of concerns may upset the proposed ESP. Three in particular stand out. First, the plan has a French stamp upon it, which may cause nervousness amongst transatlanticists. Second, much of the ESP's success is dependent upon the continuation of the Maastricht process leading to European Union. Although the ESP does not exclude North American membership, it drastically changes the US's role and influence within the new security structure. It also gives NATO a far less significant role and heightens that of the EC and the CSCE. Whether Washington will readily accept its new role in Europe is open to doubt, particularly bearing in mind Washington's ambivalent attitude towards European integration. Third, the proposed ESP will establish a common machinery for conciliation and arbitration (based on the CSCE's machinery) and the Pact will establish the legal basis for enforcement action. However, the proposed ESP bureaucracy outlined in Table 10.3 may prove to be excessively bureaucratic and unmanageable. Even if it is not, the question of whether there is the *will* to support the inducements and supporting measures of the Pact remains a problem. Since this appears to be the primary responsibility of the EU, the familiar questions of Germany's role and British preferences for transatlantic involvement may come to the fore, as may concerns from the Mediterranean members of the EC who may perceive financial inducements to the east as a blow to their chances for further development.

The ESP also assumes that the EC continues on its path towards European Union and that the ESP will be incorporated under the general provisions of Article J.3 of the Maastricht Treaty. Progress towards European Union has received a number of serious setbacks, such as the virtual collapse of EMU and the less than enthusiastic endorsement of European Union in the referendums or votes held in Denmark, France and Britain. European Union may still be an attainable objective, but it will take more time and patience than was foreseen – which is exactly what the Eastern Europeans cannot spare.

Charges will inevitably arise that the Pact is self-serving for the French. While the ESP has an unmistakable French imprimatur and thus serves to promote a European design with France playing a key role, it also relies upon key institutions and other players collaborating, and moves responsibility for European security primarily, but not exclusively, into European hands. In spite of the ESP's flaws, it is a move which must be welcomed, since it is one of the few attempts to address security concerns in the pan-European context.

PEACE BY PIECES

Given the uncertain status of the ESP as well as reactions to it, the likelihood of a pan-European security organization appears remote, as is the possibility of widespread membership of the EC or NATO for other European countries. The CSCE remains the only existent pan-European organization, but it lacks dedicated forces or the ability to enforce decisions. In the absence of any formal security guarantees, what can be done to help these countries?

The only apparent solution would seem to call for *ad hoc* solutions that would be primarily aimed at economic stabilization, as well as efforts to increase the effectiveness of the military for defensive purposes (some of which exist in the various institutions). These solutions may include the following:

(1) The institution of Low profile military programmes, such as the training of specialists and officers. This could be carried out under the aegis of either the WEU or NATO. The importance of this

lies partly in the military realm but mainly in the political. Such training schemes could be used to imbue officers with democratic values and ensure the loyalty of the military to the democratization process in their countries of origin.

(2) The organization of joint military training for crisis prevention and peace-keeping operations between the European countries.

(3) The provision of certain armaments at a reduced cost to Central and Eastern European countries based on carefully controlled assessments of their defensive needs. Although much of the feasibility of this rests upon the democratization process within the region, it would have the benefit of enhancing the ability of these countries, individually or collectively, to defend their borders against attack. Any such sales would have to be complemented initially by training and instruction from Western sources.

(4) Expansion of dialogue through NACC by extending Article 4 to NACC members,[47] which would have the effect of making NATO members more aware of their security preoccupations.

(5) An increase in technical assistance in areas such as nuclear safety, the conversion of defence industries to domestic manufacturing, and the inspection of items limited under present arms-control treaties.

(6) The stocking of military equipment, on the model of NATO's POMCUS stocks, in NACC countries. The content of these stocks should be made known to Russia to remove any suspicion that NATO was merely being moved eastward. This equipment should be at the disposal of the CSCE, the UN or the WEU and would be funded through the NACC.

(7) Expansion of economic assistance to include better access to technology, investment guarantees, and greater accessibility to Western markets for Eastern goods. The collapse of the Soviet Union and the Council for Mutual Economic Assistance (CMEA) has deprived many Eastern European countries of their markets. The opening of Western markets to these countries in areas where they already have relative efficiency would greatly aid their process of economic recovery. Better access to technology would incur substantial revision, or even scrapping, of COCOM restrictions.

(8) Initiation of negotiations on the level of immigration to Western Europe. The general economic assistance referred to above could be tied to tighter controls in Eastern and Central Europe on immigration. Tighter controls would help alleviate the problems of immigrants using Eastern Europe to gain access to Western Europe illegally. It is in the EC's own interest to promote economic re-

covery in Eastern Europe, since this would remove much of the incentive to migrate westwards.

Although these are only suggestions and other alternatives may be offered, all would require time to negotiate and implement. Undoubtedly, if any were adopted they could lead to significant improvements in Central and Eastern Europe. These measures *do not* address short-term threats to security or instability. They may, however, provide much-needed stability and security in the long term.

Part of the reason that no solutions seem to have arisen to these difficult problems is that, unlike in the 1945 world, there is no decisive leader, figure or country to define an agenda. In 1945 one country, the US, clearly had the political, economic and military requisites to lead the Western world. In the post-Cold War world these essential ingredients are no longer possessed by one power; instead they are divided unequally between a number of powers.

CONCLUSION

There are a number of constructive actions that NATO and other organizations could take, in the attempt to build a genuinely collective security system; some of these have been suggested above. They are essentially ad hoc responses to the issue of security in Eastern Europe. These measures could be extended to the CIS. Objections that the cost will be too high, that Western Europe and North America have enough problems of their own, and that these countries cannot and should not be expected to provide panaceas for every security threat to Europe, are valid; they nevertheless have to be balanced by long-term consideration of the costs to Western Europe of instability elsewhere in Europe.

Ad hoc responses will also call for all of the current European security institutions to play a role in pan-European security. The CSCE is clearly the only institution open to all of Europe; as such, it must assume prime responsibility for arbitration and attempts to settle disputes amicably. The role of the CSCE beyond this depends largely upon its ability to act under current voting rules, and the development of its constituent organs, such as the Crisis Prevention Centre. The WEU clearly does not have the attractiveness of the CSCE as an arbitration centre. Yet it may assume increased significance in the event that military intervention is called for. Unlike NATO, the WEU is not constrained by geographical limitations upon its area of security interests; it is, however, constrained by its ability physically to move forces and to provide support. The WEU also leaves open the possibility of European action in the event of US indecisiveness or non-involvement.

NATO is of questionable significance as long as its geographical limitations and membership restrictions apply. It could assume an important military function in some of the activities suggested above, such as military training and technical assistance. Although the NACC contributes to the post-Cold War security dialogue, it has been argued that there is an element of tokenism to such extensions to the Alliance. As a forum for advancing the dialogue, the CSCE may eventually prove of more significance then the NACC.

The pursuit of *ad hoc* solutions suggests the eventual need for a new organization. It is possible that a European Security Organization, based conceptually upon the WEU and the CSCE, would give more institutional coherence to the problems of pan-European security. Whatever the name of the institution(s), the dilemmas pertaining to security will remain the same. If the political consensus does not exist in Western Europe to treat the security problems of Eastern Europe as *their* security problems, any institution be it new or old will be inadequate. To simply ignore these countries is short-sighted, since there can be no security and stability in Western Europe without matching stability to the east. If crises in Eastern Europe are stemmed early, confidence in the new security structure will be built and the democratization process will be promoted and safeguarded, as will the attractiveness of Eastern Europe as a potentially lucrative market.

To underestimate the lack of urgency and to wait for another Yugoslav-type crisis is to misunderstand the most important change of all since 1989: for the lands of former foes are now those of friends. Although the series of reforms in Eastern Europe have yet to produce much that is tangible, in part due to expectations that were too high, it remains obvious that Eastern Europe will require assistance and encouragement from its Western neighbours. Currently Eastern Europe is in limbo, especially from the security viewpoint. So long as this remains the case, talk of 'victory' in the Cold War and of a 'Europe whole and free' will remain, respectively, premature and empty.

11 Lessons for European Security from the Yugoslav Conflict

At the time of writing the irreparable dissolution of Yugoslavia was assured; all that remains unclear is the eventual shape and composition of the new states that now make up the former country. Although reflection at this point may be somewhat premature, the constant references to the former Yugoslavia throughout this book and elsewhere indicate the need to consider what lessons have been learnt for the future of European security, both in terms of leadership and issues of institutional structure.

The crisis in Yugoslavia has upset many of the comfortable assumptions made about the end of the Cold War. Some, like Francis Fukuyama's much publicized views on the end of history, which posited the final victory of liberalism over communism, have proven to be dramatically wrong.[1] While this is not the place to debate the intricacies of Fukuyama's argument, a brief consideration of his precepts does reveal the general Western cultural assumption that with the demise of communism, those states formerly under its yoke would behave and act like their Western counterparts. Thus, it was assumed that the route to democracy and economic stability was assured. It was also assumed that Western legal norms, such as the inviolability of borders and frontiers, would be upheld.

Many of these Western assumptions turned out to be quite wrong, if only for conceptual reasons which, as it turned out, were to have important political ramifications. For instance, 'democracy' to many Western minds meant removing all vestiges of authoritarian or dictatorial regimes and replacing them with multi-party systems. Once multi-party systems were in place, the country in question could then proceed to build a market economy. The transition from various types of authoritarian regimes to democratic ones is difficult enough in itself; when the added burden of making a second transition (to a market economy) is added, the enormity of the task becomes almost overwhelming. However, notions of 'democracy' and the exercise of democratic rights was, in reality, to have a vastly different meaning for many Central

347

and Eastern Europeans, as well as those living in the newly independent ex-Soviet republics. For these people, democracy signalled fore-
most the right to *national* sovereignty as a precondition for political
democracy.

The differences in fundamental ideas about democracy were soon to
undermine cherished Western assumptions and norms regarding the way
democratic states behave. Obviously, if national sovereignty is a precondition for political democracy, the chances of supposedly inviola-
ble borders being violated is high. Nor were Central or Eastern Europeans
prepared to accept that claims to national sovereignty could only be
accepted if the nations were already recognized subjects under international law – such as the Czechs and Slovaks. The essential differences between the Western world and the East at the end of the Cold
War explains in part why Western Europe and North America have
been shocked by events in Yugoslavia and elsewhere. For Western
Europe, seemingly set on a course of ever-intensifying integration, the
prospect of the new-found freedoms of the peoples to their east being
channelled into ethnic and nationalistic conflict seems almost counterintuitive.

The unwillingness, or inability, of the post-Cold War hegemons to
exercise their power and influence in the Balkan area has led to the
reawakening of competing historical claims. The lack of established
civil societies in this area, unlike in the countries of Central Europe,
encouraged the pursuit of nationalist claims.[2] These claims were based
upon unresolved historical antagonisms dating from the inter-war period
that were suppressed, but never forgotten, during the Cold War period.[3]
In the case of Yugoslavia, the waning influence of the Soviet Union
over Eastern Europe led to a recrudescence of aspirations for national
sovereignty amongst the Yugoslav (non-Serbian) nations. The Serbian
regime attempted to centralize the government of the entire country
and to rescind the autonomy of the republics, which had been granted
under the 1974 constitution. The gradual disintegration of Yugoslavia,
as well as the secessionist movements elsewhere in Eastern Europe
and the former Asian Soviet republics, provided an awkward conun-
drum for Western governments:

(1) It was difficult for Western governments to condemn efforts of
national unification and to uphold the inviolability of frontiers, in
light of their warm and rapid endorsement of German reunification.
(2) On the one hand, open support of democratic movements by the
West often implied a rejection of the territorial *status quo* and

thus tacit support for the splintering of the state. On the other hand, to support the *status quo* would more likely than not involve supporting conservative or repressive elements.

(3) Intervention or strong condemnation was also difficult for Western European governments, nearly all of whom have had to cope with their own secessionist movements.[4]

The bind in which many Western governments found themselves explains their tendency to turn away from the conflict in question or to wait for a resolution of the situation merely to evolve. While it would be untrue to claim that the Western European or the North American governments supported the June 1991 use of force by the Federal Army in Slovenia, following the declaration of independence by Croatia and Slovenia, they did not actively oppose it either. The actions of the Western governments from this time on show a tension between their own interests in Eastern Europe – stability and prosperity – and those of the Central and Eastern Europeans, which in some cases involved the breaking up of a country, with resultant security problems for Western Europe. Most Western governments were prepared to put order and stability at the top of their list of priorities, even if this meant the suppression of democratic secessionist movements.

Amongst the many confusing issues to come out of the conflicts that engulfed Yugoslavia, was the question of the implementation of the principle of national self-determination. Specifically, the question of who should exercise this right became a critical issue: Croatia and Slovenia claimed the right should be exercised by the Yugoslav republics, while Serbia argued it should be the Yugoslav people. The application of either solution spelt trouble for Bosnia and Herzegovina, since it was the only Yugoslav republic with no clearly identifiable ethnic group upon which to base a claim to statehood – unlike with Serbia and Croatia. The Serbo-Croatian-speaking Muslims constituted the largest ethnic group, at around 44 per cent of the population, having enjoyed recognition as one of Yugoslavia's nations since 1971.[5] Serbs and Croats comprised 31 per cent and 17 per cent of Bosnia's population respectively.[6]

The dissolution of the Yugoslav federation set the stage for the rival Bosnian, Serbian and Muslim claims to Bosnia's territory. During the course of 1990–91 discussions were held on the future of Yugoslavia. Many ideas were explored, including some form of cantonization of Bosnia; independent statehood for the individual republics, but with some central control over foreign and security policy; or a new Yugoslav association to include Bosnia, Croatia, Serbia and Macedonia. In 1991 the Serbs and Croatians formed autonomous provinces within Bosnia, which marked the first step towards the eventual break-up of Bosnia. In early March 1992 a referendum was held and a vast majority voted in favour of Bosnian independence. However, the referendum was boycotted by the Serbs and, as a result, it was argued that the referendum had no effect unless agreed to by Bosnia's three constituent nations. In spite of attempts at international mediation in March 1992, various plans for an independent Bosnia divided up between the three constituent nations (equal portions being allotted to Serbs and Muslims, with a lesser portion to Croats) were rejected as unworkable. Further attempts to reach an agreement broke down later the same month. The breakdown of another attempt to mediate led the state presidency of Bosnia and Herzegovina to order the mobilization of its territorial defence forces. This followed in the wake of clashes between Serbian paramilitary forces, the Yugoslav army, and the Croatian armed forces in mid-March. In mid-May the Yugoslav army was officially withdrawn from Bosnia and Herzegovina. However, many Serbian officers and soldiers of Bosnian extraction remained and were incorporated into the Serb armed forces in Bosnia.

By September 1993 the break-up of Bosnia had become all but inevitable. In the middle of that month Bosnia's President Izetbegović agreed to negotiations in Geneva with the country's Serbs, Croats and Muslims. The Owen–Stoltenberg[7] agreement accepted the dissolution of Bosnia, to be replaced by three ethnic mini-states; the Bosnian Muslims were to receive 30 per cent of the territory, Bosnian Serbs 52.5 per cent and Bosnian Croats 17.5 per cent. Under this plan the Muslims would end up with less territory than they wanted, but more than they possessed at that time. The proposed Muslim area also contained much of Bosnia's (heavily damaged) industrial potential, but was completely surrounded by Croats and Serbs who could, at whim, put a stranglehold on the Muslims. The siege of the city of Mostar, shortly after the agreement was signed, served as a brutal reminder of this fact. The Owen–Stoltenberg plan collapsed when the Croats and the Serbs refused to yield another 4 per cent of Bosnia to the Muslims. Radovan Karadžić, the leader of the Bosnian Serbs, coldly observed that, in the absence of an agreement, the Croats and the Serbs would simply divide Bosnia between themselves.

Following the collapse of the Geneva negotiations, Izetbegović presented his case to both the UN Security Council and to Washington. Neither showed any inclination to implement resolutions or to give substance to rhetoric. On 12 September US Secretary of Defence Les

Aspin made it clear that the US would send up to 25 000 troops to Bosnia but only on the condition that the Europeans contribute forces of the same size and that a command structure (by which was meant NATO) be agreed upon beforehand. Both issues are problematical in London and Paris. In the absence of any willingness to enforce the Owen–Stoltenberg agreement, Bosnia will be divided between the Croats and Serbs. The Muslims will be displaced, killed or subjugated. This grim scenario may not be the end of the story as violence may also follow elsewhere as Bosnia dissolves in the midst of competing demands for autonomy from Zagreb. Serbia may also face severe problems resulting from ethnic pressures applied by Albanian Muslims in Kosovo and Hungarians to the north.

In spite of further attempts at international mediation, especially the Vance–Owen and the later Owen–Stoltenberg plans, the brutal war in Bosnia has continued unabated. Even the imposition of UN sanctions against Serbia and humanitarian aid efforts seemed to have little effect in slowing down the war or the horrendous casualty rates. Most of the civilian casualties were Muslims who were killed in the process of 'ethnic cleansing' – a term which refers to attempts to create ethnically homogenous areas through the purging of those of different ethnicity. Reliable estimates for the number of civilian casualties are scarce; suggestions that over 100 000 have died seem reasonable and probably on the low side.[8] In addition there have been enormous upheavals of civilians, which have contributed to a massive refugee problem for Europe (see Chapter 2).

All parties to the conflict have exhibited blatant violation of human rights and international law, and have shocked many Europeans. In spite of the horrendous images that have come out of Bosnia, ranging from emaciated detainees in Serbian detention camps, to the aftermath of a Croatian massacre where women and children were raped and killed, the likelihood of massive international armed intervention seems small although not out of the question. Bosnia poses some of the hardest questions regarding the future of European security. It should also prompt soul-searching about the values that Western Europe and other parts of the developed world profess to uphold.

LEADERSHIP AND RESPONSIBILITY

Among the many questions raised by the Bosnia imbroglio is that of leadership and responsibility. Attempts have been made to reach settlements, backed by various institutions and countries; but all seem to lack the will or conviction actually to make a settlement stick. The Serbs in particular have been disinclined to take Western cajoling seriously. There has also been a lack of coordination; for example, Germany forced the early recognition of Croatia and Slovenia as a means of drawing international attention to their plight. This, in turn, met with accusations of German attempts at reviving influence in Western Yugoslavia and caused serious rifts within the EC.[9] The premature German recognition of Croatia and Slovenia jumped the gun, since the EC had already decided to recognize their independence. With their recognition by all of the EC's members, Yugoslavia ceased, *de facto*, to exist. Britain and France made the appropriate condemnatory noises but otherwise declined to push for further action, apart from supporting the UN arms embargo. The US threw its weight and support behind the UN embargoes which, paradoxically, cut off arms to *all* parties, thus emphasizing the advantage enjoyed by the Serbs in terms of manpower and resources and also guaranteeing Bosnia's defencelessness.

The Bosnian crisis has illustrated much about the fragility and shortcomings of any CFSP for Europe. The crisis has also demonstrated that the US cannot be relied upon to demonstrate leadership and resolve when it feels that its vital interests are not at stake. The normal retort to this line of argument is that Bosnia is in Europe and therefore is a European problem. As an addendum it is observed that the US has enough problems of its own and is actively involved in several other UN operations, and that it is about time the affluent European allies stopped expecting the US to fix everything. However, the *expectation* that the US will provide leadership is one that has been emphasized by successive post-war US administrations, the current one being no exception. Warren Christopher, US Secretary of State, stated that, 'The end of the Cold War is making American leadership even more important – and we accept the challenge'.[10] In Bosnia's case, the US has been reluctant to accept the challenge, preferring instead to remind its European allies that Yugoslavia is after all in Europe's 'back yard' and that a European solution should therefore be forthcoming. For their part, the European allies anticipated US leadership and initiative and in its absence have shown a remarkable lack of direction and resolve. This can only have deleterious effects on US–European relations.

For its part, Western Europe, in mid-1991, was preoccupied with the EC's progress toward 'Europe 1992' and was slow to realize the significance of events in Yugoslavia for the rest of Europe. Just as the 1948 Berlin crisis had been the first real test of post-World War II stability, the unfolding crisis in Yugoslavia was to test the mettle and resolve of the Western leaders in the post-Cold War world. Yugoslavia marked a rude awakening for several reasons. One, the assumptions about the progress towards democracy, stability and prosperity in Central and Eastern Europe had to be rethought in light of developments in Yugoslavia. Two, subsequent actions would alter the timetable by which the EC was to advance to political union, which included the construction of a common foreign and defence policy. As differing positions emerged on the Yugoslav question, the European integration process slowed. Three, the theory that somehow the crisis could be contained so that surrounding countries would not be dragged into a conflict, underestimated the gravity of the spin-off from the fighting and, in particular, the floods of refugees dislocated by the fighting. The refugee problem came to play a major role in Germany and led to more restrictive policies being adopted vis-à-vis immigration and asylum. This, in turn, widened the gulf between those who supported more lenient policies toward refugees and those on the Right and Extreme Right who supported harsh exclusionary policies against refugees. In political terms, the refugee dilemma contributed to the polarization of Western European politics. For instance, Warren Christopher's shuttle diplomacy around the European capitals unintentionally made clearer the differences between the stance of various European countries on the issue, including, unusually, those of Britain and the US. Diplomatic attempts by Washington to build European consensus, by working initially through London, met with resistance. The lack of closeness between Clinton and Major, accompanied by mutual criticisms, would appear to have eroded the special relationship to a point below the 'close relationship' of the Wilson–Johnson years.[11]

The dithering in the early days of the Clinton administration about the most suitable course of action, accompanied by a more general uncertainty about what America's foreign-policy interests are, led to an uneasy questioning of the US's ability to fulfil its self-proclaimed leadership role in the post-Cold War world. The apparent inability of the Clinton administration to act decisively and coherently was compounded by the situation in Somalia – a legacy from the last months of the Bush administration. Grandiose promises by the Bush administration that the US would be out of Somalia by 20 January 1993 (Clinton's inauguration day) now seem, in retrospect, hoplessly optimistic or ill-informed. The subsequent search for General Aidid, the commitment of armoured forces to help patrol the streets of Mogadishu, and the imposition of a deadline for the withdrawal of US forces (which has led other countries to decide to withdraw as well) have not created an image of leadership to complement the rhetoric. Perhaps the most significant lesson for the Bosnian crisis, arising out of the US's involvement in Somalia, is the rationale for involvement in a country that seemingly effects America's national interest in no way at all. The extensive involvement in Somalia and the less than extensive involvement in Bosnia sit uneasily beside each other.

The above argument is not meant to belittle what has been done in Bosnia by UN, NATO, WEU and other forces. But, even when impressive-sounding action appeared to have been taken, it proved in practice to be far more vague and problematical. For instance, the outcome of the NATO Council meeting in Brussels on 9 August 1993 outlined plans for air strikes in Bosnia, unless the Bosnian Serbs lifted their siege of Sarajevo immediately and the surrounding heights use put under UN control. But, air strikes would be limited to the 'support of humanitarian relief and must not be interpreted as a decision to intervene militarily in the conflict'.[12] It was made clear at the NAC meeting that only the UN Secretary General, Boutros Boutros-Ghali, who was reportedly unenthusiastic about air strikes while negotiations were pending, could order the air strikes. Control of the air strikes would fall under NATO's Southern Commander. Questions about whether there is the necessary intelligence to carry out such strikes effectively and about the safety of the UN forces in Bosnia may also make air strikes less than desirable.

Two broad lessons would appear to have emerged for the Western Europeans from the Yugoslav crisis. The first is that the US has yet to define a clear foreign policy for the post-Cold War world. This includes the question of when and why the US may intervene in a given incident, as well as the question of whether the US is willing to commit some of its resources to make collective security effective – especially its willingness to alleviate the fiscal pressures on the UN's peace-keeping operations. As self-proclaimed leader of the post-Cold War world, the US has failed to give the leadership or to back up promises with action. The US, along with its European allies, has betrayed almost every principle that it claimed its domestic and foreign-policy values were based upon. Furthermore, by standing by and watching the subjugation of the Bosnian Muslims, the clear message has been sent out to every aspiring despot that there is no new world order and that the use of force will not necessarily be challenged.

US actions, or non-actions, during the course of the Yugoslav crisis may also serve as a warning to the European allies that the US was willing to put domestic concerns first and to adopt a more parochial view of foreign policy. If, as the message seemed to be from Washington, the major European powers are to take more responsibility for pan-European security problems, US leadership in NATO and in security issues should not be counted upon; nor may it be desirable. The inadequacy of both the US and European responses seem to indicate the clear need for the US to clarify its foreign-policy goals and for the major European powers to be prepared and able to assume more responsibility for security issues beyond the immediate confines of the EC or NATO.

For its part, the US seems to be driven largely by *Realpolitik*, whereby national self-interest is the motivating factor. Unlike the Gulf War, where precious natural resources were the issue, nothing is at stake for the US in Yugoslavia. This must prompt questions in the European allies' minds about where the common interests lie between themselves and the US. If it is not in the US's interests to intervene in Yugoslavia, would it intervene in the Czech and Slovak Republics, or for that matter the Baltic states where vital German interests are seen to be at stake? The failure of the Europeans to act coherently in Yugoslavia *coupled with* the lack of US interest, may do more for forming a coherent European security identity than anything else, or alternatively kill any such notions once and for all. The open disagreements between the US and its European allies must also challenge the notion that the US shares common values and assumptions with Europe and that the post-Cold War world will be a 'new commonwealth of freedom . . . rest[ing] on shared principles . . . that constitute our common values'.[13] The second lesson is a more general one regarding the role of institutions during the Bosnian conflict.

Institutional Inertia

The crisis in Yugoslavia erupted when many Western European countries were preoccupied with the negotiations leading up to the Maastricht Summit of December 1991 (one of the items on the agenda was whether to strengthen the political aspects of the EC, with the eventual aim of moving toward a common foreign and security policy). Fighting began in Yugoslavia almost as soon as Slovenia and Croatia declared their independence on 25 June 1991. Within seventy-two hours two EC-backed missions had been sent to Yugoslavia.[14] In spite of promises from Dimitrij Rupel, Slovenia's foreign minister, to join a conference to discuss independence and to delay any declaration thereof, the EC mission was unsuccessful in achieving any meaningful promises. It was

356 *Pan-European Security?*

at this juncture that the European Council, consisting of EC leaders of government, called for an emergency meeting of the CSCE.

Like the EC, the CSCE was also going through a transition from an organization designed to maintain crisis stability, to something approaching a standing collective security body. The CSCE immediately called for a meeting of the Consultative Committee of the newly established Conflict Prevention Centre. On 1 July 1991, the chair of the Consultative Committee called for the cessation of all hostilities and 'the immediate return of all relevant units of the JNA, as well as the territorial defense forces of Slovenia'.[15] On 3 July another of the new organs established by the Charter of Paris, the Committee of Senior Officials, assumed responsibility. They promptly made an appeal for an immediate ceasefire, stating also that 'any recourse to the use of force in the present crisis in Yugoslavia continues to be absolutely inadmissable'.[16]

Soon after this decision, the EC banned all arms sales to Yugoslavia and suspended almost $1 billion in economic aid. On 7 July, the EC negotiators reached the first of many agreements, (the Brioni ceasefire) which provided for the withdrawal of the JNA forces from Slovenia and the disarmament of the Slovenian militia. Civilian monitoring missions were sent to check compliance with the 7 July agreement, which was ratified by the Slovenian parliament on 10 July. The agreement was never fully implemented since hostilities erupted in the Croatian territories of Slavonia and Krajina. It was not until August that Luxembourg's foreign minister, Jacques Poos, suggested the possibility of sending military 'interposition' forces.[17] He was backed in this proposal by the Netherlands, France and Germany. William van Eekelen, Secretary-General of the WEU, suggested that any use of force should be used to isolate the source of conflict. However, the EC was forced to abandon any notion of interposition when Serbia rejected the plan and escalated their military action against Croatia.

Thereafter the EC contented itself with condemnation of Serbian violence, made some attempts at arbitration, and threatened the imposition of further sanctions against those parts of Yugoslavia that failed to accept its proposals by the 1 September 1991 deadline. In spite of several ceasefires that ensued, none of which had actually achieved a complete end to the fighting at the time of writing, and an agreement by the CSCE to suspend all arms shipments to Yugoslavia, the matter was transferred to the UN Security Council on 25 September 1991.[18] Yet this was not the end of EC involvement; further EC-backed attempts at brokering a settlement were made by Hans van den Broek and Lord Carrington and later by Lord David Owen. On 8 October

1991, the UN Secretary-General appointed Cyrus Vance as his personal envoy. After several trips to Yugoslavia, Vance negotiated a ceasefire that was signed in Geneva on 23 November 1991. This ceasefire, like others before it and others to follow, did not hold. With the obvious failure of European efforts, the UN Security Council, on the recommendation of the secretary-general, decided on 21 February 1992 to commit a 14 000-person peace-keeping force to Yugoslavia – after ten months of war there were around 700 000 displaced people and over 10 000 dead.

The recognition of Slovenia and Croatia by the EC on 15 January 1992 was prompted by Germany's earlier recognition and occurred just after the UN dispatched liaison officers to Yugoslavia. EC recognition was intended to facilitate a political settlement of the crisis, since amongst the conditions of recognition was a commitment to 'settle by agreement, including where appropriate by recourse to arbitration, all questions concerning State succession and regional disputes', and a pledge that none of the republics had a 'territorial claim against a neighbouring EC state' – a clear response to Greek nervousness about suspected Macedonian claims.[19] Arguably, Macedonia was as deserving of recognition as the other republics and the failure of the EC to recognize it reflected the extreme reluctance of Greece to establish diplomatic relations with Macedonia. Subsequent involvement of the EC and the CSCE followed in the Bosnia-Herzegovina crisis when Serb militia, supported by JNA units, gained control of significant portions of Bosnian territory. President Alija Izetbegović of Bosnia-Herzegovina appealed to the CSCE, the EC and the UN for assistance. All three responded, albeit cautiously.

The history of the crisis thus far offers several tentative conclusions:

(1) The crisis caught both the EC and the CSCE at a point of transition. In spite of this, both organizations did what they could to reach a settlement in virtually every field, except military action for which they are ill-equipped.

(2) The CSCE collaborated with the EC; the former included Yugoslavia as a member and could therefore bring political pressure to bear (of the non-binding type) while the EC could use its economic muscle to reinforce the CSCE's views, although Yugoslavia is not an EC member.

(3) The UN initially avoided early involvement in the crisis based upon the argument that it was forbidden to intervene in the internal matters of a member state.

(4) Military intervention was discussed on several occasions and, when it was, the WEU was the vehicle for coordinating any such action. NATO remained uninvolved.

The crisis has demonstrated much about the lack of interventionary capability on the part of EC or CSCE countries, and made the general aim of working toward a common European foreign and security policy look overly ambitious if not utopian. At the same time it has also pointed out the essential irrelevance of NATO to wider European security policies, alongside the US's extreme reluctance to be avoided in a situation where it either perceived no direct interests to be at stake, or where it was not certain of a relatively easy victory. It has become almost fashionable to blame NATO for the failure of the international community to resolve the Bosnian crisis. These criticisms are certainly justified on the grounds that NATO was the *only* institution with the military potential to make a decisive difference; the non-use of that potential reflects badly upon NATO's members and damages the credibility of the institution. As one journalist put it, NATO has 'stayed in its bunk with its boots on'.[20]

Manfred Wörner, Secretary-General of NATO, has, along with others, justified NATO's role by observing that, 'No one asked NATO to take over, certainly none of today's critics'.[21] Wörner went on to outline NATO's contribution to the United Nations operations in Bosnia:

> NATO has offered its support to the United Nations and it has done everything the UN has asked, and has done so efficiently. We are enforcing the embargo at sea and the no-fly zone in the air. We have supplied UNPROFOR with command and control equipment and we have coordinated our military planning with the United Nations. We have also offered the UN our protective air power in case of attack against UNPROFOR and we are prepared to use air strikes, if necessary, to relieve strangulation of Sarajevo and other areas . . . These missions are thus a demonstration of NATO's vitality rather than of its irrelevance.[22]

NATO's North Atlantic Council decided in March 1993 to support peace-keeping activities under either a CSCE mandate or a UN one. In spite of NATO's historical willingness to extend its treaty-defined geographical area of interest, any meaningful intervention has been prevented by political and practical problems. Basic issues, such as the size of the forces, command issues, who should supply what, and rules of engagement, remained unresolved. Some, having watched

UNPROFOR's difficulties in disarming militia forces in parts of Croatia, concluded that military operations in Bosnia would be even more hazardous and difficult. As the Vance–Owen plan appeared to be wavering it became obvious that without a meaningful military threat there could be little incentive to surrender territory as part of an agreement.

With a lack of consensus on whether NATO should intervene or not, demands for the relaxation of the arms embargo to the Bosnian Muslims intensified; amongst the advocates of this course of action were Jeane Kirkpatrick, Senator Joseph Biden, Margaret Thatcher and Governor Bill Clinton, campaigning for the US presidency (since his election, his position on this issue has become more opaque). With the rejection of the Vance–Owen plan in May 1993, the Clinton administration pressed for air strikes against Serb military positions. On 2 August the North Atlantic Council agreed to threaten to bomb Serbian forces if they failed to lift their stranglehold on Sarajevo. The question of command and control was clumsy; operations could be initiated only by the UN commanders on the ground (Frenchman General Jean Cot and Belgian General Francis Briquemont). Thereafter control of the forces would fall under NATO's Southern Command. Up until this point NATO had contented itself with the enforcement of a no-fly ban that precluded NATO aircraft from firing on Serbian aircraft; nor was retaliation possible against surface-to-air missile sites or anti-aircraft positions. Sensing the reluctance of the US and Western Europe actually to use aircraft, and also noting opposition to the idea of air strikes by Lord Owen, Stoltenberg and Boutros Boutros-Ghali, the Serbians made the virtually meaningless gesture of withdrawing their forces from Mount Izman.

NATO's role in Bosnia has not been impressive. Throughout the conflict there has been an unwillingness actually to use NATO's military might although such use was threatened on several occasions. As a result, NATO, the US and Western European countries have lost much credibility. This loss of stature is all the more marked when NATO's marginal role in Bosnia is compared to its extremely active and vigorous role in the Gulf War. For instance, the rules of engagement applied to the no-fly zone over Iraq permitted the instant engagement of any hostile aircraft within the zone, unlike the exclusion zone over Bosnia. The argument that NATO did all that was asked of it by the UN, thus exculpating NATO from major responsibility for the fate of Bosnia, is not persuasive. In truth, NATO was anxious to *appear* to be playing an active role while leaving the onus for failure in the hands of the UN. On virtually every occasion that direct air, sea or land actions have been proposed in Bosnia, qualifications and contingencies have been expressed to the point where action became well-nigh impossible. Far from being the 'only serious security game in town', NATO has proven itself to be insular and hollow.

Other institutions also fared badly, such as the CSCE, which was the first to call for a ceasefire when the Slovenian and Croatian republics attempted to turn away from the Yugoslav federation. However, the CSCE failed to censure its own members, some of whom had an open role in aiding Slovenian and Croatian separatism. In a rather disconcerting reminder of 1912–13, Austria and Hungary are deeply involved in illegal but open arms supply, including heavy equipment to Slovenian and Croatian separatist paramilitary forces.

The EC assumed primary responsibility for generating a diplomatic resolution of the crisis, but there was no agreement on what policy to follow. As a result of disagreement, the EC was split into two: Germany, with historical ties to the region, supported the rebels and prematurely recognized their independence; while Britain, France, Italy and Spain were anxious to avoid a precedent which could exacerbate the problems with their own minorities seeking independence. Yet, in spite of differing opinions there were factors that should have mitigated for a more active and coherent EC role, such as the fact that half of Yugoslavia's trade was with the EC and many Yugoslavs wished to join the EC.

Perhaps the most worrying aspect of the institutional responses, or lack thereof, to the crisis in the former Yugoslavia has been that the confidence of the Central and Eastern Europeans, as well as that of the CIS countries, has been undermined both as regards Western Europe's potential to help its weaker neighbours and, more generally, the rule of international law. Thus, for those who have been watching Serbia's actions, the lesson would seem to be that the use of force is permissible, given the lack of any effective institutional restraints or leadership. Furthermore, the principles of the Helsinki Final Act, which seemed to provide the foundations for the 'New World Order' and the new European security architecture, have been undermined. The Helsinki Final Act states:

The participating states will respect each other's sovereign equality and individuality as well as all the rights inherent in and encompassed by its sovereignty, including in particular the right of every State to juridical equality, to territorial integrity and to freedom and political independence.[23]

The Helsinki Final Act is also unambiguous on its stipulations regarding the right of self-determination; these must be exercised in compliance with the relevant norms of international law, 'including those relating to the territorial integrity of states'.[24] In spite of the fact that the Helsinki Final Act has no legally binding effect, it is frequently cited in NATO, CSCE and WEU documents as the basis for conduct and guidance in the post-Cold War world.[25] By deciding to give priority to the principle of self-determination, some EC members have in effect placed that principle above established norms and rules of international law and respect for the sovereignty of people and territorial integrity. This may have set an unfortunate and dangerous precedent since, as was observed in Chapter 2, there are many other 'Croatias' and 'Serbias' throughout Europe and the former Soviet Union.

The respected *Eurobarometer* carried out a survey in Central and Eastern Europe and the CIS countries, to ascertain how effective people there thought the European institutional responses had been to the Yugoslav crisis. The figures show that of those surveyed a majority thought that all of the institutions were ineffective. Although the UN was seen as the most ineffective, it was also seen as the most effective. Of more interest is the way in which individual countries assessed the effectiveness of the institutions involved.

People from the PHARE and the TACIS countries agree on the ineffectiveness of the EC, NATO and the CSCE; however the TACIS countries are inclined to view the UN more favourably. Unsurprisingly, the countries most critical of the efforts of the various bodies are the adjoining countries (Albania, the Former Yugoslav Republic of Macedonia, and Slovenia). The countries most inclined to view the organizations favourably, especially the UN, are those that are currently embroiled in conflicts of their own and thus appreciative of the extreme difficulty in finding a solution. Georgia, embroiled in a conflict against separatist Abkhazia, and Moldova, on the Trans-Dniester battlefront, deserve special mention.

One of the interesting paradoxes to arise from the survey data above is that, on the one hand, there seems to be the general impression that the institutions are ineffective, but, on the other, many of the countries in Central and Eastern Europe are queuing up to join the very same institutions that they see as ineffective. For example, the Czech Republic, Hungary, Poland and Slovakia have all signed Europe Agreements and would ultimately like full membership of the EU. NATO is in the same boat. NATO has no real enemy, has a hazy military doctrine, is noticeably smaller than its Cold War version, and failed to

Table 11.1 Do you feel that the following bodies have been on the whole rather effective or rather ineffective in trying to help resolve the conflict in former Yugoslavia? (%)

	Effective	Ineffective	Neither
United Nations	23	33	11
European Community	17	31	12
CSCE	14	28	11
NATO	12	30	12

Source: Central and Eastern Eurobarometer No. 3 (Brussels: Commission of the European Communities, February 1993).

intervene in Yugoslavia. Yet it too has no shortage of countries itching to join it. The CSCE, which used to be the main forum for East–West relations, also lost much of its rationale with the demise of the Cold War. Presently the CSCE is attempting to demonstrate its relevance to the post-Cold War world by acting as a peacemaker; however it has failed conspicuously in both the Caucasus and Yugoslavia.

What explains this apparent paradox of having no confidence in the institutions but nevertheless being eager to join them? One explanation would be that although the institutions have conspicuously failed in Yugoslavia this need not undermine the utility or attractiveness of the various institutions to the PHARE and TACIS countries who see their situations as distinct from those of former Yugoslavia. A second explanation would be that, ineffective as the institutions may be, they remain the only security organizations that serve potentially to link Central and Eastern Europe with Western Europe. Which institutions these countries eventually accede to may not be the most significant fact. That they feel 'tied' to Western Europe and North America, and by extension Western Europe and the US feel tied to Central and Eastern Europe and the CIS countries, is the important factor.

A further paradox that is difficult to explain is the fact that the UN was seen as the most effective institution in the Yugoslav crisis, yet also the most ineffective. This presumably can be explained by the fact that the UN assumed a higher profile than any of the other institutions. Frustration with the other organizations has given the UN the Central role in the crisis; but it is also the institution with most to lose in terms of reputation.

That the crisis in Bosnia has given rise to a serious credibility crisis for all of the institutions is evident. Not so evident is the question of why, in the event of membership of these institutions, countries in

Table 11.2 Do you feel that the following bodies have been on the whole rather effective or rather ineffective in trying to help resolve the conflict in former Yugoslavia? (%)

E: effective; I: ineffective; N: neither.

	UN			EC			CSCE			NATO		
	E	I	N	E	I	N	E	I	N	E	I	N
Albania	10	56	16	15	53	14	15	52	10	5	38	28
Armenia	20	27	14	14	29	13	15	23	13	13	25	15
Belarus	22	28	16	11	26	18	9	24	16	7	26	16
Bulgaria	15	33	16	15	31	16	12	26	13	10	30	14
Czech Republic	23	58	8	20	55	7	15	53	9	9	56	8
Estonia	17	34	16	10	31	16	9	31	16	7	31	17
Georgia	48	8	9	32	9	8	27	9	9	35	11	8
Hungary	20	54	9	17	49	11	16	48	9	9	51	12
Latvia	11	47	7	6	42	8	5	41	7	7	39	9
Lithuania	14	35	4	11	33	3	11	30	4	9	32	4
(Macedonia)	11	67	8	10	71	7	11	62	8	9	56	8
Moldova	39	19	4	20	21	5	16	22	7	17	23	8
Poland	24	56	7	19	53	8	13	52	6	10	56	6
Romania	29	28	18	26	24	16	23	25	16	23	24	15
Russia (European)	21	24	12	14	22	13	12	19	12	10	21	14
Slovakia	29	53	8	21	55	9	21	49	10	11	52	12
Slovenia	16	61	16	23	51	16	16	53	16	7	62	14
Ukraine	27	26	11	16	25	11	12	23	10	11	23	10
Region Total	23	33	11	17	31	12	14	28	11	12	30	12

Source: *Central and Eastern Eurobarometer* no. 3 (Brussels: Commission of the European Communities, February 1993).

Eastern or Central Europe should believe in Western security guarantees? There are numerous examples in the past of other unfulfilled security guarantees that have left Eastern European in limbo, such as the 1925 Locarno Pact, the pre-World War II French guarantees to Czechoslovakia, and the guarantee to Poland by Britain. The West's credibility problem can only be overcome with concerted action that will arrest potentially fractious nationalist or ethnic conflicts at an early stage. This, needless to say, will require a considerable investment by the Western world and involve an emphasis upon peace-making, peace-enforcement and peace-keeping, not upon collective defence. It is easy to malign the progressive failure of institutions to deal with the unfolding tragedy in the former Yugoslavia. Perhaps the greatest failure was that of the main powers to work through *any* of the institutions available to them, including NATO.

RAMIFICATIONS OF THE BOSNIAN CRISIS FOR EUROPEAN SECURITY

A further area of weakness in the US and European responses to Yugoslavia was their failure to recognize the potentially inflammatory nature of the crisis. While trying not to use the benefit of hindsight unfairly, it seems the failure to act effectively at an early stage of the crisis has made the task of stopping the conflict from becoming a Balkan imbroglio much more difficult.

One of the underplayed results of the Western reaction to the crisis has been that it has encouraged the revival of pan-Slavism. Pan-Slavism appeals particularly to the conservative opposition in Russia who have, on the one hand, never wholly accepted the loss of the Soviet empire and, on the other, are immensely buoyed by the ineffectiveness of the Western response. Today's defence of Serbian aspirations could become tomorrow's rallying point for the revival of the Soviet empire through the medium of orthodox pan-Slavism. Russia has begun to play a major role in the Bosnian crisis since it is widely perceived as the only major power that can exert influence over the Serbs, largely because of the historically close relations with Serbia – a fellow Eastern Orthodox state. In one of the more unexpected developments of the post-Cold War period, Russia has emerged as a major influence in European security affairs. The close ties that have been formed between the Russian administration plus the high visibility of Vitaly Churkin (the Presidential envoy to Yugoslavia) and Foreign Minister Andrei

Kozyrev, have led to the impression that it is Russia that is coordinating efforts to secure a settlement of the conflict. The visits of Kozyrev to the WEU in the spring of 1993 also outlined the acceptance by the Western Europeans of Russia's critical role in negotiating a settlement between the Bosnian, Croatian and Serbian leaders. Although it would be far-fetched to claim that Western Europe is seeking a new line-up of Europeans and Russia, to the detriment of US–European relations, the Russian initiative serves to illustrate the potential for Russia to play an important role in finding solutions to European security problems.

The chances of reconciling the Yugoslav crisis depend, in part, upon the future stability of the Russian regime. The Russian government could bring influence to bear on the Serbs, but so too could the conservative opposition – in a different, more destructive, sense. In spite of Russian efforts at mediation, the conflict remains unresolved and potentially dangerous in several ways:

(1) The inadequacy of the Western response may send a clear message out to other secessionist groups, or those who wish to right historical wrongs, that the use of military force will go unchecked.
(2) By failing to contain the conflict at an early stage, Serbia has been encouraged in its territorial ambitions, which go far beyond the reacquisition of historically Serbian lands – for example, the expansion of Serbia Westward from the Drina river cannot be justified on these grounds since this was never Serbian territory.
(3) Western non-intervention in Yugoslavia may drive moderate Muslim regimes to adopt more fundamentalist stances in defence of Muslim people. The massive intervention against Iraq following their invasion of Kuwait, in support of the restoration of territorial sovereignty, followed by relative inaction in the Yugoslav case, has set a puzzling double standard that could be construed as anti-Muslim.
(4) The failure to halt Serbia's territorial aggrandizement may have encouraged other states to seek to correct perceived historical injustices, amongst them being: the potential expansion of Serb ambitions into Kosovo and Macedonia; collusion on the part of Greece in Serbia's territorial ambitions regarding Macedonia, with a possible territorial division. Although there is no direct evidence for this, it may be partially supported by Greece's extreme reluctance to recognize the independence of the Former Yugoslav republic of Macedonia. Bulgaria has its own historical interests in Macedonia

but has shown no appetite or interest to participate in any division of the country. Interestingly, Bulgaria's president has recognized the independence of Macedonia but has refused to recognize the existence of an independent Macedonian nationality.[26] An attack on Kosovo by Serbia and an attempt to oust the Albanians from Kosovo would drag Albania into the war, and probably Turkey as well, since Albania has a defence agreement with Turkey. If Turkey's defence pact with Albania were invoked to protect ethnic Albanians in Kosovo and Turkey responded, this could well lead to Greek intervention with horrific consequences for not only the region but Europe as a whole. The rekindling of Greek–Turkish animosities in the Balkans would destroy NATO and make it impossible for the WEU to intervene without appearing to take sides (Turkey is not a WEU member).

Although the scenarios outlined above are purely conjectural, they do serve to show the relative ease with which the current Yugoslav crisis could once again slide into a generalized Balkan war.

CONCLUSION

The fate of former Yugoslavia has done much to illustrate the failings of leadership in Europe as well as the US. It has also shown much about the inadequacy of various institutions to cope with the first major security challenge to post-Cold War European security. Rather than reiterate the negative lessons learned from both Europe's and the international community's efforts to halt the conflict in Yugoslavia, there are some positive lessons that can be drawn from the Yugoslav case.

The first is that the fate of Yugoslavia should have the effect of refocusing Western thinking regarding the parameters of European security. The artificial debate about what should, and what should not, fall within the various institutional areas of purview has historically had the effect of leaving the south of Europe as an area of secondary concern. The fate of Yugoslavia and the potential for a general Balkan war serve as a reminder of the critical importance of this part of the world.

Second, many of the unrealistic and somewhat complacent Western ideas about other parts of Europe following the defeat of communism, encapsulated in the rhetoric of the 'New World Order', have been shaken by the Yugoslav conflict. The fate of Yugoslavia has illustrated that the progress toward democracy will not only be difficult but will often be accompanied by divisions of existing states. It has also pointed to the awkward choice that many Western governments were forced to make between supporting democracy, with the risk of dissolution and instability, or supporting the status quo, which could entail supporting conservative and repressive regimes. Western predilections had been towards supporting unity, and hence it was hoped stability, while not examining too closely how democratic the regimes are. Democracy is a far more tangible and fragile concept in the former communist bloc than many Western leaders had realized.

Third, the lack of coherent leadership may have the effect of not just underscoring the need for more responsibility for their own security on the part of the major European powers, but of stressing the need for the support of international efforts aimed at solving disputes at the earliest stage possible. For the US, the Yugoslav crisis may start some long overdue soul-searching about the nature of US foreign policy and its global responsibilities. As the only superpower to survive the Cold War intact, the US may quite naturally assume the role of global leadership. But this is a role that has commensurate international responsibilities and cannot be fulfilled on a selective basis. The difficult balancing act that President Clinton has to address between domestic and foreign priorities may also lead to more transparency in US foreign policy, so that allies, in particular, know when it is and when is not appropriate to look to the US for leadership.

Fourth, Russia's mediation in the crisis in May 1993, whether successful or not, has reminded all the Western nations that Russia is an important power with a major role to play in European and international security. The collaboration between Kozyrev, Kinkel and WEU members may act as an encouraging development leading towards the adoption of a pan-European security agenda and, in time, effective institutions.

There are positive lessons to be extracted from the Bosnian tragedy. However, failure to take these lessons on board will lead to a far less palatable: the disintegration of Yugoslavia may have been unavoidable, but much of the bloodshed and human-rights abuses that followed in Bosnia were avoidable. That the US and the Western European failed to act in a concerted manner is embarrassing and a betrayal of the very values that these countries claim to uphold. Amongst the negative lessons that may be drawn from this sad episode is that these same countries care little about despots and abuses of human dignity that do not effect them directly. Europe cannot afford, and should not tolerate another Bosnia.

12 Conclusions

The security environment in Europe has changed radically since 1989 with the collapse of the Soviet Union, the attempted August 1991 coup, reunification of Germany, the disintegration of the states created by the 1918 Versailles Treaty (Czechoslovakia and Yugoslavia), the developments in Western Europe as a result of the Maastricht Treaty, the emergence of fledgling democracies in Eastern Europe accompanied by economic instability, ethnic violence in parts of the former Soviet Union, and refugee movements generated by numerous civil wars. These and many other security concerns have presented Europe with the tremendously difficult task of designing a coherent response.

In designing a response there has to be a clear understanding of what is being responded to. It has been argued that there are still threats, in the military sense of the word; but there are more challenges to Europe's security that demand non-traditional responses. The presence of an unstable Russia or Ukraine, alongside nuclear aspirant states in the Persian Gulf, calls for the retention of a smaller but effective nuclear and conventional defence. However, the problems with refugees, support of fragile democracies and economies, human rights, environmental problems and other twenty-first-century ailments, are most suited to non-military solutions. Since national security is still tinged with Cold War associations, it is difficult to persuade Western powers that the less obvious post-Cold War security concerns deserve serious attention. This is especially so when these powers are deeply involved in addressing domestic woes of their own.

The problems of addressing the security concerns of post-Cold War Europe have been compounded by a lack of leadership and initiative. The US has assumed, at least rhetorically, the mantle of leader. In practice, the Clinton administration has proven indecisive in both Somalia and Bosnia, as well as exhibiting a greater proclivity toward addressing America's domestic woes. Western Europe, also preoccupied with domestic issues, has no clear leader. Statesmen of the stature of Jean Monnet, Winston Churchill, Ernesto Rossi or Konrad Adenauer (to name but a few), who guided Europe in the aftermath of the Second World War, seem to be lacking in post-Cold War Europe. Disillusionment with politicians seems to be rife. Introversion seems to characterize many of the European publics. The lack of leadership at the transatlantic and European levels may, in part, be due to the lack of vision. This, in turn, may be due to the way in which the Cold War ended: with a hiss rather than a bang. The trauma of the Second World War and the denial of liberty to those in POW camps inspired the 1941 Ventotene Manifesto and later the European Federalist movement.[1] The experience of war was to have a far-reaching influence upon the shape of post-war Europe. The end of the Cold War sees no equivalent vision or dynamism in European politics; these, above all, motivate and provide leadership. The question of leadership cannot simply be attributed to lack of resources or political differences. It is at root a lack of will to think beyond the divisions of the Cold War – which may have disappeared physically, but remains in many other less apparent ways.

The lack of leadership, where individual states or groups of states are unwilling to shoulder substantial burdens for the sake of long-term peace and stability in Europe, has led to a vain search for answers in institutions. Solutions, though, are not to be found *in* institutions but *through* institutions. Those who advocate structural solutions to Europe's myriad of security problems either oversimplify the challenges facing these institutions or downplay the fractious tendencies between the members. For security collaboration to occur, the German role has to be defined and agreed upon, the US has to decide what level of involvement it anticipates for itself and its European partners, the French have to identify institutions that they can work through while safeguarding their concerns vis-à-vis Germany and the US, and the British have to make a clear-cut decision about whether wholeheartedly to endorse the political aspects of European union, which includes the murky commitment to a 'common defence'. Those outside the formal Western European institutional structure have to be given guidance as to what criteria are acceptable for full integration into the select Western European 'clubs' (the EC and NATO).

The common usage of the term security 'architecture', which consists of a framework of 'interlocking institutions', is misleading; the system is far from being architecture. Rather than being conceived, designed and constructed, it was cobbled together in an attempt to give substance to the hyperbole of a Europe 'whole and free', the 'common house of Europe' and a 'European confederation'. Nor is the architecture solid and unmovable; it resembles a tent rather than a building of stone. Such images are bandied about with little regard for how they can be realistically interpreted in structural terms. In fact, there is little agreement about the design, let alone the structure of European security. Again, in common with the League and the United Nations, what has been created since the end of the Cold War in Europe has shown a tendency to try and capture and preserve Cold War hierarchies, both between and within the various institutions. The lessons from the League and the United Nations show that building a new security architecture based on the power relations of the old one is a cause for resentment and maybe instability in the long term.

Over the course of the next few years some institutions may well grow in importance, such as the WEU and the CSCE, while others may fade completely or be incorporated. The resultant shape of European security will most likely *not* be the result of meticulous design; it will emerge from a long process of trial and error. Institutions will thrive or weaken as a result of their successes or failures. The possibility of institutional rivalry between those institutions with similar mandates has also been touched upon. The emergence of new institutions cannot be completely dismissed, but if new institutions do emerge they will more likely than not be built upon the ashes of old institutions. Competition between institutions, new or old, with the potential for inertia will have to be guarded against. The same result may be achieved due to the sheer number of security and related institutions, where one institution looks to the other to assume leadership or responsibility, as in Yugoslavia's case.

Whether Europe's security will or will not be catered for by a series of haphazard responses is a matter of choice, not fate. It ceases to be a matter of fate where vision and leadership exist. The vision should be to construct guarantees for peace and stability on a *pan-European* basis. These have been notably absent, with the exception of the somewhat ponderous CSCE and clip-on additions to NATO and the WEU. There remains a profound reluctance on the part of the Western Europeans and the US to think of the security problems of other parts of Europe, or indeed North Africa, as their problems. Even where institutions exist on a pan-European level there is a reluctance to vest real power in the institutions or to give any binding commitments to the weaker countries in Central and Eastern Europe, or to the CIS. This is immensely short-sighted for several reasons:

(1) Given the nature of the security threats facing Europe (outlined in Chapter 2), pan-European responses are demanded. The problems of migratory movements or nationalism are no respecters of frontiers or borders. The solution to these problems rests initially in dialogue and then concerted action at the earliest possible stage and not, as is the case now, in reactionary responses.

(2) The fate of Western Europe is intimately bound up with that of other parts of Europe. 'Western' Europe only adopted this adage because of the exigencies of the Cold War, which is reflected in the institutional structures but now has very little real relevance.

(3) Insistence on stability and democratic reforms as prerequisites for full membership of the EC, NATO, the European Stability Pact and so forth, are counter-intuitive. *Now* is the time that these institutions and the major European powers should be reaching out and providing membership and support. If there is stability and democracy, what use would the institutions then be and what would relations between the major European powers and North America be like with these countries when, in their hour of need, they stood by with their hands in their pockets?

(4) The question of whether the more affluent powers can afford (in all senses) to take on the problems of the Central Europeans, the Eastern European countries and the CIS countries should not be an excuse for inaction. The question makes more sense in reverse: can they afford *not* to make their problems their own? The crisis in Yugoslavia provides one lesson in this regard. Try as the international community might to point fingers of responsibility at others or at institutions, an untreated problem will eventually become a problem for all and a far bigger one.

(5) Fears that the Western Europeans may face numerous 'East Germanies' and become involved in countless nationalist struggles are greatly exaggerated. The type of massive economic effort that has been sunk into the former East Germany is not typical of the aid that could be given to other countries – such would clearly be unrealistic. East Germany's case was a unique one. Clearly, in economic terms Europe will operate at many different levels for some time to come. There are, however, considerable benefits to pump-priming, which may not make the economy fantastically affluent but at least contributes to growth and stability. In this context the Southern European countries provide a lesson, and point to a level of hypocrisy on the part of the major European powers. Greece, Portugal, Spain and Turkey were granted NATO membership at a time when they could scarcely be considered as particularly democratic; and all but the last were granted EC membership when they were certainly not particularly affluent or advanced economically. The growth potential in Central Europe may well be better than that of these countries.

(6) The longer the Western Europeans and the US prevaricate about whether or how to construct pan-European security institutions,

the more difficult it will be to avoid the renationalization of military forces following the break-up of the Warsaw Pact, and maybe, in time to come, of NATO. The reversion of military forces to serve essentially nationalist aspirations would be a loss for all, not just for Central and Eastern Europe. There are structures that could impede or stop this development, such as the integrated military command of NATO or the Franco–German 'Euro' corps. These should be maintained, even if not in their current institutional configuration, and extended to include other parts of Europe. The EU has a valuable role to play in this respect since, as has been argued, it need not be contradictory to pursue a strategy of *both* deepening and widening.

Working towards pan-European peace and stability should be the vision; this, in turn, requires initiative to make it reality. Since there is only tacit agreement about the shape of Europe generally and, more specifically, about the need for a (hitherto ill-defined) 'common defence' to support the Maastricht goal of European Union, the answers to Europe's security concerns will only evolve gradually and as the result of an intense negotiating process. The French leadership role in Europe has to be squared with Britain's suspicion of continental European initiatives, as well as Germany's historical and legal constraints, and with the Mediterranean countries' concerns about being excluded from a northern 'Fortress Europe'. These, and many other, differences have to be addressed in a cooperative and constructive way. The first step, which has been taken by the CSCE, is to recognize that there are many security challenges to Europe that *demand* cooperative strategies to combat them; they are beyond the scope of any one country or organization to address. *Ad hoc* responses undoubtedly work some of the time, but the glaring occasions where they haven't, as in Bosnia, testify to the need for organized, coordinated and swift responses.

Initiative will have to come largely from the Western Europeans themselves, with the support of the US. A constructive US role is essential since it could do much to aid the development of a pan-European security order in which it would play a significant role. Alternatively, if there is a refusal to realign the US's role in Europe to the new realities of post-Cold War Europe, the US could be a brake on the development of a coherent pan-European security identity. With the decline in US force levels in Europe, it is obvious that the amount of influence Washington can exert on decisions by European governments will also decline. With a largely introspective American population the interest in maintaining US forces in Europe and in other overseas locations may also decline. There are three tentative options that seems to offer themselves to the question of the US's future role in Europe:

(1) *Business as usual*. While it may be tempting to imagine that the US is willing to assume its mantle of Alliance leadership and able to pay for it, this is clearly illusory. Even if the US adapts to the new security environment, it is clear that the Allies have changed in several critical ways so that the roles will not be the same. The predominant role in the Alliance was afforded to the US in large part because of the nuclear element to the Cold War world in which NATO operated. While not insignificant now, it is clearly not as relevant. Furthermore, the growing European self-assertiveness and the development of European consultative bodies on security questions have diminished the US's potential influence. The traditional US ploy of communicating with its European allies through Britain, its most erstwhile ally, no longer has the same leverage since Britain is not on the cutting edge of European security developments, preferring instead to hold on grimly to the vestiges of the special relationship. Perhaps the most important and obvious factor precluding a return to the *status quo* is the absence of an overt threat to European security. This threat was the glue that held the Alliance together.

(2) *Nominal US involvement*. The solution put forward in some circles is to have a nominal US involvement in Europe. In practical terms this would involve the preservation of the POMCUS supply depots and technical support facilities, communications and lift capability, which would be 'on-call'. The objections are obvious: the US would not accept any solution which gave them an indecisive role and which appeared to leave them at the beck and call of their allies. The proposal also confines the US to a military role at a time when the Alliance is ostensibly moving towards a far more political role. Any such scheme would, presumably, make existing and future debates about economic and political issues more divisive.

(3) *Goodbye, and thank you*. The third option is *gradually* to phase out US military forces in Europe, with all the accolades appropriate to a job well done (after all, the Bush administration claimed, almost single-handedly, to have 'won' the Cold War). The gradual phasing out of the North American military presence in Europe would be accompanied by growing responsibilities being vested in a European defence entity, most probably built around the WEU or the CSCE.

Although it is early days in terms of post-Cold War developments, the Bush and Clinton administrations have pursued a course that is potentially injurious to European interests; this is the almost natural propensity of Washington to cling to NATO as *the* institution that ties North America to Europe. NATO was a product of the Cold War and also reflected the clear hegemony of the US within that structure. From this point of view, Washington clearly has vested interests in maintaining NATO as their vehicle of influence in Europe. This has become an unwise strategy for several reasons:

(1) The US's European allies have shown a tendency to vest resources and energy into other institutions, such as the WEU. To interpret this as being anti-American or anti-NATO would be a mistake, and to attempt to block these developments may be counter-productive and could, ironically, produce anti-Americanism.

(2) The book started by suggesting that the currency of power in the international system has changed in the post-Cold War environment. For example, more emphasis is put on economic factors. For the US to continue to attempt to exert influence on its European allies through a primarily military institution would be inappropriate. Other ways can be found to symbolize the close links between the US and Europe.

(3) There is much that the US could do to aid stability in Europe since it is, as the Gulf War demonstrated, the pre-eminent military power. If the US were to vest its considerable forces and influence behind the CSCE, at least for the medium term until other institutions emerge, not only would pan-European stability be enhanced but so too would the ties across the Atlantic – many of the Central European countries are pro-American, some more so than the Western allies. Again, the lessons of Yugoslavia should be taken on board at this point: NATO remained bogged down in wrangling about whether Yugoslavia was in NATO's area of interest; the US has shown no particular fondness for working through the UN except where it is in their direct self-interest to do so, and it remains the organization's largest debtor. This would suggest that if the American public remain convinced that Europe is broadly of concern and that the institutional structures somehow serve their interests, the CSCE may be a far wiser institution to US resources and energy in.

It has been argued that the Western Europeans have not yet demonstrated sufficient leadership qualities to assume all the burdens of security, but this does not preclude the possibility in the future. The fact that there is no coherent European leadership in security matters necessitates the need for a US military presence in Europe, until such time as the Europeans are in a position to assume the main responsibility for their security affairs. A continued US presence in Europe is, for the immediate future, necessary as a balancer for British and French concerns about Germany's new role and position in Europe, as well as to overcome British reticence about involvement in the development of a European security identity. Britain's 1993 defence white paper makes it clear that Britain will continue to define its security interests with half an eye to Washington. France meanwhile regards the US as a counterweight to overbearing German influence in Europe until such time as a European security organization (with a strong French component) comes into being.

The rationale behind the argument that the primary responsibility for Europe's security should rest with the Europeans themselves leads to the conclusion that the US should *eventually* phase out its forces in Europe. Two arguments support this notion: first, the US military presence in Europe was never intended to be permanent (President Roosevelt foresaw at the Yalta conference that the US would be out of Europe in a couple of years). In the event of the continuing decline of US military forces in Europe in response to budgetary stringencies, the European allies will have to take over some of the functions hitherto provided by the US, as well as investing in lift capacity.

Second, a continued US presence in Europe, beyond the phasing-out period, could be counterproductive. It seemed natural to the Bush administration and, thus far, to the Clinton administration, to assume that the US *is* European and therefore deserves legroom under the European table. However, the extent to which the US is European is debatable, from the standpoint of demographic trends, which seem to be dragging US interests towards the Pacific Rim, as well as from evidence of the serious internal problems that will divert attention from foreign-policy concerns. The understandable need to address the urgent domestic issues that beset America, alongside a general lack of resolve and purpose in US foreign policy (such as in Bosnia, Somalia and Haiti), may encourage the growth of a European security identity.

There are also pressures in the US that are altering American perceptions of Europe and the need to regard it as a region worthy of considerable time and attention. For instance, the dispute in the GATT Uruguay Round has had a wholly negative effect on European–American relations, especially those between Paris and Washington. Thus, it is a matter of prudence for the Europeans to take seriously the notion of providing for their own defence, as well as being in the interests of the United States to encourage its European allies to do so. However, the development of a European security identity is still in its infancy and needs to be allowed to develop at its own rate until such time as it can stand by itself. There will be inevitable difficulties and disputes en route, but the desire to create a European security identity has been clearly expressed and it is one that need not preclude the US. This latter depends largely upon American perceptions of whether their interests are represented in new or adapted security organizations, but the new arrangement would involve a new role for the US as *pares* and not necessarily *primus*. This is a new and unfamiliar role for the US and one that may be problematical.

If the vision is pan-European and the leadership is to stem from Europe, the question arises as to which are the appropriate institutions to work through. The institutions that comprise the 'new security architecture' – the CSCE, the WEU, the Council of Europe, the EC and NATO – have largely been thrown together in a haphazard manner and are all flawed in various ways. It would be overly optimistic at this stage to expect any one institution to provide all of the answers. Clearly the immediate answer lies in task-sharing, with some institutions assuming responsibility for certain eventualities and others doing so in different circumstances. This is not altogether a happy solution; it makes the eventual task of designing an appropriate and efficient security organization immensely complicated since all can claim to have some *raison d'être*. To let the institutions specialize in their areas of expertise may sound appealing, but it scarcely amounts to a long-term solution due to the fact that the current architecture has a large amount of overlapping responsibilities built into it, resulting in needless duplication of resources and effort. In the worst-case analysis, the lack of clear institutional responsibility leads to paralysis and mutual finger-pointing, as has been the case in Bosnia.

The architecture is often presented as being built around a pillar, NATO, which provides stability for the rest of the structure. Too often NATO is presented as a sacred cow that may not be touched or cajoled. It is time to think openly and frankly about whether NATO has a role in post-Cold War European security. This study has suggested that NATO has a crucial *transitional* role to play, by fostering the development of new institutions or adaptation of existing ones that can eventually represent pan-European security interests, but that its long-term utility is questionable. Purely defensive ties between states will become less relevant for dealing with the new security environment. The geographical confines of areas of security interest have to be extended to include 'out-of-area' concerns and more peace-keeping roles. Arguments that Articles 2 and 4 of the North Atlantic Treaty make any redefinition of NATO's area of responsibility unnecessary are unconvincing. A vague promise that NATO *might* intervene is of little comfort to the threatened and of little threat to the oppressor. Nor is the continuation of second-class membership for much of Eastern Europe, through NACC, an answer to the membership issue. Carrots work for so long, but unless there is a reasonable chance of reaching them, disillusionment follows.

The pan-European aspects of the CSCE make it a vital institution and, so far, the only one that can really claim to represent Europe. The importance of creating a truly pan-European structure was stressed by Miodrag Mihajlovic, the former minister plenipotentiary of the Yugoslav Federal Secretariat for Foreign Affairs, in what could now be interpreted as a *cri de coeur*:

> Anything less than an unreserved investment by the CSCE in a new security concept may condemn Eastern Europe – and thereby the whole of the Continent – to recurrent trauma and national tragedy. Such an investment is not merely financial. It upholds the notion that the West can no longer find security by assuming military power within a common defensive alliance. Western security is now imperiled by the same environment that endangers Eastern Europe. To abate these threats, and to reinforce non-military – and hence non-threatening capacities of the post-communist systems, requires dispensing with the Cold War notions of force, power and security. The instability in Yugoslavia is, however, only one of the examples that Europe is facing on its very long and difficult road to peace, stability and prosperity.[2]

However, the CSCE remains an institution with no military forces specifically dedicated to it, and its decisions are not binding. The process of strengthening the CSCE must be accompanied by the deepening and widening of the European Community, to provide the economic underpinnings of stability through access to markets. The 1990 Paris Charter and the 1992 Stockholm Council meeting have given the CSCE a coherent stucture while, hopefully, the addition of a Secretary-General will give the CSCE a face as well. Weaknesses aside, the CSCE has the potential to develop into an immensely important European security organization, if not *the* security organization. Needless duplication is one potential danger of the growth of institutions. There is clearly a need to reach decisions at an early stage about apportionment of responsibilities and even the complete merger of institutions. For instance, the Council of Europe's responsibilities could feasibly be absorbed by the CSCE. The type of division of responsibilities suggested by Edouard Balladur's European Security Pact is a useful tool for addressing these problems.

There are no easy answers or prescriptions to the challenges that will face Europe; even if there were, they should not be trusted. The institutions are mere tools with no life of their own. It is the developments in and around Europe that will provide shape and form to the institutions, not the other way around. Some shapes are already discernible; one is the emergence of a set of European security concerns that are in some cases distinct from North American preoccupations. Washington's preoccupation with domestic issues and its shaky ventures in Somalia and Bosnia have not inspired confidence and have highlighted differences in perspective between the European capitals and Washington. By extension, the undermining of European confidence in US leadership may encourage the development of an increasingly independent European security role. However, any such role must assume as an integral function the promotion and protection of liberal democracies throughout Europe, not just the protection of Western Europe.

Thus far, it has been argued, the Western European and American response to the post-Cold War security environment has been slow, cautious and primarily based on national interest. The general failure to include Central and Eastern Europeans in the economic structures of Western Europe or to advance security guarantees to the Eastern Europeans has left ideas of 'common houses' or that of a Europe 'free and whole', as hollow abstractions. The idea of Western and Eastern Europe divided by an Iron Curtain, may have disappeared, but Europe remains divided economically and institutionally.

This is a situation that is not without hope since the existing institutions, *given the will*, have a valuable role to play in Europe as a whole – the EC economically, the CSCE as a guardian of democracy and human rights, the WEU militarily, NATO as a transition manager, and the Council of Europe preserving the rich cultures of Europe. If the inefficiencies and overlapping mandates between these institutions could be reduced, then Europe would have the foundations for a security system that could be extended to become truly European. The need for a pan-European security identity makes the CSCE a strong candidate to become the nucleus of a new post-Cold War security order which includes North America and Russia. Although there are detractors from the idea of building a European security order around the CSCE,[3] it is an idea that has a considerable constituency in Central and Eastern Europe and even some popularity in Western Europe. Hans-Dietrich Genscher's advocacy of a new European security structure based on the CSCE serves as a reminder that Germany has strong interests in Central and Eastern Europe and that any new or adapted security order must bear these in mind, given both Germany's geographical position and its strong economic influence upon that region. The CSCE could play a valuable role in not only helping to stabilize Central, Eastern and southeastern Europe; it could easily be augmented with a series of sub-regional security arrangements, such as the Conference on Security and Cooperation in the Mediterranean. Furthermore the CSCE incorporates the CIS countries and is not laden with the same historical baggage as NATO. A greater role for the CSCE would presumably have cause fewer ripples in Moscow than an extension of NATO's influence into Eastern Europe.

The fate of the former Yugoslavia has illustrated inadequacies in all of the institutions involved in aspects of European security, including the CSCE. However, many of the problems associated with the CSCE have to do with the newness of much of the permanent machinery. One challenge the CSCE will clearly have to cope with is the problem of minority rights. These should be tackled by a specialized permanent institution within the framework of the CSCE. To avoid the recurrence of particular conflicts, it may also be helpful to move towards the establishment of a peace-keeping mechanism.[4]

Amongst the objections to the idea of giving the CSCE pride of place are two that deserve attention. First, the neo-realist fondness for trotting out historical analogies with past attempts to establish security orders, such as The Concert of Europe in the early nineteenth century and the League of Nations, to name but two, which do not provide auspicious examples. They are, however, inaccurate in the sense that in each case there was at least one major power with a vested interest in upsetting the status quo. Unlike in previous periods, there is no major power (except perhaps *in extremis* the Ukraine) with any interest in upsetting the applecart. Indeed, the opposite seems to be true, whereby there are vested interests in enhancing and preserving interdependence.

The second argument goes back to the CSCE's cumbersome procedures. The unanimity-minus-one voting procedure clearly needs revising in the light of the divergent interests between the fifty-three members. The CSCE could, for example, adopt some form of qualified voting procedure, subject to agreement amongst the major powers and different numbers of votes being allotted to members. Although this too would create wrangling and malaise, the current voting procedure is clearly in need of overhaul.

Europe stands at a historical crossroads. No road that may be chosen is without its perils, but the opportunity decisively to influence events in post-Communist Europe, to encourage the growth of healthy economies and democracy, to rid Europe of the scourge of major war as well as the adages 'East' and 'West', must be taken. For the developed countries of Europe and North America to ignore the rest of Europe, including Russia, is short-sighted and may ultimately be foolish. There need be nothing munificent or overtly ideological about supporting fragile regimes in Eastern Europe or the CIS; it is after all a question of the future peace and prosperity of Europe as a whole. It is time that the foreign and security policies of the more affluent and strong countries of Europe and North America began to reflect this. Only when that happens can the institutions be adapted or designed to reflect truly pan-European concerns.

Finally, the fate of the former Yugoslavia and the inadequate response to the crisis present some lessons for European security. The crisis underscores the need for a redefinition of the parameters of 'European security'. Prior to the crisis there had been a general tendency to think of Europe in security terms as being defined by the NATO area and, by extension, the non-NATO area. The Yugoslav crisis, and the involvement of Britain, Canada and France, may have the effect of extending Europe in security terms away from parochial Cold War definitions. For all practical purposes the idea of 'out-of-area' operations has been dropped, but nothing definitive seems to have taken its place. If anything, the fate of Yugoslavia illustrated that NATO's out-of-area stipulation has been replaced by an even narrower concept of extent of interest, which focuses on national security with only a vague case by-case acknowledgment of wider regional or international security issues.

The Yugoslav crisis also forced Germany to begin to address its constitutional debate with a judgement from the Federal Constitutional Court (FCC) reminding Germany of its international obligations and duties. The FCC judgements have, thus far, only applied to AWACS operations over Bosnia and to humanitarian relief operations in Somalia, but they have opened the way to a later FCC decision on the issue in general. The resolution of this issue will be of critical importance for the development of a European Security Identity. In the event of a reinterpretation of the Basic Law which allows a greater German role in UN sanctioned peace-keeping operations, Germany can begin to play a constructive role that befits its influence and status.

The lack of leadership from Washington during the Yugoslav crisis and several notable differences of opinion between the US and its European allies may encourage the Western Europeans to act more decisively on their own without waiting for a nod from Washington. It may also have the effect of pushing Britain towards greater European security collaboration with the French in particular, and thus alleviate French concerns about facing Germany alone. The hesitancy of the Bush and Clinton administrations in the Yugoslav crisis, when contrasted to the decisiveness in the Gulf in 1990–91, or to the apparent dangers to regional security stemming from the Somali situation, have left many allies puzzled. The inadequacy of the US response and the failure to provide leadership may lead to a clarification of the US role and intentions in the post-Cold War world. If the crisis really is in 'Europe's back yard' and therefore of little interest to the US, there are important and urgent lessons that the European allies should learn. Two in particular stand out: don't rely upon the US for leadership in all circumstances, and don't rely upon NATO.

The slow and inadequate response to developments in the former Yugoslavia will permit a fresh look at European security issues. The image of NATO in particular has been tarnished, which will, hopefully, prompt a frank assessment of the utility of all the institutions and the performance of their members. The fate of the former Yugoslavia alongside the risk of destabilization in the Balkans may also refocus attention from the east to the south where, as has been argued, many of Europe's post-Cold War security concerns emanate from.

The security challenges outlined in Chapter 2 should serve as a reminder that many of the threats facing Europe are in fact regional manifestations of wider international problems that have emerged since the end of the Cold War. This suggests that any effective response to the challenges facing Europe should also concentrate on vesting the United Nations with effective power and funding to be able to carry out its intended role. Whatever institutional structure emerges in Europe should be a complement to, not a substitute for, the UN.

For inspiration we should, ironically, return to the defunct Warsaw Treaty Organization, which in its founding treaty reaffirmed the 'desire to create a system of collective security in Europe based on the participation of all European states, irrespective of their social and political structure, whereby the said States may be enabled to combine their efforts in the interests of ensuring peace in Europe'.[5]

Appendix I

The following figures are taken from the chart *European Security Institutions* prepared by the National Technical Information Service, Virginia, published in April 1993.

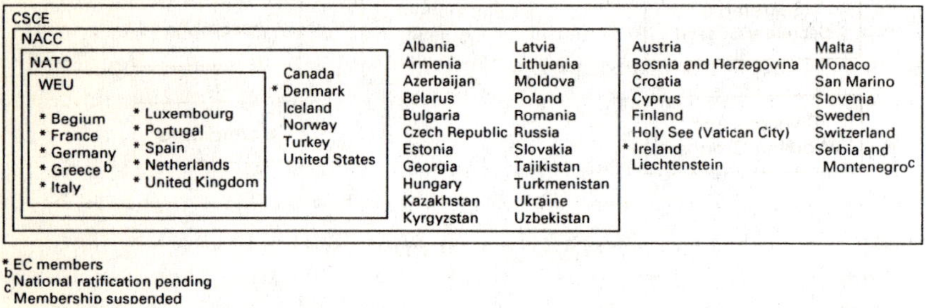
CSCE
NACC
NATO
WEU
* Begium
* France
* Germany
* Greece b
* Italy
* Luxembourg
* Portugal
* Spain
* Netherlands
* United Kingdom
Canada
* Denmark
Iceland
Norway
Turkey
United States
Albania
Armenia
Azerbaijan
Belarus
Bulgaria
Czech Republic
Estonia
Georgia
Hungary
Kazakhstan
Kyrgyzstan
Latvia
Lithuania
Moldova
Poland
Romania
Russia
Slovakia
Tajikistan
Turkmenistan
Ukraine
Uzbekistan
Austria
Bosnia and Herzegovina
Croatia
Cyprus
Finland
Holy See (Vatican City)
* Ireland
Liechtenstein
Malta
Monaco
San Marino
Slovenia
Sweden
Switzerland
Serbia and Montenegro c
* EC members
b National ratification pending
c Membership suspended

Figure A.1 Overlapping membership in Europe's security institutions

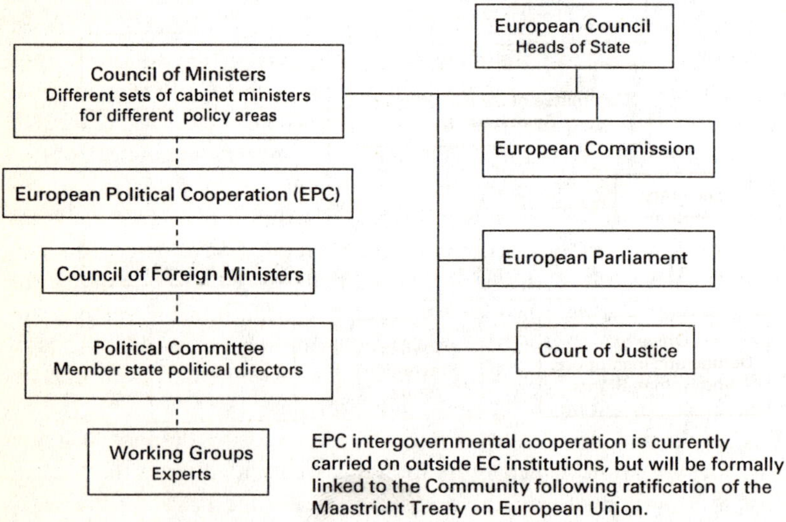
European Council
Heads of State
Council of Ministers
Different sets of cabinet ministers for different policy areas
European Commission
European Political Cooperation (EPC)
European Parliament
Council of Foreign Ministers
Court of Justice
Political Committee
Member state political directors
Working Groups
Experts
EPC intergovernmental cooperation is currently carried on outside EC institutions, but will be formally linked to the Community following ratification of the Maastricht Treaty on European Union.

Figure A.2 EC (Common Foreign and Security Policy – CFSP)

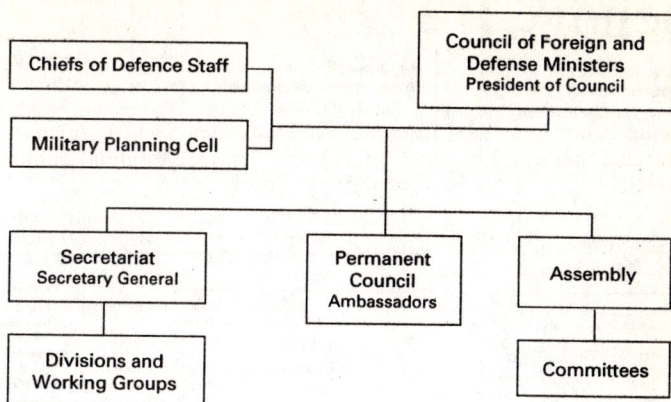

Figure A.3 WEU

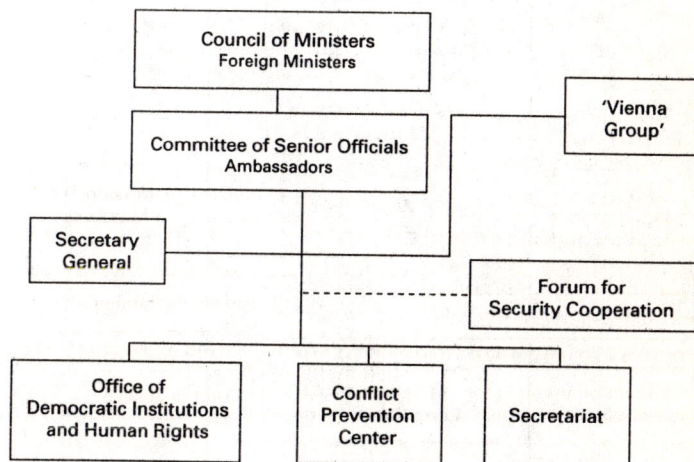

Figure A.4 CSCE

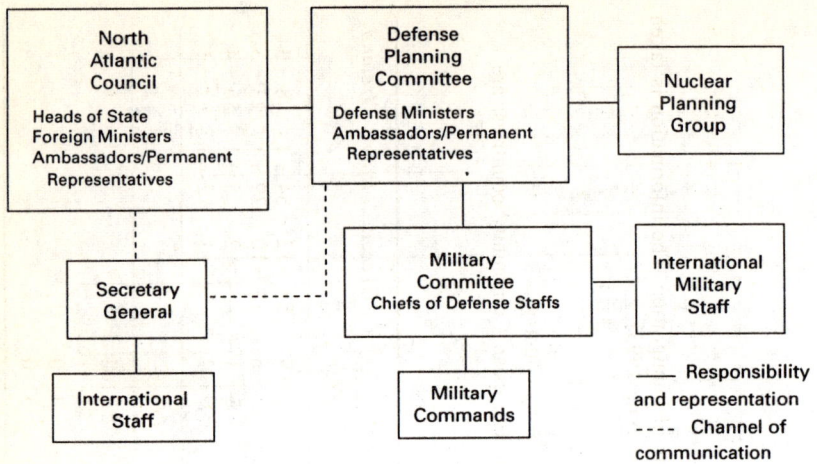

Figure A.5 NATO

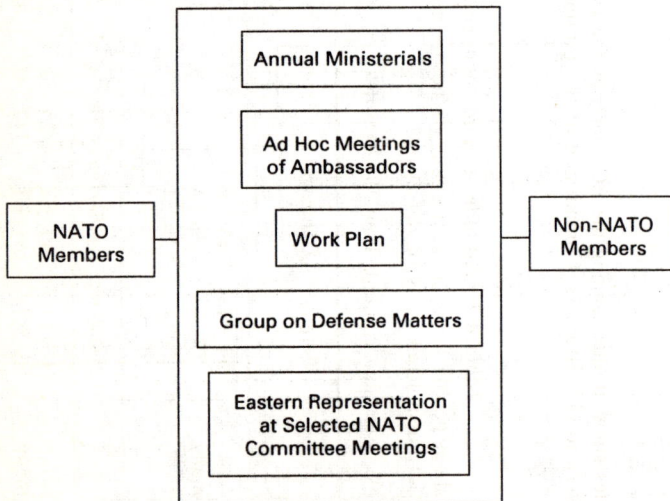

Figure A.6 NACC

Appendix II

The following tables show attitudes among the EC countries towards various aspects of immigration. The information is taken from *Eurobarometer*, no. 39 (Brussels: Commission of the European Communities, June 1993).

Table A.1 Attitudes towards non-nationals of the EC (% by country)

How do you feel about people living in your country who are not nationals of the European Community countries: are there too many, a lot but not too many or not many?

1st column: June 1993 result; 2nd column: June 1992 result.

	Belgium	Denmark	France	Germany		Greece	Italy	Ireland
				West	East			
Too many	54 +1	43 −8	56 +4	60 +3	57 +9	57 +12	64 −1	8 −3
A lot but not too many	35 +2	38 +4	32 −3	32 −3	32 −6	32 −10	29 +1	23 −3
Not many	5 −1	16 −2	5 −3	4 −1	5 −1	4 −2	5 +1	56 +4
Don't know	6 −2	4 +1	7 +1	4 +1	6 −2	6 +1	2 −1	2 −1

	Luxemburg	Netherlands	Portugal	Spain	UK	EC + 12
Too many	21 −11	47 −2	25 −3	25 +2	50 0	52 +2
A lot but not too many	53 +7	41 +3	42 0	44 +1	33 +2	34 −1
Not many	19 +4	7 −2	19 −2	20 −2	11 −2	9 0
Don't know	8 +1	4 0	14 +4	12 0	6 −1	6 0

Table A.2 Presence of people of another nationality, race or religion (% by country)

Some people are disturbed by the opinions, customs and way of life of people different from themselves.
(a) Do you find the presence of people of another nationality disturbing?
(b) Do you find the presence of people of another race disturbing?
(c) Do you find the presence of people of another religion disturbing?

1st column: disturbing; 2nd column: not disturbing.

	Belgium	Denmark	France	Germany West	Germany East	Greece	Italy	Ireland	Luxemburg
Nationality	16 80	21 77	18 76	12 82	13 80	28 70	11 86	6 91	8 90
Race	22 73	20 78	24 70	15 79	15 77	25 74	13 84	9 88	6 92
Religion	19 76	39 58	18 77	13 80	9 81	30 69	11 84	4 93	6 92

	Netherlands	Portugal	Spain	UK	EC + 12
Nationality	13 82	6 93	7 91	14 84	13 83
Race	7 89	9 90	11 87	15 84	16 81
Religion	4 93	8 90	8 88	12 86	13 82

Table A.3. Acceptance of people coming from the south of the Mediterranean

Spring 1992: Some people from different countries of the South of the Mediterranean wish to work here in the European Community. For this type of immigration, what do you think should be done here in the European Community: accept them without restrictions, accept them but with restrictions or not accept them?

Spring 1993: If people from countries of the South of the Mediterranean wish to work here in the European Community, do you think that they should . . . (as above)?

1st column: spring 1992 results; 2nd column: spring 1993 results.

	Belgium	Denmark	France	Germany West	Germany East	Greece	Italy	Ireland
Without restrictions	10 +1	6 +3	10 +2	16 +1	9 +1	9 +1	22 +3	21 −2
With restrictions	54 +2	63 +3	50 −5	57 +6	52 −9	56 −5	58 −5	58 −1
Not accept them	31 −1	30 −7	37 +3	22 −8	36 +9	32 +4	16 +2	16 +2
Don't Know	4 −2	1 0	3 0	4 −1	4 0	4 0	3 −1	3 −1

	Luxemburg	Netherlands	Portugal	Spain	UK	EC + 12
Without restrictions	10 +2	12 +5	24 −8	25 −11	8 +1	15 10
With restrictions	68 +6	62 +6	55 +8	57 +10	63 0	57 +1
Not accept them	18 −3	23 −1	9 −2	13 +3	28 +1	24 −1
Don't know	3 0	3 0	12 +3	5 −3	2 +3	4 −1

Table A.4. Acceptance of people coming from the Eastern Europe

Spring 1992: Some people from Eastern Europe wish to work in the West. For this type of immigration, what do you think should be done here in the European Community: accept them without restrictions, accept them but with restrictions or not accept them?

Spring 1993: And what about people coming from Eastern Europe who wish to work in the West?

1st column: spring 1992 result; 2nd column: spring 1993 results.

	Belgium	Denmark	France	Germany West	Germany East	Greece	Italy	Ireland
Without restrictions	9 +1	8 +3	11 +1	7 −3	8 −1	8 +2	19 +1	18 −3
With restrictions	59 +1	65 0	58 −5	56 +3	49 −11	57 −4	60 −4	61 +2
Not accept them	28 +1	26 −3	29 +5	32 −1	39 +11	31 +1	17 +3	13 +3
Don't know	3 −4	1 0	3 0	5 +1	4 0	3 −1	4 −1	9 −1

	Luxemburg	Netherlands	Portugal	Spain	UK	EC + 12
Without restrictions	7 −3	10 +2	21 −11	26 −12	8 −1	12 −2
With restrictions	69 +9	64 +4	55 +6	60 +13	63 0	59 0
Not accept them	19 −4	23 −6	11 +1	10 +3	28 +2	25 +2
Don't know	6 0	3 −1	13 +3	5 −3	1 −2	4 −1

Table A.5. Acceptance of people seeking political asylum

Spring 1992: Some people, suffering from human rights violations in their country, are seeking political asylum. For this type of immigration, what do you think should be done here in the European Community: accept them without restrictions, accept them but with restrictions, or not accept them?

Spring 1993: And what about people suffering from human rights violations in their country, who are seeking political asylum?

1st column: spring 1992 results; 2nd column: spring 1993 results.

	Belgium	Denmark	France	Germany West	Germany East	Greece	Italy	Ireland
Without restrictions	15 +13	38 +8	21 +6	19 +1	31 −5	15 −6	27 +1	18 +1
With restrictions	57 −7	55 −6	46 −5	54 +5	53 +4	57 0	47 +1	54 −1
Not accept them	25 −4	8 −2	30 +1	23 −6	12 0	24 +5	18 +1	16 +3
Don't Know	4 −5	2 +1	4 −1	4 −1	4 +1	5 +1	9 −2	13 −2

	Luxemburg	Netherlands	Portugal	Spain	UK	EC + 12
Without restrictions	16 −3	31 +12	23 −10	43 −4	18 +3	24 +1
With restrictions	67 +12	56 −5	50 +6	44 +9	57 −2	51 +1
Not accept them	11 −8	11 −7	11 +1	7 −1	19 −1	19 −2
Don't know	6 0	3 +1	15 +1	6 −4	5 −1	6 −1

Table A.6. Acceptance of people from other EC countries

Spring 1993 on: And what about citizens of other countries of the European Countries who wish to settle in (your country)?

	Belgium	Denmark	France	Germany West	Germany East	Greece	Italy	Ireland
Accept without restrictions	33	41	29	30	21	28	46	47
Accept with restrictions	48	51	49	49	51	51	39	38
Not accept them	16	7	18	14	21	19	10	6
Don't know	4	2	4	6	3	3	5	9

	Luxemburg	Netherlands	Portugal	Spain	UK	EC + 12
Accept without restrictions	16	28	46	52	28	35
Accept with restrictions	68	52	37	37	50	46
Not accept them	9	16	5	5	19	14
Don't know	8	4	12	6	2	5

Notes and References

Introduction

1. For an excellent and persuasive iteration of this point see Gwyn Prins, 'Politics and the Environment', *International Affairs*, vol. 66, no. 4 (October 1990) pp. 711–30.
2. Jessica Tuchman Mathews, 'Redefining Security', *Foreign Affairs*, vol. 68, no. 2 (Spring 1989) p. 174.
3. London Declaration on a transformed North Atlantic Alliance, Issued by the Heads of State and Government participating in the meeting of the North Atlantic Council in London, 5–6 July 1990, Para. 2.
4. Hans J. Morgenthau, *Politics Among Nations: The Struggle for Power and Peace*, 6th edn (New York: Alfred A. Knopf, 1985) p. 11.
5. Joseph S. Nye, Jr., *Bound to Lead: The Changing Nature of American Power* (New York: Basic Books, 1990) p. 188.
6. See for instance Joseph Nye, Jr., who argues that 'war has been the ultimate indicator of national military strength', in ibid., p. 78, or E.H. Carr who argued that, since potential war is always present in the international system, 'military strength becomes a recognized standard of political values', in *The Twenty Years Crisis* (New York: St Martin's Press, 1939) p. 102.
7. For a stimulating discussion of power in the international system, see John M. Rothberg, Jr. *Defining Power: Influence and Force in the Contemporary International System* (New York: St Martin's Press, 1993) pp. 17–46.
8. Examples would include Armand Clesse and Lothar Rühl (eds), *Beyond East–West Confrontation: Searching for a New Security Structure in Europe* (Baden-Baden: Nomon Verlagsgesellschaft, 1990); Mathias Jopp, Reinhardt Rummel and Peter Schmidt (eds), *Integration and Security in Western Europe* (Colorado: Westview, 1991); Alpo M. Rusi, *After the Cold War: Europe's New Political Architecture* (London: Macmillan, 1992); Adrian Hyde-Price, *European Security Beyond the Cold War* (London: Royal Institute for International Affairs/Sage, 1991); John Leech, *Halt! Who Goes Where?* (London: Brassey's Defence, 1992); and Richard Ullman, *Securing Europe* (Princeton NJ: Princeton University Press, 1991).
9. Ullman, *Securing Europe*, pp. 63–82.
10. Hans Bennendijk, 'European Security Alternatives', in Clesse and Rühl (eds) *Beyond East–West Confrontation*, p. 176.
11. James Baker III spoke of a 'Europe whole and free and a Euro-Atlantic community that extends east from Vancouver to Vladivostok'. President Bush spoke in Prague about 'A new commonwealth of freedom ... resting on shared principles ... that constitute our common values' in 'The Euro-Atlantic Architecture: From East to West', a speech delivered to the Aspen Institute, Berlin, Germany, 18 June 1991, *Vital Speeches of the Day*, 15 July 1991, vol. LVII, no. 19, p. 1.

12. Mikhail Gorbachev, *New Thinking for Our Country and the World* (New York: Harper and Row, 1987) pp. 197–8.

1 The Nature of Post-Cold War Security

1. John Mearsheimer, 'Why we will soon miss the Cold War', *The Atlantic Monthly*, August 1990, p. 35. The idea of anarchy in international relations is one that seems to point to its inherent instability, since there is a lack of 'government' or legal enforcement agencies at the international level. However, the absence of domestic political analogies at the international level means that the system may well be anarchical, but at the same time may show patterns on collaboration and cooperation. See Hedley Bull, *The Anarchical Society: A Study of Order in World Politics* (London: Macmillan, 1977) pp. 46–52. In an extended version of 'Why we will soon miss the Cold War', Mearsheimer observes that, 'Each state living under anarchy faces the ever-present possibility that another state will use force or harm to conquer it. Offensive military action is always a threat to all states in the system.' See John Mearsheimer, 'Back to the Future,' *International Security*, vol. 15, no. 1 (Summer 1990) pp. 12–13.
2. Mearsheimer, 'Why we will soon miss the Cold War', p. 35.
3. See Lawrence Freedman, *The Evolution of Nuclear Strategy* (New York: St Martin's Press, 1989) pp. 76–119.
4. At the time of writing the START treaties had not been ratified.
5. For a wide-ranging discussion of the security threats in the post-Cold War era, see Michael Klare and Daniel Thomas, *World Security: Trends and Challenge at Century's End*, 2nd edn, (New York: St Martin's Press, 1993).
6. Athens and Sparta, the supreme maritime and land powers respectively, pursued a mutual rivalry based upon the pursuit of their 'world interests'. Both had shared in the defeat of the Persian Great Kings early in the fourth century B.C. After the defeat both developed massive alliance systems over which each enjoyed prestige and decision-making capacity in its respective alliance. Athens dominated the Delian League, comprised mainly of island states, and Sparta the Peloponnesian land mass. Each, like the US and the USSR in the Cold War, enjoyed predominant influence over its alliance system. The lines were thus drawn for conflict which eventually broke out over the issue of Athenian aid to Corcyra (Corfu) in 431 B.C. As Peter Fleiss suggests, the Peloponnesian War is an early example of bipolar politics which broke down into war. For further details, see Peter J. Fliess, *Thucydides and the Politics of Bipolarity* (Louisiana: Louisiana State University, 1966).
7. Article 231 of the Versailles Treaty compelled the German people to accept collective guilt for beginning World War I. Gathorne-Hardy commented that, 'the imputation of war guilt . . . was the cause not only of abiding irritation in Germany, but of most laborious and voluminous documentary efforts to disprove it'. *A Short History on International Affairs 1920–39* (Oxford: Oxford University Press, 1950) p. 33.
8. In one of the large neo-Nazi marches in November 1992, a demonstrator carried a banner that read: '5 minutes to 1933'. In spite of the resur-

gence of neo-Nazis in Germany, they do not represent a major political force and no extreme right-wing party has yet reached the 5 per cent limit necessary to claim a seat in the Bundestag. In political terms, Jean Marie Le Pen's National Front in France is far more significant. Unlike their 1933 counterparts, the neo-Nazi movement of the early 1990s is not concerned with redrawing Germany's frontiers but with expelling immigrants.

9. Mearsheimer, 'Why we will soon miss the Cold War', p. 35. Also see 'Back to the Future,' for a fuller discussion of Mearsheimer's ideas. In particular see his critique of those who hold that Europe is more stable than he assumes, as well as being less prone to violence (pp. 8–9, 40–51).

10. See Bull, *The Anarchical Society*, pp. 23–77.

11. Leon T. Haddar, 'What Green Peril?', *Foreign Affairs*, vol. 72, no. 2 (Spring 1993) p. 27.

12. David B. Rivkin, Jr., 'Winning the Peace – Dilemmas of Post-Soviet European Security', *Problems of Communism*, vol. 41, no. 1–2 (January 1992) p. 151.

13. For a discussion on this issue, see Hadar, 'What Green Peril?', and Judith Miller, 'The Challenge of Radical Islam', both in *Foreign Affairs*, vol. 72, no. 2 (Spring 1993) pp. 27–57.

14. Rémy Leveau, 'Maghrebi Immigration to Europe: Double Insertion or Double Exclusion?', *ANNALS, AAPSS*, vol. 524 (November 1992) p. 175. In numerical terms this means around 6 million people: 2.5 million in France, 2 million in Britain, 1 million in Germany, and a few hundred thousand in Belgium and Holland.

15. The Central Asian republics are sensitive to the 'Islamic state' issue. President Nazarbayev has been especially anxious to safeguard Russian sensibilities about the emergence of an Islamic state in Kazakhstan. So too is President Askar Akayev of Kyrgyzstan sensitive to the issue, since his support comes largely from the Russian minority. The remaining three republics, Tajikistan, Turkmenistan and Uzbekistan, are more inclined to pursue pro-Islamic policies. For more details, see Martha Brill Olcott, 'Central Asia's Catapult to Independence', *Foreign Affairs*, vol. 71, no. 3 (Summer 1992) pp. 108–31.

16. Even here, doubt can be cast upon Iran and Pakistan as being truly Islamic states since in both cases there is a significant change in Islamic practices in the modern regimes, unlike in Morocco and Saudi Arabia. Iran and Pakistan exist primarily as modern nation-states that are nominally Islamic states but whose Islamic identity exists primarily in political terms and not necessarily in the moral or traditional Muslim sense. Since the turn of the century more Islamic states have disappeared than have been created, Egypt, Iraq, Jordan, Tunisia and Turkey serving as cases in point.

17. See Robin Wright, 'Islam, Democracy and the West', *Foreign Affairs*, vol. 71, no. 3 (Summer 1992) pp. 131–146.

18. Ibid., p. 132.

19. Ibid.

20. For example, Saudi Arabia, which contends that its constitution is the *Quran* and its source of legislation the *shari'a*, has shown remarkable

flexibility in adapting these sources with the needs of a modernizing society. Innovation, or *itjihad*, had been tolerated to the extent that there is a quasi-secular system of courts (Mazalim courts) that coexists with the *shari'a* courts. In the case of Pakistan under former President Zia ul-Haq, which saw Pakistan at its most developed in Islamic terms (due mainly to Zia's backing of the Jama'at-i-Islami party), the *shari'a* was never fully enforced since critical areas of law were excluded from its purview, such as the constitution and martial law offences, family and fiscal law. For further details, see Graham E. Fuller, 'Islamic Fundamentalism in Pakistan: Its Character and Prospects', *RAND*, R-3964-USDP (1991) p. 38.

21. Graham E. Fuller, 'Islamic Fundamentalism in the Northern Tier Countries: An Integrative View', *RAND*, R-3966-USDP (1991) p. 41.
22. Ibid., p. 36.
23. Mansour Farhanq, 'The United States and the Question of Democracy in the Middle East', *Current History*, vol. 92, no. 570 (January 1993) p. 3.
24. Ibid.
25. Ibid., p. 2.
26. *New York Times*, 31 December 1992, A.5.
27. Charles E. Butterworth, 'Political Islam: The Origins,' *ANNALS, AAPSS*, vol. 524 (November 1992) p. 37.
28. Ira M. Lapidus, 'The Golden Age: The Political Concepts of Islam', ibid., p. 25.
29. Vitaly Naumkin, 'Islam in the States of the Former USSR', ibid., p. 141.
30. *The Middle East*, no. 215 (September 1992) p. 5.
31. Wright, 'Islam, Democracy and the West', pp. 144–5.

2 Security Challenges Facing Europe in the post-Cold War World

1. The four are Russia, Belarus, the Ukraine and Kazakhstan.
2. Russian nuclear forces will be reduced from 27 000 to 4406 warheads by the year 2000. The US will reduce from 13 800 warheads (on 1842 launch systems) to 500 Minuteman III missiles, 18 Trident submarines and 212 nuclear-capable bombers (which means 4700 warheads on 1144 potential launch systems) by 1997. As of July 1992, the four CIS republics with nuclear weapons had 15 000 active warheads and a further 12–15 000 warheads that are awaiting dismantling and disposal. Figures quoted in *Bulletin of The Atomic Scientists*, July/August 1992, p. 49.
3. Figures from *SIPRI Yearbook 1992: World Armaments and Disarmament* (Oxford: Oxford University Press, 1992) p. 33.
4. The majority of the warheads are deployed on almost 3000 tactical missiles (the Scud-B, Frog 3/7 and the SS-21), and a further 2000 warheads are reserved for use in the 7000 nuclear-capable artillery systems. For further details, see *SIPRI Yearbook 1992*, pp. 76–7.
5. The official reason was that Russia would 'temporarily suspend' the withdrawal of some of its troops from the Baltic States because there was nowhere for the returning troops to live. Russia has requested that the states build housing for the returning troops. See *New York Times*, 21 October 1992, A 12.

6. The START I agreement assigned certain values to the number of war-heads deployable on a given delivery system. Since the assigned num-bers were in some cases below the actual number of warheads that could be carried by a delivery system, such as strategic bombers, the *real* number of warheads could be above the 6000 level, although the *ac-countable* level would be 6000.
7. See S. Meyer, 'The Post-Soviet nuclear menace is being hyped', *Inter-national Herald Tribune*, 16 December 1991, p. 8.
8. President Bush of the United States, State of the Union Address to Con-gress, 28 January 1992, quoted in *SIPRI Yearbook 1992*, p. 82.
9. President of the Russian Federation, Boris Yeltsin, record of televised statement, 29 January 1992. Also in *SIPRI Yearbook 1992*, pp. 89–92.
10. START 1, signed in July 1991, allowed for 8556 strategic warheads, split between bombers, submarine-launched ballistic missiles SLBMs, and Intercontinental ballistic missile (ICBM) warheads, for the US. The corresponding figure for the USSR was 6450. As a result of the Janu-ary 1992 accords between Yeltsin and Bush, these figures were reduced to 4700 and 4456 for the US and CIS respectively. The June 1992 accords, which formed the basis of START II in January 1993, pro-vided for a first-stage reduction in the number of warheads to 3800–4200 within the first seven years of START I's duration. Further reductions, to 3000–3500, were stipulated by the year 2003.
11. For a stimulating debate on the wider question of whether the Ukraine should surrender all of its nuclear weapons to the RSFR for destruc-tion, see John J. Mearsheimer, 'The Case. for a Ukrainian Nuclear De-terrent', and Steven E. Miller, 'The Case Against a Ukrainian Nuclear Deterrent', both in *Foreign Affairs*, vol. 72, no. 3, pp. 50–81.
12. The US proposal to put the nuclear weapons based in the Ukraine under international control forms part of a four-pronged effort aimed at securing Ukrainian ratification of the START treaties while also answering the Ukraine's security concerns. In conversations between the Ukraine's defence minister, General Konstantin Morozov, and US defence minis-ter, Les Aspin, held on 7 June 1993 it was agreed to: (i) strengthen military ties between the countries; (ii) enhance confidence-building meas-ures (including the proposal to put nuclear warheads under international control; (iii) support for the Ukraine's independent status; (iv) improve the quality of the Ukraine's conventional armed forces.
13. FBIS-SOV-91-237, 10 December 1991, pp. 56–7.
14. FBIS-SOV-91-240, 13 December 1991, pp. 84–5.
15. The non-nuclear status reflects the fact that the 1968 Non-Proliferation Treaty only permits five nuclear weapon states – Britain, China, France, the Soviet Union (since 10 February 1992 the RSFR has taken on all obligations assumed in international treaties by the former Soviet Union) and the US.
16. FBIS-SOV-91-246, 23 December 1991, pp. 30–31 (emphasis added).
17. Shaposhnikov, with the support of Yeltsin, and the five Central Asian republics, Belarus and Armenia, has included under the joint strategic forces not only the strategic nuclear attack systems (which includes their air and missile defence forces) but almost all of the naval surface vessels,

military transportation, and airborne assets.

18. Edward L. Warner III, 'The Decline of the Soviet Military: Downsizing, Fragmentation and Possible Disintegration', *RAND Paper*, P-7762, p. 17.
19. Edward L. Warner III, 'The Decline of the Soviet Military: Downsizing, Fragmentation and Possible Disintegration,' *RAND Paper*, P-7762, p. 19.
20. Ibid., p. 13.
21. The full texts of the *Declaration on the State Sovereignty of the Ukraine* and the *Act Proclaiming Independence of Ukraine* can be found in 'Ukraine's Non-Nuclear Option', United Nations Institute for Disarmament Research, Research Paper No. 14 (New York: United Nations, 1992) pp. 17–22.
22. Ibid., p. 15.
23. Anatoly Zlenko, 'Ukrainian security and the nuclear dilemma', *NATO Review*, vol. 41, no. 4 (August 1993) p. 12.
24. Ibid. Statement to the Press Service by Leonid Kravchuk, Kiev, 12 March 1992, pp. 26–7.
25. Of the 176 strategic nuclear weapons in the Ukraine, 130 are older SS-19s and are not the object of contention. The 46 SS-24s are more modern and accurate, each equipped with 10 warheads. The launchers for the SS-24s were assembled in the Ukraine. There are also 20 Blackjack bombers but the Ukraine does not have control of their nuclear bombs. The SS-24s are the missiles that the Ukraine may wish to retain.
26. Zlenko, *NATO Review*, August 1993, p. 14.
27. Quoted in *The Economist*, 3–9 April 1993, p. 52.
28. Michael R. Gordon, 'Ukrainian Official Backs U.S. Plan on Atom Arms', *New York Times*, 8 June 1993, A7.
29. John J. Mearsheimer, 'The Case for a Ukrainian Nuclear Deterrent', *Foreign Affairs*, vol. 72, no. 3 (Summer 1993) p. 52.
30. North Atlantic Assembly, Defence and Security Committee, Report on Nuclear Weapons in the former Soviet Union, DSC (93) 9, October 1993.
31. A report in the *Washington Post* by Ann Devroy and Margaret Shapiro suggested that there is a secret schedule that has a three-year deadline for the removal of all weapons from the Ukraine's soil. 15 January 1994, p. A.1.
32. One report by Sonni Efron in the *Los Angeles Times* suggested that Britain had also agreed to security guarantees. 15 January 1994, p. A.5.
33. John Lloyd, 'Yeltsin Ushers out Cold War with N-accord', *Financial Times*, 15 January 1994, p. 2.
34. Anatol Lieven and Michael Evans, 'Kravchuk faces Kiev battle over nuclear arsenal', *The Times*, 15 January 1994, p. 1.
35. A Socis-Gallup poll published in the Ukraine on 13 January 1994 showed that 17.4 per cent of the Ukraine would agree unconditionally to exchange the weapons in return for oil and gas and 31.4 per cent would agree to such a deal if 'absolutely necessary.' 36 per cent opposed giving up the weapons. Published in the *Los Angeles Times*, 15 January 1994, p. A5.
36. Quoted in *The Economist*, 3–9 April 1993, p. 52.
37. For details, see 'Red-Tape and Mistrust Slow US–Russia Nuclear Ef-

fort', *The Wall Street Journal*, 8 March 1993; and 'Red-tape and Suspicion Slow Nuclear Dismantling to a Crawl,' *The Independent*, 15 March 1993.

38. Yegor Gaidar, the architect of Russia's economic reform programme, announced his resignation on 16 January 1994. His decision was motivated by his feeling that 'He didn't feel that the government would pursue a sensible economic policy.' See Steven Erlanger, 'Leading Russian Reformer Quits: Questioning the Cabinet's Policies', *New York Times*, 17 January 1994, p. A.1.

39. *SIPRI Yearbook 1992*, p. 105.

40. No destruction of weapons by this method has yet taken place. Observers point out that such explosions would be in violation of the 5 October 1991 unilateral moratorium announced by Gorbachev. Chetek officials claim that 'peaceful nuclear explosions' are not covered by the moratorium.

41. *SIPRI Yearbook 1992*, p. 105.

42. Tariq Rauf, 'Cleaning up with a Bang', *Bulletin of Atomic Scientists*, January/February 1992, p. 9.

43. For example, the decision to restart one of the reactors at Chernobyl, reported in *New York Times*, 30 October 1992, was made in spite of widespread condemnation from the international community.

44. Eight CIS republic signed an agreement at Minsk in June 1992 agreeing to export controls of nuclear material. There has been little apparent progress in implementing export controls or in designing common export guidelines. See 'European Regulations Alarmed by Rise in Nuclear Smuggling', *International Herald Tribute*, 30 November 1992.

45. Ibid.

46. *SIPRI Yearbook 1992*, p. 106.

47. Gorbachev's measures do not mark the complete end of testing since President Yeltsin announced on 27 February 1992 that preparations for two to four tests would continue at the Novaya Zemlya test site, if the moratorium were broken by any other nuclear power.

48. The RBMK reactors were built only in the former Soviet Union. Fifteen are still operating in Lithuania, Russia and the Ukraine.

49. Sergei Kapitza, 'Soviet scientists: Low Pay, no pay, now insults', *Bulletin of Atomic Scientists*, May 1992, rejects this notion by arguing that, 'Those who work on nuclear weapons are personally impressed by the forces at their command. Overwhelmingly, this has a significant effect on character and attitude, and in developing a sense of personal responsibility' (pp. 8–9).

50. See Aaron Karp, 'The Frantic Third World Quest for Ballistic Missiles', *Bulletin of Atomic Scientists*, June 1988, pp. 14–22.

51. Lora Lumpe, Lisbeth Gronlund and David C. Wright, 'Third World Missiles Fall Short', *Bulletin of Atomic Scientists*, March 1992. In the article they argue, 'The spread of ballistic missiles and other advanced weapons is an important problem that merits serious attention ... An examination of current and potential ballistic missile states suggests that China – which has long had missiles capable of reaching the US – is the only developing country that could possibly pose a genuine threat

to the United States in the foreseeable future. Accordingly, fears of Third World missiles do not justify spending billions of dollars on missile defenses to protect the United States' (p. 30).

52. The original members of the MTCR are Canada, France, Germany, Italy, Japan, the United Kingdom and the United States.

53. Statement by Robert Gates, Director of the CIA, before the Senate Armed Services Committee, quoted in *SIPRI Yearbook 1992*, pp. 84 and 131.

54. China was accused of shipping components that would help Pakistan build the M-11 missile, which has a range of 300 miles and is capable of carrying a nuclear warhead. For details, see *New York Times*, 20 July 1993, A3; 26 July 1993, A2; and 26 August 1993, A15.

55. FBIS-SOV-91-237, 10 December 1991, pp. 56–7.

56. SIPRI estimates that in the period 1988–91, the production of aircraft declined by 44 per cent, tanks by 52 per cent, strategic missiles by 58 per cent, ammunition by 64 per cent, self-propelled and towed artillery by 66 per cent, and fighting landing craft and armoured carriers by 76 per cent. Production of all medium- and short-range missiles has halted. *SIPRI Yearbook 1992*, p. 383.

57. For an excellent discussion of the changes in the Soviet defence industries, see Alexei Kireyev, 'Arms Production: The Former Soviet Union', in *SIPRI Yearbook 1992*, pp. 380–90.

58. Edward Mortimer, 'Continent of Conflicts', *Financial Times*, 29 July 1992, p. 6.

59. On 21 September 1993 Boris Yeltsin dissolved parliament following a prolonged struggle between hard-line communists, nationalists and re-form opponents within the parliament and those who supported Yeltsin's reforms, particularly economic ones. The parliament's staff were suspended until new elections were held. Within an hour of the dissolution of parliament, a rump parliament, assembled by Ruslan Khasbulatov, had stripped Yeltsin of all of his powers and sworn in Alexandr Rutskoi, the vice-president, as Russia's president. A protracted struggle ensued for physical control of the White House (the parliament building) in which many in the parliament opposing Yeltsin were killed. Eventually, the remains of the rump parliament surrendered.

60. Karl Kaiser, 'Patterns of Partnership', in Steven Muller and Gebhard Schweigler, eds, *From Occupation to Cooperation: The United States and United Germany in a Changing World Order* (New York: Norton, 1992) p. 158.

61. See *SIPRI Yearbook 1992*, p. 541.

62. Ibid., p. 540.

63. Paul B. Henze, 'Ethnic Dynamics and Dilemmas of the Russian Republic', *RAND NOTE*, N-3219-USDP, p. 18.

64. As was noted earlier, the withdrawal of Russian troops from the Baltic states was temporarily suspended in October 1992 on the grounds that there were no facilities for returning troops. There are still 6000 support (non-combat) troops who will remain in Poland until the end of 1993 to assist with the pull-out from Eastern Germany.

65. 'La Sécurité européenne dans les années 90: Problèmes de l'Europe du Sud-Est', Rhodes, Greece, 6–7 September 1991 (New York: United

Nations, 1992); UNIDIR 92/40, pp. 27–30, 77–79.

66. For full details, see *SIPRI Yearbook 1993: World Armaments and Disarmament*, (Oxford: Oxford University Press, 1993), pp. 95–98.
67. Ibid., pp. 103–4.
68. Chechnia declared itself an independent republic in November 1991 and has been recognized by Estonia, Iran, Lithuania and Turkey.
69. Ibid., p. 99.
70. *The Economist*, April 17–23 1993, p. 51.
71. Mark Almond, 'Europe's Immigration Crisis', *The National Interest*, Fall 1992, p. 12.
72. *New York Times*, 10 August 1993, A1.
73. The use of the term 'asylum' is based on those definitions appearing in Article 1–A (2) of the Geneva Convention of 28 July 1951 on the Status of Refugees, which stated that a refugee is a person who,

> as a result of events occurring before January 1, 1951 and owing to the well-founded fear of being persecuted for reasons of race, religion, nationality, membership of a particular social group or political opinion, is outside of the country of his nationality and is unable or owing to such fear unwilling to avail himself of the protection of that country; or who, not having a nationality and being outside the country of his former habitual residence as a result of such events, is unable or, owing to such fear, unwilling to return to it.

Political refugees are also covered under the terms of the 1967 UN Protocol Relating to the Status of Refugees which, in Article 33 (1), reads:

> Prohibition of Expulsion or Return 1. No Contracting State shall expel or return (*refouler*) a refugee in any manner whatsoever to the frontiers or territories where his life or freedom would be threatened on account of his race, religion, nationality, membership of a particular social group or political opinion.

74. Figures from Henry Kamm, 'In Europe's Upheaval, Doors Close to Foreigners', *New York Times*, 10 February 1993, A.1.
75. Figures quoted in David B. Ottaway, 'Ethnic Cleansing's New Diaspora', *Washington Post: National Weekly Edition*, 23–29 August 1993, p. 11.
76. Ibid.
77. Ibid.
78. *1992 World Population Data Sheet* (Washington D.C.: Population Reference Bureau, 1992).
79. Almond, 'Europe's Immigration Crisis', p. 13.
80. Ibid.
81. Ibid.
82. Figures from *The Week in Germany*, 6 November 1992 (New York: German Information Center) p. 1.
83. *New York Times*, 10 February 1993, A.8.
84. *New York Times*, 10 August 1993, A.8.
85. The figures from the Ministry of the Interior for the number of asylum seekers for these months are: June–31 123; July–20 658; August–14 521.

Figures quoted in *The Week in Germany*, 10 September 1993, (New York: German Information Center), p. 2.

86. Figures from Henrik Bering-Jensen, 'A Flood of Strangers in Estranged Lands', *Insight*, 4 January 1993, pp. 6–11.
87. *Washington Post: Weekly National Edition*, 23–29 August 1993, p. 12.
88. Ibid., p. 8.
89. *New York Times*, 10 August 1993, A.8.
90. *Europe*, no. 321 (November 1992) pp. 38–9.
91. Ibid.
92. *El Pais* (Edición Internacional), 'Imigrantes: las diferencias económicas provocan la marginación de los extranjeros en España', 14 December 1992, p. 2.
93. *New York Times*, 10 August 1993, A.8.
94. John Fenske, 'France's Uncertain Progress toward European Union', *Current History*, vol. 90, no. 559, (November 1991) p. 360.
95. Ibid.
96. *New York Times*, 10 August 1993, A.8.
97. *The Economist*, 18–24 September 1993, pp. 63–4.
98. Ibid.
99. Ibid.
100. World Bank, *World Development Report 1992* (Washington D.C.: World Bank, 1992).
101. The members of the Arab Maghreb Union are Algeria, Libya, Mauritania, Morocco and Tunisia.
102. The Schengen agreement was signed in 1990 by nine of the twelve EC countries (Denmark, Eire and the United Kingdom are outside the agreement). The accord was supposed to remove physical barriers, such as customs posts, between these countries. Concern about immigration and crime (such as terrorism and narcotics) has delayed the implementation of the accords. The 1986 Single European Act and the 1991 Maastricht Agreement, between them, aim to guarantee the free movement of goods, services, capital and people. The removal of any one of these 'pillars' endangers the structure of the whole.
103. PHARE, originally 'Aid for the Economic Reconstruction of Poland and Hungary', is the EC's assistance programme to Albania, Bulgaria, the Czech Republic, Estonia, Hungary, Latvia, Lithuania, the former Yugoslav Republic of Macedonia, Poland, Romania, Slovakia and Slovenia. TACIS is the name of the EC's programme for 'Technical Assistance to the Commonwealth of Independent States', including Armenia, Belarus, Moldova, Russia (west of the Urals), the Ukraine and Georgia.
104. The security ramifications are not completely clear but they include increased costs of policing the borders (and quelling racially motivated incidents and demonstration), possible reinforcement of vulnerable borders in France, Italy and Spain, increased coastguard patrols, undercover work and so forth. The added costs and use of paramilitary or military forces obviously removes personnel from other duties.
105. See *SIPRI Yearbook 1993*, pp. 86–7.
106. UN Security Council Resolution 688, 5 April 1991, called for Iraq to allow 'immediate access by international humanitarian organizations to

all those in need of assistance in all parts of Iraq'.

107. Boutros-Boutros Ghali, *An Agenda for Peace, Report of the Secretary-General pursuant to the statement adopted by the Summit Meeting of the Security Council on 31 January 1992*, UN Doc No. A/47/277, 17 June 1992, Section 1, para. 17.

108. *UN Yearbook 1974*, General Assembly Resolutions, 29th session, vol. 1., Agenda Item 86, 3314 (XXIX) Report of the Special Committee on the question of defining aggression, A/9890, Article 3, 14 December 1974.

109. Article 1 referred not only to 'acts of aggression', but to 'other breaches of the peace'. The latter was never defined specifically, though, and thus makes it an unreliable base for UN intervention.

110. See *SIPRI Yearbook 1992*, pp. 421–2.

3   European Leadership: A Ship without a Rudder

1. See John Mearsheimer, 'Back to the Future: Instability in Europe after the Cold War', *International Security*, vol. 15, no. 1 (Summer 1990) pp. 5–56.

2. Jean Lacouture, *De Gaulle: The Ruler 1945–1970* (New York: W.W. Norton, 1992) p. 367.

3. M. Harrison, *The Reluctant Ally: France and Atlantic Security* (Baltimore: The Johns Hopkins University Press, 1981) p. 12.

4. Lacouture, *De Gaulle*, p. 376.

5. Ibid., p. 377.

6. See Stephen George, *An Awkward Partner: Britain in the European Community* (Oxford: Oxford University Press, 1990).

7. For a full description, see Richard Ullman, 'The Covert French Connection', *Foreign Policy*, no. 75 (Summer 1989).

8. Thomas-Durell Young and Samuel Newland, 'Germany, France, and the Future of Western European Security', *Parameters*, September 1991, p. 76.

9. *Europa-Archiv*, vol. 41, no. 9 (May 1986) D236.

10. Ministère de la défense, *La défense de la France* (Paris: 1988) p. 101.

11. Speech at the Institut des Hautes Études de Défense Nationale, Paris, 21 May 1990, quoted in David Yost, 'France in the New Europe', *Foreign Affairs*, vol. 69, no. 5 (Winter 1990/91) p. 114.

12. Jean Klein, 'France and the New Security Order in Europe', in Armand Clesse and Lothar Rühl, eds, *Beyond East–West Confrontation: Searching for a New Security Structure in Europe* (Baden-Baden: Nomos Verlagsgesellschaft, 1990) p. 294.

13. Ronald Tiersky, 'France in the New Europe', *Foreign Affairs*, vol. 71, no. 2 (Spring 1992) pp. 132–3.

14. Klein, 'France and the New Security Order in Europe', p. 293.

15. This would presumably be done through the European Council which is a semi-official EC body and consists of heads of state who meet, on average, twice a year.

16. Karl Lowe, 'US Armed Forces in the New Europe', in Jeffrey Simon, ed., *European Security Policy after the Revolutions of 1989* (Washington D.C.: National Defense University, 1991) p. 122.

17. The S-4 is the new generation intermediate-range ballistic missile. It has met with substantial cost overruns. The programme has been put on hold although Mitterrand has promised to continue its development.
18. London Declaration on a Transformed North Atlantic Alliance, issued by the heads of state and government participating in the meeting of the North Atlantic Council, London, 5–6 July 1990, para. 18.
19. *Le Monde*, 13 March 1990.
20. Jacques Chirac, 'Discours devant l'IHEDN, le 12 December 1987', quoted in Olivier Debouzy, *Anglo-French Nuclear Cooperation: Perspectives and Problems* (London: Royal United Services Institute/Whitehall Paper Series, 1991) p. 47.
21. Signed in Rome, 21 February 1991, subtitled 'Security cooperation in the framework of the Common Foreign and Security Policy of Political Union'. Full text can be found in Auke P. Venema and Henriëtte Romijn, *Documents on International Security Policy May 1989–December 1991* (Brussels: Netherlands Atlantic Commission).
22. The following points are based on those appearing in Yost, 'France in the New Europe', p. 116.
23. In spite of the oft-proclaimed French hostility to US foreign and security policy, there is a surprising amount of Franco–US cooperation. For a detailed account of this, see Ullman, 'The Covert French Connection', pp. 3–33.
24. Communiqué of the Ministerial meeting of the North Atlantic Council in Oslo, 4 June 1992, para. 7, in *NATO Review*, vol. 40, no. 3 (June 1992) p. 31.
25. *Le Monde*, 30 September 1992.
26. *Agence France Presse*, 28 November 1992, and *Le Monde*, 13 May 1993.
27. France has observer status in the Military Committee and liaison officers at SHAPE, SACLANT, AFCENT and CENTAG.
28. *Le Monde*, 13 May 1993.
29. London Declaration, para. 14.
30. Yost, 'France in the New Europe', p. 119.
31. London Declaration, para. 15.
32. Ibid., para. 18.
33. France's pre-strategic systems include the Pluton and Hadès missiles and the Mirage 2000 and Super-Etendard aircraft.
34. 'La Force d'Euro-frappe', *The Economist*, 18 January 1992, p. 48.
35. Ibid.
36. See Peter Jenkins, 'Tribune Europenée Feu La Doctrine nucleaire Gaulliste', *Le Monde*, 8 June 1992.
37. Ibid.
38. Interview with Jacques Isnard, *Le Monde*, 13 May 1993.
39. Yost, 'France in the New Europe', p. 122.
40. *Le Monde*, 10 June 1993.
41. Ibid.
42. Pierre Lellouche, 'France in Search of Security', *Foreign Affairs*, vol. 72, no. 2 (Spring 1993) p. 128.
43. For details, see *Le Monde*, 21 June 1993.
44. *L'Usine Nouvelle*, 16 May 1991.

45. Philip Jacobson and Michael Evans, 'Delors wants French nuclear force for EC', *The Times*, 6 January 1992.

46. Gregory F. Treverton, 'The New Europe', in *Foreign Affairs: America and the World 1991/92* vol. 71, no. 1, p. 106.

47. For instance in relation to Libyan raid of April 1986 where the Thatcher government offered the use of airbases in England, contrary to the non-cooperation and condemnation of the raid by other European allies.

48. See Paul Kennedy, *Strategy and Diplomacy 1870–1945* (London: George, Allen and Unwin, 1984) pp. 91–3.

49. For a comprehensive survey of early Anglo-American security relations, see John Baylis, *Anglo-American Defence Relations 1939–1980* (London: Macmillan, 1981).

50. For a full discussion of the British reaction to the McMahon Bill, see Margaret Gowing, *Independence and Deterrence: Britain and Atomic Energy 1945–52* (London: Macmillan, 1974) pp. 104–22.

51. Baylis, *Anglo-American Defence Relations 1939–1980*, p. 33.

52. For details of the agreement, see Simon Duke, *US Defence Bases in the United Kingdom* (London: Macmillan/St Antony's, 1987) pp. 41–4.

53. See ibid., pp. 123–50.

54. Sir Anthony Eden, *Full Circle* (London: Cassell, 1960) p. 166.

55. See Baylis, *Anglo-American Defence Relations 1939–1980*, pp. 77–99.

56. Simon Duke, *The Burdensharing Debate: A Reassessment* (London: Macmillan, 1993) pp. 72–6.

57. Hugo Young: *The Iron Lady: A Biography of Margaret Thatcher* (New York: Farrar Straus Giroux, 1989) pp. 190–1.

58. Stephen George, *An Awkward Partner: Britain in the European Community* (Oxford: Oxford University Press, 1990) pp. 194–5.

59. *Statement on Defence Estimates*, Cmnd. 9430-1 (London: HMSO, 1985) vol. 1, p. 18.

60. Stephen George, p. 202.

61. Ibid.

62. Geoffrey Smith, 'Britain and the New Europe', *Foreign Affairs*, vol. 71, no. 4, p. 166.

63. See Statement issued by the Defence Planning Committee and the Nuclear Planning Group of the North Atlantic Treaty Organization, Brussels, 28–9 May 1991, which states in paragraph 9 that 'We have agreed [to] the creation of a Rapid Reaction Corps for Allied Command Europe, under United Kingdom command with a multinational headquarters.'

64. Margaret Thatcher: *The Downing Street Years* (New York: HarperCollins, 1993) p. 727.

65. Ibid., p. 760.

66. For details of the Anglo-French nuclear collaboration see Ian Smart, *In Future Conditional: The Prospect for Anglo-French Nuclear Cooperation*, Adelphi Paper, no. 78 (London: IISS, 1971), and D. Fairhall, 'Younger in talks on Arms Link with France', *Guardian*, 16 September 1986, p. 5.

67. In the July 1992 Statement on Defence Estimates, the government committed itself to the acquisition of a fourth Trident SSBN, as well as a more general goal of stabilizing the defence budget at twenty-four billion pounds for the next three years, which means a reduction in real terms

of around five per cent. For details see Carole A. Shifrin, 'UK's New Defense Strategy Stresses Role in Preserving International Stability', *Aviation Week and Space Technology*, 13 July 1992, p. 72.

68. Figures from *SIPRI Yearbook 1992* (Oxford: OUP/SIPRI, 1992) p. 264. Figures for 1991 reflected less dramatic cuts on account of the increased defence expenditure entailed by the Gulf War.

69. *Options for Change* was announced in July 1990 and detailed plans, based on that paper, were elaborated upon in the 1991 Statement on Defence Estimates and *Britain's Army for the '90s*, Cm. 1595 (London: HMSO, 1991).

70. *Statement on the Defence Estimates 1990*, Cmnd. 675–1 (London: HMSO, 1990), vol. 1, p. 16.

71. Carole Shifrin, 'UK New Defense Strategy Stresses Role in Preserving International Stability', *Aviation Week and Space Technology*, 13 July 1992, p. 72.

72. *Defending Our Future*, Statement on Defence Estimates 1993, Cm. 2270 (London: HMSO, July 1993).

73. Malcolm Rifkind quoted in *The Times*, 6 July 1993, p. 8; see also *Defending Our Future*, p. 8.

74. From 1994 on a total of 100 Tornado F-3s are to be dedicated to the defence of the UK's airspace, down from the 122 projected in 'Options for Change'. In addition, four new Upholder class conventional submarines are to be scrapped or leased, leaving the Navy dependent upon nuclear powered submarines. The destroyer/frigate fleet is to shrink from 40 to 35, while minesweepers will be reduced to 25. Apart form the growth in the size of the army, the white paper also announced that the army's capability would be enhanced by the addition of the new Challenger-2 tanks, to replace the two regiments of Chieftain tanks (leaving open the question of how to equip the army's other six tank regiments).

75. *The Times*, 6 July 1993, p. 8.

76. *Defending Our Future*, para. 115, p. 10.

77. Ibid., para. 116.

78. The 1993 White Paper casts doubt on the idea of 'earmarking' forces for UN operations, since the nature of a given crisis makes it difficult to determine the nature and number of forces that may be required. In addition, 'it seems probable that no government will give the UN an unconditional call on their forces: nations will wish to reserve the right to decide whether or not forces be committed'. Concern was also expressed about the potential for UN operations to become 'open-ended commitments'. (Para. 5, p. 48.)

79. See for instance the comments by David Clark, Labour's defence spokesman, in *The Times*, 6 July 1993, p. 8.

80. 1993 white paper, 'Defending Our Future', (London: HMSO) para 2, p. 15.

81. It should, however, be pointed out that, although the ARRC command may be considered an accolade, there was very little choice since the Germans could not assume it, due to constitutional restrictions, the French were not interested for obvious reasons, and the Italians did not compare in terms of military assets with those of Britain. Early on, Britain sought to take the lead in providing the First UK Corps as the nucleus of the

force. This also explains the location of the force in NATO's central region, since most of the contributions come from that area.

82. 'Defending Our Future', p. 15.
83. Ibid., p. 16.
84. Provisions on a Common Foreign and Security Policy, agreed upon by the European Council, Maastricht, 9–10 December 1991, Article D, paras 1 and 3.
85. Ibid., para. 1.
86. 'Defending Our Future', p. 17.
87. *The Economist*, 'Survey: Business in Eastern Europe', 21–27 September 1991, p. 25.
88. For instance, in a speech at the Aspen Institute in August 1990 Mrs Thatcher called for unequivocal support for EC membership for the emerging democracies. Quoted in Louise Richardson, 'British State Strategies after the Cold War', in Robert O. Keohane, Joseph S. Nye and Stanley Hoffmann, eds, *After the Cold War: International Institutions and State Strategies in Europe, 1989–91* (Cambridge, MA: Harvard University Press, 1993), p. 158.
89. See 'Defending Our Future', paras 127–30, 304–7 and 410.

4 Germany, Security and Post-Cold War Europe

1. Hans J. Morgenthau, *Politics Among Nations: The Struggle for Power and Peace*, 6th edn (New York: Alfred A. Knopf, 1985) p. 555.
2. Federal president, Richard von Weizsäcker, who attended the dedication of the Holocaust Memorial Museum on 22 April 1993, commented that the museum is not only of signal importance 'as a place of remembrance elucidating the past; it is at the same time a warning for the future'. Quoted in *The Week in Germany*, 23 April 1993 (New York: German Information Center) p. 1. Since the dedication leading figures in German political and cultural life, such as Günter Grass, have called for a similar memorial in Germany.
3. *New York Times*, 15 November 1990, A16.
4. The term 'unification' is used to denote the creation of a new state in new borders, rather than a return to the status quo antebellum. Others have used the term 'reunification' (*Wiedervereingung*) which refers to the creation of a unitary Germany composed of the two nation-states created after World War II. The latter is the formal, legal terminology, while the former is the popularly preferred term.
5. Amongst the remarks made by Nicholas Ridley to *The Spectator*, 14 July 1990, were, '[The EMS] is all a German racket designed to take over the whole of Europe. It has to be thwarted. This rushed take-over by the Germans on the worst possible basis, with the French behaving like poodles to the Germans is absolutely intolerable.' And on the European Community he commented, 'the idea that one says, "OK, we'll give this lot our sovereignty", is unacceptable to me. I'm not against giving up sovereignty in principle, but not to this lot. You might just as well give it to Adolf Hitler, frankly' (p. 8).
6. This book was written at the time of the particularly vicious arson attack

on a Turkish woman and two children in Mölln (Schleswig-Holstein) on 22 November 1992, all of whom died. This case marked a significant change in the violent attacks which had hitherto been directed towards asylum-seekers, who are seen by some as being openly abusive of Germany's relatively lax constitutional right to asylum for the politically persecuted. The Mölln attacks were directed against residents. One of the children who died was born in Germany, and the 51-year-old woman had lived in Germany for years. The Mölln murders were perpetrated by skinheads with neo-Nazi leanings.

A second serious attack took place on 29 May 1993, in the North Rhine-Westphalia town of Solingen. In this attack five Turkish residents died. The attack was followed by a spate of other racially motivated attacks.

In party-political terms most right-wingers are members of one of three parties: the Nationaldemokratische Partei Deuschlands, the Deutsche Volksunion (DVU, German People's Union) and the Republikaner. The latter aroused public attention in April 1992 when they gained 10.9 per cent of the vote and fifteen seats in the state parliament in Baden-Württemberg. At the same time the DVU gained 6.3 per cent and six seats in Schleswig-Holstein. One of the four who carried out the Solingen attack was a member of the DVU.

7. Figures from *The Economist*, 6–12 March 1993, p. 13.
8. Figures quoted in Thomas Kielinger and Max Otte, 'Germany: The Pressured Power', *Foreign Policy*, vol. 91, no. 91 (Summer 1993) p. 45.
9. See *Eurostat: Basic Statistics of the Community* (Luxembourg: Office for Official Publications of the European Communities, 1990) 27th edn, p. 51.
10. For details, see Stephen George, *An Awkward Partner: Britain in the European Community* (Oxford: Oxford University Press, 1990) pp. 190–208.
11. See Josef Joffe, 'Reunification II: This time, no hob-nail boots', *New York Times*, 7 September 1990.
12. Simon Rich, *The Fruits of Fascism* (Ithaca: Cornell University Press, 1990). The process of *Historikerstreit* would also support this argument, where some historians have relativized German war crimes and atrocities in an attempt to point out that other cultures and peoples have their dark periods in history. An even smaller group is claiming that the Jewish holocaust never happened. The histories, although written by a small number, are worrying since if they are read by, for instance, rightist groups, they may serve as the justification for more violence.
13. See Kielinger and Otte, 'Germany: The Pressured Power', pp. 44–63.
14. *Mitteleuropa* is the nineteenth-century idea of forming a common German political, economic and cultural area.
15. *The Economist*, 15 December 1990.
16. Kielinger and Otte, 'Germany: The Pressured Power', p. 52.
17. Under Article 2 of the Unity Treaty the seat of the presidency is to be moved to Berlin while the location of the parliament and government was left in Bonn until post-unification. The subsequent decision to move all to Berlin has met with criticism, particularly in the light of the recent opening of Bonn's expensive new parliament building.

18. In a poll quoted in *Die Zeit*, 25 January 1991 (p. 43) which was just over a week after the first air strikes against Iraq, 79 per cent of those questioned believed the use of force was wrong. On 29 January 1991, *Süddeutsche Zeitung* (p. 10) conducted a poll which showed that 71 per cent of those surveyed supported the action.

19. MC 14/3 was adopted at the ministerial meeting of the North Atlantic Council, 14 December 1967.

20. For a good analysis of the German reactions to SDI, see Thomas Risse-Kappen, 'Star Wars Controversy in West Germany', *Bulletin of the Atomic Scientists*, 43, July–August 1987.

21. For an excellent discussion of European reactions to the Reagan years, see Michael Howard, 'A European Perspective on the Reagan Years', *Foreign Affairs,* vol. 66, no. 3.

22. Article 25 of the *Grundegesetz* (Basic Law) of the Bundesrepublik Deutschland, of 23 May 1949, states: 'Acts tending to and undertaken with the intent to disturb the peaceful relations between nations, especially to prepare for aggressive war, shall be unconstitutional. They shall be made a punishable offense.'

23. The pledge appeared in the Declaration by the German Federal Republic and was included in the Final Act of the Nine Power Conference, London, of 3 October 1954. The document was subsequently ratified at the Paris Summit shortly afterwards. For details of the meeting, see *Documents agreed on by the Conference of Ministers held in Paris, 20–22 October 1954*, Cmd 304 (London: HMSO, November 1954); and for the communiqué recommending German membership of NATO, see *NATO Final Communiqués* 1949–70 (Brussels: NATO Information Service) pp. 84–86.

24. Hans-Joachim Falenski, 'Peace Keeping Missions with the German Armed Forces', *German Comments: UN Peace Keeping Missions for the Bundeswehr*, no. 30, April 1993, p. 11.

25. Article 24, paras 1–2 (emphasis added).

26. See Article 5 of the North Atlantic Treaty, 4 April 1949.

27. The argument presented here is based on those put forward by Lothar Ruehl, 'Limits of Leadership: Germany', and Karl Kaiser, 'Patterns of Partnership: Security Relationship: Germany', in Steven Muller and Gebhard Schweigler, *From Occupation to Cooperation: The United States and United Germany in a Changing World Order* (New York: W.W. Norton, 1992) pp. 108–110, 169–70.

28. On 15 July 1992 the Bonn cabinet approved the sending of a destroyer (*Bayern*) and three Breguet Atlantic reconnaissance aircraft to the Adriatic to help enforce the no-flight ban over Bosnia. The decision to send non-combat forces to help in the aftermath of 'Operation Restore Hope' in Somalia was announced to the press by Chancellor Kohl on 17 December 1992. Agreement was reached in mid-January 1993 to draft an amendment to the constitution that would allow German troops to take part in international peace-keeping operations sanctioned by the UN and other international bodies. See *New York Times*, 14 January 1993, A7, and *The Week in Germany*, 15 January 1993 (New York: German Information Center) p. 1.

29. Now replaced by the frigate *Niedersachsen*.
30. Tyler Marshall, 'Germany Mulls Role in Global Peacekeeping', *Los Angeles Times*, 14 January 1993, A5.
31. *The Week in Germany*, 18 December 1992 (New York: German Information Center) p. 1.
32. Craig Whitney, 'Kohl and Partners in Accord on Peacekeeping', *New York Times*, 14 January 1993, A.7.
33. 'Germany clarifies constitutionality of out-of-area missions', *International Defense Review*, vol. 25, no. 1 (February 1993) pp. 89–90 (emphasis added).
34. At the 1991 SPD Conference it was agreed that German military forces could be involved in UN peace-keeping operations and that any such forces could be used only in self-defence. The involvement of German forces in military action, conducted under UN auspices, was specifically rejected.
35. See Volker Rühe, 'Die Zunkuft der Bundeswehr in einem veränderten Europa', *Soldat und Technik*, August 1992, pp. 513–17.
36. *The Week in Germany*, 29 January 1993 (New York: German Information Center) p. 1.
37. *New York Times*, 25 February 1993, A.8.
38. See *The Economist*, 30 January 1993, p. 46.
39. *New York Times*, 24 September 1992, A.1.
40. Figures from *Politbarometer*, Mannheim, Germany, March 1991.
41. Figure from *The Economist*, 23 May 1992, p. 24.
42. UN troops witnessed the Serbs shooting at the plane with a 23mm anti-aircraft gun operating from a Serbian occupied swathe of Croatia under UN protection. *New York Times*, 9 February 1993, A.15.
43. Security Council Resolution 816, 31 March 1993, authorized UN members, 'seven days after the adoption of this resolution, acting nationally or through regional organizations or arrangements, to take, under the authority of the Security Council and subject to close coordination with the Secretary-General and the United Nations Protection Force, all necessary measures in the airspace of the Republic of Bosnia and Herzegovina, in the event of further violations, to ensure compliance with the ban on flights.' Prior to Resolution 816, Resolution 781 of 9 October 1992 applied. Resolution 781 called for the United Nations Protection Force only to 'monitor compliance with the ban on all military flights', and called on 'States to take nationally or through regional agencies or arrangements all measures necessary to provide assistance to the United Nations Protection Force, based on technical monitoring and other capabilities.' US Department of State, *Dispatch*, vol. 3, no. 42 (19 October 1992) p. 777. The naval counterpart to the AWACS operations commenced on 16 July 1992 (Operation 'Maritime Monitor' in support of UN Security Council Resolutions 713 and 757. This subsequently became Operation 'Maritime Guard' in support of Resolution 787 on 22 November 1992.
44. The FCC was critical of inconsistencies in the FDP and SPD's positions since they called for the withdrawal only of the 'flight crews' from AWACS operations. Thus, in principle, they appeared to favour the participation of German ground crews in such operations and thus associate Germany

with the enforcement of UN Security Council Resolution 816.

45. The Bundeswehr detachments are deployed at Belet Huen, some 180 miles from Mogadishu.

46. *Rebus sic stantibus* cases are based upon Article 62 of the Vienna Convention on the Law of Treaties which states:

   A fundamental change of circumstances which has occurred with regard to those existing at the time of the conclusion of a treaty, and which was not foreseen by the parties, may not be involved as a ground for terminating or withdrawing from the treaty unless:

   (a) the existence of those circumstances constituted an essential basis of consent of the parties bound by the treaty: and

   (b) the effect of change is radically to transform the extent of obligations still to be performed under the treaty . . .

47. *NATO Review*, vol. 39, no. 6, (December 1991) p. 30.

48. *NATO Review*, vol. 40, no. 6, (December 1992) p. 29.

49. *Financial Times*, 20 June 1992, p. 3.

50. 'A "Bundeswehr" for a new security situation', *Information Bulletin of the Federal Government*, 8 January 1993, North America.

51. The CRF would consist of 50 000 men by the year 2006 and will include two airborne brigades. The air force will provide two fighter squadrons, five anti-aircraft squadrons, and the navy will provide six frigates, fifteen minesweepers and eight submarines.

52. Interview with General Klaus Naumann, chief of staff of the German armed forces, in *Armed Forces Journal International*, February 1993, p. 45.

53. For details of relative lift capacity as well as more general information on the size and composition of armed forces, see *The Military Balance* (annual) (London: Brassey's/International Institute for Strategic Studies 1992–3 and IISS, 1993).

54. For details of the START Agreements, see Dunbar Lockwood, 'The Panchant for peace', *The Bulletin of the Atomic Scientists*, vol. 48, no. 8 (October 1992) pp. 10–11.

55. Chancellor Konrad Adenauer, first chancellor of the Federal Republic of Germany, declared in 3 October 1954 that the Federal Republic of Germany would not manufacture in its territory atomic, biological or chemical weapons alongside other prohibited weapons systems. This pledge appeared as Annex 1 to Protocol No. III on the Control of Armaments, signed at Paris on 23 October 1954.

56. Ustashi is the name given to the Croatian forces established by the Nazis, who were then used to mount genocidal campaigns against the Serbs.

57. Karl Kaiser in Muller and Schweigler, *From Occupation to Cooperation*, p. 151.

58. *The Week in Germany*, 29 May 1992, (New York: German Information Center, p. 1) quoting Chancellor Helmut Kohl speaking at the University of Heidelberg.

59. The adoption of a constitutional amendment by the Bundestag in May 1993, which severely limits the eligibility requirements for political asylum, has solved some of the refugee problem but has provoked demonstrations

and criticism from the German public. The amendment has also left the door open for many of the three million ethnic Germans living outside Germany, provoking racial charges.

60. Figures from *Eurostat: Basic Statistics of the Community*, 27th edn (Luxembourg: Office for Official Publications of the European Communities, 1990) pp. 268–71.
61. *Frankfurter Allgemeine Zeitung*, 3 December 1992.

5   Where Does the US Fit In?

1. President George Bush, State of the Union Address, delivered before a joint session of Congress, Washington D.C., 28 January 1992. For full text, see *Vital Speeches of the Day*, vol. LVII, 15 February 1992, pp. 258–63.
2. The same assumptions can be found in the speeches of US Secretary of Defense Dick Cheyney. He said on one occasion, 'The pace of change has been so great that we're almost taking unprecedented events for granted... These shifts didn't just happen. They are a direct result of America's leadership role in the world and our willingness over the last 40 years to deploy sufficient military capability to defend freedom and to guarantee our security.' Speech to the Economic Club of Indianapolis, Indianapolis, Indiana, 4 September 1992. Quoted in *Vital Speeches of the Day*, vol. 59, 15 October 1992, pp. 12–15.
3. General Colin L. Powell, 'U.S. Forces: Challenges Ahead', *Foreign Affairs*, vol. 72, no. 5 (Winter 1992/3) p. 33.
4. The EEA is comprised of the EC and EFTA.
5. Quoted in the *New York Times*, 8 March 1992, A.1.
6. Quoted in Simon Duke, *The Burdensharing Debate: A Reassessment* (London: Macmillan, 1993) p. 29.
7. Earl Ravenal, 'Disengagement from Europe: The Framing of an Argument', in Ted Galen Carpenter, ed., *NATO at 40: Confronting a Changing World* (Lexington MA: Lexington Books/CATO Institute, 1990) p. 233.
8. North Atlantic Treaty Organization public data service, NAA Report: AK 224, 14 September 1993, p. 3.
9. 'US Forces Cut', *Jane's Defence Weekly*, 15 August 1992, p. 7.
10. Warren Christopher, 'Towards a NATO Summit', *NATO Review*, August 1993, vol. 41, no. 4, p. 4.
11. President Bush, 'Historic Steps Toward Unity by European Community', released by the Office of the White House Press Secretary, 11 December 1991 in US Department of State *Dispatch*, 16 December 1991, p. 901.
12. Alan Cowell, 'Bush challenges partners in NATO over role of U.S.', *New York Times*, 8 November 1991, A.1.
13. The twin concepts of transparency and complementarily are to be found in the 'Rome Declaration on Peace and Cooperation' issued by the heads of state and government participating in the meeting of the North Atlantic Council, Rome, 7–8 November 1991; also in the 'Declaration of the member states of the Western European Union which are also members

of the European Union on the Role of the WEU and its relations with the European Union and with the Atlantic Alliance', Maastricht 9–10 December 1991, Section B, para. 4.

14. US Department of State, *Foreign Relations of the United States*, Statement by Secretary of State John Foster Dulles to the North Atlantic Council, 14 December 1953, p. 462. For a detailed analysis of this, see Brian R. Duchin, 'The "Agonizing Reappraisal": Eisenhower, Dulles and the European Defence Community', *Diplomatic History*, vol. 16, no. 2 (Spring 1992) pp. 201–21.

15. For a detailed discussion of Dulles approach to the EDC, see Duchin, 'The "Agonizing Reappraisal"' pp. 201–21.

16. Henry A. Kissinger, *Years of Upheaval* (Boston: Little Brown and Company, 1982) p. 713.

17. *The Washington Post*, 7 June 1991, A17. It is worth noting that the month before, May, NATO had agreed to create its own rapid-reaction force which was designed as a pre-emptive move against the WEU proposal. The NATO RDF would seem to be of little practical value since it is limited to intervention in the NATO area.

18. *National Military Strategy of the United States*, January 1992 (Washington D.C.: GPO, 1992) p. 6.

19. Michael Vlahos, 'The Atlantic Community', in Nils Wessell, ed., *The New Europe: Revolution in East–West Relations* (New York: The Academy of Political Science, 1991) p. 189.

20. *National Military Strategy of the United States*, January 1992, p. 6.

21. Ibid., p. 4.

22. See John Lewis Gaddis, *Strategies of Containment* (New York: Oxford University Press, 1982) p. 89–90.

23. *National Military Strategy of the United States*, January 1992, p. 20.

24. Ibid.

25. *National Military Strategy of the United States*, January 1992, pp. 8–9.

26. Edward C. Luck, 'Making Peace', *Foreign Policy*, no. 89 (Winter 1992/3) p. 137.

27. For a detailed discussion of the UN's financial plight and the US role in it, see Simon Duke, 'The UN Financial Crisis: A History and Analysis', *International Relations*, vol. XI, no. 2 (August 1992) pp. 127–51.

28. Samuel F. Wells, Jnr, 'Nuclear Weapons and European Security during the Cold War', *Diplomatic History*, vol. 16, no. 2 (Spring 1992) pp. 278–86.

29. Gregory F. Treverton, 'The Year of European (Dis)Unification', *Current History*, vol. 91, no. 568 (November 1992) p. 358.

30. Even this role was de-emphasized by President Bush, who was reluctant to involve the US directly in the Yugoslavian conflict, claiming that the US is 'not the world's policeman'. *New York Times*, 12 June 1992, A1. However, the *New Military Strategy of the United States* (Washington D.C.: GPO, 1992) states that, as a nation that seeks 'neither territory, hegemony, nor empire, the United States is in a unique position of trusted leadership on the world scene, (p. 2).

31. Warren Christopher, 'Towards a NATO Summit', p. 4.

32. The US wishes for a reduction in EC agricultural subsidies administered

through CAP and Europe; in return, the EC wishes for a reduction in the amount of US grain exports made beneath the EC price levels. The longevity of the talks has led to the quip that GATT now stands for the General Agreement to Talk and Talk.

33. The central irritant in US–EC trade relations is the question of agricultural subsidies that are administered through the Common Agricultural Policy (CAP). CAP not only protects EC agriculture; it also represents very powerful agricultural interests in France and Germany. This is particularly so in France where the role of the farmer may be compared to that of the miner in England or the steel worker in the US. Mittterrand's fragile hold over the Socialist Party in France depends largely upon the continued good health of the agricultural sector. The US itself insisted in the 1950s that agriculture be exempt from GATT regulations, but in 1987 it changed its course and advocated a phasing out of agricultural subsidies over a ten-year period. When Europe declined to respond to the proposal, it was the US who walked out of the Uruguay Round that had started in 1986. Attempts to put pressure on the agricultural lobbies have been greeted with little enthusiasm in France, Germany or even Britain. Although there was nothing particularly new in the US objections to the EC's CAP, the circumstances under which the debate took place were new.

    Prior to the wrangling of December 1990, the US had accommodated the EC's tight guarding of the agricultural subsidies issues, in return for EC backing on another trade issue. From December 1990 on, the absence of the Cold War, which had exercised a moderating influence on the GATT rounds, was absent. The US felt that it could leave the issue open largely because of resentment at the Europeans and especially Germany who, it was believed, would be the voice of reason in the dispute; instead of providing the expected leadership, Bonn remained preoccupied with unification and was reluctant to take on France in an area of immense sensitivity.

34. *The Week in Germany* (New York: German Information Center) 27 March 1992, p. 1.

35. This argument is not new and is merely a version of the burden-sharing debate which has been a consistent feature of US–European relations since the early 1950s. See Duke, *The Burdensharing Debate.*

36. Joseph Brand, 'The New World Order: Regional Trading Blocs', speech delivered to the Annual Meeting of the American Society of Agricultural Consultants, Alexandria, Virginia, 17 October 1991, in *Vital Speeches of the Day*, vol. 58, 15 December 1991, p. 156.

37. Christopher Hill, 'The Foreign Policy of the European Community', in Roy C. Macridis, ed., *Foreign Policy in World Politics* (New Jersey: Prentice Hall, 1992) p. 130.

38. Jennone Walker, 'The United States and a Future European Security Order', in William Wharton, ed., *Security Arrangements for a New Europe* (Washington D.C.: National Defense University Press, 1992) p. 69.

39. *Die Welt*, 23 March 1992.

40. The elections on 22 March 1992, were held in France's twenty-two regional councils. The Socialists won 16.4 per cent of the vote, but were

overtaken by Jean-Marie Le Pen's National Front in five regions, which gave the FN 13.9 per cent of the vote (lower than the estimated 20 per cent). The two green parties (Vert and Génération Ecologie) captured 14.4 per cent of the vote.

41. Richard M. Nixon, 'Is America Part of Europe?', *National Review*, 2 March 1992, p. 28.
42. Ibid., p. 31.
43. Lt. General William E. Odom, *America's Military Revolution: Strategy and Structure after the Cold War*, (Washington D.C.: The American University Press, 1993) p. 84.
44. Christopher Layne and Benjamin Schwartz, 'American Hegemony – Without an Enemy', *Foreign Policy*, vol. X, no. 92 (Fall 1993) p. 20.
45. See Secretary of Defense's *Annual Report to the President and Congress* (Washington D.C.: GPO, 1991).
46. The Clinton administration plans to cut the number of US troops in Europe to 100 000 no later than fiscal year 1996, which begin on 1 October 1995. These cuts are deeper than the ones planned by President George Bush, who anticipated cutting US force levels in Europe to 15 000 by 1996.
47. Richard L. Kugler, *RAND* R-4194-EUCOM/NA, p. 45.
48. Ibid.
49. Carl H. Builder and Steven C. Bankes, 'The Etiology of European Change', RAND document P-7693, December 1990, p. 23.
50. Traditionally this point was countered by the observation that there are significant geographical asymmetries between the US presence in Europe and those of the Soviet Union in Eastern Europe. The greater distance between the US and its European allies was forwarded as an argument in favour of retaining a large US military presence.
51. Kugler, *RAND* R-4194-EUCOM/NA, p. 37.
52. Article 2 of the North Atlantic Treaty obliges all allies to 'contribute toward the further development of peaceful and friendly international relations by promoting conditions of stability and well-being'. Article 4 commits all parties to the treaty to 'consult together whenever, in the opinion of any of them, the territorial integrity, political independence or security of any of the Parties is threatened'.

6 The 'New Security Architecture'

1. Hans J. Morgenthau, 'Another Great Debate: The National Interest of the United States, *American Political Science Review*, LXVI (December 1952) p. 961, quoted in James E. Dougherty and Robert L. Pfaltzgraff, Jr., *Contending Theories of International Relations*, 3rd edn (Philadelphia: Harper and Row, 1990) p. 96.
2. See Robert D. Blackwill, 'Conventional and Theatre Nuclear Forces in Europe', in *American Defense Annual*, edited by Joseph Kruzel (New York: Lexington Books, 1992) pp. 79–80.
3. Richard Ullman, *Securing Europe* (Princeton NJ: Princeton University Press, 1991) pp. 23–83.
4. Mikhail Gorbachev, *Perestroika: New Thinking for Our Country and the*

World (New York: Harper & Row, 1987) pp. 194–5. For a detailed background account of the origins of the concept, see Eugene B. Rumer, 'The German Question in Moscow's "Common European Home": A Background to the Revolutions of 1989', *RAND Note*, N-3220-USDP.

5. Ibid.
6. See for instance, Emilio Colombo, 'European Security at a time of Radical Change', *NATO Review*, vol. 40, no. 3 (June 1992) p. 3.
7. Quoted in Adam Rotfeld and Wather Stützle, eds, *Germany and Europe in Transition* (Oxford: Oxford University Press, 1991) p. 96.
8. Ibid.
9. James Baker III, 'The Euro-Atlantic Architecture: From East to West', speech delivered to the Aspen Institute, Berlin, Germany, 18 June 1991, in *Vital Speeches of the Day*, vol. LVII, 15 July 1991, p. 579.
10. Johan Jorgen Holst, 'Uncertainty and Opportunity in an Era of East–West Change', *The Strategic Implications of Change in the Soviet Union*, Adelphi Paper 247 (London: Brassey's for the International Institute for Strategic Studies, 1989) p. 8.
11. For a detailed description of this problem, see Simon Duke, *International Relations*, vol. XI, no. 2, August 1992, pp. 127–51.
12. Ibid.
13. James Baker III, 'Uncertainty and Opportunity' speech, p. 579.
14. See Ted Galen Carpenter, ed., *NATO at 40: Confronting a Changing World* (Lexington, MA: Lexington, Books, 1990); Jonathan Dean, *Watershed in Europe: Dismantling the East–West Military Confrontation* (Lexington, MA: Lexington Books 1987); Keith Dunn and Stephen Flanagan, eds, *NATO in the 5th Decade* (Washington D.C.: National Defense University, 1990); Lawrence Kaplan, S. Victor Papacosma, Mark Rubin and Ruth Young, eds., *NATO After Forty Years* (Wilmington, DE: Scholarly Resources, 1990); Robert A. Levine, ed., *Transition and Turmoil in the Atlantic Alliance* (New York: Crane Russak 1992); Stanley Sloan, *NATO's Future: Towards a New Transatlantic Bargain*, (Washington D.C.: National Defense University 1985); Stanley Sloan, ed., *NATO in the 1990s* (New York: Pergamon-Brassey's, 1989); and Gregory Treverton, *Making the Alliance Work: The United States and Western Europe*, (Ithaca, NY: Cornell University Press, 1985).
15. An excellent example of this is Maj-Gen. Edward Fursdon, *The European Defence Community: A History* (London: Macmillan, 1980).
16. See for example David Garnham, *The Politics of European Defence Cooperation: Germany, Britain, France and America* (Cambridge, MA: Ballinger Publishing Company, 1988); and Geoffrey Lee Williams and Alan Lee Williams, *The European Defence Initiative: Europe's Bid for Equality* (New York: St Martin's Press, 1986).
17. See *The Economist*, 6–12 June 1992, p. 51. The Treaty of Maastricht states that the European Community members agree to 'define and implement common defence and security policies', accompanied by the hope that this might eventually lead to a 'common defence' and that the Western European Union should be developed as the 'defence component of the European Union and as a means to strengthen the European pillar of the Atlantic Alliance'.

18. Richard Ullman, *Securing Europe* (Princeton NJ: Princeton University Press, 1991) p. 63.
19. See Adrian Hyde-Price, *European Security Beyond the Cold War* (London: Royal Institute of International Affairs/Sage, 1991) pp. 203–13.

7 Institutional Confusion

1. The early post-war plans drawnup by the Joint Planning Staff and the Joint War Plans Committee, for the Joint Chiefs of Staff, assumed that continental Europe would be overrun relatively quickly and that NATO would have to rely upon massive strategic bombing offensives against the Soviet Union launched from Britain and other areas.
2. Major-General Edward Fursdon, *The European Defence Community: A History* (London: Macmillan, 1980) p. 89.
3. Ibid.
4. Sir Anthony Eden, *Full Circle*, (London: Cassell, 1960) pp. 32–3.
5. The Nine Powers were the six EDC nations (Belgium, Netherlands, Luxembourg, Germany, Italy and France), and Canada, the United Kingdom and the United States.
6. For details of the Paris meeting, see *Documents agreed on by the Conference of Ministers held in Paris, 20–22 October 1954*, Cmd 9304 (London: HMSO, November 1954); and for the communiqué recommending German membership of NATO, see *NATO Final Communiqués 1949–1974* (Brussels: NATO Information Service) pp. 84–6.
7. Eden, *Full Circle*, p. 168.
8. Rome Declaration on Peace and Cooperation, Issued by the Heads of State and Government participating in the meeting of the North Atlantic Council in Rome, 7–8 November 1991, paras 3 and 6 (emphasis added). This was reaffirmed at the Ministerial Meeting of the North Atlantic Council in Oslo, 4 June 1992 (emphasis added).
9. *NATO's Core Security Functions in the New Europe*, statement issued by the North Atlantic Council meeting in ministerial session, Copenhagen 6–7 June 1991, para. 7.
10. Ibid., para. 1.
11. Greece was formally admitted as full member of the WEU by the Protocol of Accession, signed on 20 November 1992. At the same time associate membership was granted to Iceland, Norway and Turkey. Observer status was granted to Denmark and Ireland.
12. Figures vary on the exact size to the proposed corps; some estimates are high as 100 000.
13. The Alliance's New Strategic Concept, agreed upon by the Heads of State and Government participating in the meeting of the North Atlantic Council, Rome 7–8 November 1991, Part II, paras 17, 21, 22.
14. Ibid., Article 52.
15. *The Economist*, 14 December 1991, p. 52.
16. Ibid.
17. *Provisions on a Common Foreign and Security Policy*, agreed upon by the European Council, Maastricht 9–10 December 1991, Article J.1, para. 4.
18. Ibid., Article J.2, para. 1.

19. Final Communiqué following the Ministerial meeting of the North Atlantic Council, Oslo, 4 June 1992, para. 7.
20. Ibid.
21. *The Week in Germany*, 29 May 1992 (New York: German Information Center) p. 1.
22. David Garnham, *The Politics of European Defence Cooperation: Germany, France, Britain and America*, (Cambridge, MA: Ballinger Publishing Company, 1988) p. 130.
23. *Treaties revising the Treaties establishing the European Communities and Acts relating to the Communities*, (Single European Act), 11 June 1986, Title III, Treaty Provisions on European Cooperation in the sphere of foreign policy, Article 30, paras 1–2.
24. Title 1, Article B, of the Maastricht Treaty, entitled 'Common Provisions', defines European Union as comprising the following: economic and social progress; common foreign and security policy; citizenship of the Union; cooperation on justice and home affairs; enhanced effectiveness of the mechanisms and institutions of the Community.
25. The EBRD was established in 1990 with funds from the EC, fourteen other developed countries including Japan and the US, and eight Eastern European states. The capitalization of the EBRD is around $14 billion. The EBRD has so far concentrated on lending on private sector and productive investment in the former CMEA countries.
26. Farm products accounted for approximately 25 per cent of the exports from Eastern Europe to the EC (only for Czechoslovakia was the proportion smaller). In the absence of EC protective measures this trade would be substantially bigger. The Hungarians and the Poles have expressed interest in trading with the EC, especially in the agricultural area, and have pointed out that the EC has given the East Germans preferential access for agricultural products for a long time. If greater access were granted to the Eastern Europeans to the EC markets this would entail a drastic restructuring of CAP since the goods coming from the east would be produced substantially lower costs than the heavily subsidized CAP goods. Alternatively, the EC could decide to let the Eastern Europeans exercise their comparative advantage in producing agricultural goods. This is, however, highly unlikely, since the agricultural sectors in most of the EC countries, especially in France and the mediterranean countries, are jealously guarded. For a discussion of the problems that will have to be faced, see John Pinder, *The European Community and Eastern Europe* (London: Royal Institute of International Affairs, 1991) pp. 59–73.
27. The European Council is a meeting of the heads of state and government and the president of the Commission, assisted by the foreign ministers and a commissioner. There are normally two meetings per annum. The first meeting was launched by President Giscard d'Estaing in 1974 at Fontainbleau. The Council quickly became more influential than had been intended since it compensated for the political vacuum at the centre of the Community caused by the Council of Ministers' failure to take decisions. The European Council was formally incorporated into the EC structure in Article 2 of the 1986 Single European Act.

28. The EC had a team of fifty observers in Yugoslavia by the end of July 1991, and two hundred by October. However, serious differences became evident once the EC tried to act. Germany wanted to support the sovereignty of Slovenia and Croatia and to condemn Serbia as the aggressor. France, by way of contrast, found itself unusually closer to the US view, which remained in favour of some form of federation. The idea of moving from peace-keeping to peace-making was suggested by the Dutch, but soon died as an idea when it was realized that this could involve a commitment of up to 30 000 troops. Opposition was strong from Germany, which was undecided about whether troops could intervene beyond NATO's frontiers. Britain was presumably afraid of another Irish-type situation, which would involve not only bloodshed but an indefinite commitment. German insistence on recognizing Slovenia and Croatia in January 1992, effectively made EC observers and representatives in Serbia *personae non gratae*.

29. For instance, Britain reserved the right at the Masstricht Summit to opt out of the monetary system and the social/welfare stipulation of the Maastricht Treaty, known collectively as the Social Charter.

30. For an interesting discussion of this problem, see Nicole Gnesotto, 'European Union after Minsk and Maastricht', *International Affairs*, vol. 68, no. 2 (1992) pp. 223–31.

31. Ibid.

32. Trevor Salmon, 'Testing Times for European Political Cooperation: The Gulf and Yugoslavia, 1990–92', ibid., p. 244.

33. Ibid., p. 244.

34. Ibid., p. 250.

35. 'Declaration on the Role of the WEU and its relations with the European Union and with the Atlantic Alliance', 10 December 1991. Quoted in Auke P. Venema & Henriëtte Romijn, *Documents on International Security Policy May* 1989–December 1991 (Brussels: Netherlands Atlantic Commission: NATO's Office of Information and Press, February 1992) pp. 72–3.

36. *Platform on European Security Interests*, statement by the WEU Council resulting from the WEU Council meeting at The Hague, 26–27 October 1987, Section 1, para. 4.

37. Ibid., Preamble, para. 4.

38. *Convention of the Presence of Foreign Forces in the Federal Republic of Germany*, Article IV, TIAS 3426, 23 October 1954, p. 5707.

39. North Atlantic Treaty: Accession of the Federal Republic of Germany, Article II, TIAS 3428, 1 April 1955, p. 5698.

40. *NATO's Core Security Functions in the New Europe.*

41. Alessandro Politi, 'Alliance, WEU may command Rapid Reaction Force', *Defense News*, 6 May 1991.

42. On 19 June 1992 the foreign and defence ministers of the nine WEU countries met under the presidency of Klaus Kinkel in Bonn and adopted the Petersberg Declaration, named after the mansion in Bonn where the meeting took place.

43. Text of the Petersberg Declaration from Reuters Textline, Agence Europe, 23 June 1992. Petersberg Declaration, 19 June 1992, Section 1, 'On WEU and European Security', para. 1.

44. Ibid., Section 1, para. 3.
45. Ibid., Loc cit.
46. Ibid., Section 7.
47. Ibid., Section II, para. 2.
48. Ibid., Section II, para. 6.
49. Ibid., Section I, para. 3.
50. Ibid., Section II, para. 8.
51. Ibid., Section III, 'On Relations Between WEU and the other European members of the European Union or the Atlantic Alliance', para. A–B.
52. The IEPG was established by the 1976 Rome Resolution and was intended to further the attainment of standardization and interoperability, to build a solid industrial and technological base and to strengthen, for the benefit of both sides of the Atlantic, the European identity in relations with the United States and Canada.
53. The IEPG agreed at the Defence Ministers' meeting in Oslo, 6 March 1992. The Eurogroup Defence Ministers agreed at their meeting in Brussels on 25 May 1992.
54. Petersberg Declaration, Section I, para. 15.
55. France's former defence minister, Jean-Pierre Chevenement, called the Franco–German corps 'a language laboratory masquerading as a fighting force'. *Washington Post*, 17 May 1992, A31.
56. The 1963 Elysée Treaty provided for Franco–German cooperation in many different fields. As far as defence was concerned, it provided for the eventual harmonization of military doctrines, the establishment of combined operational research, military exchanges (particularly from the general staff schools), joint armament projects and an examination of the potential for Franco–German collaboration in the civil defence area. Traité entre la République française et la République fédérale d'Allemagne sur la coopération franco-allemande, 22 January 1963.
57. For a detailed analysis of Franco–German security relations, see Robbin Laird, 'France, Germany and the Atlantic Alliance', *Proceedings of the Academy of Political Science*, vol. 38, no. 1, pp. 50–59.
58. Traité entre la République française et la République fédérale d'Allemagne sur la coopération franco-allemande, 22 Janvier 1963, Part II (Programme), Section B (Défense).
59. David Yost, 'Franco–German Defense Cooperation', *Washington Quarterly*, vol. 11 (Spring 1988) p. 173.
60. For full details, see Peter Schmidt, 'The Franco–German Defence and Security Council', *Aussenpolitik*, vol. 40, no. 4, 1989.
61. See Gérard Turbé, 'France's Rapid Deployment Force', *International Defense Review*, vol. 20, no. 8, (1987).
62. The Treaty and its supplementary protocol can be found in *25 Jahre Elsée Vertrag. Dokumente zur sicherheitspolitischen Zusammenarbeit/Le Traité de l'Elysée a 25 ans. Documents sur la cooperation en matière de politique de sécurité.* (Bonn/Paris: Presse-und Information der Bundestagierung/Service d'Information et de Diffusion du Gouvernment de la République française, 1988). For a discussion of the JDC, see Schmidt 'The Franco–German Defence and Security Council', pp. 361–71.
63. The incident is described in Schmidt, 'The Franco–German Defence and Security Council', p. 369.

64. The first commander was a French brigadier who was then replaced by a German commander, for a two-year rotational term.
65. 'M. Fabius propose d'éntendre à la RFA la Guarantie nucléaire de la France', *Le Monde*, 17 June 1987, p. 8. Quoted by David Garnham, 'U.S. Disengagement and European Defense Cooperation', in Ted Galen Carpenter, *NATO at 40: Confronting a Changing World* (Lexington MA: Lexington Books/CATO, 1990) p. 80.
66. See 'L'equation Allemande: Entretien avec Helmut Schmidt', *Politique Internationale*, 27 (Spring 1985) pp. 147–59; and Helmut Schmidt, 'La France, L'Allemagne et la défence européenne', *Commentaire*, 27 (1984) pp. 411–17.
67. 'Déclaration concernant un accord entre le Président de la République française et le Chancelier Fédéral de la RFA', Palais de l'Elysée, 27–28 February 1986. Quoted in Olivier Debouzy, *Anglo–French Nuclear Cooperation: Perspectives and Problems* (London: Royal United Services Institute, 1991) p. 44,
68. Address of the Prime Minister to the Institut des Hautes Études de Défense Nationale, at the opening of their 39th session, 12 September 1986, 'La Politique de défense la France', *Revue de Défense Nationale*. November 1986, p. 11.
69. Jacques Chirac, address of the Prime Minister to the Institut des Hautes Études de Défense Nationale 'La France et les enjeux de la sécurité européenne', 12 December 1987, *Revue de Défense Nationale*, February 1988, pp. 15–16.
70. François Heisbourg, 'The British and French Nuclear Forces: Current Roles and New Challenges', *Survival* 31, July–August 1985, pp. 301–20.
71. See Chancellor Helmut Kohl, 'Europe Still Needs North America: An Alliance must be maintained', *Vital Speeches of the Day*, vol. 58, June 1992, p. 484.
72. In spite of the undoubted significance of this, the German contribution remains a small one compared to the overall size of its armed forces. The Bundeswehr will be reduced from its current level of 665 000 to 370 000 by the end of 1994.
73. 'French and Germans plan an Army Corps despite NATO fears', *New York Times*, 23 May 1992, A.4.
74. 'U.S., Bonn Clash over Pact with France', *Wall Street Journal*, 27 May 1992, A.9.
75. 'The Alliance's Strategic Concept', agreed by the Heads of State and Government participating in the meeting of the North Atlantic Council in Rome, 7–8 November 1991, Part II, para 22.
76. 'U.S., Bonn Clash over Pact with France', *Wall Street Journal*, 27 May 1992, A.9.
77. 'Paris and Bonn Planning a Big Joint Army Force', *New York Times*, 23 May 1992, A.4.
78. 'Esprit de Korps', *National Review*, 22 June 1992, p. 18.
79. The European members of NATO have been attempting to forge a common European arms market through the Independent European Programme Group (IEPG) which was founded in 1976 and based on free-market principles. The IEPG includes all NATO members (and France) except Iceland. Since 1985 the IEPG meetings have included defence ministers rather

than just lower level officials. The IEPG lies outside NATO's integrated military command structure. IEPG decisions are not legally binding. In November 1988 the IEPG established a permanent secretariat and adopted new objectives and guidelines which included: the opening of international markets to European competition by establishing international industrial consortia, the principle of '*Juste Retour*' (whereby benefits are proportional to contributions) is to be observed, technology transfer between members should be encouraged in order to improve the industrial base of the members, and cooperation and collaboration in research and development should be encouraged.

80. For details, see *Aviation Week and Space Technology*, 6 May 1991, p. 68. For a more general examination of the future of European defence industries, see James B. Steinberg, 'The Transformation of the European Defence Industry: Emerging Trends and Prospects for Future US–European Competition and Collaboration', *RAND*, R-4141-ACQ (Santa Monica CS: RAND, 1992).

81. In June 1992 NATO's foreign ministers 'agreed in private to use of NATO forces in peace-keeping roles beyond their borders. This dispatch of such troops would be subject to unanimous agreement.' *Aviation Week and Space Technology*, 1 June 1992, p. 24.

82. Alan Riding, 'Paris and Bonn Seek to End Unease over New Joint Force', *New York Times*, 30 November 1992, A.8.

8 Pan-European Options

1. See Harald Müller, 'A United Nations of Europe and North America', *Arms Control Today*, vol. 21, no. 1 (January/February 1991).

2. Charter of Paris for a New Europe; a new era of democracy, peace and unity, Paris, 19–21 November 1990.

3. See Jiří Dienstbier, 'Central Europe's Security', *Foreign Policy*, no. 83 (Summer 1991) pp. 119–27.

4. *Financial Times*, 11 May 1990, p. 2.

5. London Declaration on a transformed North Atlantic Alliance issued by the Heads of State and Government participating in the meeting of the North Atlantic Council, London, 5–6 July 1990, paras 21–22.

6. Ibid., para. 22.

7. The Paris Charter provides very little detail of the exact shape and functions of the Assembly.

8. Charter of Paris for a New Europe, Prologue.

9. Ibid. (emphasis added).

10. Statement issued by the North Atlantic Council meeting in ministerial session, Copenhagen, 6–7 June 1991 (emphasis added).

11. Membership increased from 48 to 51 on 24 March 1992, with the induction of Slovenia, Georgia and Croatia.

12. Helsinki Document 1992: The Challenges of Change, Helsinki, 10 July 1992, Extracts in *SIPRI Yearbook 1993: World Armaments and Disarmament* (Oxford: SIPRI/Oxford University Press, 1993) pp. 190–218.

13. At the Stockholm meeting of the Council of the CSCE, 14–15 December 1992, the Council appointed Mr Max van der Stoehl as the High Com-

missioner on National Minorities. He was encouraged to 'analyze carefully potential areas of tension, to visit any participating state and undertake wide-ranging discussions at all levels with the parties involved in the issues', Summary of Conclusions of the Stockholm Council meeting, 15 December 1992, Section 3, quoted in *SIPRI Yearbook 1993* p. 212.

14. The Challenges of Change, Helsinki Summit Declaration, Annex, Section VI, paras 5–6, 10 July 1992.

15. Helsinki Final Document, quoted in *SIPRI Yearbook 1993*, p. 201.

16. Fact Sheet released by the White House, Office of the Press Secretary, Helsinki, Finland, 10 July 1992, quoted in *US Department of State Dispatch*, 13 July 1992, vol. 3, no. 28, p. 559.

17. Charter of Paris for a New Europe. Supplementary document to give effect to certain provisions contained in the Charter of Paris for a New Europe, Section F, para. 1.

18. Ibid., Section F, para. 3.

19. Erika B. Schlager, 'Does CSCE spell "Stability" for Europe?', *Cornell International Law Journal*, vol. 24, no. 3 (1991 Symposium) pp. 508–9.

20. Decision on Peaceful Settlement of Disputes, Stockhom, 15 December 1992, para. 3. Principle V of the Helsinki Final Act states that, 'The participating States will settle disputes among them by peaceful means in such a manner as no to endanger international peace and security, and justice . . . For this purpose they will use arbitration, judicial settlement or other peaceful means of their own choice including any settlement procedure agreed to in advance of disputes to which they are parties.'

21. Stockholm Convention on Conciliation and.Arbitration, 14 December 1992, Article 18.

22. The first CSCE secretary general is Ambassador Wilhelm Hoynck of Germany who was appointed for a three-year term commencing 15 June 1993.

23. Conclusions of the Stockholm Council Meeting, Stockholm, 15 December 1992, Annex. 1.

24. See Adrian Hyde-Price, *European Security beyond the Cold War: Four Scenarios for the Year 2010* (London: Sage/Royal Institute of International Affairs, 1991) pp. 217–18.

25. This is enshrined in the Centre for the Prevention of Conflict (CPC) established during the Paris meeting of November 1990. For further details, see Victor-Yves Gehbaldi, 'The CSCE Conflict Prevention Centre', *International Defense Review*, vol. 24, no. 3 (March 1991) p. 219.

26. In the CSCE any country can exercise a veto (except the accused on human rights issues) and prevent action from occurring. In the UN only there has to be a two-thirds majority of the fifteen-member Security Council, including the concurring vote of all five permanent members.

27. The provisions agreed to in the CSCE are divided into Baskets, the third probably being the most publicized. The Baskets are: (i) General Principles and Security Issues (including CSBMs). (ii) Economics, Science and Technology, the Environment. (iii) Humanitarian Issues.

28. Quoted in Richard Weitz, 'The CSCE and the Yugoslav Conflict', *Radio Free Europe/Radio Liberty Research Report*, vol. 1, no. 5, 31 January 1992, p. 26.

29. Principle VI of the Helsinki Final Act, signed on 1 August 1974, recognized that, 'The participating States will refrain from any intervention, direct or indirect, individual or collective, in the internal or external affairs falling within the domestic jurisdiction of another participating State, regardless of their mutual relations.' 14 I.L.M. 1292 (1975).

30. Article 2 (7) states: 'Nothing contained in the present Charter shall authorize the United Nations to intervene in matters which are essentially within the domestic jurisdiction of any state or shall require the Members to submit such matters to settlement under the present Charter . . .'

31. For elaboration on these ideas, see 'The Future of European Security and Defense Cooperation', Annex to The Declaration of the WEU Council, Paris, 22 February 1991.

32. Initially NACC comprised the foreign ministers of the Republic of Bulgaria, the Czech and Slovak Federal Republic, the Republic of Estonia, the Republic of Hungary, the Republic of Latvia, the Republic of Lithuania, the Republic of Poland, the Republic of Romania, and the Soviet Union. The initial meeting was held in December 1991 and NACC now has thirty-seven members, the latest to join being Georgia and Albania.

33. Statement issued at the Meeting of the North Atlantic Cooperation Council, Oslo, 5 June 1992, para 3.

34. It is the oldest of the European institutions, stemming from the 1948 Hague Congress, and was officially founded the following year.

35. See Catherine Lalumière, 'The Council of Europe's place in the new European architecture', *NATO Review*, vol. 40, no. 5 (October 1992) pp. 8–12.

36. Richard H. Ullman, *Securing Europe* (Princeton NJ: Princeton University Press, 1991) p. 63.

37. Richard Ullman argues that the US will have a diminished role and will change from 'onshore organizer of security to offshore guarantor. Air and naval forces will be at the center of that guarantee.' He also observes that the Europeans will continue to be heavily reliant upon US intelligence, communication and logistical facilities (see *Securing Europe*, pp. 79–82.). To the author it remains unclear that the US would wish to furnish such support for economic and political reasons. The use of such facilities could bring demands for the continuation of US leadership as well as an implied expectation that the European allies would cooperate in collective security operations that may be of concern to the US but of little or no relevance to the Europeans.

38. A reminder contained in several NATO communiqués, such as the Communiqué of the Ministerial meeting of the North Atlantic Council, Oslo, 4 June 1992, para 13.

9   The Transatlantic Option

1. Warren Christopher, 'Towards a NATO Summit', *NATO Review*, vol. 41, no. 4 (August 1993) p. 3.

2. See for instance, London Declaration on a transformed North Atlantic Alliance, issued by the Heads of State and Government participating in the meeting of the North Atlantic Council, 5–6 July 1990, para. 2.

3. Warren Christopher, 'Towards a NATO Summit', p. 3 (emphasis added).
4. Manfred Wörner, 'NATO's Major Political Tasks: Europe Needs America', in a speech delivered before the Economic Club of Detroit, 26 June 1991. In *Vital Speeches of the Day*, vol. LVII, 15 August 1991, p. 643. See also Speech by the Secretary-General of NATO to the IISS, Brussels, 10 September 1993; 'A New NATO for a New Era', Speech by the Secretary-General of NATO at the National Press Club, Washington D.C., 6 October 1993; 'NATO: A Changing Alliance for a Changing World', Foreign Policy Association, New York, 7 October 1993 (Brussels: NATO Information Service). All of these speeches repeated the same points.
5. Wörner, 'A New NATO for a New Era'.
6. London Declaration, para. 4.
7. Ibid., para. 5.
8. For full details of the CFE and CFE-1A Agreements, see Jane Sharp, 'Conventional Arms Control in Europe', *SIPRI Yearbook 1993: World Armaments and Disarmaments* (Oxford: Oxford University Press/SIPRI, 1993) pp. 591–617.
9. London Declaration, para. 18.
10. Richard L. Kugler, 'NATO's Future Conventional Defense Strategy in Central Europe: Theater Employment Doctrine for the Post-Cold War Era, RAND, Arroyo Center, R-4084-A, p. V.
11. London Declaration, para. 14.
12. Ibid., para. 14.
13. Ibid., Article 22, para. 2.
14. Ibid., Article 2, para. 4.
15. Article 23 of the New Strategic Concept states: 'In defining the core functions of the Alliance in the terms set out above, member states confirm that the scope of the Alliance as well as their rights and obligations as provided for in the Washington Treaty remain unchanged.'
16. Jed Snyder, 'Challenges for NATO's Southern Region in the 1990s', in William Wharton, ed., *Security Arrangements for a New Europe* (Washington D.C.: National Defense University Press, 1992) p. 135.
17. The Group of Nine consists of France, Italy, Portugal and Spain and the five Union of the Arab Maghreb members – Algeria, Libya, Mauritania, Morocco and Tunisia.
18. Ankara did receive more security assistance and trade benefits from the US as a result of its role in the Gulf War. Turkey also received assistance in recouping its war costs.
19. Ozal himself had been elected to a seven-year post as president in 1989.
20. The Military Staff Committee is composed of the chiefs of the defence staff of each NATO country except France, which is represented by a military mission, and Iceland, which has no indigenous defence forces.
21. See Wharton ed., *Security Arrangements for A New Europe*, pp. 81–135.
22. Gregory Treverton, 'The New Europe', *Foreign Affairs: America and the World 1991/2* vol. 7, no. 1, p. 110.
23. NATO has for example involved itself in environmental, cultural and scientific concerns. See Paul C. Rambault, 'Environmental Challenges: The Role of NATO', in *NATO Review*, vol. 40, no. 2 (April 1992) pp. 24–7.

24. The Alliance's New Strategic Concept, agreed upon by the Heads of State and Government participating in the Meeting of the North Atlantic Council, Rome, 7–8 November 1991, para 31.
25. Ibid., para. 32.
26. See *Financial Times*, 30 August 1991, p. 4.
27. *NATO Review*, vol. 39, no. 3 (June 1991) p. 34.
28. New Strategic Concept, para. 40.
29. Ibid., para. 46.
30. Agreed to by the Heads of State and Government participating in the meeting of the North Atlantic Council in Rome, 7–8 November 1991.
31. See 'The Rome Summit: NATO Transformed', *NATO Review*, vol. 39, no. 6 (December 1991) p. 29.
32. Forward defence has been a troublesome and slippery concept in NATO, since no agreement on exactly what it means exists. To Germany it meant that, Because of the lack of depth, the high population density, and heavy industrialization, of the Federal Republic of Germany, there is no military operational alternative to immediate initiation of a cohesive defence closer to the border.' *White Paper 1985: The Situation and Development of the Federal Armed Forces* (Bonn: The Federal Minister of Defence, June 1985) p. 35. To the other allies, a degree of manoeuvre space was considered more of possibility.
33. The layer-cake concept was not officially part of MC 14/3's forward defence strategy. The strategy merely called for 'forward defence', but beyond that did not specify how that was to be implemented. The 1960s emphasized mobility, the 1970s moved towards linear defence with high firepower, and the 1980s began to shift away from this towards a more mobile concept.
34. There are currently four multinational main defence corps in existence: one Danish–German, one German–Dutch, and two German–US. In addition the Franco–German 'Eurocorps' may also be called upon.
35. The canceling of REFORGER exercises and some tactical air training in Germany suggests that public opposition to such exercises could be overwhelming.
36. The new corps meant the demise of the 1st British Corps and the merging of Britain's troops in Germany into the new ARRC, under the command of Lieutenant-General Sir Jeremy Mackenzie.
37. Norway, Iceland, Luxembourg and France do not contribute.
38. 'New Corps Launched by NATO', *The Times*, 3 October 1992, p. 10. See also Ian Kemp, 'Reaction force HQ activated', *Janes's Defence Weekly*, 10 October 1992, p. 11.
39. New Strategic Concept, para. 47.
40. See US Army *Field Manual FM 100-5* (Washington D.C.: Headquarters, Dept. of the Army, 1982).
41. The Harmel Report (1967), issued by NATO, stressed that the success of détente rested not only upon military stability, but also upon the ability of each side to reduce tensions by enganging in constructive dialogue, arms control, and building up domestic consensus for these military and political measures. The Report marked both an acceptance of the status quo and an explicit acknowledgement that stability had to have a politi-

cal context, not merely a military one.

42. New Strategic Concept, paras 8–15.
43. Ibid., para. 15.
44. Communiqué of the ministerial meeting of the North Atlantic Council in Oslo, 4 June 1992, para. 9.
45. Defence Planning Committee Communiqué, 27 May 1992, para. 5.
46. London Declaration, para. 15.
47. Ibid., para. 18.
48. Flexible response was adopted by NATO in 1967 and was designed to lend credibility to NATO's nuclear deterrent posture which had hitherto relied upon a massive nuclear response to aggression. Systematic criticism of the 'mutual assured destruction' strategy led to the adoption of flexible response, which allowed for a graduated response matching the level of aggression. Thus, if NATO were attacked with conventional weapons, the response would be similar; but if aggression could not be halted at that level, NATO reserved the right of Europe escalation dominance', that is, the right to got to the next level of aggression. The levels ranged from conventional, battlefield nuclear, theatre nuclear, to strategic nuclear exchanges. It was also designed with a political purpose in mind, the reassurance of the US's European allies, whereby instead of relying on a massive nuclear response, which the French had come to believe was incredible, the reliance would be upon a graduated response which was more credible in the sense that the US would actually use nuclear weapons in the defence of Europe.
49. New Strategic Concept, para. 40.
50. NATO Nuclear Planning Group Communiqué, 18 October 1991, p. 33.
51. *NATO Review*, vol. 39, no. 6 (December 1991) p. 13. Cuts amounting to 80 per cent of NATO's substrategic nuclear stockpile were announced in October 1991 by the Nuclear Planning Group.
52. New Strategic Concept, para. 56.
53. Ibid.
54. This makes President Bush's assertion at the Rome Summit that, 'whoever might contemplate aggression against any ally will face the power of a united alliance with a full range of options', seem slightly fanciful. President Bush, 'A Time of Decision for the NATO Alliance', in *US Department of State Dispatch*, 11 November 1991, p. 823.
55. New Strategic Concept, para. 56.
56. There has been some informal cooperation on out-of-area activities, such as that during the Gulf War, where NATO's AWACS aircraft were present in the region.
57. See Robert E. Hunter, 'NATO's Future: The Out-of-Area Problem', in Stanley R. Sloan, ed., *NATO in the 1990s* (Washington: Pergamon-Brassey's, 1989) pp. 317–18.
58. The territorial limits are explicitly delineated in Article 6, as amended, but there still is room for some equivocation since Article 4 commits the signatories to 'consult together *whenever*, in the opinion of any of them, the territorial integrity, political independence or security of any of the Parties in threatened' (emphasis added).
59. It is worth noting that the WEU was used during the Gulf War as the

main coordinating body for Western European actions in the Gulf area as well as in the UN economic blockade against Iraq.

60. Some of these arguments presented in William H. Lewis, 'NATO and Out-of-Area Concerns: A Different Paradigm', in William D. Wharton, ed., *Security Arrangements for a New Europe* (Washington D.C.: National Defense University Press, 1992) p. 101.

61. London Declaration, para. 4.

62. New Strategic Concept, para. 41.

63. Ibid., para. 9.

64. Ibid., para. 10.

65. Ibid., Part V.

66. Article 4 states: 'The Parties will consult together whenever, in the opinion of any of them, the territorial integrity, political independence or security of any of the Parties is threatened.' Under this article a plausible case could be made for NATO involvement in an out-of-area contingency, based upon the argument that the political independence or security of a member is threatened. Against this have to be considered the obligations of Articles 5 and 6. Article 5 states that, 'The Parties agree than armed attack against one or more of them in *Europe or North America* shall be considered an attack against them all . . .'; and Article 6 defines the territories covered as, 'The territory of any of the Parties in Europe or North America, Turkey, or the islands under the jurisdiction of any of the Parties on the North Atlantic area north of the Tropic of Cancer', and it also included the 'forces, vessels, or aircraft of any one of the Parties, when in or over these territories . . .'

67. Communiqué of the ministerial meeting of the North Atlantic Council in Oslo, 4 June 1992, para 11. The North Atlantic Cooperation Council issued a statement in Oslo on 5 June 1992, and this read, 'We are committed to working with all the CSCE participating states to ensure that the Helsinki Summit opens a significant new chapter in the CSCE process. In this respect, we attach particular importance to enhancing the CSCE's operational and institutional capacity to contribute to conflict prevention, crisis management and the peaceful settlement of disputes, including peace-keeping, making use of the potential support of CSCE countries and other organizations which are prepared to contribute. In this context, we have noted with interest yesterday's statement by Alliance Foreign Ministers in paragraph 11 regarding support for peace-keeping activities under the responsibility of the CSCE' (para. 4).

68. Final Communiqué following the North Atlantic Council Ministerial session in Brussels, 9–10 December 1992.

69. France and Britain did not participate in the WEU force and Germany did not participate in the blockade enforcement.

70. The problem is also compounded by German reservations concerning the overseas commitment of its forces. Chancellor Kohl would have to summon a two-thirds majority in order to change the Basic Law. Such a majority is unlikely given SPD opposition and Germany's preoccupation with post-unification tasks. There is a minority in the SPD who would sanction a change in the Basic Law, but only strictly UN 'blue helmet' peace-keeping operations.

71. For a detailed description of European capabilities, see James W. Becker, *European Civil Air: Can NATO Count On it?* (Washington D.C.: National Defense University, 1989). Amongst his conclusions, Becker points out the severe shortage of European cargo planes, as opposed to passenger planes, and the unpreparedness of civilian airline pilots to use military air-traffic control procedures.
72. The C-17 programme will, according to the US budget, cost $30 billion for 120 C-17 aircraft. The C-17 is not without its critics, since some prefer the C-5B with its larger airlift capacity. See Jeffrey Record, 'The US Air Force in the Post-Cold War Era', *Strategic Review*, vol. 19, no. 2 (Spring 1991).
73. Statement issued at the Meeting of the North Atlantic Cooperation Council in Oslo, 5 June 1992. Text in *NATO Review*, vol. 40, no. 3 (June 1992) pp. 32–4.
74. The NACC Athens meeting, 11 June 1993, endorsed NATO's role in peace-keeping in support of the UN and CSCE. Peace-keeping included conflict prevention, peace-making, peace-keeping, peace-enforcement and peace-building.
75. *The United States and NATO in an Undivided Europe*, A Report by the Working Group on Changing Roles and Shifting Burdens in the Atlantic Alliance (Washington D.C.: The Johns Hopkins Foreign Policy Institute, SAIS, 1991) p. 11.
76. Opening statement, Special Meeting of the North Atlantic Council with Participation of Heads of State or government, 10 January 1994 (Brussels: NATO Information Service).
77. Ibid.; emphasis added.
78. Ibid.; emphasis added.
79. Declaration of the Heads of State and Government Participating in the Meeting of the North Atlantic Council, Brussels, 11 January 1994, para. 13 (Brussels: NATO Information Service).
80. Partnership for Peace: Invitation issued by the Heads of State and Government participating in the Meeting of the North Atlantic Council, Brussels, 10–11 January 1994 (Brussels: NATO Information Service).
81. Ibid.
82. Annex to NATO Document M-1(94)2.
83. Ibid., para. 6.
84. Ibid., para. 8.
85. Senator Richard G. Lugar, Speech to the Altantic Council of the United States, 'NATO's "Near Abroad": New Membership, New Missions', 9 December 1993, p. 10.
86. Declaration of the Heads of State and Government Participating in the Meeting of the North Atlantic Council, Brussels, 10–11 January 1994, para. 25.

10 Democracy without Security

1. James Baker III, US Secretary of State, 'The Euro-Atlantic Architecture: From East-to-West', *Vital Speeches of the Day*, vol. LVII, 15 July 1991, p. 579.
2. Edward Mortimer, 'Creating a New Alliance', *Financial Times*, 17 April

1990, p. 19, quoted in Richard Ullman. *Securing Europe* (Princeton NJ: Princeton University Press, 1991) p. 74.

3. Eduard Shevardnadze, 'Georgia's Security Outlook', *NATO Review*, August 1993, vol. 41, no. 4, p. 9.

4. *United Nations Treaty Series*, vol. 219, no. 2962, Treaty of Friendship, Co-operation and Mutual Assistance between the People's Republic of Albania, The People's Republic of Bulgaria, The Hungarian People's Republic. The German Democratic Republic, The Polish People's Republic, The Romanian People's Republic, The Union of Soviet Socialist Republics and the Czechoslovak Republic, Warsaw, 14 May 1955, p. 24 (unofficial translation).

5. Ullman, *Securing Europe*, p. 74.

6. Hans-Dietrich Genscher, Minister for Foreign Affairs of the FRG, 'A World Community Sharing Responsibility on the Basis of Law, speech delivered at the 46th session of the General Assembly of the UN, New York, 25 September 1991, *Vital Speeches of the Day*, vol. 58, p. 10.

7. Warren Christopher, 'Towards a NATO Summit', *NATO Review*, vol. 41, no. 4 (August 1993) p. 3.

8. Adrian Hyde-Price, *European Security Beyond the Cold War* (London: Sage Publications/Royal Institute for International Affairs, 1991) p. 215.

9. Jiri Dienstbier, 'Central Europe's Security', *Foreign Policy*, no. 83 (Summer 1991) p. 222.

10. Szubiszewski's address to the Royal Institute of International Affairs, *Guardian*, 10 January 1991, quoted in Thomas S. Szayna, 'The Military in Postcommunist Poland', *RAND Note*, N-3309-USDP, p. 45.

11. Alfred A. Reisch, 'Hungary Sees Common Goals and Bilateral Issues', *Radio Free Europe/Radio Liberty Research Report*, vol. 1, no. 23 (5 June 1991) p. 27.

12. Sylvie Kauffmann, '"Visegrad" frappe à la porte', *Le Monde*. 22 June 1993.

13. These arguments are drawn from Trevor Taylor, 'NATO and Central Europe', *NATO Review*, vol. 39, no. 3 (October 1991) pp. 17–20.

14. Thomas Friedman, 'Yeltsin Says Russia Seeks to Join in NATO', *New York Times*, 21 December 1991, A 4–5. Yevgeni Kozhokin, 'A view from Russia on the Creation and Strengthening of the New European Security Order'. Working Report on the New European Security Order, North Atlantic Assembly, stated that, 'Although Russia does not consider joining NATO as a short – or even medium-term prospect, an equal partnership between the Russian Federation and NATO has become a reality' (para. 22).

15. Roger Cohen, 'Yeltsin Opposes Expansion of NATO in Eastern Europe', *New York Times*, 2 October 1993, p. 4.

16. *New York Times*, 26 August 1993, A.3.

17. There are approximately 700 000 Hungarians living mainly in the southern part of Slovakia.

18. Douglas L. Clarke, 'Arms Control and Security: After the Warsaw Pact', *Radio Free Europe/Radio Liberty*, vol. 1, no. 1 (3 January 1992) p. 108.

19. London Declaration on a Transformed North Atlantic Alliance, issued by the Heads of State and Government participating in the meetings of

the North Atlantic Council, London 5–6 July 1990, para. 7.

20. Statement made on behalf of the North Atlantic Council by the secretary-general, Manfred Wörner, on the occasion of the visit to NATO by Vàclav Havel, president of the Czech and Slovak Republic, 21 March 1991. See *NATO Review* vol. 39, no. 2 (April 1991) pp. 29–30 for full text.

21. Speech made before the North Atlantic Council by the president of the Czech and Slovak Federal Republic Vàclav Havel, 21 March 1991, *NATO Review*, vol. 39, no. 2 (April 1991) p. 33.

22. Text of President Lech Waťesa's speech given on the occasion of his visit to NATO headquarters, Brussels, 3 July 1991, in *NATO Review*, vol. 39, no. 4 (August 1991), pp. 33–5.

23. Senate Concurrent Resolution 90 – Relative to the Role of the North Atlantic Treaty Organization, submitted by Senator William Roth. International: NATO 10.21:S42, AJ 59, SEM (92) 4, Annex IX.

24. London Declaration, Article 7 stated that, '[The NAC] invites the governments of the Union of Soviet Socialist Republics, the Czech and Slovak Republic, the Hungarian Republic, the Republic of Poland, and the People's Republic of Bulgaria and Romania to come to NATO, not just to visit, but to establish regular diplomatic liaison with NATO.'

25. The Alliance's New Strategic Concept, agreed upon by the Heads of State and Government participating in the meeting of the North Atlantic Council, Rome, 7–8 November 1991, para. 29.

26. Ibid.

27. Ibid., para. 30.

28. Ibid.

29. Ibid., para. 34.

30. Ibid., para. 36 (emphasis added).

31. Article 10 of the North Atlantic Treaty states, 'The Parties may, by unanimous agreement, invite any other European state in a position to further the principles of this Treaty and to contribute to the security of the North Atlantic area to accede to this Treaty . . .'

32. Bruce George, *European and Transatlantic Security in a Revolutionary Age*, North Atlantic Assembly, Political Committee, Draft Report, no. NAA – AK 224-PC(93)6, 13 September 1993 (Brussels: NATO Information Service) para. 35.

33. Charter of Paris for a New Europe; a new era of democracy, peace and unity, Paris, 21 November 1990, section entitled 'Security' (emphasis added).

34. For instance, see those of Hans Binnendijk, 'NATO can't be Vague About Commitment to Eastern Europe', *International Herald Tribune*, 8 November 1991, p. 6.

35. For a brief description of the political structures that have arisen in these countries, see 'Democracy in Europe', *The Economist*, 1 February 1992, pp. 52–3.

36. Figures from *Central and Eastern Eurobarometer* no. 3 (Brussels: Commission of the European Communities) February 1993, p. 13.

37. Géza Jeszenszky, Minister of Foreign Affairs of the Republic of Hungary, 'Nothing Quiet on the Eastern Front', *NATO Review*, vol. 40, no. 3, (June 1992) p. 13.

38. The Alliance's New Strategic Concept, Rome, 8 November 1991, para. 29.
39. James P. McCarthy, Deputy Commander in Chief, US European Command, 'opportunities for Strengthening Security in Central and Eastern Europe: The Atlantic Community after Communism', speech delivered at the Eighth Annual US Mission NATO Conference for Directors of strategic Studies Institutes, Knooke Heist, Belgium 24 September 1992, *Vital Speeches of the Day*, vol. 59, no. 3 (15 November 1992), pp. 66–9.
40. Jiří Dienstbier, 'Central Europe's Security', *Foreign Policy*, (Summer 1991) p. 126.
41. Christopher Bobinski, 'Clinton fails to impress Poland', *Financial Times*, 11 January 1994, p. 3.
42. The 'near-abroad', or, as Foreign Minister Kozyrev said, 'the zone of good neighbourliness', are terms applied to those areas of the former Soviet Union where Russia claims to have legitimate security interests. The protection of the 'near-abroad' has become one of Russia's top foreign policy goals. Amongst the republics that appear to fall within this area are Belorus and the Ukraine.
43. Interview with Volker Rühe, *Magyar Hirlap*, 1 April 1993.
44. Maurice Blin, *Enganging the New Democracies*, North Atlantic Assembly, Sub-Committee on Eastern Europe and the former Soviet Union, Draft enterim Report, October 1993, NAA Report No. AK245 PC/EE(93)5 (Brussels: NATO Information Office) para. 46.
45. Ibid.
46. Ibid., (emphasis added).
47. Article 4 of the North Atlantic Treaty states, 'The Parties will consult together whenever, in the opinion of any of them, the territorial integrity, political independence or security of any of the Parties is threatened.'

11 Yugoslavia

1. Francis Fukuyama, 'The End of History', *The National Interest*, (Summer 1989).
2. See Zbigniew Brezinski, 'Post-Communist Nationalism', *Foreign Affairs*, vol. 68, no. 5 (Winter 1989/90) pp. 1–25.
3. See Barbara Jelavich, *History of the Balkans* (2 vols) (Cambridge: Cambridge University Press, 1983); and Hugh Seton-Watson, *Eastern Europe Between the Wars 1918–1941* (New York: Harper Torchbooks, 1967).
4. For instance, Belgium is deeply divided over Walloon–Flemish issues, Britain has its historical problems with Northern Ireland and to a lesser extent with the Welsh and Scottish, France has problems with the Alsatians, Bretons, and Corsicans, The Netherlands has the Frisian question, Portugal has that of the Azores, and Spain the problems posed by ETA (the Basque) terrorists.
5. The other nations being serbs, Croats, Slovenes, Macedonians and Montenegrines who, with the Muslims, constituted the Yugoslav Federation.
6. M. Andrejevich, 'Bosnia and Herzegovina: A Precarious Peace', *RFE/RL Research Report*, 28 February 1992, p. 7.
7. Thorvald Stoltenberg of Norway replaced Cyrus Vance as the UN-appointed

envoy on 27 July 1993. Lord Owen continued to negotiate on behalf of the European powers.

8. *SIPRI Yearbook 1993: World Armaments and Disarmament* (Oxford: Oxford University Press/SIPRI, 1993) pp. 91–2.

9. The EC had decided on 16 December 1991 that the Yugoslav case would be dealt with on 15 January 1992. Germany recognized Croatia on 25 December 1991. Macedonia declared its independence on 15 September 1991. Bosnia-Herzegovina proclaimed its independence on 3 March 1992, while Montenegro voted for union with Serbia in a referendum held on 1 March 1992.

10. Warren Christopher, 'Toward a NATO Summit', *Nato Review*, vol. 41, no. 4 (August 1993) p. 3.

11. See John Baylis, *Anglo-American Defence Relations, 1939–80: The Special Relationship* (London: Macmillan, 1981) pp. 77–97.

12. *The Economist*, 14–20 August 1993, p. 45; and *NATO Review*, vol. 41, no. 4 (August 1993) p. 26.

13. President George Bush, quoted by James Baker III in his speech, 'The Euro–Atlantic Architecture: From West to East', delivered to the Aspen Institute, Berlin, 18 June 1991. In *Vital Speeches of the Day*, vol. LVII, 15 July 1991, p. 578.

14. The mission consisted of the foreign ministers of Italy, Luxembourg and the Netherlands.

15. Chairman's Statement on the results of the meeting of the Consultative Committee of the Conflict Prevention Center, 1 July 1991, quoted in Marc Weller, 'The International Response to the Dissolution of the Socialist Federal Republic of Yugoslavia', *The American Journal of International Law*, vol. 86, no. 3, pp. 572–3.

16. 'Urgent Appeal for a Cease Fire', 3 July 1991, in *American Journal of International Law*, vol. 86, no. 3.

17. As the name suggests, the forces were intended to provide a barrier between conflicting forces. However, the plan soon became bogged down in discussion about the number that would be needed, contributions, rules of engagement, command arrangements and, above all, feasibility.

18. In UN Security Council Resolution 713 the UN expressed its support for European efforts and imposed a general arms embargo on Yugoslavia.

19. Quoted in Weller, 'The International Response', p. 588.

20. Neal Ascherson, *The Independent*, 16 August 1992, quoted in Jane Sharp, 'If not NATO, Who?', *The Bulletin of the Atomic Scientists*, October 1992, p. 30.

21. Speech by Manfred Wörner to IISS in Brussels, 10 September 1993 (Brussels: NATO Information Service).

22. Ibid.

23. Helsinki Final Act Conference on Security and Cooperation in Europe, Section A: Declaration on Principles Guiding Relations between Participating States, para. 1, 1 August 1975, 14 I.L.M. 1292 (1975).

24. Ibid., Section VIII, 'Equal Rights and Self-Determination of Peoples'.

25. For instance, the Charter of Paris for a New Europe, adopted by the CSCE Heads of State on 21 November 1990, contained the pledge to the 'full commitment of the Ten Principles of the Helsinki Final Act, and

that, 'We reaffirm the equal rights of peoples and their rights to self-determination in conformity with the Charter of the United Nations and with the relevant norms of international law, including those relating to territorial integrity of States.'

26. Bulgaria, Greece and Serbia have already fought wars over Macedonia in 1912 and again in 1913. the first Balkan war erupted on 8 October 1912, when Montenegro declared war on Turkey, to be quickly followed by Bulgaria, Greece and Serbia. In May 1913 the Treaty of London ended the first Balkan war. The Bulgarians failed to take Constantinople and the Austrians managed to persuade the parties to the conference of ambassadors to agree to the an independent Albania, which cut off Serbia from the sea. Russian interests had thus been served, by denying Bulgaria Constantinople, and Austrian interests had been served through denying Serbia access to the sea. The second Balkan war was a result of disagreements over the spoils from the first war. The Serbians wanted railways both to Salonika a well as to the Macedonian territory it had conquered, while Bulgaria attacked Andrianople. In response to these demands the Bulgarians attacked both Greece and Serbia in June 1913, shortly to be followed by a Romanian attack against Bulgaria (to seize Dobrudja) and a Turkish attack to recover Andrianople. The second Balkan war was ended on 10 August 1913 with the Peace of Bucharest, by which Bulgaria lost almost everything that it had gained in the first war.

12   Conclusion

1. See Ghiţa Ionescu (ed.) *The New Politics of European Integration* (London: Macmillan, 1972) pp. 6 and 17.
2. Miodrag Mihajlovic, 'Internal Changes in South-East European Countries', in La sécurité européenne dans les années 90: Problèmes de L'Europe du Sud-Est, Rhodes, Greece, 6–7 September 1991 (New York: United Nations, 1992). UNIDIR/92/40, p. 34.
3. See, for instance, 'The Dream of Europax', *The Economist*, 7 April 1990, pp. 14–15.
4. An idea put forward by Stephen S. Larrbee, 'Long memories and Short Fuses: Change and Stability in the Balkans', *International Security*, vol. 15, no. 3 (Winter 1990/91) p. 89.
5. Treaty of Friendship, Co-operation and Mutual Assistance, Signed at Warsaw, 14 May 1955. *United Nations Treaties Series*, vol. 219, no. 2962 (1955) p. 24.

Bibliography

FULL-LENGTH STUDIES

Allison, G. and G.F. Treverton (eds), *Rethinking America's Security: Beyond Cold War to the New World Order* (New York: W.W. Norton, 1992)

Buzan, B., M. Kelstrup, P. Lemaitre, E. Tromer, and O. Waever, *The European Security Order Recast: Scenarios for the Post-Cold War Era* (London: Pinter, 1990)

Calleo, D. and P. Gordon, *From the Atlantic to the Urals: National Perspectives on the New Europe* (Washington D.C.: Seven Locks Press, 1992)

Carpenter, T.G., *NATO at 40: Confronting a Changing World* (Lexington, MA: Lexington Books/CATO Institute, 1990)

Cerruti, F. and R. Ragioieri (eds), *Rethinking European Security* (New York: Crane Russak, 1990)

Clark, T. and S. Serfaty (eds) *New Thinking and Old Realities: America, Europe and Russia* (Washington D.C.: Seven Locks, 1991)

Clarke, M. and R. Hague (eds), *European Defence Cooperation: America, Britain and NATO* (Manchester; Manchester University Press, 1990)

Clesse, A. and L. Rühl, *Beyond East–West Confrontation: Searching for a New Security Structure in Europe* (Baden-Baden: Nomos Verlagsgesellschaft, 1990)

Danspeckgruber, W.F., *Emerging Dimensions of European Security Policy* (Boulder, CO: Westview, 1991)

Harrison, M., *The Reluctant Ally: France and Atlantic Security* (Baltimore: Johns Hopkins University Press, 1981)

Heuser, B. and R. O'Neill (eds) *Securing Peace in Europe: 1945–62* (London: Macmillan, 1992)

Hyde-Price, A., *European Security Beyond the Cold War* (London: Royal Institute for International Affairs/Sage Publications, 1991)

Jopp, M., R. Rummel, and P. Schmidt (eds) *Integration and Security in Western Europe: Inside the European Pillar* (Boulder CO: Westview, 1991)

Kaplan, L. S.V. Papacosma, M. Rubin and R. Young (eds) *NATO After Forty Years* (Wilmington, DE: Scholarly Resources, 1990)

Keohane, R.O., J.S. Nye, and S. Hoffmann, *After the Cold War: International Institutions and State Strategies in Europe 1989–91* (Cambridge, MA: Harvard University Press, 1993)

Kissinger, H.A., *Years of Upheaval* (Boston: Little Brown and Company, 1982)

Klare, M., and D. Thomas (eds) *World Security: Trends and Challenges at Century's End* (New York: St Martin's Press, 1991)

Kommers, D.P., *The Constitutional Jurisprudence of the Federal Republic of Germany* (Durham NC: Duke University Press, 1989)

Kruzel, J. (ed.) *American Defense Annual 1991–2* (New York: Lexington Books, 1992)

Laird, R., *The Europeanization of the Alliance* (Boulder, CO: Westview, 1991)

Leech, J., *Halt! Who Goes Where?* (London: Brassey's Defence, 1991)

Lepgold, J., *The Declining Hegemon: The United States and European Defense, 1960–90* (New York: Praeger Publishers, 1990)

Levine, R.A., *Transition and Turmoil in the Atlantic Alliance* (New York: Crane Russak, 1992)

Macridis, R.C. (ed.) *Foreign Policy in World Politics* (New Jersey: Prentice Hall, 1992)

Mattox, G.A. and A.B. Shingleton, *Germany at the Crossroads: Foreign and Domestic Policy Issues* (Boulder, CO: Westwview, 1992).

Morgenthau, H.J., *Politics Among Nations: The Struggle for Power and Peace,* 6th edn (New York: Alfred A. Knopf, 1985)

Muller, S. and G. Schweigler (eds) *From Occupation to Cooperation: The United States and United Germany in a Changing World Order* (New York: W.W. Norton, 1992)

Nelson, D.N., *Balkan Imbroglio: Politics and Security in South-Eastern Europe* (Boulder, CO: Westview, 1991)

Nye, J.S., *Bound To Lead: The Changing Nature of America Power* (New York: Basic Books, 1990)

Perle, R. (ed.) *Reshaping Western Security: A United States Faces a United Europe* (Washington D.C., The American Enterprise Institute, 1991)

Pinder, J., *The European Community and Eastern Europe* (New York: Council on Foreign Relations Press, 1991)

Randle, M. and P. Rogers (eds), *Alternatives in European Security* (Aldershot: Dartmouth, 1990)

Rotfeld, A.D. and W. Stützle, (eds) *Germany and Europe in Transition* (Oxford: Oxford University Press/SIPRI, 1991)

Rusi, A.M., *After the Cold War: Europe's New Political Architecture* (London: Macmillan, 1991)

Sharp, J.M.O., *Europe After an American Withdrawal: Economic and Military Issues* (Oxford: Oxford University Press, 1990)

Sherwood, E., *Allies in Crisis: Meeting the Global Challenges to Western Security* (New Haven: Yale University Press, 1990)

Simon, J. (ed.) *European Security Policy after the Revolutions of 1989* (Washington D.C.: National Defense University Press, 1991)

Sloan, S.R., *NATO's Future: Towards a New Transatlantic Bargain* (Washington D.C.: National Defense University Press, 1985)

Sloan, S.R., *NATO in the 1990s* (New York: Pergamon-Brassey's, 1989)

Stockhom International Peace Research Institute, *SIPRI Yearbook: World Armaments and Disarmament* (Annual) (Oxford: Oxford University Press)

Stuart, D. and W. Tow, *The Limits of Alliance: NATO Out-of-Area Problems since 1949* (Baltimore: Johns Hopkins University Press, 1990)

Treverton, G., *The Shape of the New Europe* (New York: Council on Foreign Relations, 1992)

Treverton, G., America, Germany and the Future of Europe (Princeton NJ: Princeton University Press, 1992)

Ullman, R.H., *Securing Europe* (Princeton: Princeton University Press, 1991)

Wallace, W. (ed.) *The Dynamics of European Integration* (New York: Columbia University Press, 1991)

Wessell, N.H., *The New Europe: Revolution in East–West Relations* (Montpelier, VT: Capital City Press, 1991)

Wharton, W.D. (ed.) *Securing Arrangements for a New Europe* (Washington D.C.: National Defense University Press, 1992)

Williams A.L. and G.L. Williams, *The European Defence Initiative: Europe's Bid for Equality* (New York: St Martin's Press, 1986)

ARTICLES AND PAPERS

Ahlstrom, R.P., 'The European Community Faces 1992', *Current History*, vol. 90, no. 559 (November 1991) pp. 374–8.

Almond, M., 'National Pacifism: Germany's New Temptation', *European Security Studies*, no. 12 (London: Institute for European Defence and Strategic Studies, 1991)

Clarke, D.L. 'Arms Control and Security: After the Warsaw Pact', *Radio Free Europe/Radio Liberty Research Report*, vol. 1, no. 1 (3 January 1992) pp. 105–8.

Cooper, M.H., 'NATO's Changing Role', *Congressional Quarterly Researcher*, vol. 2, no. 31 (21 August 1992) pp. 713–36.

DeHaven, M.J., 'Internal and External Determinants of Foreign Policy: West Germany and Great Britain During the Two-Track Missile Controversy', *International Studies Quarterly*, vol. 35, no. 2 (1991) pp. 87–108.

Dienstbier, J., 'Central Europe's Security', *Foreign Policy*, no. 83 (Summer 1991) pp. 119–27.

Duchin, B.R., 'The "Agonizing Reappraisal": Eisenhower, Dulles, and the European Defense Community', *Diplomatic History*, vol. 16, no. 2 (Spring 1992) pp. 201–21.

'European Security: Still Divided', *The Economist*, 12 October 1991, pp. 54–5.

'Qu'est-ce qu'on fait? Ich Weiss nicht', *The Economist*, 23 May 1992, pp. 51–3.

Feinstein, L., 'Commonwealth Members Offer Early Support for CFE Treaty', *Arms Control Today*, vol. 22, no. 1 (January/February 1992) p. 44.

Fenske, J., 'France's Uncertain Progress toward European Union', *Current History*, vol. 90, no. 559 (November 1991) pp. 358–62.

Flanagan, S.J., 'NATO and Central and Eastern Europe: From Liaison to Security Partnership', *The Washington Quarterly*, vol. 15, no. 2 (Spring 1992) pp. 141–51.

Germroth, D.S. and R.J. Hudson, 'German–American Relations in the Post-Cold War World', *Journal of Social, Political and Economic Studies*, vol. 16, no. 2 (Summer 1991) pp. 131–57.

Gnesotto, N., 'European Union after Minsk and Maastricht', *International Affairs*, vol. 68, no. 2 (1992) pp. 223–31.

Gronimus, A., 'Allied Security Services in Germany: The NATO SOFA and Supplementary Agreement seen from a German Perspectives', *Military Law Review*, vol. 136, (Spring 1992) pp. 43–67. Dept. of Army Pankleb 27–100–136

Gronlund, L., L. Lumpe and D.C. Wright, 'Third World Missiles Fall Short',

Bulletin of the Atomic Scientists (march 1992) p. 30–32.

Hartley, A., 'The Irrelevance of Maastricht: Redefining the Atlantic Community', Institute for European Defence and Strategic Studies, Occasional Paper 53, (1992).

Hettne, B., 'Security and Peace in Post-Cold War Europe', *Journal of Peace Research*, vol. 28, no. 3 (1991) pp. 279–94.

Kaldova, J., 'Czechoslovakia's Return to Europe', *Ukranian Quarterly*, vol. 47, no. 4 (Winter 1991) pp. 399–409.

Kapitza, S., 'Soviet Scientists: Low Pay, No Pay, Now Insults', *Bulletin of the Atomic Scientists* (May 1992) pp. 8–9.

Kelleher, C.M. 'Arms Control in Revolutionary Future: Europe', *Daedalus*, vol. 20, no. 1 (Winter 1991) pp. 111–31.

Kershaw, I., 'Germany's Present, Germany's Past', The 1992 Bithell Memorial Lecture, Institute of Germanic Studies, University of London, 1992.

Klare, M., 'Challenges to Peace in the Post-Cold War Era: An Agenda for Peace', *Nuclear Times* (Fall/Winter 1992) pp. 6–10.

Laird, R., 'France, Germany, and the Future of the Atlantic Alliance', *Proceedings of the Academy of Political Science*, vol. 38, no. 1 (1991) pp. 50–59.

Latter, R., 'National Defence Policies of the NATO Allies: Internal Tensions and Out-of-Area Problems', *Wilton Park Papers* no. 5 (London: HMSO, 1988)

Lepgold, J., 'The United States and Europe: Redefining the Relationship', *Current History*, vol. 90, no. 559 (November 1991) pp. 353–7.

Malcolm, N., 'Heads in the Sand', *National Review*, 20 July 1992, pp. 34–5.

Markovits, A.S. and S. Reich, 'Model Deutschland and the New Europe', *Telos*, vol. 24, no. 3 (1991) pp. 45–63.

Mearsheimer, J.L., 'Back to the Future: Instability in Europe after the Cold War', *International Security*, vol. 15, no. 1 (Summer 1990) pp. 5–56.

Mecham, M., 'Security of Eastern Europe Shifts Strategy Issues for Western Powers', *Aviation Week and Space Technology*, 13 May 1991, pp. 92–3.

Mecham, M., 'Signing NATO's New Strategy May be the Easy Part for the Summit', *Aviation Week and Space Technology*, 4 November 1991, p.27.

Mecham, M., 'NATO Strategy Review Moves Faster on Political Rather than Military Front', *Aviation Week and Space Technology*, 11 November 1991.

Mora, M., 'Heeding the Weimar Factor: Germany Steps out of the Shadows', *The New Leader*, 10–24 February 1992, pp. 12–14.

'Esprit de Korps', *National Review*, 18 November 1991, pp. 18–19.

'The German Delusion', *The New Republic*, 11 November 1991, pp. 8–9.

Nelson, D.N., 'NATO – means, but no ends', *Bulletin of the Atomic Scientists*, January/February 1992, pp. 10–11.

Nelson, D.N., 'Snatching Defeat From the Jaws of Victory', *Bulletin of the Atomic Scientists*, October 1992, pp. 24–8.

Nixon, R., 'Is America a Part of Europe?', *National Review*, 2 March 1992, pp. 27–31.

Noël, E., 'Reflections on the Maastricht Treaty', *Government and Opposition*, vol. 27, no. 2 (Spring 1992) pp. 148–57.

Obrman, J., 'Slovakia Declares Sovereignty', *Radio Free Europe/Radio Liberty Research Report*, vol. 1, no. 31 (31 July 1992) pp. 25–9.

Obrman, J., 'Czechoslovakia: A Messy Divorce After All', *Radio Free Europe/*

Radio Liberty Research Report, vol. 1, no. 41 (16 October 1992) pp. 1–5.

Pick, O., 'Eastern Europe II: Czechoslovakia's divisions', *The World Today*, vol. 48, no. 5, 5 (January 1992) pp. 83–5.

Rauf, T., 'Cleaning Up with a Big Bang', *Bulletin of the Atomic Scientists*, January/February 1992, pp. 9–11.

Rayner, T., 'The Best Farytale of All', *New Statesman and Society*, 12 June 1992, pp. 14–15.

Reisch, A.A., 'Hungary sees common goals and bilateral issues', *Radio Free Europe/Radio Liberty Research Report*, vol. 1, no. 23 (June 1992) p. 25–32.

Rivkin, D.B., Jr., 'Winning the Peace – Dilemmas of Post-Soviet European Security', *Problems of Communism* vol. 41, no. 1–2 (January–April 1992) pp. 150–3.

Ross, G., 'After Maastricht : Hard Choices for Europe', *World Policy Journal*, vol. 9, no. 3 (Summer 1992) pp. 487–513.

Rupieper, H-J., 'After the Cold War: The United States, Germany and European Security', *Diplomatic History*, vol. 16, no. 2 (Spring 1992) pp. 262–8.

Pehe, J., 'Scenarios for Disintegration: The Breakup of Czechoslovakia', *Radio Free Europe/Radio Liberty Research Report*, vol. 1, no. 31 (31 July 1992) pp. 30–33.

Salmon, T.C. 'Testing Times for European Political Cooperation: The Gulf and Yugoslavia, 1990–1992', *International Affairs*, vol. 68, no. 2 (1992) pp. 233–53.

Sayari, S., 'Turkey: The Changing European Security Environment and the Gulf Crisis', *Middle East Journal*, vol. 46, no. 1 (Winter 1992) pp. 9–21.

Schlager, E.B. 'Does CSCE Spell "Stability" for Europe?', *Cornell International Law Journal*, vol. 24, no. 3 (1991 Symposium) pp. 503–15.

Schmähling, E., 'German Security Policy Beyond American Hegemony', *World Policy Journal*, vol. 6, no. 2 (Spring 1989) pp. 371–84.

Schmidt, P., 'The Franco–German Defence and Security Council', *Aussenpolitik*, vol. 40, no. 4 (1989) pp. 316–71.

Sharp, J., 'If Not NATO, Who?', *The Bulletin of the Atomic Scientists*, October 1992, pp. 29–32.

Smith, G., 'Britain in the New Europe', *Foreign Affairs*, vol. 71, no. 4 (Fall 1992) pp. 155–70.

Steel, R., 'NATO's Afterlife', *The New Republic*, 2 December 1991, pp. 18–19.

Stromseth, J.E., 'The North Atlantic Treaty and European Security after the Cold War', *Cornell International Law Journal*, Vol. 24, no. 3 (1991 Symposium) pp. 479–502.

Svec, M., 'Czechoslovakia's Velvet Divorce', *Current History*, vol. 91, no. 569 (November 1992) pp. 376–80.

Thränert, O., 'Germans Battle over Blue Helmets', *Bulletin of the Atomic Scientists* (october 1991) PP. 33–5.

Tiersky, R., 'France in the New Europe', *Foreign Affairs*, vol. 71, no. 2 (Spring 1992) pp. 131–46.

Treverton, G.F., 'The Year of European (Dis)Unification', *Current History*, vol. 91, no. 568 (November 1992) pp. 353–8.

Treverton, G.F., 'The New Europe', *Foreign Affairs*, vol. 71, no. 1 (America and the World 1991/2) pp. 94–112.

Vysny, P., 'Slovakia: The Scotland of Central Europe', *Coexistence*, no. 29 (1992) pp. 137–44.

Walker, D.B., 'Germany Searches for a New Role in World Affairs', *Current History*, vol. 90. no. 559 (November 1991) pp. 368–73.

Weitz, R., 'The CSCE and the Yugoslav Conflict', *Radio Free Europe/ Radio Liberty Research Report*, vol. 1, no. 5 (31 January 1992) pp. 24–6.

Weitz, R., 'The CSCE's New Look', *Radio Free Europe/Radio Liberty Research Report*, vol. 1, no. 6 (7 February 1992) pp. 27–31.

Weller, M., 'The International Response to the Dissolution of the Socialist Republic of Yugoslavia', *The American Journal of International Law*, vol. 86, no. 3 (July 1992) pp. 569–607.

Wells, S.F. Jr, 'Nuclear Weapons and European Security during the Cold War', *Diplomatic History*, vol. 16, no. 2 (Spring 1992) pp. 278–86.

Wright, R., 'Islam, Democracy and the West', *Foreign Affairs*, vol. 71, no. 3 (Summer 1992) pp. 131–45.

Young, T-D. and S.J. Newland 'Germany, France, and the Future of Western European Security', *Parameters* (September 1990) pp. 71–84.

Zielonka, J., 'Europe's Security: A Great Confusion', *International Affairs*, vol. 67, no. 1 (1991) pp. 127–37.

OFFICIAL SOURCES

US Department of State Dispatch (Various) (Washington: US Government Printing Office).

Vital Speeches of the Day (Various) (Mt, Pleasant, S.C.: City News Publishing).

RAND Reports

Asmus, R., J.F. Brown and K. Crane, 'Soviet Foreign Policy and the Revolutions of 1989 in Eastern Europe', 1991, R-3903-USDP.

Asmus, R. and T.S. Szayna, 'Polish National Security Thinking in a Changing World: A Conference Report', 1991, R-4056-FF.

Asmus, R., 'German Perceptions of the United States at Unification', 1991, R-4069-AF.

Bitzinger, R., 'Reconstructing NATO Strategy for the 1990s: A Conference Report', August 1989, R-3803-FF.

Builder, C. and S.C. Bankes, 'The Etiology of European Change', December 1990, P-7693

Crane, K. and K.C. Yeh, 'Economic Reform and the Military in Poland, Hungary and China', 1991, R-3961-PCT.

Crane, K., 'The Economic Implications of Reductions in Military Budgets and Force Levels in Eastern Europe', 1991, *RAND Note*, R-3208-USDP.

Fuller, G.E., 'Central Asia: The New Geopolitics', 1992, R-4129-USDP.

Henze, P.B., 'Ethnic Dynamics and Dilemmas of the Russian Republic', 1991, *RAND Note*, N-3219-USDP.

Hirschfeld, T.J., 'Helsinki II: The Future of Arms Control in Europe', 1992, R-4174-FF/RC.

Kugler, R.L., 'NATO's Future Role in Europe: Toward a More Political Alliance in a Stable "1 1/2" Bloc System', May 1990, R-3923-FF.

Kugler, R.L., 'The Future U.S. Military Presence in Europe', 1992, R-4194-EUCOM/NA.

Kugler, R.L., 'NATO's Future Conventional Defense Strategy in Central Europe: Theater Deployment for the post-Cold War era', 1992, R-4084-A.

Kugler, R.L., 'NATO Military Strategy for the Post-Cold War Era', 1992, R-4217-AF.

Lesser, I.O., 'Southern Region Perspectives on Security and International Affairs', 1991, R-3269-AF.

Levine, R.A., 'What If the Russians aren't coming and the Americans aren't staying?', 1991, *RAND Note*, N-3331-CC.

Nation, J.E., 'German, British, and French Military Requirements and Resources to the Year 2005', 1992, N-2982-RGSD

Rumer, E.B., 'The German Question in Moscow's "Common European Home"', 1992, *RAND Note* N-3220-USDP

Rumer, E.B., 'The End of a Monolith: The Politics of Military Reform in the Soviet Armed Forces', 1991, R-3993-USDP.

Scouras, J., 'U.S. Strategic Forces Under the Prospective START Treaty', 1991, *RAND Note* N-3193-AF.

Steinberg, J., 'Integration and Security in an all European order', 1991, P-7733.

Szayna, T.S., 'The Ethnic Factor in the Soviet Armed Forces: The Muslim Dimension', 1991, R-4002-A.

Szayna, T.S., 'The Military in a Postcommunist Poland', 1991, RAND Note, N-3309-USDP.

Szayna, T.S. and J.B. Steinberg, 'Civil–Military Relations and National Security Thinking in Czechoslovakia: A Conference Report', 1992, R-4195-OSD/A/FF.

van Heuven, M., 'Europe 1991: The Grail of Unity', May 1991, P-7724.

Webb, S., 'NATO and 1992: Defense Acquisition and Free Markets', July 1989, R-3758-FF.

NEWSPAPERS

Christian Science Monitor
Die Zeit
El Pais
The European
The Independent
Le Monde
The New York Times
The Times

Index

Abkhazia   see Georgia
Adenauer, Konrad   97, 179, 368, 409n
Adriatic   240, 269
Afghanistan   122
Agenda for Peace   see Boutros
   Boutros-Ghali
Aidid, Gen. Mohammed Farah   359
AIDS   84
Air–land battle   291
Albania   59, 80, 334, 361, 363
   disputes with Serbia   62, 366
   disputes with Greece   62, 366
Algeria   25, 54, 78, 99
*Allied Command Europe Rapid Reaction
   Corps* (ARRC)   *see* NATO
Alma-Ata Agreement   31, 37, 88
Amoto, Guiliano   331
Antall, Jozsef   322
Arab Maghreb Union   78
Armenia   59, 64, 66, 80, 263
Arms control agreements
   Anti-Ballistic Missile Treaty   292
   Chemical Weapons Convention   5
   Conference on Disarmament   292
   Conventional Forces in Europe   112,
      170, 189, 190, 207, 253, 260, 278,
      292
   Intermediate-range Nuclear Force
      Treaty   18, 292
   Non-Proliferation Treaty   35, 37, 38,
      48, 52, 54
   START I   5, 18, 30–1, 35, 39, 47,
      49, 50, 88, 106, 155, 292, 395n
   START II   5, 18, 31, 35, 39, 49, 88,
      106, 125, 155, 292
Aquinas, Thomas   85
Arzamas 16   51
Ashkhabad Declaration   31, 37
Aspin, Les   49, 149, 194, 196, 306,
   350–1
Athens Guidelines (1962)   247, 279
Atlantic Nuclear Force   119
Atomic Energy Act (1954)   118
Attlee, Clement   118, 119
Augustine   85
Austria   71, 74–5, 225, 267, 360
   Freedom Party   71
   migratory pressures   74–5

AWACS   150–2,m 299
Azerbaijan   56, 64, 65, 283, 285

Baker, James III   52, 182, 209, 210,
   214, 317
BAOR   see United Kingdom
Balance of Power system   206
Balkan Pact   282
Balladur, Edouard   111, 113, 340–3,
   378
   European Stability Pact   113, 321,
      328, 329
Bartholomew memorandum   172
Bayern   146, 407n
Belarus   30, 33, 35, 37, 38, 48, 56,
   113, 333, 334, 363
   ethnic disputes   58, 62, 64, 80
Belgium   68, 121, 205, 213, 225, 227
   Flemish separatists   68
   migratory pressures   77
   Vlaams Blok   71
Berlin   140
Berlin Wall   135
Bessarabia   332
Biden, Senator Joseph   359
Black Sea Economic Cooperation
   Region   203
Bombers
   Bear   30, 43, 48
   Blackjack   34, 43
Bosnia   3, 129, 149, 186–7, 233, 263,
   349–67, 375, 408n
   and migration   69–70
   and Muslims   27, 28
   US role in   168–9, 186, 198–99
   war in   349–68
Boutros Boutros-Ghali   86, 310, 354,
   359
Brandt, Willy   157, 168
Bratislava process   320, 321
Britain   see United Kingdom
Brussels Treaty (1954)   144
Bukovina   332
Bulgaria   29, 59, 80, 237, 261, 326,
   331, 332, 334, 363
   dispute with Greece   62
   dispute with Macedonia   365, 432n
   dispute with Romania   62

dispute with Turkey 65
Bundesbank 141
Bundeswehr see Germany
Burdensharing 98, 180
Burdenshedding 98
Burt, Richard 174
Bush, George 17–18, 33, 34, 35, 165,
    170, 171–5, 181, 183, 184, 194–6,
    198, 286, 411n

C-17 Transport aircraft 301, 427n
Callaghan, James 121
Cambodia 150
Canada 113, 210, 273, 278, 281
Canning, George 118
CAP 182, 412n, 416n
Carrington, Lord Peter 233, 356
Carter, Jimmy 121, 142
    long-term defence plan 121
    neutron bomb debate 184
Caucasus 33, 64–5, 70, 94, 285
Ceausescu, Nicolae 63
CENTCOM 301
CFSP see European Union
Chechen-Igush 59
Chechina 65, 399n
Chernobyl 5, 41, 53
Chetek 51
Chevènement, Jean-Pierre 101, 102,
    105, 109
Cheyney, Dick 109, 410n
China 54–55
Chirac, Jacques 75–6, 105, 110,
    112–13, 246, 247, 249
Christopher, Warren 149, 170, 180,
    184, 214, 275, 306, 352, 353
Chronovil, Vyacheslav 46
Churchill, Winston 10, 119, 368
Churkin, Vitaly 364
Clark, David 404n
Clinton, President Bill 36, 44, 46,
    49, 161, 169, 177, 180, 185, 187,
    190, 194–5, 286, 307, 324, 353,
    359
    Baghdad raid 184
Cold War, stability of 17–19
Colombey meeting (1958) 97
Commonwealth of Independent States
    (CIS)
    establishment of 37
    future of 58, 60
    military and 30, 33, 35–41, 55–7,
    319
Confédération see Mitterrand

Conference on Security and
    Cooperation in Europe
    (CSCE) 10, 11, 132, 153, 164,
    211, 255–69, 320, 345, 370, 377–9
    Caucasus and 362
    Charter of Paris 152, 256–8, 319, 330
    Committee for Conflict
        Prevention 256, 263, 267
    Committee of Senior Officials 262,
        263, 265, 267
    Court of Conciliation and
        Arbitration 261, 262
    effectiveness of 362–3, 377–8
    Forum for Security Cooperation 260
    Geneva Experts Meeting 260, 261
    Georgia and 67
    Helsinki Summit (1992) 255, 258
    High Commission on National
        Minorities 259
    Moldovia 67
    Office for Free Elections 256, 259
    Prague Meeting 263–4
    Stockhom Convention on Conciliation
        and Arbitration 262–3
    Vienna Meeting 260
    Yugoslavia and 267–9
Conference on Security and
    Cooperation in the
    Mediterranean 78
Conversion programmes 57
Cot, General Jean 359
Council for Mutual Economic
    Assistance 11
Council of the Baltic States 203
Council of Europe 10, 270–1, 378
Cresson, Edith 75
Cyprus 207, 283
Czechoslovakia 18, 58, 68
Czech Republic 59, 68, 80, 156, 237,
    261, 307, 325, 327–8, 334, 363

Dagetan 60
Danube 150
Dawa 24
De Gaulle, Charles 96, 97, 124, 130,
    174, 244
Delors, Jacques 117, 228, 231
Demirel, Suleiman 27, 284
Denmark 213, 225, 227, 229, 239,
    272, 281
Department of Defense 167
Détente 142, 244
Dien Bien Phu 99
Dienstbier, Jirí 256, 318, 321, 337

Drina 365
Dual-Track decision *see* NATO
Dulles, John Foster 173
Dumas, Roland 102

Economic Security Council 198
Eden, Anthony 119, 216, 217
Eisenhower, Dwight 184, 216
Eliasson, Nils 268
Elysée Treaty (1963) 244, 245,
 418n
Engholm, Björn 146, 148
Estonia 58, 80, 113, 237, 264, 270,
 334, 336, 363
Eurocorps 108, 219, 223–4
Eurasia 11
Eurofighter 2000 127
Europe Agreements 333
European Bank for Reconstruction and
 Development (EBRD) 11, 133,
 228, 416n
European Commission on Human
 Rights 270
European Community 10, 77, 106,
 119, 136, 152, 159–61, 164
 CAP and 228, 416n
European Council 113, 228, 340
 Rome Conference (1991) 107
European Community
 Commission 132, 228
European Community Council of
 Ministers 228
European Court of Human Rights 270
European Defence Community 120,
 173, 212, 215–6, 224
European Defence Organization 10,
 214
European Energy Community 228
European Environmental Agency 228
European Free Trade Area 10, 119,
 228, 230
European Monetary System 99, 229
European Political Community 215,
 224
European Security Identity 221–4
European Security Organization 10,
 171, 214, 271, 346
European Stability Pact *see*
 Balladur
European Union 94, 106, 132, 152,
 352
 CFSP 107–8, 173, 224–31, 234
 Council 226, 416n
 effectiveness of 362–3

membership 230
 Yugoslavia and 355–6, 357
Exchange Rate Mechanism 106, 111

Fabius, Laurent 246
Fadlallah, Muhammad 27
Falin, Valentin 319
Falklands conflict 295
Faraj, Abd al-Salam 26
Farhanq, Mansour 26
Federal Constitutional Court *see*
 Germany
Finland 225
Flexible Response *see* NATO
Force d'Action Rapide *see* France
Foreign and Commonwealth
 Office 129
Former Yugoslav Republic of
 Macedonia 264, 333, 261, 365
France
 Algerians and 72
 backing for CFSP 107–8
 force d'action rapide 101, 245
 force de frappe 96–7, 99, 101, 104,
  114
 lead in European security 95–117,
  341–2
 migratory pressures 75
 Rafale fighter 104
 relations with FRG 97–108, 114,
  136, 141, 155
 relations with NATO 96–113, 115,
  179, 241
 relations with Russia 106, 107
 relations with UK 99, 111, 130,
  132–4
 relations with US 96, 103–4,
  114–16, 171, 325
 role in EC Rome meeting 107–8
 role in WEU 104, 107–8, 232
 nuclear collaboration with the
  UK 124–5, 134
 Plan Armée 2000 109, 281
 population growth 72
 proportional deterrence 97
 S-4 missile 104
 see also Mitterrand *and* Balladur
Franco-German Brigade/Corps 100,
 103–4, 108–9, 115, 142, 197,
 219–20, 241–254
Franco-Prussian War 20
Front National *see* Le Pen
Fukuyama, Francis 347
Functionalism 229
Fyodorov, Boris 51

Gaddafi, Muammar 295
Gaidar, Yegor 50
Gallois, General Pierre 97
GATT Uruguay Round 108, 172,
    180–1, 182, 197, 240, 375,
    411–12n
Genscher–Colombo Plan 224
Genscher, Hans-Dietrich 144, 156,
    158, 245, 247, 319, 321, 328,
    329, 379
Georgia 59, 60, 64, 80, 94
    dispute with Abkhazia 65–6, 285,
    361
    dispute with South Ossetia 264,
    269, 285, 333, 334, 336, 363
German Democratic Republic
    (GDR) 135
Germany
    Basic Law 73, 143–154
    Bosnia and 145–6, 150–2
    Bundeswehr 143, 148, 154–6, 251
    CRF 154–6
    current role in Europe 82–3,
    135–64, 353
    defence cooperation with
    France 244–54
    European security 95, 156–63, 225,
    281
    Federal Constitutional Court 144–56
    Gulf War and 140–1
    historical role in Europe 19–21, 156
    migratory pressures on 71, 73–4,
    77, 158–9
    Mitteleuropa 20, 82, 106, 136, 140,
    162, 163
    Neo-Nazis 135–6
    Ostpolitik 21, 98, 157, 168
    population growth 72
    public opinion 150
    racially inspired incidents 21, 71,
    136, 406n
    recognition of Croatia and
    Slovenia 83, 156–8, 213
    reunification 135, 138, 405n
    role in Somalia 152–4
    Two plus Four talks 137
    US military and 160–2
Ghannouchi, Rached 27
Giscard d'Estaing, Valéry 99, 104,
    244
Glasnost 59
Gorbachev, Mikhail 12, 30, 33, 53,
    57–8, 98, 103, 142, 159, 168, 170,
    209, 249

GPALS 49
Grachev, General Pavel 44, 49, 56
Gramm–Rudman–Hollings Bill 190
Greece 207, 225, 227, 229–30, 281,
    285, 331
    dispute with Albania 62
    dispute with Bulgaria 62
    migratory pressures on 75, 77
    relations with Macedonia 365
    relations with WEU 239, 415n
Grundgesetz see Germany, Basic Law
Gulf War (1991) 54, 145, 168, 190,
    213, 225, 272, 283
    Operations Desert Shield/Storm 178,
    179, 225, 232, 298–99

Haiti 375
Harmel Report (1967) 210, 286, 424n
Havel, Václav 168, 256, 319, 320,
    327
Heath, Edward 120–1
Heidelberg 170
Helios I & II 116
Helsinki Accords (1975) 69, 331,
    360–1
Hernu, Charles 246, 248
Hexagonal initiative 203
Highly enriched uranium 46
Hintze, Peter 147
Hizbollah 24
Hobbes, Thomas 21
Hoffmann, Stanley 209
Honecker, Erich 102, 135
Holst, Johan Jorgen 210
Howe, Geoffrey 122
Humanitarian intervention 89
Hungary 18, 59, 61, 80, 156, 228,
    237, 261, 308, 319, 320–1, 326,
    331–2, 334, 360, 363
    dispute with Romania 62
    dispute with Slovakia 325
Hurd, Douglas 131
Hussein, Saddam 26, 272
Hyde Park Agreement (1944) 118

Iceland 261
Iliescu, Ion 331
*Independent European Programme
    Group* see NATO
INF forces 98–9, 106, 142
Ingush Republic 65
International Atomic Energy
    Authority 37, 54
Iran 24–5, 28, 146

Iraq 86, 115, 146, 229, 232 (*see also* Gulf War)
Iran-contra 188
Ireland (Northern) 233
Ireland (Republic) 225, 227, 229, 234, 239, 261
Irkutsk 60
Islamic fundamentalism 22–8
Italy 194, 225, 227, 232, 251, 281, 331
  Albanians and 72
  Northern League 71
  population growth 72
Izetbegovic, Alija 350

Japan 198
Jeszensky, Géza 429
Jihad 22, 24
Joffe, Josef 139
Joint Defence Council (Franco–German) 245, 246
Joxe, Pierre 109, 116
Jus sanguinis 73
Jus soli 73

Kabardin-Balkar 60
Kaliningrad 323
Karadzic, Radovan 350
Kashani, Ayatollah 28
Kazakhstan 283
  future of 64, 264
  nuclear weapons and 30, 35, 38, 39, 47, 48
Kennedy, John F. 97, 129, 174, 209
Khahn, Herman 141
Khasbulatov, Ruslan 66
Khomeini, Ayatollah 27
Kinkel, Klaus 149, 158
King, Tom 125, 126, 367
Kirkpatrick, Jeane 359
Kishk, Saykh 26
Klaus, Vàclav 322
Klose, Hans-Ulrich 146
Kohl, Helmut 83, 101, 102, 103, 138, 144, 147, 156, 158, 159, 170, 181, 183, 220, 223, 245, 250, 254
Kolodziejczyk, Admiral Piotr 321
Kosovo 28, 29, 62, 67, 94, 264, 332, 365
Kozyrev, Andrei 38, 49, 364–5, 367
Krajina 356
Kravchenko, Pytor 49
Kravchuk, Leonid 40–2, 43, 44, 46
  opposition to 46–8
Krenz, Egon 135

Kuchma, Leonid 44
Kurds *see* Iraq
Kuwait 184, 225, 229, 232, 272, 299
Kyrgzstan 52, 60, 64, 283, 264
Kyshtym 53

Lacouture, Jean 97
Lambsdorff, Count Otto von 149
La Rochelle 223, 250
Latvia 59, 80, 113, 237, 266, 333, 334, 336, 363
League of Nations 188, 208
Lellouche, Pierre 114
Léotard, François 109, 402n
Le Pen, Jean-Marie 23, 71, 75
Libya 54, 187
Lisbon Protocols (1992) 38, 47, 48
Lithuania 58, 62, 80, 113, 237, 266, 334, 336, 363
Lombardi League 11
Lomé Convention 229
Lowe, Karl 103
Lundzhev, Dimitar 326
Lugar, Senator Richard 308
Lukaszewski, Jerzy 322
Luxembourg 77, 205, 225, 227, 250

Maastricht Summit (1991) 100, 108, 171–2, 176, 219, 222, 224–31, 234, 318
Maastricht Treaty (1991) 116, 122, 123, 131–2, 156, 184, 213, 221, 225–31
Macedonia 61, 62, 334, 350, 357, 363
Macmillan, Harold 97
Maghreb 75, 78
Major, John 117, 123–5, 126, 173, 183, 223, 251, 353
Manhattan Project 118
MAPI 51
Marshall Plan 90
Mathews, Jessica 5
Matrix-Churchill 54
McCarthy, James 337
McMahon Act (1946) 118
McNamara, Robert 279
Mearsheimer, John 17, 22, 44
Mendès-France, Pierre 217
Middle East War (1973) 174
Minsk Agreement (1991) 31, 37, 48, 55–6
Missiles
  Frog 33
  GLCM 98, 249

Hadès 101, 105, 106, 248
Lance 184
Pershing II 98
Pluton 248
Scud 33, 115
SS-18 30, 35, 48, 49
SS-19 30, 43, 45
SS-21 33
SS-24 30, 33, 43, 46
SS-25 30, 33, 48
Trident D-5 125, 129
Missile Technology Control Regime
    (MTCR) 54–55
Mitteleuropa see Germany
Mitterrand, François 100, 101, 102,
    103, 104, 110, 112, 172, 220, 223,
    245, 247, 248, 250, 254
and *confédération* 102, 106, 109,
    114, 256
MLF 97, 119
Mogadishu 152, 353
Moldavia 29
Moldova 60, 64, 334, 336, 363
Monnet, Jean 119, 368
Montenegro 69, 146
Morgenthau, Hans 6, 135, 203
Morocco 75, 78
Morozov, General Konstantin 44, 45
Moscow 135
Moscow Declaration (1994) 50
Mostar 350
Mölln 21, 71, 406n
Musitelli, Jean 113
Mutual Assured Destruction
    doctrine 97

NAFTA 181
Nagorno-Karabakh 60, 65, 264, 269,
    285 (*see also* Armenia *and*
    Azerbaijan)
Nassau Meeting (1963) 97
National interest 9
Nationalism 57–69
National Security Council 167
Naumann, General Klaus 154
NAVSTAR 115
Nazarbayev, Nursultan 37, 47
Neo-realism 7
Netherlands 121, 205, 213, 225, 227,
    232, 252, 281
Nicaragua 188
Nine Power Conference (1954) 216
Nixon, Richard 184
North Africa 69, 72

North Atlantic Cooperation Council 11,
    269, 285, 301–4, 328, 336–7, 377
North Atlantic Council 6, 98, 217
Athens Meeting (1993) 304
Brussels Meeting (1992) 153, 298, 302
Brussels Meeting (1993) 354
Brussels Meeting (1994) 196, 338
Copenhagen Meeting (1991) 219–20,
    327
London Meeting (1990) 6, 110, 134,
    183, 214–22, 252, 256, 278, 293,
    297
Oslo Meeting (1992) 108, 222, 297,
    301, 302
Rome Meeting (1991) 153, 172,
    175, 218, 269, 286, 297, 301, 327,
    329, 330, 410n
North Atlantic Treaty 194–5, 330
North Atlantic Treaty Organization 211,
    212, 275–92, 346
ARRC 108–9, 123, 130, 290, 304,
    404n
Bosnia and 276, 310, 358–60
Command and control 304–5
Defence College 303
Defence Planning committee 287,
    292
dual-track decision 98, 121, 244
effectiveness of 362–3, 370
Eurogroup 131, 239
European pillar 100, 108, 130–2,
    196–9, 201, 238–9
European Security Identity 109
flexible response 116, 141, 293,
    425n
IEPG 239, 240, 253
New Strategic Concept 153, 219,
    288–94
out-of-area problems 194–5,
    295–300
Partnership for Peace 196, 305–11
relations with 'Eurocorps' 247–54
SHAPE College 303
North Korea 194
North Ossetia 60, 65
Norway 210, 281
Nott, John 125
Nuclear Suppliers Group 52
Nuclear weapons 17–18, 29–36
and PALs 33

Odom, Lt-General William 185
Omnibus Trade and Competitiveness
    Act (1988) 180

Operation Deny Flight 147, 151
Operation Desert Shield/Storm *see*
   Gulf War
Operation Granby 128, 129
Operation Maritime Guard 408n
Operation Maritime Monitor 408n
Operation Restore Hope *see* Somalia
Operation Sky Monitor 151
Organization for Economic Cooperation
   and Development (OECD) 111,
   228
Organization of the Islamic
   Conference 28
Organization of Petroleum Exporting
   Countries (OPEC) 6, 181
Osh 60
Ostpolitik see Germany
Owen, David 233, 256, 259, 300
Owen–Stoltenberg Agreement 350,
   351
Özal, Turgut 283–4

Pakistan 23, 24, 54
Papendreou, Andreas 283
Pasqua, Charles 76
Peace dividend 93, 279
Peloponnesian War 19, 392n
Persian Gulf 194
Perestroika 59
Petersberg Declaration see WEU
PHARE 79, 333–5, 361, 400n
Pleven Plan 206, 215
Poland 59, 80, 156, 228, 261, 307,
   319, 321, 326, 334, 363
   dispute with Belarus 62
   relations with Germany 137
Polaris Agreement (1962) 119
Pompidou, Georges 99
Poos, Jacques 356
Portugal 227, 281, 285, 331
Powell, General Colin 166, 194
Power, definition of 3–7
Prepositioned organizational material
   configured to unit sets
   (POMCUS) 194
Proliferation 29–55

Quebec Agreement (1943) 118
Quran 27

RAF Greenham Common 121
RAF Molesworth 121
Rassemblement pour la République see
   Chirac

Reagan, Ronald 98, 121, 126, 142,
   181, 184, 249
   follow-on-to Lance dispute 184
   Libyan Raid 184, 187
Reich, Simon 139
Reverse-realism 94
Reykjavik Summit (1986) 98, 122,
   142, 187, 249
Reynaud, Jean 114
Ridley, Nicholas 138
Rifkind, Malcolm 127, 128–9, 223,
   251, 404n
Romania 29, 59, 61, 63, 80, 237, 261,
   331, 332, 336, 363
   dispute with Bulgaria 62
   dispute with Hungary 62
Roosevelt, Franklin Delano 166, 184,
   375
Rossi, Ernesto 119, 368
Roth, Senator William 328
Russian Soviet Federative Socialist
   Republic (RSFR)
   arms control and 49, 50
   Black Sea fleet 45–7
   Bosnia and 364–5, 367
   CSCE and 273
   ethnic disputes within 59–62, 64–7
   military of 31, 37, 39, 49, 159
   Nagorno-Karabakh 64–5
   NATO and 307–9, 323–4, 338
   'near abroad' 339
   nuclear material 30, 37, 51–55, 60
   relations with Georgia 65–66
   relations with Yakuts 31, 60
   relations with Tartars 31
Rupel, Dimitrij 355
Rutskoi, Aleksandr 59
Rühe, Volker 148, 149, 154, 340

Salmon, Trevor 233
Sanjak 264
Sarajevo 168, 310, 354, 358–9
Saudia Arabia 24
Shaposhnikov, Marshal Yevgeni 38–9
Scharping, Rudolph 152
Schengen Accords 79, 229, 400n
Schmidt, Helmut 99, 244, 247
Schuman, Robert 119
Scowcroft, Brent 250
Security, definition of 5–10
Seiters, Rudolf 158
Seks, Vladimir 71
Semipalatinsk 48, 53
Serbia 58, 69, 146, 150, 349

dispute with Albania 62
Kosovo and 365
Macedonia and 365
Shaposhnikov, Marshal Yevgeni
38-9, 65
Shari'a 23
Shevardnadze, Eduard 66, 319
Shiite 23-6, 28
Shushkevich, Stanislav 49
Siberian Gas pipeline dispute 181
Silesia 67
Single European Act (SEA) 224-5,
230
Skopje 264
Skubiszewski, Krzysztof 321
Skybolt Agreement 119
Slavonia 356
Slovakia 59, 68, 80, 261, 307, 325,
334, 363
Slovenia 59, 80, 233, 334, 349,
355-6, 360, 363
recognized by EC 357
Snyder, Jed 281
Socialist Unity Party (SED) 135
Solingen 71, 406n
Somalia 146, 169, 178, 272,
375, 407n
Spaak, Paul-Henri 119
Spain 227, 232, 233, 250, 281,
285, 331
Falangists 71
migratory pressures on 75
SPOT (satellites) 115
Srebrenica 310
State Department 182
Stoltenberg, Gerhard 246, 350, 359
Suez crisis (1956) 120
Sunni 23-5
Sverdlosk 60
Sweden 225, 261
Syria 54

TACIS 79, 333-5, 361, 400n
Tajikistan 52, 64, 264
Tarasov, Lt-General Boris 49
Tartar see RSFR
Tbilisi 337
Technabexport 51-2
Thatcher, Margaret 117, 121, 122,
124, 126, 139, 287, 359
Tiger attack helicopter 253
Torrejon 240
Trans-Dniester see Moldova
Transylvania 61, 67, 332

Treaty on European Union see
Maastricht Treaty
Treverton, Gregory 286
Truman, Harry 176
Turkey 65, 145, 194, 207, 281,
282-5, 331
dispute with Bulgaria 62
Turkmenistan 56, 64, 264, 283
Tuzla 310
Tyrolians 11

Ukraine
anti-Russian sentiment 58-9, 62, 64
Black Sea Fleet dispute 45-7
control of nuclear weapons 44-5,
46, 261
conventional forces of 55-7
European security and 113, 363
nuclear weapons and 30, 33, 35,
37-42, 47, 52
see also Kravchuk
Ullman, Richard 206, 271
Union pour la Démocratie
Française 110
United Kingdom
BAOR 125, 130
British National Party (BNP) 71, 76
'Defending our Future' 127-8, 404n
Economy of 125-7
European leadership and 95,
117-34, 225, 250
migratory pressures on 76, 77
nuclear collaboration 124-5, 134, 155
'Options for Change' 126, 404n
relations with US 117-20, 122, 124,
129, 133, 173, 188
'The Way Forward' 125
United Nations 84-5, 86-7, 134,
150-1, 152, 177, 188, 209, 211,
213, 408n
effectiveness of 342-3
Register for Conventional Arms 261
UNPROFOR 277, 310, 358
United States
CSCE and 270-1
Gulf War and 168, 178
leadership by 165, 166, 185-6,
196-9, 273, 368
Marine Corps 195
military presence in 170-86, 189-94
military strategy of 176-7, 189, 194
NATO and 170-180, 188
relations with Europe 93, 113-17,
165-99, 250-1, 373-5

United States *cont.*
relations with UN   177–9, 188
Somalia and   178, 368
Yugoslavia and   168, 178, 179, 352,
354–5
Universal Declaration of Human Rights
(1948)   85
Uruguay Round   see GATT
USECOM   190
US Enrichment Corporation   46
US Holocaust Museum   136
Ustashi   159, 409n
Uzbekistan   52, 56, 64, 264, 283

Vance, Cyrus   233, 300, 357
Vance–Owen Plan   351, 359
Vancouver Summit (1993)   36
Van den Brande, Luc   68
Van den Broek, Hans   356
Van Eekelen, William   356
Ventotene Manifesto   369
Versailles, Treaty (1918)   137, 323,
392n
Vienna Convention on the Law of
Treaties   153, 409n
Visegrad   320–5
Vladivostock   11, 60
Vlahos, Michael   175
Voigt, Karsten   147
Vojvodina   264

Walesa, Lech   168, 270, 323, 324,
327–8, 338
Warsaw Treaty Organization   10, 12,
55, 159, 320, 381
Watanabe, Michio   149
Watergate   188
West European Treaty Organization   131

Western European Union (WEU)   10,
11, 106, 108, 117, 120, 122,
130–1, 164, 172, 174, 211, 217,
221, 229, 230, 231–41, 249,
272–3, 370
IEPG and   239–40
Petersberg Declaration   152, 237–9
Platform on Security Interests   232,
249
Rapid Reaction Force   237
relations with CSCE   237
relations with EU   231–5
relations with NATO   235–41, 300–1
satellite centre   240
Westphalia, Treaty (1648)   84
Wilson, Harold   120
World Bank   111
Wörner, Manfred   276, 327, 330, 358
Wright, Robin   24

Yakuts   see RSFR
Yalta, Treaty   137
Yassin, Ahmad   27
Yeltsin, Boris   30, 33, 35, 36, 39, 45,
49, 50, 56, 323–4, 339
Yugoslavia   21, 88, 95, 113, 156, 168,
179, 184, 213, 229, 232, 272, 282,
299, 347–68
Brioni Accord   356
CSCE and   267–9
EU and   232, 352, 417n
WEU and   109, 112
Yost, David   109, 112
Young, Hugo   121

Zagreb   351
Zhirinovsky, Vladimir   47, 50, 338
Zlenko, Anatoly   41, 42